Fodor's

NORTHERN
CALIFORNIA

Welcome to Northern California

It's easy to tap into the good life in Northern California. Indulge in rounds of golf at Pebble Beach, and then follow scenic trails through Yosemite National Park. Sip wine at picturesque Napa and Sonoma vineyards, and then dine in stellar locavore restaurants. Urban pleasures await, too. San Francisco's cable cars zip you through vibrant neighborhoods filled with chic boutiques and cutting-edge museums. As you plan your upcoming travels, please confirm that places are still open and let us know when we need to make updates at editors@ fodors.com.

TOP REASONS TO GO

★ **San Francisco:** This diverse city beguiles with natural beauty and contagious energy.

★ **Wine Country:** Top-notch whites and reds in Napa, Sonoma, and beyond.

★ **Feasts:** Cutting-edge cuisine, food trucks, fusion flavors, farmers' markets.

★ **Stunning Scenery:** Picture-perfect backdrops from the Golden Gate Bridge to redwoods.

★ **Hiking Adventures:** The trails—inland or coastal—are sublime.

★ **Road Trips:** The Pacific Coast Highway offers spectacular views and thrills aplenty.

Contents

MAPS

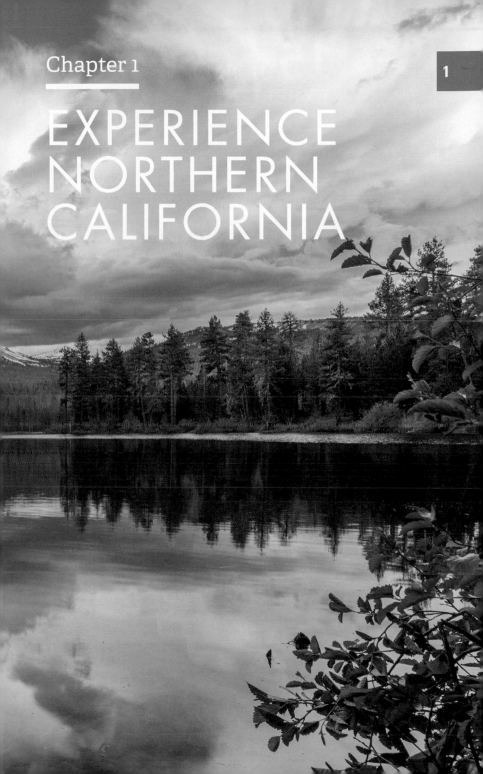

Chapter 1

EXPERIENCE NORTHERN CALIFORNIA

1

15 ULTIMATE EXPERIENCES

Northern California offers terrific experiences that should be on every traveler's list. Here are Fodor's top picks for a memorable trip.

1 Crane your neck at Redwood National and State Parks

Redwood National and State Parks have the tallest trees on Earth (300–400 feet), and hug 40 miles of California coastline. There are countless things to see and do, including camping, hiking, fishing, and kayaking. *(Ch. 14)*

2 Enjoy the view from a hot-air balloon

It's worth rising early for a balloon ride at dawn over vineyards in either Napa or Sonoma. *(Ch. 12)*

3 Ogle General Sherman

Sequoia National Park's General Sherman tree is the largest living tree in the world, at 275 feet tall and 36 feet in diameter at its roots. *(Ch. 5)*

4 Hike the Pacific Crest Trail

The Pacific Crest Trail stretches 2,659 miles along the U.S. coast from Mexico to Canada. It peaks at Forester Pass in Kings Canyon National Park, at 13,153 feet. *(Ch. 5)*

5 Commune with nature at Yosemite National Park

Nestled in the Sierra Nevada, Yosemite National Park is known for its giant sequoia trees, epic waterfalls, and abundant wildlife. *(Ch. 6)*

6 Witness greatness in sport

Sports fans have their pick of great Northern California teams, including the Giants or '49ers in San Francisco and the Golden State Warriors in Oakland. *(Chs. 10-11)*

7 Spot whales in Monterey

Depending on the season, you can charter boats to view migrating gray, humpback, and blue whales. Monterey is also prime territory for killer whales, bottlenose dolphins, and more. *(Ch. 4)*

8 Get an adrenaline rush at Lake Tahoe

Straddling California and Nevada, Lake Tahoe is a wonderland for adventure enthusiasts year-round, with world-class skiing in winter and lake sports in summer. *(Ch. 9)*

9 Drink all the wine

Don't tell the French, but the best wine is from Napa and Sonoma Counties. Only a few hours away from each other, both are flush with world-class wineries. *(Ch. 12)*

10 Dive into history in San Francisco's Chinatown

San Francisco's Chinatown is the largest outside of Asia and the oldest in the U.S. Don't miss the Dragon Gate, Golden Gate Fortune Cookie Factory, and the Old Telephone Exchange. *(Ch. 10)*

11 Take the scenic 17-Mile Drive

This stretch of road in Pebble Beach takes you past enchanting sights, like Fanshell Beach, Point Joe, the Lone Cypress, and more. *(Ch. 4)*

12 Eat your way through Berkeley

Explore Berkeley's campus, and then dine along nearby Shattuck Avenue, where chef Alice Waters got her start. *(Ch. 11)*

13 Play arcade games at Musée Mécanique

This quirky "museum" at Fisherman's Wharf in San Francisco has more than 200 antique arcade games, including coin-operated fortune tellers, moving dioramas, and stereoscopes. *(Ch. 10)*

14 Ski at Mammoth

Mammoth Mountain (a dormant volcano) is the largest ski resort in California; its 3,500 acres of skiable area hosts millions of skiers and snowboarders each year. *(Ch. 7)*

15 Cross the Golden Gate Bridge

Opened in 1937, the Golden Gate Bridge is one of the most iconic symbols of San Francisco. Visitors can cross the mile-long suspension bridge by foot, bicycle, or car. *(Ch. 10)*

California Today

"Has the Golden State Lost Its Luster?" "Is the California Dream Dead?" So read the inevitable rueful headlines in stories detailing the supposedly insurmountable obstacles—most notably a declining population, the high cost of living (especially housing), wildfires, drought, crime, traffic congestion, homelessness, and high taxes. So dire are some of the assessments that one might assume there's no reason to stay here, let alone come for a visit. This despite the fact that everything that has lured settlers and tourists from the get-go—breathtaking scenery, scintillating sightseeing, abundant natural resources, agricultural bounty, and a mostly hospitable climate—remains well in evidence.

Although California, like the rest of the nation and world, faces daunting challenges, the same gloomy predictions (often bearing precisely the same "lost its luster" and "dream dead" headlines) have appeared before: in the middle of the Great Recession (2009), after the first dot-com implosion (2000), all the way back to the gold and silver busts of the 19th century. And guess what? In every instance, the state bounced back, sometimes brilliantly.

Each allegedly ruinous calamity required reinvention, and each time residents rose to the occasion. Based on the past, there's no reason to think that the Golden State won't regain its luster—if it's even been lost.

POPULATION, POTENTIAL

California's birth rate and the pace of migration may have slowed, but they're hardly stagnant. For perspective, consider that the current population of about 39 million (about an eighth of the U.S. total) represents a net increase of nearly 2 million since 2010, albeit a pace behind Texas and Florida. While many residents departing California cite the high cost of living, recent transplants tend to perceive the same potential here as previous settlers.

HISTORICAL CONTEXT

By most accounts, the ancestors of California's indigenous peoples migrated from Asia, traversing a land bridge across the Bering Strait that formerly joined what's now Russia and Alaska. Some of these trailblazers continued south to California, flourishing off the fertile land for centuries. Many famous place names—Malibu, Napa, Ojai, Shasta, Sonoma—reflect this heritage.

Millennia later, Spanish explorers ventured north from Mexico searching for gold, with converts to Christianity the quest of 18th-century missionaries. Nineteenth-century miners rushed here from the world over also seeking gold—the state achieved statehood two years after the precious metal's 1848 discovery.

During the 20th century, successive, sometimes overlapping, waves of newcomers followed in their footsteps: real-estate speculators, would-be motion-picture actors and producers, Dust Bowl farmers and migrant workers, Asians fleeing poverty or chasing opportunity, sexual and gender pioneers, artists, dot-commers, venture capitalists, and these days AI practitioners.

POLITICS

The result is a population that leans toward idealism (some say utopianism)—without necessarily being as liberal as voter-registration statistics might lead one to think. California is Ronald Reagan's old stomping ground, after all. Herbert Hoover also thrived here, and Richard Nixon was a native son. Democrats hold a 2–1 registration advantage over

Republicans, the latter essentially tied with "no party preference," but wander into some inland counties, and you may see signs proposing a breakaway, more conservative 51st State of Jefferson. Many residents in these areas supported a 2021 effort to recall Governor Gavin Newsom, a liberal Democrat. Early polls indicated the special-election race might be tight, but the governor prevailed by a substantial margin and was reelected to a second term in 2022.

DEMOGRAPHICS
As with politics, despite the stereotype of the blue-eyed, blond surfer, California's population isn't homogeneous either. Latino residents outnumber whites 40%–35%, with Asians (16%) and African Americans (6.5%) the next-largest groups. Residents here speak more than 220 languages, making California by far the nation's most linguistically diverse state.

ECONOMICS
Back to California's supposedly desperate situation: keep in mind that, in 2022, the Golden State reported a $98 billion budget *surplus,* hardly numbers to prompt despair and proving the Great Recession doomsayers predicting economic catastrophe way off the mark. (For the record, 2023 saw the state in the red to the tune of $30-plus billion.) California, responsible for 15% of the gross domestic product, leads all other states in income generated by agriculture, tourism, entertainment, and industrial activity. With a gross state product of approximately $3.6 trillion (median household income of about $79,000), by many estimates, California would have the world's fifth-largest economy—some say the fourth—were it an independent nation.

STILL DREAMIN'
A few years ago, dueling state-of-the-state analyses appeared within days of each other. A historian's *New York Times* opinion piece described California's declining population and loss of a congressional seat as among negative "firsts" for the state that had "sapped the collective sense of zealous optimism." The historian also predicted "decades of pain" if politicians didn't quickly produce solutions to California's pressing problems.

Two days before the *Times* piece ran, the University of California published a study suggesting pretty much the opposite: that the rate of residents moving out of state is neither unusual nor something to fret over; that residents by a 2–1 majority still believe in the California Dream; and that the state attracts more than half the nation's venture-capital investments, a sign that favorable economic conditions persist.

The naysayers may well be right about California's demise, but if history is any indication, the populace will likely shift gears as necessary. And again the next time it's required. In the meantime, the state's brigade of bucket-list attractions continues to supply the essentials for a dream vacation.

WHAT'S WHERE

1 Monterey Bay Area. Postcard-perfect Monterey, Victorian-flavored Pacific Grove, and exclusive Carmel all share this stretch of California coast. To the north, Santa Cruz has a UC campus, a boardwalk, and lots of surfers.

2 Sequoia and Kings Canyon National Parks. Breathtaking—with towering redwoods and jagged mountains.

3 Yosemite National Park. Immortalized by Ansel Adams, the granite monoliths, verdant valleys, and lofty waterfalls are still camera-ready.

4 Eastern Sierra. In the Mammoth Lakes region, sawtooth mountains and deep powdery snowdrifts beckon skiers and snowboarders.

5 Sacramento and the Gold Country. The 1849 gold rush began here, and the former mining camps strung along 185 miles of Highway 49 replay this past.

6 Lake Tahoe. High Sierra peaks reflected in crystalline waters make Lake Tahoe the perfect setting for year-round outdoor activities.

7 San Francisco. To see why many have left their hearts here, you need only explore the city's iconic neighborhoods.

8 The Bay Area. The area that rings San Francisco is home to some of the nation's great universities, fabulous water views, Silicon Valley, and Alice Waters's Chez Panisse.

9 Napa and Sonoma. Acclaimed vintages, luxe lodgings, and epicurean eats—these counties still comprise the California Wine Country.

10 The North Coast. Secluded beaches, wave-battered bluffs, and towering redwoods are top attractions.

11 Redwood National and State Parks. More than 200 miles of trails, ranging from easy to strenuous, travel amid the redwoods.

12 The Far North. Snowcapped Mt. Shasta, pristine wilderness, and backwoods character are highlights here.

What to Eat and Drink in Northern California

Oysters

SOURDOUGH BREAD
In California, sourdough history is tied to the Gold Rush, when French bakers set up shop in San Francisco to feed the miners. For the perfect loaf, head to Boudin Bakery in San Francisco where they've been perfecting their sourdough recipe since 1849.

WINE
You could throw a rock and hit a world-class wine up and down the coast of California. Monterey, Napa, and Sonoma all have some of the best vintages on the planet.

FRESH PACIFIC SEAFOOD
You don't have to go far to find seafood, most of it freshly sourced from the waters off California. Always check out the day's catch—shucked and placed on ice or served in a sandwich, salad, or other dish.

Sourdough bread

IRISH COFFEE
Inspired by a drink in Ireland, the owner of the Buena Vista in San Francisco set out to re-create the concoction and stumbled upon what we now know as an Irish Coffee. The mixture of coffee, whiskey, and floating cream can still be enjoyed out of a chalice at the same Buena Vista location since its humble beginnings.

BURGERS
If there's any debate about the home of the burger, just ask Fat Burger, Carl's Jr, McDonald's, In-N-Out, Umami Burger, The Habit Burger Grill, Hamburger Mary's, Johnny Rockets, The Counter, Original Tommy's, and Jack in the Box, which all started in the Golden State.

SUSHI
Outside of Japan, there is no better place to eat raw fish than in California. At Akiko in San Francisco, you can find the freshest, most savory cuts of fish that rivals any place in the world.

CHEESE
Wisconsin? Please. The best cheese is clearly from California. Have you heard of Humboldt Fog? That comes from Cypress Grove in Humboldt County. How about Red Hawk, that gooey triple-crème that melts in your mouth? Marin County. And cheddar? Sorry Wisconsin, but Fiscalini Bandaged Cheddar from Modesto has you beat any day of the week.

VEGETARIAN FOOD
Californians are known to be health conscious, eating lots of fresh local produce (including adding avocado to everything). There are plentiful vegetarian and vegan options throughout the state.

BEER
California is a hotbed of beer-making, and craft brewers are dominating the beer scene like never before. Check out 21st Amendment in San Francisco.

MAI TAIS
White rum, dark rum, Curaçao liqueur, orgeat syrup, and lime juice makes the perfect Mai Tai. The drink was invented (allegedly) by Victor Bergeron in 1944 of the famed restaurant Trader Vic's in Oakland, California, though Donn Beach (of Don the Beachcomber fame) claims he invented it in the 1930s in Hollywood.

10 Best Photo Ops in San Francisco

THE PALACE OF FINE ARTS

This stirringly lovely terra-cotta–color domed structure on a lagoon near the Marina's yacht harbor has an otherworldly quality about it. Built in 1915 for an exposition, the palace is a San Francisco architect's version of a Roman ruin, and it's been eliciting gasps ever since. It's a popular wedding spot, which is good if you like happy couples in your photos.

THE PAINTED LADIES

Familiar to fans of the TV show *Full House,* the so-called Painted Ladies or Seven Sisters are a row of seven colorful and beautifully maintained Queen Anne–style houses just off Alamo Square Park. Take photos at midday for clear city views.

LANDS END COASTAL TRAIL

This 4-mile trail winds and twists along the rugged cliffs of San Francisco Bay, offering stunning views of the Golden Gate Bridge and surprisingly woodsy forest. At the 1.3-mile mark, turn left at the wooden staircase to explore Mile Rock Beach and the Lands End Labyrinth. On a clear day, you can see the Golden Gate Bridge in the distance.

TWIN PEAKS

These two adjacent peaks near Noe Valley are at the near geographic center of San Francisco, with an elevation of 925 feet. Especially pretty (and popular, but chilly) at sunrise and sunset, the peaks provide sweeping 180-degree views of the Bay Area, with a great perspective on downtown San Francisco, the Bay Bridge, and the tips of the Golden Gate Bridge.

THE PRESIDIO

As the gateway to the Golden Gate Bridge, San Francisco's 1,500-acre Presidio offers incredible views of the bridge and the sprawling landscape that surrounds it. Enjoy spectacular bridge photo opportunities from Crissy Field or the Presidio Tunnel Tops. The Presidio also abuts Baker Beach, a stretch of sand with an alternative perspective.

MUIR WOODS NATIONAL MONUMENT

Naturalist John Muir wrote, "Most people are on the world, not in it—have no conscious sympathy or relationship to anything about them …" It's hard not to feel connected as you walk the shaded paths of Muir Woods amid the towering majesty of the redwood groves.

UNION SQUARE

This lively spot is the place to capture the cable cars as they rumble by. The towering Dewey Monument pillar, topped triumphantly by Nike, the Greek goddess of victory, is a beautiful sculpture. Relax on the steps and photograph what many call the heart of the city.

TREASURE ISLAND

Tiny, man-made Treasure Island is generally off the tourist track, so your photos won't be crowded with selfie-takers. Sitting right in the middle of San Francisco Bay, it offers gorgeous views of the San Francisco skyline, especially at night when everything is lit up.

HAWK HILL

At a high point on the south-facing Marin Headlands, Hawk Hill lies opposite the city with vistas of the Pacific and of the Golden Gate Bridge as it enters San Francisco. True to its name, it's also a great spot for nature-watching. Hawk Hill is the site of the autumnal raptor migration and also serves as a habitat for the Mission Blue Butterfly.

BERNAL HEIGHTS

This somewhat stumpy-looking mound rises unenthusiastically above the houses of the surrounding neighborhood. But, pictures taken *from* Bernal Heights Hill offer 360-degree panoramic views. Take a sunset stroll here for stunning San Francisco shots.

What to Read and Watch

WINE COUNTRY WOMEN OF NAPA VALLEY BY MICHELLE MANDRO AND DONA KOPOL BONIK

Winemakers, chefs, executives, and other women holding key positions share insights and recipes in this large-format volume filled with photography.

THE MALTESE FALCON BY DASHIELL HAMMETT

There was a time when San Francisco's most notorious antiheroes weren't billionaires in T-shirts, but rather chain-smoking, hard-boiled detectives. In *The Maltese Falcon,* detective Sam Spade criss-crosses an atmospheric 1930s San Francisco to locate a jeweled statue. Dashiell Hammett's novel is a legendary piece of noir fiction, but the film, which starred an in-his-prime Humphrey Bogart, is also a classic.

THE GIRLS BY EMMA CLINE

In this nuanced coming-of-age story set in the Sonoma County town of Petaluma, the 14-year-old narrator yearns for excitement, attention, and beauty—and falls into the violent, psychological mind-trip of a Charles Manson–like cult. Beautiful and gripping, Cline's novel shares a gritty, late 1960s Sonoma County—one that couldn't be further from today's world of Cabernets and Pinots.

GUN, WITH OCCASIONAL MUSIC BY JONATHAN LETHEM

Lethem started his career with a captivating but decidedly weird novel set in San Francisco and Oakland. In this sci-fi noir detective story, people rub elbows with talking, man-sized, genetically engineered animals, and everyone lives under a monetized "karma" system like that used in modern-day China to track and influence its citizens.

BURMA SUPERSTAR BY DESMOND TAN AND KATE LEAHY

Burmese food is increasingly popular in San Francisco, where the Burma Superstar restaurant is a hit. This cookbook offers a look into the flavor-packed southeast Asian cuisine.

THE MAYOR OF CASTRO STREET BY RANDY SHILTS

Randy Shilts's biography of gay civil rights icon Harvey Milk is perhaps the most well-regarded and authoritative reckoning of his life to date. Milk was a bombastic, iconic figure whose advocacy and brutal murder permanently shaped the political landscape of not just San Francisco, but the entire country.

MR. PENUMBRA'S 24-HOUR BOOKSTORE BY ROBIN SLOAN

This novel about a quirky used-book store in San Francisco does double duty. Not only is it a story of mystery, love, code-breaking, secret societies, and adopted and inherited culture, but it's also a narrative about the dangers of rapid technological advancement (and of rejecting technology), tribalism, and other timely issues.

NOSE: A NOVEL BY JAMES CONAWAY

A fictitious Northern California wine-making region—couldn't be Napa or Sonoma, could it?—is the setting for a mystery.

THE BIRDS

Alfred Hitchcock's 1963 *The Birds* centers around a small Northern Californian town under attack by swarming, possessed birds. Although, you'll never again look at a crow in quite the same way after watching this graphic thriller, it also showcases the beauty of Sonoma County's coast and the charm of Bodega Bay, the town where most of the movie was filmed.

Chapter 2

TRAVEL SMART

Updated by
Daniel Mangin

★ **CAPITAL:**
Sacramento

👥 **POPULATION:**
39.5 million

💬 **LANGUAGE:**
English

$ **CURRENCY:**
U.S. dollar

☎ **COUNTRY CODE:**
1

⚠ **EMERGENCIES:**
911

🚗 **DRIVING:**
On the right

⚡ **ELECTRICITY:**
120–240 v/60 cycles;
plugs have two or three
rectangular prongs

🕑 **TIME:**
Three hours behind New
York

🌐 **WEB RESOURCES:**
www.visitcalifornia.com,
www.parks.ca.gov,
dot.ca.gov/travel,
travel.state.gov

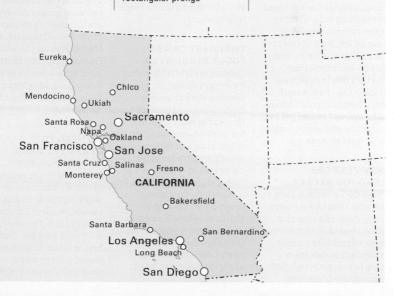

Know Before You Go

To help you prepare for a visit to the vast, diverse, unique state of California, below are tips about driving, destinations, the weather, saving money at restaurants and hotels, wildlife, cannabis tourism, and things to see and do that might save you time or money or increase peace of mind.

ROAD TRIPS TAKE TIME
California has some of the most scenic drives in the world. It's also the third-largest state behind Alaska and Texas and, in square miles, is similar in size to Sweden, Japan, or Paraguay. So, if you want to see all its beaches, deserts, mountains, and forests, you'll need a car—and, perhaps, a bit of patience.

A road trip through even half of the state takes several hours in the best of traffic (frequently not the case), and this doesn't count contending with winding, mountainous terrain, or coastal fog. Rule of thumb: factoring in an extra 20% or 25% more time than the GPS driving estimate lessens the chance you'll miss events or connections. Who knows? You might be surprised and arrive early—or at least on time.

DON'T LET GPS LEAD YOU ASTRAY
"Your GPS is Wrong: Turn Around," warns a sign on a steep dead-end road that some smartphone mapping apps mistake for a small mountain town's main drag below. Although GPS is generally reliable in cities and suburbs, it's less so in coastal, mountain, and desert areas, including some national and state parks. In addition to referencing the maps in this book, back yourself up with old-school atlases or fold-out paper maps.

If you plot out a trip and begin navigation while reception is good, you should still receive turning directions even if you move out of range. If you're already out of range when initiating a search, you won't be able to access route information.

THE COAST CAN BE FOGGY IN SUNNY CA
California rightfully earns its sunny reputation: on average, the sun shines more than two-thirds of the year in most regions, but with deserts, beaches, mountains, and forests, you should prepare for wide variations in temperature and conditions. This is especially true along the coast and at higher altitudes, where it's best to dress in layers year-round. On a day when it's 85° or 95° inland, the temperature along the coast can be 55° and windy.

In July and August, hot inland temperatures often cause cooler Pacific Ocean air—in the form of fog—to blanket areas nearest the shore. As a rule along the coast: the farther south you go, the drier and hotter the weather tends to be. The farther north you go, the cooler and wetter you'll likely find it.

"WINE COUNTRY" IS MORE THAN NAPA AND SONOMA
Modern California wine making got its start in Sonoma County, and Napa Valley wines raised the state's profile worldwide, but with about 4,800 bonded wineries from the Oregon border to San Diego County—the world's fourth-largest producer, making 80-plus percent of U.S. wines—the whole state's pretty much "Wine Country." Tasting rooms abound, even in unlikely places.

The state's most-planted red-wine grapes, in order, are Cabernet Sauvignon, Pinot Noir, Zinfandel, and Merlot. Among the whites, Chardonnay is by far the most grown, with French Colombard, Sauvignon Blanc, and Pinot Gris the runners-up.

NO NEED TO BREAK THE BANK
Away from coastal California or the eastern mountains on summer weekends or during ski season, much of California is affordable. In some cases, it's even a bargain. Tasting fees in lesser-known wine regions, for example, are at least half the price of those

in high-profile ones, and some wineries even provide sips for free. In many inland areas, except for the fanciest bed-and-breakfasts, room rates trend lower than by the shore.

AVOIDING STICKER SHOCK AT RESTAURANTS

Even if you're not dining at temples of haute cuisine, eating out in California can induce sticker shock. There are several ways to avoid this. Have the day's fancy meal at brunch or lunch, when prices tend to be lower. Happy hour, when a restaurant might serve a signature appetizer or smaller version of a famous plate at a lower price, is another option. Even small towns in the interior are likely to have a purveyor or two of gourmet food to go, making picnicking in a park or eating back at your lodging a viable strategy.

AVOIDING STICKER SHOCK AT HOTELS

California's hotels, inns, and resorts are the most expensive from late spring to early fall. The easiest way to avoid sticker shock is to come during winter when prices are the least expensive except at ski resorts and a few desert hot spots. Year-round, you can save money by traveling midweek, when rates tend to drop. Visiting during the shoulder seasons of mid-to-late spring and mid-to-late fall, when the weather can be nice and the crowds less formidable, can also save you money.

Many travelers cut costs by booking a big-city business hotel on the weekend, when rates trend lower (with Sunday often the cheapest night of the week at such places). Conversely, weekend prices at beach or countryside resorts are generally high but sometimes drop midweek.

MAKERS AND MUSEUMS

The state's early-21st-century DIY types birthed what's come to be known as the maker movement, and throughout California you'll see evidence of this artisanal activity. Blue jeans, lasers, Apple computers, sourdough bread, Popsicles, McDonald's, Barbie Dolls, Hollywood movie glamour, and television all emerged from California. Nearly 3,000 museums (more than any other state) honor such accomplishments and more—if you can think of it, a museum here probably celebrates it.

PLAY BALL

Because the weather is basically great year-round, there's a dynamic sports culture in the Golden State. Spectacular (and often free) recreation areas and parks offer opportunities for surfing, skiing, hiking, and biking, among other activities.

If you're more into spectating, California supports more professional sports teams than any other state, including five MLB, four NBA (plus one WNBA), three NFL and NHL franchises, and several (men's and women's) soccer squads. You can witness

athletic greatness at the highest levels any day of the week.

CALL OF THE WILDLIFE

Off the coast, creatures from gray and humpback whales to blue whales and orcas might come into view, along with sea lions, elephant seals, dolphins, and the occasional shark. Inland forests contain black bears, mountain lions, bobcats, beavers, and foxes. The desert supplies no end of reptiles, and the entire state is a birder's paradise.

Wild animals generally avoid interacting with humans, but contact is not unheard of. Most state and national parks post advice about steering clear of potentially dangerous encounters and what to do if you find yourself in one.

POT IS LEGAL, BUT...

Marijuana is legal in California for medical and recreational purposes. If you're 21 (or 18 with a doctor's order) and have proof of age or medical status, you can acquire and use marijuana, albeit not always in public. The California Cannabis Portal website maintains a searchable database (⊕ *search. cannabis.ca.gov/retailers*) of licensed dispensaries, where cannabis might come as flowers, edibles, and concentrates, among other things. The Cannabis Travel Association (⊕ *cannabistravelassociation.org*) promotes "safe and responsible cannabis tourism" and provides general information.

Getting Here and Around

Air

Most national and many international airlines fly to California. Flying time to the state is about 6 hours from New York and 4½ hours from Chicago. Travel from London to either Los Angeles or San Francisco is 10½ hours and from Sydney approximately 15 hours. Flying between San Francisco and Los Angeles takes about 90 minutes.

Bus

Greyhound is the primary bus carrier in California. Regional bus service is available in metropolitan areas.

Car

All passengers must wear a seat belt at all times. A child must be secured in a federally approved child passenger restraint system and ride in the back seat until at least eight years of age or until the child is at least 4 feet 9 inches tall. Unless indicated, right turns are allowed at red lights after you've come to a full stop. Drivers with a blood-alcohol level higher than 0.08 are subject to arrest.

You must turn on your headlights whenever weather conditions require the use of windshield wipers. Texting on a wireless device is illegal. If using a mobile phone while driving, it must be hands-free and mounted (i.e., it's not

From San Francisco to:	By Air	By Car
San Jose	No flights	U.S. 101; 50 miles; 1 hr
Monterey	N/A (no nonstops)	U.S. 101 to Hwy. 156 to Hwy. 1; 120 miles; 2 hrs
Los Angeles	90 mins	I–80 to I–580 to I–5; 382 miles; 5 hrs 40 mins
Portland, OR	1 hr 50 mins	I–80 to I–505 to I–5; 635 miles; 10 hrs
Mendocino	No flights	U.S. 101 to Hwy. 128 to Hwy. 1; 174 miles; 3 hrs
Yosemite NP/ Fresno	1 hr	I–80 to I–580 to I–205 to Hwy. 120 east; 184 miles; 3 hrs
Lake Tahoe/ Reno	1 hr	I–80; 220 miles; 3.5 hrs

legal having it loose on the seat or your lap). For more driving rules, refer to the Department of Motor Vehicles driver's handbook at

CAR RENTAL
When you reserve a car, ask about cancellation penalties, taxes, drop-off charges (to drop off in another city), and surcharges (for age, additional drivers, or driving across state or country borders).

ROAD CONDITIONS

View current road conditions online, or download the easier-to-use Caltrans QuickMap smartphone app. Rainy weather can make driving along the coast or in the mountains treacherous. Some smaller routes over mountain ranges and in the deserts are prone to flash flooding. Many smaller roads over the Sierra Nevada are closed in winter, and if it's snowing, tire chains may be required on routes that are open. Note, though, that most rental-car companies prohibit chain installation on their vehicles. If you disregard this rule, your insurance likely won't cover chains-related damage.

Standard chains or cables generally cost $55–$80. On some highways and freeways, uniformed chain installers charge around $40 to apply chains ($20 later to remove them) but aren't allowed to sell or rent chains. On lesser roads, you're on your own. It's less expensive to purchase chains before you get to the mountains.

RULES OF THE ROAD

All passengers must wear a seat belt at all times. A child must be secured in a federally approved child passenger restraint system and ride in the back seat until at least eight years of age or until the child is at least 4 feet 9 inches tall. Unless indicated, right turns are allowed at red lights after you've come to a full stop. Drivers with a blood-alcohol level higher than 0.08 are subject to arrest.

You must turn on your headlights whenever weather conditions require the use of windshield wipers. Texting on a wireless device is illegal. If using a mobile phone while driving, it must be hands-free and mounted (i.e., it's not legal having it loose on the seat or your lap). For more driving rules, refer to the Department of Motor Vehicles driver's handbook at ⊕ *www.dmv.ca.gov.*

Train

Amtrak provides rail service within California. On some trips, passengers board motor coaches part of the way.

Essentials

Activities

Athletic Californians often boast that it's possible to surf in the morning and ski in the afternoon (or vice versa) in the Golden State. With thousands of hiking, biking, and horse-riding trails and hundreds of lakes, rivers, and streams for fishing, swimming, and boating—not to mention sandy coastal strands for sunning and surfing and other beaches with dunes or rocks to explore—there's no shortage of outdoor fun to be had. One challenge on many a hiker's bucket list is the Pacific Crest Trail, which travels the length of the state. The National Park Service operates numerous parks and sites in California, and the state park system is robust. If you're interested in Native American heritage, Visit California's website (visitcalifornia.com/native) has a section devoted to indigenous cultural travel.

Dining

California has led the pack in bringing natural and organic foods to the forefront of American dining. Though rooted in European cuisine, California cooking sometimes has strong Asian and Latin influences. Wherever you go, you're likely to find that dishes are made with fresh produce and other local ingredients.

The restaurants we list are the cream of the crop in each price category. Restaurant reviews have been shortened. For full information, visit Fodors.com. For price information, see the Planning sections in each chapter.

DISCOUNTS AND DEALS

The better grocery and specialty-food stores have grab-and-go sections, with prepared foods on par with restaurant cooking, perfect for picnicking.

MEALS AND MEALTIMES

Lunch is typically served from 11 or 11:30 to 2:30 or 3, with dinner service starting at 5 or 5:30 and lasting until 9 or later. Restaurants that serve breakfast usually open by 7, sometimes earlier, with some serving breakfast through the lunch hour. Most weekend brunches start at 10 or 11 and go at least until 2.

PAYING

Most restaurants take credit cards. Some accept cash, but others operate cashless. In most establishments tipping is the norm, but some include the service in the menu price or add it to the bill. For guidelines on tipping see Money, below.

RESERVATIONS AND DRESS

It's a good idea to make a reservation when possible. Where reservations are indicated as essential, book a week or more ahead in summer and early fall. Large parties should always call ahead to check the reservations policy. Except as noted in individual listings, dress is informal.

Health/Safety

If you have a medical condition that may require emergency treatment, be aware that many rural and mountain communities have only daytime clinics, not hospitals with 24-hour emergency rooms. Take the usual precautions to protect your person and belongings. In large cities, ask at your lodging about areas to avoid, and lock valuables in a hotel safe when not using them. Car break-ins are common in some larger cities, but it's always a good idea to remove valuables from your car or at least keep them out of sight.

COVID-19

Most travel restrictions, including vaccination and masking requirements, have been lifted across the United States except in health-care facilities and nursing homes. Some travelers may still wish to wear a mask in confined spaces, including on airplanes, on public transportation, and at large indoor gatherings, but that is increasingly a personal choice. Be aware that some local mandates still exist and should be followed.

THE OUTDOORS

At beaches, heed warnings about high surf and deadly rogue waves, and don't fly within 24 hours of scuba diving. When hiking, stay on trails, and heed all warning signs about loose cliffs, predatory animals, and poison ivy or oak.

Before heading into remote areas, let someone know your trip route, destination, and estimated time and date of return. Make sure your vehicle is in good condition and equipped with a first-aid kit, snacks, extra water, jack, spare tire, tools, and a towrope or chain. Mind your gas gauge, keeping the needle above half if possible and stopping to top off the tank whenever you can.

In arid regions, stay on main roads, and watch out for wildlife, horses, and cattle. Don't enter mine tunnels or shafts. Not only can such structures be unstable, but they might also have hidden dangers such as pockets of bad air. Be mindful of sudden rainstorms, when floodwaters can cover or wash away roads and quickly fill up dry riverbeds and canyons. Never place your hands or feet where you can't see them: rattlesnakes, scorpions, and black widow spiders may be hiding there.

Sunscreen and hats are musts, and layered clothing is best as desert temperatures can fluctuate greatly between dawn and dusk. Drink at least a gallon of water a day (three gallons if you're hiking or otherwise exerting yourself). If you have a headache or feel dizzy or nauseous, you could be suffering from dehydration. Get out of the sun immediately, dampen your clothing to lower your body temperature, and drink plenty of water.

Although you might not feel thirsty in cooler, mountain climes, it's important to stay hydrated (drinking at least a quart of water during activities) at high altitudes, where the air is thinner, causing you to breathe more heavily. Always bring a fold-up rain poncho to keep you dry and prevent hypothermia. Wear long pants, a hat, and sturdy, closed-toe hiking boots with soles that grip rock. If you're going into the backcountry, bring a signaling device (such as a mirror), emergency whistle, compass, map, energy bars, and water purifier.

⊞ Lodging

California has inns, motels, hotels, and specialty accommodations to suit every traveler's fancy and finances. Retro motels recalling 1950s roadside culture but with 21st-century amenities are a popular trend, but you'll also see traditional motels and hotels, along with luxury resorts and boutique properties.

The state's more than 1,000 bed-and-breakfasts offer everything from simple home-stay options to lavish lodgings in historic hotels or homes. The California Association of Boutique and Breakfast Inns represents more than 200 member properties that you can locate and book through its website. In addition, you'll find listings for Airbnb and similar rentals throughout California.

Essentials

The lodgings we review are the top choices in each price category. We don't specify whether the facilities cost extra; when pricing accommodations, ask what's included and what costs extra.

CHILDREN

Most hotels allow children under a certain age to stay in their parents' room at no extra charge, but others charge for them as additional adults; find out the cutoff age for discounts. Conversely, some accommodations aren't suitable for children, so check before you book.

RESERVATIONS AND CANCELLATIONS

Reservations are a good idea throughout the year, especially in summer. On week-ends at smaller lodgings, minimum-stay requirements of two or three nights are common, though some places are flexible about this in winter.

Some properties allow you to cancel without a penalty—even if you prepaid to secure a discounted rate—if you cancel at least 24 hours in advance. Others require you to cancel a week in advance or penalize you the cost of one night. Small inns and B&Bs are most likely to require you to cancel far in advance.

$ Money

On the coast, you'll pay top dollar for everything from gas and food to lodging and attractions. Aside from desert and ski resorts, inland prices tend to be lower.

In terms of gratuities, obviously the amount you tip (or if you tip at all) is a

Tipping Guidelines for California	
Bartender	$1–$3 per drink, or 15%–20% per round
Bellhop	$2–$5 per bag, depending on the level of the hotel
Hotel Concierge	$5–$10 for advice and reservations, more for difficult tasks
Hotel Doorman	$3–$5 for hailing a cab
Valet Parking Attendant	$3–$5 when you get your car
Hotel Maid	$4–$6 per day (either daily or at the end of your stay, in cash)
Waiter	18%–22% (20%–25% is standard in upscale restaurants); nothing additional if a service charge is added to the bill
Skycap at Airport	$2 per bag
Hotel Room-Service Waiter	15%–20% per delivery, even if a service charge was added since that fee goes to the hotel, not the waiter
Tasting-room server	$5–$10 per couple basic tasting, $5–$10 per person hosted seated tasting
Taxi Driver	15%–20%, but round up the fare to the next dollar amount
Tour Guide	15% of the cost of the tour, more depending on quality

matter of personal preference. Remember, though, that in California, as in the rest of the United States, many people who work in the service industry rely on tips to earn a living wage. The degree and quality of service also come into play when considering what to tip.

TAXES

Depending on the city or county, you'll pay from 7.25% to 10.75% in sales tax, with larger urban areas toward the higher end. Exceptions include grocery-store food items and some takeout. Hotel taxes vary from 4% to 15%.

🖸 Packing

The California lifestyle emphasizes casual wear, and with the generally mild climate you needn't worry about packing cold-weather clothing unless you're going into mountainous areas. Jeans, walking shorts, and T-shirts are acceptable in most situations. Few restaurants require men to wear a jacket or tie, though a collared shirt is the norm at upscale establishments.

Summer evenings can be cool, especially near the coast, where fog often rolls in. Always pack a sweater or light jacket. If you're headed to state or national parks, packing binoculars, clothes that layer, long pants and long-sleeve shirts, sunglasses, and a wide-brimmed hat is wise. Pick up insect repellent, sunscreen, and a first-aid kit once in-state.

🗓 When to Go

Expect high summer heat in the desert areas and low winter temperatures in the Sierra Nevada and other inland mountain ranges.

HIGH SEASON $$$–$$$$

High season lasts from late May through early September (a little later in wine regions and well into winter in desert resorts and ski areas). Expect higher hotel occupancy rates and prices.

LOW SEASON $$

From December to March, tourist activity slows. Except in the mountainous areas, which may see snowfall and an influx of skiers, winters here are mild, and hotels are cheaper.

VALUE SEASON $$–$$$

From April to late May and from late September to mid-November the weather is pleasant and hotel prices are reasonable.

Contacts

Air

AIRLINES

CONTACTS **Air Canada.** ☎ 888/247–2262 ⊕ www. aircanada.com. **Alaska Airlines/Horizon Air.** ☎ 800/252–7522 ⊕ www. alaskaair.com. **American Airlines.** ☎ 800/433–7300 ⊕ www.aa.com. **Delta Airlines.** ☎ 800/221–1212 for U.S. reservations, 800/241–4141 for international reservations ⊕ www.delta.com. **Frontier Airlines.** ☎ 801/401–9000 ⊕ www.flyfrontier.com. **JetBlue.** ☎ 800/538–2583 ⊕ www.jetblue.com. **Southwest Airlines.** ☎ 800/435–9792 ⊕ www. southwest.com. **United Airlines.** ☎ 800/864–8331 ⊕ www.united.com.

AIRLINE SECURITY ISSUES

CONTACTS **Transportation Security Administration.** (*TSA*). ☎ 866/289–9673 ⊕ www.tsa.gov.

AIRPORTS

CONTACTS **Oakland International Airport.** ☎ 510/563–3300 ⊕ www. oaklandairport.com. **Sacramento International Airport.** ☎ 916/929–5411 ⊕ www. sacramento.aero/smf.

San Francisco International Airport. ☎ 650/821–8211, 800/435–9736 ⊕ www. flysfo.com. **San Jose Mineta International Airport.** ☎ 408/392–3600 ⊕ www. flysanjose.com.

Bus

CONTACTS **Greyhound.** ☎ 800/231–2222 ⊕ www. greyhound.com.

Car

ASSISTANCE **American Automobile Association.** (*AAA*). ☎ 800/222–4357 ⊕ www.aaa.com.

INFORMATION **Caltrans Current Highway Conditions.** ☎ 800/427–7623 ⊕ quickmap.dot.ca.gov. **511 Traffic/Transit Alerts.** ☎ 511.

MAJOR RENTAL AGENCIES **Alamo.** ☎ 800/462–5266 ⊕ www.alamo.com. **Avis.** ☎ 800/633–3469 ⊕ www.avis.com. **Budget.** ☎ 800/218–7992 ⊕ www. budget.com. **Hertz.** ☎ 800/654–3131 ⊕ www. hertz.com. **National Car Rental.** ☎ 844/382–6875 ⊕ www.nationalcar.com.

SPECIALTY CAR AGENCIES **Enterprise Exotic Car Rentals.** ☎ 866/458–9227 ⊕ www. enterprise.com.

Lodging

CONTACTS **California Association of Boutique and Breakfast Inns.** (*CABBI*). ☎ 800/373–9251 ⊕ www. cabbi.com.

Train

CONTACTS **Amtrak.** ☎ 800/872–7245 ⊕ www. amtrak.com.

Chapter 3

NORTHERN CALIFORNIA'S BEST ROAD TRIPS

Updated by
Daniel Mangin

A California visit wouldn't be complete without taking a spin through the state's spectacular scenery. However, adding a road trip to your itinerary is not just a romantic idea: it's often a practical one, too—perhaps linking one urban area with another, say, or sampling some of this massive state's remote areas. Whether you have just a few days or longer to spare, these itineraries will help you hit the road.

Monterey Bay to San Francisco, 4 Days

Another glorious section of Highway 1 stretches north from Monterey Bay to San Francisco. The drive to San Francisco only takes three hours, but there's enough history and scenery to fill three leisurely days. Book two nights at a Monterey or Carmel-by-the-Sea hotel or inn, arriving the evening before to maximize your time here. Occupying prime bayside real estate, the **Monterey Plaza Hotel & Spa** is the gateway to Cannery Row, with the less-expensive **Casa Munras** winning bonus points for the tapas at its Estéban Restaurant. Head to inland Carmel Valley to splurge at **Bernardus Lodge**; Carmel's **Pine Inn** and **Tally Ho Inn** are less showy but well located.

DAY 1: MONTEREY
15 mins by car, less than an hr by foot.

Monterey is the perfect spot to kick off a coastal tour. Start with a visit to the enthralling **Monterey Bay Aquarium.** Exhibits such as the dramatic three-story kelp forest near the entrance give you a true sense of the local marine environment, much of it federally protected. Take to the water on a kayak or whale-watching tour for an even closer encounter. While undoubtedly touristy, the shops and galleries of **Cannery Row** still make for an interesting diversion, and it's fun to watch the colony of sea lions at **Fisherman's Wharf.** Enjoy a seafood dinner downtown and an evening stroll before hitting the road the following day.

DAY 2: 17-MILE DRIVE AND CARMEL-BY-THE-SEA

The 17-Mile Drive's Pacific Grove entrance gate is 20 mins by car from Monterey.

Begin your drive with a spin along the shoreline in the Victorian town of **Pacific Grove.** Pick up Ocean View Boulevard near the aquarium and head northwest. If your visit falls between October and March, detour off Ocean View to see the migrating monarch butterflies at the **Monarch Grove Sanctuary.**

Enter the **17-Mile Drive** through the tollgate off Sunset Drive in Pacific Grove. This scenic road winds along the coast through a hushed and refined landscape of stunning homes and the celebrated golf links at **Pebble Beach.** Perhaps the most famous (and photographed) resident is the **Lone Cypress,** which has come to symbolize the coast's solitude and natural beauty. Even though the drive is only 17 miles, take your time. If you stop for lunch or souvenir shopping, inquire about a refund on the entry toll.

Upon exiting the drive, continue south to **Carmel-by-the-Sea.** Spend the afternoon browsing its boutiques and galleries before walking to **Carmel Beach** for sunset, followed by dinner at one of Carmel's many fine restaurants.

DAY 3: SANTA CRUZ

A little less than 1 hr by car from Monterey or Carmel-by-the-Sea.

Depart your hotel midmorning, and pick up Highway 1, following its curve around Monterey Bay north toward Santa Cruz. For a magical experience, book an **Elkhorn Slough Safari Nature Boat Tour.** You'll see otters and plenty of other creatures up close. From the tour, head to **Seacliff State Beach,** a strand in Aptos known for its tall sandstone bluffs. The 1½-mile walk to adjacent New Brighton State Beach is highly scenic.

From the beaches, continue to Santa Cruz, and check into your hotel. If it fits your budget, the **Dream Inn Santa Cruz,** the city's only lodging directly on the beach, is the most convenient choice, with the **Hotel Paradox** another good option. Once settled in, stroll the **Santa Cruz Boardwalk,** and catch the sunset over cocktails, dinner, or both. If time permits, walk or drive a bit of **West Cliff Drive,** which winds around to a lighthouse.

DAY 4: SANTA CRUZ TO SAN FRANCISCO

90 mins by car in light traffic, not counting stops.

Highway 1 darts up the coast 77 miles to San Francisco, occasionally so close to the Pacific that a section collapses into the sea and requires rebuilding. Although not as dramatic as Big Sur to the south or Mendocino to the north, the landscape still is fetching.

Let your desire to arrive in San Francisco control your pace. At **Año Nuevo State Park,** you can hike a short way to the dunes to observe the resident elephant seals. If you're getting hungry, knotty-pine-paneled **Duarte's Tavern,** in business in **Pescadero** since 1894, delivers a blast from the past along with stick-to-your-ribs American standards like deep-fried calamari and pork chops with old-school applesauce. To reach the restaurant, head east 2 miles on Pescadero Creek Road. **Half Moon Bay,** 17 miles north, has more updated fare.

Suburban encroachment becomes more evident as you approach San Francisco. Head east on Highway 92 to I–280 north to get to San Francisco more quickly; otherwise, continue on Highway 1 and enjoy the coastal scenery.

San Francisco's Greatest Hits, 3 Days

DAY 1: UNION SQUARE, CHINATOWN, NORTH BEACH
30–45 mins on public transport.

Head to your hotel straight from the airport, staying above the fray at the **Hotel Drisco** in tony Pacific Heights or amid the south of Market Street (SoMa) action at the lighthearted **Hotel Zetta.** From the Drisco, drive or ride-share to **Union Square** (a short walk north from the Zetta), which packs a wallop of people-watching, window-shopping, and architecture viewing. **Chinatown**—chock-full of dim sum shops, storefront temples, and open-air markets—promises authentic bites for lunch or a late-afternoon snack. Catch a Powell Street **cable car** to the end of the line, and get off to see the bay views and the antique arcade games at **Musée Mécanique,** the hidden gem of otherwise mindless **Fisherman's Wharf.** No need to go any farther than cosmopolitan **North Beach** for cocktail hour, dinner, and live music.

DAY 2: THREE ICONIC SIGHTS
About 1 hr by car, taxi, or rideshare, 2½ hrs by public transport.

Today's all about iconic sights. Begin the morning with a brief, brisk bay cruise to **Alcatraz,** the famous island prison in the middle of San Francisco Bay. Start as early as possible (the first boat departs at 8:45 am in summer), and plan on spending at least three hours round-trip. If you're staying at the Drisco, inquire the night before about the free chauffeur-driven car the hotel provides 7 am–11 am for one-way in-town trips.

Back on land, head to **Golden Gate Bridge's** southern (San Francisco) side. If the weather's nice, walk at least to the orange wonder's south tower; the parking lot at the bridge's northern end yields textbook SF selfies.

From the bridge, zip south to **Golden Gate Park.** Choose your initial stops based on your interests, lingering amid the flora of the **Conservatory of Flowers** or the **San Francisco Botanical Garden at Strybing Arboretum,** soaking up the art at the **de Young Museum,** or being enchanted by the well-conceived exhibits at the **California Academy of Sciences.** Afterward, find serene refreshment at the **San Francisco Japanese Tea Garden.**

A late-afternoon cocktail at the **Beach Chalet** will whet your appetite for dinner back in Pac Heights or SoMa.

DAY 3: ROAMIN' AROUND
About 1 hr of driving total, not counting traffic, 2 hrs by public transport.

Begin the day with a dose of culture at the **San Francisco Museum of Modern Art,** visiting one or two of the other nearby downtown museums on Wednesday, when SFMOMA is closed. Walk, drive, ride-share, or hop on a public bus heading less than a mile east to the **Ferry Building,** browsing the bodegas and lunching here before strolling the **Embarcadero.**

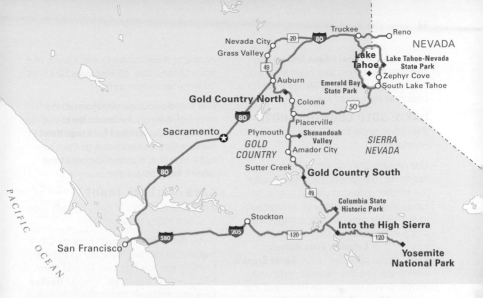

If you haven't ridden a cable car yet, catch one on California Street up to Nob Hill. If you've been driving, retrieve your vehicle, and proceed to **Japantown.** Otherwise, ride-share or switch to public transit (on Sacramento Street); if on the bus, alight at Webster Street and walk south a few blocks.

Visit the gay **Castro District** if you have time, in any case bidding the City by the Bay adieu on Market Street at the Palace Hotel's wood-paneled **Pied Piper Bar,** where Maxfield Parrish's storied painting *The Pied Piper of Hamelin* has anchored the lounge for more than a century.

Sierra Riches: Yosemite, Gold Country, and Tahoe, 7 Days

This tour of some of California's most inspiring terrain serves up gold-rush-era history and offers a chance to hike a trail or two. Particularly in summer, book a room within Yosemite National Park (the Ahwahnee Hotel and the Wawona Hotel being the two historic choices) well ahead of your visit. Gateway towns such as Oakhurst and Mariposa can be less expensive, but you'll have to drive more.

DAY 1: INTO THE HIGH SIERRA
4–5 hrs by car from San Francisco.

First thing, head for the hills. Arriving in **Yosemite National Park, Bridalveil Fall,** and **El Capitan,** the 350-story granite monolith, greet you en route to **Yosemite Village.** Ditch the car, and pick up information and refreshment before boarding the shuttle to explore. Famous sights cram Yosemite Valley: massive **Half Dome** and **Sentinel Dome,** thundering **Yosemite Falls,** and wispy **Ribbon Fall** and **Nevada Fall.** Short hikes off the shuttle route lead to numerous vantage points. Even if you're not staying at the **Ahwahnee Hotel,** stop in for a cocktail.

DAY 2: YOSEMITE NATIONAL PARK
Yosemite shuttles run every 10–30 mins.

Ardent hikers consider **John Muir Trail to Half Dome** a must-do, tackling the rigorous 12-hour round-trip to the top of Half Dome. Mere mortals hike downhill from Glacier Point on **Four-Mile** or **Panorama trails,** the latter an all-day trek past waterfalls. Less demanding still is a drive to Wawona to the **Mariposa Grove of Big Trees,** followed by lunch at the 19th-century **Wawona Hotel Dining Room.** Take shelter in the **Ansel Adams Gallery** and **Yosemite Museum** in bad weather. If conditions permit, head to **Glacier Point** for a breathtaking sunset view.

DAY 3: GOLD COUNTRY SOUTH

2½–3 hrs by car from Yosemite Valley to Plymouth.

Get an early start driving west from Yosemite to Highway 49, which traces the mother lode that yielded many fortunes in gold (and plenty of heartaches) in the 1800s. You can ride a stagecoach and pan for riches in the living-history town at **Columbia State Historic Park.** About 46 miles north, **Sutter Creek's** well-preserved downtown bursts with shops, or you can explore history at the outdoor **Miners' Bend** park and **Knight Foundry.** Switch focus in the Shenandoah Valley, the heart of the Sierra Foothills Wine Country. Taste your way through Zinfandels at **Turley Wine Cellars,** that varietal plus Cabernets and Rhône-style wines at **Terre Rouge and Easton Wines,** or Barbera and more at **Andis Wines.** Retire in modest boutique comfort at **Rest Hotel Plymouth,** whose owners also operate nearby **Taste** restaurant.

DAY 4: GOLD COUNTRY NORTH

1½–2 hrs by car from Plymouth to Nevada City, not counting stops.

From Plymouth, drive north on Highway 49. Once in El Dorado County, detour east on U.S. 50 to learn about **Placerville**-area wines at **Starfield Vineyards** or **Lava Cap Winery,** or continue north on Highway 49 to **Marshall Gold Discovery State Historic Park.** Encompassing most of **Coloma,** the park preserves the spot where James Marshall's 1848 find set off the California gold rush. If you went to the winery, backtrack to Highway 49, continuing north past Coloma, and stop in Old Town **Auburn** for lunch. The **Auburn Alehouse** is open daily, but there are other choices in the historic district. After lunch, continue north to Grass Valley's **Empire Mine State Historic Park,** which

closes at 5 pm, so try to arrive by 3. The drive to the mine, off Highway 20, takes 35 minutes in light traffic.

The same company transformed the mid-19th-century **Holbrooke Hotel** in Grass Valley and the **National Exchange Hotel** in Nevada City into boutique gems. Overnight at either, but have dinner at the latter's **Lola** restaurant.

DAYS 5–7: LAKE TAHOE

About 75 mins by car from Nevada City or Grass Valley to Tahoe City.

If you didn't stroll through Nevada City's historic district on Day 4, do so before heading east on Highway 20 and then I-80 toward Lake Tahoe. Stop in **Truckee** for lunch and walk its historic downtown. From there, continue south on Highway 89 to **Tahoe City,** on the northern shore of jewel-like **Lake Tahoe.**

Where you stay and the time of year will determine the order in which you explore the 72-mile shoreline of Lake Tahoe, bisected north–south by the California–Nevada border. Regardless, some backtracking is inevitable. Two noteworthy North Lake Tahoe lodgings are the **Sunnyside Restaurant and Lodge** (Tahoe City, California side) and the **Hyatt Regency Lake Tahoe Resort, Spa and Casino** (Nevada side). **Desolation Hotel Lake Tahoe** and the **Black Bear Lodge** are good South Lake Tahoe (California) choices; **The Lodge at Edgewood Tahoe** provides the classiest, albeit most expensive, stay in Stateline (Nevada), where the casino hotels are active 24/7.

Clockwise from South Lake Tahoe, the top sights and activities include riding the **Heavenly Gondola** to see the lake from up high; hopping aboard a vintage **Tahoe Tastings** boat to (seasonally) sip wines; paddling a clear (see-through) kayak on a tour led by **Clearly Tahoe's** expert crew; or visiting the three magnificent estates in the **Pope-Baldwin Recreation Area.** Farther along, the lake views from **Emerald Bay State Park** inspire year-round; season and stamina permitting, hike down to the **Vikingsholm** Scandinavian-style castle.

Continuing clockwise, **North Lake Tahoe**'s pleasures include more boat rides from **Tahoe City** (also more history and ample dining); outdoor sports in **Incline Village** plus tours of **Thunderbird Lodge;** and Tahoe cruises aboard the stern-wheeler MS *Dixie II* departing from **Zephyr Cove.** Continue south to **Stateline** to try your luck at the casinos, or head to the beaches and bays of **Lake Tahoe–Nevada State Park**.

Ultimate Napa and Sonoma Wine Trip, 4 Days

On this loop north from San Francisco into the Wine Country, you'll taste well-known and under-the-radar wines, bed down in plush hotels, and dine at celebrity-chef restaurants. Reservations are required for most tasting-room visits and advised for dinner.

DAY 1: SOUTHERN SONOMA
About 90 mins total by car from San Francisco.

Head north from San Francisco to **Sonoma.** Less than an hour after crossing the Golden Gate Bridge, you'll be holding a glass of Chardonnay at **Sangiacomo Family Wines,** also known for Pinot Noir. The outdoor tasting areas here overlook land the Sangiacomos have farmed since 1927. Alternatively, book a tasting a few miles west at **Schug Carneros Estate Winery,** which makes Chardonnay and Pinot Noir plus Cabernet Sauvignon and other wines from Bordeaux varietals.

Next, explore the shops bordering or near Sonoma Plaza, and have lunch at the **Girl and the Fig** or the **Sausage Emporium.** Then, head north to **Glen Ellen,** whose famous writer-residents have included M.F.K. Fisher, Hunter S. Thompson, and, most

notably, Jack London. Visit **Jack London State Historic Park,** the writer's memorabilia-filled estate, or enjoy a tasting at **Benziger Family Winery** or **Lasseter Family Winery.** Dine at **Glen Ellen Star,** and stay at the **Gaige House** or the **Olea Hotel.**

DAY 2: NORTHERN SONOMA
About 75 mins total by car.

From Glen Ellen, drive 40 minutes northwest on Highway 12 and north on U.S. 101 to **Healdsburg.** Start your tasting outside town amid rolling vineyards at **Ridge Vineyards** (Zinfandel, Cabernet, Petite Sirah) or **MacRostie Estate House** (Chardonnay and Pinot Noir). Have an informal lunch at **Dry Creek General Store,** in business since 1881.

After lunch, drive to the French-style chateau at **Jordan Vineyard & Winery** to taste Chardonnay and Cabernet Sauvignon. If you're staying at the luxurious 250-acre **Montage Healdsburg** (book dinner at the resort's **Hazel Hill** restaurant), you're just minutes away. Two in-town lodgings, the **Harmon Guest House** and the **River Belle Inn,** are highly recommended. Have dinner at **Bravas Bar de Tapas** or **The Matheson,** both near the plaza. For a splurge, reserve a table (well ahead) at **SingleThread Farms Restaurant.**

DAY 3: NORTHERN NAPA VALLEY
About 75 mins total by car.

Head into the northern Napa Valley via Alexander Valley Road and Highway 128, which winds east to **Calistoga** through dairy pasture and the vineyards of the Knights Valley appellation. **Chateau Montelena** made history in the 1970s when its Chardonnay took top honors at a famous Paris tasting. After a sample here or at nearby **Bennett Lane Winery** (Cabernet and other Bordeaux-style reds), continue south 15 minutes on Highway 29 to St. Helena.

Much Napa Valley history unfolded at **Charles Krug Winery,** which began operations in 1861. Taste Cabernets and other Bordeaux-style reds here, then have lunch at nearby **Brasswood Bar + Kitchen** (or Brasswood's bakery) or downtown at **Cook St. Helena** (weekdays only) or **Market.** Afterward, poke through Main Street shops before continuing south on Highway 29 to **Hall St. Helena** (high-scoring Cabernets, impressive art collection) or its homey neighbor **Prager Winery & Port Works.** Backtrack to Calistoga to stay at the small but hospitable **Brannan Cottage Inn,** or **Solage,** an upscale-casual resort. The latter's **Solbar** is a top Calistoga restaurant; **Lovina** and **Sam's Social Club** are also fine options.

DAY 4: SOUTHERN NAPA VALLEY
45 mins driving in Napa Valley, 1 hr back to San Francisco.

After breakfast, head south on Highway 29 to Oakville, where sipping wine at **Far Niente** or **Silver Oak** makes clear why collectors covet Oakville Cabernet Sauvignons. Far Niente is west of Highway 29 off Oakville Grade Road; Silver Oak is east of the highway on Oakville Cross Road. After tasting, stop for lunch just north of Yountville at Cindy Pawlcyn's **Mustards Grill** (on Highway 29) or in **Yountville** at Thomas Keller's **Bouchon Bistro.** Even offseason, make a reservation at either. Afterward, explore intriguing shops on downtown Yountville's Washington Street.

From Yountville, pop back on Highway 29 and head south to Highway 121. Turn west (right) to reach **Domaine Carneros,** world-famous for its sparkling wines. There's hardly a more elegant way to bid a Wine Country adieu than on the vineyard-view terrace of this winery's splendid chateau. If you can't tear yourself away from the Wine Country, extend your stay at the **Archer Hotel Napa,** the **Inn on First** in downtown Napa, or the **Carneros Resort & Spa,** a short drive east of Domaine Carneros.

Best of the North Coast, 5 Days

Hit coastal Northern California's highlights in one Highway 1 itinerary: scenic coastal drives, windswept towns, wine tasting, culinary delights, and redwood forests. You can also make this route part of a longer trip north to the Oregon border, or loop back to San Francisco.

DAY 1: MARIN COUNTY AND POINT REYES NATIONAL SEASHORE
Without stops, Point Reyes National Seashore is about 1½ hrs by car from San Francisco on Hwy 1. Point Reyes Lighthouse is 45 mins by car from the visitor center.

Heading to San Francisco on the Golden Gate Bridge, pull over at the **scenic lookout** on the north side, and take in the classic skyline view. If you haven't yet checked out the picturesque harbor community of **Sausalito,** just north of the bridge, now is your chance. It will be hard

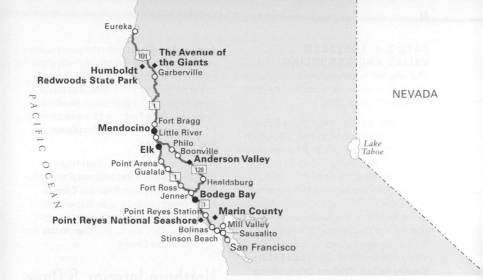

not to linger, but there's still much to see. Bidding San Francisco farewell, you will quickly find yourself amid the natural splendor of Marin County. Exit U.S. 101 onto Highway 1 at **Mill Valley** and head to **Muir Woods National Monument.** Amid the tall coastal redwoods, you may forget that San Francisco lies less than a dozen miles away. However, the proximity to the city means that Muir Woods attracts throngs; be sure to make a mandatory parking or shuttle reservation a day or two ahead (more in summer).

From Muir Woods, continue on Highway 1 past the laid-back towns of **Stinson Beach** and **Bolinas** to **Point Reyes National Seashore.** Spend the rest of the day tide pooling, kayaking, hiking one of the many trails, or exploring the **Point Reyes Lighthouse.** Watch for migrating gray whales in winter and early spring. **Point Reyes Station** has shops and restaurants, including **Tomales Bay Foods.** Spend a quiet evening in town and stay overnight at one of the nearby inns.

DAY 2: BODEGA BAY TO ELK
Point Reyes Station to Elk via Highway 1 is 3 hrs by car, not counting stops.

Continue north on Highway 1 past the town of **Bodega Bay,** which starred in the

1963 Alfred Hitchcock movie *The Birds.* At **Jenner,** known for its resident harbor seals, stop for lunch at **River's End.**

Drive north to **Fort Ross State Historic Park,** a restored remnant of Russia's 19th-century fur-trapping era. The highway continues winding past small towns like Gualala and **Point Arena,** the latter worth a stop for its windswept lighthouse east of town. (The town's few restaurants are good, but their hours and days open are variable.) From Point Arena, continue north up the coast to the quirky but increasingly upscale town of **Elk,** where you can choose between three cliffside resorts, all of which have good restaurants.

Note: the highway twists dramatically between Marin and Mendocino. Take precautions if anyone in your party is prone to car sickness. For a less winding route, albeit 40 or so miles longer, turn east at Jenner on Highway 116, north on U.S. 101 at Santa Rosa. Stop for lunch in Healdsburg, then get back on U.S. 101 heading north to Highway 128, following it northwest to Highway 1, on which you'll turn south (left).

DAYS 3–4: ANDERSON VALLEY AND MENDOCINO

The nearest Anderson Valley wineries are about 30 mins by car from Elk, the two farthest about 45 mins.

Drive north on Highway 1 from Elk, and turn east (right) on Highway 128, which follows the Navarro River through several miles of breathtaking redwood forest before entering the Anderson Valley, famous for Pinot Noir and Chardonnay (also Gewürztraminer and other Alsace white varietals). The laid-back atmosphere of its tasting rooms makes them refreshing alternatives to those in Napa Valley. From east to west, **Lula Cellars, Handley Cellars, Roederer Estate, Lichen Estate, Foursight Wines,** and **Pennyroyal Farm** are all recommended. The small towns of **Boonville** and **Philo** have high-quality restaurants.

Backtrack west on Highway 1 and head south back to Elk or north to **Mendocino** and **Little River,** which have noteworthy restaurants and inns, too. Continue north 10 miles past Mendocino to **Fort Bragg,** where some reasonably priced motels and inns have full ocean views. Spend the next day and a half exploring the area. Opportunities for stunning coastal walks abound, including the **Mendocino Headlands State Park, Van Damme State Park,** and the **Fort Bragg Coastal Trail.** Save time to explore Mendocino village, with its galleries, boutiques, and New England–style architecture.

DAY 5: HUMBOLDT REDWOODS STATE PARK AND THE AVENUE OF THE GIANTS

Mendocino to Eureka via The Avenue of the Giants is 3 hrs by car.

Heading north, Highway 1 eventually curves inland, joining U.S. 101 near Leggett. Continue north on U.S. 101 to reach the redwoods. A drive through **The Avenue of the Giants** will take your breath away. The 32-mile stretch of road, also signed as Highway 254, runs alongside some of the planet's tallest trees as it weaves through a portion of **Humboldt Redwoods State Park.** Try to make time for a short hike through **Founders Grove** or **Rockefeller Forest.**

From here, continue up the coast through **Redwood National and State Parks** and on to the Oregon border. Alternatively, head south on U.S. 101 and either return to **San Francisco** or combine this itinerary with a trip to the **Napa Valley** and inland **Sonoma County.**

Northern Interior, 5 Days

Mountain peaks, alpine lakes, a lush waterfall, and a volcanic landscape are all part of this tour. The drive packs a big scenic punch in a short amount of time and without the crowds found elsewhere in California's national parks. The remote roads and high elevations make parts of this route subject to snow closures well into the spring, so check road conditions.

DAY 1: SACRAMENTO TO CHICO

1½ hrs by car.

Start your trip touring the highlights of California's capita, **Sacramento.** Wander the cobblestone streets of the **Old Sacramento Waterfront** for a sense of the gold-rush era. Enjoy the walk-through exhibits at the **California State Railroad Museum,** and tour the magnificent **Capitol** building or **Leland Stanford Mansion State Historic Park** (both free) if there's time.

Departing Sacramento, drive north on Highway 99 to **Chico.** Overnighting here gets you a jump-start on the next day's drive. Stop at **Sierra Nevada Brewing Company** for a tour and/or a brewpub meal.

DAYS 2–3: LASSEN VOLCANIC NATIONAL PARK

1½–2 hrs by car from Chico.

Follow Highway 32 northeast from Chico toward Chester, branching northwest at Highway 36 to reach the southern entrance of **Lassen Volcanic National Park.** Spend the next two days exploring geothermal features and dramatic landscapes. Highlights include a hike alongside the bubbling mud pots and hot springs of **Bumpass Hell Trail,** views of **Lassen Peak** from Manzanita Lake, or an ascent of the peak itself. On your second day, drive part of the **Volcanic Legacy Scenic Byway**'s, southern loop, which winds through Lassen national park and forest.

Plan far ahead to score a reservation at the **Highlands Ranch Resort** or one of the park's campgrounds. Otherwise, bunk in Chester. In winter, portions of Lassen are closed to vehicles. If so, skip the park and drive to **McArthur-Burney Falls Memorial State Park** from Chico via Highway 299.

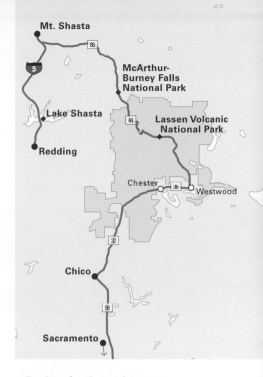

DAY 4: MCARTHUR-BURNEY FALLS NATIONAL PARK AND MT. SHASTA

McArthur-Burney Falls is about 45 mins by car from Manzanita Lake; the start of Everitt Memorial Highway is 70 mins from the falls.

Follow Highway 89 north out of Lassen to **McArthur-Burney Falls Memorial State Park.** Arrive early on summer holidays and weekends—rangers close the entrance when the park gets too crowded. The 129-foot-high falls are a sight to behold: water cascades over moss-covered rocks, and a trail leads down to the base.

Continue north on Highway 89 to **Mt. Shasta.** Drive up the mountain on Everitt Memorial Highway for incredible views, perhaps hiking one of the trails along the route. In winter, hit the slopes at nearby **Mt. Shasta Ski Park.** Mount Shasta City is a great place to stay overnight. Alternatively, venture 10 miles south to **Dunsmuir** and stay at the **Railroad Park Resort,** a collection of antique cabooses transformed into a motel. In Dunsmuir's small downtown, the **Mossbrae Hotel** exudes boutique charm.

DAY 5: LAKE SHASTA AND REDDING

The exit for Lake Shasta Caverns is 50 mins by car from Mount Shasta City, 40 mins from Dunsmuir. It's another 30 mins by car to Redding.

Drive south on I–5 to Lakehead, taking Exit 695 to **Lake Shasta Caverns.** Two-hour tours of the glittering caverns also include a boat ride. Make reservations in summer. From the caverns, head to **Shasta Dam,** the country's second-largest concrete dam. Drive south and conclude your tour in **Redding** for the best dining and lodging options.

Chapter 4

MONTEREY BAY AREA

4

Updated by
Cheryl Crabtree

● Sights	⑪ Restaurants	🛏 Hotels	⑤ Shopping	⑨ Nightlife
★★★★★	★★★★☆	★★★★★	★★☆☆☆	★☆☆☆☆

WELCOME TO THE MONTEREY BAY AREA

TOP REASONS TO GO

★ **Marine life:** Monterey Bay is the location of the world's third-largest marine sanctuary, home to whales, otters, and other underwater creatures.

★ **Getaway central:** For more than a century, urbanites have come to the Monterey Bay area to unwind, relax, and have fun. It's a great place to browse unique shops and galleries, ride a giant roller coaster, or play a round of golf on a world-class course.

★ **Nature preserves:** The region has nearly 30 state parks, beaches, and preserves—all of them fantastic places for walking, jogging, hiking, or biking.

★ **Wine and dine:** The area's rich agricultural bounty translates into abundant fresh produce, great wines, and fabulous dining. It's no wonder more than 300 culinary events take place here every year.

★ **Small-town vibes:** Even the cities here are friendly, walkable places where you'll feel like a local.

1 Carmel-by-the-Sea. Galleries and cobblestone streets are among its charms.

2 Carmel Valley. An esteemed wine region marks this celebrity enclave.

3 Pebble Beach. This world-class golf destination also has the stunning 17-Mile Drive.

4 Pacific Grove. A picturesque city known for its migrating butterflies.

5 Monterey. The state's first capital is rich in history and marine life.

6 Salinas. The heart of Steinbeck country is also known for its fruits and veggies.

7 Pinnacles National Park. A volcano with jagged spires and caves.

8 Moss Landing. This tiny fishing port is near marine preserves.

9 Aptos. A charming village that edges redwood forests and stellar beaches.

10 Capitola and Soquel. Seaside gateways to mountain wine country.

11 Santa Cruz. World-famous surf and a university are among its draws.

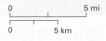

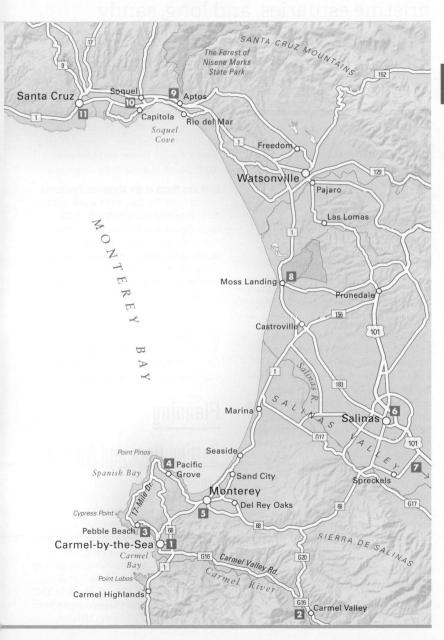

North of Big Sur, the coastline softens into lower bluffs, windswept dunes, pristine estuaries, and long, sandy beaches bordering one of the world's most amazing marine environments—Monterey Bay.

The bay itself is protected by the Monterey Bay National Marine Sanctuary, which holds the nation's largest undersea canyon—bigger and deeper than the Grand Canyon. Sunny coastal communities such as Aptos, Capitola, Soquel, and Santa Cruz offer miles of sand and surf. On-the-water activities abound, from whale-watching and kayaking to sailing and surfing. Bay cruises from Monterey and Moss Landing almost always encounter other enchanting sea creatures, among them sea otters, sea lions, and porpoises.

Land-based activities include hiking, ziplining in the redwood canopy, and wine tasting along urban and rural trails. Golf has been an integral part of the Monterey Peninsula's social and recreational scene since the Del Monte Golf Course opened in 1897. Today, Pebble Beach's championship courses host prestigious tournaments. Quaint, walkable towns such as Carmel-by-the-Sea and Carmel Valley Village are dotted with smart restaurants and galleries that encourage culinary and cultural immersion. Monterey's well-preserved waterfront invites historical exploration. Of course, whatever activity you pursue, natural splendor appears at every turn.

MAJOR REGIONS
The Monterey Peninsula. On the peninsula at the bay's southern end are Carmel-by-the-Sea—a good jumping-off point for the Carmel Valley wine region—Pebble Beach, Pacific Grove, and Monterey itself, home to a world-famous aquarium.

East and North of the Monterey Peninsula. Inland from the bay, amid a rich agricultural area that many refer to as Steinbeck Country, is Salinas, with Pinnacles National Park farther to the southeast. North of Monterey, Highway 1 cruises along the curving coastline, passing windswept beaches piled high with dunes, as well as wetlands and artichoke and strawberry fields. Here you'll find Moss Landing, where otters and seals play; classic seaside villages such as Aptos, Soquel, and Capitola; and Santa Cruz, home of surf legends, a historic boardwalk, and UC Santa Cruz.

Planning

Getting Here and Around

AIR
Monterey Regional Airport, 3 miles east of downtown Monterey off Highway 68, is served by Alaska, Allegiant, American, JSX, and United. Taxi service costs from $14 to $16 to downtown and from $23 to $25 to Carmel. Monterey Airbus service between the region and the San Jose and San Francisco airports starts at $53; the Early Bird Airport Shuttle costs from $220 to $250 ($270 from Oakland).

AIRPORT CONTACTS Monterey Regional Airport. (*MRY*) ✉ *200 Fred Kane Dr., at Olmsted Rd., off Hwy. 68, Monterey* ☎ *831/648–7000* ⊕ *www.montereyairport.com.*

GROUND TRANSPORTATION Central Coast Cab Company. ☎ *831/626–3333.* **Early Bird Airport Shuttle.** ☎ *831/462–3933* ⊕ *www.earlybirdairportshuttle.com.* **Monterey Airbus.** ☎ *831/373–7777* ⊕ *www.montereyairbus.com.* **Yellow Cab.** ☎ *831/333–1234* ⊕ *www.yellowcab1234.com.*

BUS

Greyhound serves Santa Cruz and Salinas from San Francisco (4½ hours) and San Jose (3 hours). Monterey-Salinas Transit (MST) provides frequent service in Monterey County (from $2; day pass $6), and Santa Cruz METRO ($2; day pass from $6 to $14) buses operate throughout Santa Cruz County. You can switch between the lines in Watsonville.

BUS CONTACTS Monterey-Salinas Transit. ☎ *888/678–2871* ⊕ *mst.org.* **Santa Cruz METRO.** ☎ *831/425–8600* ⊕ *scmtd.com.*

CAR

Highway 1 runs south–north along the coast, linking the towns of Carmel-by-the-Sea, Monterey, and Santa Cruz; some sections have only two lanes. The freeway, U.S. 101, lies to the east, roughly parallel to Highway 1. The two roads are connected by Highway 68 from Pacific Grove to Salinas; Highway 156 from Castroville to Prunedale; Highway 152 from Watsonville to Gilroy; Highway 129 from near San Juan Bautista to Watsonville, and Highway 17 from Santa Cruz to San Jose.

■**TIP→** **Traffic near Santa Cruz can crawl to a standstill during commuter hours. Avoid traveling between 7 and 9 am and between 4 and 7 pm.**

The drive south from San Francisco to Monterey can be made comfortably in three hours or less. The most scenic way is to follow Highway 1 down the coast.

A generally faster route is I–280 south to Highway 85 to Highway 17 to Highway 1. The drive from the Los Angeles area takes five or six hours. Take U.S. 101 to Salinas, and head west on Highway 68. You can also follow Highway 1 up the coast.

TRAIN

Amtrak's *Coast Starlight* runs between Los Angeles, Oakland, and Seattle. You can also take the *Pacific Surfliner* to San Luis Obispo and connect to Amtrak buses to Salinas or San Jose. From the train station in Salinas you can connect with buses serving Carmel and Monterey, and from the train station in San Jose with buses to Santa Cruz.

Hotels

Accommodations in the Monterey area range from no-frills motels to luxurious hotels. Pacific Grove, amply endowed with ornate Victorian houses, is the region's bed-and-breakfast capital; Carmel also has charming inns. Lavish resorts cluster in exclusive Pebble Beach and pastoral Carmel Valley.

High season runs from May through October. Rates in winter, especially at the larger hotels, may drop by 50% or more, and smaller inns often offer midweek specials. Whatever the month, some properties require a two-night stay on weekends.

■**TIP→** **Many of the fancier accommodations aren't suitable for children; if you're traveling with kids, ask before you book.**

Restaurants

The Monterey Bay area is a culinary paradise. The surrounding waters are full of fish, wild game roams the foothills, and the inland valleys are some of the most fertile in the country. Local chefs draw on this bounty for their fresh, truly Californian cuisine. Except at beachside stands and inexpensive eateries, where anything goes, casual but neat dress is the norm.

⇨ *Restaurant and hotel reviews have been shortened. For full information, visit Fodors.com. Restaurant prices are the average cost of a main course at dinner, or if dinner is not served, at lunch. Hotel prices are the lowest cost of a standard double room in high season*

What It Costs			
$	$$	$$$	$$$$
RESTAURANTS			
under $20	$20–$30	$31–$40	over $40
HOTELS			
under $200	$200–$350	$351–$500	over $500

Tours

Ag Venture Tours & Consulting

GUIDED TOURS | Crowd-pleasing half-day wine tasting, sightseeing, walking, and agricultural tours are Ag Venture's specialty. Tastings are at Monterey and Santa Cruz Mountains wineries; sightseeing opportunities include the Monterey Peninsula, Big Sur, and Santa Cruz; and the agricultural forays take in the Salinas and Pajaro valleys. Customized and full-day itineraries can be arranged. ☎ *831/761–8463* ⊕ *agventuretours.com* ◷ *From $65 (½-day walking tour) and $100 (½-day van tour).*

California Pacific Excursions

BUS TOURS | This outfit operates motor-coach tours in Monterey and Carmel, and from those towns and San Jose to Big Sur. The company's two-day San Jose–Los Angeles tours include stops in Monterey and Carmel. ☎ *415/228–9865* ⊕ *californiapacificexcursions.com* ◷ *From $278 (day) and $418 (overnight).*

Monterey Guided Wine Tours

SPECIAL-INTEREST TOURS | The company's guides lead customized wine tours in Monterey, Carmel, and Carmel Valley, along with the Santa Lucia Highlands, the Santa Cruz Mountains, and the Paso Robles area. Tours, which typically last from four to six hours, take place in a town car, a Lincoln Navigator, or a party bus and can accommodate groups of one to 100. ☎ *831/920–2792* ⊕ *www.montereyguidedwinetours.com* ◷ *From $175.*

Visitor Information

CONTACTS Monterey County Convention & Visitors Bureau. ✉ *419 Webster St., Suite 100, Monterey* ☎ *888/221–1010* ⊕ *www.seemonterey.com.* **Monterey Wine Country.** ✉ *Monterey* ☎ *831/375–9400* ⊕ *montereywines.org.* **Santa Cruz Mountains Winegrowers Association.** ✉ *335 Spreckels Dr., Suite B, Aptos* ☎ *831/685–8463* ⊕ *winesofthesantacruzmountains.com.* **Visit Santa Cruz County.** ✉ *303 Water St., Suite 100, Santa Cruz* ☎ *831/425–1234, 800/833–3494* ⊕ *www.santacruz.org.*

When to Go

Summer is peak season; mild weather brings in big crowds. In this coastal region a cool breeze generally blows and fog often rolls in from offshore; you will frequently need a sweater or windbreaker. Off-season, from November through April, fewer people visit and the mood is mellower. Rainfall is heaviest in January and February. Fall and spring days are often clearer than those in summer.

FESTIVALS AND EVENTS

Carmel Bach Festival. This three-week, mid-July festival has presented the works of Johann Sebastian Bach and his contemporaries since 1935. ⊕ *bachfestival.org*

Jazz Bash by the Bay. Bands play early jazz, big band, swing, ragtime, blues, zydeco, and gypsy jazz at waterfront venues during this festival, held on the first full weekend of March. ⊕ *jazzbashmonterey. com*

Monterey Jazz Festival. The world's oldest jazz festival, held the third full weekend in September, attracts top-name performers and their fans to the Monterey Fairgrounds. ⊕ *montereyjazzfestival.org*

Santa Cruz Shakespeare. This six-week festival in July and August occasionally includes a modern dramatic performance. Most performances are outdoors under the redwoods in Delaveaga Park. ⊕ *santacruzshakespeare.org*

Carmel-by-the-Sea

26 miles north of Big Sur.

Even when its population quadruples with tourists on weekends and in summer, Carmel-by-the-Sea, commonly referred to as Carmel, retains its identity as a quaint village. Self-consciously charming, the town is populated by many celebrities, major and minor, and has its share of quirky ordinances. For instance, women wearing high heels do not have the right to pursue legal action if they trip and fall on the cobblestone streets, and drivers who hit a tree and leave the scene are charged with hit-and-run.

Buildings have no street numbers— street names are written on discreet white posts—and consequently no mail delivery. One way to commune with the locals: head to the post office. Artists started this community, and their legacy is evident in the numerous galleries.

GETTING HERE AND AROUND

From north or south follow Highway 1 to Carmel. Head west at Ocean Avenue to reach the main village hub.

TOURS
Carmel By-the-Sea Wine Walk

SPECIAL-INTEREST TOURS | Download a free, mobile Wine Walk Guide with a map to tasting rooms and other venues where you can redeem exclusive offers like discounted flights and free tapas plates. (It's not an app—it's downloaded via text or email.) Check in at each tasting room (just pull up the venue in the guide) to redeem the offers. ⊠ *Carmel Chamber of Commerce Visitor Center, San Carlos St., between 5th and 6th Aves., Carmel* ☎ *831/624–2522* ⊕ *www.carmelcalifornia.com/carmel-by-the-sea-wine-walk. htm* ⊠ *$100.*

Carmel Food Tours

SPECIAL-INTEREST TOURS | Taste your way through Carmel-by-the-Sea culinary delights on this guided walking tour to restaurants and shops that serve small portions of standout offerings, from empanadas and ribs to honey and chocolate. Along the way, guides share colorful tales about local culture, history, and architecture. The Classic Tour (which departs from the Sunset Cultural Center) includes five to six tasting stops and lasts three hours. The five-hour Bikes, Bites, & Bevs Tour combines a morning e-bike tour from Carmel through Pebble Beach with four food and wine/cocktail destinations in the afternoon. Tickets must be purchased in advance. ⊠ *Sunset Cultural Center, 9th Ave. at San Carlos St., Carmel* ☎ *831/216–8161 tickets* ⊕ *carmelfoodtour.com* ⊠ *From $119.*

Carmel Walks

WALKING TOURS | For insight into Carmel's history and culture, join one of these guided two-hour ambles through hidden courtyards, gardens, and pathways. Tours depart from the Pine Inn courtyard, on Lincoln Street. Call or visit the website to reserve a spot. ⊠ *Lincoln St. at 6th Ave., Carmel* ☎ *831/223–4399* ⊕ *gaelgallagher. com/carmel-walks.html* ⊠ *From $35.*

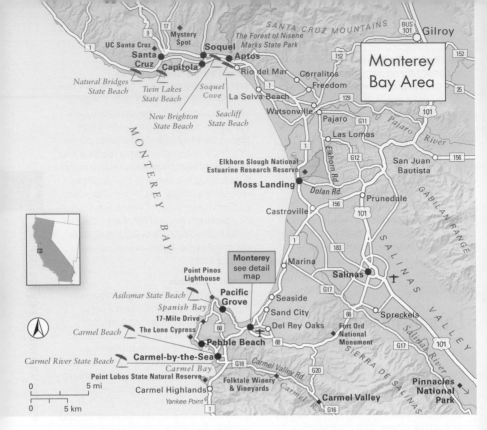

ESSENTIALS

VISITOR INFORMATION Carmel Chamber of Commerce. ✉ *Visitor center, in Carmel Plaza, Ocean Ave. between Junípero and Mission Sts., Carmel* ☎ *831/624–2522* ⊕ *carmelchamber.org.*

⦿ Sights

Carmel Mission

RELIGIOUS BUILDING | FAMILY | Long before it became a shopping and browsing destination, Carmel was an important religious center during the establishment of Spanish California. That heritage is preserved in the Mission San Carlos Borroméo del Rio Carmelo, more commonly known as the Carmel Mission. Founded in 1771, it served as headquarters for the mission system in California under Father Junípero Serra. Adjoining the stone church is a tranquil garden planted with California poppies. Museum rooms at the mission include an early kitchen, Serra's spartan sleeping quarters and burial shrine, and the first college library in California. ✉ *3080 Rio Rd., at Lasuen Dr., Carmel* ☎ *831/624–1271* ⊕ *carmelmission.org* ⛁ *$13* ⊘ *Closed Mon. and Tues.*

★ Ocean Avenue

STREET | FAMILY | Downtown Carmel's chief lure is shopping, especially along its main street, Ocean Avenue, between Junípero Avenue and Camino Real. The architecture here is a mishmash of ersatz Tudor, Mediterranean, and other styles. ✉ *Carmel.*

★ Point Lobos State Natural Reserve

NATURE PRESERVE | FAMILY | A 350-acre headland harboring a wealth of marine life, the reserve lies a few miles south of Carmel. The best way to explore here is to walk along one of the many trails.

The Cypress Grove Trail leads through a forest of Monterey cypress (one of only two natural groves remaining) that clings to the rocks above an emerald-green cove. Sea Lion Point Trail is a good place to view sea lions. From those and other trails, you might also spot otters, harbor seals, and (in winter and spring) migrating whales. An additional 750 acres of the reserve is an undersea marine park open to qualified scuba divers. No pets are allowed. **■ TIP→ Arrive early (or in late afternoon) to avoid crowds; the parking lots fill up.** ✉ *Hwy. 1, Carmel* ☎ *831/624–4909* 🌐 *www.pointlobos.org* 🎫 *$10 per vehicle.*

Tor House

HISTORIC HOME | Scattered throughout the pines of Carmel-by-the-Sea are houses and cottages originally built for the writers, artists, and photographers who discovered the area decades ago. Among the most impressive dwellings is Tor House, a stone cottage built in 1919 by poet Robinson Jeffers on a craggy knoll overlooking the sea. Portraits, books, and unusual art objects fill the low-ceilinged rooms. The highlight of the small estate is Hawk Tower, a detached edifice set with stones from the Carmel coastline—as well as one from the Great Wall of China. The docents who lead tours (six people maximum) are well informed about the poet's work and life. Reservations (by phone or online) are required. ✉ *26304 Ocean View Ave., Carmel* ☎ *831/624–1813 direct docent office line, Mon.–Thurs. only* 🌐 *www.torhouse.org* 🎫 *$15* ☞ *No children under 12.*

Beaches

Carmel Beach

BEACH | FAMILY | Carmel-by-the-Sea's greatest attraction is its rugged coastline, with pine and cypress forests and countless inlets. Carmel Beach, an easy walk from downtown shops, has sparkling white sands and magnificent sunsets. **■ TIP→ Dogs are allowed to romp off-leash here. Amenities:** parking (no fee); toilets. **Best for:** sunset; surfing; walking. ✉ *End of Ocean Ave., Carmel* ☎ *831/620–2020.*

Restaurants

Anton and Michel

$$$$ | AMERICAN | Carefully prepared California cuisine is the draw at this airy restaurant, where the rack of lamb is carved at the table, the grilled Halloumi cheese and tomatoes are meticulously stacked and served with basil and Kalamata olive tapenade, and the desserts are set aflame before your eyes. For lighter fare with a worldwide flair, head to the bar, where small plates such as Dungeness crab ravioli and brochette of filet mignon with chimichurri sauce are served. **Known for:** romantic courtyard with fountain; elegant interior with fireplace lounge; flambé desserts. [$] *Average main: $46* ✉ *Mission St. and 7th Ave., Carmel* ☎ *831/624–2406* 🌐 *www.antonandmichel.com.*

★ Aubergine

$$$$ | AMERICAN | To eat and sleep at luxe L'Auberge Carmel is an experience in itself, but even those staying elsewhere can splurge at the inn's intimate restaurant, which was awarded a Michelin star in 2022. Chef Justin Cogley's eight-course prix-fixe tasting menu (your only option at dinner, $265 per person) is a gastronomical experience unrivaled in the region. **Known for:** exceptional chef's choice tasting menu; expert wine pairings (extra fee); intimate nine-table dining room. [$] *Average main: $265* ✉ *Monte Verde at 7th Ave., Carmel* ☎ *831/624–8578* 🌐 *auberginecarmel.com* 🕒 *Closed Mon. and Tues. No lunch.*

★ Basil

$$ | AMERICAN | Eco-friendly Basil was Monterey County's first restaurant to achieve a green-dining certification, recognition of its commitment to using organic, sustainably cultivated ingredients in creative dishes such as black

Point Lobos State Natural Reserve offers stunning vistas of sea and sky.

squid linguine with sea urchin sauce, charred octopus, and smoked venison and other house-made charcuterie. **Known for:** organic ingredients; creative cocktails; year-round patio dining. [$] *Average main: $30* ✉ *Paseo Sq., San Carlos St., between Ocean Ave. and 7th Ave., Carmel* ☎ *831/626–8226* 🌐 *basilcarmel.com.*

Casanova

$$$ | MEDITERRANEAN | This restaurant inspires European-style celebration and romance in an intimate French-country setting. Feast on authentic dishes from southern France and northern Italy—think beef tartare and escargot. **Known for:** house-made pastas and gnocchi; private dining at antique Van Gogh's table; romantic candlelight dining room and outdoor patio. [$] *Average main: $34* ✉ *5th Ave., between San Carlos and Mission Sts., Carmel* ☎ *831/625–0501* 🌐 *www.casanovacarmel.com.*

The Cottage Restaurant

$ | AMERICAN | FAMILY | This family-friendly spot serves sandwiches, pizzas, and homemade soups at lunch, but the best meal is breakfast (good thing it's served all day). The menu offers six variations on eggs Benedict and all kinds of crepes. **Known for:** artichoke soup; sweet or savory crepes; daily specials. [$] *Average main: $17* ✉ *Lincoln St. between Ocean and 7th Aves., Carmel* ☎ *831/625–6260* 🌐 *www.cottagerestaurant.com* 🕒 *No dinner.*

Flying Fish Grill

$$ | SEAFOOD | Simple in appearance yet bold with its flavors, this Japanese–California seafood restaurant is one of Carmel's most inventive eateries. The warm, wood-lined dining room is broken up into very private booths. **Known for:** almond-crusted sea bass served with Chinese cabbage and rock shrimp stir-fry; clay pot dinners for two cooked at the table; authentic Asian decor. [$] *Average main: $30* ✉ *Carmel Plaza, Mission St. between Ocean and 7th Aves., Carmel* ☎ *831/625–1962* 🌐 *www.flyingfishgrill.com* 🕒 *No lunch.*

Grasing's Coastal Cuisine
$$$ | AMERICAN | Chef Kurt Grasing draws from fresh Carmel Coast and Central Valley ingredients to whip up contemporary adaptations of European-provincial and American dishes. Longtime menu favorites include fresh farm-raised abalone, a savory sausage and seafood paella, and grilled steaks and chops. **Known for:** artichoke and fontina ravioli; grilled steaks; bar, patio lounge, and rooftop deck. [$] *Average main: $39 ✉ 6th Ave. and Mission St., Carmel ☎ 831/624–6562 🌐 grasings.com.*

★ The Pocket
$$$ | MODERN ITALIAN | In surf lingo, "the pocket" is a perfect riding spot within a barrel-shape wave, and this Italian–Californian restaurant is likewise a perfect (casual and unfussy) gathering spot for those who seek first-rate food, wine, and cocktails. The chefs craft seasonal menus that focus on seafood, fresh pastas, curries, steaks, and braised meats. **Known for:** sleek marble, wood, and slate dining room, spacious garden seating; full bar, extensive list of more than 400 wines; lively atmosphere, especially during the daily happy hour. [$] *Average main: $35 ✉ Lincoln St., between 5th and 6th Ave., Carmel ☎ 831/626–8000 🌐 www.thepocketcarmel.com 🕒 Closed Mon. and Tues. No lunch.*

Stationaery
$$ | ECLECTIC | This cozy neighborhood restaurant serves one of Carmel's most popular brunches every day, plus dinner several nights a week. The eclectic seasonal menu focuses on elegant comfort food with an international flair—options vary, but might include caviar with crème fraiche and kettle chips, shakshuka, chilaquiles, or poke bowls for brunch and soft-shell crab with fava bean puree for dinner. **Known for:** specialty coffee, natural wines; fresh, locally sourced ingredients; takeout window. [$] *Average main: $30 ✉ San Carlos St., between 5th and 6th Aves., Carmel ☎ 831/250–7183 🌐 www.thestationaery.com 🕒 No dinner Sun.–Wed.*

Vesuvio
$$$ | ITALIAN | Chef and restaurateur Rich Pèpe heats up the night with this lively trattoria downstairs and swinging rooftop terrace, the Star Bar. Pèpe's elegant take on traditional Italian cuisine yields dishes such as risotto made with local seafood, spicy Calabrian sausage, and lobster reduction sauce, crab ravioli, and velvety limoncello mousse cake. **Known for:** traditional cuisine of Campania, Italy; two bars with pizzas and small plates; live music on rooftop terrace in summer. [$] *Average main: $32 ✉ 6th and Junipero Aves., Carmel ☎ 831/625–1766 🌐 chefpepe.com/restaurants/vesuvio 🕒 No lunch ☞ Cash not accepted.*

Hotels

Carmel Mission Inn
$ | HOTEL | A multimillion-dollar renovation completed in the early 2020s transformed this 1970s motel, conveniently located near the intersection of Highway 1 and Rio Road, into a hip haven that evokes the region's natural environment (sand, sea, mountains, pines) and artsy past (mosaic floors, local art, vintage doors). **Pros:** near two shopping centers with many services; fitness center with Peleton bikes; pool and hot tub, free parking. **Cons:** some rooms have limited storage space; no guest laundry; noise from outdoor gathering areas filters to some rooms. [$] *Rooms from: $191 ✉ 3665 Rio Rd., Carmel ☎ 855/235–3915, 831/624–1841 🌐 www.carmelmissioninn.com 🛏 165 rooms 🍴 No Meals.*

Cypress Inn
$$ | B&B/INN | This luxurious inn has a fresh, Mediterranean ambience with Moroccan touches. **Pros:** luxury without snobbery; popular lounge and restaurant; live music on the patio. **Cons:** not for the pet-phobic; some rooms and baths are tiny; basic amenities. [$] *Rooms*

*from: $299 ✉ Lincoln St. and 7th Ave.,
Carmel ☎ 831/624–3871, 800/443–7443
⊕ cypress-inn.com ⇌ 44 rooms ⓄⅠ Free
Breakfast.*

Hyatt Carmel Highlands

$$$ | HOTEL | High on a hill overlooking the
Pacific, this place has superb views and
accommodations that include king rooms
with fireplaces, suites with personal
whirlpool tubs, and full town houses
with many perks. **Pros:** killer views;
romantic getaway; great food. **Cons:** thin
walls; must drive to the center of town;
some rooms and buildings need update.
Ⓢ *Rooms from: $499 ✉ 120 Highlands
Dr., Carmel ☎ 831/620–1234 ⊕ www.
hyatt.com ⇌ 48 rooms ⓄⅠ No Meals.*

La Playa Carmel

$$$$ | HOTEL | A historic complex of lush
gardens and Mediterranean-style buildings, La Playa has light and airy interiors
done in Carmel Bay beach-cottage
style. **Pros:** historical restaurant and bar;
manicured gardens; two blocks from the
beach. **Cons:** four stories (no elevator);
busy lobby; some rooms are on the small
side. Ⓢ *Rooms from: $549 ✉ Camino
Real at 8th Ave., Carmel ☎ 800/582–
8900, 831/293–6100 ⊕ laplayahotel.com
⇌ 75 rooms ⓄⅠ Free Breakfast.*

★ L'Auberge Carmel

$$$$ | B&B/INN | Stepping through the
doors of this elegant inn is like being
transported to a little European village.
Pros: in town but off the main drag; four
blocks from the beach; full-service luxury.
Cons: touristy area; not a good choice
for families; no a/c. Ⓢ *Rooms from:
$549 ✉ Monte Verde at 7th Ave., Carmel
☎ 831/624–8578 ⊕ laubergecarmel.com
⇌ 20 rooms ⓄⅠ Free Breakfast.*

Mission Ranch

$$ | HOTEL | Movie star Clint Eastwood
owns this sprawling property where
accommodations include rooms in a
converted barn and several cottages,
some with fireplaces. **Pros:** farm setting;
pastoral views; great for tennis buffs.

Cons: busy parking lot; must drive to the
heart of town; old buildings. Ⓢ *Rooms
from: $270 ✉ 26270 Dolores St., Car-
mel ☎ 831/624–6436, 800/538–8221,
831/625–9040 restaurant ⊕ www.
missionranchcarmel.com ⇌ 31 rooms
ⓄⅠ No Meals.*

Pine Inn

$$ | HOTEL | A favorite with generations
of visitors, the Pine Inn is four blocks
from the beach and has Victorian-style
furnishings, complete with a grandfather
clock, padded fabric wall panels, antique
tapestries, and marble tabletops. **Pros:**
elegant; close to shopping and dining;
Carmel institution. **Cons:** on the town's
busiest street; public areas a bit dark;
limited parking. Ⓢ *Rooms from: $289
✉ Ocean Ave. and Monte Verde St.,
Carmel ☎ 831/624–3851, 800/228–3851
⊕ www.pineinn.com ⇌ 49 rooms ⓄⅠ No
Meals.*

Tally Ho Inn

$$ | B&B/INN | This inn is nearly all suites,
many of which have fireplaces and
floor-to-ceiling glass walls that open
onto ocean-view patios. **Pros:** within
walking distance of shops, restaurants,
and beach; free parking; spacious
rooms. **Cons:** small property; busy area;
basic breakfast. Ⓢ *Rooms from: $299
✉ Monte Verde St. and 6th Ave., Carmel
☎ 831/624–2232, 800/652–2632 ⊕ www.
tallyho-inn.com ⇌ 12 rooms ⓄⅠ No
Meals.*

Tickle Pink Inn

$$$$ | B&B/INN | Atop a towering cliff, this
inn has views of the Big Sur coastline,
which you can contemplate from your private balcony. **Pros:** close to great hiking;
intimate; dramatic views. **Cons:** close to
a big hotel; lots of traffic during the day;
basic breakfast. Ⓢ *Rooms from: $429
✉ 155 Highland Dr., Carmel ☎ 831/624–
1244, 800/635–4774 ⊕ www.ticklepink-
inn.com ⇌ 34 units ⓄⅠ Free Breakfast.*

ⓨ Nightlife

Barmel

BARS | Al Capone and other Prohibi-tion-era legends once sidled up to this hip nightspot's carved wooden bar. Rock to DJ music and sit indoors, or head out to the pet-friendly patio. Some menu items pay homage to California's early days. ✉ *San Carlos St., between Ocean and 7th Aves., Carmel* ☎ *831/626–3400* ⊕ *barmel.com* ☾ *Closed Mon.*

Mulligan Public House

PUBS | A sports bar with seven TV screens, 12 beers on tap, and extensive menu packed with hearty American pub food, Mulligan usually stays open until midnight. ✉ *5 Dolores St. at Ocean* ☎ *831/250–5910* ⊕ *www.mulliganscarmel.com.*

⬤ Shopping

ART GALLERIES

Carmel Art Association

ART GALLERIES | Carmel's oldest gallery, established in 1927, exhibits original paintings and sculptures by local artists. ✉ *Dolores St., between 5th and 6th Aves., Carmel* ☎ *831/624–6176* ⊕ *carmelart.org* ☾ *Closed Tues. and Wed.*

★ Weston Gallery

ART GALLERIES | Run by the family of the late Edward Weston, this is hands down the best photography gallery around, with contemporary color photography and classic black-and-whites. ✉ *6th Ave., between Dolores and Lincoln Sts., Carmel* ☎ *831/624–4453* ⊕ *www.westongallery.com* ☾ *Open by appointment only.*

MALLS

Carmel Plaza

MALL | FAMILY | Tiffany & Co. and Anthropologie are among the name brands doing business at this mall on Carmel's east side, but what makes it worth a stop are homegrown enterprises such as Carmel Honey Company for local honey; Monterey Design Center for home decor;

and J. Lawrence Khaki's for debonair menswear. Flying Fish Grill, Alvarado Street Brewery, and several other restaurants are here, along with Wrath, Hahn, and Blair Estate wine tasting rooms. The Carmel Visitor Center (open daily) is on the second floor. ✉ *Ocean Ave. and Mission St., Carmel* ☎ *831/624–1385* ⊕ *carmelplaza.com.*

SPECIALTY SHOPS

elizabethW

SOUVENIRS | Named after the designer and owner's pioneering great-grandmother, elizabethW handcrafts fragrances, essential oils, candles, silk eye pillows, and other soul-soothing goods for bath, body, and home. ✉ *Ocean Ave., between Monte Verde and Lincoln, Carmel* ☎ *831/626 3892* ⊕ *www.elizabethw.com.*

★ Foxy Couture

SECOND-HAND | Shop for one-of-a-kind treasures at this curated collection of gently used luxury couture and vintage clothes and accessories—think Chanel, Hermes, and Gucci—without paying a hefty price tag. ✉ *San Carlos St., in Vanervort Court, between Ocean and 7th Aves., Carmel* ☎ *831/625–9995* ⊕ *foxycouturecarmel.com* ☾ *Closed Tues. and Wed.*

Jan de Luz

HOUSEWARES | This shop monograms and embroiders fine linens (including bathrobes) while you wait. ✉ *Dolores St., at 6th Ave. NE, Carmel* ☎ *831/622–7621* ⊕ *jandeluzlinens.com.*

Carmel Valley

10 miles east of Carmel.

Carmel Valley Road, which heads inland from Highway 1 south of Carmel, is the main thoroughfare through this valley, a secluded enclave of horse ranchers and other well-heeled residents who prefer the area's sunny climate to coastal fog and wind. Once thick with dairy farms, the valley has evolved into an esteemed wine appellation. Carmel Valley Village has crafts shops, art galleries, and the tasting rooms of numerous local wineries.

GETTING HERE AND AROUND

From U.S. 101 north or south, exit at Highway 68 and head west toward the coast. Scenic, two-lane Laureles Grade winds southwest over the mountains to Carmel Valley Road west of the village.

An incredible bargain ($6 for an all-day pass), the Carmel Valley Grapevine Express—aka MST's Bus 24—travels between Carmel Valley Village and downtown Monterey, with stops near wineries, restaurants, and shopping centers.

Sights

Bernardus Tasting Room

WINERY | At the tasting room of Bernardus—known for its Bordeaux-style red blend, called Marinus, and its Chardonnays—you can sample current releases and reserve wines. ✉ *5 W. Carmel Valley Rd., at El Caminito Rd., Carmel Valley* ☎ *831/298–8021, 800/223–2533* 🌐 *www.bernardus.com* 🎟 *Tastings from $30.*

Earthbound Farm

FARM/RANCH | **FAMILY** | Pick up fresh vegetables, ready-to-eat meals, gourmet groceries, flowers, and gifts at Earthbound Farm, the world's largest grower of organic produce. You can also take a romp in the kids' garden, cut your own herbs, and stroll through the chamomile aromatherapy labyrinth. ✉ *7250 Carmel Valley Rd., Carmel* ☎ *831/625–6219* 🌐 *www.earthboundfarm.com* 🎟 *Free.*

★ **Folktale Winery & Vineyards**

WINERY | The expansive winery on a 15-acre estate offers daily tastings, live music on weekends (plus Friday in summer and fall), and special events and programs such as Sunday yoga in the vineyard. Best-known wines include the estate Pinot Noir, Sparkling Rosé, and Le Mistral Joseph's Blend. Chefs in the on-site restaurant cook up small plates with wine pairing suggestions. Tours of the winery and organically farmed vineyards are available by appointment. ✉ *8940 Carmel Valley Rd., at Schetter Rd.* ☎ *831/293–7500* 🌐 *www.folktalewinery.com* 🎟 *Tastings from $40; tours $30 (includes tasting)* 🕓 *Closed Tues. and Wed.*

★ **Holman Ranch Vineyards Tasting Room**

WINERY | Estate-grown Chardonnay and Pinot Noir are among the standout wines made by Holman Ranch, which pours samples in its chic tasting room and on two patios in the historic Will's Fargo tavern building. The 15-acre ranch itself is just up the road, set amid rolling hills that were once part of the Carmel mission's land grant. You can take winery and vineyard tours by appointment ✉ *18 W. Carmel Valley Rd., Carmel Valley* ☎ *831/659–2640* 🌐 *www.holmanranch.com* 🎟 *Tastings from $35* 🕓 *Closed Tues. and Wed.*

Restaurants

Café Rustica

$$$ | **EUROPEAN** | European country cooking is the focus at this lively roadhouse, where specialties include roasted meats, seafood, pastas, and thin-crust pizzas from the wood-fired oven. It can get noisy inside; for a quieter meal, request a table outside. **Known for:** Tuscan-flavored dishes from Alsace; open kitchen with wood-fired oven; outdoor patio seating. [$] *Average main: $34* ✉ *10 Delfino Pl., at Pilot Rd., off Carmel Valley Rd., Carmel Valley* ☎ *831/659–4444* 🌐 *caferusticacv.com* 🕓 *Closed Mon. No lunch Tues. and Wed.*

Corkscrew Café

$$ | **MODERN AMERICAN** | Farm-fresh food is the specialty of this casual, Old Monterey–style bistro, where the herbs and seasonal produce come from its own organic gardens, the catch of the day comes from local waters, and the meats are hormone-free. Don't miss the collection of corkscrews dating from the 17th century to the present. **Known for:** wood-fired pizzas; fantastic regional wine list; garden patio. $ *Average main: $23* ✉ *55 W. Carmel Valley Rd., Carmel Valley* ☎ *831/659–8888* 🌐 *www.corkscrewcafe.com* 🕓 *Closed Jan.*

Roux

$$$$ | **MODERN FRENCH** | Chef Fabrice Roux, who hails from France, worked at lauded Parisian restaurants for more than a decade before coming to Carmel Valley to wow diners with his contemporary takes on traditional French-Mediterranean cuisine. The eclectic menu, with mostly small and large plates meant for sharing, focuses on local ingredients procured that week—perhaps crispy duck leg confit, tuna tartare, or braised wild-boar bourguignon. **Known for:** expert food and wine pairings; European-style cottage with private room for dining and tastings; extensive wine list with more than 400 labels. $ *Average main: $41* ✉ *6 Pilot Rd., Carmel Valley* ☎ *831/659–5020* 🌐 *rouxcarmel.com* 💳 *No credit cards* 🕓 *Closed Tues. No lunch Wed. and Thurs.*

🛏 Hotels

★ Bernardus Lodge & Spa

$$$$ | **RESORT** | The spacious guest rooms at this luxury spa resort have vaulted ceilings, French oak floors, featherbeds, fireplaces, patios, and bathrooms with heated-tile floors and soaking tubs for two. **Pros:** exceptional personal service; outstanding food and wine; serene, cushy full-service spa. **Cons:** hefty rates; can feel a little snooty; resort fee. $ *Rooms from: $535* ✉ *415 W. Carmel Valley Rd., Carmel Valley* ☎ *831/658–3400* 🌐 *www.bernarduslodge.com* 🛏 *73 rooms* 🍴 *No Meals.*

★ Carmel Valley Ranch

$$$$ | **RESORT** | **FAMILY** | The activity options at this luxury ranch are so varied that the resort provides a program director to guide you through them. **Pros:** stunning natural setting; upscale on-site restaurant, Valley Kitchen; River Ranch center with a pool, splash zone, boccie courts, and fitness center. **Cons:** must drive several miles to shops and nightlife; high rates; footsteps from neighboring rooms easy to hear in some buildings. $ *Rooms from: $707* ✉ *1 Old Ranch Rd., Carmel* ☎ *831/625–9500, 855/687–7262 toll-free reservations* 🌐 *carmelvalleyranch.com* 🛏 *181 suites* 🍴 *No Meals.*

Quail Lodge & Golf Club

$$$ | **HOTEL** | **FAMILY** | A sprawling collection of ranch-style buildings on 850 acres of meadows, fairways, and lakes, Quail Lodge offers luxury rooms and outdoor activities at surprisingly affordable rates. **Pros:** on the golf course; on-site restaurant; spacious rooms. **Cons:** service sometimes spotty; 5 miles from the beach and Carmel Valley Village; basic amenities. $ *Rooms from: $395* ✉ *8205 Valley Greens Dr., Carmel* ☎ *866/675–1101 reservations, 831/624–2888* 🌐 *www.quaillodge.com* 🛏 *93 rooms* 🍴 *No Meals.*

★ Stonepine Estate

$$$ | **RESORT** | Set on 407 pastoral acres, the former estate of the Crocker banking family has been converted to a luxurious inn. **Pros:** supremely exclusive; close to Carmel Valley Village; attentive, personalized service. **Cons:** not suitable for children under 12; far from the coast; expensive rates. $ *Rooms from: $375* ✉ *150 E. Carmel Valley Rd., Carmel Valley* ☎ *831/659–2245* 🌐 *stonepineestate.com* 🛏 *16 units* 🍴 *Free Breakfast.*

Activities

GOLF
Quail Lodge & Golf Club

GOLF | Robert Muir Graves designed this championship, semiprivate, 18-hole course that provides challenging play for golfers of all skill levels. The scenic course, which is set next to Quail Lodge and incorporates five lakes and edges the Carmel River, was completely renovated in 2015 by golf architect Todd Eckenrode to add extra challenge to the golf experience, white sand bunkers, and other enhancements. For the most part flat, the walkable course is well maintained, with stunning views, lush fairways, and ultrasmooth greens. ⊠ *8000 Valley Greens Dr., Carmel* ☎ *831/620–8808 golf shop, 831/620–8866 club concierge* ⊕ *www.quaillodge.com/golf* ⊠ *$236* ⚲ *18 holes, 6500 yards, par 71.*

SPAS
★ Refuge

SPAS | At this coed, European-style center on 2 serene acres you can recharge without breaking the bank. Heat up in the eucalyptus steam room or cedar sauna, plunge into cold pools, and relax indoors in zero-gravity chairs or outdoors in Adirondack chairs around firepits. Repeat the cycle a few times, then lounge around the thermal waterfall pools. Talk is not allowed, and bathing suits are required. ⊠ *27300 Rancho San Carlos Rd., south off Carmel Valley Rd., Carmel* ☎ *831/620–7360* ⊕ *www.refuge.com* ⊠ *$44* ⚲ *$55 admission; $175 50-min massage (includes Refuge admission), $12 robe rental, hot tubs (outdoor), sauna, steam room. Services: aromatherapy, hydrotherapy, massage.*

Pebble Beach

Off North San Antonio Ave. in Carmel-by-the-Sea or off Sunset Dr. in Pacific Grove.

In 1919, the Pacific Improvement Company acquired 18,000 acres of prime land on the Monterey Peninsula, including the entire Pebble Beach coastal region and much of Pacific Grove. Pebble Beach Golf Links and The Lodge at Pebble Beach opened the same year, and the private enclave evolved into a world-class golf destination with three posh lodges, five golf courses, hiking and riding trails, and some of the West Coast's ritziest homes. Pebble Beach has hosted major international golf tournaments, including the U.S. Open in 2019. The annual Pebble Beach Food & Wine, a four-day event in late April with 100 celebrity chefs, is one of the West Coast's premier culinary festivals.

GETTING HERE AND AROUND
If you drive south from Monterey on Highway 1, exit at 17-Mile Drive/Sunset Drive in Pacific Grove to find the northern entrance gate. Coming from Carmel, exit at Ocean Avenue and follow the road almost to the beach; turn right on North San Antonio Avenue to the Carmel Gate. You can also enter through the Highway 1 Gate off Highway 68. Monterey–Salinas Transit (MST) buses provide regular service in and around Pebble Beach.

 Sights

★ The Lone Cypress
NATURE SIGHT | FAMILY | The most-photographed tree along 17-Mile Drive is the weather-sculpted Lone Cypress, which grows out of a precipitous outcropping above the waves about 1½ miles up the road from Pebble Beach Golf Links. You can't walk out to the tree, but you can stop for a view of it at a small parking area off the road. ⊠ *Pebble Beach.*

★ **17-Mile Drive**

SCENIC DRIVE | FAMILY | Primordial nature resides in quiet harmony with palatial, mostly Spanish Mission–style estates along 17-Mile Drive, which winds through an 8,400-acre microcosm of the Pebble Beach coastal landscape. Dotting the drive are rare Monterey cypresses, trees so gnarled and twisted that Robert Louis Stevenson described them as "ghosts fleeing before the wind." The most famous of these is the Lone Cypress.

Other highlights include Bird Rock and Seal Rock, home to harbor seals, sea lions, cormorants, and pelicans and other sea creatures and birds, and the Crocker Marble Palace, inspired by a Byzantine castle and easily identifiable by its dozens of marble arches. **■TIP→ If you spend $35 or more on dining in Pebble Beach and show a receipt upon exiting, you'll receive a refund off the drive's $11.75 per-car fee.** ✉ *Hwy. 1 Gate, 17-Mile Dr., at Hwy. 68, Pebble Beach* 🎟 *$12 per car, free for bicyclists.*

Hotels

★ **Casa Palmero**

$$$$ | RESORT | This exclusive boutique hotel evokes a stately Mediterranean villa, where rooms are decorated with sumptuous fabrics and fine art. **Pros:** ultimate in pampering; sumptuous decor; more private than sister resorts. **Cons:** rates out of reach for most visitors; not the best views compared to sister lodges; some showers on the small side. [$] *Rooms from: $1,290* ✉ *1518 Cypress Dr., Pebble Beach* ☎ *831/622–6650, 800/877–0597 reservations* 🌐 *www.pebblebeach.com* 🛏 *24 rooms* 🍴 *Free Breakfast.*

The Inn at Spanish Bay

$$$$ | RESORT | This resort sprawls along a breathtaking stretch of shoreline and has plush, 600-square-foot rooms. **Pros:** attentive service; many amenities; spectacular views. **Cons:** huge hotel; 4 miles from other Pebble Beach Resorts facilities; atmosphere too snobbish for some. [$] *Rooms from: $960* ✉ *2700 17-Mile Dr., Pebble Beach* ☎ *831/647–7500, 800/877–0597* 🌐 *www.pebblebeach.com* 🛏 *269 rooms* 🍴 *No Meals.*

The Lodge at Pebble Beach

$$$$ | RESORT | Most rooms have wood-burning fireplaces, and many have wonderful ocean views at this circa-1919 resort, which includes the much newer, 38-room Fairway One complex. **Pros:** world-class golf; borders the ocean and fairways; fabulous facilities. **Cons:** some rooms are on the small side; very pricey; not many activities if you don't golf. [$] *Rooms from: $1,100* ✉ *1700 17-Mile Dr., Pebble Beach* ☎ *831/624–3811, 800/877–0597* 🌐 *www.pebblebeach.com* 🛏 *199 rooms* 🍴 *No Meals.*

Activities

GOLF

The Hay

GOLF | The only 9-hole, par-3 course on the Monterey Peninsula open to the public attracts golfers of all skill levels. It's an ideal place for warm-ups, practicing short games, and for those who don't have time to play 18 holes. ✉ *17-Mile Dr. and Portola Rd., Pebble Beach* ☎ *800/877–0597* 🌐 *www.pebblebeach.com* 🎟 *$65* 🏌 *9 holes, 725 yards, par 27.*

Links at Spanish Bay

GOLF | This course, which hugs a choice stretch of shoreline, was designed by Robert Trent Jones Jr., Tom Watson, and Sandy Tatum in the rugged manner of traditional Scottish links, with sand dunes and coastal marshes interspersed among the greens. A bagpiper signals the course's closing each day. **■TIP→ Nonguests of the Pebble Beach Resorts can reserve tee times up to two months in advance.** ✉ *17-Mile Dr., north end, Pebble Beach* ☎ *800/877–0597* 🌐 *www.pebblebeach.com* 🎟 *$335* 🏌 *18 holes, 6821 yards, par 72.*

★ Pebble Beach Golf Links

GOLF | Each February, show-business celebrities and golf pros team up at this course, the main site of the glamorous AT&T Pebble Beach National Pro-Am tournament. On most days the rest of the year, tee times are available to guests of the Pebble Beach Resorts who book a minimum two-night stay. Nonguests can reserve a tee time only one day in advance on a space-available basis; resort guests can reserve up to 18 months in advance. ✉ 17-Mile Dr., near The Lodge at Pebble Beach, Pebble Beach ☎ 800/877–0597 ⊕ www.pebblebeach.com ⌬ $625 🏌 18 holes, 6828 yards, par 72.

Poppy Hills

GOLF | An 18-hole course designed in 1986 by Robert Trent Jones Jr., Poppy Hills reopened in 2014 after a yearlong renovation that Jones supervised. Each hole was restored to its natural elevation along the forest floor, and all 18 greens were rebuilt with bent grass. Individuals may reserve up to a month in advance. ■TIP→ Poppy Hills, owned by a golfing nonprofit, represents good value for this area. ✉ 3200 Lopez Rd., at 17-Mile Dr., Pebble Beach ☎ 831/622–8239 ⊕ poppyhillsgolf.com ⌬ $300 🏌 18 holes, 7002 yards, par 73.5.

Spyglass Hill

GOLF | With three holes rated among the toughest on the PGA tour, Spyglass Hill, designed by Robert Trent Jones Sr. and Jr., challenges golfers with its varied terrain but rewards them with glorious views. The first 5 holes border the Pacific, and the other 13 reach deep into the Del Monte Forest. Reservations are essential and may be made up to one month in advance (18 months for resort guests). ✉ Stevenson Dr. and Spyglass Hill Rd., Pebble Beach ☎ 800/877–0597 ⊕ www.pebblebeach.com ⌬ $465 🏌 18 holes, 6960 yards, par 72.

Pacific Grove

3 miles north of Carmel-by-the-Sea.

This picturesque town, which began as a summer retreat for church groups more than a century ago, recalls its prim and proper Victorian heritage in a host of tiny board-and-batten cottages and stately mansions. However, long before the church groups flocked here the area received thousands of annual pilgrims—in the form of bright orange-and-black monarch butterflies. They still come, migrating south from Canada and the Pacific Northwest to take residence in pine and eucalyptus groves from October through March. In Butterfly Town USA, as Pacific Grove is known, the sight of a mass of butterflies hanging from the branches like a long, fluttering veil is unforgettable.

A prime way to enjoy Pacific Grove is to walk or bicycle the 3 miles of city-owned shoreline along Ocean View Boulevard, a cliff-top area landscaped with native plants and dotted with benches meant for sitting and gazing at the sea. You can spot many types of birds here, including the web-footed cormorants that crowd the massive rocks rising out of the surf. Two Victorians of note along Ocean View are the Queen Anne–style Green Gables, at No. 301—erected in 1888, it's now an inn—and the 1909 Pryor House, at No. 429, a massive, shingled, private residence with a leaded- and beveled-glass doorway.

GETTING HERE AND AROUND

Reach Pacific Grove via Highway 68 off Highway 1, just south of Monterey. From Cannery Row in Monterey, head north until the road merges with Ocean Boulevard and follow it along the coast. MST buses travel within Pacific Grove and surrounding towns.

Sights

Lovers Point Park
CITY PARK | FAMILY | The coastal views are gorgeous from this waterfront park whose sheltered beach has a children's pool and a picnic area. The main lawn has a volleyball court and a snack bar. ✉ *Ocean View Blvd., northwest of Forest Ave., Pacific Grove* 🌐 *www.cityofpacificgrove.org.*

Monarch Grove Sanctuary
NATURE PRESERVE | FAMILY | The sanctuary is a reliable spot for viewing monarch butterflies between November and February. ■ **TIP→ The best time to visit is between noon and 3 pm.** ✉ *250 Ridge Rd., off Lighthouse Ave., Pacific Grove* 🌐 *www.pgmuseum.org/monarch-viewing* 🎫 *Free.*

Pacific Grove Museum of Natural History
HISTORY MUSEUM | FAMILY | The museum, a good source for the latest information about monarch butterflies, has permanent exhibitions about the butterflies, birds of Monterey County, biodiversity, and plants. There's a native plant garden, and a display documents life in Pacific Grove's 19th-century Chinese fishing village. ✉ *165 Forest Ave., at Central Ave., Pacific Grove* ☎ *831/648–5716* 🌐 *www.pgmuseum.org* 🎫 *$10* 🕒 *Closed Mon. and Tues.*

Point Pinos Lighthouse
LIGHTHOUSE | FAMILY | At this 1855 structure, the West Coast's oldest continuously operating lighthouse, you can learn about the lighting and foghorn operations and wander through a small museum containing U.S. Coast Guard memorabilia. ✉ *Asilomar Ave., between Lighthouse Ave. and Del Monte Blvd., Pacific Grove* ☎ *831/648–5722* 🌐 *www.cityofpacificgrove.org* 🎫 *$5* 🕒 *Closed Mon.–Thurs.*

Beaches

Asilomar State Beach
BEACH | FAMILY | A beautiful coastal area, Asilomar State Beach stretches between Point Pinos and the Del Monte Forest. The 100 acres of dunes, tidal pools, and pocket-size beaches form one of the region's richest areas for marine life—including surfers, who migrate here most winter mornings. Leashed dogs are allowed on the beach. **Amenities:** none. **Best for:** sunrise; sunset; surfing; walking. ✉ *Sunset Dr. and Asilomar Ave., Pacific Grove* ☎ *831/646–6440* 🌐 *www.parks.ca.gov.*

Restaurants

Beach House
$$$ | AMERICAN | Patrons of this bluff-top perch sip classic cocktails, sample California fare, and watch the otters frolic on Lovers Point Beach below. The sunset discounts between 4 and 5:30 (reservations recommended) are a great value. **Known for:** sweeping bluff-top views; heated patio; seafood and organic pastas. [$] *Average main: $31* ✉ *620 Ocean View Blvd., Pacific Grove* ☎ *831/375–2345* 🌐 *beachhousepg.com* 🕒 *No lunch.*

★ **Fandango**
$$$ | MEDITERRANEAN | The menu here is mostly Mediterranean and southern French, with such dishes as osso buco and paella. The decor follows suit—stone walls and country furniture lend the restaurant the earthy feel of a European farmhouse. **Known for:** wood-fire-grilled rack of lamb, seafood, and beef; convivial residential vibe; traditional European flavors. [$] *Average main: $38* ✉ *223 17th St., south of Lighthouse Ave., Pacific Grove* ☎ *831/372–3456* 🌐 *fandangorestaurant.com* 🕒 *No lunch Mon.–Sat.*

★ **Passionfish**
$$$ | MODERN AMERICAN | South American artwork and artifacts decorate Passionfish, and Latin and Asian flavors infuse

the dishes. The chef shops at local farmers' markets several times a week to find the best produce, fish, and meat available and then pairs it with creative sauces like a caper, raisin, and walnut relish. **Known for:** sustainably sourced and organic ingredients; reasonably priced wine list that supports small producers; slow-cooked meats. $ *Average main: $32* ✉ *701 Lighthouse Ave., Pacific Grove* ☎ *831/655–3311* ⊕ *www.passionfish.net* ⊘ *No lunch.*

Red House Café

$$ | **AMERICAN** | **FAMILY** | When it's nice out, sun pours through the big windows of this cozy restaurant and across tables on the porch; when fog rolls in, the fireplace is lit. The American menu changes with the seasons, but grilled lamb chops atop mashed potatoes are often on offer for dinner, and a grilled calamari steak might be served for lunch, either in a salad or as part of a sandwich. **Known for:** cozy homelike dining areas; comfort food; stellar breakfast and brunch. $ *Average main: $24* ✉ *662 Lighthouse Ave., at 19th St., Pacific Grove* ☎ *831/643–1060* ⊕ *redhousecafe.com* ⊘ *Closed Mon. No dinner Sun.*

Wild Fish

$$$ | **SEAFOOD** | Inventive dishes—made with 100% organic and locally sourced ingredients—live music, and a friendly staff are among the reasons why this intimate, ocean-to-table eatery is packed on weekends. Everything is fresh as it gets, from fish-and-chips, Monterey Bay bouillabaisse, and whole roasted fish of the day to local greens with spicy vinaigrette. **Known for:** cured house-smoked sablefish; jazz quartet on Friday and Saturday nights; smoked fish chowder. $ *Average main: $34* ✉ *545 Lighthouse Ave., Pacific Grove* ☎ *831/373–8523* ⊕ *www.wild-fish.com.*

Hotels

Gosby House Inn

$$ | **B&B/INN** | This turreted Queen Anne Victorian was completely remodeled and updated in early 2023, and although rooms still have things like vintage armoires and headboards, they now also have a swanky, contemporary vibe and modern amenities. **Pros:** peaceful; homey; within walking distance of shops and restaurants. **Cons:** not cozy enough for some; area is busy during the day; limited parking. $ *Rooms from: $200* ✉ *643 Lighthouse Ave., Pacific Grove* ☎ *831/375–1287* ⊕ *www.gosbyhouseinn.com* ⌗ *22 rooms* ⦿ *Free Breakfast.*

★ Green Gables Inn

$$$ | **B&B/INN** | Stained-glass windows, ornate interior details, and sophisticated modern amenities (the inn completed a top-to-bottom remodel in early 2023) compete with spectacular ocean views at this Queen Anne–style mansion. **Pros:** exceptional views; impeccable attention to historic detail; afternoon wine and cheese served in the parlor. **Cons:** some rooms are small; thin walls; breakfast room can be crowded. $ *Rooms from: $365* ✉ *301 Ocean View Blvd., Pacific Grove* ☎ *831/375–2095* ⊕ *www.greengablesinnpg.com* ⌗ *11 rooms* ⦿ *Free Breakfast.*

Martine Inn

$$ | **B&B/INN** | The glassed-in parlor and many guest rooms at this 1899 Mediterranean-style villa have stunning ocean views. **Pros:** romantic; exquisite antiques; ocean views. **Cons:** not child-friendly; sits on a busy thoroughfare; inconvenient parking. $ *Rooms from: $309* ✉ *255 Ocean View Blvd., Pacific Grove* ☎ *831/373–3388* ⊕ *www.martineinn.com* ⌗ *25 rooms* ⦿ *Free Breakfast.*

★ Seven Gables Inn

$$$ | **B&B/INN** | This luxe collection of seven buildings and flower-filled gardens on a bluff overlooking Monterey Bay includes the main mansion, built in 1886, a carriage house, guesthouse, and beach house. **Pros:** great location across from Lover's Point, a short walk to area restaurants, and a short drive to Cannery Row and Monterey aquarium; cooked-to-order breakfast in solarium; concierge services. **Cons:** small parking lot; not pet-friendly; most rooms aren't child-friendly. [$] *Rooms from: $390* ✉ *555 Ocean View Blvd., Pacific Grove* ☎ *831/372–4341* 🌐 *thesevengablesinn.com* 🛏 *25 rooms* 🍴 *Free Breakfast* ☞ *2-night minimum on weekends.*

Activities

GOLF

Pacific Grove Golf Links

GOLF | One of the best golf values in the region, this course has spectacular ocean views on its links-style back nine, which borders 17-Mile Drive. Jack Neville designed this section in 1960. Golfers with a sense of history will appreciate that H. Chandler Egan, a giant of early-20th-century course architecture, designed the front nine. Tee times may be reserved up to 60 days in advance. ✉ *77 Asilomar Ave., Pacific Grove* ☎ *831/648–5775* 🌐 *www.playpacificgrove.com* 🎟 *From $62* ⛳ *18 holes, 5800 yards, par 70.*

Monterey

2 miles southeast of Pacific Grove, 2 miles north of Carmel.

Monterey is a scenic city filled with early California history: adobe buildings from the 1700s, Colton Hall, where California's first constitution was drafted in 1849, and Cannery Row, made famous by author John Steinbeck. Thousands of visitors come each year to mingle with otters and other sea creatures at the world-famous Monterey Bay Aquarium and in the protected waters of the national marine sanctuary that hugs the shoreline.

GETTING HERE AND AROUND

From San Jose or San Francisco, take U.S. 101 south to Highway 156 West at Prunedale. Head west about 8 miles to Highway 1 and follow it about 15 miles south. From San Luis Obispo, take U.S. 101 north to Salinas and drive west on Highway 68 about 20 miles.

Many MST bus lines connect at the Monterey Transit Center, at Pearl Street and Munras Avenue. In summer (daily from 10 until at least 7), the free MST Monterey Trolley travels from downtown Monterey along Cannery Row to the Aquarium and back.

TOURS

Old Monterey Walking Tour

WALKING TOURS | **FAMILY** | Learn all about Monterey's storied past by joining a guided walking tour through the historic district. Tours begin at the Custom House in Custom House Plaza, across from Fisherman's Wharf and are typically offered Thursday through Sunday at 11, 1, and 3. ✉ *Monterey* 🌐 *www.parks.ca.gov/?page_id=951* 🎟 *$10.*

The Original Monterey Walking Tours

WALKING TOURS | **FAMILY** | Learn more about Monterey's past, primarily the Mexican period until California statehood, on a guided tour through downtown Monterey. You can also join a guided walking tour of Cannery Row in the morning. Tours last 1½ to 2 hours and are offered Thursday–Sunday at 10 am and 2. Reservations are essential. ✉ *Monterey* ☎ *831/521–4884* 🌐 *walkmonterey.com* 🎟 *From $25.*

ESSENTIALS

VISITOR INFORMATION Monterey Peninsula Chamber of Commerce. ✉ *353 Camino El Estero, Monterey* ☎ *831/648–5350* 🌐 *www.montereychamber.com.*

👁 Sights

Cannery Row

STREET | FAMILY | When John Steinbeck published the novel *Cannery Row* in 1945, he immortalized a place of rough-edged working people. The waterfront street, edging a mile of gorgeous coastline, once was crowded with sardine canneries processing, at their peak, nearly 200,000 tons of the smelly silver fish a year. During the mid-1940s, however, the sardines disappeared from the bay, causing the canneries to close. Through the years the old tin-roof canneries have been converted into restaurants, art galleries, and malls with shops selling T-shirts, fudge, and plastic sea otters. Recent tourist development along the row has been more tasteful, however, and includes stylish inns and hotels, wine tasting rooms, and upscale specialty shops. ⊠ *Between Reeside and David Aves., Monterey* ⊕ *canneryrow.com.*

Colton Hall

HISTORY MUSEUM | FAMILY | A convention of delegates met here in 1849 to draft the first state constitution. The stone building, which has served as a school, a courthouse, and the county seat, is a city-run museum furnished as it was during the constitutional convention. The extensive grounds outside the hall surround the Old Monterey Jail. ⊠ *570 Pacific St., between Madison and Jefferson Sts., Monterey* ☎ *831/646–5640* ⊕ *www.monterey.org/museums* ☜ *Free* ⊗ *Closed Mon.–Wed.*

Cooper-Molera Adobe

HISTORIC HOME | FAMILY | The restored 2-acre complex includes a house dating from the 1820s, a gift shop, bakery, and a large garden enclosed by a high adobe wall. The mostly Victorian-era antiques and memorabilia that fill the house provide a glimpse into the life of a prosperous sea merchant's family. The museum is open weekends for self-guided tours; docents are available to answer questions. If the house is closed, you can still pick up walking-tour maps and stroll the grounds. ⊠ *Monterey State Historic Park, 506 Munras Ave., Monterey* ☎ *800/944–6847* ⊕ *coopermolera.org* ☜ *$5 tour* ⊗ *Museum closed weekdays.*

Fisherman's Wharf

PEDESTRIAN MALL | FAMILY | The mournful barking of sea lions provides a steady soundtrack all along Monterey's waterfront, but the best way to actually view the whiskered marine mammals is to walk along one of the two piers across from Custom House Plaza. Lined with souvenir shops, the wharf is undeniably touristy, but it's lively and entertaining. At Wharf No. 2, a working municipal pier, you can see the day's catch being unloaded from fishing boats on one side and fishermen casting their lines into the water on the other. The pier has a couple of low-key restaurants, from whose seats lucky customers might spot otters and harbor seals. ⊠ *At end of Calle Principal, Monterey* ⊕ *www.montereywharf.com.*

Fort Ord National Monument

NATIONAL PARK | FAMILY | Scenic beauty, biodiversity, and miles of trails make this former U.S. Army training grounds

Steinbeck's Cannery Row

"Cannery Row in Monterey in California is a poem, a stink, a grating noise, a quality of light, a tone, a habit, a nostalgia, a dream. Cannery Row is the gathered and scattered, tin and iron and rust and splintered wood, chipped pavement and weedy lots and junk heaps, sardine canneries of corrugated iron, honky tonks, restaurants and whore houses, and little crowded groceries, and laboratories and flophouses." — John Steinbeck, *Cannery Row*

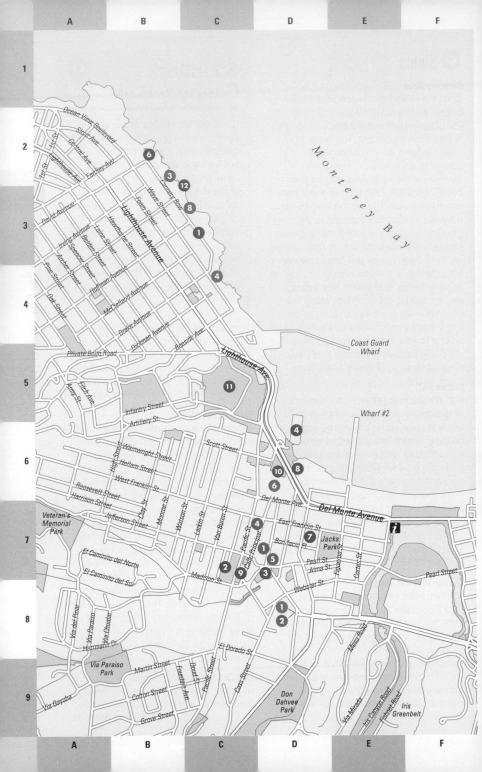

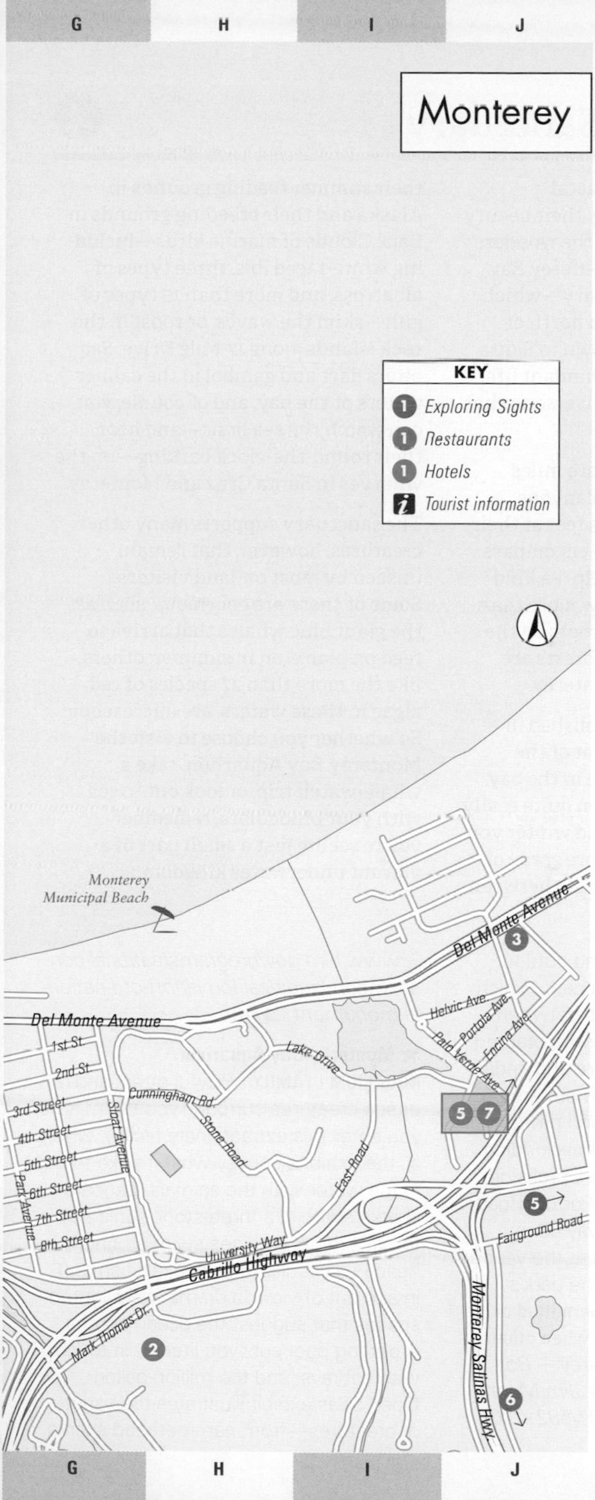

Monterey

KEY

1 *Exploring Sights*

1 *Restaurants*

1 *Hotels*

i *Tourist information*

4

Monterey Bay Area MONTEREY

Monterey Municipal Beach

Del Monte Avenue

Del Monte Avenue

1st St
2nd St
3rd Street
4th Street
5th Street
6th Street
7th Street
8th Street

Cunningham Rd.
Stone Road
Sloat Avenue
Park Avenue

Lake Drive

Helvic Ave.
Palo Verde Ave.
Portola Ave.
Encina Ave.

East Road

Fairground Road

University Way
Cabrillo Highway

Mark Thomas Dr.

Monterey Salinas Hwy.

Del Monte Avenue

3
5 7
5
2
6

The Marine Sanctuary

Although Monterey's coastal landscapes are stunning, their beauty is more than equaled by the wonders that lie offshore. The Monterey Bay National Marine Sanctuary—which stretches 276 miles, from north of San Francisco almost down to Santa Barbara—teems with abundant life, and has topography as diverse as that aboveground.

The preserve's 5,322 square miles include vast submarine canyons, which reach down 10,663 feet at their deepest point. They also encompass dense forests of giant kelp—a kind of seaweed that can grow more than a hundred feet from its roots on the ocean floor. These kelp forests are especially robust off Monterey.

The sanctuary was established in 1992 to protect the habitat of the many species that thrive in the bay. Some animals can be seen quite easily from land. In summer and winter you might glimpse the offshore spray of gray whales as they migrate between their summer feeding grounds in Alaska and their breeding grounds in Baja. Clouds of marine birds—including white-faced ibis, three types of albatross, and more than 15 types of gull—skim the waves, or roost in the rock islands along 17-Mile Drive. Sea otters dart and gambol in the calmer waters of the bay; and of course, you can watch the sea lions—and hear their round-the-clock barking—on the wharves in Santa Cruz and Monterey.

The sanctuary supports many other creatures, however, that remain unseen by most on-land visitors. Some of these are enormous, such as the giant blue whales that arrive to feed on plankton in summer; others, like the more than 22 species of red algae in these waters, are microscopic. So whether you choose to visit the Monterey Bay Aquarium, take a whale-watch trip, or look out to sea with your binoculars, remember you're seeing just a small part of a vibrant underwater kingdom.

a haven for nature lovers and outdoor enthusiasts. The 7,200-acre park, which stretches east over the hills between Monterey and Salinas, is also protected habitat for 35 species of rare and endangered plants and animals. There are 86 miles of single-track, dirt, and paved trails for hiking, biking, and horseback riding. The main trailheads are the Creekside, off Creekside Terrace near Portola Road, and Badger Hills, off Highway 68 in Salinas. Maps are available at the various trail-access points and on the park's website. ■TIP➔ Dogs are permitted on trails, but should be leashed when other people are nearby. ✉ Monterey ✛ Bordered by Hwy. 68 and Gen. Jim Moore and Reservation Rds. ☎ 831/582–2200

⊕ www.blm.gov/programs/national-conservation-lands/california/fort-ord-national-monument ✉ Free.

★ Monterey Bay Aquarium
AQUARIUM | FAMILY | Playful otters and other sea creatures surround you the minute you enter this extraordinary facility, where all the exhibits convey what it's like to be in the water with the animals. Leopard sharks swim in a three-story, sunlit kelp forest exhibit; sardines swim around your head in a circular tank; and jellyfish drift in and out of view in dramatically lighted spaces that suggest the ocean depths. A petting pool puts you literally in touch with bat rays, and the million-gallon Open Seas exhibit illustrates the variety of creatures—from hammerhead sharks

to placid-looking turtles—that live in the eastern Pacific. Splash Zone's 45, interactive, bilingual exhibits let kids commune with African penguins, clownfish, and other marine life. The only drawback to the aquarium experience is that it must be shared with the throngs that congregate daily, but most visitors think it's worth it. ⊠ *886 Cannery Row, Monterey* ☎ *831/648–4800 info* ⊕ *www.montereybayaquarium.org* ⊒ *$60.*

Monterey County Youth Museum
(*MY Museum*)
CHILDREN'S MUSEUM | FAMILY | Monterey Bay comes to life from a child's perspective in this fun-filled, interactive indoor exploration center. The seven galleries showcase the science and nature of the Big Sur coast, theater arts, Pebble Beach golf, and beaches. Also here are a live performance theater, a creation station; a hospital emergency room; and an agriculture corner where kids follow artichokes, strawberries, and other fruits and veggies on their evolution from sprout to harvest to farmers' markets. ⊠ *425 Washington St., between E. Franklin St. and Bonifacio Pl., Monterey* ☎ *831/649–6444* ⊕ *mymuseum.org* ⊒ *$10* ⊗ *Closed Mon. and Tues.*

Monterey History and Art Association at Stanton Center
ART MUSEUM | This two-story museum in Custom House Plaza showcases works by well-known contemporary artists, as well as artifacts relating to Monterey's maritime history. Featured artists include Salvador Dali, Armin Hansen, Paul Whitman, and Jo Mora. Exhibits focusing on a local artist rotate every three months. ⊠ *5 Custom House Plaza, Monterey* ☎ *831/372–2608* ⊕ *montereyhistory.org/stanton-center* ⊒ *$20* ⊗ *Closed Fri.*

Monterey Museum of Art at Pacific Street
ART MUSEUM | Photographs by Ansel Adams and Edward Weston and works by other artists who have spent time on the peninsula are on display here, along with international folk art, from Kentucky hearth brooms to Tibetan prayer wheels.

⊠ *559 Pacific St., across from Colton Hall, Monterey* ☎ *831/372–5477* ⊕ *montereyart.org* ⊒ *$15* ⊗ *Closed Mon.–Wed.*

★ **Monterey State Historic Park**
HISTORY MUSEUM | FAMILY | You can glimpse Monterey's early history in several well-preserved adobe buildings in Custom House Plaza and the downtown area. Although most are only open via guided tours (check ahead for details), some also have beautiful gardens to explore. Set in what was once a hotel and saloon, the Pacific House Museum now houses a visitor center and exhibits of gold-rush relics; photographs of old Monterey; and Native American baskets, pottery, and other artifacts. The adjacent Custom House, built by the Mexican government in 1827 and now California's oldest standing public building, was the first stop for sea traders whose goods were subject to duties. (In 1846 Commodore John Sloat raised the American flag over this adobe structure and claimed California for the United States.)

Exhibits at Casa Soberanes (1842), once a customs-house guard's residence, survey Monterey life from Mexican rule to the present. A veranda encircles the second floor of Larkin House (1835), whose namesake, an early California statesman, brought many of the antique furnishings inside from New Hampshire. Stevenson House was named in honor of author Robert Louis Stevenson, who boarded here briefly in a tiny upstairs room that's now furnished with items from his family's estate. Other rooms include a gallery of memorabilia and a children's nursery with Victorian toys.

■ **TIP→ If the buildings are closed, you can access a cell-phone tour 24/7** (☎ *831/998–9458*) **or download an app.** ⊠ *10 Custom House Plaza, Pacific House Museum visitor center, Monterey* ☎ *831/649–2907* ⊕ *www.parks.ca.gov/?page_id=575* ⊒ *Free–$5, 1-hr history walk $10.*

4

Monterey Bay Area MONTEREY

California sea lions are intelligent, social animals that live (and sleep) close together in groups.

Presidio of Monterey Museum

HISTORY MUSEUM | **FAMILY** | This spot has been significant for centuries. Its first incarnation was as a Native American village for the Rumsien tribe. The Spanish explorer Sebastián Vizcaíno landed here in 1602, and Father Junípero Serra arrived in 1770. Notable battles fought here include the 1818 skirmish in which the corsair Hipólito Bruchard conquered the Spanish garrison that stood on this site and claimed part of California for Argentina. The indoor museum tells the stories; plaques mark the outdoor sites. ✉ *Corporal Ewing Rd., Monterey* ✥ *Off Lighthouse Ave.* ☎ *831/646–3456* 🌐 *www.monterey.org/museums* 🎟 *Free* 🕒 *Closed weekdays.*

A Taste of Monterey

WINERY | Without driving the back roads, you can taste the wines of nearly 100 area vintners (craft beers, too) while taking in fantastic bay views. Bottles are available for purchase, and food is served from 11:30 until closing. ✉ *700 Cannery Row, Suite KK, Monterey* ☎ *831/646–5446* 🌐 *atasteofmonterey.com* 🎟 *Tastings from $23.*

🍴 Restaurants

Alejandro's

$$ | **MEXICAN** | **FAMILY** | A stylish Mexican eatery in the heart of downtown, Alejandro's is designed to feel like a Yucatán holiday getaway. Options, many of them cooked in the wood-fired oven, include seafood tostadas and ceviches, *birria* (meat stew), bone-marrow tacos, and roast chicken wrapped in banana leaves. **Known for:** housemade tortillas; extensive salsa selection; creative cocktails and list of wines from Baja and Alta California. [$] *Average main: $30* ✉ *474 Alvarado St., Monterey* ☎ *831/717–4781* 🌐 *www.alejandros.co* 🕒 *No lunch.*

Estéban Restaurant

$$$ | **SPANISH** | **FAMILY** | A festive dining room with a fireplace at the Casa Munras hotel is the setting for meals featuring modern and classic versions of empanadas, crispy Spanish octopus, flash-fried wild Gulf prawns, and five types of paella. Midweek specials abound—on Tuesday night, feast on a three-course prix-fixe paella dinner ($38 per person), bottles of wine are half off on Monday, and Wednesday wine flights are just $16 for three tastes. **Known for:** daily tapas happy hour from 4:30 to 6; patio with firepit; special menus for kids and pups. [$] *Average main: $35* ✉ *700 Munras Ave., Monterey* ☎ *831/375–0176* 🌐 *www.hotelcasamunras.com/dining* ⏲ *No lunch.*

Monterey's Fish House

$$ | **SEAFOOD** | Casual yet stylish and always packed, this seafood restaurant is removed from the hubbub of the wharf. The bartenders and waitstaff will gladly advise you on the perfect wine to go with your poached, blackened, or oak-grilled seafood. **Known for:** seafood, steaks, house-made pasta; festive atmosphere; oyster bar. [$] *Average main: $25* ✉ *2114 Del Monte Ave., at Dela Vina Ave., Monterey* ☎ *831/373–4647* 🌐 *montereyfishhouse.com.*

★ Montrio Bistro

$$$$ | **AMERICAN** | This quirky converted firehouse, with its rawhide walls and iron indoor trellises, has a wonderfully sophisticated menu. Organic produce and meats and sustainably sourced seafood are used in imaginative dishes that reflect the area's agriculture—crispy artichoke hearts with Mediterranean baba ghanoush, for instance, and hamachi crudo with passion-fruit vinaigrette. **Known for:** green-certified restaurant; extensive international wine list; inventive cocktails. [$] *Average main: $44* ✉ *414 Calle Principal, at W. Franklin St., Monterey* ☎ *831/648–8880* 🌐 *www.montrio.com* ⏲ *No lunch.*

Old Monterey Café

$ | **AMERICAN** | **FAMILY** | Breakfast here gets constant local raves thanks to familiar favorites such as a dozen kinds of omelets and pancakes options that range from blueberry to cinnamon-raisin-pecan. The lunch menu has good soups, salads, and sandwiches. **Known for:** seven types of eggs Benedict; upbeat, team-style service; all meals cooked to order. [$] *Average main: $16* ✉ *489 Alvarado St., at Munras Ave., Monterey* ☎ *831/646–1021* 🌐 *www.oldmontereycafeca.com* ⏲ *No dinner.*

Tarpy's Roadhouse

$$$ | **AMERICAN** | **FAMILY** | Fun, dressed-up American favorites—a little something for everyone—are served in this renovated early-1900s stone farmhouse several miles east of town. The kitchen cranks out everything from Cajun-spiced prawns to meat loaf with marsala-mushroom gravy to grilled ribs and steaks. **Known for:** American comfort food with a California twist; rustic dining near an indoor fireplace or out in a garden courtyard; generous portions. [$] *Average main: $34* ✉ *2999 Monterey–Salinas Hwy., Hwy. 68, Monterey* ☎ *831/647–1444* 🌐 *www.tarpys.com.*

Hotels

Casa Munras Garden Hotel & Spa

$ | **HOTEL** | **FAMILY** | A cluster of Spanish-theme buildings in the heart of downtown, Casa Munras pays homage to Monterey's roots and the legacy of Spanish diplomat Don Estéban Munras, who built a residence on the site in 1824. **Pros:** full-service spa and salon, heated pool, and fitness room; excellent tapas restaurant; walk to downtown sights and restaurants; rate includes bike usage. **Cons:** $17 parking fee; pool area can get noisy; thin walls. [$] *Rooms from: $199* ✉ *700 Munras Ave., Monterey* ☎ *831/375–2411, 800/222–2446* 🌐 *www.hotelcasamunras.com* 🛏 *154 rooms* 🍴 *No Meals.*

Hyatt Regency Monterey

$$ | **RESORT** | **FAMILY** | A 22-acre resort amid cypress forests on the Del Monte Golf Course, the Hyatt Regency Monterey is a good choice for business travelers and families (especially those with pets)

seeking relatively affordable lodgings with numerous on-site services. **Pros:** half the rooms overlook the golf course; six tennis courts, firepits, two pools and hot tubs, hammocks, and swings on property; restaurant with live weekend entertainment. **Cons:** not in heart of downtown; sprawling resort that can seem packed during busy seasons; not ideal for pet-phobic guests. [$] *Rooms from: $264* ✉ *1 Old Golf Course Rd., Monterey* ☎ *831/372–1234* 🌐 *www.hyatt.com* 🛏 *560 rooms* 🍴 *No Meals.*

InterContinental the Clement Monterey
$$$ | **HOTEL** | **FAMILY** | Spectacular bay views, upscale amenities, assiduous service, and a superb location next to the aquarium propelled this luxury hotel to immediate stardom. **Pros:** a block from the aquarium; fantastic waterfront views from some rooms; great for families. **Cons:** a tad formal; not budget; Cannery Row crowds everywhere on weekends and holidays. [$] *Rooms from: $365* ✉ *750 Cannery Row, Monterey* ☎ *831/375–4500* 🌐 *www.ictheclementmonterey.com* 🛏 *208 rooms* 🍴 *No Meals.*

Monterey Plaza Hotel & Spa
$$ | **HOTEL** | Guests at this Cannery Row hotel can see frolicking sea otters from its wide outdoor patio and many room balconies. **Pros:** on the ocean; many amenities; attentive service. **Cons:** touristy area; heavy traffic; parking fee. [$] *Rooms from: $306* ✉ *400 Cannery Row, Monterey* ☎ *831/920–6710* 🌐 *montereyplazahotel.com* 🛏 *290 rooms* 🍴 *No Meals.*

Monterey Tides
$$ | **RESORT** | One of the area's best values, this hotel has a great waterfront location—2 miles north of Monterey, with views of the bay and the city skyline—and offers a surprising array of amenities. **Pros:** on the beach; large pool; family-friendly. **Cons:** several miles from major attractions; big-box mall neighborhood; most rooms on the small side. [$] *Rooms from: $249* ✉ *2600 Sand Dunes Dr., Monterey* ☎ *831/394–3321, 800/242–8627* 🌐 *montereytides.com* 🛏 *196 rooms* 🍴 *No Meals.*

Portola Hotel & Spa at Monterey Bay
$$ | **HOTEL** | **FAMILY** | One of Monterey's largest hotels, and locally owned and operated for more than 40 years, the coastal-theme Portola anchors a prime city block between Custom House Plaza and the Monterey Conference Center. **Pros:** walk to sights and downtown restaurants and shops; three on-site restaurants and coffee shop; pet- and family-friendly. **Cons:** crowded when conferences convene; no limit on dog size; parking fee. [$] *Rooms from: $316* ✉ *2 Portola Plaza, Monterey* ☎ *831/649–4511, 888/222–5851* 🌐 *www.portolahotel.com* 🛏 *379 rooms* 🍴 *No Meals.*

The Sanctuary Beach Resort
$$$ | **HOTEL** | **FAMILY** | Walk to the sand from spacious, luxurious bungalows furnished in contemporary, ocean-theme style at this 19-acre, wellness-centered resort next to Marina Dunes Preserve and a secluded stretch of Marina State Beach. **Pros:** easy access to hiking and biking trails; heated pool, on-site spa services; each bungalow has two rooms that can combine for families and groups. **Cons:** not in the heart of town; parking lot relatively far from rooms; area weather is often cooler than other parts of the bay. [$] *Rooms from: $429* ✉ *3295 Dunes Dr., Seaside* ☎ *855/693–6583* 🌐 *www.thesanctuarybeachresort.com* 🛏 *60 rooms* 🍴 *No Meals.*

Spindrift Inn
$$ | **HOTEL** | This boutique hotel on Cannery Row has beach access and a rooftop garden that overlooks the water. **Pros:** close to aquarium; steps from the beach; friendly staff. **Cons:** throngs of visitors outside; can be noisy; not good for families. [$] *Rooms from: $315* ✉ *652 Cannery Row, Monterey* ☎ *831/646–8900, 800/841–1879* 🌐 *www.spindriftinn.com* 🛏 *45 rooms* 🍴 *Free Breakfast.*

Nightlife

BARS

Cibo

LIVE MUSIC | An Italian restaurant and event venue with a big bar area, Cibo brings live jazz and other music to downtown five nights a week. ⊠ *301 Alvarado St., at Del Monte Ave., Monterey* ☎ *831/649–8151* ⊕ *cibo.com.*

LindaRose Bar & Grill

BARS | Head up to the rooftop bar at Hotel 1110 for sweeping bay views, craft cocktails, local wine and beer, and an array of Mediterranean-centric dishes—from kebabs and lamb fries to mezze. Check the event schedule for live music and other special happenings. ⊠ *1110 Del Monte Ave., Monterey* ☎ *831/655–0515* ⊕ *www.hotel1110.com/lindarose.*

Turn 12 Bar & Grill

BARS | The motorcycles and vintage photographs at this downtown watering hole pay homage to nearby 11-turn Laguna Seca Raceway. The large-screen TVs, heated outdoor patio, happy-hour specials, and live entertainment keep the place jumpin' into the wee hours. ⊠ *400 Tyler St., at E. Franklin St., Monterey* ☎ *831/372–8876* ⊕ *www.turn12barandgrill.com.*

BREWPUBS

Alvarado Street Brewery & Grill

BREWPUBS | Housed in an historic Beaux Arts building that dates from 1916, this craft brewery lures locals and visitors alike with a full bar and 20 craft beers on tap, decent gastropub menu, beer garden, and shaded sidewalk patio. The company also has a brewery, bistro, and wine bar in Carmel Plaza in Carmel-by-the-Sea. ⊠ *426 Alvarado St., Monterey* ☎ *831/655–2337* ⊕ *www.alvaradostreetbrewery.com.*

Peter B's Brewpub

BREWPUBS | House-made beers, 18 HDTVs, a decent pub menu, and a pet-friendly patio ensure lively crowds at this craft brewery in back of the Portola Hotel & Spa. ⊠ *2 Portola Plaza, Monterey* ☎ *831/649–2699* ⊕ *www.portolahotel.com/dining/peter-bs-brewpub* ⊘ *Closed Mon. and Tues.*

PUBS

Crown & Anchor

PUBS | An authentic British pub, downtown Crown & Anchor has 20 beers on tap, classic cocktails, and a full menu, including 18 daily specials available in the restaurant and heated patio until midnight. ⊠ *150 W. Franklin St., Monterey* ☎ *831/649–6496* ⊕ *crownandanchor.net.*

Shopping

Alvarado and nearby downtown streets are good places to start a Monterey shopping spree, especially if you're interested in antiques and collectibles.

Cannery Row Antique Mall

ANTIQUES & COLLECTIBLES | Bargain hunters can sometimes find little treasures at the mall, which houses more than 100 local vendors under one roof. ⊠ *471 Wave St., Monterey* ☎ *831/655–0261* ⊕ *www.canneryrowantiquemall.com.*

Activities

Monterey Bay waters never warm to the temperatures of their Southern California counterparts—the warmest they get is the low 60s. That's one reason why the marine life here is so diverse, which in turn brings out the fishers, kayakers, and whale-watchers. During the rainy winter, the waves grow larger, and surfers flock to the water. On land pretty much year-round, bikers find opportunities to ride, and walkers have plenty of waterfront to stroll.

BIKING

Adventures by the Sea

BIKING | **FAMILY** | You can rent surreys plus tandem, standard, and electric bicycles from this outfit that also conducts bike and kayak tours, and rents kayaks and stand-up paddleboards. There are multiple locations along Cannery Row and Custom House Plaza as well as branches at Lovers Point in Pacific Grove and 17-Mile Drive in Pebble Beach. ⊠ *299 Cannery Row, Monterey* ☎ *831/372–1807, 800/979–3370 reservations* ⊕ *adventuresbythesea.com.*

FISHING
J&M Sport Fishing
FISHING | FAMILY | This outfit takes beginning and experienced fishers out to sea to catch rock cod, ling cod, sand dabs, mackerel, halibut, salmon (in season), albacore, squid, Dungeness crab, and other species. ⊠ *66 Fisherman's Wharf, Monterey* ☎ *831/372–7440* ⊕ *jmsportfishing.com* 🖥 *Trips from $115.*

GOLF
Del Monte Golf Course
GOLF | Though overshadowed by its higher-profile Pebble Beach siblings, this classic course that golf champion Johnny Miller once described as "sneaky hard" predates them all. Designed by Charles Maud in 1897 (the first nine) and 1903 (the back nine) and redesigned in 1920 by W. Herbert Fowler, the course has wide fairways—many of them with wicked doglegs—flanked by oak, pine, and cypress trees. Many golfers find the par-5 13th hole their unluckiest: long (512 yards) and straight, it narrows sharply just before the green. ⊠ *1300 Sylvan Rd., Monterey* ☎ *800/877–0597* ⊕ *pebblebeach.com* 🖥 *$125* ⅄ *18 holes, 6365 yards, par 72.*

HIKING
Monterey Bay Coastal Recreation Trail
HIKING & WALKING | FAMILY | From Custom House Plaza, you can walk along the coast in either direction on this 18-mile-long trail and take in spectacular views of the sea. The trail runs from north of Monterey in Castroville south to Pacific Grove, with sections continuing around Pebble Beach. Much of the path follows an old Southern Pacific Railroad route. *Easy–moderate.* ⊠ *Monterey* ☎ *888/221–1010*

⊕ *www.seemonterey.com/things-to-do/outdoors/hiking/coastal-trail.*

KAYAKING
★ Monterey Bay Kayaks
KAYAKING | FAMILY | For many visitors the best way to see the bay is by kayak. This company rents equipment and conducts classes and natural-history tours. ⊠ *693 Del Monte Ave., Monterey* ☎ *831/373–5357* ⊕ *www.montereybaykayaks.com* 🖥 *4-hr rentals from $35 per person.*

WHALE-WATCHING
Thousands of gray whales pass close by the Monterey Coast on their annual migration between the Bering Sea and Baja California, and a whale-watching cruise is the best way to see these magnificent mammals close up. The migration south takes place from December through March; January is prime viewing time. The whales migrate north from March through June. Blue whales and humpbacks also pass the coast; they're most easily spotted in late summer and early fall.

Fast Raft Ocean Safaris
RAFTING | FAMILY | Naturalists lead whale-watching and sightseeing tours of Monterey Bay aboard the 33-foot *Ranger,* a six-passenger, rigid-hull, inflatable boat. The speedy craft slips into coves inaccessible to larger vessels, and its quiet engines enable intimate marine experiences without disturbing wildlife. Children ages eight and older are welcome to participate. From April to November, the boat departs from Moss Landing Harbor North Boat Launching Ramp. ⊠ *32 Cannery Row, Suite F2, Monterey* ☎ *408/659–3900* ⊕ *www.fastraft.com* 🖥 *From $195.*

Monterey Bay Whale Watch
WILDLIFE-WATCHING | FAMILY | The marine biologists here lead three- to five-hour whale-watching tours. ⊠ *84 Fisherman's Wharf, Monterey* ☎ *831/375–4658* ⊕ *montereybaywhalewatch.com* 🖥 *From $79.*

Princess Monterey Whale Watching
WILDLIFE-WATCHING | FAMILY | Tours are offered daily on a 100-passenger high-speed cruiser and a large 100-foot boat. ⊠ *96 Fisherman's Wharf, Monterey* ☎ *831/372–2203* ⊕ *montereywhale-watching.com* ⌑ *From $70.*

Salinas

17 miles east of Monterey on Hwy. 68.

Salinas, a hardworking city surrounded by vineyards and fruit and vegetable fields, honors the memory and literary legacy of John Steinbeck, its most famous native, with the National Steinbeck Center. The facility is in Old Town Salinas, where renovated turn-of-the-20th-century stone buildings house shops and restaurants.

GETTING HERE AND AROUND

From San Francisco, take Highway 101 south to Salinas, exit at Market Street for downtown/Old Town Salinas. Highway 68 connects Salinas to Monterey; Highway 183 is the main route to Castroville and Santa Cruz County. Both routes eventually connect with Highway 1.

Greyhound buses stop at the main depot (⊠ *11 Station Pl. at Market St.*), as does Amtrak's *Coast Starlight.* From there it's a short walk to the Salinas Transit Center (⊠ *110 Salinas St. at Central Ave.*), with connections to public transit throughout Monterey Bay and Central California. You can purchase day passes for Monterey-Salinas Transit (MST) buses here.

ESSENTIALS

TRAIN INFORMATION Salinas Amtrak Station. ⊠ *11 Station Pl., Salinas* ☎ *800/872–7245* ⊕ *www.amtrak.com.*

VISITOR INFORMATION California Welcome Center. ⊠ *1A Station Pl., Salinas* ☎ *831/757–8687* ⊕ *www.visitcalifornia.com.*

Sights

★ **National Steinbeck Center**
HISTORY MUSEUM | FAMILY | The center's exhibits document the life of Pulitzer- and Nobel-prize winner John Steinbeck and the history of the nearby communities that inspired novels such as *East of Eden.* Highlights include reproductions of the green pickup-camper from *Travels with Charley* and the bunk room from *Of Mice and Men.* Steinbeck House, the author's Victorian birthplace, is two blocks from the center at 132 Central Avenue. Now a popular (lunch-only) restaurant and gift shop with docent-led tours, it also displays memorabilia. ⊠ *1 Main St., Salinas* ☎ *831/775–4721* ⊕ *www.steinbeck.org* ⌑ *$15.*

San Juan Bautista State Historic Park
HISTORIC SIGHT | FAMILY | With the low-slung, colonnaded Mission San Juan Bautista as its drawing card, this park 20 miles northeast of Salinas is about as close to early-19th-century California as you can get. Historic buildings ring the wide green plaza, among them an adobe home furnished with Spanish-colonial antiques, a hotel frozen in the 1860s, a blacksmith shop, a pioneer cabin, and a jailhouse. The mission's cemetery contains the unmarked graves of more than 4,300 Native American converts. ■TIP→ **On the first Saturday of the month, costumed volunteers engage in quilting bees, tortilla making, and other frontier activities, and sarsaparilla and other non-alcoholic drinks are served in the saloon.** ⊠ *19 Franklin St., San Juan Bautista* ☎ *831/623–4881* ⊕ *www.parks.ca.gov* ⌑ *$3 park, $4 mission* ◔ *Mission closed Tues.*

Pinnacles National Park

38 miles southeast of Salinas.

It was Teddy Roosevelt who recognized the uniqueness of this ancient volcano—its jagged spires and monoliths thrusting upward from chaparral-covered mountains—when he made it a national monument in 1908. Though only about two hours from the bustling Bay Area, the outside world seems to recede well before you even reach the park's gates.

GETTING HERE AND AROUND

One of the first things you need to decide when visiting Pinnacles is which entrance—east or west—you'll use, because there's no road connecting the two rugged peaks separating them. Entering from Highway 25 on the east is straightforward. The gate is only a mile or so from the turnoff. From the west, once you head east out of Soledad on Highway 146, the road quickly becomes narrow and hilly, with many blind curves. Drive slowly and cautiously along the 10 miles or so before you reach the west entrance.

ESSENTIALS

Pinnacles Visitor Center

VISITOR CENTER | At the park's main visitor center, near the eastern entrance, you'll find a helpful selection of maps, books, and gifts. The adjacent campground store sells light snacks. ⊠ *5000 Hwy. 146, Paicines* ☎ *831/389–4485* ⊕ *www.nps. gov/pinn.*

West Pinnacles Visitor Contact Station

VISITOR CENTER | This small ranger station is just past the park's western entrance, about 10 miles east of Soledad. Here you can get maps and information, watch a 13-minute film about Pinnacles, and view interpretive exhibits. No food or drink is available here. ⊠ *Hwy. 146, Soledad* ☎ *831/389–4427* ⊕ *www.nps.gov/pinn.*

 Sights

Pinnacles National Park

NATIONAL PARK | FAMILY | The many attractions at Pinnacles include talus caves, 30 miles of hiking trails, and hundreds of rock-climbing routes. A mosaic of diverse habitats supports an amazing variety of wildlife species: 160 birds, 48 mammals, 70 butterflies, and nearly 400 bees. The park is also home to some of the world's remaining few hundred condors in captivity and release areas. Fourteen of California's 25 bat species live in caves and other habitats in the park. President Theodore Roosevelt declared this remarkable 26,000-acre geologic and wildlife preserve a national monument in 1908. President Barack Obama officially designated it a national park in 2013.

The pinnacles are believed to have been created when two major tectonic plates collided and pushed a smaller plate down beneath the earth's crust, spawning volcanoes in what's now called the Gabilan Mountains, southeast of Salinas and Monterey. After the eruptions ceased, the San Andreas Fault split the volcanic field in two, carrying part of it northward to what is now Pinnacles National Park. Millions of years of erosion left a rugged landscape of rocky spires and crags, or pinnacles. Boulders fell into canyons and valleys, creating talus caves and a paradise for modern-day rock climbers.

Spring is the most popular time to visit, when colorful wildflowers blanket the meadows; the light and scenery can be striking in fall and winter; the summer heat is often brutal. The park has two entrances—east and west—but they are not connected. Amenities and attractions on the park's east side include the Pinnacles Visitor Center, Bear Gulch Nature Center, the park headquarters, Pinnacles Campground, and the Bear Gulch Cave and Reservoir. The Chaparral Parking Area is on the west side, where you can feast on fantastic views of the Pinnacles High

Peaks from the parking area. Dogs are not allowed on hiking trails.

■ **TIP→ The east entrance is 32 miles southeast of Hollister via Highway 25. The west entrance is about 12 miles east of Soledad via Highway 146.** ⊠ *5000 Hwy. 146, Paicines* ☎ *831/389–4486* ⊕ *www. nps.gov/pinn* ⊠ *$30 per vehicle, $15 per visitor if biking or walking.*

 Activities

HIKING

Hiking is the most popular activity at Pinnacles, with more than 30 miles of trails for every interest and level of fitness. Because there isn't a road through the park, hiking is also the only way to experience its interior, including the High Peaks, the talus caves, and the reservoir.

★ Balconies Cliffs–Cave Loop

TRAIL | FAMILY | Grab your flashlight before heading out from the Chaparral Trailhead parking lot for this 2.4-mile loop that takes you through the Balconies Caves. This trail is especially beautiful in spring, when wildflowers carpet the canyon floor. About 0.6 mile from the start of the trail, turn left to begin ascending the Balconies Cliffs Trail, where you'll be rewarded with close-up views of Machete Ridge and other steep, vertical formations; you may run across rock climbers testing their skills before rounding the loop and descending back through the cave. *Easy–Moderate.* ⊠ *Pinnacles National Park* ⊕ *Trailhead: Chaparral Parking Area.*

★ Bear Gulch Cave–Moses Spring–Rim Trail Loop

TRAIL | FAMILY | Perhaps the most popular hike at Pinnacles, this relatively short (2.2-mile) loop trail is fun for kids and adults. It leads to the Bear Gulch cave system, and if your timing is right, you'll pass by several seasonal waterfalls inside the caves (flashlights are required). If it's been raining, check with a ranger, as the caves can flood. The upper side of the cave is usually closed in spring and

early summer to protect the Townsend's big-ear bats and their pups. *Easy.* ⊕ *Trailhead: Bear Gulch Day Use Area.*

Moss Landing

12 miles northwest of Salinas.

Moss Landing is not much more than a couple of blocks of cafés and restaurants, art galleries, and studios, plus a busy fishing port, but therein lies its charm. It's a fine place to overnight or stop for a meal and get a dose of nature.

GETTING HERE AND AROUND

From Highway 1 north or south, exit at Moss Landing Road on the ocean side. MST buses serve Moss Landing.

TOURS

Elkhorn Slough Safari Nature Boat Tours

BOAT TOURS | FAMILY | This outfit's naturalists lead two-hour tours of Elkhorn Sough aboard a 27-foot pontoon boat. Reservations are required. ⊠ *Moss Landing Harbor, Moss Landing* ☎ *831/633–5555* ⊕ *elkhornslough.com* ⊠ *From $43.*

ESSENTIALS

VISITOR INFORMATION Moss Landing Chamber of Commerce. ⊠ *Moss Landing* ☎ *831/633–4501* ⊕ *mosslandingchamber. com.*

 Sights

Elkhorn Slough National Estuarine Research Reserve

NATURE PRESERVE | FAMILY | The reserve's 1,700 acres of tidal flats and salt marshes form a complex environment that supports some 300 species of birds. A walk along the meandering waterways and wetlands can reveal hawks, white-tailed kites, owls, herons, and egrets. Also living or visiting here are sea otters, sharks, rays, and many other animals. ⊠ *1700 Elkhorn Rd., Watsonville* ☎ *831/728–2822* ⊕ *www.elkhornslough. org* ⊠ *Free* ⊙ *Closed Mon. and Tues.*

🍴 Restaurants

Haute Enchilada

$$ | **SOUTH AMERICAN** | **FAMILY** | Part of a complex that includes art galleries and an events venue, the Haute adds bohemian character to the seafaring village of Moss Landing. The inventive Latin American–inspired dishes include shrimp and black corn enchiladas topped with a citrus cilantro cream sauce, and roasted *pasilla* chilies stuffed with mashed plantains and caramelized onions. **Known for:** extensive cocktail and wine list; many vegan and gluten-free options; artsy atmosphere. [$] *Average main: $26* ✉ *7902 Moss Landing Rd., Moss Landing* ☎ *831/633–5843* 🌐 *www.hauteenchilada.com* ⏲ *Closed Tues. and Wed.*

🛏 Hotels

Captain's Inn

$ | **B&B/INN** | Commune with nature and pamper yourself with upscale creature comforts at this green-certified complex in the heart of town. **Pros:** walk to restaurants and shops; tranquil natural setting; closest Monterey Bay hotel to Pinnacles National Park. **Cons:** rooms in historic building don't have water views; far from urban amenities; not appropriate for young children. [$] *Rooms from: $129* ✉ *8122 Moss Landing Rd., Moss Landing* ☎ *831/889–0815* 🌐 *www.captainsinn.com* 🛏 *10 rooms* 🍽 *No Meals.*

🏃 Activities

KAYAKING

Monterey Bay Kayaks

KAYAKING | **FAMILY** | Rent a kayak to paddle out into Elkhorn Slough for up-close wildlife encounters. ✉ *2390 Hwy. 1, at North Harbor, Moss Landing* ☎ *831/373–5357* 🌐 *www.montereybaykayaks.com* 🎟 *4-hr rentals from $35 per person.*

Aptos

17 miles north of Moss Landing.

Backed by a redwood forest and facing the sea, downtown Aptos—known as Aptos Village—is a place of wooden walkways and false-fronted shops, as well as a "new" village complex of restaurants, shops, and services. Antiques dealers cluster along Trout Gulch Road, off Soquel Drive east of Highway 1.

GETTING HERE AND AROUND

Use Highway 1 to reach Aptos from Santa Cruz or Monterey. Exit at State Park Drive to reach the main shopping hub and Aptos Village. You can also exit at Freedom Boulevard or Rio del Mar. Soquel Drive is the main artery through town.

ESSENTIALS

VISITOR INFORMATION Aptos Chamber of Commerce. ✉ *7605–A Old Dominion Ct., Aptos* ☎ *831/688–1467* 🌐 *aptoschamber.com.*

⛱ Beaches

★ Seacliff State Beach

BEACH | **FAMILY** | Sandstone bluffs tower above this popular beach, whose long fishing pier was, unfortunately, demolished in 2023 following devastating winter storm damage. The 1.5-mile walk north to adjacent New Brighton State Beach in Capitola is one of the nicest on the bay. Leashed dogs are allowed on the beach. **Amenities:** food and drink; lifeguards; parking (fee); showers; toilets. **Best for:** sunset; swimming; walking. ✉ *201 State Park Dr., Aptos* ☎ *831/685–6500* 🌐 *www.parks.ca.gov* 🎟 *$10 per vehicle.*

🍴 Restaurants

Bittersweet Bistro

$$$ | **MEDITERRANEAN** | A large old tavern with cathedral ceilings houses this popular bistro, where the Mediterranean–California menu changes seasonally, but

regular highlights include paella, seafood puttanesca, and pepper-crusted rib-eye steak with Cabernet demi-glace. **Known for:** value-laden happy hour; seafood specials; house-made desserts. $ *Average main: $38 ⊠ 787 Rio Del Mar Blvd., off Hwy. 1, Aptos ☎ 831/662–9799 ⊕ www. bittersweetbistro.com ⊙ Closed Mon. and Tues. No lunch, but open at 2 for dinner.*

★ Mentone

$$ | **ITALIAN** | This spacious restaurant with soaring ceilings and floor-to-ceiling windows serves dishes featuring the authentic flavors of the French/Italian Riviera, from Nice to Genoa. The menu changes often, depending on ingredients acquired from local purveyors, but, in addition to house-made pizzas and traditional pastas, it might offer black-truffle cappellini in an Armagnac and truffle butter sauce, Dungeness crab gnocchi, or pork belly with squash and fennel in a scallop sauce. **Known for:** seasonal cocktails; wood-oven-fired pizzas; house-made pastas. $ *Average main: $30 ⊠ 174 Aptos Village Way, Aptos ☎ 831/708–4040 ⊕ www. mentonerestaurant.com ⊙ Closed Tues. No lunch weekdays.*

 Hotels

Seacliff Inn, Tapestry Collection by Hilton

$ | **HOTEL** | **FAMILY** | Families and business travelers like this 6-acre property near Seacliff State Beach that's more resort than hotel. **Pros:** walking distance to the beach; family-friendly; on-site restaurant and bar. **Cons:** close to freeway; occasional nighttime bar noise; no elevator. $ *Rooms from: $180 ⊠ 7500 Old Dominion Ct., Aptos ☎ 831/688–7300, 800/367–2003 ⊕ www.seacliffinn.com ⥂ 158 rooms ⦿ No Meals.*

Seascape Beach Resort

$$$ | **RESORT** | **FAMILY** | It's easy to unwind at this full-fledged resort on a bluff overlooking Monterey Bay. The spacious suites sleep from two to eight people. **Pros:** time share–style apartments; access to miles of beachfront; superb views. **Cons:** far from city life; most bathrooms are small; some rooms need updating. $ *Rooms from: $387 ⊠ 1 Seascape Resort Dr., Aptos ☎ 831/662–7171, 866/867–0976 ⊕ www.seascaperesort. com ⥂ 285 suites ⦿ No Meals.*

Capitola and Soquel

4 miles northwest of Aptos.

On the National Register of Historic places as California's first seaside resort town, the village of Capitola has been in a vacation mood since the late 1800s. Casual eateries, surf shops, and ice-cream parlors pack its walkable downtown. Inland, across Highway 1, antiques shops line Soquel Drive in the town of Soquel. Wineries dot the Santa Cruz Mountains beyond.

GETTING HERE AND AROUND

From Santa Cruz or Monterey, follow Highway 1 to the Capitola/Soquel (Bay Avenue) exit about 7 miles south of Santa Cruz and head west to reach Capitola and east to access Soquel Village. On summer weekends, park for free in the lot behind the Crossroads Center, a block west of the freeway, and hop aboard the free Capitola Shuttle to the village.

ESSENTIALS

VISITOR INFORMATION Capitola-Soquel Chamber of Commerce. ⊠ *1855 41st Ave., Suite J06, Capitola ☎ 831/475–6522 ⊕ www.capitolachamber.com.*

 Beaches

★ New Brighton State Beach

BEACH | **FAMILY** | Once the site of a Chinese fishing village, New Brighton is now a popular surfing and camping spot. Its Pacific Migrations Visitor Center traces the history of the Chinese and other peoples who settled around Monterey Bay. It also documents the migratory patterns of the area's wildlife, such as monarch

Did You Know?

Soquel Cove in Santa Cruz is surrounded by New Brighton State Beach and Seacliff State Beach, where a WWI concrete ship sits partially submerged in the water.

butterflies and gray whales. Leashed dogs are allowed in the park. New Brighton connects with Seacliff Beach, and at low tide you can walk or run along this scenic stretch of sand for nearly 16 miles south (though you might have to wade through a few creeks). ■TIP→ The 1½-mile stroll from New Brighton to Seacliff's concrete ship is a local favorite. **Amenities:** parking (fee); showers; toilets. **Best for:** sunset; swimming; walking. ⊠ *1500 State Park Dr., off Hwy. 1, Capitola* ☎ *831/464–6329* ⊕ *www.parks.ca.gov* 🖃 *$10 per vehicle.*

🍴 Restaurants

Carpo's

$ | SEAFOOD | FAMILY | Locals love this casual restaurant where seafood predominates, but you can also order burgers, salads, and steaks. Baskets of battered snapper are among the favorites, along with calamari, prawns, seafood kebabs, fish-and-chips, and homemade olallieberry pie. **Known for:** large portions of healthy comfort food; lots of options under $14; soup and salad bar. $ *Average main: $14* ⊠ *2400 Porter St., at Hwy. 1, Soquel* ☎ *831/476–6260* ⊕ *www.carposrestaurant.com.*

Gayle's Bakery & Rosticceria

$$ | CAFÉ | FAMILY | Whether you're in the mood for an orange-olallieberry muffin, a wild rice and chicken salad, or tri-tip on garlic toast, this bakery-deli's varied menu is likely to satisfy. Munch on your lemon meringue tartlet or chocolate brownie on the shady patio, or dig into the daily blue-plate dinner—teriyaki grilled skirt steak with edamame-shiitake sticky rice, perhaps, or roast turkey breast with Chardonnay gravy—amid the whirl of activity inside. **Known for:** prepared meals to go; on-site bakery and rosticceria; deli and espresso bar. $ *Average main: $23* ⊠ *504 Bay Ave., Capitola* ☎ *831/462–1200* ⊕ *www.gaylesbakery. com.*

Shadowbrook

$$$ | EUROPEAN | To get to this romantic spot overlooking Soquel Creek, you can take a cable car or walk the stairs down a steep, fern-lined bank beside a running waterfall. Dining room options include the rooftop Redwood Room, the wood-paneled Wine Cellar, the creekside, glass-enclosed Greenhouse, the Fireplace Room, and the airy Garden Room. **Known for:** romantic creek-side setting; prime rib and grilled seafood; local special-occasion favorite for nearly 70 years. $ *Average main: $38* ⊠ *1750 Wharf Rd., at Lincoln Ave., Capitola* ☎ *831/475–1511* ⊕ *www.shadow-brook-capitola.com.*

VinoCruz Wine Bar & Kitchen

$ | AMERICAN | In a lively contemporary space with a patio in the heart of Soquel Village, VinoCruz offers more than 50 wines by the glass, with a focus on Santa Cruz Mountains but also other California and international regions; it also has local cider and beer on tap. Nosh on artisanal burgers, tacos, flatbread pizzas, salads, and cheese and charcuterie plates. **Known for:** weekend brunch; weekday happy hour and weekly live music; fresh food, made in-house. $ *Average main: $18* ⊠ *4901 Soquel Dr., Soquel* ☎ *831/426–8466* ⊕ *vinocruz.com* 🕐 *No lunch weekdays.*

🛏 Hotels

Inn at Depot Hill

$$ | B&B/INN | This inventively designed B&B in a former rail depot views itself as a link to the era of luxury train travel, and each double room or suite, complete with fireplace and featherbeds, is inspired by a different destination— Italy's Portofino, France's Côte d'Azur, Japan's Kyoto. **Pros:** short walk to beach and village; historic charm; excellent service. **Cons:** fills quickly; hot-tub conversation audible in some rooms; not suitable for children. $ *Rooms from: $319* ⊠ *250 Monterey Ave., Capitola*

☎ 831/462–3376, 800/572–2632 ⊕ www.
innatdepothill.com ⇨ 13 rooms ⦁⦁ Free
Breakfast.

Santa Cruz

*5 miles west of Capitola, 48 miles north
of Monterey.*

The big city on this stretch of the California coast, Santa Cruz (pop. 63,364) is less manicured than Carmel or Monterey. Long known for its surfing and its amusement-filled beach boardwalk, the town is an eclectic mix of grand Victorian-era homes, beachside inns, and multimillion-dollar compounds owned by tech gurus. The opening of the University of California campus in the 1960s swung the town sharply to the left politically, and the counterculture more or less lives on here. At the same time, a revitalized downtown and an insane real-estate market reflect the city's proximity to Silicon Valley, which is just a 30-minute drive to the north, and to a growing wine region in the surrounding mountains.

Amble around downtown's Santa Cruz Farmers' Market (Wednesday afternoon year-round) to experience the local culture, which derives much of its character from close connections to food and farming. The market covers a city block and includes not just the expected organic produce, but also live music and booths with local crafts and prepared food.

GETTING HERE AND AROUND

From the San Francisco Bay area, take Highway 17 south over the mountains to Santa Cruz, where it merges with Highway 1. Use Highway 1 to get around the area. The Santa Cruz Transit Center is at 920 Pacific Avenue, at Front Street, a short walk from the wharf and boardwalk, with connections to public transit throughout the Monterey Bay and San Francisco Bay areas. You can purchase day passes for Santa Cruz METRO buses here.

ESSENTIALS

VISITOR INFORMATION Visit Santa Cruz County. ⊠ 303 Water St., Suite 100, Santa Cruz ☎ 831/425–1234, 800/833–3494 ⊕ www.santacruz.org.

Sights

Monterey Bay National Marine Sanctuary Exploration Center

VISITOR CENTER | FAMILY | The interactive and multimedia exhibits at this fascinating interpretive center reveal and explain the treasures of the nation's largest marine sanctuary. The two-story building, across from the main beach and municipal wharf, has films and exhibits about migratory species, watersheds, underwater canyons, kelp forests, and intertidal zones. The second-floor deck has stellar ocean views and an interactive station that provides real-time weather, surf, and buoy reports. ⊠ 35 Pacific Ave., near Beach St., Santa Cruz ☎ 831/421–9993 ⊕ montereybay.noaa.gov/vc/sec ▣ Free ⊙ Closed Mon. and Tues.

Mystery Spot

OTHER ATTRACTION | FAMILY | Hokey tourist trap or genuine scientific enigma? Since 1940, curious throngs baffled by the Mystery Spot have made it one of the most visited attractions in Santa Cruz. The laws of gravity and physics don't appear to apply in this tiny patch of redwood forest, where balls roll uphill and people stand on a slant. ■TIP➔ **On weekends and holidays, it's wise to purchase tickets online in advance.** ⊠ 465 Mystery Spot Rd., off Branciforte Dr. (north off Hwy. 1), Santa Cruz ☎ 831/423–8897 ⊕ www. mysteryspot.com ▣ $10, parking $5.

Pacific Avenue

STREET | FAMILY | When you've had your fill of the city's beaches and waters, take a stroll in downtown Santa Cruz, especially on Pacific Avenue between Laurel and Water streets. Vintage boutiques and mountain-sports stores, sushi bars, and Mexican restaurants, day spas, and nightclubs keep the main drag and the surrounding streets hopping from mid-morning until late evening.

★ Santa Cruz Beach Boardwalk

AMUSEMENT PARK/CARNIVAL | FAMILY | This boardwalk has entertained beachgoers for more than a century. Its Looff carousel and classic wooden Giant Dipper roller coaster, both dating from the early 1900s, are surrounded by high-tech thrill rides and easygoing kiddie rides with ocean views. Video and arcade games, a minigolf course, and a laser-tag arena pack one gigantic building, which is open daily even if the rides aren't running. You have to pay to play, but you can wander the entire boardwalk for free while sampling carnival fare such as corn dogs and garlic fries. ⊠ *Along Beach St., Santa Cruz* ☎ *831/423–5590 info line* ⊕ *beach-boardwalk.com* ✉ *$40 day pass for unlimited rides, or pay per ride* ☉ *Some rides closed Sept.–May.*

Santa Cruz Mission State Historic Park

HISTORY MUSEUM | FAMILY | On the northern fringes of downtown is the site of California's 12th Spanish mission, built in the 1790s and destroyed by an earthquake in 1857. A museum in a restored 1791 adobe and a half-scale replica of the mission church are part of the complex. ⊠ *144 School St., at Adobe St., Santa Cruz* ☎ *831/425–5849* ⊕ *www.parks. ca.gov* ✉ *Free* ☉ *Closed Tues. and Wed.*

Santa Cruz Municipal Wharf

MARINA/PIER | FAMILY | Jutting half a mile into the ocean near one end of the boardwalk, the century-old Municipal Wharf is lined with seafood restaurants, a wine bar, souvenir shops, and outfitters offering bay cruises, fishing trips, and boat rentals. A salty soundtrack drifts up from under the wharf, where barking sea lions lounge in heaps on the crossbeams. ⊠ *Beach St. and Pacific Ave., Santa Cruz* ☎ *831/420–5725* ⊕ *www.santacruzwharf.com.*

Santa Cruz Surfing Museum

HISTORY MUSEUM | FAMILY | This museum inside the Mark Abbott Memorial Lighthouse chronicles local surfing history. Photographs show old-time surfers, and a display of boards includes rarities such as a heavy redwood plank predating the fiberglass era and the remains of a modern board chomped by a great white shark. Surfer docents reminisce about the good old days. ⊠ *Lighthouse Point Park, 701 W. Cliff Dr. near Pelton Ave., Santa Cruz* ☎ *831/420–6289* ⊕ *www.facebook. com/santacruzsurfingmuseum* ✉ *$3 suggested donation* ☉ *Closed Tues. and Wed. except open Tues. July–early Sept.*

Seymour Marine Discovery Center

AQUARIUM | FAMILY | Part of the Long Marine Laboratory at the University of California Santa Cruz's Institute of Marine Sciences, the center looks more like a research facility than a slick aquarium. Interactive exhibits demonstrate how scientists study the ocean, and the aquarium displays creatures of interest to marine biologists. The 87-foot blue whale skeleton is one of the world's largest. ⊠ *100 Shaffer Rd., end of Delaware Ave., west of Natural Bridges State Beach, Santa Cruz* ☎ *831/459–3800* ⊕ *seymourcenter.ucsc. edu* ✉ *$12* ☉ *Closed Mon.*

Surf City Vintners

WINERY | A dozen tasting rooms of limited-production wineries occupy renovated warehouse spaces west of the beach. MJA, Sones Cellars, Santa Cruz Mountain Vineyard, and Equinox are good places to start. Also here are the Santa Cruz Mountain Brewing Company and El Salchichero, popular for its homemade sausages, jams, and pickled and candied vegetables. ⊠ *Swift Street Courtyard, 334 Ingalls St., at Swift St., off Hwy. 1 (Mission St.), Santa Cruz* ☎ ⊕ *www. surfcityvintners.com.*

UC Santa Cruz

COLLEGE | FAMILY | The 2,000-acre University of California Santa Cruz campus nestles in the forested hills above town.

Its sylvan setting, ocean vistas, and redwood architecture make the university worth a visit, as does its arboretum ($10, open daily from 9 to 5), whose walking path leads through areas dedicated to the plants of California, Australia, New Zealand, and South Africa. ■ **TIP→ Free shuttles help students and visitors get around campus, and you can join a guided tour (online reservation required).** ✉ *Santa Cruz* ✣ *Main entrance at Bay and High Sts. (turn left on High for arboretum)* ☎ *831/459–0111* 🌐 *www.ucsc.edu/visit.*

★ West Cliff Drive

SCENIC DRIVE | FAMILY | The road that winds along an oceanfront bluff from the municipal wharf to Natural Bridges State Beach makes for a spectacular drive, but it's even more fun to walk or bike the paved path that parallels the road. Surfers bob and swoosh in Monterey Bay at several points near the foot of the bluff, especially at a break known as **Steamer Lane.** Named for a surfer who died here in 1965, the nearby Mark Abbott Memorial Lighthouse stands at Point Santa Cruz, the cliff's major promontory. From here you can watch pinnipeds hang out, sunbathe, and frolic on Seal Rock. ✉ *Santa Cruz.*

Beaches

Natural Bridges State Beach

BEACH | FAMILY | At the end of West Cliff Drive lies this stretch of soft sand edged with tide pools and sea-sculpted rock bridges. ■ **TIP→ From September to early January a colony of monarch butterflies roosts in the eucalyptus grove. Amenities:** lifeguards; parking (fee); toilets. **Best for:** sunrise; sunset; surfing; swimming. ✉ *2531 W. Cliff Dr., Santa Cruz* ☎ *831/423–4609* 🌐 *www.parks.ca.gov* 🎟 *Beach free, parking $10.*

Twin Lakes State Beach

BEACH | FAMILY | Stretching ½ mile along the coast on both sides of the small-craft jetties, Twin Lakes is one of Monterey Bay's sunniest beaches. It encompasses Seabright State Beach (with access in a residential neighborhood on the upcoast side) and Black's Beach on the downcoast side. Families often come here to sunbathe, picnic, and hike the nature trail around adjacent Schwann Lake. Parking is tricky from May through September—you need to pay for a $10 day-use permit at a kiosk and the lot fills quickly—but you can park all day in the harbor pay lot and walk here. Leashed dogs are allowed. **Amenities:** food and drink; lifeguards (seasonal); parking; showers; toilets; water sports (seasonal). **Best for:** sunset; surfing; swimming; walking. ✉ *7th Ave., at East Cliff Dr., Santa Cruz* ☎ *831/427–4868* 🌐 *www.parks.ca.gov.*

Restaurants

Bad Animal

$$ | ECLECTIC | By day, Bad Animal mostly sells rare and used books, but, at 5 pm, it morphs into a wine bar and restaurant, where you're encouraged to order a glass of wine while browsing the stacks. The menu depends on who is the current Culinary Artist in residence, a position that rotates every year or so. **Known for:** extensive list of natural, primarily French and California wines; interesting intellectual staff and clientele; emphasis on local, organic ingredients. [$] *Average main: $29* ✉ *1011 Cedar St., Santa Cruz* ☎ *831/900–5031* 🌐 *www.badanimalbooks.com* 🕓 *Closed Mon. and Tues. No lunch.*

Crow's Nest

$$ | SEAFOOD | FAMILY | Vintage surfboards and local surf photography line the walls, and nearly every table overlooks sand and surf at this restaurant on the Santa Cruz Harbor. For sweeping ocean views and fish tacos, burgers, and other casual fare, head upstairs to the Breakwater Bar & Grill. **Known for:** house-smoked salmon and calamari apps; crab-cake eggs Benedict and olallieberry pancakes; on-site market with pizzas, sandwiches, soups, and salads. [$] *Average main: $29* ✉ *2218 E. Cliff Dr., west* *of 7th Ave., Santa Cruz* ☎ *831/476–4560* 🌐 *crowsnest-santacruz.com.*

★ Laili Restaurant

$$ | MEDITERRANEAN | Exotic Mediterranean flavors with an Afghan twist take center stage at this artsy, stylish space with soaring ceilings. In the evening, locals come to relax over wine and soft jazz at the blue-concrete bar, on the seasonal heated patio with twinkly lights, or at a communal table near the open kitchen. **Known for:** house-made pastas and numerous vegetarian and vegan options; fresh naan, chutneys, and dips with every meal; traditional dishes like pomegranate eggplant and maushawa soup. [$] *Average main: $24* ✉ *101–B Cooper St., near Pacific Ave., Santa Cruz* ☎ *831/423–4545* 🌐 *lailirestaurant.com* 🕒 *Closed Sun. and Mon. No lunch.*

La Posta Via

$$ | ITALIAN | Authentic Italian fare made with fresh local produce lures diners into this cozy, modern-rustic restaurant. Nearly everything is made in-house, from the pizzas and breads baked in the brick oven to the pasta and the vanilla-bean gelato. **Known for:** seasonal wild-nettle lasagna; braised lamb shank; in the heart of the Seabright neighborhood. [$] *Average main: $30* ✉ *538 Seabright Ave., at Logan St., Santa Cruz* ☎ *831/457–2782* 🌐 *www.lapostarestaurant.com* 🕒 *Closed Mon. and Tues. No lunch.*

Oswald

$$$ | EUROPEAN | Sophisticated yet unpretentious European-inspired California cooking is the order of the day at this intimate and stylish bistro, whose seasonal menu might include such items as seafood risotto or crispy duck breast in a pomegranate reduction sauce. The creative concoctions poured at the slick marble bar include whiskey mixed with apple and lemon juice or tequila with celery juice and lime. **Known for:** excellent burgers and fries; crab appetizers; dark-chocolate soufflé and other tasty desserts. [$] *Average main: $34* ✉ *121 Soquel Ave., at Front St., Santa Cruz* ☎ *831/423–7427* 🌐 *www.oswaldrestaurant.com* 🕒 *Closed Sun.–Tues.*

🛏 Hotels

Babbling Brook Inn

$$ | B&B/INN | Though it's in the middle of Santa Cruz, this inn has lush gardens, a running stream, and tall trees that make you feel as if you're in a secluded wood. **Pros:** close to UCSC; within walking distance of downtown shops; woodsy feel. **Cons:** near a high school; some rooms close to a busy street; many stairs and no elevator. [$] *Rooms from: $280* ✉ *1025 Laurel St., Santa Cruz* ☎ *831/427–2437* 🌐 *www.babblingbrookinn.com* 🚪 *13 rooms* 🍴 *No Meals.*

★ Chaminade Resort & Spa

$$ | RESORT | FAMILY | Secluded on 300 hilltop acres of redwood and eucalyptus forest laced with hiking trails, this Mission-style complex also features a lovely terrace restaurant with expansive views of Monterey Bay. Guest rooms are furnished in an eclectic, bohemian style that pays homage to the artsy local community and the city's industrial past. **Pros:** peaceful, verdant setting; full-service spa and large pool; ideal spot for romance and rejuvenation. **Cons:** not within walking distance of downtown; not near the ocean; resort fee. [$] *Rooms from: $289* ✉ *1 Chaminade La., Santa Cruz* ☎ *800/283–6569, 831/475–5600* 🌐 *www.chaminade.com* 🚪 *156 rooms* 🍴 *No Meals.*

Courtyard by Marriott Santa Cruz

$$ | HOTEL | FAMILY | This sparkling hotel, set in the heart of the tourist district and opened in fall 2022, is a warm, welcoming, haven filled with custom-designed furnishings and local art that reflects the beachy Santa Cruz vibe. **Pros:** two blocks from the beach and boardwalk, easy walk to the wharf and downtown; on-site café; spa with four treatment rooms. **Cons:** no rooms with beach views; valet parking only (fee); summer traffic may cause slow arrival to hotel. [$] *Rooms from:*

$249 ✉ 313 Riverside Ave., Santa Cruz ☎ 831/419–8700 🌐 www.marriott.com 🛏 151 rooms 🍴 No Meals.

★ Dream Inn Santa Cruz

$$$ | **HOTEL** | A short stroll from the boardwalk and wharf, this full-service luxury hotel is the only lodging in Santa Cruz directly on the beach, and its rooms all have private balconies or patios overlooking Monterey Bay. Accommodations have contemporary furnishings, muted retro-chic colors, and upscale linens, but the main draw here is having the ocean at your doorstep. **Pros:** restaurant with sweeping bay views; cool mid-century modern design; walk to boardwalk and downtown. **Cons:** expensive; area gets congested on summer weekends; pool area and hallways can be noisy. [$] *Rooms from: $499 ✉ 175 W. Cliff Dr., Santa Cruz ☎ 831/740–8069 🌐 www.dreaminnsantacruz.com 🛏 165 rooms 🍴 No Meals.*

Hotel Paradox

$$ | **HOTEL** | About a mile from the ocean and two blocks from Pacific Avenue, this stylish, forest-theme complex (part of the Marriott Autograph Collection) is among the few full-service hotels in town. **Pros:** close to downtown and main beach; spacious pool area with cabanas, firepits, hot tub, and dining and cocktail service; farm-to-table restaurant. **Cons:** pool area can get crowded; some rooms on the small side; thin walls. [$] *Rooms from: $297 ✉ 611 Ocean St., Santa Cruz ☎ 831/425–7100, 888/236–2427 reservations 🌐 www.hotelparadox.com 🛏 172 rooms 🍴 No Meals.*

★ West Cliff Inn

$$$ | **B&B/INN** | On bluffs across from Cowell Beach, this three-story, Italianate property, built in 1877, exudes classic California beach style. **Pros:** killer bay and boardwalk views; walking distance of the beach; close to downtown. **Cons:** boardwalk noise; outdoor hot tub has limited privacy; street traffic. [$] *Rooms from: $348 ✉ 174 W. Cliff Dr., Santa Cruz ☎ 831/457–2200 🌐 www.westcliffinn.com 🛏 9 units 🍴 Free Breakfast.*

Nightlife

Catalyst

LIVE MUSIC | This huge, grimy, and fun club books rock, indie rock, punk, death-metal, reggae, and other acts. *✉ 1011 Pacific Ave., Santa Cruz ☎ 831/713–5492 🌐 catalystclub.com.*

Moe's Alley

LIVE MUSIC | Blues, salsa, reggae, funk: delightfully casual Moe's presents it all (and more). *✉ 1535 Commercial Way, Santa Cruz ☎ 831/479–1854 🌐 moesalley.com ⏲ Closed Mon.*

Performing Arts

Kuumbwa Jazz Center

MUSIC | The center draws top performers such as Lee Ritenour, Chris Potter, and the Dave Holland Trio. A café serves meals an hour before most shows. *✉ 320–2 Cedar St., Santa Cruz ☎ 831/427–2227 🌐 www.kuumbwajazz.org.*

Tannery Arts Center

ARTS CENTERS | The former Salz Tannery now contains nearly 30 studios and live-work spaces for artists whose disciplines range from ceramics and glass to film and digital media; most have public hours of operation. Performances also take place at the on-site Colligan Theater, and the center hosts assorted arts events on weekends and, occasionally, on weekdays. *✉ 1060 River St., at intersection of Hwys. 1 and 9, Santa Cruz 🌐 www.tanneryartscenter.org.*

Shopping

Bad Animal Books

BOOKS | An eclectic independent shop in downtown Santa Cruz, Bad Animal has shelves packed with rare and used books, mostly representing the humanities: literature, philosophy, and theology,

among them the favorite picks of the owner, a friend of famed poet Lawrence Ferlenghetti who earned a PhD in the History of Consciousness from UC Santa Cruz. ⊠ *1011 Cedar St., Santa Cruz* ☎ *831/900–5031* ⊕ *www.badanimalbooks.com* ⊗ *Closed Mon. and Tues.*

Bookshop Santa Cruz

BOOKS | FAMILY | In 2021, the town's best and most beloved independent bookstore celebrated its 55th anniversary of selling new, used, and remaindered titles. The children's section is especially comprehensive, and the shop's special events calendar is packed with readings, social mixers, book signings, and discussions. ⊠ *1520 Pacific Ave., Santa Cruz* ☎ *831/423–0900* ⊕ *www.bookshopsantacruz.com.*

Botanic + Luxe

OTHER SPECIALTY STORE | Come here to browse a carefully curated collection of goods, many from local craftspeople, including items for the home, jewelry, personal care, and plants—all that you need to inspire soulful living. ⊠ *110 Cooper St., Suite 100F, Santa Cruz* ☎ *831/515–7710* ⊕ *botanicandluxe.com.*

O'Neill Surf Shop

SPORTING GOODS | FAMILY | Local surfers get their wetties (wet suits) and other gear at this O'Neill store or the one in Capitola (⊠ *1115 41st Ave.*). There's also a satellite shop on the Santa Cruz Boardwalk. ⊠ *110 Cooper St., Santa Cruz* ☎ *831/469–4377* ⊕ *us.oneill.com.*

Santa Cruz Downtown Farmers' Market

MARKET | FAMILY | Santa Cruz is famous for its long tradition of organic growing and sustainable living, and its downtown market (one of five countywide) reflects the incredible diversity and quality of local agriculture and the synergistic daily life of community-minded residents. The busy market, which always has live music, happens every Wednesday from 1 to 6, rain or shine. The stalls cover much of an entire city block near Pacific Avenue and include fresh produce plus everything from oysters, beer, bread, and charcuterie to arts and crafts to prepared foods made from ingredients sourced from on-site vendors. ⊠ *Cedar St. at Lincoln St., Santa Cruz* ☎ *831/454–0566* ⊕ *santacruzfarmersmarket.org.*

🏃 Activities

BICYCLING

Another Bike Shop

BIKING | FAMILY | Mountain bikers should head here for tips on the best area trails and to browse cutting-edge gear made and tested locally. ⊠ *2361 Mission St., at King St., Santa Cruz* ☎ *831/427–2232* ⊕ *www.anotherbikeshop.com.*

BOATS AND CHARTERS

Chardonnay Sailing Charters

BOATING | The 70-foot *Chardonnay II* departs year-round from Santa Cruz yacht harbor on whale-watching, sunset, and other cruises around Monterey Bay. Most regularly scheduled excursions cost $75; food and drink are served on many of them. Reservations are essential. ⊠ *Santa Cruz West Harbor, 790 Mariner Park Way, Santa Cruz* ☎ *831/423–1213* ⊕ *www.chardonnay.com.*

Stagnaro Sport Fishing, Charters & Whale Watching Cruises

BOATING | FAMILY | Stagnaro (aka Santa Cruz Whale Watching) offers salmon, albacore, and rock-cod fishing expeditions (fees include bait) as well as whale-watching, dolphin, and sea-life cruises year-round. ⊠ *1718 Brommer St., near Santa Cruz Harbor, Santa Cruz* ☎ *831/427–0230* ⊕ *stagnaros.com* 🎫 *From $48.*

GOLF

DeLaveaga Golf Course

GOLF | Woodsy DeLaveaga, a public course set in a hilly park, overlooks Santa Cruz and the bay. With its canyons, tree-lined fairways, and notoriously difficult par-5, dogleg 10th hole, the course challenges novices and seasoned golfers. ⊠ *401 Upper Park Rd., Santa Cruz*

☎ 831/423–7214 ⊕ www.delaveagagolf.
com ✉ $60 weekdays, $80 weekends/
holidays ⚲. 18 holes, 5700 yards, par 70.

Pasatiempo Golf Club

GOLF | Designed by famed golf archi-
tect Dr. Alister MacKenzie in 1929, this
semiprivate course, set amid undulating
hills just above the city, is among the
nation's top championship courses.
Golfers rave about the spectacular views
and challenging terrain. According to the
club, MacKenzie, who designed Pebble
Beach's exclusive Cypress Point course
and Augusta National in Georgia, the
home of the Masters Golf Tournament,
declared this his favorite layout. ✉ 20
Clubhouse Rd., Santa Cruz ☎ 831/459–
9155 ⊕ www.pasatiempo.com ✉ From
$345 ⚲. 18 holes, 6125 yards, par 72.

KAYAKING

Kayak Connection

KAYAKING | **FAMILY** | From March through
May, participants in this outfit's tours
mingle with gray whales and their calves
on their northward journey to Alaska.
Throughout the year, the company rents
kayaks and paddleboards and conducts
tours of Natural Bridges State Beach, Capitola, and Elkhorn Slough. ✉ Santa Cruz
Harbor, 413 Lake Ave., Suite 3, Santa Cruz
☎ 831/479–1121 ⊕ kayakconnection.com
✉ From $85 for scheduled tours.

Venture Quest Kayaking

KAYAKING | **FAMILY** | Explore hidden coves
and kelp forests on guided two-hour
kayak tours that depart from Santa Cruz
Wharf. The tours include a kayaking
lesson. Venture Quest also rents kayaks
(and wet suits and gear) and arranges
tours at other Monterey Bay destinations,
including Elkhorn Slough. ✉ 2 Santa
Cruz Wharf, Santa Cruz ☎ 831/427–2267
kayak hotline, 831/425–8445 rental office
⊕ www.santacruzkayak.com ✉ From $40
for rentals, $70 for tours.

SURFING

Club-Ed Surf School and Camps

SURFING | **FAMILY** | Find out what all the
fun is about at Club-Ed. Your first private
or group lesson ($120 and up) includes all
equipment. ✉ Cowell's Beach, at Dream
Inn Santa Cruz, Santa Cruz ☎ 831/464–
0177 ⊕ club-ed.com.

Cowell's Surf Shop

SURFING | **FAMILY** | This shop sells gear,
clothing, and swimwear; rents surf-
boards, stand-up paddleboards, and wet
suits; and offers lessons. ✉ 30 Front St.,
Santa Cruz ☎ 831/427–2355 ⊕ www.
facebook.com/cowellssurfshop.

Richard Schmidt Surf School

SURFING | **FAMILY** | Since 1978, Richard
Schmidt has shared the stoke of surfing
and the importance of ocean aware-
ness with legions of
students of all ages. Today, the outfit
offers surfing and stand-up paddleboard
lessons (equipment provided) as well as
marine adventure tours in Santa Cruz and
elsewhere on the bay. Locations depend
on where the waves are breaking or the
wind's a'blowing, but outings typically
convene at Cowell's Beach or Pleasure
Point. ✉ Santa Cruz ☎ 831/423–0928
⊕ richardschmidt.com ✉ From $120.

ZIPLINING

Mount Hermon Adventures

ZIP LINING | **FAMILY** | Zipline through the
redwoods at this adventure center in
the Santa Cruz Mountains. On some
weekends there's an aerial adventure
course with obstacles and challenges
in the redwoods. ■**TIP➜ To participate
(reservations essential), you must be at
least 10 years old and at least 54 inches tall, and weigh between 75 and 250
pounds.** ✉ 17 Conference Dr., 9 miles
north of downtown Santa Cruz near
Felton, Mount Hermon ☎ 831/430–4357
⊕ mounthermonadventures.com ✉ From
$90 ☉ Closed Tues.–Thurs.

SEQUOIA AND KINGS CANYON NATIONAL PARKS

Updated by
Cheryl Crabtree

⛺ **Camping**
★★★★☆

🛏 **Hotels**
★★★★☆

🏃 **Activities**
★★★★☆

👁 **Scenery**
★★★★★

👥 **Crowds**
★★★☆☆

WELCOME TO SEQUOIA AND KINGS CANYON NATIONAL PARKS

TOP REASONS TO GO

★ **Gentle giants:** You'll feel small—in a good way—walking among some of the world's largest living things in Sequoia's Giant Forest and Kings Canyon's Grant Grove.

★ **Because it's there:** You can't even glimpse it from the main part of Sequoia, but the sight of majestic Mt. Whitney is worth the trip to the eastern face of the High Sierra.

★ **Underground exploration:** Far older even than the giant sequoias, the gleaming limestone formations in Crystal Cave will draw you along dark, marble passages.

★ **A grander-than–Grand Canyon:** Drive the twisting Kings Canyon Scenic Byway down into the jagged, granite Kings River canyon, deeper in parts than the Grand Canyon.

★ **Regal solitude:** To spend a day or two hiking in a subalpine world of your own, pick one of the many trailheads at Mineral King.

1 **Giant Forest–Lodgepole Village.** One of Sequoia's most visited areas has major sights such as Giant Forest, General Sherman Tree, Crystal Cave, and Moro Rock.

2 **Mineral King.** In Sequoia's southeast section, the highest road-accessible part of the park is a good place to hike, camp, and soak up the grandeur of the Sierra Nevada.

3 **Mt. Whitney.** The highest peak in the Lower 48 stands on the eastern edge of Sequoia; to get there from Giant Forest you must either backpack eight days through the mountains or drive nearly 300 miles around the park to its other side.

4 **Grant Grove Village–Redwood Canyon.** The "thumb" of Kings Canyon is its busiest section, where Grant Grove, General Grant Tree, Panoramic Point, and Big Stump are the main draws.

5 **Cedar Grove.** The drive through the high-country of Kings Canyon to Cedar Grove Village, on the canyon floor, reveals magnificent granite formations of varied hues. Rock meets river in breathtaking fashion at Zumwalt Meadow.

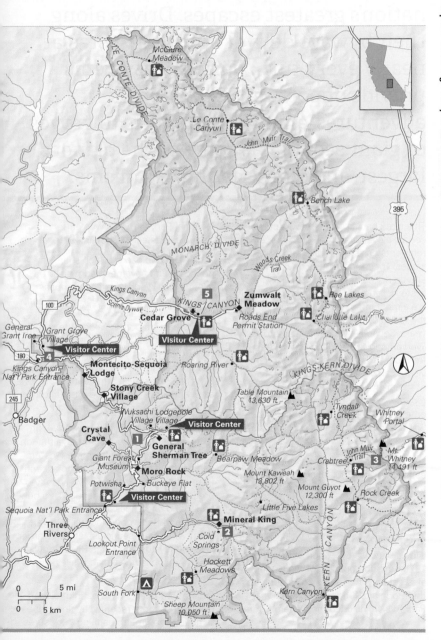

McClure Meadow

Le Conte Canyon

John Muir Trail

Bench Lake

395

MONARCH DIVIDE

Woods Creek Trail

Kings Canyon Scenic Byway

100

KINGS CANYON

Zumwalt Meadow

Rae Lakes

Charlotte Lake

Cedar Grove

Roads End Permit Station

Visitor Center

General Grant Tree

Grant Grove Village

Visitor Center

180

4

Kings Canyon Nat'l Park Entrance

245

Badger

Montecito-Sequoia Lodge

Roaring River

KINGS KERN DIVIDE

Stony Creek Village

Table Mountain 13,630 ft

Tyndall Creek

Whitney Portal

Wuksachi Lodgepole Village Village

Visitor Center

Crystal Cave

1

General Sherman Tree

Bearpaw Meadow

Crabtree

John Muir Trail

Mt. Whitney 14,491 ft

3

Giant Forest Museum

Moro Rock

Mount Kaweah 13,802 ft

Mount Guyot 12,300 ft

Rock Creek

Potwisha

Buckeye Flat

Little Five Lakes

Visitor Center

Sequoia Nat'l Park Entrance

Mineral King

2

KERN CANYON

Three Rivers

Lookout Point Entrance

Cold Springs

Hockett Meadows

0   5 mi

South Fork

Kern Canyon

0   5 km

Sheep Mountain 10,050 ft

The word "exceptional" best describes these two parks, which offer some of the nation's greatest escapes. Drives along their byways deliver stunning vistas at nearly every turn. Varied ecosystems provide opportunities for repeat adventures, among them hikes to groves of giant sequoias—some of the planet's largest, and oldest, living organisms.

This rare species of tree grows only at certain elevations and in particular environments on the Central Sierra's western slopes. Their monstrously thick trunks and branches, remarkably shallow root systems, and neck-craning heights really are almost impossible to believe, as is the fact they can live for more than 2,500 years. Several Native American groups lived among these magnificent trees for thousands of years before modern visitors arrived. By the late 1800s, word of the giant sequoias (*Sequoiadendron giganteum*) had spread, attracting logging enterprises and mobilizing those who wanted to protect these living treasures.

Sequoia National Park—the nation's second oldest after Yellowstone—was established in 1890, officially preserving the world's largest sequoia groves in the Giant Forest and other areas of the park. At first, visitors traveled along a pack road to view the towering marvels. In 1903, a road into the Giant Forest allowed access by wagon. It wasn't until 1926, with the opening of the General's Highway, that autos could chug up the mountain. Kings Canyon National Park, which included the General Grant

National Park formed a week after Sequoia, was established in 1940.

Today, the two parks, which share a boundary and have been administered jointly since World War II, encompass 865,964 wild and scenic acres between the foothills of California's Central Valley and its eastern borders along the craggy ridgeline of the Sierra's highest peaks. Next to or a few miles off the 46-mile Generals Highway are most of Sequoia National Park's main attractions, as well as Grant Grove Village, the orientation hub for Kings Canyon National Park.

Sequoia includes Mt. Whitney, the highest point in the lower 48 states (although it is impossible to see from the western part of the park and is a chore to ascend from either side). Kings Canyon has two portions: the smaller is shaped like a bent finger and encompasses Grant Grove Village and Redwood Mountain Grove (both with many sequoias), and the larger is home to stunning Kings River Canyon, where unspoiled peaks and valleys are a backpacker's dream.

Of late, both parks have been damaged by fire and, more recently, by flood (due to heavy snowmelt) resulting in closures.

Areas greatly affected by floods in 2023, for instance, included Giant Forest–Lodgepole Village and Mineral King in Sequoia and Kings Canyon Scenic Byway (Route 180) and Cedar Grove in Kings Canyon. Though repair work began immediately, some amenities or attractions within these areas might still be closed. Check for updates, which are provided weekly on the park website.

Planning

Getting Here and Around

AIR
The closest airport to Sequoia and Kings Canyon national parks is Fresno Yosemite International Airport (FAT).

AIRPORT CONTACTS Fresno Yosemite International Airport. (*FAT*) ⊠ *5175 E. Clinton Way, Fresno* ☎ *800/244–2359 automated info, 559/621–4500* ⊕ *flyfresno.com.*

CAR
Sequoia is 36 miles east of Visalia on Route 198; Grant Grove Village in Kings Canyon is 56 miles east of Fresno on Route 180. There is no automobile entrance on the eastern side of the Sierra. Routes 198 and 180 are connected by Generals Highway, a paved two-lane road (also signed as Highway 198) that sometimes sees delays at peak times due to ongoing improvements. The road is extremely narrow and steep from Route 198 to Giant Forest, so keep an eye on your engine temperature gauge, as the incline and congestion can cause vehicles to overheat; to avoid overheated brakes, use low gears on downgrades.

If you are traveling in an RV or with a trailer, study the restrictions on these vehicles. Do not travel beyond Potwisha Campground on Generals Highway (Route 198) with an RV longer than 22 feet; take straighter, easier Route 180

through the Kings Canyon park entrance instead. Maximum vehicle length on Generals Highway is 40 feet, or 50 feet combined length for vehicles with trailers. For current road and weather conditions, call ☎ *559/565–3341* or visit the park website (⊕ *www.nps.gov/seki*).

Generals Highway between Lodgepole and Grant Grove is sometimes closed by snow. The Mineral King Road from Route 198 into southern Sequoia National Park is closed 2 miles below Atwell Mill either on November 1 or after the first heavy snow. The Buckeye Flat–Middle Fork Trailhead road is closed from mid-October to mid-April when the Buckeye Flat Campground closes. The lower Crystal Cave Road is closed when the cave closes (typically in November). Its upper 2 miles, as well as the Panoramic Point and Moro Rock–Crescent Meadow roads, close with the first heavy snow. Because of the danger of rockfall, the portion of Kings Canyon Scenic Byway east of Grant Grove closes in winter.

■TIP→ **Snowstorms are common from late October through April. Unless you have a four-wheel-drive vehicle with snow tires, you should carry chains and know how to install them.**

Hotels

Hotel accommodations in Sequoia and Kings Canyon are limited, and, although they are clean and comfortable, they tend to lack much in-room character. Keep in mind, however, that the extra money you spend on lodging here is offset by the time you'll save by being inside the parks. You won't be faced with a 60- to 90-minute commute from the less-expensive motels in Three Rivers (by far the most charming option), Visalia, or Fresno. Reserve as far in advance as you can, especially for summertime stays.

AVERAGE HIGH/LOW TEMPERATURES (MID-LEVEL ELEVATIONS)					
Jan.	Feb.	Mar.	Apr.	May	June
42/24	44/25	46/26	51/30	58/36	68/44
July	Aug.	Sept.	Oct.	Nov.	Dec.
76/51	76/50	71/45	61/38	50/31	44/27

Park Essentials

ACCESSIBILITY

All the visitor centers, the Giant Forest Museum, and Big Trees Trail are wheelchair accessible, as are some short ranger-led walks and talks. General Sherman Tree can be reached via a paved, level trail near a parking area. None of the caves is accessible, and wilderness areas must be reached by horseback or on foot. Some picnic tables are extended to accommodate wheelchairs. Many of the major sites are in the 6,000-foot range, and thin air at high elevations can cause respiratory distress for people with breathing difficulties. Carry oxygen if necessary. Contact the park's main number for more information.

PARK FEES AND PERMITS

The admission fee is $35 per vehicle, $30 per motorcycle, and $20 per person for those who enter by bus, on foot, bicycle, horse, or any other mode of transportation; it is valid for seven days in both parks. U.S. residents over the age of 62 pay $80 for a lifetime pass, and permanently disabled U.S. residents are admitted free.

If you plan to camp in the backcountry, you need a permit, which costs $15 for hikers or $30 for stock users (e.g., horseback riders). One permit covers the group, plus $5 per person. Availability of permits depends upon trailhead quotas. You must reserve and pay for your permit at Recreation.gov. from six months to one week in advance. Without a reservation, you may still get a permit on a first-come, first-served basis starting at 1 pm the day before you plan to hike. For more information on backcountry camping or travel with pack animals (horses, mules, burros, or llamas), contact the Wilderness Permit Office (☎ 530/565–3766).

PARK HOURS

The parks are open 24/7 year-round. They are in the Pacific time zone.

CELL PHONE RECEPTION

Cell phone reception is poor to nonexistent in the higher elevations and spotty even on portions of Generals Highway, where you can (on rare clear days) see the Central Valley. Public telephones may be found at the visitor centers, ranger stations, some trailheads, and at all restaurants and lodging facilities in the park.

EMERGENCIES

Call 911 from any telephone within the park in an emergency. Rangers at the Cedar Grove, Foothills, Grant Grove, and Lodgepole visitor centers, the Giant Forest Museum, and the Mineral King ranger station are trained in first aid. National park rangers have legal jurisdiction within park boundaries: contact a ranger station or visitor center for police matters. For less urgent matters, call the parks' main number, ☎ 559/565–3341 (you can also choose an emergency option on this line).

RESTROOMS

Public restrooms may be found at all visitor centers and campgrounds. Additional locations include Big Stump, Columbine, Grizzly Falls, Hospital Rock, Wolverton, Crescent Meadow, Giant Forest Museum, and Crystal Cave.

Restaurants

In Sequoia and Kings Canyon national parks, you can treat yourself (and the family) to a high-quality meal in a wonderful setting in the Peaks restaurant at Wuksachi Lodge, but otherwise you should keep your expectations modest. You can grab bread, spreads, drinks, and fresh produce at one of several small grocery stores for a picnic, or get takeout food from the Grant Grove Restaurant, the Cedar Grove Grill, or one of the two small Lodgepole eateries.

⇨ *Hotel and restaurant reviews have been shortened. For full information visit Fodors.com. Hotel prices are the lowest cost of a standard double room in high season. Restaurant prices are the average cost of a main course at dinner, or if dinner is not served, at lunch.*

What It Costs

	$	$$	$$$	$$$$
RESTAURANTS				
	under $20	$20–$30	$31–$40	over $40
HOTELS				
	under $200	$200–$350	$351–$500	over $500

Tours

★ **Sequoia Parks Conservancy Adventures**
SPECIAL-INTEREST TOURS | The Sequoia Parks Conservancy's highly regarded educational division conducts half-, single-, and multiday tours that include backpacking hikes, natural-history walks, astronomy programs, snowshoe treks, and custom adventures. ⊠ *47050 Generals Hwy., Suite 10, Three Rivers* ☎ *559/565–4251* ⊕ *www.sequoiaparksconservancy. org* 🖭 *From $230 for 2-hr guided tour.*

Sequoia Sightseeing Tours
GUIDED TOURS | This locally owned operator's friendly, knowledgeable guides conduct daily interpretive sightseeing tours in Sequoia and Kings Canyon. Reservations are essential. The company also offers private tours. ⊠ *Three Rivers* ☎ *559/561–4189* ⊕ *www.sequoiatours. com* 🖭 *From $79 tour of Sequoia; from $169 tour of Kings Canyon.*

Visitor Information

NATIONAL PARK SERVICE Foothills Visitor Center. ⊠ *47050 Generals Hwy., Rte. 198, 1 mile north of Ash Mountain entrance, Sequoia National Park* ☎ *559/565–3341.* **Sequoia and Kings Canyon National Parks.** ⊠ *47050 Generals Hwy. (Rte. 198), Three Rivers* ☎ *559/565–3341* ⊕ *nps.gov/seki.*

When to Go

The best times to visit are spring and fall, when temperatures are moderate and crowds thin. Summertime can draw hordes of tourists to see the giant sequoias, and the few, narrow roads mean congestion at peak holiday times. If you must visit in summer, go during the week. By contrast, in wintertime you may feel as though you have the parks all to yourself. But because of heavy snows, sections of the main park roads can be closed without warning, and low-hanging clouds can move in and obscure mountains and valleys for days. From early October to late April, check road and weather conditions before venturing out.

■TIP➔ **Even in summer, you can escape hordes of people just walking ¼ to ½ mile off the beaten path on a less-used trail.**

Plants and Wildlife Canyon

The parks can be divided into three distinct zones. In the west (1,500–4,500 feet) are the rolling, lower-elevation foothills, covered with shrubby chaparral vegetation or golden grasslands dotted with oaks. Chamise, red-barked manzanita, and the occasional yucca plant grow here. Fields of white popcorn flower cover the hillsides in spring, and the yellow fiddleneck flourishes. In summer, intense heat and absence of rain cause the hills to turn golden brown. Wildlife includes the California ground squirrel, noisy blue-and-gray scrub jay, black bears, coyotes, skunks, and gray fox.

At middle elevation (5,000–9,000 feet), where the giant sequoia belt resides, rock formations mix with meadows and huge stands of evergreens—red and white fir, incense cedar, and ponderosa pines, to name a few. Wildflowers like yellow blazing star and red Indian paintbrush bloom in spring and summer. Mule deer, golden-mantled ground squirrels, Steller's jays, and black bears (most active in fall) inhabit the area, as does the chickaree.

The high alpine section of the parks is extremely rugged, with a string of rocky peaks reaching above 13,000 feet to Mt. Whitney's 14,494 feet. Fierce weather and scarcity of soil make vegetation and wildlife sparse. Foxtail and whitebark pines have gnarled and twisted trunks, the result of high wind, heavy snowfall, and freezing temperatures. In summer, you can see yellow-bellied marmots, pikas, weasels, mountain chickadees, and Clark's nutcrackers.

Sequoia National Park

Sequoia National Park is all about the trees, and to understand the scale of these giants you must walk among them. If you do nothing else, get out of the car for a short stroll through one of the groves. In addition, try to access one of the vista points that provide a panoramic view over the forested mountains.

Generals Highway (which connects Routes 198 and 180) will be your route to most of the park's sights. A few short spur roads lead from the highway to some sights, and Mineral King Road branches off Route 198 to enter the park at Lookout Point, winding east from there to the park's southernmost section.

Giant Forest— Lodgepole Village

Giant Forest is 16 miles from the Sequoia National Park Visitor Center.

The Sequoia National Park entrance at Ash Mountain is the main gateway to the Giant Forest and many of the park's major sights. From there, the narrow, twisty General's Highway snakes up the mountain from a 1,700-foot elevation through the Giant Forest (a 45-minute drive from the entrance) up to 6,720 feet at Lodgepole Village.

Note that, in this area of the park, flooding in spring of 2023 resulted in attraction and amenity closures both short term (e.g., Crystal Cave) and long (e.g., Little Baldy and John Muir trails). Check with the park and/or the park conservancy for updates.

◎ Sights

HISTORIC SIGHTS

Giant Forest Museum

OTHER MUSEUM | FAMILY | Well-imagined and interactive displays at this worthwhile stop provide the basics about sequoias, of which there are 2,161 with diameters exceeding 10 feet in the approximately 2,000-acre Giant Forest. ⊠ *Sequoia National Park ⊹ Generals Hwy., 4 miles south of Lodgepole Visitor Center* ☎ *559/565–4436* 🖼 *Free* ⌖ *Shuttle: Giant Forest or Moro Rock–Crescent Meadow.*

SCENIC DRIVES

★ Generals Highway

SCENIC DRIVE | FAMILY | One of California's most scenic drives, this 46-mile road (also signed as Route 198) is the main asphalt artery between Sequoia and Kings Canyon national parks. Named after the landmark Grant and Sherman trees that leave so many visitors awestruck, Generals Highway runs from Sequoia's Foothills Visitor Center north to Kings Canyon's Grant Grove Village. Along the way, it passes the turnoff to Crystal Cave, the Giant Forest Museum, Lodgepole Village, and other popular attractions. The lower portion, from Hospital Rock to the Giant Forest, is especially steep and winding. If your vehicle is 22 feet or longer, avoid that stretch by entering the parks via Route 180 (from Fresno) rather than Route 198 (from Visalia or Three Rivers). Take your time on this road—there's a lot to see, and wildlife can scamper across at any time. ⊠ *Sequoia National Park.*

SCENIC STOPS

Auto Log

FOREST | FAMILY | Before its wood showed signs of severe rot, cars drove right on top of this giant fallen sequoia. Now it's a great place to pose for pictures or shoot a video. ⊠ *Sequoia National Park ⊹ Moro Rock–Crescent Meadow Rd., 1 mile south of Giant Forest.*

★ Crystal Cave

CAVE | One of more than 200 caves in Sequoia and Kings Canyon, Crystal Cave is composed largely of marble, the result of limestone being hardened under heat and pressure. It contains several eye-popping formations. There used to be more, but some were damaged or obliterated by early-20th-century dynamite blasting. You can see the cave only on a tour. The Daily Tour ($17), a great overview, takes about 50 minutes. To immerse yourself in the cave experience—at times you'll be crawling on your belly—book the exhilarating Wild Cave Tour ($140). Availability is limited—reserve tickets at least 48 hours in advance at or stop by either the Foothills or Lodgepole visitor center first thing in the morning to try to nab a same-day ticket; they're not sold at the cave itself. ⊠ *Crystal Cave Rd., off Generals Hwy., Sequoia National Park* ☎ *877/444–6777* ⊕ *www.sequoiaparksconservancy.org/ crystalcave.html* 🖼 *$17* ⊘ *Closed Oct.– late May* ⌖ *Fires and flooding have led to temporary closures of the cave; check for updates on the conservancy website.*

★ General Sherman Tree

NATURE SIGHT | FAMILY | The 274.9-foot-tall General Sherman is one of the world's tallest and oldest sequoias, and it ranks No. 1 in volume, adding the equivalent of a 60-foot-tall tree every year to its approximately 52,500 cubic feet of mass. The tree doesn't grow taller, though—it's dead at the top. A short, wheelchair-accessible trail leads to the tree from Generals Highway, but the main trail (½ mile) winds down from a parking lot off Wolverton Road. The walk back up the main trail is steep, but benches along the way provide rest for the short of breath. ⊠ *Sequoia National Park ⊹ Main trail Wolverton Rd. off Generals Hwy. (Rte. 198)* ⌖ *Shuttle: Giant Forest or Wolverton–Sherman Tree.*

★ Moro Rock

NATURE SIGHT | FAMILY | This sight offers panoramic views to those fit and determined enough to mount its 350 or so

Sequoia National Park in One Day

After overnighting in Visalia or Three Rivers, take off early on Route 198 to the **Sequoia National Park entrance.** Pull over at the **Hospital Rock** picnic area to gaze up at the imposing granite Moro Rock, which you later will climb. Heed signs that advise "10 mph" around tight turns as you climb 3,500 feet on **Generals Highway** to the **Giant Forest Museum.** Spend a half hour here, then examine trees firsthand by circling the lovely **Round Meadow** on the **Big Trees Trail,** to which you must walk from the museum or its parking lot across the road.

Get back in your car, and continue a few miles north on Generals Highway to see the jaw-dropping **General Sherman Tree.** Then set off on the **Congress Trail** so that you can be further awed by the Senate and House big-tree clusters. Buy lunch at the **Lodgepole** complex, 2 miles to the north, and eat at the nearby **Pinewood** picnic area. Now you're ready to climb **Moro Rock.**

You can drive there or, if it is summer, park at the museum lot and take the free shuttle. Count on spending at least an hour for the 350-step ascent and descent, with a pause on top to appreciate the 360-degree view. Next, proceed past the **Tunnel Log** to **Crescent Meadow.** Spend a relaxing hour or two strolling on the trails that pass by, among other things, **Tharp's Log.** By now you've probably renewed your appetite; head to **Lodgepole Grill & Market** or the restaurant at **Wuksachi Lodge.**

steps. In a case where the journey rivals the destination, Moro's stone stairway is so impressive in its twisty inventiveness that it's on the National Register of Historic Places. The rock's 6,725-foot summit overlooks the Middle Fork Canyon, sculpted by the Kaweah River and approaching the depth of Arizona's Grand Canyon, although smoggy, hazy air often compromises the view. ⊠ *Sequoia National Park* ✛ *Moro Rock–Crescent Meadow Rd., 2 miles east off Generals Hwy. (Rte. 198) to parking area* ☞ *Shuttle: Moro Rock–Crescent Meadow.*

Tunnel Log

NATURE SIGHT | **FAMILY** | This 275-foot tree fell in 1937, and soon a 17-foot-wide, 8-foot-high hole was cut through it for vehicular passage (not to mention the irresistible photograph) that continues today. Large vehicles take the nearby bypass. ⊠ *Sequoia National Park* ✛ *Moro Rock–Crescent Meadow Rd., 2 miles east of Generals Hwy. (Rte. 198)* ☞ *Shuttle: Moro Rock–Crescent Meadow.*

TRAILS
★ Big Trees Trail

TRAIL | **FAMILY** | The 0.7-mile, wheelchair-accessible portion of this path is a must, as it does not take long, and the setting is spectacular: beautiful Round Meadow, surrounded by many mature sequoias. Well-thought-out interpretive signs along the way explain the ecology on display. Parking at the trailhead lot off Generals Highway is for cars with handicap placards only. The full, round-trip loop from the Giant Forest Museum is about a mile long. *Easy.* ⊠ *Sequoia National Park* ✛ *Trailhead: Off Generals Hwy. (Rte. 198), near the Giant Forest Museum* ☞ *Shuttle: Giant Forest.*

★ Congress Trail

TRAIL | **FAMILY** | This 2-mile trail, arguably the best hike in the parks in terms of natural beauty, is a paved loop that begins near General Sherman Tree. You'll get close-up views of more big trees here than on any other Sequoia hike. Watch for the clusters known as the House and Senate. The President Tree, also on the trail, supplanted the General Grant Tree in 2012 as the world's second largest in volume (behind the General Sherman). An offshoot of the Congress Trail leads to Crescent Meadow, where, in summer, you can catch a free shuttle back to the Sherman parking lot. *Easy.* ✉ *Sequoia National Park* ✣ *Trailhead: Off Generals Hwy. (Rte. 198), 2 miles north of Giant Forest* ☞ *Shuttle: Giant Forest.*

Crescent Meadow Trails

TRAIL | FAMILY | A sea of ferns signals your arrival at what John Muir called the "gem of the Sierra." A 1-mile trail loops around meadow to Tharp's Log, a cabin built from a fire-hollowed sequoia. From there you can embark on a 60-mile trek to Mt. Whitney, if you're prepared and have the time. Brilliant wildflowers bloom here in midsummer. *Easy.* ✉ *Sequoia National Park* ✣ *Trailhead: The end of Moro Rock–Crescent Meadow Rd., 2.6 miles east off Generals Hwy. (Rte. 198)* ☞ *Shuttle: Moro Rock–Crescent Meadow.*

Marble Falls Trail

TRAIL | The 3.7-mile trail to Marble Falls crosses through the rugged foothills before reaching the cascading water. Plan on three to four hours one-way. *Moderate.* ✉ *Sequoia National Park* ✣ *Trailhead: Off dirt road across from concrete ditch near site 17 at Potwisha Campground, off Generals Hwy. (Rte. 198).*

Tokopah Falls Trail

TRAIL | This trail with a 500-foot elevation gain follows the Marble Fork of the Kaweah River for 1¾ miles one-way and dead-ends below the impressive granite cliffs and cascading waterfall of Tokopah Canyon. The trail passes through a mixed-conifer forest. It takes 2½ to 4 hours to make the round-trip journey. *Moderate.* ✉ *Sequoia National Park* ✣ *Trailhead: Off Generals Hwy. (Rte. 198), ¼ mile north of Lodgepole Campground* ☞ *Shuttle: Lodgepole-Wuksachi-Dorst.*

VISITOR CENTERS

Lodgepole Visitor Center

VISITOR CENTER | Along with exhibits on the area's history, geology, and wildlife, the center screens an outstanding 22-minute film about bears. You can buy books, maps, wilderness permits, and tickets to cave tours here. ✉ *Sequoia National Park* ✣ *Generals Hwy. (Rte. 198), 21 miles north of Ash Mountain entrance* ☎ *559/565–3341* 🕘 *Closed Oct.–Apr.* ☞ *Shuttle: Giant Forest or Wuksachi-Lodgepole-Dorst.*

🍴 Restaurants

Lodgepole Market and Café

$ | CAFÉ | FAMILY | The choices here run the gamut from simple to very simple, with several counters only a few strides apart in a central eating complex. The café, which is next to the Lodgepole Visitor Center, also sells fresh and prepackaged salads, sandwiches, and wraps. **Known for:** quick and convenient dining; many healthful options; grab-and-go items for picnics. [$] *Average main: $12* ✉ *Sequoia National Park* ☎ *559/565–3301* 🌐 *www.visitsequoia.com/shop/lodgepole-market.*

The Peaks

$$ | MODERN AMERICAN | FAMILY | Huge windows run the length of the Wuksachi Lodge's high-ceilinged dining room, and a large fireplace on the far wall warms both body and soul. The diverse dinner menu—by far the best at both parks—reflects a commitment to locally sourced and sustainable products. **Known for:** seasonal menus with fresh local ingredients; great views of sequoia grove; box lunches. [$] *Average main: $28* ✉ *Wuksachi Lodge, 64740 Wuksachi Way, Wuksachi Village* ☎ *559/625–7700* 🌐 *www.visitsequoia.com.*

Hotels

★ Wuksachi Lodge

$$ | **HOTEL** | **FAMILY** | The striking cedar-and-stone main building is a fine example of how a structure can blend effectively with lovely mountain scenery. **Pros:** best place to stay in the parks; lots of wildlife; easy access to hiking and snowshoe/ski trails. **Cons:** rooms can be small; main lodge is a few-minutes' walk from guest rooms; slow Wi-Fi. $ *Rooms from: $267* ✉ *64740 Wuksachi Way, Wuksachi Village* ☎ *559/625–7700, 866/807–3598 reservations* ⊕ *www.visitsequoia.com/lodging/wuksachi-lodge* ⮩ *102 rooms* ⦿ *No Meals.*

Shopping

Wuksachi Gift Shop

SOUVENIRS | **FAMILY** | Souvenir clothing, Native American crafts, postcards, and snacks are for sale at this tasteful shop off the Wuksachi Lodge lobby. ✉ *64740 Wuksachi Way, Wuksachi Village* ☎ *559/625–7700.*

Mineral King

25 miles east of Generals Hwy. (Rte. 198) via Mineral King Rd.

A subalpine valley of fir, pine, and sequoia trees with myriad lakes and hiking trails, Mineral King sits at 7,500 feet at the end of a steep, winding road. This is the highest point to which you can drive in the park. It is open only from Memorial Day through late October.

Note that damage to roads caused by floods in spring of 2023 prevented public access to this entire area of the park. Check the park website to see if there are any attractions or amenities that might still be closed.

Sights

SCENIC DRIVES
Mineral King Road

SCENIC DRIVE | **FAMILY** | Vehicles longer than 22 feet are prohibited on this side road into southern Sequoia National Park, and for good reason: it's smaller than a regular two-lane road, some sections are unpaved, and it contains 589 twists and turns. Anticipating an average speed of 20 mph is optimistic. The scenery is splendid as you climb nearly 6,000 feet from Three Rivers to the Mineral King Area. In addition to maneuvering the blind curves and narrow stretches, you might find yourself sharing the pavement with bears, rattlesnakes, and even softball-size spiders. Allow 90 minutes each way. ✉ *Sequoia National Forest* ✛ *East off Sierra Dr. (Rte. 198), 3½ miles northeast of Three Rivers* ⊙ *Road typically closed Nov.–late May.*

TRAILS
Mineral King Trails

TRAIL | Many trails to the high country begin at Mineral King. Two popular day hikes are Eagle Lake (6.8 miles round-trip) and Timber Gap (4.4 miles round-trip). At the Mineral King Ranger Station (☎ *559/565–3341*) you can pick up maps and check about conditions from late May to late September. *Difficult.* ✉ *Sequoia National Park* ✛ *Trailheads: At end of Mineral King Rd., 25 miles east of Generals Hwy. (Rte. 198).*

VISITOR CENTERS
Mineral King Ranger Station

VISITOR CENTER | The station's small visitor center has exhibits on area history. Wilderness permits and some books and maps are available. ✉ *Sequoia National Park* ✛ *Mineral King Rd., 24 miles east of Rte. 198* ☎ *559/565–3341* ⮕ *Typically closed mid-Sept.–mid-May.*

🛏 Hotels

Silver City Mountain Resort

$$$ | RESORT | FAMILY | High on Mineral King Road, this privately owned resort has rustic cabins and deluxe chalets—all with a stove, refrigerator, and sink—plus three hotel rooms with private baths. **Pros:** rustic setting; friendly staff; great location for hikers. **Cons:** long, winding road is not for everybody; not much entertainment except hiking; some units have shared baths. $ *Rooms from: $396* ✉ *Mineral King Rd., Sequoia National Park* ✛ *21 miles southeast of Rte. 198* ☎ *559/242–3510, 559/561–1322 reservations* ⊕ *www.silvercityresort. com* ⊘ *Closed Nov.–late May* 🔁 *16 units* 🍽 *No Meals.*

Mt. Whitney

276 miles by car from Sequoia National Park/Foothills Visitor Center (looping around the Sierra Nevada) on U.S. 395, 60 miles on foot (an 8-day trek) along Mt. Whitney Trail.

At 14,494 feet, Mt. Whitney is the highest point in the contiguous United States and the crown jewel of Sequoia National Park's wild eastern side. The peak looms high above the tiny, high-mountain desert community of Lone Pine, where numerous Hollywood Westerns have been filmed. The high mountain ranges, arid landscape, and scrubby brush of the eastern Sierra are beautiful in their vastness and austerity.

Despite the mountain's scale, you can't see it from the more traveled west side of the park because it is hidden behind the Great Western Divide. The only way to access Mt. Whitney from the main part of the park is to circumnavigate the Sierra Nevada via a 10-hour, nearly 400-mile drive outside the park. No road ascends the peak; the best vantage point from which to catch a glimpse of

the mountain is at the end of Whitney Portal Road. The 13 miles of winding road leads from U.S. 395 at Lone Pine to the trailhead for the hiking route to the top of the mountain. Whitney Portal Road is closed in winter.

◉ Sights

TRAILS

Mt. Whitney Trail

TRAIL | The most popular route to the summit, the Mt. Whitney Trail can be conquered by very fit and experienced hikers. If there's snow on the mountain, this is a challenge for expert mountaineers only. All overnighters must have a permit, as must day hikers on the trail beyond Lone Pine Lake, about 2½ miles from the trailhead. From May through October, permits are distributed via a lottery run each February. The Eastern Sierra Interagency Visitor Center (☎ 760/876–6200), on Route 136 at U.S. 395 about a mile south of Lone Pine, is a good resource for information about permits and hiking. ✉ *Kings Canyon National Park* ☎ *760/873–2483 trail reservations* ⊕ *www.fs.usda.gov/inyo.*

Activities

BIKING

Steep, winding roads and shoulders that are either narrow or nonexistent make bicycling here more of a danger than a pleasure. Outside of campgrounds, you are not allowed to pedal on unpaved roads.

BIRD-WATCHING

More than 200 species of birds inhabit Sequoia and Kings Canyon national parks. Not seen in most parts of the United States, the white-headed woodpecker and the pileated woodpecker are common in most mid-elevation areas here. There are also many hawks and owls, including the renowned spotted owl. Due to the changes in elevation, both parks

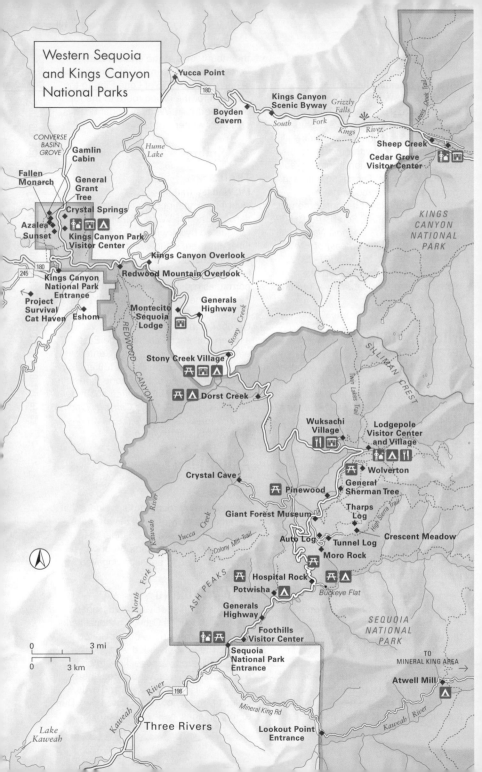

Western Sequoia and Kings Canyon National Parks

Yucca Point

Kings Canyon Scenic Byway

Boyden Cavern

Grizzly Falls

South Fork Kings River

Sheep Creek

Cedar Grove Visitor Center

CONVERSE BASIN GROVE

Gamlin Cabin

Hume Lake

Lewis Creek Trail

KINGS CANYON NATIONAL PARK

Fallen Monarch

General Grant Tree

Crystal Springs

Kings Canyon Park Visitor Center

Azalea Sunset

Kings Canyon National Park Entrance

Kings Canyon Overlook

Redwood Mountain Overlook

Project Survival Cat Haven

Eshom

Generals Highway

Montecito Sequoia Lodge

Stony Creek

REDWOOD CANYON

Stony Creek Village

Dorst Creek

SILLIMAN CREST

Twin Lakes Trail

Wuksachi Village

Lodgepole Visitor Center and Village

Crystal Cave

Wolverton

Pinewood

General Sherman Tree

Kaweah River

Yucca Creek

Giant Forest Museum

Tharps Log

High Sierra Trail

Crescent Meadow

Colony Mill Trail

Auto Log

Tunnel Log

Moro Rock

North Fork

ASH PEAKS

Hospital Rock

Buckeye Flat

SEQUOIA NATIONAL PARK

Potwisha

Generals Highway

Foothills Visitor Center

Sequoia National Park Entrance

TO MINERAL KING AREA

Lake Kaweah

Three Rivers

Mineral King Rd

Lookout Point Entrance

Atwell Mill

Kaweah River

0   3 mi
0   3 km

180

245

198

have diverse species ranging from warblers, kingbirds, thrushes, and sparrows in the foothills to goshawk, blue grouse, red-breasted nuthatch, and brown creeper at the highest elevations. The Sequoia Parks Conservancy (☎ 559/565–4251 ⊕ www.sequoiaparksconservancy. org) has information about bird-watching in the southern Sierra.

CAMPING

Some campgrounds are open year-round, others only seasonally. Except for Bearpaw (around $450 a night including meals), site range from $32 to $50, depending on location and size. There are no RV hookups at any of the campgrounds. Expect a table and a fire ring with a grill at standard sites.

You must make reservations at Bearpaw (☎ 877/436–9726 ⊕ www.visitsequoia. com), as well as Atwell Mill, Buckeye Flat, Dorst Creek, and Lodgepole (☎ 877/444–6777 ⊕ www.recreation. gov). Even if they're not required at other campgrounds, they're a good idea. Book as far ahead as possible, particularly for the Lodgepole and Dorst Creek campgrounds, which are quite popular with families.

Carefully follow all posted instructions about food storage. Bear-proof metal containers are provided at many campgrounds, as black bears are prevalent.

EDUCATIONAL PROGRAMS

Educational programs in Sequoia include museum-style exhibits, ranger- and naturalist-led talks and walks, film screenings, and sightseeing tours, most of them conducted by either the park service or the nonprofit Sequoia Parks Conservancy. Exhibits at the visitor centers and the Giant Forest Museum focus on different aspects of the park: its history, wildlife, geology, climate, and vegetation—most notably the giant sequoias. Weekly notices about programs are posted at the visitor centers and elsewhere.

Free Nature Programs

WILDLIFE-WATCHING | FAMILY | Almost any summer day, ½-hour to 1½-hour ranger talks and walks explore subjects such as the life of the sequoia, the geology of the park, and the habits of bears. Giant Forest Museum, Lodgepole Visitor Center, and Wuksachi Village are frequent starting points. Look for less frequent tours in the winter from Grant Grove. Check bulletin boards throughout the park for the week's offerings. ⊕ www. sequoiaparksconservancy.org.

Junior Ranger Program

HIKING & WALKING | FAMILY | Children over age five can earn a patch upon completion of a fun set of age-appropriate tasks outlined in the Junior Ranger booklet. Pick one up at any visitor center. ☎ 559/565–3341.

Sequoia Parks Conservancy Evening Programs

STARGAZING | FAMILY | The Sequoia Parks Conservancy offers hikes and evening lectures during the summer and winter. The popular Wonders of the Night Sky programs celebrate the often stunning views of the heavens experienced at both parks year-round. ⊠ Sequoia National Park ☎ 559/565–4251 ⊕ www. sequoiaparksconservancy.org.

Sequoia Parks Conservancy Seminars

WILDLIFE-WATCHING | Expert naturalists lead seminars on a range of topics, including birds, wildflowers, geology, botany, photography, park history, backpacking, and pathfinding. Reservations are required. Information about times and prices is available at the visitor centers or through the Sequoia Parks Conservancy. ⊠ Sequoia National Park ☎ 559/565–4251 ⊕ www.sequoiaparksconservancy.org.

FISHING

There's limited trout fishing in the creeks and rivers from late April to mid-November. The Kaweah River is a popular spot; check at visitor centers for open and closed waters. Some of the park's

Did You Know?

Sequoias once grew throughout the northern hemisphere but were almost wiped out by glaciers. Some fossils in Arizona's Petrified Forest National Park are extinct sequoia species.

secluded backcountry lakes have good fishing. A California fishing license, required for persons 16 and older, costs about $19 for one day, $29 for two days, and $59 for 10 days (discounts are available for state residents and others). For park regulations, closures, and restrictions, call the parks (☎ 559/565–3341) or stop at a visitor center. Licenses and fishing tackle are usually available at Hume Lake.

California Department of Fish and Game
FISHING | FAMILY | The department supplies fishing licenses and provides a full listing of regulations. ☎ 916/928–5805 ⊕ www.wildlife.ca.gov.

HIKING
The best way to see the park is to hike it. The grandeur and majesty of the Sierra is best seen up close. Carry a hiking map and plenty of water. Visitor center gift shops sell maps and trail books and pamphlets. Check with rangers for current trail conditions, and be aware of rapidly changing weather. As a rule of thumb, plan on covering about a mile per hour.

HORSEBACK RIDING
Grant Grove Stables
HORSEBACK RIDING | FAMILY | Grant Grove Stables isn't too far from parts of Sequoia National Park and is perfect for short rides from June to September. Reservations are recommended. ⊠ Rte. 180, Hume ☎ 559/335–9292 summer ⊕ www.nps.gov/seki/planyourvisit/horseride.htm ☑ From $60.

SLEDDING AND SNOWSHOEING
The Wolverton area, on Generals Highway (Route 198) near Giant Forest, is a popular sledding spot, where sleds, inner tubes, and platters are allowed. You can buy sleds and saucers, with prices starting at $20, at the Lodgepole Visitor Center. The shop also rents snowshoes (from $20). Naturalists lead snowshoe walks around Giant Forest and Wuksachi Lodge, conditions permitting, on Saturday and holidays. Make reservations

and check schedules at Giant Forest Museum (☎ 559/565–3341) or Wuksachi Lodge (⊕ www.visitsequoia.com).

SWIMMING
Drowning is the number-one cause of death in both Sequoia and Kings Canyon parks. Though it is sometimes safe to swim in the parks' rivers in the late summer and early fall, it is extremely dangerous to do so in the spring and early summer, when the snowmelt from the high country causes swift currents and icy temperatures. Stand clear of the water when the rivers are running, and stay off wet rocks to avoid falling in. Check with rangers for safety information.

Kings Canyon National Park

Kings Canyon National Park consists of two sections that adjoin the northern boundary of Sequoia National Park. The western portion, covered with sequoia and pine forest, contains the park's most visited sights, such as Grant Grove. The vast eastern portion is remote high country, slashed across half its southern breadth by the deep, rugged Kings River canyon. Separating the two is Sequoia National Forest, which encompasses Giant Sequoia National Monument. The Kings Canyon Scenic Byway (Route 180) links the major sights within and between the park's two sections.

Grant Grove Village— Redwood Canyon

56 miles east of Fresno on Rte. 180, 26 miles north of Lodgepole Village in Sequoia National Park.

Grant Grove Village, home to the Kings Canyon Visitor Center, Grant Grove Cabins, John Muir Lodge, a market, and two restaurants, anchors the northwestern

Kings Canyon National Park in One Day

Enter the park via the **Kings Canyon Scenic Byway** (Route 180), having spent the night in Fresno or Visalia. Or wake up already in **Grant Grove Village**, perhaps in the **John Muir Lodge.** Stock up for a picnic with takeout from the **Grant Grove Restaurant** or with food from the nearby market. Drive east a mile to see the **General Grant Tree** and compact **Grant Grove's** other sequoias. If it's no later than mid-morning, walk up the short trail at **Panoramic Point,** for a view of Hume Lake and the High Sierra. Either way, return to Route 180, and continue east. Stop at Junction View to take in several peaks towering over Kings Canyon. From here, visit **Boyden Cavern** or continue to **Cedar Grove Village,** pausing along the way at **Grizzly Falls.** Eat at a table by the **South Fork of the Kings River** or on the Cedar Grove Snack Bar's deck. Now you are ready for the day's highlight: strolling **Zumwalt Meadow,** which lies a few miles past the village.

After you have enjoyed that short trail and its views of **Grand Sentinel** and **North Dome,** head to **Roads End,** where backpackers embark for the High Sierra wilderness. Make the return trip—with a stop at **Roaring River Falls**—past Grant Grove and briefly onto southbound **Generals Highway.** Stop at **Redwood Mountain Overlook,** and use binoculars to look down upon the world's largest sequoia grove. Drive another couple of miles to the **Kings Canyon Overlook** to survey some of what you have done today. Make reservations for a late dinner at **Wuksachi Lodge.**

section of the park. Nearby attractions include the General Grant Tree and Redwood Canyon sequoia grove.

The Kings Canyon Scenic Byway (Route 180) begins here and travels 30 miles down to the Kings River Canyon and Cedar Grove. Note, though, that this byway was closed in spring 2023 after a section was damaged by flooding. Check the park website to see if there are still any area attraction closures or traffic delays due to ongoing roadwork.

Sights

HISTORIC SIGHTS
Fallen Monarch
NATURE SIGHT | FAMILY | This toppled sequoia's hollow base was used in the second half of the 19th century as a home for settlers, a saloon, and even a U.S. Cavalry stable. As you walk through it (assuming entry is permitted, which is not always the case), notice how little the wood has decayed, and imagine yourself tucked safely inside, sheltered from a storm or protected from the searing heat. ⊠ *Kings Canyon National Park ⊹ Grant Grove Trail, 1 mile north of Kings Canyon Park Visitor Center.*

Gamlin Cabin
NOTABLE BUILDING | FAMILY | Despite being listed on the National Register of Historic Places, this replica of a modest 1872 pioneer cabin is only borderline historical. The structure, which was moved and rebuilt several times over the years, once served as U.S. Cavalry storage space and, in the early 20th century, a ranger station. It's along the Grant Grove Trail. ⊠ *Kings Canyon National Park.*

SCENIC DRIVES
★ **Kings Canyon Scenic Byway**
SCENIC DRIVE | FAMILY | The 30-mile stretch of Route 180 between Grant Grove Village and Zumwalt Meadow delivers

eye-popping scenery granite cliffs, a roaring river, waterfalls, and Kings River canyon itself—much of which you can experience at vista points or on easy walks. The canyon comes into view about 10 miles east of the village at Junction View. Five miles beyond, at Yucca Point, the canyon is thousands of feet deeper than the more famous Grand Canyon. Canyon View, a special spot 1 mile east of the Cedar Grove Village turnoff, showcases evidence of the area's glacial history. Here, perhaps more than anywhere else, you'll understand why John Muir compared Kings Canyon vistas with those in Yosemite. ■ TIP→ Without any stops, this out-and-back drive takes about two hours, but check ahead to see if there are any roadwork delays. ⊠ *Kings Canyon National Park* ✛ *Rte. 180 north and east of Grant Grove village.*

SCENIC STOPS

Boyden Cavern

CAVE | FAMILY | The Kings River has carved out hundreds of caverns, including Boyden, which brims with stalagmite, stalactite, drapery, flowstone, and other formations. In summer, the Bat Grotto shelters a slew of bats. If you can't make it to Crystal Cave in Sequoia, Boyden is a reasonable substitute. Regular tours take about 45 minutes and start with a steep walk uphill. ⊠ *74101 E. Kings Canyon Rd. (Rte. 180), Sequoia National Forest, between Grant Grove and Cedar Grove* ☎ *888/965–8243* ⊕ *boydencavern.com* ⊠ *$18.*

General Grant Tree

NATURE SIGHT | FAMILY | President Coolidge proclaimed this to be the "nation's Christmas tree," and, 30 years later, President Eisenhower designated it as a living shrine to all Americans who have died in wars. Bigger at its base than the General Sherman Tree, it tapers more quickly. It's estimated to be the world's third-largest sequoia by volume. A spur trail winds behind the tree, where scars from a long-ago fire remain visible. ⊠ *Kings Canyon*

National Park ✛ *Trailhead: 1 mile north of Grant Grove Visitor Center.*

Project Survival Cat Haven

ZOO | FAMILY | Take the rare opportunity to glimpse a Eurasian lynx, a clouded leopard, a jaguar, and other endangered wild cats at this conservation facility that shelters more than 30 big cats. A guided hour-long tour along a ¼-mile walkway leads to fenced habitat areas shaded by trees and overlooking the Central Valley. ⊠ *38257 E. Kings Canyon Rd. (Rte. 180), 15 miles west of Kings Canyon National Park, Dunlap* ☎ *559/338–3216* ⊕ *cathaven.com* ⊠ *$16* ◷ *Closed Tues. May–Sept. Closed Tues. and Wed. Oct.–Apr.*

TRAILS

Big Baldy Trail

TRAIL | This hike climbs 600 feet and 2.2 miles up to the 8,209-foot summit of Big Baldy. Your reward is the view of Redwood Canyon. Round-trip, the hike is 4.4 miles. *Moderate.* ⊠ *Kings Canyon National Park* ✛ *Trailhead: 8 miles south of Grant Grove on Generals Hwy. (Rte. 198).*

Big Stump Trail

TRAIL | FAMILY | From 1883 until 1890, logging operations (there was even a mill) were conducted in this area. The 2-mile loop, whose unmarked beginning is a few yards west of the Big Stump entrance, passes by many enormous stumps. *Easy.* ⊠ *Kings Canyon National Park* ✛ *Trailhead: Near Big Stump Entrance, Generals Hwy. (Rte. 180).*

★ Grant Grove Trail

TRAIL | FAMILY | Grant Grove is only 128 acres, but it's a big deal. More than 120 sequoias here have a base diameter that exceeds 10 feet, and the General Grant Tree is the world's third-largest sequoia by volume. Nearby is the Robert E. Lee Tree, recognized as the world's 11th-largest sequoia. Also along the easy-to-walk trail are the Fallen Monarch and the Gamlin Cabin, built by 19th-century pioneers. *Easy.* ⊠ *Kings Canyon National*

Park ✥ Trailhead: Off Generals Hwy. (Rte. 180), 1 mile north of Kings Canyon Park Visitor Center.

Panoramic Point Trail

TRAIL | FAMILY | You'll get a nice view of whale-shape Hume Lake from the top of this Grant Grove path, which is paved and only 300 feet long. It's fairly steep—strollers might work here, but not wheelchairs. Trailers and RVs are not permitted on the steep and narrow road that leads to the trailhead parking lot. *Moderate.* ✉ *Kings Canyon National Park* ✥ *Trailhead: At end of Panoramic Point Rd., 2.3 miles from Grant Grove Village.*

VISITOR CENTERS

Kings Canyon Visitor Center

VISITOR CENTER | The center's 15-minute film and various exhibits provide an overview of the park's canyon, sequoias, and human history. Books, maps, and weather advice are dispensed here, as are (if available) $15 wilderness permits. ✉ *Kings Canyon National Park* ✥ *Grant Grove Village, Generals Hwy. (Rte. 198), 3 miles northeast of Rte. 180, Kings Canyon National Park entrance at Big Stump* ☎ *559/565–3341.*

🍴 Restaurants

Grant Grove Restaurant

$ | AMERICAN | FAMILY | Gaze at giant sequoias and a verdant meadow while enjoying a meal in this eco-friendly restaurant's spacious dining room with a fireplace or on its expansive deck. The menu is heavy on standard American fare, with dishes often made using locally sourced natural and organic ingredients. **Known for:** takeout service year-round; walk-up window for pizza, sandwiches, coffee, ice cream; picnic tables on outdoor deck. [$] *Average main: $16* ✉ *Grant Grove Village, Kings Canyon National Park* ☎ *559/335–5500* 🌐 *www.visitsequoia.com/dine.*

🛏 Hotels

Grant Grove Cabins

$ | HOTEL | FAMILY | Some of the wood-panel cabins here have heaters, electric lights, and private baths, but most have woodstoves, battery lamps, and shared baths. **Pros:** warm, woodsy feel; clean; walk to Grant Grove Restaurant. **Cons:** can be difficult to walk up to if you're not in decent physical shape; costly for what you get; only basic amenities. [$] *Rooms from: $135* ✉ *Kings Canyon Scenic Byway in Grant Grove Village, Kings Canyon National Park* ☎ *866/807–3598* 🌐 *www.visitsequoia.com/lodging/grant-grove-cabins* 🛏 *50 units* 🍴 *No Meals.*

John Muir Lodge

$$ | HOTEL | FAMILY | In a wooded area in the hills above Grant Grove Village, this modern, timber-sided lodge has rooms and suites with queen- or king-size beds and private baths. **Pros:** open year-round; common room stays warm; quiet. **Cons:** check-in is down in the village; spotty Wi-Fi; remote location. [$] *Rooms from: $210* ✉ *Kings Canyon Scenic Byway, ¼ mile north of Grant Grove Village, 86728 Hwy. 180, Kings Canyon National Park* ☎ *866/807–3598* 🌐 *www.visitsequoia.com/lodging/john-muir-lodge* 🛏 *36 rooms* 🍴 *No Meals.*

Montecito Sequoia Lodge

$ | HOTEL | FAMILY | Outdoor activities are what this year-round family resort is all about, including many that are geared toward teenagers and small children. **Pros:** friendly staff; great for kids; lots of fresh air and planned activities. **Cons:** can be noisy with all the activity; no TVs or phones in rooms; not within national park. [$] *Rooms from: $179* ✉ *63410 Generals Hwy., 11 miles south of Grant Grove, Sequoia National Forest* ☎ *559/565–3388, 800/227–9900* 🌐 *www.mslodge.com* 🕒 *Closed 1st 2 wks of Dec.* 🛏 *52 rooms* 🍴 *All-Inclusive.*

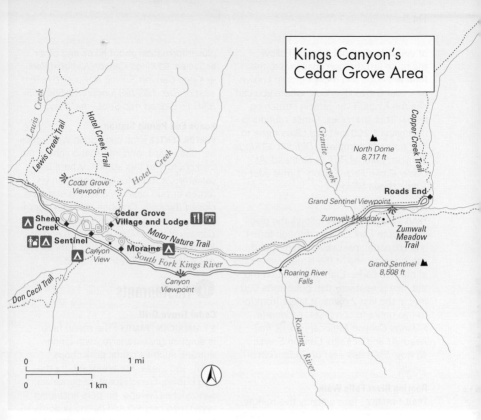

Kings Canyon's Cedar Grove Area

North Dome
8,717 ft

Copper Creek Trail

Granite Creek

Lewis Creek

Lewis Creek Trail

Hotel Creek Trail

Cedar Grove Viewpoint

Hotel Creek

Roads End

Grand Sentinel Viewpoint

Zumwalt Meadow

Sheep Creek

Cedar Grove Village and Lodge

Zumwalt Meadow Trail

Sentinel

Motor Nature Trail

Moraine

Canyon View

South Fork Kings River

Grand Sentinel 8,508 ft

Don Cecil Trail

Canyon Viewpoint

Roaring River Falls

Roaring River

0 ___ 1 mi

0 ___ 1 km

Cedar Grove

35 miles east of Grant Grove Village.

The Cedar Grove section of Kings Canyon National Park bears many similarities to Yosemite Valley: a mighty river flowing through a verdant valley, ringed by massive glacier-hewn granite cliffs that loom several thousand feet above. Drive along the Kings Canyon Scenic Byway (Route 180) to access this relatively uncrowded wonderland, where you can hike excellent backcountry trails, stroll around lush Zumwalt Meadows, and take a break in Cedar Grove Village.

Prior to the 2023 season, portions of Route 180 were severely damaged by floods, so there was no access to this area, and its attractions and amenities were closed. Check ahead for updates on any ongoing roadwork or closures.

◉ Sights

HISTORIC SIGHTS
Knapp's Cabin

NOTABLE BUILDING | FAMILY | Stop here not so much for the cabin itself, but as an excuse to ogle the scenery. George Knapp, a Santa Barbara businessman, stored gear in this small wooden structure when he commissioned fishing trips into the canyon in the 1920s. ⊠ *Kings Canyon National Park* ⊹ *Kings Canyon Scenic Byway, 2 miles east of Cedar Grove Village turnoff.*

TRAILS
Hotel Creek Trail

TRAIL | For gorgeous canyon views, take this trail from Cedar Grove up a series of switchbacks until it splits. Follow the route left through chaparral to the forested ridge and rocky outcrop known as Cedar Grove Overlook, where you can see the Kings River canyon stretching below. This strenuous, 5-mile round-trip hike gains 1,200 feet and takes three to four hours to complete. *Difficult.* ✉ *Kings Canyon National Park* ⊕ *Trailhead: At Cedar Grove Pack Station, 1 mile east of Cedar Grove Village.*

Mist Falls Trail

TRAIL | This sandy trail follows the glaciated South Fork Canyon through forest and chaparral, past several rapids and cascades, to one of the largest waterfalls in the two parks. Eight miles round-trip, the hike is relatively flat, but climbs 600 feet in the last 2 miles. It takes from four to five hours to complete. *Moderate.* ✉ *Kings Canyon National Park* ⊕ *Trailhead: At end of Kings Canyon Scenic Byway, 5½ miles east of Cedar Grove Village.*

Roaring River Falls Walk

TRAIL | **FAMILY** | Take a shady five-minute walk to this forceful waterfall that rushes through a narrow granite chute. The trail is paved and mostly accessible. *Easy.* ✉ *Kings Canyon National Park* ⊕ *Trailhead: 3 miles east of Cedar Grove Village turnoff from Kings Canyon Scenic Byway.*

★ Zumwalt Meadow Trail

TRAIL | **FAMILY** | One of the most popular day hikes in the Cedar Grove area is just 1.6 miles long and takes in not only the lush meadow, but also the South Fork of the Kings River and the high granite walls above, including those of Grand Sentinel and North Dome. *Easy.* ✉ *Kings Canyon National Park* ⊕ *Trailhead: 4½ miles east of Cedar Grove Village turnoff from Kings Canyon Scenic Byway.*

VISITOR CENTERS

Cedar Grove Visitor Center

VISITOR CENTER | Off the main road and behind the Sentinel Campground, this small ranger station has books and maps, plus information about hikes and other activities. ✉ *Kings Canyon National Park* ⊕ *Kings Canyon Scenic Byway, 30 miles east of Rte. 180/198 junction* ☎ *559/565–3341* ⏲ *Closed mid-Sept.–mid-May.*

Roads End Permit Station

VISITOR CENTER | You can obtain wilderness permits, maps, and information about the backcountry at this station, where bear canisters, a must for campers, can be rented or purchased. When the station is closed (typically October–mid-May), complete a self-service permit form. ✉ *Kings Canyon National Park* ⊕ *Eastern end of Kings Canyon Scenic Byway, 6 miles east of Cedar Grove Visitor Center* ☎.

🍴 Restaurants

Cedar Grove Grill

$ | **AMERICAN** | **FAMILY** | The menu here is surprisingly extensive, with dinner entrées such as pasta, pork chops, trout, and steak. For breakfast, try the egg burrito, French toast, or pancakes; sandwiches, wraps, burgers (including vegetarian patties) and hot dogs dominate the lunch choices. **Known for:** scenic river views; extensive options; alfresco dining on balcony overlooking the Kings River. [$] *Average main: $16* ✉ *Cedar Grove Village, Kings Canyon National Park* ☎ *866/807–3598* 🌐 *www.visitsequoia.com/dine/cedar-grove-grill* ⏲ *Closed Oct.–May.*

🛏 Hotels

Cedar Grove Lodge

$ | **HOTEL** | Backpackers like to stay here on the eve of long treks into the High Sierra wilderness, so bedtimes tend to be early. **Pros:** a definite step up from camping in terms of comfort; great base camp for outdoor adventures; on-site snack bar. **Cons:** impersonal; not everybody agrees it's clean enough; remote location. [$] *Rooms from: $148* ✉ *Kings Canyon Scenic Byway, Kings Canyon National Park* ☎ *866/807–3598* 🌐 *www.*

visitsequoia.com/lodging/cedar-grove-lodge ◷ Closed mid-Oct.–mid-May ⚑ 21 rooms ◯ No Meals.

Activities

BIKING

Bicycles are allowed only on the paved roads in Kings Canyon. Cyclists should be extremely cautious along the steep highways and narrow shoulders.

CAMPING

Campgrounds in Kings Canyon occupy wonderful settings, with lots of shade and nearby hiking trails. Reservations (🕾 *877/444–6777* ⊕ *www.recreation. gov*) are a good idea; at some campgrounds, they're required. Make them as far ahead as possible, particularly for stays around Grant Grove, an area that's popular with vacationing families.

Keep in mind that this is black-bear country and carefully follow posted instructions about storing food. Bear-proof metal containers are provided at many campgrounds.

CROSS-COUNTRY SKIING

Roads to Grant Grove are accessible even during heavy snowfall, making the trails here a good choice over Sequoia's Giant Forest when harsh weather hits.

Grant Grove Ski Touring Center

SKIING & SNOWBOARDING | The Grant Grove Market doubles as the ski-touring center, where you can rent cross-country skis or snowshoes in winter. This is a good starting point for a number of marked trails, including the Panoramic Point Trail and the General Grant Tree Trail. *⊠ Grant Grove Market, Generals Hwy. (Rte. 198), 3 miles northeast of Rte. 180, Big Stump entrance, Kings Canyon National Park* 🕾 *559/335–5500* ⊕ *www.visitsequoia. com/cross-country-skiing.aspx* ⚑ *From $15.*

EDUCATIONAL PROGRAMS

Grant Grove Visitor Center has maps of self-guided park tours. Ranger-led walks and programs take place throughout the year in Grant Grove. Cedar Grove and Forest Service campgrounds have activities from Memorial Day to Labor Day. Check bulletin boards or visitor centers for schedules.

FISHING

There is limited trout fishing in the park from late April to mid-November, and catches are minor. Still, Kings River is a popular spot. Some of the park's secluded backcountry lakes have good fishing. Licenses are available, along with fishing tackle, in Grant Grove and Cedar Grove.

HIKING

You can enjoy many of Kings Canyon's sights from your car, but the giant gorge of the Kings River canyon and the sweeping vistas of some of the highest mountains in the United States are best seen on foot. Carry a hiking map—available at any visitor center—and plenty of water. Check with rangers for current trail conditions, and be aware of rapidly changing weather. Except for one trail to Mt. Whitney, permits are not required for day hikes.

HORSEBACK RIDING

One-day destinations by horseback out of Cedar Grove include Mist Falls and Upper Bubb's Creek. In the backcountry, many equestrians head for Volcanic Lakes or Granite Basin, ascending trails that reach elevations of 10,000 feet. Costs per person range from $60 for a one-hour guided ride to around $300 per day for fully guided trips for which the packers do all the cooking and camp chores.

Cedar Grove Pack Station

HORSEBACK RIDING | **FAMILY** | Take a day ride or plan a multiday adventure along the Kings River canyon with Cedar Grove Pack Station. Popular routes include the Rae Lakes Loop and Monarch Divide. Closed early September–late May.

✉ *Kings Canyon National Park* ✢ *Kings Canyon Scenic Byway, 1 mile east of Cedar Grove Village* ☎ *559/565–3464 summer, 559/802–7626 off-season* ⊕ *www.nps.gov/seki/planyourvisit/horseride.htm* ✉ *From $50 per hr or $90 per day.*

Grant Grove Stables

HORSEBACK RIDING | FAMILY | A one- or two-hour trip through Grant Grove leaving from the stables provides a taste of horseback riding in Kings Canyon. The stables are closed October–early June. ✉ *Kings Canyon National Park* ✢ *Rte. 180, ½ mile north of Grant Grove Visitor Center* ☎ *559/335–9292* ⊕ *www.nps.gov/seki/planyourvisit/horseride.htm* ✉ *From $50 per hr, $90 for 2 hrs.*

SLEDDING AND SNOWSHOEING

In winter, Kings Canyon has a few great places to play in the snow. Sleds, inner tubes, and platters are allowed at both the Azalea Campground area on Grant Tree Road, ¼ mile north of Grant Grove Visitor Center, and at the Big Stump picnic area, 2 miles north of the lower Route 180 entrance to the park.

Snowshoeing is good around Grant Grove, where you can take occasional naturalist-guided snowshoe walks from mid-December through mid-March as conditions permit. Grant Grove Market rents sleds and snowshoes.

What's Nearby

Three Rivers

7 miles south of Sequoia National Park's Foothills Visitor Center.

Three Rivers is a good spot to find a room when park lodgings are full. Either because residents here appreciate their idyllic setting or because they know that tourists are their bread and butter, you'll find them eager to share tips about

the best spots for "Sierra surfing" the Kaweah's smooth, moss-covered rocks or where to find the best cell reception (it's off to the cemetery for Verizon customers).

GETTING HERE AND AROUND

Driving is the easiest way to get to and around Three Rivers, which straddles a stretch of Highway 198. In summer, the Sequoia Shuttle connects Three Rivers to Visalia and Sequoia National Park.

CONTACTS Sequoia Shuttle. ☎ *877/287–4453* ⊕ *www.sequoiashuttle.com.*

 Sights

Sequoia National Forest and Giant Sequoia National Monument

FOREST | FAMILY | Delicate spring wildflowers, cool summer campgrounds, and varied winter-sports opportunities—not to mention more than half of the world's giant sequoia groves—draw outdoorsy types year-round to this sprawling district surrounding the national parks. Together, the forest and monument cover nearly 1,700 square miles, south from the Kings River and east from the foothills along the San Joaquin Valley. The monument's groves are both north and south of Sequoia National Park. One of the most popular is the **Converse Basin Grove,** home of the Boole Tree, the forest's largest sequoia. The grove is accessible by car on an unpaved road.

The Hume Lake Forest Service District Office, at 35860 Kings Canyon Scenic Byway (Route 180), has information about the groves, along with details about recreational activities. In springtime, diversions include hiking among the wildflowers that brighten the foothills. The floral display rises with the heat as the mountain elevations warm up in summer, when hikers, campers, and picnickers become more plentiful. The abundant trout supply attracts anglers to area waters, including 87-acre **Hume Lake,** which is also ideal for swimming and nonmotorized boating. By fall, the turning leaves provide the visual delights, particularly in the Western Divide, Indian Basin, and the Kern Plateau. Winter activities include downhill and cross-country skiing, snowshoeing, and snowmobiling. ⊠ *Sequoia National Park ✦ Northern Entrances: Generals Hwy. (Rte. 198), 7 miles southeast of Grant Grove; Hume Lake Rd. between Generals Hwy. (Rte. 198) and Kings Canyon Scenic Byway (Rte. 180); Kings Canyon Scenic Byway (Rte. 180) between Grant Grove and Cedar Grove. Southern Entrances: Rte. 190 east of Springville; Rte. 178 east of Bakersfield* ☎ *559/784–1500 forest and monument, 559/338–2251 Hume Lake* ⊕ *www.fs.usda.gov/sequoia.*

Restaurants

Gateway Restaurant and Lodge
$$$ | AMERICAN | The view's the draw at this roadhouse that overlooks the Kaweah River as it plunges out of the high country. The Gateway serves everything from osso buco and steaks to shrimp in Thai chili sauce; dinner reservations are essential on summer weekends. **Known for:** scenic riverside setting; fine dining in otherwise casual town; popular bar. $ *Average main: $33* ⊠ *45978 Sierra Dr., Three Rivers* ☎ *559/561–4133* ⊕ *gateway-sequoia. com.*

Hotels

Buckeye Tree Lodge
$$$ | B&B/INN | FAMILY | Every room at this two-story motel has a patio facing a sun-dappled grassy lawn, right on the banks of the Kaweah River; individually decorated cottages and cabins across the river have private outdoor spaces with barbecue grills. **Pros:** near the park entrance; fantastic river views; kitchenette in some rooms. **Cons:** can fill up quickly in the summer; could use a little updating; some rooms are tiny. $ *Rooms*

from: $458 ⊠ *46000 Sierra Dr., Hwy. 198, Three Rivers* ☎ *559/561–5900* ⊕ *www. buckeyetreelodge.com* ⇆ *22 units* ⧖*| Free Breakfast* ⛄ *2-night minimum on summer weekends.*

★ Rio Sierra River Resort
$$$ | B&B/INN | Guests at Rio Sierra come for the river views, the sandy beach, and the proximity to Sequoia National Park (6 miles away), but invariably end up raving equally about the warm, laid-back hospitality of proprietress Mars Roberts. **Pros:** seductive beach; river views from all rooms; contemporary ambience. **Cons:** books up quickly in summer; some road noise audible in rooms; long walk or drive to restaurants. $ *Rooms from: $400* ⊠ *41997 Sierra Dr., Hwy. 198, Three Rivers* ☎ *559/561–4720* ⊕ *rio-sierra. com* ⇆ *3 rooms, 1 cottage* ⧖*| No Meals* ⛄ *2-night minimum stay on summer weekends. Closed Jan.–mid-Mar.*

Activities

RAFTING
Kaweah Whitewater Adventures
RAFTING | FAMILY | Kaweah's trips include a two-hour excursion (good for families) through Class III rapids, a longer paddle through Class IV rapids, and an extended trip (typically Class IV and V rapids). ⊠ *40443 Sierra Dr., Three Rivers* ☎ *559/202–3103* ⊕ *www.kaweahadventures.com* ⛵ *From $50 per person.*

Visalia

35 miles west of the Sequoia National Park entrance.

Visalia's combination of a reliable agricultural economy and civic pride has produced the Central Valley's most vibrant downtown, with numerous restaurants, craft breweries, and cafés. If you're into history, drop by the visitor center and pick up a free map of a self-guided historic downtown walking tour. A clear day's view of the Sierra from Main

Street is spectacular, and even Sunday night can find the streets bustling with pedestrians. Visalia provides easy access to Sequoia National Park and the serene Kaweah Oaks Preserve.

GETTING HERE AND AROUND

Highway 198, just east of its exit from Highway 99, cuts through town (and proceeds up the hill to Sequoia National Park). Greyhound stops here, but not Amtrak. KART buses serve the locals, and, in summer, the Sequoia Shuttle ($20) travels among Visalia, Three Rivers, and Sequoia National Park with a stop in Three Rivers.

VISITOR INFORMATION

CONTACTS Visalia Convention & Visitors Bureau. ✉ *112 E. Main St., Visalia* ☎ *559/334–0141, 800/524–0303* 🌐 *www.visitvisalia.com.*

Sights

Bravo Farms

OTHER ATTRACTION | FAMILY | For one-stop truck-stop entertainment, pull off the highway in Traver, where at Bravo Farms you can try your luck at an arcade shooting gallery, watch cheese being made, munch on barbecue and ice cream, play a round of minigolf, peruse funky antiques, buy produce, visit a petting zoo, and climb a multistory tree house. Taste a few "squeekers" (fresh cheese curds, so named because chewing them makes your teeth squeak), and then be on your way. ✉ *36005 Hwy. 99, 9 miles north of Hwy. 198 and Visalia, Traver* ☎ *559/897–5762* 🌐 *bravofarms.com* 🎟 *Free.*

★ **Colonel Allensworth State Historic Park**

HISTORY MUSEUM | FAMILY | It's worth the slight detour off Highway 99 to learn about and pay homage to the dream of Allen Allensworth and other Black pioneers who, in 1908, founded Allensworth, the only California town settled, governed, and financed by African Americans. At its height, the town prospered as a key railroad transfer point, but after cars and trucks reduced railroad traffic and water was diverted for Central Valley agriculture, the town declined and was eventually deserted. Today, the restored and rebuilt schoolhouse, library, and other structures commemorate Allensworth's heyday, as do festivities that take place each October. ✉ *4129 Palmer Ave., 48 miles south of Visalia, Allensworth* ✣ *From Visalia, take Hwy. 99 south to Earlimart, and then turn west toward Allensworth* ☎ *661/849–3433* 🌐 *www.parks.ca.gov* 🎟 *Free.*

★ **Farmer Bob's World** (*McKellar Family Farms*)

FARM/RANCH | FAMILY | Taste, touch, and feel your way through orange and mandarin groves on a guided tour of this 180-acre working citrus farm. Tours last 60 minutes; tractor-pulled wagon tours are also available, as are more expensive walking tours. Kids and adults love the challenge of navigating the nation's only orange-grove maze, answering questions at a series of checkpoints to earn a prize at the end. You must book tours in advance online. ✉ *32985 Rd. 164, north of Hwy. 216, Ivanhoe* ☎ *559/798–0557* 🌐 *farmerbobsworld.com* 🎟 *Farm Tour $15; Tractor Tour $15; Walking Tour $100 for up to 2 persons, $10 for each additional person* 🕒 *Closed Sun.–Tues.* ✍ *Tour reservations required.*

Restaurants

Fugazzi's Bistro

$$ | ITALIAN | An upscale restaurant in Visalia's downtown hub, Fugazzi's serves up Italian-American and international-fusion dishes in a slick, contemporary space with leather booths and shiny metal tables. The extensive lunch and dinner menus feature everything from quinoa-and-kale salad and Thai chicken wraps to traditional Italian dishes and grilled lamb chops. **Known for:** full bar with classic and creative cocktails; house-made sauces; upscale yet casual vibe. [$] *Average main: $22* ✉ *127 W. Main St., Visalia*

☎ 559/625–0496 ⊕ www.fugazzishistro.com ✆ Closed Sun.

★ The Vintage Press

$$$$ | EUROPEAN | Established in 1966, this is one of the best restaurants in the Central Valley. The California–continental cuisine includes dishes such as French escargot with a white-wine sauce and filet mignon with a cognac-mustard sauce. **Known for:** wine list with more than 900 selections; chocolate Grand Marnier cake and other house-made desserts; sophisticated vibe. $ Average main: $49 ✉ 216 N. Willis St., Visalia ☎ 559/733–3033 ⊕ www.thevintage-press.com.

Hotels

★ The Darling Hotel

$ | HOTEL | Developers meticulously restored a dilapidated, three-story, 1930s building to create this hotel, where rooms have a modern take on art deco style, with plush furnishings, 12-foot ceilings, and spacious bathrooms with period accents. **Pros:** in the heart of downtown; outdoor pool; rooftop lounge and restaurant with panoramic mountain and city views. **Cons:** some rooms on the small side; fronts a busy street; vintage single-pane glass windows don't block urban noise. $ Rooms from: $179 ✉ 210 N. Court St., Visalia ☎ 559/713–2113 ⊕ thedarlingvisalia.com ⟿ 32 rooms ꙳⊙꙳ No Meals.

Fresno

44 miles north of Visalia, 53 miles west of Kings Canyon National Park, 77 miles northwest of Sequoia National Park, 62 miles south of Yosemite National Park.

Fresno, with half a million people, is the center of the richest agricultural county in the United States. Cotton, grapes, and tomatoes are among the major crops; poultry and milk are also important. About 75 ethnic groups, including Armenians, Laotians, and Indians, live here. The city has a relatively vibrant arts scene, several public parks, and many low-price restaurants. The Tower District—with its restaurants, coffeehouses, and performance venues—is the town's arts and nightlife nexus.

Although Fresno is the closest large city to Sequoia and Kings Canyon, it's not that close. Nevertheless, it's an option if there's nothing available in the park itself, Three Rivers, or Visalia. It can also serve as a gateway to Yosemite National Park.

GETTING HERE AND AROUND

Highway 99 is the biggest road through Fresno. Highways 41 and 180 also bisect the city. Amtrak trains stop here daily (and often).

VISITOR INFORMATION

Fresno / Clovis Convention & Visitors Bureau. ✉ 1180 E. Shaw Ave., Fresno ☎ 559/981–5500, 800/788–0836 ⊕ www.visitfresno-county.org.

Sights

★ Forestiere Underground Gardens

GARDEN | FAMILY | Sicilian immigrant Baldassare Forestiere spent four decades (1906–46) carving out an odd, subterranean realm of rooms, tunnels, grottoes, alcoves, and arched passageways that once extended for more than 10 acres between Highway 99 and busy, mall-pocked Shaw Avenue. Though not an engineer, Forestiere called on his memories of the ancient Roman structures he saw as a youth and on techniques he learned digging subways in New York and Boston. Only a fraction of his prodigious output is on view, but you can tour his underground living quarters, including bedrooms (one with a fireplace), the kitchen, living room, and bath, as well as a fishpond and auto tunnel. Skylights allow exotic full-grown fruit trees to flourish more than 20 feet belowground. ✉ 5021 W. Shaw Ave., 2 blocks east of Hwy. 99, Fresno ☎ 559/271–0734

🌐 *undergroundgardens.com* 🎟 *$23* ⏲ *Closed Dec.–Mar. Closed Tues. and Wed. in fall and early spring.*

🍴 Restaurants

School House Restaurant & Tavern
$$$ | **MODERN AMERICAN** | A Wine Country–style establishment that sources ingredients from the on-site gardens and surrounding farms and orchards, this popular restaurant occupies a redbrick 1921 schoolhouse in the town of Sanger. Chef Ryan Jackson, who grew up on local fruit farms, creates seasonal menus from the bounty of familiar backyards, mostly filled with classic American dishes with a contemporary twist. **Known for:** ingredients from neighboring farms and orchards; historical country setting; convenient stop between Kings Canyon and Fresno. [$] *Average main: $35* ✉ *1018 S. Frankwood Ave., at Hwy. 180 (King's Canyon Rd.), 20 miles east of Fresno, Sanger* ☎ *559/787–3271* 🌐 *schoolhousesanger.com* ⏲ *Closed Mon. and Tues. No lunch.*

🛏 Hotels

Best Western Plus Fresno Inn
$ | **HOTEL** | **FAMILY** | With a location near Highway 41 (the main route to Yosemite), Fresno State, and a big mall, this well-run hotel is popular with families, businesspeople, and parents with offspring at the university. **Pros:** convenient location; attentive staff; 24-hour business center. **Cons:** mildly sterile feel; on a busy street; small pool. [$] *Rooms from: $140* ✉ *480 E. Shaw Ave., Fresno* ☎ *559/229–5811* 🌐 *www.bestwestern.com* 🔑 *55 rooms* 🍽 *Free Breakfast.*

Chapter 6

YOSEMITE NATIONAL PARK

Updated by
Cheryl Crabtree

Camping
★★★★★

Hotels
★★★★☆

Activities
★★★★★

Scenery
★★★★★

Crowds
★★★★☆

WELCOME TO YOSEMITE NATIONAL PARK

TOP REASONS TO GO

★ **Scenic falls:** An easy stroll brings you to the base of Lower Yosemite Fall, where roaring springtime waters make for misty photo filters and lasting memories.

★ **Tunnel vision:** Approaching Yosemite Valley, Wawona Road passes through a mountainside and emerges before one of the park's most heart-stopping vistas.

★ **Inhale the beauty:** Pause to take in the light, pristine air as you travel about the High Sierra's Tioga Pass and Tuolumne Meadows, where 10,000-foot granite peaks just might take your breath away.

★ **Walk away:** Leave the crowds behind—but do bring along a buddy—and take a hike somewhere along Yosemite's 800 miles of trails.

★ **Winter wonder:** Observe the snowflakes and stillness of winter in the park.

1 Yosemite Valley. At an elevation of 4,000 feet, in roughly the center of the park, beats Yosemite's heart. This is where you'll find the park's most famous sights and biggest crowds.

2 Wawona. The park's southern tip holds Wawona, with its grand old hotel and pioneer history center, and the Mariposa Grove of Giant Sequoias. These are closest to the south entrance, 35 miles (a one-hour drive) south of Yosemite Village.

3 Tuolumne Meadows. The highlight of east-central Yosemite is this wildflower-strewn valley that's laced with hiking trails and nestled among sharp, rocky peaks. It's a 1½-hour drive northeast of Yosemite Valley along Tioga Road (closed mid-October–late May).

4 Hetch Hetchy. The most remote, least visited part of Yosemite accessible by automobile, this glacial valley is dominated by a reservoir and veined with wilderness trails. It's near the park's western boundary, about a half-hour drive north of the Big Oak Flat entrance.

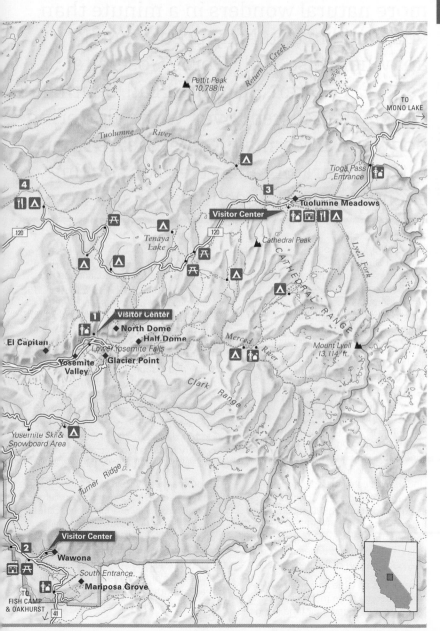

TO
MONO LAKE

Pettit Peak
10,788 ft

Tuolumne   River

Return   Creek

Tioga Pass
Entrance

Tuolumne Meadows

Visitor Center

120

120

Tenaya
Lake

Cathedral Peak

CATHEDRAL RANGE

Lyell Fork

Visitor Center

El Capitan

North Dome

Half Dome

Lower Yosemite Falls

Glacier Point

Yosemite
Valley

Merced   River

Mount Lyell
13,114 ft

Clark   Range

Yosemite Ski &
Snowboard Area

Turner Ridge

Visitor Center

Wawona

South Entrance

Mariposa Grove

TO
FISH CAMP
& OAKHURST

41

By merely standing in Yosemite Valley and turning in a circle, you can see more natural wonders in a minute than you could in a full day pretty much anywhere else. Half Dome, Yosemite Falls, El Capitan, Bridalveil Fall, Sentinel Dome, the Merced River, white-flowering dogwood trees, maybe even bears ripping into the bark of fallen trees or sticking their snouts into beehives—it's all here.

Native American nations—including the Miwok, Paiute, Mono, and Ahwahneechee tribes—roamed this wonderland long before other cultures. Indeed, some of the footpaths used by Native Americans to cross mountains and valleys are still used as park hiking trails today.

In the mid-1800s, the valley's special geologic qualities and the giant sequoias of Mariposa Grove 30 miles to the south began attracting visitors. The two areas so impressed a group of influential Californians that they lobbied President Abraham Lincoln to grant them to the state for protection, which he did on June 30, 1864. Further lobbying efforts by naturalist John Muir and Robert Underwood Johnson, editor of The Century Magazine, led Congress to set aside an additional 1,500 square miles for Yosemite National Park on October 1, 1890. The valley and Mariposa Grove, which had remained under state control, also became part of the park in 1906.

Yosemite is so large and diverse, it almost seems to be multiple parks. Many visitors spend their time along the southwestern border, between Wawona, which is open all year and is where the giant sequoias stand, and the Big Oak Flat entrance. Also very popular are Yosemite Valley, famous for its waterfalls and cliffs and also open year-round, and the Badger Pass Ski Area, a winter-only destination. The seasonal, east–west Tioga Road spans the park north of the valley and bisects Tuolumne Meadows, the subalpine high country that's open for summer hiking and camping; in winter, it's accessible only via cross-country skis or snowshoes. The northwestern Hetch Hetchy district, home of less-used backcountry trails, is most accessible from late spring through early fall.

Photographers, hikers, and nature enthusiasts visit again and again, lured by the seasonally changing landscapes. In spring, waterfalls are robust thanks to abundant snowmelt. In early summer, wildflowers blanket alpine meadows. In fall, the trees showcase glorious explosions of color. In winter, snows provide a magical setting for activities like ice skating in the valley or cross-country skiing to Glacier Point.

Planning

Getting Here and Around

AIR

The closest airport to the south and west entrances is Fresno Yosemite International Airport (FAT). Mammoth Yosemite Airport (MMH) and Eastern Sierra Regional Airport (BIH) in Bishop are closest to the east entrance. Sacramento International Airport (SMF) is also close to the north and west entrances.

United has seasonal flights from to and from Denver and San Francisco (fly into MMH or BIH and take a shuttle). Advanced Airlines flies from Hawthorne and Carlsbad into MMH.

BUS AND TRAIN

Greyhound buses and Amtrak's daily *San Joaquins* train stop in Merced, connecting with YARTS buses that travel to Yosemite Valley along Highway 140 from there. Seasonal YARTS buses (typically mid-May to late September) also travel along Highway 41 from Fresno, Highway 120 from Sonora, and Highway 395 and Tioga Road from Mammoth Lakes with scheduled stops at towns along the way.

Once you're in Yosemite Valley, you can take advantage of the free, low-emission shuttle buses that make 19 stops and run from 7 am to 10 pm year-round. Buses run about every 10 minutes in summer, a bit less frequently in winter. The free Mariposa Grove shuttle takes you from the Mariposa Grove Welcome Plaza to the sequoia grove trails (April–November). Also in summer, you can pay to take the "hikers' bus" from Yosemite Valley to Tuolumne or to ride a tour bus up to Glacier Point. During the snow season, buses run regularly between Yosemite Valley and Badger Pass Ski Area.

CAR

Roughly 200 miles from San Francisco, 300 miles from Los Angeles, and 500 miles from Las Vegas, Yosemite takes a while to reach—and its many sites and attractions merit much more time than what rangers say is the average visit: four hours.

Of the park's four entrances, Arch Rock is the closest to Yosemite Valley. The road that goes through it, Route 140 from Merced and Mariposa, is a scenic western approach that snakes alongside the boulder-packed Merced River. Route 41, through Wawona, is the way to come from Los Angeles (or Fresno, if you've flown in and rented a car). Route 120, through Crane Flat, is the most direct route from San Francisco. The only way in from the east is Tioga Road, which may be the best route in terms of scenery—though due to snow accumulation it's open for a frustratingly short amount of time each year (typically early June through mid-October).

Once you enter Yosemite Valley, park your car in one of the two main day-parking areas, at Yosemite Village and Yosemite Falls, and then visit the sights via the free shuttle bus system. Or walk or bike along the valley's 12 miles of paved paths.

There are few gas stations within Yosemite (Crane Flat and Wawona, none in the valley), so fuel up before you reach the park. EV charging stations are available at The Ahwahnee, The Village Store, and Yosemite Valley Lodge. From late fall until early spring, the weather is especially unpredictable, and driving can be treacherous. You should carry chains during this period as they are required when roads are icy and when it snows.

Hotels

Indoor lodging options inside the park appear more expensive than initially seems warranted, but that premium pays off big-time in terms of the time you'll save—unless you are bunking within a few miles of a Yosemite entrance, you will face long commutes to the park when you stay outside its borders (though the Yosemite View Lodge, on Route 140, is within a reasonable half-hour's drive of Yosemite Valley).

Because of the park's immense popularity—not just with tourists from around the world but with Northern Californians who make weekend trips here—reservations are all but mandatory. Book up to one year ahead.

■ TIP➔ If you're not set on a specific hotel or camp but just want to stay somewhere inside the park, call the main reservation number to check for availability and reserve (☎ 888/413–8869 or ☎ 602/278–8888 international). Park lodgings have a seven-day cancellation policy, so you may be able to snag last-minute reservations.

Park Essentials

ACCESSIBILITY

Yosemite's facilities are continually being upgraded to make them more accessible. Many of the valley floor trails—particularly at Lower Yosemite Fall, Bridalveil Fall, and Mirror Lake—are wheelchair accessible, though some assistance may be required. The Valley Visitor Center is fully accessible, as are the park shuttle buses. A sign-language interpreter is available for ranger programs. Visitors with respiratory difficulties should take note of the park's high elevations—the valley floor is approximately 4,000 feet above sea level, but Tuolumne Meadows and parts of the high country hover around 10,000 feet.

PARK FEES AND PERMITS

The admission fee, valid for seven days, is $35 per vehicle, $30 per motorcycle, or $20 per individual.

All trails inside Yosemite National Park are subject to a daily trailhead quota, and wilderness permits ($10 reservation plus $5/person via ⊕ www.recreation.gov) are required for all overnight backcountry treks.

For hiking or climbing dates in late April through late October, you can enter the weekly permit reservation lottery from 24 weeks to three days in advance of the start of your trip (lotteries happen from mid-November to mid-May). Sixty percent of the reservations are distributed in these weekly lotteries. Of this portion, any reservations that remain become available on a first-come, first-served basis after the lottery process is complete for that week's reservations up until seven days in advance.

Seven days before a wilderness entry date, the remaining 40% of the reservation spots are released. Popular trailheads fill very quickly. Be ready to reserve promptly at 7 am (PDT) on Recreation.gov. The latest you can make a reservation is three days before a trip, subject to remaining availability.

From late October until late April, a wilderness permit is still required, but you can obtain it via self-registration at the Yosemite Valley Wilderness Center in Yosemite Village (in winter this is your only option), Tuolumne Meadows Wilderness Center on Tioga Road, Wawona Visitor Center at Hill's Studio on Wawona Road/Forest Drive, Big Oak Flat Information Station on Highway 120, and Hetch Hetchy Entrance Station on Hetch Hetchy Road.

All of these stations also rent food-storage canisters, which are required for wilderness travel. Those who hold valid permits can camp at designated backpacker campgrounds the night before and after their wilderness trip (no additional reservations are required.)

PARK HOURS

The park is open 24/7 year-round. All entrances are open at all hours, except for the Hetch Hetchy entrance, which is open roughly dawn to dusk. Yosemite is in the Pacific time zone.

AUTOMOBILE SERVICE STATIONS

There are gas stations at Crane Flat, Wawona, and El Portal (a few miles west of the Arch Rock entrance). There's one garage (☎ 209/372-8320) in Yosemite Village, but it performs only basic repairs, and no gas is available there. Electric vehicles can charge up at The Ahwahnee, The Village Store, and Yosemite Valley Lodge.

CELL PHONE RECEPTION

Cell phone reception can be hit or miss everywhere in the park. There are public telephones at entrance stations, visitor centers, all park restaurants and lodging facilities, gas stations, and in Yosemite Village.

Restaurants

Yosemite National Park has a couple of moderately priced restaurants in lovely (which almost goes without saying) settings: the Mountain Room at Yosemite Valley Lodge and the dining room at the Wawona Hotel. The Ahwahnee hotel provides one of the finest dining experiences in the country.

Food served by park concessionaire services at cafeterias, snack bars, and most lodge restaurants ranges from standard burgers and chips to poke bowls and healthful Mediterranean fare. Most dining options are geared to convenience rather than culinary fireworks.

Yosemite Valley Lodge's Base Camp Eatery is the valley's best lower-cost, hot-food option, with Italian, classic American, and world-cuisine counter

options. In Curry Village, the offerings at Seven Tents are overpriced and usually fairly bland, but you can get decent pizzas on the adjacent outdoor deck. In Yosemite Valley Village, the Village Grill whips up burgers and fries and Degnan's Kitchen has made-to-order sandwiches and salads.

The White Wolf Lodge and Tuolumne Meadows Lodge—both off Tioga Road and therefore guaranteed open only from early June through September—have small restaurants where meals are competently prepared. Tuolumne Meadows also has a grill, and the gift shop at Glacier Point sells premade sandwiches, snacks, and hot dogs. During ski season, you'll also find one at the Badger Pass Ski Area, off Glacier Point Road.

⇨ *Hotel and restaurant reviews have been shortened. For full information, visit Fodors.com. Hotel prices are the lowest cost of a standard double room in high season. Restaurant prices are the average cost of a main course at dinner, or if dinner is not served, at lunch.*

What It Costs			
$	$$	$$$	$$$$
RESTAURANTS			
under $20	$20–$30	$31–$40	over $40
HOTELS			
under $200	$200–$350	$351–$500	over $500

Tours

★ Ansel Adams Photo Walks

SPECIAL-INTEREST TOURS | Photography enthusiasts shouldn't miss these guided, 90-minute walks offered Tuesday and Thursday each week from April to December by professional photographers. All are free, but participation is limited to 10 people so reservations are essential and can be made starting three days before the walk. Meeting points vary. ⊠ *Yosemite National Park* ☎ *209/372–4413* ⊕ *www.anseladams. com* ⊠ *Free.*

Discover Yosemite

GUIDED TOURS | **FAMILY** | This outfit operates daily tours to Yosemite Valley, Mariposa Grove, and Glacier Point in 14- and 29-passenger vehicles. The tour travels along Highway 41 with stops in Bass Lake, Oakhurst, and Fish Camp; rates include lunch. Sunset tours to Sentinel Dome are additional summer options. ⊠ *Yosemite National Park* ☎ *559/642–4400* ⊕ *discoveryosemite.com* ⊠ *From $200.*

Glacier Point Tour

GUIDED TOURS | **FAMILY** | This four-hour trip takes you from Yosemite Valley to the Glacier Point vista, 3,214 feet above the valley floor. Some people buy a $29 one-way ticket and hike down. Shuttles depart from the Yosemite Valley Lodge three times a day. ⊠ *Yosemite National Park* ☎ *888/413–8869* ⊕ *www.travelyosemite.com* ⊠ *From $57* ⊘ *Closed Nov.–late May.*

Grand Tour

GUIDED TOURS | **FAMILY** | For a full-day tour of Yosemite Valley, the Mariposa Grove of giant Sequoias, and Glacier Point, try the Grand Tour, which departs from the Yosemite Valley Lodge in the valley. The tour stops for a picnic lunch (included) at the historic Wawona Hotel. ⊠ *Yosemite National Park* ☎ *888/413–8869* ⊕ *www. travelyosemite.com* ⊠ *$110.*

Tuolumne Meadows Hikers Bus

BUS TOURS | **FAMILY** | For a full day's outing to the high country, opt for this ride up Tioga Road to Tuolumne Meadows. You'll stop at several overlooks, and you can connect with another shuttle at Tuolumne Lodge. This service is mostly for hikers and backpackers who want to reach high-country trailheads, but everyone is welcome. ⊠ *Yosemite National Park* ☎ *209/372–1240* ⊕ *www.travelyosemite. com* ⊠ *$15 one-way, $23 round-trip* ⊘ *Closed Labor Day–mid-June.*

Valley Floor Tour

GUIDED TOURS | **FAMILY** | Take a two-hour tour of Yosemite Valley's highlights, complete with narration on the area's history, geology, and flora and fauna. Tours (offered year-round) are either in trams or enclosed motor coaches, depending on weather conditions. ⊠ *Yosemite National Park* ☎ *888/413–8869* ⊕ *www.travelyosemite.com* ⊠ *From $40.*

Visitor Information

PARK CONTACT INFORMATION Yosemite National Park. ⊠ *Yosemite National Park* ☎ *209/372–0200* ⊕ *www.nps.gov/yose.*

When to Go

During extremely busy periods—such as weekends and holidays throughout the year—you will experience delays at the entrance gates. For smaller crowds, visit midweek. Or come January through March, when the park is a bit less busy, and the days usually are sunny and clear.

Summer rainfall is rare. In winter, heavy snows occasionally cause road closures, and tire chains or four-wheel drive may be required on the routes that remain open. The road to Glacier Point beyond the turnoff for the Badger Pass Ski Area is closed after the first major snowfall. Tioga Road is closed from late October through May or mid-June. Mariposa Grove Road is typically closed for a shorter period in winter.

Yosemite Valley

Yosemite Valley Visitor Center is 12 miles from the Arch Rock entrance and 15 miles east of El Portal.

The glacier-carved Yosemite Valley stretches nearly 8 miles along the Merced River. It holds many of the park's major sights, including El Capitan, Half

AVERAGE HIGH/LOW TEMPERATURES					
Jan.	Feb.	Mar.	Apr.	May	June
48/29	53/30	55/32	61/36	69/43	78/49
July	Aug.	Sept.	Oct.	Nov.	Dec.
85/55	84/55	79/49	70/42	56/34	47/29

Dome, Glacier Point, and famous waterfalls. The valley is accessible year-round. Park your car at Yosemite Village (home of the visitor center, museum, market, and other services), Curry Village, or near Yosemite Falls. Free shuttle buses loop through the eastern and western sections of the valley.

 ## Sights

HISTORIC SITES

★ The Ahwahnee

HOTEL | Gilbert Stanley Underwood, architect of the Grand Canyon Lodge, also designed The Ahwahnee hotel. Opened in 1927, it is generally considered his best work. You can stay here (for about $500 or more a night), or simply explore the first-floor shops and perhaps have breakfast or lunch in the bustling and beautiful Dining Room or more casual bar. The Great Lounge, 77 feet long with magnificent 24-foot-high ceilings and all manner of artwork on display, beckons with big, comfortable chairs and relative calm. ⊠ *Yosemite Valley, Ahwahnee Rd., Yosemite Village* ✛ *About ¾ mile east of Yosemite Valley Visitor Center* ☎ *888/413–8869* ⊕ *www.travelyosemite.com/lodging/the-ahwahnee.*

Curry Village

HOTEL | **FAMILY** | A couple of schoolteachers from Indiana founded Camp Curry in 1899 as a low-cost option for staying in the valley, which it remains today. Curry Village's 400-plus lodging options, many of them tent cabins, are spread over a large chunk of the valley's southeastern side. This is a very family-friendly place, but it's more functional than attractive.

⊠ *Southside Dr., Yosemite National Park* ✛ *About ½ mile east of Yosemite Village* ☎ *888/413–8869* ⊕ *www.travelyosemite.com/lodging/curry-village.*

Indian Village of Ahwahnee

MUSEUM VILLAGE | **FAMILY** | This solemn smattering of structures, accessed by a short loop trail behind the Yosemite Museum, offers a look at what Native American life might have been like in the 1870s. One interpretive sign points out that the Miwok people referred to the 19th-century newcomers as "Yohemite" or "Yohometuk," which have been translated as meaning "some of them are killers." ⊠ *Northside Dr., Yosemite Village* ⊒ *Free.*

Yosemite Museum

HISTORY MUSEUM | **FAMILY** | This small museum consists of a permanent exhibit that focuses on the history of the area and the people who once lived here. An adjacent gallery promotes contemporary and historic Yosemite art in revolving gallery exhibits. A docent demonstrates traditional Native American basket-weaving techniques a few days a week. ⊠ *Yosemite Village* ☎ *209/372–0299* ⊕ *www.nps.gov/yose/learn/historyculture/yosemite-museum.htm* ⊒ *Free.*

SCENIC STOPS

Bridalveil Fall

WATERFALL | **FAMILY** | This 620-foot waterfall is often diverted dozens of feet one way or the other by the breeze. It is the first marvelous site you will see up close when you drive into Yosemite Valley. ⊠ *Yosemite Valley, access from parking area off Wawona Rd., Yosemite National Park.*

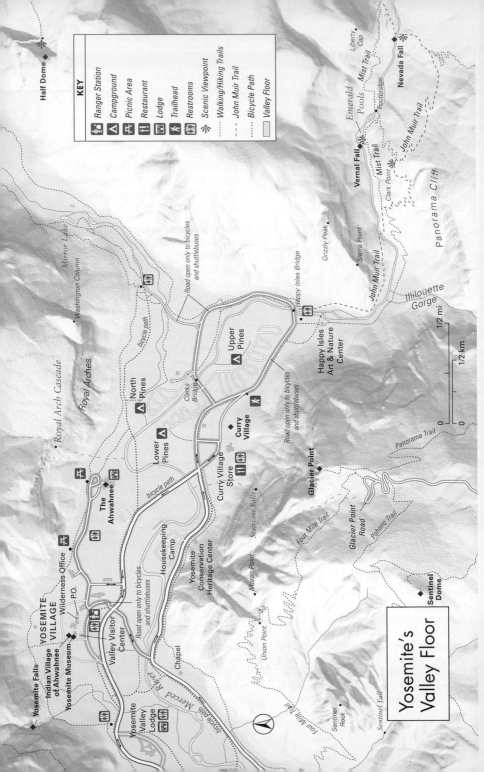

Yosemite's Valley Floor

KEY

![Ranger Station]	Ranger Station
![Campground]	Campground
![Picnic Area]	Picnic Area
![Restaurant]	Restaurant
![Lodge]	Lodge
![Trailhead]	Trailhead
![Restrooms]	Restrooms
![Scenic Viewpoint]	Scenic Viewpoint
⋯⋯	Walking/Hiking Trails
– – –	John Muir Trail
········	Bicycle Path
	Valley Floor

Half Dome

Liberty Cap

Nevada Fall

Mist Trail

Emerald Pools

Footbridge

Vernal Fall

John Muir Trail

Mist Trail

Clark Point

Panorama Cliff

Grizzly Peak

Sierra Point

John Muir Trail

Illilouette Gorge

Happy Isles Bridge

Happy Isles Art & Nature Center

Mirror Lake

Washington Column

Royal Arch Cascade

Royal Arches

bicycle path

North Pines

Upper Pines

Clarks Bridge

Lower Pines

Road open only to bicycles and shuttlebuses

Curry Village

Curry Village Store

1/2 mi

1/2 km

0   0

Panorama Trail

Glacier Point

The Ahwahnee

bicycle path

Housekeeping Camp

Yosemite Conservation Heritage Center

Staircase Falls

Four Mile Trail

Glacier Point Road

Pohono Trail

Sentinel Dome

Wilderness Office

P.O.

YOSEMITE VILLAGE

Valley Visitor Center

Yosemite Museum

Indian Village of Ahwahnee

Road open only to bicycles and shuttlebuses

Chapel

Moran Point

Union Point

Yosemite Falls

Merced River

Yosemite Valley Lodge

bicycle path

Four Mile Trail

Sentinel Rock

Sentinel Fall

Yosemite in One Day

Begin at the **Valley Visitor Center** and go to the nearby Yosemite Theater, where you can watch the documentary *Spirit of Yosemite*. A minute's stroll from there is the **Indian Village of the Ahwahnee**, which recalls Native American life circa 1870. Take another 20 minutes to see the **Yosemite Museum.** Then, hop aboard the free shuttle to Yosemite Falls, and hike the **Lower Yosemite Fall Trail** to the base of the falls. Have lunch at **Yosemite Valley Lodge**, which you can access via a shuttle or a 20-minute walk.

Afternoon choices include spending time in **Curry Village**—perhaps swimming or ice-skating, shopping, renting a bike, or having a beer on the deck; checking out the family-friendly

Happy Isles Art and Nature Center and the adjacent nature trail; or hiking up the **Mist Trail** to the Vernal Fall footbridge to admire the view.

Hop back on the shuttle, then disembark at **The Ahwahnee.** The Great Lounge here has a magnificent fireplace and Native American artwork; have a meal in the Dining Room if you're up for a splurge. Or take the shuttle to **Yosemite Village** where you can grab some fixings, then drive to **El Capitan picnic area** and enjoy an outdoor evening meal. At this time of day, "El Cap" should be sun-splashed. (You will have also gotten several good looks at world-famous **Half Dome** throughout the day.) If the sun hasn't set yet, drive to the base of **Bridalveil Fall** to take a short hike.

El Capitan

NATURE SIGHT | FAMILY | Rising 3,593 feet—more than 350 stories—above the valley, El Capitan is the largest exposed-granite monolith in the world. Since 1958, people have been climbing its entire face, including the famous "nose." You can spot adventurers with your binoculars by scanning the smooth and nearly vertical cliff for specks of color. ⊠ *Yosemite National Park ⊹ Off Northside Dr., about 4 miles west of Valley Visitor Center.*

★ Glacier Point

VIEWPOINT | FAMILY | If you lack the time, desire, or stamina to hike more than 3,200 feet up to Glacier Point from the Yosemite Valley floor, you can drive here—or take a bus from the valley—for a bird's-eye view. You are likely to encounter a lot of day-trippers on the short, paved trail that leads from the parking lot to the main overlook. Take a moment to veer off a few yards to the Geology Hut,

which succinctly explains and illustrates what the valley looked like 10 million, 3 million, and 20,000 years ago. ⊠ *Yosemite National Park ⊹ Glacier Point Rd., 16 miles northeast of Rte. 41* ☎ *209/372–0200* ⊘ *Closed late Oct.–mid-May.*

★ Half Dome

NATURE SIGHT | Visitors' eyes are continually drawn to this remarkable granite formation that tops out at more than 4,700 feet above the valley floor. Despite its name, the dome is actually about three-quarters intact. You can hike to the top of it on an 8½-mile (one-way) trail whose last 400 feet must be ascended while holding onto a steel cable. Permits, available only by lottery, are required and are checked on the trail. (Call ☎ *877/444–6777* or visit ⊕ *recreation.gov* well in advance of your trip for details.) Back down in the valley, see Half Dome reflected in the Merced River by heading to Sentinel Bridge just before sundown. The brilliant orange light on Half Dome is a stunning sight. ⊠ *Yosemite National Park* ⊕ *www.nps.gov/yose/planyourvisit/halfdome.htm.*

Nevada Fall

WATERFALL | FAMILY | Climb Mist Trail from Happy Isles for an up-close view of this 594-foot cascading beauty. If you don't want to hike (the trail's final approach is quite taxing), you can see it—albeit distantly—from Glacier Point. Stay safely on the trail, as there have been fatalities in recent years after visitors have fallen and been swept away by the water. ⊠ *Yosemite National Park.*

Ribbon Fall

WATERFALL | FAMILY | At 1,612 feet, this is the highest single fall in North America. It's also the first waterfall to dry up in summer; the rainwater and melted snow that create the slender fall evaporate quickly at this height. Look just west of El Capitan for the best view of the fall from the base of Bridalveil Fall. ⊠ *Yosemite National Park.*

Sentinel Dome

VIEWPOINT | FAMILY | The view from here is similar to that from Glacier Point, except you can't see the valley floor. A moderately steep, 1.1-mile path climbs to the viewpoint from the parking lot. Topping out at an elevation of 8,122 feet, Sentinel is more than 900 feet higher than Glacier Point. ⊠ *Glacier Point Rd., off Rte. 41, Yosemite National Park.*

Vernal Fall

WATERFALL | FAMILY | Fern-covered black rocks frame this 317-foot fall, and rainbows play in the spray at its base. You can get a distant view from Glacier Point, or hike to see it close up. You'll get wet, but the view is worth it. Access is via the Mist Trail from the nature center at Happy Isles ⊠ *Yosemite National Park.*

★ Yosemite Falls

WATERFALL | FAMILY | Together these three cascades constitute the highest combined waterfall in North America and the fifth highest in the world. The water

from the top descends a total of 2,425 feet, and when the falls run hard, you can hear them thunder across the valley. If they dry up—that sometimes happens in late summer—the valley seems naked without the wavering tower of spray. If you hike the mile-long loop trail (partially paved) to the base of the Lower Fall in spring, prepare to get wet. You can get a good full-length view of the falls from the lawn of Yosemite Chapel, off Southside Drive. ⊠ *Yosemite National Park.*

TRAILS

Cook's Meadow Loop

TRAIL | FAMILY | Take this 1-mile, wheelchair-accessible, looped path around Cook's Meadow to see and learn the basics about Yosemite Valley's past, present, and future. A trail guide (available at a kiosk just outside the entrance) explains how to tell oaks, cedars, and pines apart; how fires help keep the forest floor healthy; and how pollution poses significant challenges to the park's inhabitants. *Easy.* ⊠ *Yosemite National Park* ⊹ *Trailhead: Across from Valley Visitor Center.*

Four-Mile Trail

TRAIL | If you decide to hike up Four-Mile Trail and back down again, allow about six hours for the challenging, 9½-mile round-trip. (The original 4-mile-long trail, Yosemite's first, has been lengthened to make it less steep.) The trailhead is on Southside Drive near Sentinel Beach, and the elevation change is 3,220 feet. For a considerably less strenuous experience, you can take a morning tour bus up to Glacier Point and enjoy a one-way downhill hike. *Difficult.* ⊠ *Yosemite National Park* ⊹ *Trailheads: At Glacier Point and on Southside Dr.*

★ John Muir Trail to Half Dome

TRAIL | Ardent and courageous trekkers continue on from Nevada Fall to the top of Half Dome. Some hikers attempt this entire 10- to 12-hour, 16¾-mile round-trip trek in one day; if you're planning to do this, remember that the 4,800-foot elevation gain and the 8,842-foot altitude will cause shortness of breath. Another option is to hike to a campground in Little Yosemite Valley near the top of Nevada Fall the first day, then climb to the top of Half Dome and hike out the next day. Note that the last pitch up the back of Half Dome is very steep—the only way to climb this sheer rock face is to pull yourself up using the steel cable handrails, which are in place only from late spring to early fall. Those who brave the ascent will be rewarded with an unbeatable view of Yosemite Valley below and the high country beyond.

Be sure to wear hiking boots and bring gloves. Also note that only 300 hikers and 75 overnight backpackers per day are allowed atop Half Dome, and they all must have permits (even if they already have wilderness permits), which are distributed by lottery—one in the spring before the season starts and another two days before the climb. *Difficult.* ⊠ *Yosemite National Park* ⚓ *Trailhead: At Happy Isles* ⊕ *www.nps.gov/yose/planyourvisit/halfdome.htm.*

Mirror Lake Trail

TRAIL | FAMILY | Along this trail, you'll look up at Half Dome directly from its base and also take in Tenaya Canyon, Mt. Watkins, and Washington Column. The way is paved for a mile to Mirror Lake itself (total of 2 miles out and back). The trail that loops around the lake continues from there (for a total of 5 miles). Interpretive exhibits provide insight on the area's natural and cultural history. *Easy–Moderate.* ⊠ *Yosemite Village* ⚓ *Trailhead: Shuttle bus stop #17 on the Happy Isles Loop.*

Mist Trail

TRAIL | FAMILY | Except for Lower Yosemite Fall, more visitors take this trail (or portions of it) than any other in the park. The trek up to and back from Vernal Fall is 3 miles. Add another 4 miles total by continuing up to 594-foot Nevada Fall;

this portion of the trail becomes quite steep and slippery in its final stages. The elevation gain to Vernal Fall is 1,000 feet, and to Nevada Fall an additional 1,000 feet. The Merced River tumbles down both falls on its way to a tranquil flow through the valley. *Moderate.* ⊠ *Yosemite National Park* ⚓ *Trailhead: At Happy Isles.*

★ Panorama Trail

TRAIL | Few hikes come with the visual punch that this 8½-mile trail provides. It starts from Glacier Point and descends to Yosemite Valley. The star attraction is Half Dome, visible from many intriguing angles, but you also see three waterfalls up close and walk through a manzanita grove. *Moderate.* ⊠ *Yosemite National Park* ⚓ *Trailhead: At Glacier Point.*

★ Yosemite Falls Trail

TRAIL | FAMILY | Yosemite Falls is the highest waterfall in North America. The upper fall (1,430 feet), the middle cascades (675 feet), and the lower fall (320 feet) combine for a total of 2,425 feet, and when viewed from the valley appear as a single waterfall. The ¼-mile trail leads from the parking lot to the base of the falls. Upper Yosemite Fall Trail, a strenuous 7.2-mile round-trip climb rising 2,700 feet, takes you above the top of the falls. Lower trail: *Easy.* Upper trail: *Difficult.* ⊠ *Yosemite National Park* ⚓ *Trailhead: Off Camp 4, north of Northside Dr.*

VISITOR CENTERS

Happy Isles Art and Nature Center

VISITOR CENTER | FAMILY | This family-focused center has a rotating selection of art classes for all ages, plus kid-friendly activities and hands-on exhibits that teach tykes and their parents about the park's ecosystem. Books, toys, and T-shirts are stocked in the small gift shop. ⊠ *Yosemite National Park* ⚓ *Off Southside Dr., about ¾ mile east of Curry Village* ⊕ *yosemite.org/experience/art* ▤ *Free* ☾ *Closed Oct.–Apr.*

Valley Visitor Center

VISITOR CENTER | FAMILY | Learn about Yosemite Valley's geology, vegetation, and human inhabitants at this visitor center, which is also staffed with helpful rangers and contains a bookstore with a wide selection of books and maps. A 23-minute film, *Spirit of Yosemite*, plays every half hour in the theater near the visitor center. ✉ *Yosemite Village* ☎ *209/372–0200* 🌐 *www.nps.gov/yose*.

Yosemite Conservation Heritage Center

VISITOR CENTER | This small but striking National Historic Landmark (formerly Le Conte Memorial Lodge), with its granite walls and steeply pitched shingle roof, is Yosemite's first permanent public information center. Step inside to see the cathedral-like interior, which contains a library and environmental exhibits. To find out about evening programs, check the kiosk out front. ✉ *Yosemite National Park* ✣ *Southside Dr., about ½ mile west of Half Dome Village* 🌐 *www.sierraclub.org/yosemite-conservation-heritage-center* ⏲ *Closed Mon., Tues., and Oct.–Apr.*

🍴 Restaurants

★ The Ahwahnee Dining Room

$$$$ | EUROPEAN | Rave reviews about The Ahwahnee hotel's dining room's appearance are fully justified—it features towering windows, a 34-foot-high ceiling with interlaced sugar-pine beams, and massive chandeliers. Reservations are always advised, and the attire is "resort casual." **Known for:** lavish $59 Sunday brunch; finest dining in the park; bar menu with lighter lunch and dinner fare at more affordable prices. [$] *Average main: $45* ✉ *The Ahwahnee, Ahwahnee Rd., about ¾ mile east of Yosemite Valley Visitor Center, Yosemite Village* ☎ *888/413–8869, 602/278–8888 international* 🌐 *www.travelyosemite.com*.

Base Camp Eatery

$ | AMERICAN | FAMILY | The design of this modern food court, open for breakfast, lunch, and dinner, honors the history of rock climbing in Yosemite. Choose from a wide range of menu options, from hamburgers, salads, and pizzas, to rice and noodle bowls. **Known for:** grab-and-go selections; best casual dining venue in the park; automated ordering kiosks to speed up service. [$] *Average main: $16* ✉ *Yosemite Valley Lodge, about ¾ mile west of visitor center, Yosemite Village* ☎ *888/413–8869* 🌐 *www.travelyosemite.com*.

★ Mountain Room

$$ | AMERICAN | Gaze at Yosemite Falls through this dining room's wall of windows—almost every table has a view—as you nosh on steaks, seafood, and classic California salads and desserts. The Mountain Room Lounge, a few steps away in the Yosemite Valley Lodge complex, has about 10 beers on tap. **Known for:** locally sourced, organic ingredients; very busy—might have to wait for a table, even with reservations; vegetarian and vegan options. [$] *Average main: $29* ✉ *Yosemite Valley Lodge, Northside Dr., about ¾ mile west of visitor center, Yosemite Village* ☎ *888/413–8869* 🌐 *www.travelyosemite.com* ⏲ *No lunch except Sun. brunch.*

Seven Tents Pavilion

$ | AMERICAN | FAMILY | Formerly Curry Village Pavilion, this casual eatery serves everything from roasted meats and salads to pastas, burritos, rice bowls, and beyond. Alternatively, order a pizza from the stand on the deck, and take in the views of the valley's granite walls. **Known for:** convenient eats; cocktails at Bar 1899; additional venues (Meadow Grill, Pizza Deck, Coffee Corner). [$] *Average main: $18* ✉ *Curry Village, Yosemite National Park* ☎ *888/413–8869* 🌐 *www.travelyosemite.com* ⏲ *Closed mid-Oct.–mid-Apr. No lunch.*

Village Grill Deck
$ | **FAST FOOD** | **FAMILY** | If a burger joint is what you've been missing, head to this bustling eatery that serves veggie, salmon, and a few other burger varieties in addition to the usual beef patties. Order at the counter, then take your tray out to the deck, and enjoy your meal under the trees. **Known for:** burgers, sandwiches, and hot dogs; crowds; outdoor seating on expansive deck. [$] *Average main: $16* ✉ *Yosemite Village* ✥ *100 yards east of Yosemite Valley Visitor Center* ☎ *888/413–8869* 🌐 *www.travelyosemite.com* 🕘 *Closed Oct.–Apr. No dinner.*

Hotels

★ The Ahwahnee
$$$$ | **HOTEL** | This National Historic Landmark is constructed of sugar-pine logs and features Native American design motifs; public spaces are enlivened with art deco flourishes, Persian rugs, and elaborate iron- and woodwork. **Pros:** best lodge in Yosemite; helpful concierge; in the historic heart of the valley. **Cons:** expensive rates; some reports that service has slipped in recent years; slow or nonexistent Wi-Fi in some hotel areas. [$] *Rooms from: $581* ✉ *Ahwahnee Rd., about ¾ mile east of Yosemite Valley Visitor Center, Yosemite Village* ☎ *888/413–8869, 602/278–8888* 🌐 *www.travelyosemite.com* 🛏 *125 rooms* 🍴 *No Meals.*

Curry Village
$ | **HOTEL** | **FAMILY** | Opened in 1899 as a place for budget-conscious travelers, Curry Village has plain accommodations that include standard motel rooms, simple cabins with private or shared baths, and tent cabins with shared baths. **Pros:** close to many activities; family-friendly atmosphere; surrounded by iconic valley views. **Cons:** community bathrooms need updating; can be crowded; sometimes a bit noisy. [$] *Rooms from: $143* ✉ *South side of Southside Dr., Yosemite National Park* ☎ *888/413–8869, 602/278–8888* 🌐 *www.travelyosemite.com* 🛏 *583 units* 🍴 *No Meals.*

Yosemite Valley Lodge
$$ | **HOTEL** | This 1915 lodge near Yosemite Falls is a collection of numerous two-story, glass-and-wood structures tucked beneath the trees. **Pros:** centrally located; dependably clean rooms; lots of tours leave from out front. **Cons:** can feel impersonal; high prices; no in-room a/c. [$] *Rooms from: $260* ✉ *9006 Yosemite Valley Lodge Dr., Yosemite Village* ☎ *888/413–8869* 🌐 *www.travelyosemite.com* 🛏 *245 rooms* 🍴 *No Meals.*

Shopping

Ahwahnee Gift Shop
SOUVENIRS | This shop sells more upscale items, such as Native American crafts, photographic prints, handmade ceramics, and elegant jewelry. For less expensive gift items, browse the small book selection, which includes writings by John Muir. ✉ *The Ahwahnee, Ahwahnee Rd., Yosemite National Park* ☎ *888/413–8869* 🌐 *www.travelyosemite.com.*

Ansel Adams Gallery
ART GALLERIES | Framed prints of the famed nature photographer's best works are on sale here, as are affordable posters. New works by contemporary artists are also available, along with Native American jewelry and handicrafts. The elegant camera shop conducts photography workshops, from free camera walks a few mornings a week to five-day courses. ✉ *Northside Dr., Yosemite Village* ☎ *209/372–4413* 🌐 *anseladams.com.*

Curry Village Gift & Grocery
GENERAL STORE | **FAMILY** | You can pick up groceries and supplies at this bustling shop at the east end of the valley. ✉ *Curry Village, Yosemite National Park* ☎ *888/413–8869* 🌐 *www.travelyosemite.com.*

Housekeeping Camp General Store
GENERAL STORE | FAMILY | You'll find the basics here for picnics, campfires, and other outdoor activities. ⊠ *Southside Dr., ½ mile west of Half Dome Village, Yosemite National Park* ☎ *888/413–8869* ⊕ *www.travelyosemite.com.*

Village Store
GENERAL STORE | FAMILY | The Yosemite Valley's largest store has an extensive selection of groceries (including many organic items), household products, and personal-care items. It also has an extensive gift and souvenir shop. ⊠ *Yosemite Village* ☎ *888/413–8869* ⊕ *www.travelyosemite.com.*

Yosemite Bookstore
BOOKS | An extensive selection of maps and books is available at this store in the Valley Visitor Center. ⊠ *Valley Visitor Center, Yosemite Village* ☎ *209/379–2317* ⊕ *shop.yosemite.org.*

Yosemite Museum Shop
CRAFTS | In addition to books on California's Native Americans, this tiny shop sells traditional arts and crafts. ⊠ *Yosemite Village* ☎ *888/413–8869* ⊕ *www.travelyosemite.com.*

Yosemite Valley Lodge Gift Shop
SOUVENIRS | FAMILY | Groceries, snacks, and beverages occupy half of this large store. The other half is a gift shop. ⊠ *Yosemite Valley Lodge, Northside Dr., about ¾ mile west of visitor center, Yosemite Village* ☎ *888/413–8869* ⊕ *www.travelyosemite.com.*

Wawona

27 miles from Yosemite Valley Visitor Center, 7½ miles north of Fish Camp.

Wawona is a small village (elevation 4,000 feet) about an hours' drive south of Yosemite Valley. It's rich in pioneer history (visit the Pioneer Yosemite History Center to learn more) and is home to the Victorian-era Wawona Hotel. The park's

famous Mariposa Grove of Giant Sequoias is a few miles down the road.

 Sights

HISTORIC SIGHTS
Yosemite History Center
HISTORY MUSEUM | FAMILY | These historic buildings reflect different eras of Yosemite's history, from the 1850s through the early 1900s. They were moved to Wawona (the largest stage stop in Yosemite in the late 1800s) from various areas of Yosemite in the '50s and '60s. There is a self-guided-tour pamphlet available for 50 cents. Weekends and some weekdays in the summer, costumed docents conduct free blacksmithing and "wet-plate" photography demonstrations, and for a small fee you can take a stagecoach ride. ⊠ *Rte. 41, Wawona* ☎ *209/371–0200* ⊕ *www.nps.gov/yose/learn/historyculture/historycenter.htm* 🖾 *Free* ⊙ *Closed Mon., Tues., and mid-Sept.–early June.*

Wawona Hotel
HOTEL | Imagine a white-bearded Mark Twain relaxing in a rocking chair on one of the broad verandas of one of the park's first lodges, a whitewashed series of two-story buildings from the Victorian era. Plop down in one of the dozens of white Adirondack chairs on the sprawling lawn, and look across the road at the area's only golf course, one of the few links in the world that does not employ fertilizers or other chemicals. ⊠ *Rte. 41, Wawona* ☎ *888/413–8869* ⊕ *www.travelyosemite.com/lodging/wawona-hotel* ⊙ *Closed Dec.–Mar. except 2 wks around Christmas and New Year's.*

SCENIC DRIVES
Route 41
SCENIC DRIVE | FAMILY | Entering Yosemite National Park via this road, which follows an ultimately curvy course 55 miles from Fresno through the Yosemite gateway towns of Oakhurst and Fish Camp, presents you with an immediate, important choice: turn right to visit the Mariposa

Grove of Giant Sequoias 4 miles to the east, or turn left to travel via Wawona to Yosemite Valley, 31 miles away. Try to do both. (You can get by with an hour in Mariposa Grove if you're really pressed for time.)

As you approach the valley, you'll want to pull into the Tunnel View parking lot (it's on the east side of the mile-long tunnel) and marvel at what lies ahead: from left to right, El Capitan, Half Dome, and Bridalveil Fall. From here, the valley is another 5 miles. The drive time on Wawona Road alone is about an hour. Make a full day of it by adding Glacier Point to the itinerary; get there via a 16-mile seasonal road that shoots east from Route 41 and passes the Badger Pass Ski Area. ⊠ *Yosemite National Park.*

SCENIC STOPS

Mariposa Grove of Giant Sequoias

FOREST | **FAMILY** | Of Yosemite's three sequoia groves—the others being Merced and Tuolumne, both near Crane Flat and Hetch Hetchy well to the north—Mariposa is by far the largest and easiest to walk around. Grizzly Giant, whose base measures 96 feet around, has been estimated to be one of the world's largest. Perhaps more astoundingly, it's about 1,800 years old. Park at the grove's welcome plaza, and ride the free shuttle (required most of the year). Summer weekends are crowded. ⊠ *Yosemite National Park* ⌖ *Rte. 41, 2 miles north of south entrance station* ⊕ *www. nps.gov/yose/planyourvisit/mg.htm.*

TRAILS

Chilnualna Falls Trail

TRAIL | This Wawona-area trail runs 4 miles one-way to the top of the falls, then leads into the backcountry, connecting with other trails. This is one of the park's most inspiring and secluded—albeit strenuous—hikes. Past the tumbling cascade, and up through forests, you'll emerge before a panorama at the top. *Difficult.* ⊠ *Wawona* ⌖ *Trailhead: At Chilnualna Falls Rd., off Rte. 41.*

Restaurants

Wawona Hotel Dining Room

$$ | **AMERICAN** | Watch deer graze in the meadow while you dine in the romantic, candlelit dining room of the whitewashed Wawona Hotel, which dates from the late 1800s. The American-style cuisine favors fresh ingredients and flavors; trout and flatiron steaks are menu staples. **Known for:** Saturday-night barbecues on the lawn; historic ambience; Mother's Day and other Sunday holiday brunches. Ⓢ *Average main: $28* ⊠ *8308 Wawona Rd., Wawona* ☎ *209/375–1425* ⊘ *Closed most of Dec., Jan., Feb., and Mar.*

🛏 Hotels

Redwoods in Yosemite

$$ | **HOUSE** | **FAMILY** | This collection of more than 125 homes in the Wawona area is a great alternative to the overcrowded valley. **Pros:** sense of privacy; peaceful setting; full kitchens. **Cons:** 45-minute drive from the valley; some units have no a/c; cell phone service can be spotty. Ⓢ *Rooms from: $260* ⊠ *8038 Chilnualna Falls Rd., off Rte. 41, Wawona* ☎ *209/375–6666* ⊕ *www.redwoodsinyosemite.com* ⤵ *125 units* ⎜O⎜ *No Meals.*

Wawona Hotel

$ | **HOTEL** | This 1879 National Historic Landmark at Yosemite's southern end is a Victorian-era mountain resort, with whitewashed buildings, wraparound verandas, and pleasant, no-frills rooms decorated with period pieces. **Pros:** lovely building; peaceful atmosphere; historic photos in public areas. **Cons:** few modern amenities, such as phones and TVs; an hour's drive from Yosemite Valley; shared bathrooms in half the rooms. Ⓢ *Rooms from: $157* ⊠ *8308 Wawona Rd., Wawona* ☎ *888/413–8869* ⊕ *www. travelyosemite.com* ⊘ *Closed Dec.–Mar., except mid-Dec.–Jan. 2* ⤵ *104 rooms* ⎜O⎜ *No Meals.*

Did You Know?

In mid- to late February, when the conditions are right in the evenings (clear sky, flowing falls), Horsetail Fall, on the eastern edge of El Capitan, experiences Firefall—it looks like the falls are on fire.

Tuolumne Meadows

56 miles northeast of Yosemite Valley, 21 miles west of Lee Vining via Tioga Rd.

The largest subalpine meadow in the Sierra (at 8,600 feet) is a popular way station for backpack trips along the Pacific Crest and John Muir trails. The setting is not as dramatic as Yosemite Valley, 56 miles away, but the almost perfectly flat basin, about 2½ miles long, is intriguing, and in July it's resplendent with wildflowers. The most popular day hike is to Lembert Dome, atop which you'll have breathtaking views of the basin below.

■**TIP**➜ **It's important to check ahead for information about Tuolumne closures, both seasonal and longer term.** Tioga Road rarely opens before June and usually closes by November. Even in high season, this area can be affected by natural events. For instance, flooding from the heavy snowpack melt resulted in all of Tuolumne's hotels, restaurants, and other amenities being shuttered for the entire 2023 summer season.

Sights

SCENIC DRIVES
Tioga Road
SCENIC DRIVE | FAMILY | Few mountain drives can compare with this 59-mile road, especially its eastern half between Lee Vining and Olmstead Point. As you climb 3,200 feet to the 9,945-foot summit of Tioga Pass (Yosemite's sole eastern entrance for cars), you'll encounter broad vistas of the granite-splotched High Sierra and its craggy but hearty trees and shrubs. Past the bustling scene at Tuolumne Meadows, you'll see picturesque Tenaya Lake and then Olmsted Point, where you'll get your first peek at Half Dome. Driving Tioga Road one way takes approximately 1½ hours. Wildflowers bloom here in July and August. By November, the high-altitude road closes for the winter; it sometimes doesn't reopen until early June. ⊠ *Yosemite National Park.*

SCENIC STOPS
High Country
NATURE SIGHT | The high-alpine region east of the valley—a land of alpenglow and top-of-the-world vistas—is often missed by crowds who come to gawk at the more publicized splendors. Summer wildflowers, which pop up mid-July through August, carpet the meadows and mountainsides with pink, purple, blue, red, yellow, and orange. Hiking is the only way to get here. For information on trails and backcountry permits, check with the visitor center. ⊠ *Yosemite National Park.*

🍴 Restaurants

Tuolumne Meadows Grill
$ | FAST FOOD | FAMILY | Serving throughout the day until 5 or 6 pm, this fast-food eatery cooks up basic breakfast, lunch, and snacks. It's possible that ice cream tastes better at this altitude. **Known for:** soft-serve ice cream; crowds; fresh local ingredients. Ⓢ *Average main: $8* ⊠ *Tioga Rd. (Rte. 120), 1½ miles east of Tuolumne Meadows Visitor Center, Yosemite National Park* 🕾 *888/413–8869* ⊕ *www.travelyosemite.com* ⊘ *Closed Oct.–Memorial Day. No dinner.*

Tuolumne Meadows Lodge Restaurant
$$ | AMERICAN | In a central dining tent beside the Tuolumne River, this restaurant serves a menu of hearty American fare at breakfast and dinner. The red-and-white-checkered tablecloths and a handful of communal tables give it the feeling of an old-fashioned summer camp. **Known for:** box lunches; communal tables; small menu. Ⓢ *Average main: $24* ⊠ *Tioga Rd. (Rte. 120), Yosemite National Park* 🕾 *209/372–8413* ⊕ *www.travelyosemite.com* ⊘ *Closed late Sept.–mid-June. No lunch.*

White Wolf Lodge Restaurant

$$ | AMERICAN | FAMILY | Those fueling up for a day on the trail or famished after a high-country hike will appreciate the all-you-can-eat, family-style breakfasts and dinners in this tiny dining room. Mashed potatoes, big pots of curried vegetables, and heaps of pasta often grace the tables in this cozy out-of-the-way place. **Known for:** all you can eat; box lunches available; rustic vibe. $ *Average main: $24* ✉ *Yosemite National Park ⊹ Tioga Rd. (Rte. 120), 25 miles west of Tuolumne Meadows and 15 miles east of Crane Flat* ☎ *888/413–8869* ⊕ *www.travelyosemite. com* ⊘ *Closed mid-Sept.–mid-June. No lunch.*

 Hotels

White Wolf Lodge

$ | HOTEL | FAMILY | Set in a subalpine meadow, the White Wolf Lodge has rustic accommodations and makes an excellent base camp for hiking the backcountry. **Pros:** quiet location; near some of Yosemite's most beautiful, less crowded hikes; good restaurant. **Cons:** far from the valley; tent cabins share bathhouse; remote setting. $ *Rooms from: $138* ✉ *Yosemite National Park ⊹ Off Tioga Rd. (Rte. 120), 25 miles west of Tuolumne Meadows and 15 miles east of Crane Flat* ☎ *801/559–4884* ⊕ *www.travelyosemite. com* ⊘ *Closed mid-Sept.–mid-June* ⋑ *28 cabins* ⊙ *No Meals.*

Hetch Hetchy

18 miles from the Big Oak Flat entrance station, 43 miles north of El Portal via Hwy. 120 and Evergreen Rd.

This glacier-carved valley (now filled with water) and surrounding peaks anchor the northwestern section of the park. Drive about 2 miles west of the Big Oak Flat entrance station and turn right on Evergreen Road, which leads down to the Hetch Hetchy entrance and trails along the dam and into the mountains. Two groves of giant sequoia trees—Merced and Tuolumne—grow near Crane Flat, a tiny collection of services south of Big Oak Flat at the intersection of Highway 120 and Tioga Road.

 Sights

SCENIC STOPS

Hetch Hetchy Reservoir

BODY OF WATER | FAMILY | When Congress approved the O'Shaughnessy Dam in 1913, pragmatism triumphed over aestheticism. Some 2½ million residents of the San Francisco Bay Area continue to get their water from this 117-billion-gallon reservoir. Although spirited efforts are being made to restore the Hetch Hetchy Valley to its former, pristine glory, three-quarters of San Francisco voters in 2012 ultimately opposed a measure to even consider draining the reservoir. Eight miles long, the reservoir is Yosemite's largest body of water, and one that can be seen up close from several trails. ✉ *Hetch Hetchy Rd., about 15 miles north of Big Oak Flat entrance station, Yosemite National Park.*

Tuolumne Grove of Giant Sequoias

FOREST | FAMILY | About two dozen mature giant sequoias stand in Tuolumne Grove in the park's northwestern region, just east of Crane Flat and south of the Big Oak Flat entrance. Park at the trailhead and walk about a mile to see them. The trail descends about 500 feet down to the grove, so it's a relatively steep hike back up. Be sure to bring plenty of drinking water. ✉ *On Tioga Rd., just east of Crane Flat, about a 45-min drive from Yosemite Valley, Yosemite National Park.*

TRAILS

Merced Grove of Giant Sequoias

FOREST | FAMILY | Hike 1½ miles (3 miles round-trip, 500-foot elevation drop and gain) to the small and scenic Merced Grove and its approximately two dozen mature giant sequoias. The setting here

Half Dome at sunset

is typically uncrowded and serene. Note that you can also park here and hike about 2 miles round-trip to the Tuolumne Grove. Bring plenty of water for either outing. *Strenuous.* ✉ *Big Oak Flat Rd., Yosemite National Park* ✥ *East of Big Oak Flat entrance, about 6 miles west of Crane Flat and a 45-min drive from Yosemite Valley.*

Hotels

Evergreen Lodge at Yosemite

$$$ | **RESORT** | **FAMILY** | Amid the trees near Yosemite National Park's Hetch Hetchy entrance, this sprawling property is perfect for families. **Pros:** cabin complex includes outdoor play area, pool, nighty s'mores by an outdoor fire, disc golf, and more; no resort fees; guided tours available; great roadhouse-style restaurant. **Cons:** no in-room TVs; long, winding access road; spotty cell service. [$] *Rooms from: $390* ✉ *33160 Evergreen Rd., 30 miles east of town of Groveland, Groveland* ☎ *209/379–2606* 🌐 *www.evergreenlodge.com* 🛏 *88 cabins* 🍴 *No Meals.*

★ **Rush Creek Lodge & Spa**

$$$$ | **RESORT** | **FAMILY** | Occupying 20 acres on a wooded hillside, this sleek, nature-inspired complex has a saltwater pool and hot tubs, a restaurant and tavern with indoor and outdoor seating, a guided recreation program, a spa and wellness program, a general store, nature trails, and outdoor play areas that include a zipline and a giant slide. **Pros:** close to Yosemite's Big Oak Flat entrance; YARTS bus stops here and connects with Yosemite Valley and Sonora spring–fall; daily activities like evening s'mores are included in room rate; no resort fee. **Cons:** no in-room TVs; pricey in high season; spotty cell service. [$] *Rooms from: $515* ✉ *34001 Hwy. 120, Groveland* ✥ *25 miles east of Groveland, 23 miles north of Yosemite Valley* ☎ *209/379–2373* 🌐 *www.rushcreeklodge.com* 🛏 *143 rooms* 🍴 *No Meals.*

Activities

BIKING

One enjoyable way to see Yosemite Valley is to ride a bike beneath its lofty granite monoliths. The eastern valley has 12 miles of paved, flat bicycle paths across meadows and through woods, with bike racks at convenient stopping points. For a greater challenge, you can ride on 196 miles of paved park roads elsewhere. Note, though, that bicycles are not allowed on hiking trails or in the backcountry, and kids under 18 must wear a helmet.

Yosemite Bike Rentals

BIKING | FAMILY | You can arrange rentals at Yosemite Valley Lodge, Yosemite Village, and Curry Village bike stands. Bikes with child trailers, baby-jogger strollers, and wheelchairs are also available. ⊠ *Yosemite Valley Lodge or Curry Village, Yosemite National Park* ☎ *209/372–1268 Yosemite Village, 209/372–8323 Curry Village, 209/372–1208 Yosemite Valley Lodge* ⊕ *www.travelyosemite.com* 🖾 *$30 half day, $40 full day.*

BIRD-WATCHING

More than 250 bird species have been spotted in the park, including the sage sparrow, pygmy owl, blue grouse, and mountain bluebird. Rangers lead free bird-watching walks in Yosemite Valley a few days each week in summer; check at a visitor center or information station for times and locations. Binoculars sometimes are available for loan.

Birding Seminars

BIRD WATCHING | FAMILY | The Yosemite Conservancy organizes day- and weekend-long seminars for beginner and intermediate birders, as well as bird walks a few times a week. They can also arrange private naturalist-led walks any time of year. ⊠ *Yosemite National Park* ⊕ *www.yosemite.org* 🖾 *From $10.*

CAMPING

If you are going to concentrate solely on valley sites and activities, you should endeavor to stay in one of the "Pines" campgrounds, which are clustered near Curry Village and within an easy stroll from that busy complex's many facilities. For a more primitive and quiet experience, and to be near many backcountry hikes, try one of the Tioga Road campgrounds.

■ **TIP→ Reservations are required at all 13 of Yosemite's campgrounds April–October; first-come, first served sites are not available during this time.** You can book a site up to five months in advance, starting on the 15th of the month; some campgrounds are reservable two months or two weeks in advance. North Pines Campground in Yosemite Valley operates on an early access lottery system—visit the park website for details and a handy chart for registration windows for all campgrounds. Reservations are generally made through Recreation.gov (☎ *877/444–6777 reservations, 209/372–0266 Yosemite campsite availability*).

EDUCATIONAL OFFERINGS

CLASSES AND SEMINARS

Art Classes

LOCAL SPORTS | FAMILY | Professional artists conduct workshops (all levels, ages 12-plus, weekdays 9–11) in watercolor, etching, drawing, and other media. Bring your own materials, or purchase the basics at the Happy Isles Art and Nature Center. Children under 18 must be accompanied by an adult. The center also offers free children's art classes (ages 4–11, Monday–Thursday, June–August). ⊠ *Happy Isles Art and Nature Center, Yosemite National Park* ⊕ *www.yosemite.org/art* 🖾 *From $20* ☉ *No classes Sun. Closed Nov.–Mar.*

Yosemite Outdoor Adventures

LOCAL SPORTS | Naturalists, scientists, and park rangers lead multihour to multiday outings on topics from woodpeckers to fire management to day hikes and

Ansel Adams's Black-and-White Yosemite

What John Muir did for Yosemite with words, Ansel Adams did with photographs. His photographs have inspired millions of people to visit the park, and his persistent activism helped to ensure its conservation.

Born in 1902, Adams first came to the valley when he was 14, photographing it with a Box Brownie camera. He later said his first visit "was a culmination of experience so intense as to be almost painful. From that day in 1916 my life has been colored and modulated by the great earth gesture of the Sierra." By 1919, he was working in the valley, as custodian of LeConte Memorial Lodge (now called Yosemite Conservation Heritage Center), the Sierra Club headquarters in Yosemite National Park.

Adams had harbored dreams of a career as a concert pianist, but the park sealed his fate as a photographer in 1928, the day he shot *Monolith: The Face of Half Dome*, which remains one of his most famous works. That same year, Adams also married Virginia Best in her father's valley studio (now the Ansel Adams Gallery).

As the photographer's career took off, Yosemite began to sear itself into the American consciousness. David Brower, first executive director of the Sierra Club, later said of Adams's impact, "That Ansel Adams came to be recognized as one of the great photographers of this century is a tribute to the places that informed him."

In 1934, Adams was elected to the Sierra Club's board of directors; he would serve until 1971. As a representative of the conservation group, he combined his work with the club's mission, showing his photographs of the Sierra to influential officials such as Secretary of the Interior Harold L. Ickes, who showed them to President Franklin Delano Roosevelt. The images were a key factor in the establishment of Kings Canyon National Park.

In 1968, the Department of the Interior granted Adams its highest honor, the Conservation Service Award, and, in 1980, he received the Presidential Medal of Freedom in recognition of his conservation work. Until his death in 1984, Adams continued not only to record Yosemite's majesty on film but to urge the federal government and park managers to do right by the park.

In one of his many public pleas on behalf of Yosemite, Adams said, "Yosemite Valley itself is one of the great shrines of the world and—belonging to all our people—must be both protected and appropriately accessible." As an artist and an activist, Adams never gave up on his dream of keeping Yosemite wild yet within reach of every visitor who wants to experience it.

6

Yosemite National Park ACTIVITIES

bird-watching. Most sessions take place spring through fall with just a few in winter. ⊠ *Yosemite National Park* ⊕ *yosemite.org/experience/outdoor-adventures* 🖅 *From $105.*

RANGER PROGRAMS
Junior Ranger Program
LOCAL SPORTS | FAMILY | Children ages 3 to 13 can participate in the informal, self-guided Junior Ranger program. Park activity handbooks ($3.50 for ages 7 to 13 and $3 for Junior Cubs ages 3 to 6) are available at the Valley Visitor Center, the Happy Isles Art and Nature Center, the Tuolumne Visitor Center, and the Wawona Visitor Center. Once kids complete the book, rangers present them with a badge and, in some cases, a certificate. ⊠ *Valley Visitor Center or the Happy Isles Art & Nature Center, Yosemite National Park* ☎ *888/413–8869* ⊕ *www.travelyosemite.com.*

Ranger-Led Programs
LOCAL SPORTS | FAMILY | Rangers lead entertaining walks and give informative talks several times a day from spring to fall. The schedule is more limited in winter, but most days you can find a program somewhere in the park. In the evenings at Yosemite Valley Lodge and Curry Village, lectures, slide shows, and documentary films present unique perspectives on Yosemite. On summer weekends, campgrounds at Curry Village and Tuolumne Meadows host sing-along campfire programs. Schedules and locations are posted on bulletin boards throughout the park as well as in the indispensable *Yosemite Guide,* which is distributed to visitors as they arrive at the park. ⊠ *Yosemite National Park* ⊕ *nps.gov/yose.*

Wee Wild Ones
LOCAL SPORTS | FAMILY | Designed for kids 10 and under, this 45-minute program includes naturalist-led games, songs, stories, and crafts about Yosemite wildlife, plants, and geology. The event is held outdoors at the Curry Village Ampitheater

in summer and fall. All children must be accompanied by an adult. ⊠ *Curry Village Dr., Yosemite National Park* ☎ *209/372–1153* ⊕ *www.travelyosemite.com* 🖅 *Free.*

FISHING
The waters in Yosemite are not stocked; trout, mostly brown and rainbow, live here but are not plentiful. The park's season begins on the last Saturday in April and ends on November 15. Some waterways are off-limits at certain times; be sure to inquire at the visitor center about regulations.

A California fishing license is required; licenses cost around $19 for one day, $30 for two days, and $59 for 10 days. Full-season licenses cost $59 for state residents and $159 for nonresidents (costs fluctuate year to year). Buy your license in season online or at Yosemite Mountain Shop (☎ *209/372–1286*) in Curry Village.

GOLF
The Wawona Golf Course is one of the country's few organic golf courses; it's also an Audubon Cooperative sanctuary for birds. You can play a round or take a lesson from the pro here.

Wawona Golf Course
GOLF | This organic (one of only a handful in the United States), 9-hole course has two sets of tee positions per hole to provide an 18-hole course. ⊠ *Rte. 41, Wawona* ☎ *209/375–4386* ⊕ *www.travelyosemite.com* 🖅 *$24 for 9 holes; $39 for 18 holes* 🏌 *9 holes, 3050 yards, par 35* ☞ *Closed Nov.–early May.*

HIKING
Valley Wilderness Center
HIKING & WALKING | FAMILY | This facility provides wilderness permits, which are required for overnight camping. The staff here also provides maps and advice to hikers heading into the backcountry. If you don't have your own bear-resistant canisters, which are required, you can buy or rent them at the nearby Valley

Visitor Center. ■TIP→ **Advance reservations are $5 per person plus $5 per reservation and are required for popular trailheads April–October.** ⊠ *Between Ansel Adams Gallery and post office, Yosemite Village* ☎ *209/372–0826* ⊕ *www.nps.gov/yose.*

Yosemite Mountaineering School and Guide Service

HIKING & WALKING | From April to November, you can rent gear, hire a guide, or join a two-hour to full-day trek with Yosemite Mountaineering School. They also lead backpacking and overnight excursions. Reservations are recommended. In winter, cross-country ski programs are available at Badger Pass Ski Area. ⊠ *Yosemite Mountain Shop, Curry Village, Yosemite National Park* ☎ *209/372–8344* ⊕ *yosemitemountaineering.com* ☝ *From $195.*

HORSEBACK RIDING

Wawona Stable offers guided trail rides on mules and horses that range from two hours ($85) to a full-day trip to the Mariposa Grove of Giant Sequoias (Thursday only, ages 12-plus, late May–early September).

Wawona Stable

HORSEBACK RIDING | Two-hour rides at this stable start at $85, and a challenging full-day ride to the Mariposa Grove of Giant Sequoias (for experienced riders in good physical condition only) costs $150. Reservations are recommended. ⊠ *Rte. 41, Wawona* ☎ *209/375–6502* ⊕ *www.travelyosemite.com/things-to-do/horseback-mule-riding.*

ICE-SKATING

Curry Village Ice Skating Rink

ICE SKATING | **FAMILY** | Winter visitors have skated at this outdoor rink for decades, and there's no mystery why: it's a kick to glide across the ice while soaking up views of Half Dome and Glacier Point. ⊠ *South side of Southside Dr., Curry Village, Yosemite National Park* ☎ *209/372–8210* ⊕ *www.travelyosemite.com* ☝ *$16 per session, $6 skate rental.*

RAFTING

Rafting is permitted only on designated areas of the Middle and South forks of the Merced River. Check with the Valley Visitor Center for closures and other restrictions.

Curry Village Recreation Center

WHITE-WATER RAFTING | The per-person rental fee at Curry Village Recreation Center covers the four- to six-person raft, two paddles, and life jackets, plus a return shuttle after your trip. ⊠ *South side of Southside Dr., Curry Village, Yosemite National Park* ☎ *209/372–4386* ⊕ *www.travelyosemite.com/things-to-do/rafting* ☝ *From $31.*

ROCK CLIMBING

The granite canyon walls of Yosemite Valley are world renowned for rock climbing. El Capitan, with its 3,593-foot vertical face, is the most famous, but there are many other options here for all skill levels.

Yosemite Mountain Shop

ROCK CLIMBING | A comprehensive selection of camping, hiking, backpacking, and climbing equipment, along with experts who can answer all your questions, make this store a valuable resource for outdoors enthusiasts. This is the best place to ask about climbing conditions and restrictions around the park, as well as purchase almost any kind of climbing gear. ⊠ *Curry Village, Yosemite National Park* ☎ *209/372–8436* ⊕ *www.travelyosemite.com/things-to-do/rock-climbing.*

Yosemite Mountaineering School and Guide Service

ROCK CLIMBING | **FAMILY** | The one-day basic lesson offered by this outfit includes some bouldering and rappelling and three or four 60-foot climbs. Climbers must be at least 10 years old and in reasonably good physical condition. Intermediate and advanced classes include instruction in first aid; anchor building; and multipitch, summer-snow, and big-wall climbing. There's a Nordic program in the winter. ⊠ *Yosemite Mountain Shop, Curry Village, Yosemite National Park* ☎ *209/372–8444* ⊕ *www.travelyosemite. com* ⌂ *From $195.*

SKIING AND SNOWSHOEING
The beauty of Yosemite under a blanket of snow has long inspired poets and artists, as well as ordinary folks. Skiing and snowshoeing activities in the park center on Badger Pass Ski Area, California's oldest snow-sports resort, which is about 40 minutes away from the valley on Glacier Point Road. Here you can rent equipment, take a lesson, have lunch, and join a guided excursion.

Badger Pass Ski Area
SKIING & SNOWBOARDING | FAMILY | California's first ski resort has 10 downhill runs and 90 miles of groomed cross-country trails. Lessons, backcountry guiding, and cross-country and snowshoeing tours are also available. You can rent downhill, tele-mark, and cross-country skis, as well as snowshoes and snowboards. Note that shuttle buses run twice daily between the valley and the ski area. **Facilities:** 10 trails; 90 acres; 800-foot vertical drop; 5 lifts. ⊠ *Yosemite National Park* ✛ *Badger Pass Rd., off Glacier Point Rd., 18 miles from Yosemite Valley* ☎ *209/372–1000 conditions, weather, and ski information, 209/372–8430* ⊕ *www.travelyosemite. com/winter/badger-pass-ski-area* ⌂ *Lift ticket from $62.*

Badger Pass Ski Area School
SKIING & SNOWBOARDING | FAMILY | The gentle slopes of Badger Pass Ski Area make the ski school an ideal spot for children and beginners to learn downhill skiing or snowboarding for as little as $95 for a group lesson. ☎ *209/372–8430 spring–fall, 209/372–1000 conditions, information in winter* ⊕ *www.travelyosemite.com.*

Badger Pass Ski Area Sport Shop
SKIING & SNOWBOARDING | FAMILY | Stop here to gear (and bundle!) up for downhill and cross-country skiing, snowboarding, and snowshoeing adventures. ⊠ *Yosemite National Park* ✛ *Yosemite Ski & Snowboard Area, Badger Pass Rd., off Glacier Point Rd., 18 miles from Yosemite Valley* ☎ *209/372–8444* ⊕ *www.travelyosemite. com/winter/badger-pass-ski-area.*

Yosemite Cross-Country Ski School
SKIING & SNOWBOARDING | FAMILY | The highlight of Yosemite's cross-country skiing center is a 21-mile loop from Badger Pass Ski Area to Glacier Point. You can rent cross-country skis for $31 per day at the Cross-Country Ski School, which also rents snowshoes ($28.50 per day) and telemarking equipment ($41). ☎ *209/372–4996 Nordic Center (in season), 209/372–8444 Yosemite Mountaineering* ⊕ *www.travelyosemite.com.*

Yosemite Mountaineering School
SKIING & SNOWBOARDING | FAMILY | This branch of the Yosemite Mountaineering School, open at the Badger Pass Ski Area during ski season only, conducts snowshoeing, cross-country skiing, tele-marking, and skate-skiing classes starting at $86. ⊠ *Badger Pass Ski Area, Yosemite National Park* ☎ *209/372–8444* ⊕ *www. travelyosemite.com.*

SWIMMING
Several swimming holes with small sandy beaches can be found in mid-summer along the Merced River at the eastern end of Yosemite Valley. Find gentle waters to swim; currents are often stronger than they appear, and temper-atures are chilling. To conserve riparian habitats, step into the river at sandy beaches and other obvious entry points.

■ **TIP➜ Do not attempt to swim above or near waterfalls or rapids; people have died trying.**

Did You Know?

In the Sierra's mixed-conifer forests, telling the many types of pines apart can be difficult if you don't know the trick: sizing up the cones and examining the branches to count how many needles are in discrete clusters. If the needles are paired, you're likely looking at a lodgepole pine. If the needles are long and come in threes, chances are you've come upon a ponderosa pine.

What's Nearby

Mariposa

43 miles west of Yosemite's Arch Rock Entrance.

Mariposa marks the southern end of the Mother Lode. Much of the land in this area was part of a 44,000-acre land grant Colonel John C. Fremont acquired from Mexico before gold was discovered and California became a state. Many people stop here on the way to Yosemite National Park, about an hour's drive east on Highway 140.

GETTING HERE AND AROUND
If driving, take Highway 49 or Highway 140. YARTS (⊕ *www.yarts.com*), the regional transit system, can get you to Mariposa from the Central Valley town of Merced (where you can also transfer from Amtrak) or from Yosemite Valley. Otherwise, you'll need a car.

ESSENTIALS
VISITOR INFORMATION Mariposa County Chamber of Commerce & Visitor Center. ⊠ *5158 Hwy. 140, Mariposa* ☎ *209/966–2456.*

Sights

California State Mining and Mineral Museum
HISTORY MUSEUM | FAMILY | A California state park, the museum has displays on gold-rush history including a replica hard-rock mine shaft to walk through, a miniature stamp mill, and a 13-pound chunk of crystallized gold. ⊠ *5005 Fairground Rd., off Hwy. 49, Mariposa* ☎ *209/742–7625* ⊕ *www.parks.ca.gov/miningandmineral-museum* ☞ *$4* ۞ *Closed Mon.–Wed.*

Mariposa Museum and History Center
MUSEUM VILLAGE | FAMILY | You'll leave this small museum feeling like you just found your own gold nugget. Detailed exhibits, both indoors and out, tell the history of Mariposa County. Visit a replica of a typical miner's cabin; see a working stamp mill; tour the blacksmith shop. Artifacts, photographs, and maps, along with the knowledgeable staff, will capture your imagination and transport you back to 1849. ⊠ *5119 Jessie St., Mariposa* ☎ *209/966–2924* ⊕ *www.mariposamuseum.com* ☞ *$5.*

Yosemite Climbing Museum and Gallery
HISTORY MUSEUM | FAMILY | This small but fascinating gallery showcases area climbing history and the evolution of gear with an impressive collection of artifacts and historical photography. ⊠ *5108 Hwy. 140, Mariposa* ☎ *209/742–1000* ⊕ *www.yosemiteclimbing.org/museuminfo* ☞ *Free (donations suggested)* ۞ *Closed Mon.*

 Restaurants

Charles Street Dinner House
$$$ | AMERICAN | FAMILY | Centrally located Charles Street, its rustic decor heavy on the wood and Old West adornments, at once evokes both the gold-rush days and the 1980s, which is when it opened. The extensive straightforward menu includes hand-cut steaks, honey-barbecue baby back ribs, several pasta dishes, chicken, pork loin, lamb, a few well-adorned burgers, and some vegetarian options. **Known for:** excellent steaks; cheesecake, sundae, crème brûlée for dessert; local feel. Ⓢ *Average main: $31* ⊠ *Hwy. 140 and 7th St., Mariposa* ☎ *209/966–2366* ⊕ *www.charlesstreetdinnerhouse.com* ۞ *Closed Sun. and Mon. No lunch.*

1850 Restaurant & Brewery

$$ | **AMERICAN** | The name, decor, and menu at this lively brewpub pay homage to California's Gold Rush era and the year the state and county were officially established. Many of the craft beers on tap come from the owners' 1850 Brewing Company, and dishes include everything from traditional Bavarian pretzels and hearty baked mac and cheese to ahi nachos and salmon cakes. **Known for:** brine-marinated fried chicken; seven types of burgers; rotating local seasonal beers on tap. $ *Average main: $25* ⊠ *5114 Hwy. 140, Mariposa* ☎ *209/966–2229* ⊕ *www.1850restaurant. com* ⊘ *Closed Mon.*

Little Shop of Ramen

$ | **JAPANESE** | In a hip, modern space—alongside The Local Grape wine bar within a historic building—this unusual-for-the-region eatery serves up savory Japanese soul food. Expect home-style dishes like steaming bowls of toasted-rye ramen noodles swimming in a rich broth For dessert, there's matcha cheesecake and premium mochi ice cream. **Known for:** hand-pulled noodles and house-made stocks and sauces; vegan, vegetarian, and gluten-free options; indoor and outdoor seating. $ *Average main: $16* ⊠ *5021 Hwy. 140, Mariposa* ☎ *209/966–2695* ⊕ *littleshoptoframen.square.site* ⊘ *Closed Mon. No lunch Wed. and Thurs.*

El Portal

29 miles northwest of Mariposa, 15 miles west of Yosemite's Arch Rock Entrance on Hwy. 140.

The market in town is a good place to pick up provisions before you get to Yosemite. You'll find a post office and a gas station, but not much else.

GETTING HERE AND AROUND

The drive here on Highway 140 from Mariposa and, farther west, Merced, is the prettiest and gentlest route to Yosemite National Park. Much of the road follows the Merced River in a rugged canyon. YARTS buses are a cheap and dependable way to travel between Merced and Yosemite Valley; all stop in El Portal, where many park employees reside.

 ## Hotels

Yosemite View Lodge

$$ | **HOTEL** | Two miles outside Yosemite's Arch Rock entrance, this modern property is the most convenient place to spend the night if you are unable to secure lodgings in the valley. **Pros:** great location; good views; lots of on-site amenities. **Cons:** somewhat pricey; it can be a challenge to get the dates you want; rooms could use an update. $ *Rooms from: $249* ⊠ *11136 Hwy. 140, El Portal* ☎ *209/379–2681* ⊕ *www.yosemiteresorts.com/yosemite-view-lodge* ⊋ *335 rooms* ⊓⊘ *No Meals.*

Oakhurst

23 miles south of Yosemite's South Entrance.

Motels, restaurants, gas stations, and small businesses line Highway 41 in Oakhurst, the last sizable community before Yosemite National Park and a good spot to find provisions.

GETTING HERE AND AROUND

At the junction of highways 41 and 49, Oakhurst is about an hour's drive north of Fresno. It's the southern gateway to Yosemite, so many people fly into Fresno and rent a car to get here and beyond.

Sights

Fresno Flats Historical Village and Park
HISTORY MUSEUM | FAMILY | For a dose of colorful foothills history, make a quick stop at this engaging local museum centered on two 1870s houses. Self-guided tours are available from dawn to dusk; museum visits are by appointment. ✉ *School Rd. and Indian Springs Rd., Oakhurst* ☎ *559/683–6570* 🌐 *www.fresnoflatsmuseum.org* 🕑 *Closed Jan. and Feb.*

Restaurants

★ Elderberry House
$$$$ | EUROPEAN | This culinary oasis—stunning for its understated elegance, gorgeous setting, and impeccable service—is one of the best restaurants in the region. Earthtone walls and wood beams accent the high ceilings, and arched windows reflect the glow of candles. **Known for:** elite waitstaff; romantic setting, gorgeous garden terrace; seasonal prix-fixe menus (three-course $95, six-course $155, wine pairings add $70/$95). [$] *Average main: $95* ✉ *Château du Sureau, 48688 Victoria La., off Hwy. 41, Oakhurst* ☎ *559/683–6860* 🌐 *www.elderberryhouse.com* 🕑 *No lunch Mon.–Sat.*

★ South Gate Brewing Company
$$ | AMERICAN | Locals pack this family-friendly, industrial-chic restaurant to socialize and savor small-lot beers, crafted on-site, along with tasty meals. The creative pub fare runs a wide gamut, from thin-crust brick-oven pizzas to fish tacos, fish-and-chips, and vegan black-bean burgers. **Known for:** craft beer; house-made desserts; live-music calendar. [$] *Average main: $20* ✉ *40233 Enterprise Dr., off Hwy. 49, north of Von's shopping center, Oakhurst* ☎ *559/692–2739* 🌐 *southgatebrewco.com.*

Hotels

Best Western Plus Yosemite Gateway Inn
$$ | HOTEL | FAMILY | Perched on 11 hillside acres, Oakhurst's best motel has carefully tended landscaping and rooms with stylish contemporary furnishings and hand-painted murals of Yosemite. **Pros:** on-site restaurant; indoor and outdoor swimming pools; frequent deer and wildlife sightings. **Cons:** some rooms on the small side; Internet connection can be slow; some rooms need updating. [$] *Rooms from: $249* ✉ *40530 Hwy. 41, Oakhurst* ☎ *559/683–2378* 🌐 *www.yosemitegatewayinn.com* 🛏 *149 rooms* 🍴 *No Meals.*

★ Château du Sureau
$$$ | RESORT | Every room here is impeccably styled with European antiques, sumptuous fabrics, fresh-cut flowers, and oversize soaking tubs. **Pros:** luxurious; great views; sumptuous spa. **Cons:** expensive; cost might not seem worth it to guests not spa-oriented; can seem pretentious to some. [$] *Rooms from: $495* ✉ *48688 Victoria La., Oakhurst* ☎ *559/683–6860* 🌐 *www.chateausureau.com* 🛏 *11 rooms* 🍴 *Free Breakfast.*

Sierra Sky Ranch
$ | HOTEL | Off Highway 41 just 10 miles south of the Yosemite National Park, this 19th-century cattle ranch near a hidden grove of giant sequoia trees provides a restful, rustic retreat. **Pros:** peaceful setting; historic property; short drive to giant sequoias. **Cons:** some rooms on the small side; not in town; basic breakfast. [$] *Rooms from: $199* ✉ *50552 Rd. 632, Oakhurst* ☎ *559/683–8040* 🌐 *www.sierraskyranch.com* 🛏 *28 rooms* 🍴 *Free Breakfast.*

Bass Lake

7 miles northwest of Oakhurst via Hwy. 41 to Bass Lake Rd. 222.

Almost surrounded by the Sierra National Forest, Bass Lake is a reservoir whose waters can reach 80°F in summer. Created by a dam on a tributary of the San Joaquin River, the lake is owned by Pacific Gas and Electric Company and is used to generate electricity as well as for recreation.

GETTING HERE AND AROUND

From Oakhurst, follow Highway 41 about 3½ miles north to the Bass Lake Road/ Road 222 turnoff and head southeast another 4 miles (the road name changes to Road 274/Malum Ridge Road). Madera County Connection (MCC) provides limited bus service to the Bass Lake Government Center and the Pines Resort.

 Restaurants

Ducey's on the Lake/Ducey's Bar & Grill
$$$ | AMERICAN | FAMILY | With elaborate chandeliers sculpted from deer antlers, the lodge-style restaurant at Ducey's attracts boaters, locals, and tourists with its lake views and standard lamb, beef, seafood, and pasta dishes. It's also open for breakfast: try the lobster-crab cake eggs Benedict, huevos rancheros, or the Rice Krispies–crusted French toast. **Known for:** steaks and fresh fish; lake views; upstairs bar and grill with more affordable eats. $ *Average main: $38* ✉ *Pines Resort, 54432 Rd. 432, Bass Lake* ☎ *559/642–3121* ⊕ *www.basslake. com.*

Activities

BOATING
Bass Lake Boat Rental & Water Sports
BOATING | FAMILY | This outfit on Bass Lake Reservoir, 3 miles north and 6 miles east of Oakhurst, rents ski boats, patio boats, fishing boats, canoes, tubes, and other things that float. The folks here also conduct guided fishing and scenic tours. In summer, the noisy reservoir is packed shortly after it opens at 8 am (off-season hours are from 9 to 5). There's also a shop with snacks and gifts. ✉ *54406 Marina Dr., Bass Lake* ☎ *559/642–3200* ⊕ *basslakeboatrentals.com.*

Fish Camp

14 miles north of Oakhurst.

As you climb in elevation along Highway 41 northbound, you see nothing but trees until you get to Fish Camp, where there's a post office and general store. (For gas, head 7 miles north to Wawona, in Yosemite, or 14 miles south to Oakhurst.)

GETTING HERE AND AROUND

Highway 41 is the main drag. YARTS transit stops in Fish Camp on its route between Fresno and Yosemite Valley.

Sights

Yosemite Mountain Sugar Pine Railroad
TRAIN/TRAIN STATION | FAMILY | Travel back to a time when powerful steam locomotives hauled massive log trains through the Sierra. This 4-mile, narrow-gauge railroad excursion takes you near Yosemite's south gate. There's a moonlight special ($75), with dinner and entertainment, and you can visit the free museum. ✉ *56001 Hwy. 41, 8 miles south of Yosemite, Fish Camp* ☎ *559/683–7273* ⊕ *www.ymsprr. com* ✉ *$35* ⊗ *Closed Nov.–Mar. Closed some weekdays Apr. and Oct.*

Hotels

★ Tenaya Lodge
$$$ | RESORT | FAMILY | A stay at one of the region's largest hotels puts you amid the wilderness with all the creature comforts—from the striking lobby lounge, with its high windows and sturdy beams, to the ample lodge rooms where baths have granite countertops and

Did You Know?

The town of Bodie offers ghost tours of its abandoned village at night.

brushed-bronze fixtures. **Pros:** close to Yosemite and Mariposa Grove of Giant Sequoias; exceptional spa and exercise facility, 36 miles of mountain bike trails; activities for all ages. **Cons:** so big it can seem impersonal; pricey during summer; daily resort fee. $ *Rooms from: $379* ✉ *1122 Hwy. 41, Fish Camp* ☎ *559/683–6555, 888/514–2167* 🌐 *www.tenayalodge.com* 🛏 *352 rooms* 🍴 *No Meals.*

Lee Vining

13 miles northeast of Yosemite's Tioga Pass Entrance (near Tuolumne Meadows).

Tiny Lee Vining is known primarily as the eastern gateway to Yosemite National Park (summer only) and the location of vast and desolate Mono Lake. Pick up supplies at the general store year-round, or stop here for lunch or dinner before or after a drive through the high country. In winter, the town is all but deserted, except for the ice climbers who come to scale frozen waterfalls.

Most people enter Yosemite National Park from the west, having driven out from the Bay Area or Los Angeles. The eastern entrance on Tioga Pass Road (Highway 120 off Highway 395), however, provides stunning, sweeping views of the High Sierra. Gray rocks shine in the bright sun, with scattered, small vegetation sprinkled about the mountainside.

■ TIP→ To drive from Lee Vining to Tuolumne Meadows is an unforgettable experience, but keep in mind that the road is closed for at least seven months of the year.

GETTING HERE AND AROUND

Lee Vining is on U.S. 395, north of the road's intersection with Highway 120 and on the south side of Mono Lake. In summer, YARTS (🌐 *yarts.com*) vehicles can get you here from Yosemite Valley, but you'll need a car to explore the area.

ESSENTIALS

VISITOR INFORMATION Lee Vining Chamber of Commerce. ✉ *Lee Vining* ☎ *760/647–6629* 🌐 *www.leevining.com.* **Mono Basin National Forest Scenic Area Visitor Center.** ✉ *Visitor Center Dr., Lee Vining* ✣ *Off U.S. 395, 1 mile north of Hwy. 120* ☎ *760/647–3044* 🌐 *www.fs.usda.gov.*

Sights

June Lake Loop

SCENIC DRIVE | FAMILY | Heading south, U.S. 395 intersects the June Lake Loop. This gorgeous 16-mile drive follows an old glacial canyon past Grant, June, Gull, and Silver lakes before reconnecting with U.S. 395 on its way to Mammoth Lakes. **■ TIP→ The loop is especially colorful in fall.** ✉ *Hwy. 158 W, Lee Vining.*

★ Mono Lake

BODY OF WATER | FAMILY | Since the 1940s, Los Angeles has diverted water from this lake, exposing striking towers of tufa, or calcium carbonate. Court victories by environmentalists have meant fewer diversions, and the lake is rising again. Although to see the lake from U.S. 395 is stunning, make time to visit South Tufa, whose parking lot is 5 miles east of U.S. 395 off Highway 120. There, in summer, you can join the naturalist-guided South Tufa Walk, which lasts about 60 minutes (sign up online).

The Scenic Area Visitor Center, off U.S. 395, is a sensational stop for its interactive exhibits and sweeping Mono Lake views (closed in winter). In town, at U.S. 395 and 3rd Street, the Mono Lake Committee Information Center & Bookstore, open from 9 to 5 daily (extended hours in summer), has more information about this beautiful area. ✉ *Hwy. 120, east of Lee Vining, Lee Vining* ☎ *760/647–3044 visitor center, 760/647–6595 info center* 🌐 *www.monolake.org* 🎟 *Free.*

 Restaurants

Tioga Gas Mart & Whoa Nelli Deli

$ | AMERICAN | This might be the only gas station in the United States serving craft beers and lobster taquitos, but its appeal goes beyond novelty. Order at the counter, and grab a seat inside, or sit at one of the picnic tables on the lawn outside and take in the distant view of Mono Lake. **Known for:** fish tacos and barbecued ribs; regular live music; convenient location. $ *Average main: $18* ✉ *Hwy. 120 and U.S. 395, Lee Vining* ☎ *760/647–1088* ⊕ *www.whoanelliedeli.com* ⊘ *Closed early Nov.–late Apr.*

 Hotels

Lake View Lodge

$ | B&B/INN | FAMILY | Cottages, enormous rooms, and landscaping that includes several shaded sitting areas set this motel apart from its competitors in town. **Pros:** convenient access to Yosemite, Mono Lake, and Bodie State Historic Park; peaceful setting; on-site restaurant. **Cons:** could use updating; slow Wi-Fi in some areas; no views from some rooms. $ *Rooms from: $199* ✉ *51285 U.S. 395, Lee Vining* ☎ *760/647–6543, 800/990–6614* ⊕ *lakeviewlodgeyosemite. com* ⤶ *88 units* ⦿ *No Meals.*

Bodie State Historic Park

31 miles northeast of Lee Vining.

Bodie State Historic Park's scenery is spectacular, with craggy, snowcapped peaks looming over vast prairies. The gateway to the park (and the only supply center for miles around) is Bridgeport, whose claims to fame include a courthouse that's been in continuous use since 1880 and excellent fishing—the California state record brown trout, at 26 pounds 12 ounces, was caught in Twin Lakes. In winter, much of the town shuts down.

GETTING HERE AND AROUND
A car is the best way to reach and tour this area. Bodie lies 13 miles east of U.S. 395 off Highway 270. The last 3 miles are unpaved, and snow may close the route from late fall through early spring.

 Sights

★ Bodie Ghost Town

GHOST TOWN | FAMILY | The mining village of Rattlesnake Gulch, abandoned mine shafts, and the remains of a small Chinatown are among the sights at this fascinating ghost town. The town boomed from about 1878 to 1881; by the late 1940s, though, all its residents had departed. A state park was established here in 1962, with a mandate to preserve everything in a state of "arrested decay." Evidence of Bodie's wild past survives at an excellent museum, and you can tour an old stamp mill where ore was crushed into fine powder to extract gold and silver. ■**TIP**➜ **Bodie has no food, drink, or lodging, and snow might cause closure of the road to it from late spring through early fall, so check ahead.** ✉ *Bodie Rd., off Hwy. 270, Bodie* ☎ *760/616–5040* ⊕ *www.parks.ca.gov/bodie* ⛁ *$8.*

Chapter 7

EASTERN SIERRA

Updated by
Marlise Kast-Myers

⊙ Sights   🍴 Restaurants   🛏 Hotels   🛍 Shopping   🍸 Nightlife

★★★★★   ★★★★☆   ★★★★★   ★☆☆☆☆   ★☆☆☆☆

WELCOME TO THE EASTERN SIERRA

TOP REASONS TO GO

★ **Hiking:** Whether you walk the paved loops in the national parks or head off the beaten path into the backcountry, a hike through groves and meadows or alongside streams and waterfalls will allow you to see, smell, and feel nature up close.

★ **Winter fun:** Famous for its incredible snowpack—some of the deepest in the North American continent—the Sierra Nevada has something for every winter-sports fan.

★ **Live it up:** Mammoth Lakes is eastern California's most exciting resort area.

★ **Road trip heaven:** Legendary Highway 395 is one of California's most scenic byways, traveling to Independence, Lone Pine, Bishop, and beyond, for a glimpse of Old West history.

★ **Go with the flow:** Fish, float, raft, and row in the abundant lakes, hot springs, creeks, and rivers.

1 Lone Pine. Mount Whitney and the Alabama Hills in Lone Pine have provided authentic backdrops for hundreds of films and TV shows for nearly a century, as evidenced in the town's Museum of Western Film History.

2 Independence. The moving Manzanar National Historic Site, where 11,000 Japanese-Americans were interned during World War II, lies 6 miles south of Independence, a tiny Old West town.

3 Bishop. One of the largest towns along scenic Highway 395, Bishop is an excellent road stop and base camp for exploration in the surrounding mountains.

4 Mammoth Lakes. Easy access to year-round outdoor adventures has made Mammoth Lakes one of the Sierra Nevada's most popular destinations. The bustling town's many attractions include sprawling Mammoth Mountain Ski Area and Bike Park and nearby Mammoth Lakes Basin and Devil's Postpile National Monument.

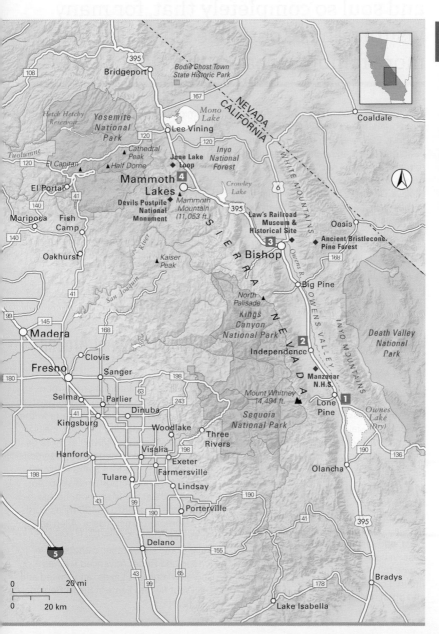

The granite peaks and ancient pines of the Eastern Sierra bedazzle heart and soul so completely that, for many visitors, the experience surpasses that at more famous urban attractions.

This rugged region offers some of the most dramatic sightseeing in California. Highway 395, one of the state's most beautiful routes and generally open year-round, is the main north–south road. It travels the length of the region, from the Mojave Desert in the south to Bridgeport in the north, and along the eastern side of the Sierra Nevada, at the western edge of the Great Basin. Main towns along the route include Lone Pine, Independence, Bishop, and Mammoth Lakes, as well as Lee Vining, a small town at the eastern endpoint of Tioga Road (open only seasonally) into Yosemite National Park.

Pristine lakes and rolling hills outside the parks offer year-round opportunities for rest and relaxation. Or not. In winter, the thrill of Mammoth Lakes slopes—and their relative isolation compared to busy Lake Tahoe—draws a hearty breed of outdoor enthusiasts. From late spring through early fall, a hike through groves and meadows or alongside streams and waterfalls allows you to see, smell, and feel nature up close.

MAJOR REGIONS

Owens Valley. In this under-visited region, the snowcapped Sierra Nevada range rises abruptly and majestically to the west, and the high desert whistles to the east. In between are a series of roadside towns full of character, history, and outfits that cater to adventurers. The dusty and often dry Owens Lake is a stopover for migratory shorebirds. Along U.S. 395 in this region are Lone Pine, Independence, and Bishop, with Lone Pine and Bishop having the best selection of dining and lodging options.

Mammoth Lakes. North of Owens Valley, en route to the gateway towns east of Yosemite National Park, is the megaresort of Mammoth Lakes, which lures skiers and snowboarders in winter and hikers and mountain bikers in warmer months.

Planning

Getting Here and Around

AIR

Fresno Yosemite International Airport (FAT) is the main gateway on the western side of the Eastern Sierra. Airports to the region's east and along U.S. 395 include Mammoth Yosemite (MMH), 6 miles east of Mammoth Lakes and mostly serves private aircraft; Eastern Sierra Regional (BIH, aka Bishop Airport) in Bishop, 45 miles southeast of Mammoth Lakes; and Reno–Tahoe (RNO), 130 miles north of Mammoth Lakes. Alaska, Allegiant, American, Delta, Southwest, United, Volaris, and a few other carriers serve Fresno and Reno. Advanced Airlines serves Mammoth Lakes, and United and SkyWest fly into Eastern Sierra Regional.

AIRPORTS Eastern Sierra Regional Airport. ✉ *703 Airport Rd., Bishop* ☎ *760/872–2971* ⊕ *www.inyocounty.us/bishop-airport.* **Fresno Yosemite International Airport.** ✉ *5175 E. Clinton Ave., Fresno* ☎ *559/621–4500* ⊕ *flyfresno.com.* **Mammoth Yosemite Airport.** ✉ *1200 Airport Rd., Mammoth Lakes* ☎ *760/965–3620, 760/934–3813* ⊕ *www.ci.mammoth-lakes.ca.us/98/Airport.* **Reno–Tahoe International Airport.** (*RNO*) ✉ *2001 E. Plumb La., Reno* ☎ *775/328–6400* ⊕ *www.renoairport.com.*

BUS

Eastern Sierra Transit Authority buses serve Mammoth Lakes, Bishop, and other Eastern Sierra towns along Highway 395, from Reno in the north to Lancaster in the south. In summer, YARTS (Yosemite Area Regional Transportation System) connects Yosemite National Park with Mammoth Lakes, June Lake, and Lee Vining, as well as Central Valley cities and towns in the west, including Fresno and Merced. This is a good option, as parking in Yosemite Valley and elsewhere in the park can be difficult in summer.

BUS CONTACTS Eastern Sierra Transit Authority. ☎ *760/872–1901 Bishop, 760/614–0030 Lone Pine, 760/924–3184 Mammoth Lakes, 800/922–1930* ⊕ *www.estransit.com.* **YARTS.** ☎ *877/989–2787* ⊕ *yarts.com.*

CAR

Interstate 5 and Highway 99 travel north–south along the western side of the Sierra Nevada. U.S. 395 follows a roughly parallel route on the eastern side. In summer, Tioga Pass Road in Yosemite National Park opens to car and bus travel, intersecting with U.S. 395 at Lee Vining.

From San Francisco: Head east on I–80 to Sacramento, then continue on I–80 to U.S. 395, east of Lake Tahoe's north shore, or take U.S. 50 to Lake Tahoe's south shore and continue on 207E to U.S. 395, then head south.

From Los Angeles: Head north on I–5, exiting and continuing north onto Highway 14 and later onto U.S. 395.

Between October and May, heavy snow may cover mountain roads. Always check conditions before driving. Carry tire chains, and know how to install them. On I–80 and U.S. 50, and at the Mammoth Lakes exit off U.S. 395, chain installers assist travelers (for $40), but elsewhere you're on your own. ■ **TIP→ Gas stations are few and far between in the Sierra, so fill your tank when you can.**

TRAIN

Amtrak's daily *San Joaquin* train stops in Fresno and Merced, where you can connect to YARTS buses for travel to Yosemite National Park and, in summer, to Mammoth Lakes, June Lake, and the Yosemite gateway town of Lee Vining.

Hotels

Book hotels everywhere in the Eastern Sierra well in advance in summer. The lodgings in Mammoth Lakes and nearest Yosemite National Park generally fill up the quickest.

Restaurants

Most small towns in the Sierra Nevada have at least one restaurant. Standard American fare is the norm, but you'll also find sophisticated cuisine. With few exceptions, dress is casual. Local grocery stores and delis stock picnic fixings, good to have on hand should the opportunity for an impromptu meal under giant trees emerge.

⇨ *Restaurant and hotel reviews have been shortened. For full information, visit Fodors.com. Restaurant prices are the average cost of a main course at dinner, or if dinner is not served, at lunch. Hotel prices are the lowest cost of a standard double room in high season.*

What It Costs			
$	$$	$$$	$$$$
RESTAURANTS			
under $20	$20–$30	$31–$40	over $40
HOTELS			
under $200	$200–$350	$351–$500	over $500

Tours

MAWS Transportation

BUS TOURS | FAMILY | This outfit (aka Mammoth All Weather Shuttle) operates summer tours from Mammoth Lakes to Yosemite; north to June Lake, Mono Lake, and Bodie Ghost Town; and around the lakes region. The company also transfers passengers from the Bishop and Mammoth Yosemite airports into Mammoth Lakes; drops off and picks up hikers at trailheads; and runs charters to Los Angeles, Reno, and Las Vegas airports—useful when inclement weather causes flight cancellations at Mammoth's airport. ⊠ *Mammoth Lakes* ☎ *760/709–2927* ⊕ *www.mawshuttle. com* ⊠ *From $65.*

Visitor Information

CONTACTS Eastern Sierra Visitor Center.
⊕ *2 miles south of Lone Pine, at junctions of U.S. Hwy. 395 and CA Hwy. 136* ☎ *760/876–6200* ⊕ *www.fs.usda. gov/recarea/inyo/recarea/?recid=20698.* **Mammoth Lakes Tourism.** ⊠ *2520 Main St., Mammoth Lakes* ☎ *760/934–2712, 888/466–2666* ⊕ *www.visitmammoth. com.* **Mono County Tourism.** ⊠ *Mammoth Lakes* ☎ *800/845–7922* ⊕ *www.mono-county.org.*

When to Go

If hiking and photography are on your agenda, aim for "off season" in the fall, when there are fewer visitors, rates are lower, and the foliage is spectacular. Outside of late September–November, the summer months offer the best weather. Come January and February, rain may hit at lower elevations but that means plenty of snow on the slopes. If your schedule allows, consider skiing midweek during early season from mid-November through mid-December when lift tickets are more affordable. April and May offer blue-sky days with plenty of space and snowpack after a good winter season.

Lone Pine

100 miles southeast of Mammoth Lakes.

Mt. Whitney towers majestically over this tiny community, which supplied nearby gold- and silver-mining outposts in the 1860s. For the past century, the town has been touched by Hollywood glamour: more than 500 movies, TV episodes, and commercials have been filmed here. From April to November, nearby rivers lure anglers in search of trout.

GETTING HERE AND AROUND

Arrive via U.S. 395 from the north or south. (If you're heading from Death Valley National Park, you can also take Highway 190 or Highway 138.) Eastern Sierra Transit buses connect Lone Pine to Reno in the north and Lancaster in the south.

ESSENTIALS

VISITOR INFORMATION Lone Pine Chamber of Commerce & Visitor Center. ⊠ *120 S. Main St., at Whitney Portal Rd., Lone Pine* ☎ *760/876–4444* ⊕ *lonepinechamber.org.*

Sights

Alabama Hills

MOUNTAIN | FAMILY | Drop by the Lone Pine Visitor Center for a map of the Alabama Hills, and drive up Whitney Portal Road (turn west at the light) to this wonderland of granite boulders. Erosion has worn the rocks smooth; some have been chiseled into arches and other formations. The hills have become a popular location for rock climbing. Tuttle Creek Campground sits among the rocks, with a nearby stream for fishing. The area has served as a scenic backdrop for hundreds of films; ask about the self-guided tour of the various movie locations at the Museum of Western Film History. ✉ *Whitney Portal Rd., Lone Pine* ✥ *4½ miles west of Lone Pine.*

Highway 395

SCENIC DRIVE | FAMILY | Travel north of Death Valley along Highway 395 for breathtaking views of Mt. Whitney, the highest mountain (14,496 feet) in the continental United States. Travel south this scenic byway, between Olancha and Big Pine, to see the massive salt-crusted Owens Lake, which was drained between 1900 and 1920 as water from the Sierra was diverted to Los Angeles.

Revered by the National Audubon Society, the lake is home to more than 240 migrating birds, including the snowy plover, American white pelican, golden eagle, and countless grebes, bitterns, blue herons, and cranes. On its northwest end are brilliant red salt flats, caused by billions of microscopic halobacteria that survive there. As tempting as it might be, don't drive onto the dry lake since tow rescues are complicated and costly. For the best views, drive the switchbacks toward Horseshoe Meadow. ✉ *Death Valley.*

Museum of Western Film History

HISTORY MUSEUM | FAMILY | Hopalong Cassidy, Barbara Stanwyck, Roy Rogers, John Wayne—even Robert Downey Jr.—are among the celebrities who have starred in the hundreds of Western films shot in the Alabama Hills and surrounding dusty terrain. This marquee-embellished, 10,000-square-foot museum relates the Hollywood-in-the-desert tale via exhibits and a rollicking 15-minute documentary. ✉ *701 S. Main St., U.S. 395, Lone Pine* ☎ *760/876–9909* 🌐 *museumofwesternfilmhistory.org* 🎟 *$5.*

Restaurants

Alabama Hills Café

$ | AMERICAN | FAMILY | The extensive breakfast and lunch menus at this eatery just off the main drag include many vegetarian items. Sandwiches are served on homemade bread; choose from up to six varieties baked fresh daily, and get a homemade pie, cake, or loaf to go. **Known for:** house-roasted turkey and beef; huge portions; on-site bakery. [$] *Average main: $18* ✉ *111 W. Post St., at S. Main St., Lone Pine* ☎ *760/876–4675* 🌐 *www.alabamahillscafe.com* 🕒 *Closed Wed. No dinner* ☞ *Pets not allowed on patio.*

The Grill

$$ | AMERICAN | FAMILY | Open for three meals a day, this small restaurant next to the Dow Villa Motel is a convenient place to stop for a break while driving along Highway 395. The extensive menu includes everything from omelets and French toast for breakfast to sandwiches and burgers for lunch to grilled steaks and fish for dinner. **Known for:** hearty meals; friendly service; house-made desserts. [$] *Average main: $21* ✉ *446 S. Main St., Lone Pine* ☎ *760/876–4240* 🌐 *www.facebook.com/TheGrillLonePine.*

Mt. Whitney Restaurant

$ | AMERICAN | FAMILY | This boisterous family-friendly restaurant with six flat-screen televisions serves the best burgers—beef, buffalo, or elk—in town. The traditional diner menu also features country-fried steak, turkey dinner, Black

Angus beef, and blueberry pie. **Known for:** burgers; John Wayne memorabilia; convenient fuel-up stop on Highway 395. [$] *Average main: $18* ✉ *227 S. Main St., Lone Pine* ☎ *760/876–5751.*

Hotels

Dow Villa Motel
$ | HOTEL | FAMILY | Built to cater to the film industry, this lodging in the center of town consists of a 1923 hotel—where John Wayne, Gene Autry, and other Western-movie greats stayed—and a late-1950s motel, where rooms (many of them updated in 2023) are more spacious. **Pros:** clean rooms; great mountain views; in-room whirlpool tubs in some motel rooms. **Cons:** some rooms in hotel share bathrooms; sinks in some rooms are in the bedroom, not the bath; on busy highway. [$] *Rooms from: $165* ✉ *310 S. Main St., Lone Pine* ☎ *760/876–5521, 800/824–9317* 🌐 *dowvillamotel.com* 🛏 *92 rooms* 🍴 *No Meals.*

Activities

Lone Pine Sporting Goods
FISHING | FAMILY | Stock up on fishing gear, bait, and sunscreen at this local shop, where the owner might just tell you where the trout are biting. You can also purchase a fishing license for the season, which runs April–November 15. ✉ *220 S. Main St., Lone Pine* ☎ *760/876–5365* 🌐 *www.facebook.com/lonepinesportinggoods.*

Independence

17 miles north of Lone Pine.

Named for a military outpost that was established near here in 1862, sleepy Independence has some wonderful historic buildings and is worth a stop for another reason: 6 miles south of the small downtown lies the Manzanar National Historic Site, one of 10 camps in the West where people of Japanese descent were confined during World War II.

GETTING HERE AND AROUND

Eastern Sierra Transit buses pass through town, but most travelers arrive by car on U.S. 395.

Sights

Ancient Bristlecone Pine Forest
FOREST | FAMILY | About an hour's drive from Independence or Bishop you can view some of the oldest living trees on Earth, a few of which date back more than 40 centuries. The world's largest bristlecone pine can be found in Patriarch Grove, while the world's oldest known living tree—over 4,800 years old—is along Methusula Trail in Schulman Grove. Getting to Patriarch Grove is slow going along the narrow dirt road, especially for vehicles with low clearance, but once there you'll find picnic tables, restrooms, and interpretive trails. ✉ *Schulman Grove Visitor Center, White Mountain Rd., Bishop* ✣ *From U.S. 395, turn east onto Hwy. 168 and follow signs for 23 miles* ☎ *760/873–2500 White Mountain Ranger Station* 🌐 *www.fs.usda.gov/recarea/inyo/recarea/?recid=70821* 🎫 *$3.*

Eastern California Museum
HISTORY MUSEUM | FAMILY | The highlights of this museum dedicated to Inyo County and the Eastern Sierra's history include photos and artifacts from the Manzanar War Relocation Center, Paiute and Shoshone baskets, and exhibits on the Los Angeles Aqueduct and mountaineer Norman Clyde. Be sure to visit the botanical garden and the outdoor exhibits as well. ✉ *155 N. Grant St., at W. Center St., Independence* ☎ *760/878–0258* 🌐 *www.facebook.com/ecmuseum* 🎫 *Free* 🕒 *Closed Wed.*

★ **Manzanar National Historic Site**
HISTORIC SIGHT | FAMILY | A reminder of an ugly episode in U.S. history, this site is where more than 10,000

Japanese-Americans were contained behind barbed-wire fences between 1942 and 1945. A visit here is both deeply moving and inspiring—the former because it's hard to comprehend that the United States was capable of confining its citizens in such a way, the latter because those imprisoned here persevered despite the adversity.

The best place to start is the outstanding interpretive center, which screens a 22-minute documentary film and displays historical photos, artifacts, and a model of the camp as it was during WWII. Although few of the original 1940s structures remain, the area known as Block 14 has a restored mess hall and reconstructions of a women's latrine as well as two barracks, where four exhibits highlight what daily life was like here. You can also drive or bike the 3.2-mile road through the site, taking a self-guided tour of Japanese rock gardens, various signposted ruins, and a small cemetery. ✉ *5001 Hwy. 395, Independence* ✣ *West side of U.S. 395 between Independence and Lone Pine* ☎ *760/878–2194* 🌐 *www.nps.gov/manz* 🎟 *Free.*

Bishop

43 miles north of Independence.

One of the biggest towns along U.S. 395, bustling Bishop has views of the Sierra Nevada and the White and Inyo mountains. Although the region was first settled by the Northern Paiute people (and Paiute and Shoshone people reside on four area reservations), the town was named in 1861 for cattle rancher Samuel Bishop, who established a camp here.

Bishop kicks off the summer season with its Mule Days Celebration. Held over Memorial Day weekend, the five-day event includes mule races, a rodeo, an arts-and-crafts show, and country-music concerts.

GETTING HERE AND AROUND

To fully enjoy the many surrounding attractions, you should get here by car. Arrive and depart via U.S. 395 or, from Nevada, U.S. 6. Eastern Sierra Transit Authority provides limited service to the town and nearby sites.

ESSENTIALS

VISITOR INFORMATION Bishop Chamber of Commerce. ✉ *690 N. Main St., at Park St., Bishop* ☎ *760/873–8405* 🌐 *bishopvisitor.com.*

👁 Sights

★ Laws Railroad Museum & Historical Site

MUSEUM VILLAGE | FAMILY | Laid-back and wholly nostalgic, this 11-acre celebrates the Carson and Colorado Railroad Company, which set up a narrow-gauge railyard here in 1883. Among the village's 50 rescued buildings—many containing the "modern amenities" of days gone by—are a post office, the original 1883 train depot, and a restored 1900 ranch house. On summer weekends and other select dates, you can also take a ride aboard Brill Car No. 5 from the Death Valley Railroad. ✉ *200 Silver Canyon Rd., off U.S. 6, 4½ miles north of town, Bishop* ☎ *760/873–5950* 🌐 *www.lawsmuseum.org* 🎟 *$10.*

🍴 Restaurants

Erick Schat's Bakkerÿ

$ | BAKERY | FAMILY | A bustling stop for motorists traveling to and from Mammoth Lakes, this shop is crammed with delicious pastries, cookies, rolls, and other baked goods. The biggest draw, though, is the sheepherder bread, a hand-shaped and stone hearth–baked sourdough that was introduced during the gold rush by immigrant Basque sheepherders in 1907. **Known for:** sheepherder bread and pastries; convenient place to stock up; hefty sandwiches. [$] *Average main: $12* ✉ *763 N. Main St.,*

near Park St., Bishop ☎ *760/873–7156* 🌐 *www.schatsbakery.com.*

Great Basin Bakery

$ | **AMERICAN** | **FAMILY** | Stop at this small, old-world-style community bakery for fresh and healthy salads, soups, sandwiches (made all day), bagels, artisan breads, cookies, pies, and pastries. Savor your goodies indoors and listen to local banter (it's a favorite gathering spot), or take them along to eat at a picnic spot while adventuring nearby. **Known for:** sandwiches on fresh-baked, house-made bread; all items made and packaged by hand; stellar pies and other desserts. [$] *Average main: $14* ✉ *275–D S. Main St., Bishop* ✣ *Corner of Lagoon St.* ☎ *760/873–9828* 🌐 *greatbasinbakerybishop.com.*

Looney Bean

$ | **CAFÉ** | **FAMILY** | Breakfast is served all day at this spot known as much for its cheerful atmosphere as for its large portions—including a breakfast burrito so packed with applewood-smoked bacon, cheddar cheese, eggs, and potatoes that it requires two hands to hold. For lunch, consider the coffeehouse burger with candied bacon or the chickpea curry bowl with roasted chicken and garnet yams over brown rice. **Known for:** vegan options; smoothies and artisan coffee; lemon-ricotta pancakes. [$] *Average main: $15* ✉ *399 N. Main St, Bishop* ☎ *760/873–3311* 🌐 *www.looneybeanbishop.com.*

🛏 Hotels

Bishop Creekside Inn

$$ | **B&B/INN** | This mountain-lodge-style hotel, where the river-rock lobby has a wonderfully large hearth, is a good base for exploring the town or going skiing and trout fishing nearby. **Pros:** nice pool; spacious and modern rooms; on-site restaurant. **Cons:** pets not allowed; faces a busy road; basic breakfast. [$] *Rooms from: $240* ✉ *725 N. Main St., Bishop* ☎ *760/872–3044, 800/273–3550* 🌐 *www.bishopcreeksideinn.com* 🛏 *87 rooms* 🍴 *Free Breakfast.*

Eastside Guesthouse & Bivy

$ | **HOTEL** | **FAMILY** | This former antiques store and car garage landed in the right hands with the Rose family, who transformed it into a boutique hotel for those on a hostel budget. **Pros:** use of full kitchen and barbecue area; picnic areas with hammocks; centrally located. **Cons:** not pet-friendly; noise carries between rooms; no blackout curtains. [$] *Rooms from: $120* ✉ *777 N. Main St., Bishop* ☎ *760/784–7077* 🌐 *eastsideguesthouse.com* 🛏 *17 rooms* 🍴 *No Meals.*

🏃 Activities

The Owens Valley is trout country; its glistening alpine lakes and streams are brimming with feisty rainbow, brown, brook, and golden trout. Good spots include Owens River, the Owens River gorge, and Pleasant Valley Reservoir. Although you can fish year-round here, some fishing is catch-and-release. Bishop is also the site of fishing derbies throughout the year, including the Blake Jones Trout Derby in March. Rock-climbing, mountain biking, and hiking are also popular Owens Valley outdoor activities.

FISHING

Reagan's Sporting Goods

FISHING | **FAMILY** | Stop at Reagan's to pick up bait, tackle, and fishing licenses and to find out where the fish are biting. The staff can also recommend guides. ✉ *963 N. Main St.* ☎ *760/872–3000* 🌐 *www.facebook.com/ReaganSportingGoods.*

MOUNTAIN CLIMBING

Sierra Mountain Center

MOUNTAIN CLIMBING | This outfitter's guided experiences include hiking, skiing, snowshoeing, rock-climbing, and mountain-biking trips for all levels of expertise. ✉ *200 S. Main St., Bishop* ☎ *760/873–8526* 🌐 *sierramountaincenter.com* 🎟 *From $150.*

Twin Lakes, in the Mammoth Lakes region, is a great place to unwind.

Sierra Mountain Guides

MOUNTAIN CLIMBING | Join expert guides on custom and scheduled alpine adventures, from backcountry skiing and mountaineering to backpacking and mountain running. Programs range from half-day forays to treks that last several weeks. ✉ *312 N. Main St., Bishop* ☎ *760/648–1122* ⊕ *sierramtnguides.com* 🎫 *From $170.*

Mammoth Lakes

43 miles northwest of Bishop, 30 miles south of the eastern edge of Yosemite National Park.

International real-estate developers joined forces with Mammoth Mountain Ski Area to transform the once sleepy town of Mammoth Lakes (elevation 7,800 feet) into an upscale ski destination. Relatively sophisticated dining and lodging options can be found at the Village at Mammoth complex, and multimillion-dollar renovations to tired motels and restaurants have revived the "downtown" area along Old Mammoth Road. Also here is the hoppin' Mammoth Rock 'n' Bowl, a two-story activity, dining, and entertainment complex. Winter is high season at Mammoth; in summer, the room rates drop.

GETTING HERE AND AROUND

The best way to get to Mammoth Lakes is by car. The town is about 2 miles west of U.S. 395 on Highway 203, signed as Main Street in Mammoth Lakes and Minaret Road west of town. In summer and early fall (until the first big snow), you can drive to Mammoth Lakes east through Yosemite National Park on scenic Tioga Pass Road. Signed as Highway 120 outside the park, this road connects to U.S. 395 north of Mammoth.

In summer, YARTS provides once-a-day public-transit service between Mammoth Lakes and Yosemite Valley. The shuttle buses of Eastern Sierra Transit Authority serve Mammoth Lakes and nearby tourist sites.

ESSENTIALS

HOTEL CONTACTS Mammoth Reservations.
✉ *Mammoth Lakes* ☎ *800/223–3032*
⊕ *mammothreservations.com.*

VISITOR INFORMATION Mammoth Lakes Visitor Center. ✉ *Welcome Center, 2510 Main St., near Sawmill Cutoff Rd., Mammoth Lakes* ☎ *760/934–2712, 888/466–2666* ⊕ *www.visitmammoth.com.*

Sights

★ Devils Postpile National Monument

NATURE SIGHT | FAMILY | Volcanic and glacial forces sculpted this formation of smooth, vertical basalt columns. For a bird's-eye view, take the short, steep trail to the top of a 60-foot cliff. To see the monument's second scenic wonder, **Rainbow Falls,** hike 2 miles past Devils Postpile. A branch of the San Joaquin River plunges more than 100 feet over a lava ledge here. When the water hits the pool below, sunlight turns the resulting mist into a spray of color. From mid-June to early September, day-use visitors must ride the shuttle bus from the Mammoth Mountain Ski Area to the monument. ✉ *Mammoth Lakes* ✛ *13 miles southwest of Mammoth Lakes off Minaret Rd. (Hwy. 203)* ☎ *760/934–2289, 760/872–1901 shuttle* ⊕ *www.nps.gov/depo* 🎫 *$10 per vehicle (allowed when the shuttle isn't running, usually early Sept.–mid-Oct.); $15 per person shuttle.*

June Lake Loop

SCENIC DRIVE | FAMILY | Heading south, U.S. 395 intersects the June Lake Loop. This gorgeous 16-mile drive follows an old glacial canyon past Grant, June, Gull, and Silver lakes before reconnecting with U.S. 395 on its way to Mammoth Lakes. ■TIP➔ **The loop is especially colorful in fall.** ✉ *Hwy. 158 W, Lee Vining.*

★ Mammoth Lakes Basin

BODY OF WATER | FAMILY | Mammoth's seven main lakes are popular for fishing and boating in summer, and a network of multiuse paths connects them to the North Village. First comes Twin Lakes, at the far end of which is Twin Falls, where water cascades 300 feet over a shelf of volcanic rock. Also popular are Lake Mary, the largest lake in the basin; Lake Mamie; and Lake George. ■TIP➔ **Horseshoe Lake is the only lake in which you can swim.** ✉ *Lake Mary Rd., off Hwy. 203, southwest of town, Mammoth Lakes.*

Mammoth Rock 'n' Bowl

OTHER ATTRACTION | FAMILY | A sprawling complex with sweeping views of the Sherwin Mountains, Mammoth Rock 'n' Bowl supplies one-stop recreation, entertainment, and dining. Downstairs are 12 bowling lanes; lounge areas; Ping-Pong and foosball tables; dartboards; and a casual bar-restaurant serving burgers, pizzas, and small plates. The upstairs floor has three golf simulators, a pro shop, and Mammoth Rock Brasserie, an upscale dining room and lounge. ■TIP➔ **If the weather's nice, sit out on the patio or the upstairs deck and enjoy the unobstructed vistas.** ✉ *3029 Chateau Rd., off Old Mammoth Rd., Mammoth Lakes* ☎ *760/934–4200* ⊕ *www.mammothrocknbowl.com* 🎫 *Bowling: from $20.*

Minaret Vista

NATURE SIGHT | FAMILY | The glacier-carved sawtooth spires of the Minarets, the remains of an ancient lava flow, are best viewed from the Minaret Vista. Pull off the road, park your car in the visitors' viewing area, and walk along the path, which has interpretive signs explaining the spectacular peaks, ridges, and valleys beyond. ✉ *Mammoth Lakes* ✛ *Off Hwy. 203, 1¼ mile west of Mammoth Mountain Ski Area and above San Joaquin Ridge, where the road from Main Lodge begins.*

★ Panorama Gondola

TRANSPORTATION | FAMILY | Even if you don't ski, ride the gondola to see Mammoth Mountain, the aptly named dormant volcano that gives Mammoth Lakes its name. The high-speed, eight-passenger gondolas—which serve skiers in winter and mountain bikers and sightseers in summer—whisk you from the chalet to the summit, where you can learn about the area's volcanic history in the interpretive center, have lunch in the café, and take in top-of-the-world views.

Standing high above the tree line, you can look west 150 miles across the state to the Coastal Range; to the east are the highest peaks of Nevada and the Great Basin beyond. You won't find a better view of the Sierra High Country without climbing. ⚠ **The air is thin at the 11,053-foot summit; carry water, and don't overexert yourself.** ✉ *Mammoth Lakes* ⊹ *Boarding area at Main Lodge, off Minaret Rd. (Hwy. 203), west of village center* ☎ *760/934–0745, 800/626–6684* ⊕ *www. mammothmountain.com* 🚡 *From $40.*

Village at Mammoth

TOWN | **FAMILY** | This huge complex of shops, restaurants, and luxury accommodations is the town's tourist center, and the venue for many special events—check the website for the weekly schedule. The complex is also the transfer hub for the free public transit system, with fixed routes throughout the Mammoth Lakes area. In winter, the free village gondola starts here and travels up the mountain to Canyon Lodge and back. ■**TIP**➔ **Unless you're staying in the village and have access to the on-site lots, parking can be very difficult here.** ✉ *100 Canyon Blvd., Mammoth Lakes* ⊕ *villageatmammoth.com.*

🍴 Restaurants

Mammoth Brewing Company

$ | **AMERICAN** | **FAMILY** | Brewing since 1995, this Village operation lures hungry patrons with 14 craft beers on tap, elevated grub from the on-site restaurant, tasting flights, a contemporary vibe at two spacious bar areas, and a beer garden. The dining menu changes constantly, but reflects a locals' twist on pub food with pork belly tacos,

black-currant-and-goat-cheese flatbread, or house-made sweet-potato tots. **Known for:** craft beer made on-site; upscale pub food; popular après-ski hangout. $ *Average main: $18* ✉ *18 Lake Mary Rd.* ⊹ *At intersection of Main St. and Minaret Rd.* ☎ *760/934–7141* ⊕ *mammothbrewingco. com.*

The Mogul

$$ | **STEAKHOUSE** | **FAMILY** | Come here for straightforward steaks—top sirloin, New York, filet mignon, prime rib, and T-bone. The only catch is that the waiters cook them, and the results vary depending on their skill level; but generally things go well, and kids love the experience. **Known for:** traditional alpine atmosphere; servers custom-grill your order; prime rib until it sell out. $ *Average main: $30* ✉ *1528 Tavern Rd., off Old Mammoth Rd., Mammoth Lakes* ☎ *760/934–3039* ⊕ *www. themogul.com* ⊗ *Closed Tues. No lunch.*

Petra's Bistro & Wine Bar

$$$ | **AMERICAN** | The ambience at Petra's—quiet, dark, and warm (there's a great fireplace)—complements its seductive meat and seafood entrées and smart selection of more than 250 wines from California and around the world. The menu impresses with duck confit, butternut squash gnocchi, and coq au vin. **Known for:** romantic atmosphere; top-notch service; lively downstairs bar. $ *Average main: $35* ✉ *Alpenhof Lodge, 6080 Minaret Rd., Mammoth Lakes* ☎ *760/934–3500* ⊕ *www.petrasbistro. com* ⊗ *No lunch. Closed Mon. and May– June 15.*

★ Restaurant at Convict Lake

$$$$ | **AMERICAN** | The lake is one of the most spectacular spots in the Eastern Sierra, and the food at this hotel restaurant lives up to the view. From pan-seared local trout and beef Wellington to rack of lamb and Long Island duck, the menu is refined, and there's an award-winning wine list to match. **Known for:** woodsy decor; homemade cheesecake; extensive wine list with reasonably priced European and California bottlings. [$] *Average main: $48* ✉ *Convict Lake Rd., Mammoth Lakes* ✣ *Off U.S. 395, 4 miles south of Mammoth Lakes* ☎ *760/934–3800* 🌐 *convictlake.com/fine-dining* 🕒 *No lunch.*

Toomey's

$$ | AMERICAN | FAMILY | A passionate baseball fan, chef Matt Toomey designed this casual space near the Village Gondola to resemble a dugout, and decorated it with baseball memorabilia. Swing by pre–outdoor adventure for coconut mascarpone pancakes or soft bagels topped with smoked trout and chipotle cream cheese. **Known for:** lobster taquitos and fish tacos; wild buffalo meat loaf; coconut mascarpone pancakes. [$] *Average main: $22* ✉ *6085 Minaret Rd., at the Village, Mammoth Lakes* ☎ *760/924–4408* 🌐 *www.toomeysmammoth.com.*

★ Vulcania

$$$ | ITALIAN | Smack in the heart of the Village, this bustling restaurant greets you with the sound of martini shakers and the smell of Italian classics prepared by Food Network/James Beard finalist/Michelin-starred brothers Michael and Bryan Voltaggio. Grab a table near the swanky bar, or nestle into one of the globe domes on the patio. **Known for:** thin-crust pizza; famous chefs; homemade pasta and creative cocktails. [$] *Average main: $31* ✉ *6201 Minaret Rd., Suite 240, Mammoth Lakes* ☎ *760/934–0669* 🌐 *www.mammothmountain.com/things-to-do/dining/vulcania* 🕒 *No lunch weekdays.*

★ The Warming Hut

$$ | AMERICAN | FAMILY | Warm up by a crackling fire in the stone fireplace while fueling up on healthy, made-from-scratch breakfast, lunch, and dinner dishes at this ski-lodge-style eatery. The flexible menu allows for lots of choice, including a DIY breakfast with more than 20 mix-and-match items, five types of hash, keto selections, grab-and-go sandwiches, salads, burgers, and soups. **Known for:** nearly everything made in-house, including ketchup; build-your-own pancake stack (batters, mix-ins, toppings); family-owned and-operated. [$] *Average main: $20* ✉ *343 Old Mammoth Rd., Mammoth Lakes* ☎ *760/965–0549* 🌐 *www.thewarminghutmammoth.com.*

Coffee and Quick Bites

Black Velvet Coffee

$ | CAFÉ | FAMILY | Start your day the way scores of locals do—with a stop at the slick Black Velvet espresso bar for Belgian waffles, baked treats, and coffee drinks made from small batches of beans roasted on-site. Then return in the afternoon to hang out in the upstairs wine bar (open 3 to 6) where tastings are offered Thursday–Sunday ($25). **Known for:** small-batch coffee roasting; small-lot wines by the glass; Belgian waffles. [$] *Average main: $6* ✉ *3343 Main St., Suite F* 🌐 *www.blackvelvetcoffee.com* 🕒 *No dinner.*

Hotels

Alpenhof Lodge

$$ | HOTEL | FAMILY | Across from the Village at Mammoth, this family-run hotel (with rooms and a couple of cabins) offers basic comforts and a few niceties such as attractive pine furniture. **Pros:** convenient for skiers; reasonable rates; excellent dinner at on-site restaurant, Petra's. **Cons:** some bathrooms are small; rooms above pub can be noisy; no elevator. [$] *Rooms from: $210* ✉ *6080 Minaret Rd., Box 1157, Mammoth Lakes* ☎ *760/934–6330, 800/828–0371* 🌐 *www.alpenhof-lodge.com* 🛏 *57 units* 🍴 *No Meals.*

★ Convict Lake Resort

$$ | RESORT | FAMILY | The cabins at this resort a 10-minute drive south from Mammoth Lakes range from rustic to modern and come with fully equipped kitchens, including coffeemakers and premium coffee. **Pros:** great views;

tranquil atmosphere; wildlife galore. **Cons:** two-night minimum stay weekdays and three nights on weekends; spotty Wi-Fi and cell service; too remote for some. [$] *Rooms from: $239 ✉ Convict Rd., Mammoth Lakes ✣ 2 miles off U.S. 395 ☎ 760/934–3800 🌐 convictlake.com 🛏 31 units 🍴 No Meals.*

★ Double Eagle Resort and Spa

$$ | RESORT | Lofty pines tower over this June Lake Loop spa retreat with rooms in four buildings overlooking a pond, as well as a three-bedroom house and knotty-pine two-bedroom cabins—all with fully equipped kitchens. **Pros:** pretty setting; spectacular indoor pool; 1½ miles from June Mountain Ski Area. **Cons:** expensive; remote; no in-room a/c. [$] *Rooms from: $299 ✉ 5587 Hwy. 158, Box 736, June Lake ☎ 760/648–7004 🌐 doubleeagle.com 🛏 34 units 🍴 No Meals.*

Juniper Springs Resort

$$ | RESORT | FAMILY | Tops for slope-side comfort, these condominium-style units have full kitchens and ski-in, ski-out access to the mountain at Eagle Lodge. **Pros:** bargain during summer; direct access to the slopes in winter; free shuttle to town in winter. **Cons:** no nightlife within walking distance; no a/c and not pet-friendly; property needs updating. [$] *Rooms from: $259 ✉ 4000 Meridian Blvd., Mammoth Lakes ☎ 760/924–1102, 800/626–6684 🌐 www.mammothmountain.com 🛏 184 units 🍴 No Meals.*

Mammoth Mountain Inn

$$ | RESORT | FAMILY | If you want to be within walking distance of the Mammoth Mountain Main Lodge, this is the place, and, in summer, the proximity to the gondola means you can hike and mountain bike to your heart's delight. **Pros:** great location; big rooms; a traditional place to stay. **Cons:** can be crowded in ski season; needs updating; not in the heart of town. [$] *Rooms from: $299 ✉ 1 Minaret Rd., Mammoth Lakes ☎ 760/934–2581, 800/626–6684 🌐 www.mammothmountain.com 🛏 266 units 🍴 No Meals.*

Sierra Nevada Resort

$$ | RESORT | FAMILY | This full-service resort has it all—Old Mammoth rustic elegance, a restaurant, bar, seasonal pool and whirlpool, and room and suite options in three buildings. **Pros:** cabins sleep up to six; walk to restaurants on property or downtown; 2022 remodel. **Cons:** must drive to the slopes; thin walls in older rooms; resort fee of $25 a night. [$] *Rooms from: $280 ✉ 164 Old Mammoth Rd., Mammoth Lakes ☎ 760/934–2515, 800/824–5132 🌐 www.thesierranevadaresort.com 🛏 149 units 🍴 No Meals.*

★ Tamarack Lodge & Resort

$$ | RESORT | FAMILY | On the edge of the John Muir Wilderness Area, where cross-country ski trails lace the woods, this 1924 lodge looks like something out of a snow globe. **Pros:** cabins are pet-friendly; rustic and eco-sensitive; many nearby outdoor activities. **Cons:** high price tag; shared bathrooms for some main lodge rooms; spartan furnishings in lodge rooms. [$] *Rooms from: $250 ✉ 163 Twin Lakes Rd., Mammoth Lakes ✣ Off Hwy. 203 ☎ 760/934–2442, 800/626–6684 🌐 www.mammothmountain.com 🛏 46 units 🍴 No Meals.*

The Village Lodge

$$ | RESORT | FAMILY | With their exposed timbers and peaked roofs, these four-story condo buildings at the epicenter of Mammoth's dining and nightlife scene pay homage to Alpine style. **Pros:** in the heart of the Village; spacious condos available in studios to three-bedrooms; underground parking garage. **Cons:** pricey; can be noisy outside; somewhat sterile decor. [$] *Rooms from: $305 ✉ 1111 Forest Trail, Mammoth Lakes ☎ 760/934–1982, 800/626–6684 🌐 www.mammothmountain.com 🛏 276 units 🍴 No Meals.*

★ Westin Monache Resort

$$$ | RESORT | FAMILY | On a hill just steps from the Village at Mammoth, the Westin provides full-service comfort and amenities close to restaurants, entertainment, and free public transportation. **Pros:** full bar, pool, 24-fitness center; prime location; free gondola to the slopes is across the street. **Cons:** long, steep stairway down to village; added resort fee; large property with confusing layout. [$] *Rooms from: $359* ✉ *50 Hillside Dr., Mammoth Lakes* ☎ *760/934–0400, 760/934–4686* 🌐 *www.marriott.com* 🛏 *230 rooms* 🍴 *No Meals.*

Nightlife

The Village at Mammoth has several rockin' bars and clubs, and concerts and other events occur throughout the year on the mountain. In mid-July, you can enjoy two nights of free live music and a Wine Walk ($45) during the Mammoth JazzFest (🌐 *mammothjazzfest.org*) in the Village. The Mammoth Lakes Festival of Beer and Bluesapalooza (🌐 *mammothbluesbrewsfest.com*) takes place over a long weekend in early August.

Bar Sierra

BARS | The upscale lounge at the Sierra Nevada Resort is where locals gather for happy hour by the fire. ✉ *202 Old Mammoth Rd., Mammoth Lakes* ☎ *760/934–2515* 🌐 *www.thesierranevadaresort.com* ⏲ *Closed Mon.–Wed.*

Clocktower Cellar

BREWPUBS | Nearly 30 beers on tap and more than 50 by the bottle—plus 160 whiskeys and an extensive pub menu—ensure plenty of variety at this lively gathering spot across from the Village Gondola. Open for three decades, this underground bar is the best spot to go for an extended après-ski. Be sure to look up at the hundreds of bottle-cap tops pressed in the ceiling by beer-consuming customers. ✉ *6080 Minaret Rd., Mammoth Lakes* ☎ *760/934–2725* 🌐 *www.clocktowercellar.com.*

Lakanuki

DANCE CLUBS | Sip mai tais at the tiki bar at Lakanuki, which is in the Village near the gondola. If you're looking for DJs and dancing, this is the closest thing to a nightclub you'll find in Mammoth. ✉ *6201 Minaret Rd., Mammoth Lakes* ☎ *760/934–7447.*

Activities

BIKING

★ Mammoth Bike Park

BIKING | FAMILY | This park at the Mammoth Mountain Ski Area opens when the snow melts, usually by July, and has 80 miles of single-track trails—from mellow to superchallenging. Chairlifts and shuttles provide trail access, and rentals are available. ✉ *10001 Minaret Rd., Mammoth Lakes* ☎ *760/934–0677, 800/626–6684* 🌐 *www.mammothmountain.com* 🎟 *$55 day pass.*

FISHING

The main fishing season runs from the last Saturday in April until November 15, but there are opportunities for catch-and-release fishing in winter. Crowley Lake is the area's top trout-fishing spot; Convict Lake, June Lake, and the lakes of the Mammoth Basin are other prime spots. One of the best trout rivers is the super-scenic Upper Owens River, near the east side of Crowley Lake. Hot Creek, a designated Wild Trout Stream, is renowned for fly-fishing (catch-and-release only).

Kittredge Sports

FISHING | FAMILY | This outfit rents rods and reels and conducts guided trips. ✉ *3218 Main St., at Forest Trail, Mammoth Lakes* ☎ *760/934–7566* 🌐 *kittredgesports.com.*

Sierra Drifters Guide Service

FISHING | FAMILY | To maximize your time on the water, get tips from local anglers, or better yet, book a guided fishing trip,

Why Is There So Much Snow?

The Sierra Nevada has some of the deepest snow anywhere in North America. In winter, houses literally get buried, and homeowners have to build tunnels to their front doors (though many install enclosed wooden walkways). In the high country, it's not uncommon for a single big storm to bring 10 feet of snow and for 30 feet of snow to accumulate at the height of the season. Record years like the 2022/23 season brought in more than 70 feet of snow. In the enormous bowls of Mammoth Mountain, you might ski past a tiny pine that looks like a miniature Christmas tree—until you remember that more than 30 feet of tree is under the snow.

To understand the weather, you have to understand the terrain. The Sierra Nevada is marked by a gentle western rise from sea level to the Sierra crest, which tops out at a whopping 14,494 feet at Sequoia National Park's Mt. Whitney, the highest point in the continental United States. On the eastern side of the crest, at the escarpment, the mountains drop sharply—as much as 5,000 feet—giving way to the Great Basin and the high-mountain deserts of Nevada and Utah.

When winter storms blow in off the Pacific, carrying vast stores of water with them, they race across the relatively flat, 100-mile-wide Central Valley. As they ascend the wall of mountains, though, the decrease in temperature and the increase in pressure on the clouds force them to release their water. Between October and April, that means snow—lots of it. Storms can get hung up on the peaks for days, dumping foot after foot of the stuff. By the time they finally cross over the range and into the Great Basin, there isn't much moisture left for the lower elevations on the eastern side. This is why, if you cross the sierra eastward on your way to U.S. 395, you'll notice that brightly colored wildflowers and forest-green trees give way to pale-green sagebrush and brown sand as you drop out of the mountains.

California's coastal cities and farmlands depend heavily on the water from the Sierra Nevada snowpack. Most of the spring and summer runoff from the melting snows is caught in lower-elevation reservoirs and routed throughout the state via a system of levees and aqueducts, which you'll no doubt see in the foothills and Central Valley, to the west of the range. But much of the water remains in the mountains, forming lakes, most notably giant Lake Tahoe to the north, Mono Lake to the east, and the thousands of little lakes along the Sierra Crest. These are an essential part of the ecosystem, providing water for birds, fish, and plant life.

contact Sierra Drifters. ✉ *Mammoth Lakes* ☎ *760/935–4250* ⊕ *sierradrifters.com.*

GOLF
Sierra Star Golf Course
GOLF | At this picture-perfect spot nestled against the forest, you might see deer and bears strolling the fairways. This is California's highest-elevation golf course. ✉ *2001 Sierra Star Pkwy., Mammoth Lakes* ☎ *760/924–4653* ⊕ *www.mammothmountain.com* ⛳ *$165* ⛳. *18 holes, 6708 yards, par 70* ☉ *Closed early Oct.– late May.*

HIKING

Hiking in Mammoth is stellar, especially along the trails that wind through alpine scenery around the Lakes Basin. Carry lots of water; and remember, the air is thin at 8,000-plus feet.

You can pick up trail maps and permits for backpacking in wilderness areas at the Mammoth Lakes Visitor Center just east of town. Wilderness permits can also be purchased online at ⊕ www. recreation.gov. For descriptions of more than 300 miles of trails—as well as maps and a wealth of information on recreation in Mammoth Lakes and the Inyo National Forest in all seasons—visit the Mammoth Lakes Trail System website (⊕ www.mammothtrails.org).

★ Convict Lake Loop

HIKING & WALKING | FAMILY | This 2.8-mile trail loops gently around deep blue Convict Lake, a popular site for anglers. Feast your eyes on stunning views of tall peaks, glistening water, and aspen and cottonwood groves while you hike. *Easy.* ⊠ *Trailhead: At Convict Lake, 9 miles south of Mammoth Lakes, Mammoth Lakes.*

Duck Lake

HIKING & WALKING | This popular and busy trail (11 miles round-trip) heads up Coldwater Canyon along Mammoth Creek, past a series of spectacular lakes and wildflower meadows over 10,797-foot Duck Pass to dramatic Duck Lake, which eventually links up with the John Muir Trail. *Difficult.* ⊠ *Trailhead: Coldwater Campground, Mammoth Lakes.*

Emerald Lake and Sky Meadows

HIKING & WALKING | The first part of this trail travels through shady pine forest along Coldwater Creek to bright-green Emerald Lake (1.8 miles round-trip). Extend the hike by climbing a trail along an inlet stream up to Gentian Meadow and Sky Meadows (4 miles round-trip), especially beautiful in July and August when various alpine wildflowers, fed by snowmelt, are at their peak splendor. *Moderate.* ⊠ *Trailhead: Coldwater Campground, Mammoth Lakes.*

Minaret Falls

HIKING & WALKING | FAMILY | Hike along portions of both the Pacific Crest and John Muir trails on this scenic trail (3 miles round-trip), which leads to Devil's Postpile, Minaret Falls, and natural volcanic springs. This is a good family hike, especially in late summer when the water has receded a bit and kids can climb boulders and splash around. *Easy.* ⊠ *Trailhead: At Devil's Postpile National Monument, Mammoth Lakes.*

HORSEBACK RIDING

Stables around Mammoth are typically open from June through September.

Mammoth Lakes Pack Outfit

HORSEBACK RIDING | FAMILY | This company runs day and overnight horseback and mule trips and will shuttle you to the high country. ⊠ *Lake Mary Rd., between Twin Lakes and Lake Mary, Mammoth Lakes* ☎ *760/934–2434* ⊕ *www.mammothpack. com* 🖃 *From $80.*

McGee Creek Pack Station

HORSEBACK RIDING | FAMILY | These folks customize pack trips or will shuttle you to camp alone. ⊠ *2990 McGee Creek Rd., Crowley Lake* ☎ *760/935–4324* ⊕ *mcgeecreekpackstation.com* 🖃 *From $65.*

ROCK CLIMBING

Via Ferrata

ROCK CLIMBING | In Europe, a Via Ferrata is a protected climbing network that allows people to experience the thrills of rock climbing and mountaineering without as much risk. Mammoth's version has six different routes of varying ability, with steel cables, iron rungs, and a suspended bridge, all permanently affixed to the rock. The fully guided tour begins with a gondola ride up the mountain. Clip yourself into a cable and climb securely to sweeping views of the Sierra Nevada range. If time and group ability allow, you can follow multiple routes during a session. No climbing experience is required. ⊠ *Mammoth Mountain, 10001 Minaret Rd., Mammoth Lakes* ☎ *800/626–6684* ⊕ *www.mammothmountain.com* ✉ *From $199.*

SKIING AND SNOWBOARDING

In winter, call the Snow Report (☎ *760/934–7669 or 888/766–9778*) for information about Mammoth weather conditions.

AREAS

June Mountain Ski Area

SKIING & SNOWBOARDING | FAMILY | Snowboarders especially dig June Mountain, a compact, low-key resort north of Mammoth Mountain. Several beginner-to-intermediate terrain areas—including the Surprise Fun Zone and Buckey's Playground—are for both skiers and boarders. There's rarely a line for the lifts here: if you must ski on a weekend and want to avoid the crowds, this is the place to come, and in a storm it's better protected from wind and blowing snow than Mammoth is. (If it starts to storm, you can use your Mammoth ticket at June.) The services include a rental-and-repair shop, a ski school, and a sports shop. There's food, but the options are better at Mammoth. **Facilities:** 35 trails on 1,400 acres, rated 35% beginner, 45% intermediate, 20% advanced; base 7,545 feet, summit 10,190 feet; 7 lifts. ■**TIP→ Kids 12 and under ski and ride free.** ⊠ *3819 Hwy. 158/June Lake Loop, June Lake* ✛ *Off U.S. 395, 22 miles northwest of Mammoth* ☎ *760/648–7733, 888/586–3686* ⊕ *www.junemountain.com* ✉ *From $129; Ikon Pass is valid at June Mountain.*

★ Mammoth Mountain Ski Area

SKIING & SNOWBOARDING | FAMILY | The views from the 11,053-foot summit of one of the West's largest and best ski areas are some of the most stunning in the Sierra. Below, you'll find a 6½-mile-wide swath of groomed boulevards and canyons, as well as pockets of tree-skiing and a dozen vast bowls. Snowboarders are everywhere on the slopes; there are seven outstanding freestyle terrain parks of varying difficulty, with jumps, rails, tabletops, and giant super pipes—this is the location of several international snowboarding competitions, and, in summer, mountain-bike meets. Mammoth's season begins in November and often lingers into July. Lessons and equipment are available, and there's a children's ski and snowboard school. Mammoth runs free shuttle-bus routes around town and to the ski area, and the Village Gondola runs from the Village complex to Canyon Lodge. However, only overnight guests are allowed to park at the Village for more than a few hours. **Facilities:** 155 trails; 3,500 acres; 3,100-foot vertical drop; 25 lifts. ⊠ *10001 Minaret Rd., Mammoth Lakes* ✛ *Rte. 203, off U.S. 395 west of Mammoth Lakes* ☎ *760/934–2571, 800/626–6684, 760/934–0687 shuttle* ⊕ *www.mammothmountain.com* ✉ *From $179* ☞ *Ikon Pass is valid at Mammoth Mountain.*

Tamarack Cross Country Ski Center

SKIING & SNOWBOARDING | FAMILY | Trails at the center, adjacent to Tamarack Lodge, meander around several lakes. Rentals are available. ⊠ *163 Twin Lakes Rd., Mammoth Lakes* ✛ *Off Hwy. 203* ☎ *760/934–5293, 760/934–2442* ⊕ *www.tamaracklodge.com* ✉ *From $99 all-inclusive day rate.*

Woolly's Tube Park & Snow Play

SNOW SPORTS | FAMILY | Ride a lift to the top of the hill, and whoosh down in a high-speed snow tube as often as you like during a 1¼-hour session. The park has six lanes, a heated deck, and a snack shop. Discounts are available for a second session if you're not ready to stop riding. Little ones can hang out in the snow play area with sleds and saucers. In 2023, the tube park added snowmaking fan guns, an elevated conveyor lift, and a larger snow-play area. ✉ *9000 Minaret Rd., Mammoth Lakes* ☎ *800/626–6684 reservations, 760/934–7533 direct line* ⊕ *www.mammothmountain.com* 🖭 *From $45; play area $25.*

RENTALS
Black Tie Ski Rentals
SKIING & SNOWBOARDING | FAMILY | Skiers and snowboarders love this rental outfit whose staffers will deliver and custom-fit equipment for free. They also offer slope-side assistance. ✉ *501 Old Mammoth Rd., Mammoth Lakes* ☎ *760/934–7009* ⊕ *mammoth.blacktieskis.com.*

Footloose
SKIING & SNOWBOARDING | FAMILY | When the U.S. Ski Team visits Mammoth and needs boot adjustments, its members head to Footloose, the best place in town—and possibly all California—for ski-boot rentals and sales, as well as custom insoles. ✉ *3043 Main St., at Mammoth Rd., Mammoth Lakes* ☎ *760/934–2400* ⊕ *www.footloosesports.com.*

Kittredge Sports
SKIING & SNOWBOARDING | FAMILY | Advanced skiers should consider this outfit, which has been around since the 1960s. ✉ *3218 Main St., Mammoth Lakes* ☎ *760/934–7566* ⊕ *kittredgesports.com.*

SNOWMOBILING
Mammoth Snowmobile Adventures
SNOW SPORTS | FAMILY | Mammoth Snowmobile Adventures conducts three guided tours along wooded trails. You can choose between a single or a double snowmobile. ✉ *10200 Minaret Rd., Mammoth Lakes* ☎ *760/934–9645, 800/626–6684* ⊕ *www.mammothmountain.com* 🖭 *From $160* ☞ *Reservations required 24 hrs in advance.*

Chapter 8

SACRAMENTO AND THE GOLD COUNTRY

8

Updated by
Daniel Mangin

⊙ Sights   🍴 Restaurants   🛏 Hotels   ⊛ Shopping   ▼ Nightlife

★★★★☆   ★★★★☆   ★★★★☆   ★★★☆☆   ★★★☆☆

WELCOME TO SACRAMENTO AND THE GOLD COUNTRY

TOP REASONS TO GO

★ **Gold rush:** Marshall Gold Discovery State Park is where it all started—it's a must-see—but there are historic and modern gems all along California Highway 49 from Nevada City to Jamestown.

★ **State capital:** Easygoing Sacramento offers sights like the Capitol and historic Old Sacramento.

★ **Bon appétit:** Sacramento has emerged as a foodie destination, but its celebrations of food, drink, and culture date back to the gold-rush parade of immigrants.

★ **Wine tasting:** With bucolic scenery and friendly tasting rooms, El Dorado County and the Shenandoah Valley are winning acclaim for their diverse offerings.

★ **Rivers, sequoias, and caverns:** Natural beauty here is rich (stream beds are still lined with gold), high (sequoias in Calaveras Big Trees State Park), and deep (the main chamber at Moaning Caverns could hold the Statue of Liberty).

The Gold Country is a sizable rural destination popular with those seeking a reasonably priced escape from Southern California and the Bay Area. Sacramento, Davis, Winters, and Lodi are in enormous valleys just west of the Sierra Nevada range. Foothills communities along Highway 49 tell the gold-rush story, support the nascent wine-growing scene, or serve as gateways to Yosemite or Lake Tahoe. A few function as all three.

1 **Sacramento.** The capital also serves as a regional hub.

2 **Davis.** Agriculture meets academics in this university town.

3 **Winters.** A foodie haven perfect for a day trip.

4 **Lodi.** "Zinfandel Capital of the World" excels at many other wines.

5 **Nevada City.** "Queen of the Northern Mines" is a real beauty.

6 **Grass Valley.** Here, the Empire Mine thrived for years.

7 **Auburn.** Old Town charms with steep hills, cobblestone streets.

8 **Coloma.** The gold rush started here.

9 **Placerville.** Over a million people visit Apple Hill each year.

10 **Plymouth.** Vines date from 1869 in nearby Shenandoah Valley.

11 **Amador City.** Shops hold this former mining town's treasures these days.

12 **Sutter Creek.** Much gold-rush history unfolded here.

13 **Volcano.** Explorable caverns lie just outside town.

14 **Jackson.** Two mines produced $70 million in gold in these parts.

15 **Angels Camp.** Mark Twain wrote about this town's famous frog-jumping contest.

16 **Murphys.** Main Street feels upscale yet unpretentious; redwoods and caverns await nearby.

17 **Columbia.** Experience gold-rush living history in this throwback village.

18 **Jamestown.** Hollywood often films in or around Railtown 1897.

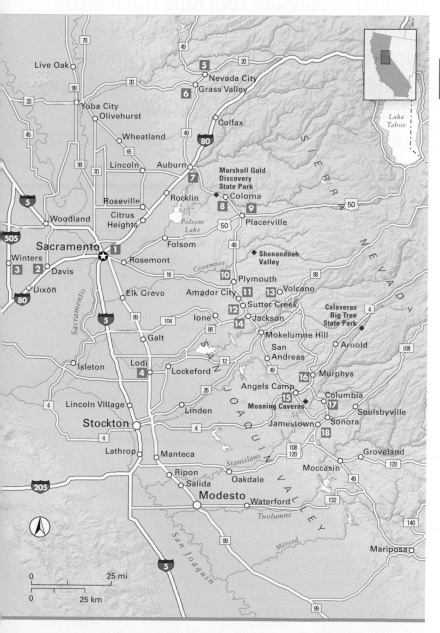

Live Oak

Yuba City
Olivehurst

Wheatland

Lincoln

Auburn

Roseville

Rocklin

Woodland

Citrus
Heights

Folsom Lake

Sacramento

Winters

Davis

Dixon

Rosemont

Elk Grove

Isleton

Lodi

Lockeford

Lincoln Village

Linden

Stockton

Lathrop

Manteca

Ripon

Salida

Oakdale

Modesto

Waterford

Nevada City
Grass Valley

Colfax

Marshall Gold
Discovery
State Park

Coloma

Placerville

Shenandoah
Valley

Plymouth

Volcano

Amador City

Sutter Creek

Jackson

Ione

Galt

Mokelumne Hill

San
Andreas

Calaveras
Big Tree
State Park

Arnold

Murphys

Angels Camp

Moaning Caverns

Columbia

Soulsbyville

Jamestown

Sonora

Moccasin

Groveland

Mariposa

Lake
Tahoe

Woodland

Folsom

Rosemont

Cosumnes

Amador City

SIERRA NEVADA

SAN JOAQUIN VALLEY

Sacramento

San Joaquin

Stanislaus

Tuolumne

Merced

0   25 mi
0   25 km

The Gold Country is one of California's less expensive destinations, a region of the Sierra Nevada foothills filled with natural and cultural pleasures. Visitors come for the boomtowns and ghost towns, art galleries and antiques shops, "farm-to-fork" cuisine and delicious wines, and atmospheric inns and historic hotels.

Spring brings wildflowers, and in fall the hills are colored by bright red berries and changing leaves. Because it offers so many outdoor diversions, the Gold Country is a great place to take kids. Sacramento is an ethnically diverse city. Many present-day immigrants are relatively recent arrivals, but the capital city has absorbed waves of newcomers since 1848, when James Marshall turned up a gold nugget in the American River. At the time, Mexico and the United States were still wrestling for ownership of what would become the Golden State. Marshall's discovery provided the incentive for the United States to tighten its grip on the region, and prospectors from all over the world came to seek their fortunes in the Mother Lode, a vein of gold-bearing quartz that stretched 150 miles across the foothills.

As gold fever seized the nation, California's population of 15,000 swelled to 265,000 within three years. The mostly young male adventurers who arrived in search of gold—the '49ers—became part of a culture that discarded many of the button-down conventions of the eastern states. It was also a violent time. Yankee prospectors chased Mexican miners

off their claims, and California's leaders initiated a plan to exterminate the local Native American population.

The gold-rush boom lasted scarcely 20 years, but it changed California forever, producing 546 mining towns, of which fewer than 250 remain. The hills of the Gold Country were alive, not only with prospecting and mining but also with business, the arts, gambling, and a fair share of crime. Opera houses went up alongside brothels, and the California State Capitol, in Sacramento, was built partly with the gold dug out of the hills.

MAJOR REGIONS

Sacramento and Ag Country. The gateway to the Gold Country, the seat of state government, and a key "ag" (agricultural) hub, Sacramento plays many contemporary roles. About 2.4 million people live in the metropolitan area, whose sunshine, mild climate, and fertile soil are responsible for the region's current riches: fresh and bountiful food and high-quality wines. There's a growing local craft-beer scene, too. Visits to Sacramento and nearby towns like Davis and Winters provide the broad agricultural perspective, Lodi the wine-making one. Wineries here earn national recognition, yet they're without the high prices of Napa and Sonoma.

Highway 49. Sacramento's museums provide an excellent introduction to the Gold Country's illustrious history, but the region's heart lies along Highway 49, which winds the approximately 300-mile north–south length of the famed Mother Lode mining area past or near the following towns: Nevada City, Grass Valley, Auburn, Coloma, Placerville, Plymouth, Amador City, Sutter Creek, Jackson, Angels Camp, Murphys, Columbia, and Jamestown. Some of these towns can be quiet early in the week, but most attractions and businesses are open from Thursday through Sunday. You can explore parts of the Gold Country as an easy day trip from Sacramento, but to immerse yourself in this storied setting, consider staying overnight for at least a day or two. On days when it's not too hot or cold, the highway—a hilly, twisting two-lane road—begs for a convertible with the top down.

Planning

Getting Here and Around

AIR

Sacramento International Airport (SMF) is served by airlines that include Aeromexico, Air Canada, Alaska, American, Delta, Frontier, Hawaiian, JetBlue, Southwest, and United. A taxi from SMF to Downtown Sacramento costs about $40; ride-sharing services often cost less. Public buses are also an option.

CONTACTS Sacramento International Airport. ⊠ 6900 Airport Blvd., Sacramento ✛ 12 miles northwest of Downtown off I–5 ☎ 916/929–5411 ⊕ sacramento.aero/smf.

BUS AND TRAIN

Greyhound serves Sacramento from San Francisco and Los Angeles. Sacramento Regional Transit serves the capital area with buses and light-rail vehicles. Yolobus public transit connects SMF airport and Downtown Sacramento, West Sacramento, and Davis. Amtrak serves Sacramento and Davis.

CONTACTS Sacramento Regional Transit. ⊠ Sacramento ☎ 916/321–2877 ⊕ www.sacrt.com. **Yolobus.** ⊠ Sacramento ☎ 530/666–2877, 916/371–2877 ⊕ yolobus.com.

CAR

Interstate 5 (north–south) and I–80 (east–west) are the two main routes into and out of Sacramento. From there, three highways fan out toward the east, all intersecting with historic Highway 49: I–80 heads northeast 34 miles to Auburn; U.S. 50 goes east 40 miles to Placerville; and Highway 16 angles southeast 45 miles to Plymouth. Two-lane Highway 49 winds and climbs through foothills and valleys, linking the principal Gold Country towns. Traveling by car is the only practical way to explore the region.

Hotels

Downtown Sacramento has boutique and full-service hotels as well as a few small inns. Chain motels predominate in Auburn, Grass Valley, and other larger towns along Highway 49, but you'll also find restored historic hotels and luxurious bed-and-breakfasts throughout the Gold Country.

Restaurants

Sacramento chefs capitalize on inland California's agricultural bounty. American, Italian, Chinese, and Mexican restaurants remain common, but Gold Country chefs also prepare ambitious international and contemporary regional cuisine. Grass

Valley's meat- and vegetable-stuffed *pasties,* introduced by 19th-century gold miners from Cornwall, England, are one of the area's more unusual treats.

⇨ *Restaurant and hotel reviews have been shortened. For full information, visit Fodors.com. Restaurant prices are the average cost of a main course at dinner, or if dinner is not served, at lunch. Hotel prices are the lowest cost of a standard double room in high season.*

What It Costs

	$	$$	$$$	$$$$
RESTAURANTS				
	under $20	$20–$30	$31–$40	over $40
HOTELS				
	under $200	$200–$350	$351–$500	over $500

Visitor Information

EVENTS AND ENTERTAINMENT Sacramento 365. ✉ *Sacramento* ⊕ *www. sacramento365.com.*

TOURISM AGENCIES Greater Grass Valley Chamber of Commerce. ✉ *128 E. Main St., Grass Valley* ☎ *530/273–4667* ⊕ *www. grassvalleychamber.com.* **Tuolumne County Visitors Bureau.** ✉ *193 S. Washington St., Sonora* ☎ *209/533–4420, 800/446–1333* ⊕ *www.visittuolumne.com.* **Visit Amador.** ✉ *109 Main St., Jackson* ☎ *209/267–9249* ⊕ *www.visitamador.com.* **Visit El Dorado.** ✉ *542 Main St., Placerville* ☎ *530/621– 5885* ⊕ *visit-eldorado.com.*

When to Go

The Gold Country is most pleasant in spring, when the wildflowers are in bloom, and in fall. Summers can be hot in the valley (temperatures of 100°F are fairly common), so head for the hills. Sacramento winters tend to be cool, with occasionally foggy or rainy days. Throughout the year, Gold Country towns stage community and cultural celebrations. In December, many towns are decked out for the holidays.

Sacramento

87 miles northeast of San Francisco, 384 miles north of Los Angeles.

All around the Golden State's seat of government you'll experience echoes of the gold-rush days, most notably in Old Sacramento, whose wooden sidewalks and horse-drawn carriages on cobblestone streets lend the waterfront district a 19th-century feel. The California State Railroad Museum and other venues hold artifacts of state and national significance, and historic buildings house shops and restaurants. River cruises and train rides are fun family diversions.

Due east of Old Sacramento is Downtown, where landmarks include the Capitol building and the surrounding Capitol Park. Golden 1 Center, a sports and concert venue, is part of DOCO, short for Downtown Commons, which also includes shops, restaurants, hotels, and grassy and concrete gathering spaces.

Farther east, starting at about 15th Street, lies Midtown, a mix of Victorian edifices, ultramodern lofts, and innovative restaurants and cozy wine bars. A few intersections are jumping most evenings when the weather's good; they include the corner of 20th and L streets in what's known as Lavender Heights, the center of the city's gay and lesbian community.

GETTING HERE AND AROUND
Most people drive to Sacramento and get around by car. Lyft and Uber tend to work out better than the cab options. Sacramento Regional Transit buses and light-rail vehicles serve the area. Bus 30 links Old Sacramento, Midtown, and Sutter's Fort.

Assuming that traffic isn't a factor (though it often is), Sacramento is a 90-minute drive from San Francisco and a seven-hour drive from Los Angeles. Parking garages serve Old Sacramento and other tourist spots; finding on-street parking Downtown can be challenging.

TRANSPORTATION CONTACTS Sacramento Regional Transit. ✉ *Sacramento* ☏ *916/321–2877* ⊕ *www.sacrt.com.*

ESSENTIALS

VISITOR INFORMATION Sacramento Visitor Center. ✉ *1000 2nd St., Sacramento* ☏ *916/808–7644* ⊕ *www.oldsacramento. com.* **Visit Sacramento.** ✉ *1608 I St., Sacramento* ☏ *916/808–7777* ⊕ *www. visitsacramento.com.*

Sights

California Automobile Museum

HISTORY MUSEUM | FAMILY | More than 150 vehicles—from Model Ts, Hudsons, and Studebakers to modern-day electric-powered ones—are on display at this museum that pays tribute to automotive history and car culture. Check out a replica of Henry Ford's 1896 Quadricycle and a 1920s roadside café and garage exhibit. The museum is south of Downtown and Old Sacramento. ✉ *2200 Front St., Downtown* ☏ *916/442–6802* ⊕ *www.calautomuseum. org* ☜ *$12* ⊘ *Closed Tues.*

California Museum

HISTORY MUSEUM | FAMILY | Showcasing longtime and temporary residents who helped elevate the Golden State, this museum contains permanent exhibits covering statehood, the experiences of California Native Americans, life for Japanese Americans in World War II internment camps, and the impact of women. The California Hall of Fame honors Walt Disney, Jackie Robinson, Bruce Lee, Amelia Earhart, writer and Sacramento native Joan Didion, and other familiar names. ✉ *1020 O St., at 11th St., Downtown* ☏ *916/653–7524* ⊕ *californiamuseum.org* ☜ *$10* ⊘ *Closed Mon.*

★ California State Railroad Museum

HISTORY MUSEUM | FAMILY | Sprawling over three floors, this museum celebrates the history of trains from their 19th-century English origins to the pre–jet age glory days of rail travel. A permanent exhibit details Chinese laborers' contributions to the transcontinental railroad's completion (Sacramento was the western terminus). Another section contains one of several gold spikes issued to commemorate the joining in Utah of the west-to-east Central Pacific and east-to-west Union Pacific lines.

Up to 21 of the museum's railroad cars and engines—among them Pullman-style cars and steam locomotives—are on exhibit, and there are interactive displays and a play area for kids. Two nearby affiliated attractions (both free) worth a peek if they're open are the re-creation of the circa-1876 Central Pacific passenger station (930 Front Street) and the Huntington, Hopkins & Company Hardware exhibit (113 I Street), a facsimile of a 19th-century hardware store. ✉ *125 I St., at 2nd St., Old Sacramento* ☏ *916/323–9280* ⊕ *www.californiarailroad.museum* ☜ *$12.*

★ Capitol

GOVERNMENT BUILDING | FAMILY | Built between 1860 and 1874 and topped by a 128-foot gilded dome, the Capitol functions as a working museum and, since 1869, the active seat of California's government. When it's open, you can wander freely past reproductions of century-old state offices or join a guided tour. Portraits of former governors on display include Arnold Schwarzenegger, Ronald Reagan, Earl Warren (later Chief Justice of the United States), and Edmund G. "Jerry" Brown, whose father was also governor. Tours of the 40-acre Capitol Park, which contains a rose garden, a fragrant display of camellias (Sacramento's city flower), and more than 1,000 types of trees from around the world, take place on Sunday and Wednesday. ✉ *1315*

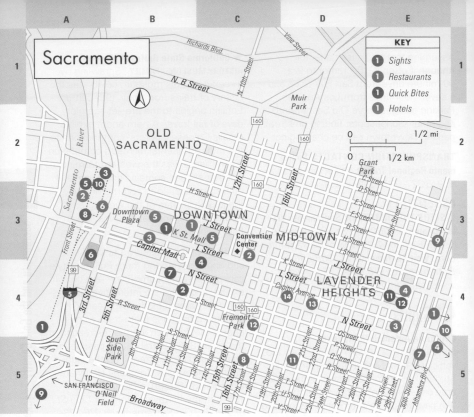

Sacramento

KEY
- 1 Sights
- 1 Restaurants
- 1 Quick Bites
- 1 Hotels

10th St., at L St., Downtown ☎ 916/324–0333 ⊕ capitolmuseum.ca.gov ◪ Free ⊙ Closed weekends.

Central Pacific Railroad Passenger Station

TRAIN/TRAIN STATION | FAMILY | At this reconstructed 1876 station there's rolling stock to admire and a typical waiting room. On some days, a train departs from the freight depot, south of the passenger station, making a 50-minute out-and-back trip that starts along the banks of the Sacramento River. ■**TIP→ Cookies and hot chocolate are served aboard sellout Polar Express rides (book way ahead) between Thanksgiving and Christmas.** ⊠ 930 Front St., at J St., Old Sacramento ☎ 916/445–5995 ⊕ www.californiarailroad.museum ◪ Train rides from $15 ⊙ Hrs vary.

★ Crocker Art Museum

ART MUSEUM | Established in 1885, Sacramento's premier fine-arts museum specializes in California art, European master drawings, and international ceramics. A highlight is the magnificent Great Canyon of the Sierra, Yosemite (1871) by Thomas Hill. Some works are displayed in two architecturally significant 19th-century structures: the original Italianate Crocker residence and a villa-like gallery. A contemporary, 125,000-square-foot space hosts outstanding traveling exhibitions. ⊠ 216 O St., at 3rd St., Downtown ☎ 916/808–1184 ⊕ crockerart.org ◪ $15 ⊙ Closed Mon. and Tues.

★ Leland Stanford Mansion State Historic Park

HISTORIC HOME | FAMILY | Leland Stanford, a railroad baron, California governor, and U.S. senator, expanded the original 1856 two-story row house on this site into a 19,186-square-foot mansion. The opulent space is open for touring except on days when California's governor hosts official events. After the death of Stanford's wife, Jane, Roman Catholic nuns transformed the mansion into an orphanage and later a home for teenage girls. Luckily for the restoration efforts, which

began in 1986 following the state acquiring the property, the sisters had stashed many original furnishings and fixtures on the fourth floor, and the renowned photographer Eadweard Muybridge had shot images in 1872 that made clear what rooms looked like and where things belonged. ■**TIP→ Guided tours (first come, first served) depart hourly from 10 to 4.** ⊠ 800 N St., at 8th St., Downtown ☎ 916/324–9266 ⊕ www.parks.ca.gov ◪ Free.

Old Sacramento Waterfront

HISTORIC DISTRICT | FAMILY | A jumble of historic attractions and bonafide tourist traps—the Sacramento History Museum and the superb California State Railroad Museum representing the former and a Ferris wheel, merry-go-round, and salt-water taffy and T-shirt concessions the latter—occupies several square blocks of the Sacramento River's eastern banks a quarter-mile west of the Capitol. Shining bright metallic gold, the Tower Bridge, designed in the art-deco Streamline Moderne style and completed in 1935, anchors the waterfront's southern flank. ⊠ Sacramento River between Tower and I St. bridges, Old Sacramento ☎ 916/442–8575 ⊕ www.oldsacramento.com.

Old Sugar Mill

WINERY | A former beet-sugar refinery a 15-minute drive south of downtown in Clarksburg now houses the tasting rooms of 14 Northern California wineries. The Clarksburg AVA (American Viticultural Area), which straddles Sacramento, Yolo, and Solano counties, is known for Chenin Blanc and Petite Sirah, though all the wineries also purchase grapes elsewhere. Clarksburg Wine Company, which owns the on-site wine-making facility, is a worthy first stop. Draconis Wines and Three Wine Company also merit investigation, with Bump City, co-owned by the Oakland-based Tower of Power's keyboard player, Roger Smith, another popular stop. ⊠ 35265 Willow Ave.,

Clarksburg ✥ Take I–5 south to Exit 510, head south on Freeport Blvd. (Hwy. 160), west onto Freeport Bridge, and south on River Rd. ☎ *916/744–1615* 🌐 *oldsugarmill.com* 🎟 *Tasting fees vary* 🕒 *Days open vary by winery.*

Sacramento History Museum
HISTORY MUSEUM | FAMILY | A pandemic-era video campaign revolving around this museum's antique printing presses went viral, making a TikTok star out of a longtime volunteer named Howard. Other exhibits investigate Sacramento's gold-rush past and agricultural, economic, and political evolution. A must-see third-floor stop provides insights into the life of a 12-year-old girl through personal belongings discovered in a trunk a century after her death in 1879. The museum's Old Sacramento Underground Tours, booked separately, explore vestiges of the city before floods wreaked havoc in the 1860s and 1870s and many buildings were raised a story or two higher. ✉ *101 I St., Sacramento* ☎ *916/808–7059* 🌐 *sachistorymuseum.org* 🎟 *$10; Underground Tours $25.*

State Indian Museum
HISTORY MUSEUM | FAMILY | Adjacent to Sutter's Fort but run separately, this small but engaging museum explores the lives and history of California's indigenous peoples. Arts-and-crafts displays and other exhibits portray the state's earliest inhabitants. ✉ *2618 K St., at 26th St., Midtown* ☎ *916/324–0971* 🌐 *www.parks.ca.gov* 🎟 *$5.*

Sutter's Fort State Historic Park
MUSEUM VILLAGE | FAMILY | Nearby office buildings tower over Sacramento's earliest Euro-American settlement, founded in 1839 by German-born Swiss immigrant John Augustus Sutter. A self-guided tour includes a blacksmith's shop, bakery, jail, living quarters, and livestock areas. Staff and docents sometimes demonstrate crafts, food preparation, and other circa-1840s activities. ✉ *2701 L St., at 27th St., Midtown* ☎ *916/445–4422* 🌐 *www.parks.ca.gov* 🎟 *From $5.*

🍴 Restaurants

★ Allora
$$$$ | MODERN ITALIAN | The husband chef at this East Sacramento restaurant recognized for its singular concept and chic, deep-green aesthetic creates nimbly plated Italian-tinged cuisine his sommelier wife and co-owner pairs with international wines from mostly Italian grapes (the California Nebbiolo selection alone is epic). Seafood is a specialty on the three- to five-course prix-fixe tasting menu, which always includes exceedingly fresh and tender oysters, alluring pasta dishes, and often voluptuous entrées. **Known for:** vegan/vegetarian tasting menu; verdant covered outdoor patio; 23% service charge added to check. [$] *Average main: $105* ✉ *5215 Folsom Blvd., Sacramento* ✥ *From downtown, take U.S. 50 west to 59th St. exit and head north* ☎ *916/538–6434* 🌐 *www.allorasacramento.com* 🕒 *No lunch.*

Cafeteria 15L
$$ | AMERICAN | The exposed brick, reclaimed wood, and natural light streaming through large-paned windows of this easygoing comfort-food hangout make a great first impression. Favorites like tater tots (in truffle oil), French onion soup, and chicken and waffles (with pecan butter, maple syrup, and pork gravy) prove simultaneously familiar and intriguing. **Known for:** two outdoor patios; nostalgic food with a modern twist; weekend brunch with bottomless mimosas. [$] *Average main: $22* ✉ *1116 15th St., at L St., Downtown* ☎ *916/492–1960* 🌐 *www.cafeteria15l.com.*

Camden Spit & Larder
$$$ | MODERN AMERICAN | Upscale London haberdasheries reportedly inspired the aesthetic of this impeccably designed, pressed-metal-ceilinged paean to spit-roasted, Brit-influenced meat dishes. Near Golden 1 Center and Downtown

Commons, it's a place to share small offerings like sausage rolls, steak tartare, and local caviar and crumpets (Sacramento is a center of caviar production) before proceeding to salmon, spit-roasted chicken, or English meat pie. **Known for:** Winston's Hour (as in Churchill) menu weekdays 3–6; wine, beer, and cider selection; craft cocktails incorporating seasonal fruits, herbs, and vegetables. $ *Average main: $39 ⊠ 555 Capitol Mall, at 6th St., Downtown ☎ 916/619–8897 ⊕ www.camdenspitandlarder.com ⊘ Closed Sun. and Mon. No lunch Sat.*

★ **Canon**

$$$ | MODERN AMERICAN | Farmhouse meets semi-industrial open-kitchen chic at this light-filled restaurant whose executive chef found success in the Midwest and the Napa Valley before returning to Sacramento, where his culinary career began. Carefully chosen produce and proteins go into shareable small plates and larger platters that might include crispy octopus, vegetables *à la plancha* (seared on a metal plate), or smoked roasted lamb. **Known for:** alfresco patio dining in good weather; seasonal cocktails with fresh herbs and fruit; vegan, vegetarian, and gluten-free options. $ *Average main: $35 ⊠ 1719 34th St., East Sacramento ☎ 916/469–2433 ⊕ canoneastsac.com ⊘ Closed Mon. and Tues. No lunch.*

★ **Ella Dining Room and Bar**

$$$$ | MODERN AMERICAN | This swank restaurant and bar near the Capitol is artfully designed and thoroughly modern. The California–French, farm-to-table cuisine changes seasonally, but typical dishes include oysters on the half shell, steak tartare, and wood-fired bone marrow and entrées like wood-fired beef tenderloin and poached or pan-roasted fish. **Known for:** fresh, seasonal local ingredients; waitstaff's attention to detail; cocktail and wine selection. $ *Average main: $48 ⊠ 1131 K St., at 12th St., Downtown ☎ 916/443–3772 ⊕ elladiningroomandbar.com ⊘ Closed Sun. and Mon. No lunch Sat.*

The Firehouse

$$$$ | AMERICAN | Sacramento's rich and famous, including California governors going back to Ronald Reagan, settle into the elegant spaces within the city's restored first brick firehouse to dine on award-winning contemporary cuisine. The creative fare ranges from carpaccio, seasonal oysters, and braised pork belly to delicately spiced fish or scallops and herb-crusted rack of lamb. **Known for:** superlative wine list; chef's tasting menu; happy-hour in bar weekdays 4–6. $ *Average main: $48 ⊠ 1112 2nd St., at L St., Old Sacramento ☎ 916/442–4772 ⊕ www.firehouseoldsac.com ⊘ No lunch (check on weekdays).*

★ **Fixins Soul Kitchen**

$$ | AMERICAN | A cheery, sometimes boisterous vibe prevails at this ode to Black cuisine and culture that former NBA star and past Sacramento mayor Kevin Johnson and his wife, Michelle, founded in a high-ceilinged, quasi-industrial space 3½ miles southeast of the Capitol. Expect heapin' helpings of soul food's greatest hits—gumbo, shrimp and grits, oxtails, and fried chicken, catfish, and pork chops among them—that you can pair with sides that include hush puppies, black-eyed peas, candied yams, and collard greens (with turkey necks). **Known for:** art on the walls, sports on bar TVs; Kool-Aid for kids and (with vodka) for adults; banana pudding for dessert. $ *Average main: $20 ⊠ 3428 3rd Ave., at Broadway, Sacramento ⊕ From Downtown or Midtown take X St. southeast to 34th St. and turn south (right) ☎ 916/999–7685 ⊕ fixinssoulkitchen.com.*

Hook & Ladder Manufacturing Company

$$ | MODERN AMERICAN | Youthful and compelling, with found-art decorative elements and exposed vents, this historic former fire station is a favorite stop for cocktails, craft beers, and farm-to-fork fare. The area's year-round farmers' markets supply ingredients for the delectable salads and soups, and the pizzas, beef,

poultry, and seafood entrées are always good. **Known for:** carefully sourced ingredients; weekend brunch; midday (2:30–4:30) menu daily, happy hour 2:30–5:30 weekdays. $ *Average main: $23* ✉ *1630 S St., at 17th St., Midtown* ☎ *916/442–4885* 🌐 *hookandladder916.com.*

★ The Kitchen

$$$$ | MODERN AMERICAN | The chefs and front-of-house staff at this perennial favorite with a prix-fixe menu pull out all the stops to deliver a multisensory gustatory experience. The flamboyant presentation of courses as a series of "Acts"—not to mention the dramatically lit, flower-bestrewn dining room's intentionally buoyant atmosphere—might distract from the modern American cuisine were it not so well conceived and prepared with such panache and precision. **Known for:** one seating each evening (plan on 3½–4 hours); optional wine pairing; impeccably sourced ingredients. $ *Average main: $195* ✉ *2225 Hurley Way, Sacramento* ✥ *6 miles east of Downtown off Hwy. 160 to Exposition Blvd.* ☎ *916/568–7171* 🌐 *thekitchenrestaurant.com* 🕒 *Closed Mon. and Tues.*

Kru

$$$ | JAPANESE | The owner-chef of this mod-Japanese restaurant fashions fresh, wildly creative sushi for patrons seated at blond-wood tables, a counter, or an open-air patio. Order a sunshine roll—spicy tuna, escolar, and shrimp tempura enlivened by the tart contribution of green apples and lemon—perhaps pairing it with cooked fare like smoked duck *kushiyaki* with plum-wine katsu sauce or hot or cold ramen. **Known for:** smart decor; nearly two-dozen rolls; impressive sake, wine, and whiskeys. $ *Average main: $37* ✉ *3135 Folsom Blvd., at Seville Way, East Sacramento* ☎ *916/551–1559* 🌐 *www.krurestaurant.com* 🕒 *No lunch.*

★ Localis

$$$$ | MODERN AMERICAN | Exquisite plating and compelling, at times piquant, flavor combinations are the trademarks of this restaurant whose chef-sommelier owner, Chris Barnum-Dann, won the debut (2021) season of the culinary-competition TV show *The Globe.* The open-kitchen choreography of Barnum-Dann and his team deftly preparing one intricate dish after another (12 courses, prix-fixe) lends the proceedings a balletic air. **Known for:** fresh ingredients from top purveyors creatively combined and presented; thoughtful menu notes; global, well-chosen wines. $ *Average main: $200* ✉ *2031 S St., at 21st St., Midtown* ☎ *916/737–7699* 🌐 *localissacramento.com* 🕒 *Closed Sun.–Tues.*

Magpie Cafe

$$ | AMERICAN | This Midtown eatery with a vaguely industrial look and a casual vibe takes its food seriously: nearly all the produce is sourced locally, and the chefs prepare only sustainable seafood. BLTs and grass-fed beef burgers (and a plant-based option) are among the staples, as are steak and fries and pan-roasted fish with seasonal vegetables. **Known for:** outdoor park-view patio; beer, cider, wine, and cocktail lineup; homemade ice-cream sandwiches. $ *Average main: $29* ✉ *1601 16th St., Midtown* ☎ *916/452–7594* 🌐 *magpiecafe.com* 🕒 *Closed Mon. No lunch Tues. and Wed.*

★ The Waterboy

$$$ | EUROPEAN | Rural French cooking with locally sourced, seasonal, high-quality, often organic ingredients is the hallmark of this upscale, white-tablecloth, corner storefront restaurant that's as appealing for a casual meal with friends as it is for a drawn-out romantic dinner for two. Among the mains, try the steak, duck breast, or seasonal seafood, and save room for one of the palate-cleansing desserts. **Known for:** exceptional French cooking; quality local ingredients; global wine list. $ *Average main: $40* ✉ *2000 Capitol Ave., at 20th St., Midtown* ☎ *916/498–9891* 🌐 *www.waterboyrestaurant.com* 🕒 *Closed Sun. and Mon. No lunch Tues. and Sat.*

Zócalo Midtown

$$ | MEXICAN | Inside a glamorously renovated Hudson Motor Car showroom from the 1920s that looks out of a movie set, Zócalo puts an upscale spin on Mexican classics. Pair the house margarita or its blackberry variation with pozole or a guac or ceviche starter before moving on to enchiladas or a burrito bowl with chicken, salmon, carne asada, or vegetarian ingredients. **Known for:** festive setting; outdoor patio; happy hour daily 3–6. $ *Average main: $20* ⊠ *1801 Capitol Ave., at 18th St., Midtown* ☎ *916/441–0303* ⊕ *www. experiencezocalo.com.*

🍵 Coffee and Quick Bites

Solomon's Vinyl Diner

$ | DINER | Named for the founder of Tower Records, this energetic diner plays the nostalgia card with an all-vinyl soundtrack and comfort classics from bagels and lox or biscuits and gravy for breakfast to pastrami on rye, two-patty burgers with melted cheddar, or the chef's take on SpaghettiOs at lunch. A few vegetarian optoins, cold-brew coffee, and craft beers in cans and on tap keep the fare current. **Known for:** zero-proof, "brunch booze," and specialty cocktails; upstairs Russ's Room listening lounge; Saturday Drag Brunch and other festivities. $ *Average main: $18* ⊠ *730 K St., at 8th St, Downtown* ☎ *916/857–8200* ⊕ *www. solomonsvinyldiner.com* ۞ *Closed Mon. and Tues. No dinner.*

🛏 Hotels

The Citizen Hotel, Autograph Collection

$$ | HOTEL | This boutique hotel within the historic 1926 Cal Western Life building is dapper and refined, with marble stairs, striped wallpaper, and plush velvet chairs, lending the place a Roaring '20s charm. **Pros:** sophisticated decor; smooth service; upscale-contemporary Grange Restaurant & Bar. **Cons:** rooms near elevator can be noisy; rates vary widely depending on conventions, legislature, and season; expensive parking. $ *Rooms from: $260* ⊠ *926 J St., Downtown* ☎ *916/447–2700* ⊕ *www.thecitizenhotel. com* ↗ *198 rooms* ⊗ *No Meals.*

Delta King

$ | HOTEL | Wake up to the sound of geese taking flight along the river when you book a stay in one of Sacramento's most unusual and historic relics, a restored riverboat hotel permanently moored on Old Sacramento's waterfront. **Pros:** unique lodgings with period feel; steps from Old Sacramento shopping and dining; often decent for the price. **Cons:** less charming than expected; cramped rooms with slanted floors and small bathrooms; some noise issues. $ *Rooms from: $109* ⊠ *1000 Front St., Old Sacramento* ⊹ *At end of K St.* ☎ *916/444–5464, 800/825–5464* ⊕ *www.deltaking.com* ↗ *44 rooms* ⊗ *Free Breakfast.*

★ Fort Sutter Hotel

$$ | HOTEL | The guest rooms in this six-story Hilton Tapestry Collection boutique property win points for their expansive windows, contemporary style, smartly designed bathrooms, and works by local artists. **Pros:** above-average food for a hotel restaurant; near Midtown dining, entertainment, and shopping; Capitol views from upper floors facing west. **Cons:** diagonally across from a hospital; no microwaves (though some rooms have small refrigerators); more than a mile walk to Downtown. $ *Rooms from: $216* ⊠ *1308 28th St, Midtown* ☎ *916/603–2301* ⊕ *www.fortsutterhotel. com* ↗ *105 rooms* ⊗ *No Meals.*

★ Hyatt House Sacramento/Midtown

$$ | HOTEL | The architects of this courtly hotel, which opened with a splash in 2023, incorporated the redbrick Romanesque Revival–style facade of the 1928 structure that preceded it. **Pros:** Historic Star Lounge for lunch, dinner, and cocktails (happy hour 3–6); full kitchens and sofa beds in suites; 3 pm check-in, noon checkout. **Cons:** bit of a hike to

Downtown; pricey on event weekends; valet parking (fee) only. $ *Rooms from: $211* ⊠ *2719 K St., Midtown* ☎ *916/894-6500* ⊕ *www.hyatt.com* ⟿ *128 rooms* ⧮ *Free Breakfast.*

★ Kimpton Sawyer Hotel

$$ | **HOTEL** | Soft shades of brown and gray and furniture milled from California oak lend this full-service hotel's spacious rooms and suites a haute-rustic feel. **Pros:** pool deck and Revival bar; "living room" lobby; convenient to Downtown and Old Sacramento. **Cons:** pricey in-season; no tubs in many rooms; may be too high-style for some guests. $ *Rooms from: $259* ⊠ *500 J St., Downtown* ☎ *916/545-7100 front desk, 877/678-6255 reservations* ⊕ *www.sawyerhotel. com* ⟿ *285 rooms* ⧮ *No Meals.*

Nightlife

Midtown BierGarten

BEER GARDENS | The neighborhood feel and selection of beers, ales, porters, stouts, sours, and ciders make a trip to this boisterous beer garden a fun occasion, with the garlic fries, fresh pretzels with mustard, old-fashioned hot dogs, and other small bites a definite bonus. A 40-foot cargo container holds the bar, and a 20-footer contains the bathrooms, with the rest of the setting alfresco. ⊠ *2332 K St., at 24th St., Midtown* ☎ *916/346-4572* ⊕ *beergardensacramento.com* ☾ *Closed when it rains.*

★ Midtown's Cantina Alley

BARS | Flavorful, colorful, fruity cocktails are the specialty of this bar and restaurant whose equally rich-hued decor and corrugated-metal ceiling intentionally evoke spots throughout Mexico. While sipping sangria, a cerveza, or the house margarita in several flavors, you can nibble on street tacos, posole, *elote* (corn on a stick), and other small plates. ⊠ *2320 Jazz Alley, Midtown* ✛ *Off 24th St.*

between *J and K Sts.* ☎ *833/232-0639* ⊕ *www.cantinaalley.com* ☾ *Closed Mon.*

Punch Bowl Social

BARS | This restaurant and entertainment complex offers bowling, billiards, karaoke, Giant Jenga, pinball, Skee-Ball, and other diversions. After you've worked up an appetite, dine on updated pub grub and sip well-chosen craft beers, wine, specialty cocktails, or boozeless beverages. ⊠ *500 J St., at 5th St., Downtown* ☎ *916/925-5610* ⊕ *punchbowlsocial.com/ location/sacramento.*

Urban Roots Brewing & Smokehouse

BREWPUBS | Two native Northern Californians are behind this microbrewery that makes beers, ales, and a dessert stout. Order brews and barbecue at the counter and choose seating indoors or out front in the spacious beer garden–like setting. ⊠ *1322 V St., Midtown* ☎ *916/706-3741* ⊕ *www.urbanrootsbrewing.com* ☾ *Closed Mon.*

🎭 Performing Arts

Broadway Sacramento

THEATER | This group presents shows like *Hamilton, Annie,* and *Les Misérables* at two Downtown venues . ⊠ *SAFE Credit Union Performing Arts Center, 1301 L St., at 13th St., Downtown* ☎ *916/557-1999* ⊕ *www.broadwaysacramento.com.*

★ The Sofia

ARTS CENTERS | The long-running B Street Theatre—known for well-staged comedies, dramas, the occasional farce, and productions for children—is the resident company at this industrial-suave performing arts center. The two theaters, plus three rehearsal spaces for workshop productions, also present musicians, solo acts, and speakers. ⊠ *2700 Capitol Ave., at 27th St., Midtown* ☎ *916/443-5300* ⊕ *bstreettheatre.org.*

🛍 Shopping

Downtown Commons (DOCO)
MALL | FAMILY | A gathering spot for locals and tourists as much as a place to shop, dine, catch a movie, or sip a cocktail, this multiblock complex adjoins the Golden 1 Center. ✉ *660 J St., at 5th St., Downtown* ☎ *916/273–8124* ⊕ *www.docosacramento.com.*

★ Kulture
SOUVENIRS | FAMILY | This vibrant shop sells Mexican art, jewelry, and gifts. Look for the pithy Keepin' It Paisa line of T-shirts, hoodies, and ball caps in the adjacent Placita MX space, where several vendors sell furniture, clothing, and other items. ✉ *2331 K St., at 24th St., Midtown* ☎ *916/442–2728* ⊕ *kulturedc.wixsite. com/kulture* 🕑 *Closed Mon.*

Strapping
SOUVENIRS | FAMILY | The people running this packed-to-the-gills shop are as jolly as the housewares, cards, knickknacks, and souvenirs on display. Sacramento socks, T-shirts, and other local products are sold here, too. ✉ *1731 L St., at 18th St., Midtown* ☎ *916/400–3922* ⊕ *strappingstore.com.*

🏃 Activities

American River Bicycle Trail
BIKING | FAMILY | The Jedediah Smith Memorial Trail, as it's formally called, runs for 32 miles from Old Sacramento to Beals Point in Folsom. Walk or ride a bit of it and you'll see why local cyclists and pedestrians adore its scenic lanes. Enjoy great views of the American River and the bluffs overlooking it. ■**TIP**➔ **Bring lunch or a snack. Parks and picnic areas dot the trail.** ✉ *Old Sacramento* ⊕ *regionalparks.saccounty.gov.*

Sacramento Brew Bike Tours
BIKING | Hop aboard this outfit's giant pedal-powered contraption, pumping away with up to a dozen or so others to tour Midtown craft-beer and wine bars.

Depending on how much beer or wine (and exercise, of course) you want, you can book a two- or three-hour guided excursion. Both start at Sac Brew Bike's own bar. ✉ *Sac Brew Bar, 1519 19th St., Sacramento* ☎ *916/952–7973* ⊕ *www. sacbrewbike.com* 🍴 *From $40.*

Davis

10 miles west of Sacramento.

Davis began as a rich agricultural area and remains one, but it doesn't feel like a cow town. It's home to the University of California at Davis, whose nearly 40,000 students hang at downtown cafés, galleries, and bookstores (most of the action takes place between Second and Fourth and B and E streets), lending the city a decidedly college-town feel.

GETTING HERE AND AROUND
Most people arrive by car via I–80, though Yolobus serves the area from Sacramento, and downtown is walkable. Touring by bicycle is also a popular option—Davis is very flat.

👁 Sights

California Agriculture Museum
HISTORY MUSEUM | FAMILY | This gigantic space north of Davis in Woodland provides a thorough historical overview of motorized agricultural vehicles through dozens and dozens of threshers, harvesters, combines, tractors, and other contraptions. A separate wing surveys the evolution of trucks, emphasizing those used for farmwork. ✉ *1958 Hays La., south off Douglas La. from East Main St., Woodland* ✛ *From Davis, take 5th St. east to Polehill Rd./ County Rd. 102 north 10 miles; from Sacramento, take I–5 for 18 miles northwest to Exit 536* ☎ *530/666–9700* ⊕ *www. californiaagmuseum.org* 🍴 *$10* 🕑 *Closed Mon. and Tues.*

University of California, Davis
COLLEGE | **FAMILY** | A top research university, UC Davis educates many Wine Country vintners and grape growers. Top majors include psychology, biological science, and economics. Campus tours depart from the welcome center, near the Mondavi Center, a striking modern glass structure that presents top-tier performing artists. Other worthy stops include the Arboretum and the Manetti Shrem Museum of Art. ✉ *Welcome Center, 550 Alumni La., Davis* 🌐 *www.ucdavis.edu/about/visit.*

🍴 Restaurants

Mustard Seed
$$$$ | **AMERICAN** | Many patrons at this restaurant serving seasonal California cuisine are attending performing-arts events at the Mondavi Center a short walk away or visiting their kids at UC Davis. With hardwood floors and soft lighting, the dining room is cozy and romantic, but when the weather's fine, the tree-shaded patio out back is the best place to enjoy dishes like tomato bisque crowned with a puff pastry or herb-crusted rack of lamb. **Known for:** less expensive salad-sandwich lunch menu; desserts aren't an afterthought; reasonably priced California wines. [$] *Average main: $45* ✉ *222 D St., Suite 11, Davis* ☎ *530/758–5750* 🌐 *www.mustardseedofdavis.com* 🕒 *No lunch Sat.–Mon.*

🛏 Hotels

Best Western Plus Palm Court Hotel
$ | **HOTEL** | **FAMILY** | Rich accents of gold and cobalt blue add boutique flair to the spacious rooms of this dependable choice for business and leisure travelers. **Pros:** off-campus but nearby; on-site Cafe Bernardo for comfort food; some rooms sleep up to six people. **Cons:** pricey during major UC Davis events; no pool; chain's usual free breakfast not offered. [$] *Rooms from: $170* ✉ *234 D St., Davis* ☎ *530/753–7100* 🌐 *www.bestwestern.com* 🔑 *27 rooms* 🍽 *No Meals.*

Hyatt Place UC Davis
$$ | **HOTEL** | **FAMILY** | A full-service hotel right on campus, the Hyatt distinguishes itself with an enthusiastic staff and well-designed rooms and suites furnished with mahogany desks, headboards, and built-in nightstands, as well as pullout sofas with beds already made up for extra guests. **Pros:** generous breakfasts; pool, fitness room, café, and bar; convenient to university and downtown restaurants and shopping. **Cons:** only rooms with queen beds have tubs; noise from campus and nearby train tracks (when booking, ask for a quieter room); only suites have microwaves. [$] *Rooms from: $210* ✉ *173 Old Davis Rd. Extension, Davis* ☎ *530/756–9500* 🌐 *www.hyatt.com* 🔑 *127 rooms* 🍽 *Free Breakfast.*

Winters

14 miles west of Davis.

Almonds, walnuts, and fruit are the main crops grown in this rural Yolo County town (population 7,600), whose several-block historic district's wine-tasting opportunities and restaurant scene lure tourists and Bay Area and Sacramento Valley day-trippers. The district's Main Street bustles on weekends, especially when music and other events close part of it.

GETTING HERE AND AROUND

It's easiest to drive to Winters, whose main drag, Grant Avenue, doubles as Highway 128 in town. From Davis, follow Russell Boulevard west until it becomes Grant Avenue, from which Railroad Avenue leads south to the historic district. Yolobus serves Winters from Davis.

Sights

Berryessa Gap Vineyards Tasting Room

WINERY | Petite Sirah, under that name and its original French one, Durif, is the flagship grape of this operation whose parent company's nursery has supplied a who's-who of Napa and Sonoma wineries with disease-free rootstock since 1969. Tempranillo and Barbera are two other successful reds, with Albariño and Verdejo the best whites. The redbrick downtown tasting room is open daily. You can visit the nearby estate and its affiliated brewery four days a week. ✉ *15 E. Main St., Winters* ☎ *539/795–3201* 🌐 *www.berryessagap.com* 🎫 *Tastings from $20* 🕓 *Estate winery closed Mon.–Wed.*

Turkovich Family Wines Tasting Room

WINERY | Third-generation farmer Chris Turkovich and his wife, Luciana, whose parents in her native Argentina are both involved in the wine business, founded this winery known for bold, balanced reds. Luciana crafts many of the wines from Spanish varietals, though Petite Sirah dominates the robust blend Tho Boss. Albariño and rosé of Grenache are among the lighter wines. The storefront tasting space's sidewalk seating is good for people-watching. The rear patio is quieter. ✉ *304 Railroad Ave., near Main St., Winters* ☎ *530/795–3842* 🌐 *turkovichwines.com* 🎫 *Tastings from $15.*

Restaurants

Preserve

$$$ | **MODERN AMERICAN** | The seasonal produce of nearby purveyors figures in nearly every dish at Preserve, which pairs elevated gastropub fare with artisanal beers, wines, and cocktails. Grilled or sautéed fish, fried chicken, and an elaborate burger that appears at lunch and dinner are typical menu items, served in the brick-walled, rustic-industrial, semi-chic bar or the plant-laden outdoor patio. **Known for:** several Italian dishes for dinner; craft cocktails; upscale-casual feel. [$] *Average main: $34* ✉ *200 Railroad Ave., near Russell St., Winters* ☎ *530/795–9963* 🌐 *www.preservewinters.com* 🕓 *No lunch Mon. and Tues. No dinner Sun.*

Putah Creek Cafe

$$ | **AMERICAN** | The wood-fired pizza oven blazing away on the sidewalk turns out this café's handmade pies, but the lunch and dinner fare extends beyond them to pan-seared fish, a tri-tip sandwich, and fresh salads with ingredients from a local farm. The brick-walled dining room has been a farmers' hangout for breakfast (you name it) for decades. **Known for:** lunchtime sandwich lineup; alfresco patio dining; sister restaurant Buckhorn Steakhouse, a Winters culinary anchor, across the street. [$] *Average main: $25* ✉ *1 Main St., at Railroad Ave., Winters* ☎ *530/795–2682* 🌐 *putahcreekcafe.com* 🕓 *No dinner Wed.*

Hotels

Hotel Winters

$$ | **HOTEL** | Works by regional artists adorn the hallways of this three-story, downtown historic district boutique property, where the first-floor public areas include a lobby that invites lingering; a spa; and Carboni's, an Italian restaurant, bar, and grab-and-go market. **Pros:** fresh look; spacious rooms with 10-foot ceilings; town and mountain views from rooftop bar. **Cons:** some street-side noise (ask for a room toward the back); shallow "water lounge" has a mesmerizing water feature, but there's no legit pool; limited hours for room service. [$] *Rooms from: $239* ✉ *12 Abbey St., Winters* ☎ *530/505–9123, 888/566–3647* 🌐 *www.hotelwinters.com* 🛏 *78 rooms* 🍴 *No Meals.*

Lodi

34 miles south of Sacramento.

Founded on agriculture and once the country's watermelon capital, Lodi additionally produces asparagus, pumpkins, beans, safflowers, sunflowers, squashes, peaches, and cherries. It's also a major grape-growing hub, with more than 100,000 acres of mostly alluvial soils planted with more than 125 grape varietals—more types than in any other California viticultural area. Eighty-five or so wineries do business in this community, the self-proclaimed Zinfandel Capital of the World, and neighboring towns. (Although plenty of Zin grows here, these days farmers devote nearly the same amount of land to Cabernet Sauvignon.)

Lodi retains an old rural charm. You can stroll downtown or visit a wildlife refuge, all the while benefiting from a Sacramento River delta breeze that keeps this microclimate cooler in summer than anyplace else in the area.

GETTING HERE AND AROUND
Most of Lodi lies west of Highway 99 and east of I-5. Amtrak trains stop here. GrapeLine (☎ 209/333–6806) buses pass by some wineries, but touring by car is more efficient.

ESSENTIALS
VISITOR INFORMATION Visit Lodi. ⊠ 25 N. School St., Lodi ☎ 209/365–1195 ⊕ visitlodi.com.

Sights

★ Acquiesce Winery
WINERY | Expect no heavy reds at this boutique operation specializing in Rhône-style whites. Owner-winemaker Susan Tipton, who sourced her grapes' vines from Château de Beaucastel in France's Châteauneuf du Pape appellation, produces Viognier, Roussanne, and Grenache Blanc but also spotlights lower-profile varietals like Bourboulenc

and Clairette Blanche. (There's also a Grenache rosé.) Tastings, by appointment only, take place in a 100-year-old barn or just outside it, in either case with vineyard views. ⊠ 22353 N. Tretheway Rd., Acampo ✛ From downtown Lodi take Hwy. 12 east, Bruella Rd. north, and E. Peltier Rd. east ☎ 209/333–6102 ⊕ www. acquiescevineyards.com ⊠ Tastings from $20 ⊙ Closed Mon.–Wed.

Berghold Vineyards & Winery
WINERY | The appointment-only tasting room at Berghold recalls an earlier wine era with its vintage Victorian interior, including restored, salvaged mantlepieces, leaded glass, and a 26-foot-long bar. The wines—among them Viognier, Cabernet Sauvignon, Syrah, and Zinfandel—pay homage to French wine-making styles. ⊠ 17343 Cherry Rd., off E. Victor Rd./Hwy. 12, Lodi ☎ 209/333–9291 ⊕ bergholdvineyards.com ⊠ Tastings $15 ⊙ Closed Mon.–Wed.

★ Bokisch Vineyards
WINERY | This operation 11 miles east of downtown comes highly recommended for its excellent Spanish varietals and warm hospitality. The Albariño white and Tempranillo and Graciano reds often receive favorable critical notice, but everything is well made, including the non-Spanish Petit Verdot and old-vine Carignane. ■TIP➡ **Bokisch welcomes picnickers; pick up fixings in town, and enjoy vineyard views while you dine.** ⊠ 18921 Atkins Rd., Lodi ✛ From Hwy. 99 head east on Hwy. 12, north on Hwy. 88, and east on Brandt Rd. ☎ 209/642–8880 ⊕ www.bokischvineyards.com ⊠ Tastings from $15.

Harney Lane Winery
WINERY | Lodi grape growers since the 1900s dawned, the Harney family only started a winery in 2006. Three Zinfandels star in a lineup that includes Albariño, Chardonnay, two rosés, Cabernet Sauvignon, Petite Sirah, Primitivo, Tempranillo, and an old-vine Zinfandel port-style dessert wine. Extend your

tasting with a glass in the "forest" garden, where three-century-old cedars supply the shade. ■TIP→ **Learn about the family and Lodi on the Home Ranch Tasting & Tour.** ✉ *9010 E. Harney La., Lodi* ✢ *About 6½ miles south of downtown, Hwy. 99 to E. Harney La. exit* ☎ *209/365–1900* ⊕ *www.harneylane.com* ✉ *Tastings from $20.*

Jeremy Wine Co.

WINERY | The downtown tasting room of owner-winemaker Jeremy Trettevik has the feel of an old-time saloon, though in good weather everyone sips in the umbrella-shaded patio out back. Creative red blends are the specialty, with sweet yet clean-on-the-palate wines like the Bluebonnet Albariño–Orange Muscat blend among the lighter options. Tastings are also held at the winery (closed Tuesday and Wednesday) in nearby Lockeford. ✉ *6 W. Pine St., at S. Sacramento St., Lodi* ☎ *209/367–3773* ⊕ *jeremywineco.com* ✉ *Tastings from $10.*

Klinker Brick Winery

WINERY | The old-vine Zinfandels of this winery named for the bricks used to construct Lodi buildings of days past score well in competitions for their smooth tannins and complex flavors. Like the Cabernet Sauvignon, they're reasonably priced considering the quality. Lighter offerings include sparkling wines, Albariño, and the Vorgänger white blend. If the weather's good, taste outside and enjoy garden and vineyard views. ■TIP→ **Request a Reserve Flight ($20) to sample top-of-the-line reds.** ✉ *15887 N. Alpine Rd., Lodi* ☎ *209/333–1845* ⊕ *www.klinkerbrickwinery.com* ✉ *Tastings from $10.*

Lodi Wine & Visitor Center

WINERY | Get a feel for Lodi wines at the center, which has a tasting bar and viticultural exhibits. You can also buy wine and pick up a free winery map. ✉ *2545 W. Turner Rd., at Woodhaven La., Lodi* ☎ *209/365–0621* ⊕ *www.lodiwine.com* ✉ *Tastings $12.*

★ Lucas Winery

WINERY | David Lucas was one of the first local producers to start making serious wine, and today the Zinfandels he and his wife, Heather Pyle-Lucas, make are among Lodi's most sought-after vintages. The Lucases, who previously worked at the Robert Mondavi Winery (she also made wine at Opus One), also craft a Chardonnay with subtle oak flavors and a Zinfandel rosé. Tastings, by appointment, often take place on a patio with a vineyard view. ✉ *18196 N. Davis Rd., at W. Turner Rd., Lodi* ☎ *209/368–2006* ⊕ *lucaswinery.com* ✉ *Tastings from $20* ⊘ *Closed Mon.–Wed.*

★ M2 Wines

WINERY | With its translucent polycarbonate panels, concrete floor, and metal framing, this winery's high-ceilinged tasting room strikes an iconoclastic, industrial-sleek pose in rural Lodi. The Soucie Vineyard old-vine Zinfandel and the Trio and Duality red blends are three to seek out, but all the wines here are good. ✉ *2900 E. Peltier Rd., Acampo* ✢ *Take Hwy. 99 north from downtown to Peltier Rd. exit and head west* ☎ *209/339–1071* ⊕ *m2wines.com* ✉ *Tastings from $20.*

McCay Cellars

WINERY | Wine critics applaud owner-winemaker Michael McCay's pursuit of balance and restraint with his flagship TruLux Zinfandel and Faith Lot 13 Zin from century-old vines. A longtime grower who started his namesake label in 2007, McCay makes several rosés and whites, plus Cabernet Franc, Cinsaut, Petite Sirah, Tempranillo, and other reds. ✉ *18817 E. Hwy. 88, Lodi* ✢ *From downtown Lodi, take E. Victor Rd./Hwy. 12 east to Hwy. 88 north* ☎ *209/759–3900* ⊕ *www.mccaycellars.com* ✉ *Tastings from $15* ⊘ *Closed Mon.–Wed.*

Michael David Winery

WINERY | Colorful tanks emblazoned with the flagship Freakshow Cabernet Sauvignon and Petite Petit (Petite Sirah and Petit Verdot) label art stand tall amid a sea of other vessels on this high-production winery's open-air back lot. Sip these wines and other intentionally accessible whites, rosés, and reds at the combination café, tasting room, and farm stand, where fifth-generation farmers turned winery owners Michael and David Philips also sell their family's produce. ✉ *4580 W. Hwy. 12, at N. Ray Rd., Lodi* ☎ *209/368–7384* 🌐 *michaeldavidwinery.com* 🎫 *Tastings from $10.*

🍴 Restaurants

The Dancing Fox Winery and Bakery
$$ | AMERICAN | A good downtown stop especially for lunch, the Dancing Fox also has a tasting room for its eponymous wines. The restaurant, whose decor shimmers with fairy-tale whimsy, serves sandwiches, salads, pizzas, burgers, and wraps and has more than a dozen beers on tap. **Known for:** Sunday brunch; wine tasting; historic downtown setting. [$] *Average main: $24* ✉ *203 S. School St., Lodi* ☎ *203/366–2634* 🌐 *www.dancingfoxlodi.com* 🕒 *Closed Mon. No dinner Sun.*

★ Guantanio's
$$ | PIZZA | FAMILY | It seems as if everybody in Lodi loves bright and chipper Guantonio's, and, after tasting the family-style restaurant's wood-fired pizzas, it's easy to see why. Placing the area's pristine seasonal produce atop naturally leavened dough from "organic non-GMO flour," the chefs turn out *cacio e pepe* (cheese and pepper), pesto and sausage, and a dozen more tour de force pies. **Known for:** pepperoni pizza "Nick's way" with ricotta and hot honey; craft beers and boutique wines; soft-serve ice cream and cannolis for dessert. [$] *Average main: $24* ✉ *600 W. Lockeford St., at N. California St., Lodi* ☎ *209/263–7152* 🌐 *www.guantonios.com* 🕒 *Closed Sun.–Tues. No lunch.*

Pietro's Trattoria
$$ | ITALIAN | Lodi's go-to spot for Italian American classics wins fans for its quality ingredients, Tuscan-courtyard ambience, and plant-filled outdoor patio (reservations essential on weekends). Expect straightforward, well-executed renditions of chicken piccata and pork Milanese, filling lasagna and seasonal risotto, pizzas, and the like, all delivered with informal good cheer by the cadre of servers. **Known for:** Italian-American classics; meatball and chicken pesto with cheese sandwiches for lunch; Lodi and Italian wines. [$] *Average main: $24* ✉ *317 E. Kettleman La., Lodi* ☎ *209/368–0613* 🌐 *www.pietroslodi.com* 🕒 *Closed Sun.*

★ Towne House Restaurant
$$$$ | MODERN AMERICAN | Special-occasion dinners often take place in the distinguished rooms of this former residence behind, and part of, the Wine & Roses hotel. Painted in rich, textured hues offset by wide white molding, the rooms exude a subtle sophistication matched by seasonal dishes that might include halibut, lamb or pork chops, or a house-made pasta plate. **Known for:** fresh seasonal local ingredients; weekend brunch with varied offerings; Town Corner Café & Market for breakfast and lunch daily. [$] *Average main: $45* ✉ *2505 W. Turner Rd., at Woodhaven La., Lodi* ☎ *209/371–6160* 🌐 *winerose.com/the-restaurant.*

🛏 Hotels

Wine & Roses Hotel
$$ | HOTEL | Set on 7 acres amid a tapestry of informal gardens and with most guest rooms decorated in rich earth tones or soothing blues and purples, this hotel has cultivated a sense of refinement typically associated with Napa or Carmel. **Pros:** luxurious setting; popular restaurant; spa treatments. **Cons:** expensive for the area; some guests mention that walls are thin; many events. [$] *Rooms from: $349* ✉ *2505 W. Turner Rd., Lodi* ☎ *209/334–6988* 🌐 *winerose.com* 🔑 *66 rooms* 🍽 *No Meals.*

Activities

★ Lodi Cyclery

BIKING | FAMILY | Lodi's flat terrain, a local group's bike-lane advocacy, and this shop's well-maintained rentals make a pedal through town a pleasure. The owner and staff are generous with tips, among them choosing a route ensuring the city's afternoon breezes are at your back. ✉ *9 N. School St., near W. Pine St., Lodi* ☎ *209/365–7433* ⊕ *www.lodicyclery. com* ✆ *From $16/hr* ⊘ *Closed Sun. and Mon.*

Nevada City

61 miles northeast of Sacramento, 93 miles northeast of Lodi.

Once known as the Queen City of the Northern Mines, Nevada City is the most attractive of the northern Mother Lode towns. The iron-shutter brick buildings lining downtown streets contain antiques shops, galleries, boutiques, B&Bs, restaurants, and a winery. Gas street lamps and historic structures like the distinctive 1861 Firehouse No. 1, at 241 Main Street (if open, the museum inside is worth a peek), and the still active 1865 Nevada Theatre, at 401 Broad Street, add to the romance.

At one point in the 1850s, Nevada City had a population of nearly 10,000—enough to support much cultural activity. About 3,000 people live here today, but the visual and performing-arts scenes remain vibrant.

GETTING HERE AND AROUND

You'll need a car to get here. From Sacramento take I–80 east to Highway 49 north; from Reno take I–80 and Highway 20 west. Nevada County Connects (☎ *530/477–0103*) provides public transit.

ESSENTIALS

VISITOR INFORMATION Nevada City Chamber of Commerce. ✉ *132 Main St., Nevada City* ☎ *530/265–2692* ⊕ *www. nevadacitychamber.com.*

Sights

Nevada City Winery

WINERY | The area's oldest operating winery, established in 1980, pours its wines, many from Sierra Foothills grapes, in a tasting room whose back patio perches over the wine-making facility. Chardonnay is a best seller, with Cabernet Sauvignon and Rhône and Italian reds among the other specialties. ✉ *321 Spring St., at Bridge St., Nevada City* ☎ *530/265–9463* ⊕ *www.ncwinery.com* ✆ *Tastings from $10/glass, $20 flight.*

Restaurants

★ Lola

$$$ | MODERN AMERICAN | Riffing off the calculated flamboyance of its namesake, the gold-rush-era celebrity Lola Montez, the National Exchange Hotel's restaurant flirts with excess—long turquoise banquette benches, wall-mounted Persian rugs, swooping brushed-bronze lighting fixtures—yet retains its composure. The chefs show a similar knack for incorporating unexpected elements that enliven but don't undermine dishes like pan-seared salmon, fried chicken, and a double-cut pork chop. **Known for:** cod and smoked-salmon chowder; many ingredients "organic, ethically raised, and locally sourced"; weekend brunch (weekday lunch served at adjoining National Bar). $ *Average main: $37* ✉ *211 Broad St., at Spring St., Nevada City* ☎ *530/362–7605* ⊕ *www.thenationalexchangehotel.com/ dining.*

Sushi in the Raw

$$$ | JAPANESE | Landlocked Nevada City might seem like an odd place for a sushi haven, but this red-walled restaurant known for offbeat items like truffle

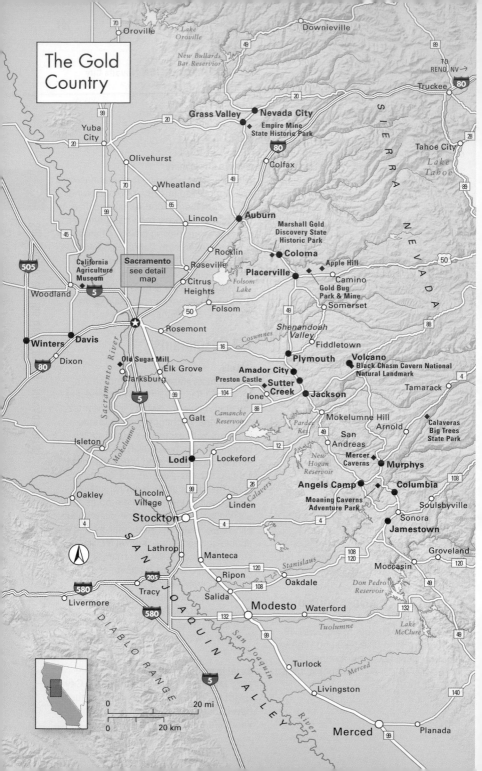

The Gold Country

Oroville
Lake Oroville
New Bullards Bar Reservoir
Downieville
TO RENO, NV →
Truckee
SIERRA
NEVADA
Tahoe City
Lake Tahoe
Grass Valley
Nevada City
Empire Mine State Historic Park
Yuba City
Olivehurst
Colfax
Wheatland
Lincoln
Auburn
Marshall Gold Discovery State Historic Park
Rocklin
Coloma
Apple Hill
Roseville
Placerville
Camino
California Agriculture Museum
Sacramento see detail map
Citrus Heights
Folsom Lake
Gold Bug Park & Mine
Somerset
Woodland
Folsom
Rosemont
Shenandoah Valley
Fiddletown
Winters
Davis
Dixon
Old Sugar Mill
Clarksburg
Elk Grove
Plymouth
Volcano
Black Chasm Cavern National Natural Landmark
Amador City
Preston Castle
Sutter Creek
Tamarack
Ione
Jackson
Galt
Camanche Reservoir
Mokelumne Hill
Arnold
Calaveras Big Trees State Park
Isleton
Pardee Res.
San Andreas
Lodi
Lockeford
New Hogan Reservoir
Mercer Caverns
Murphys
Oakley
Lincoln Village
Angels Camp
Columbia
Stockton
Linden
Moaning Caverns Adventure Park
Soulsbyville
Sonora
Jamestown
Lathrop
Manteca
Groveland
Livermore
Tracy
Ripon
Oakdale
Moccasin
Salida
Don Pedro Reservoir
Modesto
Waterford
Lake McClure
Tuolumne
DIABLO RANGE
SAN JOAQUIN VALLEY
Turlock
Merced River
Livingston
Merced
Planada

0   20 mi
0   20 km

sashimi and trout, salmon, and other "shooters" in shot glasses (quail eggs, too) consistently ranks atop local "best-of" lists for Japanese cuisine. Although Sushi in the Raw changed owners and locations in 2022, the new head chef, who trained several years under his predecessor, continues to emphasize time-honored techniques and ultrafresh ingredients. **Known for:** specialty rolls; cooked fish head in soy marinade; patio dining. [$] *Average main: $33* ✉ *California Organics, 135 Argall Way, between Zion St. and Searls Ave., Nevada City* ☎ *530/478–9503* 🌐 *sushiintheraw.net* 🕒 *Closed Sun. and Mon. No lunch.*

Three Forks Bakery & Brewing Co.

$ | **AMERICAN** | **FAMILY** | Baked goods, wood-fired pizzas, excellent coffee (teas and kombucha, too), and microbrews made on-site draw locals and tourists to this redbrick spot with a high, heavy-beamed open ceiling. The food's ingredients come from nearby organic sources; the beers on tap range from blond and pale ales to triple IPAs and several porters. **Known for:** lunch and dinner menu changes with the seasons; breads, muffins, scones, cookies, and cakes; soups and salads. [$] *Average main: $18* ✉ *211 Commercial St., Nevada City* ☎ *530/470–8333* 🌐 *www.threeforksnc.com* 🕒 *Closed Tues.*

Coffee and Quick Bites

Treats

$ | **ICE CREAM** | **FAMILY** | Careworn flooring, wainscoting, and a high tin ceiling lend an old-timey feel to this ice cream shop whose house-made offerings include quirkily contemporary ones like saffron-rose pistachio and blueberry matcha gelato. Double-chocolate, vanilla-bean, strawberry, and more conventional flavors from other brands supplement the Treats selections. **Known for:** cookies and brownies; vegan options; milk shakes, teas, and espresso drinks. [$] *Average main: $6* ✉ *210 Main St., Nevada City* ☎ *530/913–5819* 🌐 *www.treatsnevadacity.com.*

Hotels

★ Broad Street Inn

$ | **B&B/INN** | Far enough from downtown's bustle yet convenient to shops, restaurants, and performing-arts venues, this serene inn occupying a Victorian-era home is run by a couple whose sense of style informs everything from the spotless, individually decorated guest rooms to the landscaped outdoor spaces. **Pros:** step-back-in-time feel with contemporary grace notes; sensitive hosts; reasonable rates. **Cons:** no breakfast service; queen beds in all rooms; better for couples than families. [$] *Rooms from: $145* ✉ *517 W. Broad St., Nevada City* ☎ *530/265–2239* 🌐 *broadstreetinn.com* 🛏 *7 rooms* 🍴 *No Meals.*

★ The National Exchange Hotel

$ | **HOTEL** | Once more proudly anchoring the southern portion of Nevada City's historic district, this three-story boutique property, whose structure dates from 1856, underwent a multiyear makeover, and the attention to Victorian-era detail impresses throughout. **Pros:** contemporary, boutique hotel style that still evokes the past; near shops, tasting rooms, and restaurants; as in the 1800s, a swank bar. **Cons:** smaller rooms have full or queen beds and sleep only two; no elevator to third-floor rooms; expensive on summer weekends. [$] *Rooms from: $199* ✉ *211 Broad St., Nevada City* ☎ *530/362–7605* 🌐 *www.thenationalexchangehotel.com* 🛏 *38 rooms* 🍴 *No Meals.*

Outside Inn

$ | **HOTEL** | **FAMILY** | It looks like a typical one-story motel, but the Outside Inn offers a variety of accommodations inspired by nature or activities in nature. **Pros:** fun reinvention of a motel; convenient to trails and hikes; affiliated Inn Town Campground for camping and glamping. **Cons:** rooms are on the small side; might be too funky for some guests; ½-mile walk to downtown. [$] *Rooms from: $99* ✉ *575 E. Broad St., Nevada City*

☎ 530/265–2233 ⊕ outsideinn.com ⇨ 15 rooms ⋈ No Meals.

 Performing Arts

Nevada Theatre

ARTS CENTERS | This 1865 redbrick edifice reopened in 2022 after extensive renovations. The West Coast's longest continuously operating theater building, it presents film, comedy, plays, live music, and spoken-word performances. ⊠ 401 Broad St., Nevada City ☎ 530/265–6161 ⊕ nevadatheatre.com.

Grass Valley

4 miles south of Nevada City.

More than half of California's gold production was extracted from mines around Grass Valley, including the Empire-Star Mine, among the Gold Country's most fascinating attractions. The mine and the North Star Mining Museum, also worth a stop, are a few miles from the downtown historic district, which though walkable isn't as quaint as nearby Nevada City's.

GETTING HERE AND AROUND
You'll need a car to get here. Highway 49 is the north–south route into town, Highway 20 the east–west one. Nevada County Connects (☎ 530/477–0103) provides public transit.

Sights

★ **Empire Mine State Historic Park**
STATE/PROVINCIAL PARK | FAMILY | Relive the days of gold, grit, and glory, when this mine was one of North America's biggest and most prosperous hard-rock gold mines. The Empire-Star Mine complex yielded an estimated 5.8 million troy ounces of gold from 367 miles of underground passages. You can walk into a mine shaft, peer into dark, deep recesses and almost imagine what it felt like to work this vast operation. The grounds have the Bourn Cottage (exquisite redwood interior; call for tour times), picnic tables, and gentle trails—perfect for a family outing. ⊠ 10791 E. Empire St., Grass Valley ☎ 530/273–8522 ⊕ www.parks.ca.gov ⊠ $5.

Lucchesi Vineyards & Winery

WINERY | Nearly 2,600 feet up in the Sierra Foothills, this homey winery at the end of a long gravel road is known for Cabernet Franc, Cabernet Sauvignon, and Zinfandel. The lineup also includes whites, a rosé, a sparkler, and a Port-style red. After a tasting, you can walk up the hill to see how apt the estate View Forever Vineyard's name is. Bring a picnic if you'd like. ⊠ 19698 View Forever La. ✧ Follow signs off Rattlesnake Rd. ☎ 530/273–1596 ⊕ lucchesivineyards. com ⊠ Tastings from $10.

North Star Mining Museum

HISTORY MUSEUM | FAMILY | Inside a former powerhouse, the museum displays a 32-foot-high Pelton Water Wheel said to be the largest ever built. The wheel, used to power mining operations, was a forerunner of modern turbines that generate hydroelectricity. Other exhibits document life in the mines and the environmental effects mining had on the area. You can picnic nearby. ⊠ 10933 Allison Ranch Rd., Grass Valley ✧ Head south from Main St. on Mill St. ☎ 530/273–4255 ⊕ nevadacountyhistory.org ⊠ Donation requested.

⑪ Restaurants

Cirino's at Main Street

$$ | ITALIAN | FAMILY | With exposed brick walls, a tall ceiling, and a well-worn bar and floor, Cirino's serves up a vast menu of hefty Italian American favorites like Corsican rosemary chicken, steak à la Gorgonzola, and pork chop Milanese. The bar crew, which slings the signature Bloody Mary and other specialty cocktails, is as friendly as the rest of

Dancing Her Way to Fame

One of the gold-rush era's most colorful personalities was Lola Montez (1821–61), a dancer, singer, courtesan, and gender rebel who earned international notoriety for her suggestive "spider dance." By contemporary accounts, her contortions, though not universally admired, were known to inspire approving miners to toss gold nuggets onto the stage.

Countess, Mistress, Possible Witch

Born in Ireland, Montez recast herself in young adulthood as a Spanish countess, performing in Europe, where her lovers included the composer Franz Liszt and King Ludwig of Bavaria. Famous, in part, for being famous, the entertainer cooled her heels in the Gold Country not long after her calls for Bavarian democracy contributed to Ludwig's overthrow and her banishment as a witch. Or so one version goes.

Lola Lives On

For a spell, Montez resided in Grass Valley, where a reproduction of her house downtown still stands at 248 Mill Street. The house isn't accessible, but Lola's memory lives on throughout the Gold Country, most notably at Lola, the stylish restaurant of Nevada City's National Exchange Hotel, whose decor riffs off the opulence of its namesake's glory years.

---

the team. **Known for:** old-school recipes; homemade soups and sauces; family-friendly attitude. $ *Average main: $25* ⊠ *213 W. Main St., Grass Valley* ☎ *530/477–6000* ⊕ *cirinosatmainstreet. com* ⊗ *Closed Mon. and Tues.*

Grass Valley Pasty Co.

$ | **BRITISH** | Eat like a 19th-century Cornish miner at this modest takeout shop serving home-baked pasties, flaky on the outside with moist and flavorful meat, vegetable, and other fillings. Jammed with skirt steak, potatoes, and turnips, the Cousin Jack hews closest to tradition, with vegetarian and barbecued pulled pork typical of the equally satisfying updates. **Known for:** at least one vegetarian option; family-run business; closes early evening. $ *Average main: $13* ⊠ *100 S. Auburn St., at W. Main St., Grass Valley* ☎ *530/802–5202* ⊕ *grass-valley-pasty-co.business.site* ⊗ *Closed Mon. and Tues.*

South Pine Cafe

$ | **AMERICAN** | **FAMILY** | Locals flock to this always-busy diner on a Victorian's ground floor for lobster Benedict, a spiced up Mexican chicken scramble, and other dishes that are anything but your ordinary eggs and pancakes (though you can order those, too, as well as vegetarian versions of several items). Imaginative burritos, wraps, burgers, and more lobster in the form of a melt sandwich appear for lunch. **Known for:** homemade muffins; vegan and gluten-free options; local family farms supply many ingredients. $ *Average main: $16* ⊠ *102 Richardson St., Grass Valley* ☎ *707/274–0261* ⊕ *www. southpinecafe.com* ⊗ *No dinner.*

Hotels

Gold Miners Inn

$ | **HOTEL** | **FAMILY** | Just off Highway 49 and superbly run, this Ascend Collection property provides a comfortable experience, with art and artifacts reflecting the area's mining heritage gracing public areas and guest rooms. **Pros:** clean downtown hotel; art and artifacts reflecting the area's mining heritage; complimentary hot breakfast. **Cons:** no pool; despite stylish touches has a chain-like feel; some light sleepers find highway-side rooms noisy (ask for courtyard accommodations). [$] *Rooms from: $188* ✉ *121 Bank St., Grass Valley* ☎ *530/477–1700* 🌐 *www.goldminersinngrassvalley.com* 🛏 *81 rooms* 🍴 *Free Breakfast.*

Holbrooke Hotel

$ | **HOTEL** | A Main Street icon since the mid-1800s—when the A-list guest list included entertainer Lola Montez, writer Mark Twain, and Ulysses S. Grant—this two-story, historic-district hotel received a down-to-the-studs (in some cases bricks) makeover and reopened in 2020 as a boutique property. **Pros:** convenient to shops and restaurants; mix of antique, reproduction, and contemporary furnishings; ground-floor saloon is reportedly the West's oldest continuously operating bar. **Cons:** a few rooms very small; some noise from traffic in street-side rooms, restaurant patio in back rooms; books up well ahead on many weekends. [$] *Rooms from: $189* ✉ *212 W. Main St., Grass Valley* ☎ *530/460–4078* 🌐 *holbrooke.com* 🛏 *28 rooms* 🍴 *No Meals.*

Auburn

24 miles south of Grass Valley, 34 miles northeast of Sacramento.

Halfway between San Francisco and Reno, Auburn is convenient to gold-rush sites, outdoor recreation opportunities, and wineries. The self-proclaimed "endurance capital of the world" is abuzz almost every summer weekend with running, cycling, rafting, kayaking, and equestrian events. Old Town Auburn has its own gold-rush charm, with narrow climbing streets, cobblestone lanes, wooden sidewalks, and many original buildings.

GETTING HERE AND AROUND

Amtrak serves Auburn, though most visitors arrive by car on Highway 49 or I–80. Once downtown, you can tour on foot.

👁 Sights

Placer County Museum

HISTORY MUSEUM | **FAMILY** | Visible from the highway, Auburn's standout structure is the Placer County Courthouse. The classic bronze-domed building houses the Placer County Museum, which documents the area's history—Native American, railroad, agricultural, and mining—from the early 1700s to 1900. Look for the gold nuggets valued at more than $338,000 today, and don't miss the women's cell under the Maple Street staircase. **■ TIP→ Ask about other nearby county-run history museums.** ✉ *101 Maple St., Auburn* ☎ *530/889–6500* 🌐 *www.placer.ca.gov/2489/museums* 🎟 *Free.*

🍴 Restaurants

Auburn Alehouse

$ | **AMERICAN** | **FAMILY** | Inside the historic American Block building, which dates from 1856, you can see this craft operation's beers being made through glass walls behind the dining room, which serves burgers, fish-and-chips, short rib and fish tacos, salads, sandwiches, and other decent gastropub fare. Gold Country Pilsner, Old Town Brown, and Gold Digger IPA are all Great American Beer Festival award winners. **Known for:** herb-brined buttermilk fried chicken; craft whiskeys; weekend brunch. [$] *Average main: $19* ✉ *289 Washington St., Auburn* ☎ *530/885–2537* 🌐 *auburnalehouse.com.*

Awful Annie's

$ | **AMERICAN** | **FAMILY** | One of Auburn's favorite old-time breakfast and lunch spots entices patrons with waffles, pancakes, Monte Cristo French toast, and a slew of egg dishes you can wash down with an award-winning Bloody Mary or two. Feast on burgers, sandwiches, and

Almost 6 million troy ounces of gold were extracted from the Empire Mine.

more Bloody Marys for lunch. **Known for:** hearty breakfasts; Grandma's bread pudding with brandy sauce; town-hangout feel. [$] *Average main: $15* ✉ *13460 Lincoln Way, Auburn* ☎ *530/888–9857* 🌐 *www.awfulannies.com* 🕓 *No dinner.*

The Pour Choice
$ | **AMERICAN** | Black subway tiles, contemporary bistro furniture, and a gray-marble counter lit by Edison bulbs lend urban panache to this fine spot for a craft coffee or one of more than two dozen local, national, and international brews on tap. In a space once occupied by a drugstore, the Pour Choice serves light fare that might include a grilled gourmet-cheese sandwich on ciabatta with bacon. **Known for:** upbeat vibe; talented baristas; outdoor terrace in good weather. [$] *Average main: $13* ✉ *177 Sacramento St., Auburn* ☎ *530/820–3451* 🌐 *thepourchoice.com.*

★ Restaurant Josephine
$$$ | **FRENCH** | Something special transpires nightly at this ground-floor restaurant inside Auburn's 1894 redbrick Odd Fellows Hall that transcends the romantic, softly lit space and French bistro–inspired fare. Caviar, fresh oysters, steak tartare, and duck-liver mousse are typical starters, perhaps leading into *moules frites* (steamed mussels and fries), grilled Duroc pork chop, or pan-roasted fish with foraged mushrooms, all prepared from the heart by chef-owners Eric Alexander and town native Courtney MacDonald. **Known for:** simple, elegant desserts; classic cocktails and updates; French, other European, and California wines. [$] *Average main: $33* ✉ *1226 Lincoln Way, at East St., Auburn* ☎ *530/820–3523* 🌐 *www.josephineauburn.com* 🕓 *Closed Sun. and Mon. No lunch.*

Hotels

Holiday Inn Auburn Hotel
$ | **HOTEL** | **FAMILY** | Above the freeway across from Old Town, this hotel has a welcoming lobby and chain-standard but well-organized rooms with refrigerators, microwaves, and work areas. **Pros:** some rooms sleep four people; suitable

base for Gold Country exploring; on-site restaurant. **Cons:** lacks style; some traffic noise; can't walk to Old Town restaurants and shops. $ *Rooms from: $169* ✉ *120 Grass Valley Hwy., Auburn* ☎ *530/887–8787* ⊕ *www.auburnhi.com* ↩ *96 rooms* ❍❍ *No Meals.*

🛍 Shopping

Ikeda's Country Market & Pie Shop

MARKET | FAMILY | For more than a half-century a de rigueur stop between the Bay Area and Lake Tahoe, Ikeda's started as a produce stand selling fruit harvested from its Japanese-American owners' orchard and the freshly baked pies brimming with that fruit. A café known for a dozen-plus burgers, fries, shakes, and pie slices came later. ✉ *13500 Lincoln Way, Auburn* ☎ *530/885–4243* ⊕ *www.ikedas.com.*

Coloma

18 miles southeast of Auburn.

The California gold rush started in Coloma when James W. Marshall discovered flecks of metal in the bottom of a ditch. "Boys, I believe I've found a gold mine!" he exclaimed in January 1848 to colleagues at John Sutter's mill here. In short order, California's coastal communities began to empty as prospectors flocked to the hills, getting a jump on East Coasters, who didn't hear about the boom until mid-August.

GETTING HERE AND AROUND

A car is the only practical way to get to Coloma, via Highway 49. Once parked, you can walk to all the worthwhile sights.

Sights

★ **Marshall Gold Discovery State Historic Park**

STATE/PROVINCIAL PARK | FAMILY | The American River's south fork slices through this park commemorating California's mining history. Trails lead from the parking lot to a statue of James Marshall with sublime views; beyond it to the north stands a working reproduction of an 1840s mill erected near where he first spotted gold. Most of Coloma lies within the park. Though crowded with tourists in summer, the town hardly resembles the mob scene it was in 1849, when 2,000 prospectors staked out claims along the streambed. Coloma's population grew to 4,000, supporting seven hotels, three banks, and many stores and other businesses. But when reserves of the precious metal dwindled, the prospectors left as quickly as they had come. Rangers give gold-panning lessons (additional fee) on most days. ✉ *310 Back St., off Hwy. 49, Coloma* ☎ *530/622–3470* ⊕ *www. parks.ca.gov* ☜ *$10 per vehicle.*

Placerville

9 miles south of Coloma, 44 miles east of Sacramento.

It's hard to imagine now, but in 1849 about 4,000 miners staked out every gully and hillside in Placerville, turning the town into a rip-roaring camp of log cabins, tents, and clapboard houses. The area was then known as Hangtown, a graphic allusion to the nature of frontier justice. It took on the name Placerville in 1854 and became an important supply center for the miners.

Many of the downtown historic district's restaurants, shops, coffeehouses, and wine bars occupy rehabbed 19th-century buildings. A defining characteristic of nearby El Dorado AVA wineries

(⊕ *eldoradowines.org*) is its vineyards' high elevation, from 1,200 to 3,500 feet.

GETTING HERE AND AROUND
You'll need a car to get to and around Placerville, a 45-minute drive from Sacramento via U.S. 50.

Sights

Apple Hill
FARM/RANCH | FAMILY | From July to late December, Apple Hill Growers Association members open their orchards and vineyards for apple and berry picking, picnicking; and wine, cider, pressed-juice, and other tastings. Treasure hunts, pond fishing, pie making, and other activities attract families. ■**TIP→ On autumn weekends, take U.S. 50's Camino exit to avoid some of the traffic congestion.** ✉ *Placerville* ✛ *Starting 2 miles east of Hwy. 49, Exits 48–57 off U.S. 50* ☎ *530/644–7692* ⊕ *applehill.com.*

Boeger Winery
WINERY | In 1972, Greg Boeger revived a gold rush–era farm that once supported fruit and nut orchards, a winery, and a distillery. These days Boeger produces estate wines from 30 varietals grown on two parcels totaling 100 acres, with Sauvignon Blanc and Barbera the best sellers and Zinfandel and Primitivo also worth seeking out. ■**TIP→ The creek-side picnic area fronting the tasting room hosts bands on Friday evenings in summer (reserve space well ahead).** ✉ *1709 Carson Rd., Placerville* ✛ *Head north from U.S. 50, Exit 48, then northeast (right) on Carson Rd.* ☎ *530/622–8094* ⊕ *www.boegerwinery.com* 🍷 *Tastings from $15.*

★ Cappelli Wine
WINERY | Taking a cue from European shops selling everyday wines by the tap, Marco Cappelli, a respected winemaker and consultant, opened this downtown Placerville winery and tasting room in 2023. Although his wines are inexpensive, Cappelli knows where the best Northern California grapes grow. A Clarksburg Chenin Blanc and a Fair Play Barbera ranked among his early coups, all the more so given their price: less than $15 a bottle. ✉ *484 Main St., Placerville* ☎ *530/870–4372* ⊕ *facebook.com/cappelliwine* 🍷 *Tastings from $5.*

★ Edio Vineyards at Delfino Farms
WINERY | Apple growers since 1964, the Delfino family occupies one of El Dorado County's most idyllic sites. Joan Delfino's apple pies and fun farm events gained the clan early notice. In the 2010s, her grandchildren started a winery named for her husband, local agricultural icon Edio Delfino. They pour their superb whites and reds in a gleaming-silver contemporary space whose patio perches over apple trees surrounded by grapevines ringed by a forest. ■**TIP→ Wine tasting takes place year-round; bakery visits, apple events, and indie concerts occur seasonally.** ✉ *3205 N. Canyon Rd., off Carson Rd., Camino* ☎ *530/622–0184* ⊕ *delfinofarms.com* 🍷 *Tastings from $15* ⊗ *Tasting room closed Tues. and Wed.*

Element 79 Vineyards
WINERY | This winery's owner envisioned his sleek hospitality space as "a country club" for experiencing wines by the glass or flight, with or without the charcuterie and cheese sold on-site (tapas on Friday and weekends). The tasting room and adjoining patio edge the 32-acre estate vineyard, which you can hike. Winemaker Scott Johnson's red blends and Cabernets stand out, as does the unconventional, canned, dry-hopped Viognier sparkler (Johnson also brews beer). ✉ *7350 Fairplay Rd., southeast 1½ miles off Mt. Aukum Rd., Somerset* ☎ *530/497–0750* ⊕ *www.element79vineyards.com* 🍷 *Tastings from $10 glass, $15 flight.*

Gold Bug Park & Mine
MINE | FAMILY | Take a self-guided tour of this fully lighted mine shaft within a park owned by the City of Placerville. The worthwhile audio tour (included) makes clear what you're seeing. ■**TIP→ A shaded stream runs through the park, and**

there are picnic facilities. ✉ *2635 Goldbug La., Exit U.S. 50 at Bedford Ave. and follow signs, Placerville* ☎ *530/642–5207* 🌐 *www.facebook.com/GoldBugParkMine* 🎟 *Park free; mine tour $12* 🕒 *Closed weekdays late fall–early spring except for a few holidays.*

★ Holly's Hill Vineyards

WINERY | The founders of this woodsy hilltop winery 7 miles south of Apple Hill tasted Châteauneuf-du-Pape on their honeymoon, sparking a lifetime passion for Rhône wines made in classic French style. Mourvèdre is a specialty, by itself and in blends with Grenache, Syrah, or both. Carignane, Counoise, and other Rhône reds are also made, along with whites that include the Roussanne-dominant Patriarche Blanc blend. Taste these estate wines in a space with views extending 75 miles on a clear day. ✉ *3680 Leisure La., off Pleasant Valley Rd., Placerville* ✣ *From U.S. 50, Exit 49, follow Broadway east to Newtown Rd. and Pleasant Valley Rd. southeast* ☎ *530/344–0227* 🌐 *hollyshill.com* 🎟 *Tastings $10.*

★ Lava Cap Winery

WINERY | Nineteenth-century miners knew that gold was nearby if they found the type of volcanic rocks visible everywhere on this winery's property. The rocky soils and vineyard elevations as high as 2,800 feet play pivotal roles in creating Lava Cap's fruit-forward yet elegant wines. Zinfandel, Grenache, Cabernet Franc, and Petite Sirah star among the reds, Chardonnay and Viognier among the whites. **■ TIP→ After a tasting you can picnic on the patio and enjoy Sierra foothills vistas.** ✉ *2221 Fruitridge Rd., Placerville* ☎ *530/621–0175* 🌐 *www.lavacap.com* 🎟 *Tastings from $15.*

★ Starfield Vineyards

WINERY | Its many microclimates inspired owner-winemaker Tom Sinton to purchase a 67-acre hillside property he transformed into a showcase for wines from mostly Rhône and Italian varietals. With a nature trail, a 300-foot-long rose arbor, an events amphitheater, a lakeside pavilion, and an upper patio with views of trees near and far, the wines could have taken a back seat, but Sinton crafts them with such grace and precision that they more than match the setting and hospitality. ✉ *2750 Jacquier Rd., Placerville* ✣ *3 miles northeast of downtown Placerville* ☎ *530/748–3085* 🌐 *www.starfieldvineyards.com* 🎟 *Tastings from $10.*

🍴 Restaurants

★ Allez

$$ | FRENCH | The tale of how the couple running this spot for to-go or dine-in French food became husband and wife says all you need to know about their passion for beautifully crafted cuisine—he won her heart with his escargot sauce. In a casual space with ocher walls, six utilitarian stools at the wine bar, and a few tables inside and out, the two serve baguette sandwiches; salads; crepes; stews; and entrées like coq au vin, cassoulet, and pork tenderloin. **Known for:** all-day prix-fixe menu (a deal), plus à la carte; sandwich, salad, and dessert lunch boxes; many vegetarian and gluten-free items. [$] *Average main: $25* ✉ *4242 Fowler La., Diamond Springs* ✣ *Off Hwy. 49, 3 miles south of downtown Placerville* ☎ *530/621–1160* 🌐 *www.allezeldorado.com* 🕒 *Closed Sun. and Mon.*

Heyday Cafe

$$ | AMERICAN | Inside an exposed-brick 1857 former assay office where miners exchanged gold nuggets for the coin of the realm, the Heyday is a happy haven for salads, panini, and thin-crust pizzas at lunch and dinner entrées like seared salmon, hanger steak, and pasta with mushroom ragout. The mood is casual, but the food is prepared with style. **Known for:** local to international wine list; molasses gingerbread cake; affiliated The Independent nearby for fine dining. [$] *Average main: $25* ✉ *325 Main St.,*

Placerville ☎ 530/626–9700 🌐 www.heydaycafe.com ⏲ Closed Mon. No dinner Tues. and Wed.

The Place

$$ | ITALIAN | The chef-owner of this restaurant also known as The "Little Italian Place" describes the menu's influences as his East Coast grandmother's multicourse Sunday family suppers, his later culinary explorations, and his zeal to create "fresh and original" Italian cuisine. The country-road setting accentuates the just-like-home feeling, as do the calzones, pizzas, pasta dishes, and truffle risotto. **Known for:** lasagna Bolognese on Friday and Saturday evening; vegetarian and gluten-free items; live entertainment in the bar some nights. [$] *Average main: $24 ✉ 1772 Pleasant Valley Rd., 2¾ miles east of Hwy. 49, Placerville ☎ 530/621–1680 🌐 thatlittleitalianplace.com/placerville ⏲ Closed Mon. and Tues.*

★ Smith Flat House

$$$ | MODERN AMERICAN | Carefully sourced ingredients from local purveyors, meticulous execution, and the setting at a former mine site 3 miles east of downtown have made this restaurant a hit among locals, Gold Country tourists, and Tahoe travelers. Wild-mushroom Bordelaise appetizer, jambalaya risotto, and the Black and White entrée of filet mignon and perfectly grilled prawns are among the staples on the seasonally changing menu. **Known for:** Sunday brunch waffle Benedict; salads, pizzas, burgers for lunch; outdoor courtyard. [$] *Average main: $35 ✉ 2021 Smith Flat Rd., off Jacquier Rd., Placerville ☎ 530/621–1003 🌐 www.smithflathouse.com ⏲ No lunch Mon.–Thurs.*

Solid Ground Brewing

$ | ECLECTIC | The chef at this brewpub with a no-nonsense industrial decor (high ceilings, concrete floor, huge garage doors) tailors the cuisine to the namesake beers produced by two Sierra foothills natives, one with an enology degree, the other with extensive experience in European beer making. A buttermilk fried-chicken sandwich, a corned root-vegetable Reuben, and a burger with the cheese of your choice might appear among the gastropub options. **Known for:** ciders from Apple Hill; some beers aged in wine barrels; good stop for lunch on a hot day. [$] *Average main: $15 ✉ 552 Pleasant Valley Rd., Diamond Springs ✣ Off Hwy. 49, 3 miles south of downtown Placerville ☎ 530/344–7442 🌐 www.solidgroundbrewing.com.*

Sweetie Pie's Restaurant & Bakery

$ | AMERICAN | FAMILY | A circa-1865 Victorian that was expanded willy-nilly over the years houses this downtown spot known for made-from-scratch fare. Scrambles, four-egg omelets, pancakes, waffles, and French toast get things going for breakfast (served until 1 pm), with salads and well-built sandwiches the main items for lunch. **Known for:** bakery's pies, breads, cookies, cakes, muffins, and cinnamon rolls; strong coffee; breakfast-only Sunday (until 2). [$] *Average main: $13 ✉ 577 Main St., Placerville ☎ 530/642–0128 🌐 sweetiepiesrestaurant.com ⏲ No dinner.*

★ Timmy's Brown Bag

$ | SANDWICHES | The music-loving owner of this downtown shop mashes up ingredients with verve and imagination—a recent grilled purple grapes and feta specimen with micro-herbs, dry-roasted peanuts, and pear vinaigrette is but one example. Regulars rave about three frequently appearing messy-good sandwiches (ask for a fork), namely the banh mi; the chicken satay with harissa cucumber slaw; and the Spam and kimchi with grilled pineapple, chunky chili sauce, and peanut butter. **Known for:** grilled tacos ahogadas (with spicy chili sauce); top-line ingredients; mainly to-go (just a few tables). [$] *Average main: $15 ✉ Creekside Pl., 451 Main St., Suite 10, Placerville ☎ 530/303–3203 🌐 timmysbrownbag.com ⏲ Closed Wed. No dinner.*

Hotels

★ Eden Vale Inn

$$ | B&B/INN | This lavish but rustic B&B occupies a converted turn-of-the-20th-century hay barn, the centerpiece of which is a 27-foot slate fireplace that rises to a sloping ceiling of timber beams. **Pros:** exceptionally plush rooms; stunning patio and grounds; romantic setting. **Cons:** expensive for the area; summer weekends book up far ahead; weekend minimum-stay requirement. $ *Rooms from: $329* ✉ *1780 Springvale Rd., Placerville* ☎ *530/621–0901* ⊕ *edenvaleinn. com* ➦ *7 rooms* ⦿ *Free Breakfast.*

The Harper Inn

$ | MOTEL | Snappy design, full kitchens, and proximity to downtown, wineries, and Apple Hill make this small early-1940s motel renovated in 2022 into vacation rentals a delight for its price point. **Pros:** responsive Wi-Fi; aesthetically pleasing suitelike accommodations; husband-and-wife hosts. **Cons:** lacks the amenities of full-service establishments; less than scintillating location; Airbnb rental; need to call owner's cell to book a particular room. $ *Rooms from: $142* ✉ *3038 Orchard La., Placerville* ☎ *805/324–2798* ⊕ *www.facebook.com/ theharperinn* ➦ *4 rooms* ⦿ *No Meals.*

★ Lucinda's Country Inn

$ | B&B/INN | Effusive but not intrusive hospitality is the trademark of this contemporary inn between Placerville and Plymouth whose spacious light-filled suites and a cottage have views of the oaks, firs, and other trees surrounding the property. **Pros:** romantic setting; convenient for wine touring; filling buffet breakfast. **Cons:** rooms sleep only two; long drive to Placerville or Plymouth restaurants; lacks amenities of larger properties. $ *Rooms from: $180* ✉ *6701 Perry Creek Rd., Fair Play* ☎ *530/409–4169* ⊕ *www.lucindascountryinn.com* ➦ *5 rooms* ⦿ *Free Breakfast.*

Plymouth

20 miles south of Placerville.

The most concentrated Gold Country wine-touring area lies in the hills of the Shenandoah Valley, east of Plymouth—you could easily spend two or three days hitting the highlights. Zinfandel is the primary grape grown here, but area vineyards produce many other varietals, from Rhône reds like Syrah and Mourvèdre to Spanish Tempranillo and Italian Barbera and Sangiovese.

GETTING HERE AND AROUND

A car is necessary to explore the Shenandoah Valley. Highway 49 runs north–south through Plymouth; from the highway, head east and north on Shenandoah Road (also signed as E16).

Sights

Amador Cellars

WINERY | Larry and Linda Long made wine out of their home in Truckee for 15 years before opening their down-home Amador County winery. Their son Michael is head winemaker, daughter Ashley his assistant. Estate-grown Zinfandel is the biggest seller, but this small operation also does well with Syrah, Barbera, Tempranillo, the Portuguese varietal Touriga (one of the Port grapes), and a Rhône-style GSM (Grenache, Syrah, and Mourvèdre) blend. ✉ *11093 Shenandoah Rd., Plymouth* ☎ *209/245–6150* ⊕ *www. amadorcellars.com* 🍷 *Tastings from $5* ⊘ *Closed Wed.*

★ Andis Wines

WINERY | The elite Napa Valley consultant Philippe Melka oversees the wine making at Andis, whose contemporary, glass-and-metal production and hospitality buildings provide an appropriately refined setting to enjoy wines that raise the Sierra Foothills bar. The estate Barbera ranks among the region's most elegant, as do several single-vineyard Zinfandels.

On-site winemaker Mark Fowler also crafts Sauvignon Blanc and Arinto whites (the latter grape is Portuguese) and Grenache, Syrah, Petite Sirah, and several red blends. ✉ *11000 Shenandoah Rd., Plymouth* ☎ *209/245–6177* ⊕ *www.andiswines.com* 🍷 *Tastings from $15.*

★ Casino Mine Ranch

WINERY | Two brothers opened this winery named for the ranch their iconoclastic great aunt—described as a cross between Annie Oakley and Zsa Zsa Gabor—purchased in 1936. The siblings added another parcel, where tastings are held in or outside a stylish terrazzo-floored, glass-walled structure with views of the lake that fronts the property. Grenache, Mourvèdre, and Tempranillo are among the strong suits; the Greco white (from a grape either Greek or southern Italian) is among the intriguing lighter wines. ✉ *10690 Shenandoah Rd., Plymouth* ☎ *209/330–0695* ⊕ *www.casinomineranch.com* 🍷 *Tastings from $20* ⊘ *Closed Tues. and Wed.*

Helwig Winery

WINERY | Splashier than many of its neighbors and a draw as much for its restaurant and seasonal live music as its wines, family-operated Helwig occupies a hilltop steel, wood, and glass tasting space with knockout views. The winery specializes in fruit-forward reds, most notably Barbera, Graciano, and Tempranillo; the sparkling rosé of Sangiovese shines among the lighter wines. ✉ *11555 Shenandoah Rd., Plymouth* ☎ *209/245–5200* ⊕ *www.helwigwinery.com* 🍷 *Tastings from $10.*

Jeff Runquist Wines

WINERY | Known for elegant, fruit-forward wines with velvety tannins, Jeff Runquist specializes in Barbera, Zinfandel, and Petite Sirah but makes several other reds and Muscat Canelli, Verdelho, and Viognier whites. His tasting room ranks among the Shenandoah Valley's jolliest. ✉ *10776 Shenandoah Rd., Plymouth* ☎ *209/245–6282* ⊕ *www.jeffrunquistwines.com* 🍷 *Free.*

Rombauer Sierra Foothills

WINERY | Famous for its Napa Valley Chardonnays, Rombauer farmed foothills Zinfandel for years, so it wasn't a total surprise when the winery acquired an existing facility here. Inside the brightly lit tasting room or at umbrella-shaded tables, you can enjoy a flight that might include Sauvignon Blanc, Chardonnay, Cabernet Sauvignon, Merlot, and Sierra Foothills Zinfandel or sip these wines by the glass or bottle. ✉ *12225 Steiner Rd., Plymouth* ☎ *866/280–2582* ⊕ *rombauer.com* 🍷 *Tastings from $14 glass, $25 flight.*

Scott Harvey Wines

WINERY | Winemaker Scott Harvey describes the Sierra Foothills appellation as similar to Italy's Piemonte region, where Barbera originated, but with one additional benefit: it's sunnier here, which this grape loves. Barbera, Zinfandel (one from vines planted in 1869), and Syrah are his winery's focus, but you'll also find Cabernet Sauvignon and other reds along with Sauvignon Blanc, a rosé of Barbera, and sparkling wine ✉ *10861 Shenandoah Rd., Plymouth* ☎ *209/245–3670* ⊕ *www.scottharveywines.com* 🍷 *Tastings from $15.*

Sobon Estate

WINERY | You can sip fruity, robust Zinfandels—old vine and new—and learn about wine making and Shenandoah Valley pioneer life at the museum here. This winery was established in 1856 and has been run since 1989 by the owners of nearby Shenandoah Vineyards, which is open daily. ■**TIP→ To sample the best Zins, pay the modest fee for the reserve tasting.** ✉ *14430 Shenandoah Rd., Plymouth* ☎ *209/245–4455* ⊕ *sobonwine.com* 🍷 *Tastings from $10.*

★ Terre Rouge and Easton Wines

WINERY | This winery achieves success with two separate labels. Terre Rouge, which focuses on Rhône-style wines, makes some of California's most highly praised Syrahs. The Easton label specializes in high-scoring Zinfandels from old and new vines and does well with Sauvignon Blanc and Cabernet Sauvignon. ■TIP→ **You can picnic on the lawn here.** ⊠ *10801 Dickson Rd., Plymouth* ☎ *209/245–4277* ⊕ *www.terrerougewines.com* ⊠ *Tastings from $10* ⊗ *Closed Tues.*

★ Turley Wine Cellars

WINERY | Zinfandel fans won't want to miss Turley, which makes a dozen and a half single-vineyard wines (collectors love them) from old-vine grapes grown all over California. Some wines, including a few from Amador County, are available only in the tasting room. All visits are by appointment. ⊠ *10851 Shenandoah Rd., Plymouth* ☎ *209/245–3938* ⊕ *www. turleywinecellars.com/amador* ⊠ *Tastings $25* ⊗ *Closed Tues. and Wed.*

★ Vino Noceto

WINERY | Owners Suzy and Jim Gullett draw raves for their Sangioveses, which range from light and fruity to rich and heavy. They also produce Rosato di Sangiovese (aka rosé), old-vine Zinfandel, and a few other varietals. Most tastings take place in the red barn where the couple began operations in the 1980s or on a nearby patio. ⊠ *11011 Shenandoah Rd., at Dickson Rd., Plymouth* ☎ *209/245–6556* ⊕ *www.noceto.com* ⊠ *Tastings from $10, tour $25.*

 Restaurants

★ Taste

$$$$ | **MODERN AMERICAN** | A serendipitous find in downtown Plymouth, Taste serves eclectic modern dishes made from fresh local fare. The signature mushroom "cigars"—sautéed shiitake, crimini, and oyster mushrooms rolled with goat cheese in phyllo dough and served with porcini sauce and white truffle oil—are a small-plate staple, and seared day boat scallops, filet mignon, duck leg confit, and a grilled pork chop with foraged mushrooms are examples

of the sustainably sourced, creative entrées. **Known for:** superb beer and wine list; wine bar à la carte menu; three- and five-course prix-fixe dinners. Ⓢ *Average main: $75* ⊠ *9402 Main St., Plymouth* ☎ *209/245–3463* ⊕ *www.restauranttaste. com* ⊗ *Closed Tues. and Wed. No lunch weekdays.*

Coffee and Quick Bites

Fig Barn Coffee Cafe

$ | **AMERICAN** | Breakfast salads, avocado toast, and caffeine several ways are on the menu at this jovial café that's also a good stop for sandwiches and charcuterie, hummus, and bagel boards. You can eat indoors or watch Main Street's comings and goings out on the patio. **Known for:** cinnamon rolls and other baked goods; well-crafted coffee drinks; local wines and beers. Ⓢ *Average main: $15* ⊠ *9506 Main St., 1 block east of rotary, Plymouth* ☎ *530/268–9808* ⊕ *www. figbarn.com* ⊗ *Closed Sun. No dinner.*

🛏 Hotels

★ Grand Reserve Inn at Teneral Cellars Vineyard

$$$$ | **B&B/INN** | Guests typically leave this B&B gushing over just about everything—the Tuscan-villa atmosphere, the expansive vineyard vistas, the sublime hospitality, the elaborate breakfasts, the luxurious accommodations, the ultrasoft sheets. **Pros:** idyllic setting; gracious well-trained staff; marvelous special-occasion splurge. **Cons:** pricey for the area; maximum room occupancy two people except for separate two-bedroom Vineyard House; more for romance than family fun. Ⓢ *Rooms from: $549* ⊠ *19890 Shenandoah School Rd., Plymouth* ☎ *209/245–5466* ⊕ *www. grandreserveinn.com* ⊅ *5 suites* ⦿ *Free Breakfast.*

★ Rest Hotel Plymouth
$ | **B&B/INN** | The team behind Plymouth's Taste restaurant converted two adjacent run down buildings into this boutique hotel whose individually decorated rooms rank among the area's finest. **Pros:** attention to detail; breakfast buffet; evening wine hour, s'mores by the firepit. **Cons:** minimum stay requirement some weekends; lacks big-city hotel amenities; some noise in street-side rooms. *[$] Rooms from: $178 ✉ 9372 Main St., Plymouth ☎ 209/245–6315 🌐 www.hotelrest.net 🛏 16 rooms 🍴 Free Breakfast.*

Amador City

6 miles south of Plymouth.

Amador City bills itself as California's least-populated incorporated city—about 200 people live here—but within its less than ⅓ square mile, much is going on worth checking out. The town's old guard has given way to creative, energetic thirtysomethings who pride themselves on innovation and inclusivity. Most shops, restaurants, and galleries are open on Fridays and weekends, the best time to visit. In summer, an arts or music festival often takes place. In the 19th century, when the Keystone Mine ranked among the Mother Lode's most productive operations, Amador City's population soared to about 5,000. Once the miners extracted all the gold, they cleared out, and the area suffered. Artists began the current revival in the late 20th century, restoring old buildings and opening businesses; the younger newcomers are picking up where their predecessors left off.

GETTING HERE AND AROUND

Take Old Highway 49 (aka Main Street) off Highway 49. Park where you can, and walk the town.

Sights

The End of Nowhere
WINERY | Chris Walsh, a former sommelier, crafts taut natural wines, among them Pinot Gris, Zinfandel, and Primitivo. Walsh presents them three days a week at a combination tasting room, restaurant, and gallery with seating indoors and out. Some fans drive for miles for the house burger. *✉ 14204 Main St., Amador City ☎ 209/267–8345 🌐 www.endofnowhere.wine 🎫 Tastings from $5 ⏲ Closed Mon.–Thurs.*

Restaurants

Break Even Beermakers Kitchen & Beergarden
$ | **AMERICAN** | On some sunny weekends, it seems like half of Amador City has dropped by this small brewery's front porch or umbrella-shaded back patio to enjoy beers that include one made entirely from Amador County hops. The chef, who has a talent for making the familiar unusual, times seasonal items like cornmeal-breaded asparagus fries to local farmers' harvests, with pickled eggs, hot honey walnuts and dates, risotto croquettes, and a sausage-and-kraut plate counting among the year-round possibilities. **Known for:** community milieu; range of beer flavors; grab-and-go items, beers by the can. *[$] Average main: $15 ✉ 14141 Old Hwy. 49, Amador City 🌐 breakevenbeermakers.com ⏲ Closed Mon.–Wed. No lunch Thurs. and Fri.*

★ Imperial Hotel Restaurant
$$$ | **MODERN AMERICAN** | A 2023 refresh of the Imperial Hotel's ground-floor dining space made the most of its existing charms—tall ceilings, original woodwork, exposed brick walls—enhancing these elements with Gold Country memorabilia, sturdy tables, leather chairs, and metal chandeliers. More important, the owners brought in a chef capable of achieving their aspiration to create offhandedly intricate dishes based on

Did You Know?

You can still pan for gold, but any shiny stuff is usually worthless iron pyrite. Here, a young prospector tries his hand at Marshall Gold Discovery State Park.

ingredients grown as near as the culinary garden out back. **Known for:** Wednesday locals night—"limited food and live music"; wide-ranging weekend brunch; multicourse tasting menu (entire table only). ⓢ *Average main: $32* ✉ *14202 Old Hwy. 49, Amador City* ☎ *209/267–9172* ⊕ *www.imperialhotelamador.com/restaurant-bar* ⊘ *Closed Mon. and Tues. No lunch weekdays.*

☕ Coffee and Quick Bites

Small Town Food + Wine
$ | **AMERICAN** | A local success story that expanded into a second storefront after a few years in business, Small Town serves morning coffee and baked goods, by 11 am adding small bites, salads, sandwiches, and flatbreads. For a midday pick-me-up, pair affordable, well-selected wines from the area and beyond with deviled eggs, a three-cheese mac, or an artisanal charcuterie plate. **Known for:** grab-and-go gourmet sandwiches; vegan and vegetarian items; "Made in Amador" gifts and arrangements. ⓢ *Average main: $16* ✉ *14179 Main St., Amador City* ☎ *209/267–8008* ⊕ *www.smalltownfoodandwine.com* ⊘ *Closed Mon.–Wed. No lunch Thurs. No dinner Sun.*

🛏 Hotels

★ Imperial Hotel
$ | **B&B/INN** | A judicious 2023 makeover broadened the appeal of one-block Amador City's 1879 redbrick hotel without sacrificing the throwback feel of the guest rooms, two with balconies overlooking town. **Pros:** history-evoking stay; excellent restaurant and full bar; three larger cottage suites nearby. **Cons:** no phones or TVs in rooms; no staff on-site overnight; lacks pool, fitness center, and other amenities of larger properties. ⓢ *Rooms from: $155* ✉ *14202 Old Hwy. 49, Amador City* ☎ *209/267–9172* ⊕ *www.imperialamador.com* ⇥ *9 rooms* ⦿ *Free Breakfast.*

Sutter Creek

2 miles south of Amador City.

Sutter Creek is a charming conglomeration of balconied buildings, Victorian homes, and neo–New England structures. Main Street is worth a stroll for its shops selling antiques and works by local artists and craftspeople. Tasting rooms of note include Bella Grace, Scott Harvey, and Yorba Wines. Just off Main at 11 Randolph Street, peer into the Monteverde Store, hardly changed since closing in 1971.

GETTING HERE AND AROUND
Arrive here by car on Highway 49. There's no public transit, but downtown is walkable. The visitor center organizes walking tours.

ESSENTIALS
VISITOR INFORMATION Sutter Creek Visitor Center. ✉ *71A Main St., Sutter Creek* ☎ *209/267–1344* ⊕ *suttercreek.org.*

👁 Sights

Knight Foundry
FACTORY | **FAMILY** | Pivotal accomplishments in engineering history occurred at the nation's last functioning water-powered foundry and machine shop, established in 1873 and these days run by volunteers. Namesake Samuel Knight's innovations included a revolutionary system for casting iron and the one-piece Knight Water Wheel for generating power. You can tour on the second Saturday of the month or on workdays (usually Wednesday). ■**TIP→ Plaques and outdoor exhibits accessible at all hours convey some of this facility's fascinating story.** ✉ *81 Eureka St., 2 blocks east of Main St., Sutter Creek* ☎ *209/560–6160* ⊕ *knightfoundry.com* ⚐ *Tour $15, outdoor exhibits free.*

Miners' Bend Historic Gold Mining Park
CITY PARK | **FAMILY** | Volunteers converted a parking lot into a compact open-air tribute

to the area's mining legacy. Signs along the path describe 19th-century mining operations and the equipment on display used to extract or process ore. ✉ *29 Old Hwy. 49, Sutter Creek* 🌐 *suttercreekfoundation.org* 🎫 *Free.*

🍴 Restaurants

★ Element

$$ | **MODERN AMERICAN** | The menu describes this restaurant inside an ivy-covered redbrick building as "a comfort kitchen," but the term doesn't do justice to the sophistication displayed in the cuisine and presentation. Dinner items on the seasonally evolving menu have included mushroom dumplings in a shiitake ginger broth, diver scallops with pureed cauliflower and bacon jam, hanger steak with smashed fingerling potatoes, and a corn polenta bowl with asparagus and mushroom gravy. **Known for:** zesty specialty cocktails; street-side patio seating; eggs Benedict and breakfast tacos. [$] *Average main: $27* ✉ *Hanford House Inn, 61 Hanford St., Sutter Creek* ☎ *209/267–0747* 🌐 *www.hanfordhouse.com/element* 🕒 *Closed Mon. and Tues. No dinner Sun. No lunch Wed.–Fri.*

Gold Dust Pizza

$ | **PIZZA** | **FAMILY** | Zesty pies like the Miner Moe's BBQ Chicken with red onions, pineapple, bacon, and cheese make this casual spot a few steps off Main Street a fitting choice, particularly for lunch or a midafternoon snack. You can also build your own pizza or order a sandwich; there's some indoor seating, but when the weather's good most folks eat outside on the front patio or the creek-side one in back. **Known for:** ultracrispy crust; chicken wings and calzone; combo meals. [$] *Average main: $19* ✉ *20 Eureka St., off Main St., Sutter Creek* ☎ *209/267–1900* 🌐 *relicincorporated.com/gold-dust-pizza-sutter-creek.*

Sina's Backroads Café

$ | **AMERICAN** | **FAMILY** | Homemade lunches and breakfasts served with warmth and cheer are the trademarks of this restaurant and coffee shop in Sutter Creek's historic district. Egg scrambles, pancakes, bagel sandwiches, French toast, and biscuits and gravy headline at breakfast, with soups, salads, sandwiches, and wraps on the menu for lunch. **Known for:** quiches and daily-special sandwiches; good stop for coffee; cookies, muffins, and pastries. [$] *Average main: $11* ✉ *74 Main St., Sutter Creek* ☎ *209/267–0440* 🌐 *sinasbackroadscafe.com* 🕒 *Closed Wed. and Thurs. No dinner.*

🛏 Hotels

Hanford House Inn

$ | **B&B/INN** | The updated country decor of this historic district inn suggests a boutique hotel, but touches like the warm scones delivered to guest rooms each morning recall a traditional bed-and-breakfast. **Pros:** walk to shops, restaurants, and tasting rooms; spacious romantic cottages with decks; some rooms have fireplaces, balconies, or both. **Cons:** cottages and penthouse pricey for the area; sells out on summer weekends; minimum-stay requirement some weekends. [$] *Rooms from: $185* ✉ *61 Hanford St., Sutter Creek* ☎ *209/267–0747* 🌐 *www.hanfordhouse.com* 🔑 *17 rooms* 🍽 *Free Breakfast.*

Inn at 161

$ | **B&B/INN** | For many years known as the Grey Gables Inn, this property at the northern end of Sutter Creek's historic downtown received a boutique-style makeover following a 2021 change of ownership. **Pros:** gas-log fireplaces in all rooms; some rooms have a soaking or Jacuzzi tub; landscaped grounds. **Cons:** along town's busy main drag; minimum weekend-stay requirement; some bathrooms could use updating. [$] *Rooms*

from: $159 ✉ 161 Hanford St., Sutter Creek ☎ 209/267–1039 🌐 innat161.com 🛏 11 rooms 🍴 Free Breakfast.

Volcano

13 miles east of Sutter Creek.

About 100 people live in this off-the-beaten-path former mining town that's a California Historical Landmark. Many visitors come to tour Black Chasm Cavern or dine or stay at the Volcano Union Inn + Pub.

GETTING HERE AND AROUND

A car is the practical way to get to Volcano. From Sutter Creek or Jackson, pick up Highway 88 heading east. **■ TIP→ GPS can be sketchy here, so plot and save your route when you have good coverage.**

Sights

Black Chasm Cavern National Natural Landmark

CAVE | FAMILY | Guided 45-minute tours take you past stalactites, stalagmites, and rare formations of delicate helictites in three underground chambers, one of which also contains a lake. Black Chasm isn't the largest cave in the Gold Country, but its crystals dazzle both eye and camera—the Landmark Chamber, the tour's third stop, inspired a scene in the 2003 film *The Matrix Reloaded.* Outside is an area where kids can "pan" for crystals. **■ TIP→ The same outfit also conducts tours of California Cavern State Historic Landmark, 32 miles south of Volcano, though the days open are less regular.** *✉ 15701 Pioneer Volcano Rd., Volcano ✥ ¾ mile south of Volcano off Pine Grove–Volcano Rd. ☎ 209/296–5007 🌐 cavetouring.com 🎟 $20.*

Hotels

★ Volcano Union Pub + Inn

$ | B&B/INN | What began in the 1880s as a saloon and boardinghouse for miners and other long-term guests now contains four second-floor guest rooms done in pastels and furnished with high-quality linens, free Wi-Fi, and flat-screen TVs with cable. **Pros:** pub that's a worthy stop on its own; two larger rooms have king beds and balcony access; full breakfast with eggs, fresh fruit, and homemade scones. **Cons:** per website, "not suited for small children"; two rooms have a shower but no tub; lacks big-city hotel amenities. *[$] Rooms from: $165 ✉ 21375 Consolation St., Volcano ☎ 209/296–7711 🌐 www.volcanounion.com 🛏 4 rooms 🍴 Free Breakfast.*

Jackson

8 miles south of Sutter Creek.

Jackson wasn't the Gold Country's rowdiest town, but the party lasted longer here than most anywhere else: "girls' dormitories" (aka brothels) and nickel slot machines flourished until the mid-1950s. Jackson also had the world's deepest and richest gold mines, the Kennedy and the Argonaut, which together produced $70 million in gold.

Most of the miners who worked the lode were of Serbian or Italian origin, and they gave the town a European character that persists to this day. A walking-tour map of historic sites, downloadable from the city's website (*🌐 www.ci.jackson.ca.us; click on "Visit Jackson" and then "Things to Do"*), includes the town's steeply terraced Serbian cemetery.

GETTING HERE AND AROUND

Arrive by car on Highway 49. You can walk downtown but otherwise will need a car.

Sights

Kennedy Gold Mine

MINE | FAMILY | On weekends much of the year and some major holidays, docents conduct guided 90-minute surface tours of one of the gold-rush era's most prolific, and one of the world's deepest, mines. Exhibits inside the remaining buildings illustrate how gold flakes were melted for shipment to San Francisco and how "skips" were used to lower miners and materials into the mile-long shaft and carry ore to the surface. ✉ *Kennedy Mine Rd., at Argonaut La., Jackson* ✣ *½ mile east of Hwy. 49* ☎ *209/223–9542* 🌐 *www.kennedygoldmine.com* 🎟 *$7 self-guided tour, $15 guided* 🕒 *Closed most weekdays yr-round, most weekends Nov.–Feb.*

Preston Castle

NOTABLE BUILDING | FAMILY | History buffs and ghost hunters love poking around this fantastically creepy, 156-room, Romanesque Revival structure erected in 1894 to house troubled youth. Having fallen into disrepair, the building is slowly undergoing restoration. On tours, which take place on many Saturdays between April and August, you'll hear all sorts of spine-tingling tales. ✉ *909 Palm Dr., Ione* ✣ *12 miles west of Jackson via Hwys. 88 and 104* ☎ *209/256–3623* 🌐 *www.prestoncastle.org* 🎟 *From $18* 🕒 *Closed Sun.–Fri. and Sept.–Mar.*

Restaurants

Mel and Faye's Diner

$ | AMERICAN | FAMILY | Since 1956, the Gillman family has been serving up its famous two-patty "Moo Burger"—so big it presumably still makes cow sounds. The convivial diner is also known for milk shakes and floats. **Known for:** hearty breakfasts; freshly baked pies; stick with the burger and shakes advise some locals. [$] *Average main: $19* ✉ *31 Hwy. 88, Jackson* ☎ *209/223–0853* 🌐 *melandfayes.homestead.com.*

Teresa's Place

$$ | ITALIAN | Ease back in time at this rustic roadside restaurant dating from 1921, when its namesake, an Italian immigrant, opened a boardinghouse for local miners. Run by her descendants, Teresa's serves unfussy renditions of Italian-American classics—pasta dishes, wood-fired pizzas, veal and chicken dishes, and steak and seafood. **Known for:** minestrone from family recipe; local wines and microbrews, full bar; blast-from-the-past atmosphere. [$] *Average main: $28* ✉ *1235 Jackson Gate Rd., Jackson* ✣ *From downtown head north 1¼ miles on N. Main St.; from Hwy. 49 north of town take Jackson Gate Rd. east 1½ miles* ☎ *209/223–1786* 🌐 *www.teresasitalian.com* 🕒 *Closed Wed. and Thurs. No lunch Sat.–Tues.*

Angels Camp

20 miles south of Jackson.

Angels Camp is famous chiefly for its May jumping-frog contest, based on Mark Twain's short story "The Celebrated Jumping Frog of Calaveras County." The writer reputedly heard the story of the jumping frog from Ross Coon, proprietor of Angels Hotel, which opened in 1856. Sidewalk plaques downtown à la the Hollywood Walk of Fame celebrate the winning frogs in the continuing competition. Either training's gotten way better, or something else is in play—the 1929 victor jumped only 4 feet, but for the last three decades most of the leaps have been from 18- to 20-plus feet. In addition to the contests, Angels Camp's draws include its explorable subterranean caverns and river and lake fishing spots for salmon, trout, and bass.

GETTING HERE AND AROUND

Angels Camp is at the intersection of Highway 49 and Highway 4. You'll need a car to get here and around.

Sights

★ Angels Camp Museum

HISTORY MUSEUM | FAMILY | Learn a little bit about Mark Twain's "The Celebrated Jumping Frog of Calaveras County"—and Angels Camp's celebrated frog-jumping contests—at this museum's street-side facility, then head to the 3-acre spread behind it for a fascinating survey of gold rush–era mining history. The grounds include a carriage house with pre-automotive farming and passenger vehicles; another structure contains mining equipment. Outside, in its original mountings, stands the 27-foot-diameter waterwheel that powered machinery at the Angels Quartz Mine. ✉ *753 S. Main St., Angels Camp* ☎ *209/736–2963* 🌐 *gocalaveras.com/business/to-do* 🎟 *$15.*

★ Moaning Caverns Adventure Park

CAVE | FAMILY | For different sorts of underground jewels, wander into an ancient limestone cave, where stalactites and stalagmites, not gold and silver, await. Take the 235-step Spiral Tour down a staircase built in 1922 into the vast main cavern, or descend farther on the Expedition Tour caving adventure. **■TIP→ It's best to make a reservation here.** ✉ *5350 Moaning Cave Rd., off Parrotts Ferry Rd./E18, Vallecito* ✣ *Take Hwy. 4 northeast from Angels Camp (7 miles) or south from Murphys (6 miles)* ☎ *209/736–2708* 🌐 *moaningcaverns.com* 🎟 *Tours from $23* 🕓 *Closed Tues. and Wed.*

Restaurants

Pickled Porch Cafe

$ | AMERICAN | Perch yourself on this homey bungalow café's wide porch for homemade soups, salads, and sandwiches that include tuna plus three or four tri-tip, turkey, chicken, and BLT offerings. Everything from olives, jalapeños, cornichons, and celery to bacon, cheddar cheese, and shrimp—sometimes all of the above and more—accompanies the peppy "loaded" Bloody Marys (vodka and virgin), nearly a meal in themselves. **Known for:** soup and half-sandwich specials; Emerald Bay BLT with avocado and blue cheese; old-style root beer and other soft drinks. [$] *Average main: $14* ✉ *1192 S. Main St., Angels Camp* ☎ *209/890–3650* 🕓 *Closed Mon and Tues. No dinner.*

Murphys

10 miles northeast of Angels Camp.

A well-preserved hamlet of white-picket fences and Victorian houses, compact Murphys feels upscale yet unpretentious. The shops and restaurants that line several blocks of Main Street are punctuated by wine-tasting rooms, some open only on Fridays and weekends much of the year. The Calaveras Wine Alliance's staff and volunteers excel at pairing wine lovers with the right winery, in some cases providing discount passes.

Horatio Alger, Ulysses S. Grant, and other celebs passed through Murphys when they and other 19th-century tourists came to investigate the giant sequoia groves in nearby Calaveras Big Trees State Park. Both men stayed on Main Street at the Murphys Hotel, which dates from 1856. Its saloon, in business since then, has throwback appeal.

GETTING HERE AND AROUND

Murphys is 10 miles northeast of Highway 49 on Highway 4. You'll need to drive here. Parking can be difficult on summer weekends.

ESSENTIALS

VISITOR INFORMATION Calaveras Wine Alliance. ✉ *202 Main St., at Big Trees Rd., Murphys* ☎ *209/728–9467* 🌐 *calaveraswines.org.*

Sights

★ Calaveras Big Trees State Park

STATE/PROVINCIAL PARK | FAMILY | The park protects hundreds of the largest and rarest living things on the planet—magnificent giant sequoia redwood trees. Some are 3,000 years old, 90 feet around at the base, and 250 feet tall. There are campgrounds, cabin rentals, and picnic areas; wading, fishing, and sunbathing on the Stanislaus River are popular in summer. Enjoy the "three senses" trail, designated for the sight impaired, with interpretive signs in braille that guide visitors to touch the bark and encourage children to slow down and enjoy the forest in a more sensory way. ⊠ *1170 E. Hwy. 4, Arnold ✛ 15 miles northeast of Murphys, 4 miles northeast of Arnold* ☎ *209/795–2334* ⊕ *www.parks.ca.gov* ⬛ *$10 per vehicle.*

Ironstone Vineyards

WINERY | The impeccably maintained gardens at 1,150-acre Ironstone—not to mention the mining-history museum and 44-pound specimen of crystalline gold on display—make a visit here enjoyable even if you don't drink wine. Known for Cabernet Sauvignon, Cabernet Franc, old-vine Zinfandel, and whites including Albariño and Chardonnay, the winery hosts concerts and other events. Its deli has picnic items. ■**TIP→ The history-oriented estate tour, conducted on Friday and Saturday, takes in the gardens and wine caverns.** ⊠ *1894 6 Mile Rd., Murphys ✛ From Main St., head south on Scott St.* ☎ *209/728–1251* ⊕ *www.ironstonevineyards.com* ⬛ *Tastings and tour from $10* ⊙ *Closed Mon.–Wed.*

Lavender Ridge Vineyard

WINERY | A stone building dating from 1859 houses this boutique winery's tasting room, which also sells artisanal cheeses and lavender products. Lavender Ridge's longtime owner-winemaker uses traditional French methods to craft wines from organically farmed Rhône grapes. The lineup includes Viognier, Roussanne, and Grenache Blanc whites, a Grenache rosé, and Grenache, Syrah, and Mourvèdre reds, alone and in a blend. ⊠ *425 Main St., Murphys* ☎ *209/728–2441* ⊕ *lavenderridgevineyard.com* ⬛ *Tastings from $15.*

Mercer Caverns

CAVE | FAMILY | Lighthearted, well-informed guides lead 45-minute tours (208 steps down, 232 steps up) into caverns a prospector named Walter J. Mercer discovered in 1885. Millions of years in the making, the sheer, draperylike formations and aragonite crystals that resemble snowflakes are enthralling. ■**TIP→ Dress in layers (even in summer) and wear non-skid closed-toe shoes for this mildly strenuous adventure.** ⊠ *1665 Sheep Ranch Rd., Murphys ✛ Head north 1¼ miles from 400 block of Main St.* ☎ *209/728–2101* ⊕ *mercercaverns.net* ⬛ *$20.*

★ Newsome Harlow Wines

WINERY | Single-vineyard Sierra Foothills Zinfandels are the passion of Newsome Harlow's owner-winemaker Scott Klann. The ebullient Klann also makes Petite Sirah, Syrah, Carignane, and the Meritage blend of Cabernet Sauvignon and other Bordeaux varietals; whites include a Sauvignon Blanc on several local restaurants' wine lists. The in-town tasting room benefits from its upbeat staff, playful atmosphere, and indoor and outdoor tasting spaces. ⊠ *403 Main St., Murphys* ☎ *209/728–9817* ⊕ *www.nhvino.com* ⬛ *Tastings $15.*

Villa Vallecito Vineyards Tasting Room

WINERY | Winery CEO Ghee Sanchez-Hagedorn's first vineyard memories involve playing amid the Sonoma County grapevines her migrant-farmer parents tended. After successful Silicon Valley careers, she and her husband began growing Calaveras grapes, later establishing Villa Vallecito. The winery's red stars include the Barbera Reserve, the Payaso Syrah-Grenache blend, and Syrah, with Chardonnay and Viognier the whites. The downtown tasting room's Mexican style honors Sanchez-Hagedorn's heritage. ✉ *263 Main St., Suite C, Murphys* ☎ *209/890–3157* 🌐 *www.villavallecitovineyards.com* 🎫 *Tastings from $15* ⏲ *Closed Mon.–Thurs.*

★ Vina Moda

WINERY | The downtown tasting room of owner-winemaker Nathan Vader's boutique winery occupies a restored 1891 structure made of volcanic rock. Top Sierra Foothills vineyards supply grapes for his primarily reds lineup, led by best sellers Barbera and the Primitivo-based Phoenix blend. Merlot, Grenache, and the Venus red blend of Grenache, Syrah, Mourvèdre, and Cabernet Franc, rank among the other stars, served inside or on the shaded rear patio. ✉ *147 Main St., Murphys* ☎ *209/743–6226* 🌐 *vinamoda.com* 🎫 *Tastings $15* ⏲ *Closed Wed.*

🍴 Restaurants

Alchemy

$$ | **AMERICAN** | A casual spot on the eastern edge of town, Alchemy serves sturdy comfort food like meat loaf, pan-seared fish, and mushroom bourguignon over polenta. Fried calamari with roasted jalapeños and a Caesar with smoked-Gouda croutons are among the starters that pair well with the many Calaveras County wines on the list. **Known for:** Alchemy burger with blue cheese; lunch-only sandwiches; mildly pricey for dinner but reliable. [$] *Average main: $30* ✉ *191 Main St., Murphys* ☎ *209/728–0700* 🌐 *alchemymurphys.com* ⏲ *Closed Wed. No lunch Mon., Tues., and Thurs. (but check).*

★ Grounds

$$ | **AMERICAN** | From potato pancakes for breakfast to grilled rib eye for dinner, this bustling bistro with a series of wainscoted rooms and an outdoor back patio has something for all palates. Lighter grilled vegetables, chicken, sandwiches, salads, and homemade soups always shine here, as does heartier fare that might include elk medallions and prawns, forager-mushroom risotto, and cioppino with a relatively delicate yet full-flavored broth. **Known for:** full bar; wines by local producers; attentive service. [$] *Average main: $26* ✉ *402 Main St., Murphys* ☎ *209/728–8663* 🌐 *www.groundsrestaurant.com* ⏲ *Closed Mon. and Tues. No dinner Sun.*

Murphys Pourhouse

$ | **SANDWICHES** | **FAMILY** | The scene's light and lively indoors and out at this pub whose 16 taps dispense everything from pale ales to studly stouts. The kitchen turns out well-made snacks, salads, burgers, wraps, and a slew of sandwiches on various breads. **Known for:** rotating mostly West Coast beer selection; summertime trivia and movie nights on the lawn; family- and dog-friendly. [$] *Average main: $16* ✉ *350 Main St., Suite B, Murphys* ☎ *209/822–3942* 🌐 *murphyspourhouse.com.*

Rob's Place

$$ | **AMERICAN** | **FAMILY** | Comfort food crafted with care makes a trip to this low-slung restaurant on downtown's edge a pleasure whether you dine inside at linen-topped tables or on the dog-friendly, street-facing patio. Several burgers, one vegetarian, another named for a local winemaker, entice the regulars, but don't overlook dinner entrées that might include shrimp curry, lamb and grits, or grilled Indian-spice tofu with pistachios and Sriracha. **Known for:** clever appetizers; only local wines; vegetarian, vegan, and gluten-free options. [$] *Average main: $25* ✉ *140 Main St., Murphys* ☎ *209/813–7003* 🌐 *www.robsplacerestaurant.com* ⏲ *Closed Tues.–Thurs.*

Toscano's

$$ | **ITALIAN** | After paying dues at area restaurants, husband-and-wife team Oscar and Alejandra Sanchez struck out on their own in 2023, opening this tile-floored trattoria with a bar and indoor seating and a covered street-side patio. Carefully selected ingredients and a light touch with Italian sauces elevate dishes that might include shrimp scampi, cioppino, and chicken and veal piccata and marsala. **Known for:** caramel French toast and breakfast burritos and muffins; sandwiches and quesadillas for lunch; call for reservations. $ *Average main: $26* ✉ *380 Main St., Murphys* ☎ *209/728–8800* ⊘ *Closed Mon. and Tues.*

☕ Coffee and Quick Bites

Aria Bakery & Espresso Cafe
$ | BAKERY | FAMILY | For a place as small as it is, this bakery-café produces a staggering array of sweet and savory pastries, sandwiches, salads, and desserts you can enjoy with a well-brewed (if not always swiftly made) coffee, espresso drink, or tea. The croissants are golden and flaky, the quiches moist and filling, and the scones large and flavorful; the breads for lunchtime sandwiches include sourdough, focaccia, and polenta wheat. **Known for:** limited seating inside and out; blueberry muffins, savory croissants, and other baked goods; vegetarian, vegan, gluten-free options. $ *Average main: $12* ✉ *458 Main St., Suite B, Murphys* ☎ *209/728–9250* ⊕ *www.facebook.com/ ariabakery* ⊘ *Closed Tues. and Wed. No dinner.*

★ JoMa's Artisan Ice Cream
$ | AMERICAN | FAMILY | The smell of waffle cones will guide you to this town treasure whose Portuguese-Swiss namesake has been making ice cream since she was a young lass. Handcrafted flavors include Chill'n Cherry Chip (cherries and dark chocolate) and Wake Up Murphys (coffee, cocoa, and fudge). **Known for:** fruity sorbets; cookies and ice-cream cakes; gluten-free flavors. $ *Average main: $8* ✉ *386 Main St., Murphys* ☎ *209/728–8655* ⊕ *jomasicecream.com.*

Hotels

★ Dunbar House Inn
$$ | B&B/INN | The oversize rooms in this elaborate Italianate-style home have brass beds, down comforters, gas-burning stoves, and claw-foot tubs. **Pros:** delectable breakfast; colorful gardens; accommodating staff. **Cons:** books up quickly in summer; not kid-friendly; minimum-stay requirement on weekends and some holidays. $ *Rooms from: $212* ✉ *271 Jones St., Murphys* ☎ *209/728– 2897* ⊕ *www.dunbarhouse.com* ⇄ *6 rooms* ⇄ *77 suites* ⦿ *Free Breakfast.*

Murphys Suites
$ | HOTEL | FAMILY | The lobby's full-size, taxidermied bear poised to pounce and wolf on the prowl hint at a decorative sensibility that dissipates upon entering the boilerplate rooms at this motel-like property a few blocks southeast of downtown. **Pros:** free mini-doughnuts delivered to rooms each morning; pool, sauna, and hot tub; spacious accommodations. **Cons:** nondescript decor; lacks upscale amenities; built in 2001, the place could use a refresh. $ *Rooms from: $134* ✉ *134 Hwy. 4, Murphys* ☎ *209/728–2121* ⊕ *www.murphyssuites.com* ⇄ *77 rooms* ⦿ *No Meals.*

The Victoria Inn
$ | B&B/INN | Decorated with contemporary furnishings that have 19th-century accents, this inn, whose owners also manage several area vacation rentals, benefits from a prime Main Street location within walking distance of restaurants, shops, and wine-tasting rooms. **Pros:** romantic feel; many rooms with balconies; four spacious rooms with king beds. **Cons:** no TVs in rooms; minimum weekend-stay requirement; noise issues in some rooms. $ *Rooms from: $157* ✉ *420 Main St., Murphys* ☎ *209/728– 8933* ⊕ *www.victoriainn-murphys.com* ⇄ *13 rooms* ⦿ *No Meals.*

Columbia

14 miles south of Angels Camp.

Columbia is the gateway for Columbia State Historic Park, one of the Gold Country's most-visited sites. It's a great place for families to participate in living-history activities, especially on summer weekends. There are several inviting spots for a picnic in the area.

GETTING HERE AND AROUND

The only way to get here is by car, via either Highway 4 (the northern route) or Highway 49 (the southern) from Angels Camp.

Sights

★ Columbia State Historic Park

MUSEUM VILLAGE | FAMILY | Columbia, whose mines yielded $87 million in gold, is both a functioning community and a historically preserved town. Usually you can ride a stagecoach, pan for gold, and watch a blacksmith working at an anvil. Street musicians perform in summer. Restored or reconstructed buildings include a Wells Fargo Express office, a Masonic temple, an old-fashioned candy store, saloons, a firehouse, churches, a school, and a newspaper office. At times, all are staffed to simulate a working 1850s town. Also in the park is the Fallon House Theatre, a gorgeous Victorian structure that hosts plays and live music. The town's two reasonably priced historic lodgings, the Fallon Hotel and City Hotel, perch you in the past. ✉ *11255 Jackson St., Columbia* ☎ *209/588–9128* 🌐 *www.parks.ca.gov* 🎟 *Free.*

Restaurants

Diamondback Grill and Wine Bar

$ | AMERICAN | The decor signals more ambitious fare, but massive half-pound burgers and sandwiches like the Ultimate Grilled Cheese with smoked bacon and tomato between three slices of sourdough bread are what this restaurant inside a late-19th-century stone-walled building is about. Locals crowd the tables, especially after 6 pm, for the ground-meat patties, beer-battered onion rings, and veggie burgers. **Known for:** garlic fries; many local wines; homemade desserts. [$] *Average main: $16* ✉ *93 S. Washington St., Sonora* ☎ *209/532–6661* 🌐 *diamondbackgrillsonora.com.*

Performing Arts

Sierra Repertory Theater Company

THEATER | The company, established in 1979, presents dramas, comedies, and musicals at the Historic Fallon House Theatre and another venue in nearby Sonora. Recent productions include *Sunday in the Park with George* and *Jersey Boys.* ✉ *Fallon House, 11175 Washington St., Columbia* ☎ *209/532–3120* 🌐 *www.sierrarep.org.*

Jamestown

7 miles south of Columbia.

Jamestown supplies a touristy view of life during the two gold rushes in these parts. The first took place in the 1850s, the second in the 1880s. Shops in brightly colored buildings along Main Street sell antiques and gift items. Explore train history a few blocks away at Railtown 1897 State Historic Park.

GETTING HERE AND AROUND

Jamestown lies at the intersection of north–south Highway 49 and east–west Highway 108. You'll need a car to tour.

Sights

★ Railtown 1897 State Historic Park

TRAIN/TRAIN STATION | FAMILY | A must for rail enthusiasts and families with kids, this is one of North America's most intact early roundhouses (maintenance facilities). You can hop aboard a steam train for a 40-minute journey—bring the dog if you'd like. The docents entertain guests with tales about the history of locomotion. Listen to the original rotor and pulleys in the engine house and take in the smell of axle grease. Walk through a genteel passenger car with dusty-green velvet seats and ornate metalwork, where Grace Kelly and Gary Cooper filmed a scene in *High Noon.* ■ **TIP→ When offered, Polar Express excursions at Christmastime sell out quickly.** ✉ *18115 5th Ave., Jamestown* ☎ *209/984–3953* 🌐 *www.railtown1897.org* 🎟 *Park $5, rides from $20 (includes park fee)* 🕒 *No train rides Oct.–Mar. or weekdays (except Wed. in June and July).*

🍴 Restaurants

Service Station

$$ | AMERICAN | FAMILY | Exposed brick walls and a pressed-metal ceiling heighten the air of nostalgia at this restaurant whose theme is the golden age of road trips and automobile service stations. Half-pounder burgers and pulled-pork, tri-tip, and other sandwiches and wraps count among the menu's highlights, along with small plates like nacho fries and fried calamari and entrées that might include chicken, grilled salmon, or steak. **Known for:** outdoor beer garden; local wines, craft beers on tap; salads and vegetarian wraps and burgers for noncarnivores. [$] *Average main: $22* ✉ *18242 Main St., Jamestown* ☎ *209/782–5122* 🌐 *www.jamestownservicestation.com* 🕒 *Closed Mon.–Wed.*

🛏 Hotels

1859 Historic National Hotel

$ | B&B/INN | In business since 1859, the National—which has survived the gold rush, gambling, prostitution, at least two fires, a ghost named Flo, and Prohibition—stands today a well-maintained property with all the authentic character and charm its storied past implies. **Pros:** feels straight out of a Western movie; views from odd-numbered rooms (plus Room 2); popular restaurant (good brunches). **Cons:** some rooms are small; most even-numbered rooms have no view; some noise issues. [$] *Rooms from: $160* ✉ *18183 Main St., Jamestown* ☎ *209/984–3446* 🌐 *www.national-hotel.com* 🛏 *9 rooms* 🍽 *Free Breakfast.*

Jamestown Hotel

$ | HOTEL | The spacious, light-filled rooms above this century-old hotel's saloon and restaurant are decorated simply but with flair, and all have updated bathrooms with a period feel. **Pros:** convenient to shops and restaurants; balcony overlooking Main Street; on-site dining. **Cons:** rooms lack microwaves, TVs, and other amenities (though some have refrigerators); noise from restaurant and saloon bleeds through in some rooms; no elevator. [$] *Rooms from: $125* ✉ *18153 Main St., Jamestown* ☎ *209/984–3902* 🌐 *www.thejamestownhotel.com* 🛏 *8 rooms* 🍽 *No Meals.*

Chapter 9

LAKE TAHOE

Updated by
Daniel Mangin

⊙ Sights	🍴 Restaurants	🛏 Hotels	🛍 Shopping	☺ Nightlife
★★★★★	★★★★☆	★★★★★	★☆☆☆☆	★☆☆☆☆

WELCOME TO LAKE TAHOE

TOP REASONS TO GO

★ **The lake:** Blue, deep, and alpine pure, Lake Tahoe is far and away the main reason to visit this High Sierra paradise.

★ **Skiing:** Daring black-diamond runs or baby-bunny bumps—whether you're an expert, a beginner, or somewhere in between, the numerous Tahoe-area ski parks abound with slopes to suit your skills.

★ **The great outdoors:** A ring of national forests and recreation areas linked by miles of trails makes Tahoe excellent for nature lovers.

★ **Dinner with a view:** You can picnic lakeside at state parks or dine in restaurants along the shore.

★ **A date with lady luck:** Whether you want to roll dice, play the slots, or hope the blackjack dealer goes bust before you do, you'll find round-the-clock gambling at the casinos on the Nevada side of the lake and in Reno.

1 South Lake Tahoe. This small city is a gateway to nature, whether you swoosh down slopes at Heavenly Mountain, hike or bike scenic trails, or embark on a lake cruise.

2 Pope-Baldwin Recreation Area. Protected forests and several of the west shore's best beaches line the shores here; the Tallac Historic Site comprises three historic lake-view mansions.

3 Emerald Bay. Named for the glistening green waters in its shallow, emerald-shape cove, Emerald Bay State Park is a favorite recreation spot for the restored Vikingsholm mansion and trails to Eagle Falls. A hair to the north, D.L. Bliss State Park shares shoreline with Emerald Bay State Park; hike the Rubicon Trail to access white-sand beaches and spectacular views.

4 Tahoma. This serene lakeshore village reflects early Lake Tahoe, where rustic cottages housed vacationers seeking refuge from urban commotion. A mile south of town, the 2,000-acre Ed Z'berg Sugar Pine Point State Park encompasses dense forests and nearly 2 shoreline miles.

5 Tahoe City. The Truckee River begins its journey to Nevada in this small town, a convenient place to shop and dine.

6 Olympic Valley. The area that hosted the 1960 Winter Olympics is now the north shore's year-round recreation center.

7 Truckee. This Old West city is a trendy town with a historic depot.

8 Carnelian Bay to Kings Beach. Families frequent the mostly low-key motels, lodges, and cabins along this north shore stretch that includes Tahoe Vista.

9 Incline Village. This ritzy Nevada-side community's draws include Mount Rose and Diamond Peak in winter and beaches and lush hillsides in summer.

10 Zephyr Cove. This tiny Nevada resort occupies a secluded spot edging the eastern shore.

11 Stateline. Towering casinos and 24/7 action give this small city a border-town feel.

12 Reno. This city with the region's main airport has a busy downtown.

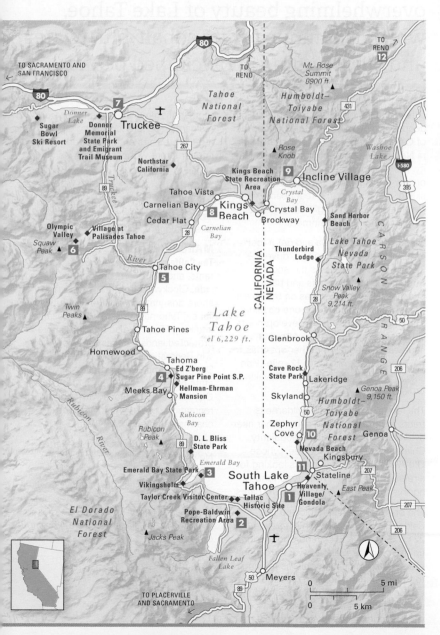

TO SACRAMENTO AND SAN FRANCISCO

TO RENO

TO RENO 12

Mt. Rose Summit 8900 ft ▲

Tahoe National Forest

Humboldt–Toiyabe National Forest

80

7 ✝ Truckee

Donner Lake

Sugar Bowl Ski Resort

Donner Memorial State Park and Emigrant Trail Museum

Northstar California

267

Rose Knob ▲

431

Washoe Lake

I-580

Kings Beach State Recreation Area

9 Incline Village

395

Tahoe Vista

Crystal Bay

Carnelian Bay

Kings Beach 8

Crystal Bay

Cedar Flat

Brockway

Sand Harbor Beach

Olympic Valley

Village at Palisades Tahoe

28

Carnelian Bay

89

Squaw Peak ▲ 6

River

Thunderbird Lodge

Lake Tahoe Nevada State Park

Tahoe City 5

89

Twin Peaks ▲

Lake Tahoe el 6,229 ft.

CALIFORNIA NEVADA

Snow Valley Peak 9,214 ft. ▲

C A R S O N   R A N G E

Tahoe Pines

Glenbrook

50

Homewood

Tahoma Ed Z'berg Sugar Pine Point S.P. 4

Cave Rock State Park

Lakeridge

206

Hellman-Ehrman Mansion

Skyland

Genoa Peak 9,150 ft. ▲

Meeks Bay

50

Humboldt–Toiyabe National Forest

Rubicon Bay

Zephyr Cove 10

Genoa

Rubicon Peak ▲

89

D. L. Bliss State Park

Nevada Beach Kingsbury

Emerald Bay State Park 3

Emerald Bay

South Lake Tahoe

11 Stateline

207

Vikingsholm

Taylor Creek Visitor Center

Tallac Historic Site

1 Heavenly Village/ Gondola

East Peak

207

El Dorado National Forest

Pope-Baldwin Recreation Area 2

206

Jacks Peak ▲

Fallen Leaf Lake

50

Meyers

TO PLACERVILLE AND SACRAMENTO

89

0   5 mi

0   5 km

TO SACRAMENTO AND SAN FRANCISCO

80

Donner Lake

Truckee

89

Rubicon River

Whether you swim, fish, sail, or simply loll on its shores, you'll be wowed by the overwhelming beauty of Lake Tahoe, which is famous for its cobalt-blue water and surrounding snowcapped peaks.

One of the world's largest, clearest, and deepest alpine lakes straddles the border of California and Nevada, giving this Sierra Nevada resort region a split personality. More than half its visitors are intent on low-key sightseeing, hiking, camping, skiing, and boating; the rest head to the Nevada side, lured by glittering casinos and showroom entertainment.

To explore the lake area and get a feel for its differing communities, drive the 72-mile road that follows the shore through wooded flatlands and past beaches, climbing to vistas on the lake's rugged southwestern side and passing through busy commercial developments and casinos on its northeastern and southeastern edges. Another option is to travel on the 22-mile-long, 12-mile-wide lake via a sightseeing cruise or kayaking trip.

The lake and the region's wilderness tracts are the main draws, but other nearby destinations are gaining popularity. Chief among these is Truckee, whose Old West feel entices visitors looking for a relaxed pace and proximity to Tahoe's north shore and Olympic Valley ski parks.

The onset of the pandemic and the Caldor Fire of 2021, which devastated 221,835 acres in El Dorado County right up to South Lake Tahoe's western edge, exacerbated ongoing problems relating to traffic, staffing, housing, and the area's ecological health. In 2023, stakeholders—including the U.S. Forest Service, various tourism boards, and groups representing businesses and year-round residents—began developing a plan to reduce pressure on the environment and infrastructure without limiting visitation.

One way travelers can contribute in the short term is to come here midweek. The bonus: with fewer fellow tourists, you'll have an easier time experiencing the lake's splendor.

MAJOR REGIONS

The California Side. Many hotels, restaurants, and ski resorts are on the California side. Clockwise from the south, lakeshore destinations include South Lake Tahoe, Tahoma, Tahoe City, Carnelian Bay, and Kings Beach. Also near the shore are protected lands such as the Pope-Baldwin Recreation Area and Emerald Bay, D.L. Bliss, and Ed Z'berg Sugar Pine Point state parks. West and north of the lake, Olympic Valley beckons with year-round recreation opportunities, and Truckee charms with its Old West feel.

The Nevada Side. Top stops along the Nevada side's southern shore counterclockwise from the south include Stateline and its casinos, Zephyr Cove, Nevada Beach, Lake Tahoe–Nevada State Park, Sand Harbor Beach, and the resort area of Incline Village. Reno's a 45-minute drive northeast.

Planning

Getting Here and Around

AIR

Reno–Tahoe International Airport (RNO), 34 miles northeast of the closest point on the lake, is served by several major and a few regional airlines. Some travelers fly into Sacramento International Airport (SMF), 112 miles from South Lake Tahoe.

North Lake Tahoe Express runs buses ($99 each way) between RNO and towns on the western and northern shores, plus Truckee and Olympic Valley. South Tahoe Airporter runs buses ($32.75 one-way, $59 round-trip) between RNO and South Lake Tahoe.

AIRPORT CONTACTS Reno Tahoe International Airport. (*RNO*) ⊠ *2001 E. Plumb La., off U.S. 395/I–580, Reno* ☎ *775/328– 6400* ⊕ *www.renoairport.com.* **Sacramento International Airport.** (*SMF*) ⊠ *6900 Airport Blvd., Sacramento* ✈ *Off I–5, 12 miles northwest of downtown* ☎ *916/929–5411* ⊕ *sacramento.aero/smf.*

TRANSFER CONTACTS North Lake Tahoe Express. ☎ *833/709–8080* ⊕ *www. northlaketahoeexpress.com.* **South Tahoe Airporter.** ☎ *866/898–2463* ⊕ *southtahoeairporter.com.*

BUS AND TRAIN

Greyhound stops in Truckee and Reno. Tahoe Transportation District (TTD) provides service (free, as of late 2023) in South Lake Tahoe, Stateline, and along the eastern shore to Sand Harbor. On the north shore, Tahoe Truckee Area Regional Transit (TART) serves Truckee and communities between Tahoma and Incline Village. RTC RIDE buses serve the Reno area. Amtrak stops in Truckee and Reno.

The app-based Lake Link provides free on-demand rides (expect a wait, though) within South Lake Tahoe and a sliver of Stateline. Mountaineer, also free and app-based, operates within Olympic Valley/Palisades Tahoe. Check with your lodging to see if it provides a ski shuttle or is served by one.

CONTACTS RTC RIDE. ☎ *775/348–7433* ⊕ *www.rtcwashoe.com.* **Tahoe Transportation District.** ☎ *775/589–5500, 530/541– 7149* ⊕ *www.tahoetransportation.org.* **Tahoe Truckee Area Regional Transit (TART).** ☎ *530/550–1212, 800/736–6365* ⊕ *tahoetruckeetransit.com.*

CAR

Lake Tahoe is 198 miles northeast of San Francisco, a drive of less than four hours in good weather and light traffic. If possible avoid leaving the San Francisco area on Friday afternoon and returning on Sunday afternoon, when traffic is heavy. The primary route is the four-lane I–80, which cuts through the Sierra Nevada about 14 miles north of the lake. From there Highway 89 and Highway 267 reach the west and north shores, respectively.

U.S. 50, parts of it two lanes with no center divider, is the more direct route to the south shore. From Reno, reach the north shore by heading south on I–580 and southwest on Highway 431. For the south shore, continue on I–580 to U.S. 50.

The scenic 72-mile route around the lake is marked Highway 89 (southwest and west shores), Highway 28 (north and northeast shores), and U.S. 50 (east and southeast shores). Interstate 80, U.S. 50, and I–580 are all-weather highways, but expect snow-removal delays during major storms. Carry tire chains from October through May. If you're renting a car, check that the agency allows their use. If not, rent a four-wheel-drive vehicle.

Hotels

Waterfront inns, slope-side lodges, old-style motels, casino hotels, and house and condo rentals constitute Tahoe's lodging choices. Reserve as far ahead as possible in summer and during ski season, especially for holiday periods, when prices skyrocket. Spring and fall see lower rates, especially at casinos.

South Lake Tahoe has the most activities and the broadest range of lodgings, particularly near California's border with Nevada. On the western and northern shores, Tahoe City has a small-town atmosphere and is accessible to several ski resorts. A few miles northwest of the lake, Palisades Tahoe has its own self-contained village, an aerial tram to the slopes, and year-round outdoor activities. Tahoe Vista and Kings Beach lodgings have a more Old Tahoe feel.

Restaurants

Straightforward American restaurants predominate in the region, but you'll also find places serving Mexican, Japanese, Thai, and other international cuisines. Most towns have a fine-dining gem, along with a pizzeria, brewpub, or both. Look to South Lake Tahoe, the Stateline casinos, Truckee, and Incline Village for the most variety.

On weekends and in high season, expect long waits at popular places. In the April–May and September–November "shoulder seasons," some close or limit their hours. Unless otherwise noted, casual dress is acceptable.

⇨ *Restaurant and hotel reviews have been shortened. For full information, visit Fodors.com. Restaurant prices are the average cost of a main course at dinner, or if dinner is not served, at lunch. Hotel prices are the lowest cost of a standard double room in high season.*

What It Costs

	$	$$	$$$	$$$$
RESTAURANTS				
	under $20	$20–$30	$31–$40	over $40
HOTELS				
	under $200	$200–$350	$351–$500	over $500

Tours

★ Clearly Tahoe

GUIDED TOURS | FAMILY | A gung-ho, well-prepared, lifeguard-certified team conducts tours in clear kayaks that let you peer into Lake Tahoe to a depth of 70 feet or more. For the signature Clearly Explorer tour, you board a tri-toon boat that whisks you across the lake to secluded coves. The kayaks are outfitted with LED lights for outings that begin at dusk. ⊠ *Clearly Explorer departures from Tahoe Keys Marina, 2435 Venice Dr. E, South Lake Tahoe* ✛ *Take Tahoe Keys Blvd. north 1½ miles off Lake Tahoe Blvd.* ☎ *530/554–4664* ⊕ *clearlytahoe. com* ☑ *Clearly Explorer from $219 single, $318 double kayak.*

★ Cruise Tahoe

BOAT TOURS | FAMILY | Once a week in summer, the *Tahoe*, a classic wooden boat, takes passengers on a six-hour cruise whose highlights are a walking tour and picnic lunch at the Thunderbird Lodge, a historic mansion. The captain also conducts private Emerald Bay cruises. ⊠ *Departures from Tahoe Keys Marina, 2435 Venice Dr. E, South Lake Tahoe* ☎ *775/230–8907* ⊕ *www.cruisetahoe. com* ☑ *$215 Thunderbird cruise.*

★ Lake Tahoe Balloons

AIR EXCURSIONS | Take a hot-air balloon flight over the lake from mid-May through mid-October with this company, which launches and lands its balloons on a boat. The four-hour excursion (the flight is 45–60 minutes) begins shortly after sunrise and ends with a traditional champagne toast. ⊠ *Tahoe Keys Marina, 2435 Venice Dr. E, South Lake Tahoe* ⊹ *Tahoe Keys Blvd. off Lake Tahoe Blvd.* ☎ *530/544–1221* ⊕ *www.laketahoeballoons.com* ⊠ *From $399.*

MS *Dixie II*

BOAT TOURS | FAMILY | The 520-passenger MS *Dixie II*, a stern-wheeler, sails year-round from Zephyr Cove to Emerald Bay on sightseeing and dinner cruises. ⊠ *Zephyr Cove Marina, 760 U.S. Hwy. 50, near Church St., Zephyr Cove* ☎ *800/238–2463* ⊕ *www.zephyrcove. com/lake-tahoe-cruises/cruise-experience* ⊠ *From $99.*

North Lake Tahoe Ale Trail

SELF-GUIDED TOURS | Bike or walk one of North Lake Tahoe's dozens of trails, then reward yourself with a craft brew at an alehouse near the end of your chosen route. A dedicated website has an interactive map, descriptions, and short videos pairing trails and drinking spots. There are also suggestions for paddleboarders and kayakers. ⊕ *www.gotahoenorth.com/ lake-tahoe-activities.*

South Tahoe Beer Trail

SELF-GUIDED TOURS | Download a handy map to find your way to nearly a dozen craft breweries along Lake Tahoe's south shore, from Tahoe Keys to Stateline. ⊕ *visitlaketahoe.com/beer-trail.*

Tahoe Cruises

BOAT TOURS | FAMILY | This outfit operates year-round Emerald Bay cruises during the day and at sunset aboard the 75-foot *Spirit of Tahoe.* Options between mid-May and mid-October include lunch, happy hour, sunset, and champagne excursions. Shuttle-bus pickup service is available. ⊠ *Ski Run Marina, 900 Ski Run Blvd., South Lake Tahoe* ☎ *775/588–1881* ⊕ *tahoecruises.com* ⊠ *From $95.*

Tahoe Gal

BOAT TOURS | FAMILY | Docked in Tahoe City, this old-style 120-passenger paddle wheeler departs from mid-May through mid-October on brunch, lunch, happy hour, and sunset tours of Emerald Bay and Lake Tahoe's north and west shores. Specialty excursions feature live music or other entertainment. ⊠ *Departures from Lighthouse Center, 952 N. Lake Blvd., Tahoe City* ☎ *530/583–0141* ⊕ *www. tahoegal.com* ⊠ *From $69.*

★ Tahoe Star Tours

SPECIAL-INTEREST TOURS | FAMILY | "Star guide and poet" Tony Berendsen brings a wealth of knowledge and enthusiasm—and a computerized Celestron telescope—to summer stargazing sessions. Typical ones start half an hour after sunset and last about 90 minutes. The emphasis isn't so much on identifying constellations as understanding and appreciating the cosmos and our place within it. ⊠ *Incline Village* ☎ *775/232–0844* ⊕ *www.tahoestartours. com* ⊠ *From $45.*

★ Tahoe Tastings

BOAT TOURS | Taste eight Northern California wines aboard the *Golden Rose*, a 1953 Chris-Craft Venetian Water Taxi, on two-hour cruises from Tahoe Keys to Emerald Bay and back. Grab-and-go sandwiches and snacks are available at the marina, or you can bring your own. Tours depart midday, later in the afternoon, and at sunset. ⊠ *Tahoe Keys Marina, Rubicon Dock, 2435 Venice Dr. E, South Lake Tahoe* ☎ *530/494–9222* ⊕ *www. tahoetastings.com* ⊠ *From $125 ($100 nondrinkers).*

Visitor Information

CONTACTS North Lake Tahoe Visitor Center. ⊠ *100 N. Lake Tahoe Blvd., Tahoe City* ☎ *530/581–6900* ⊕ *www. gotahoenorth.com.* **Travel North Tahoe Nevada.** ⊠ *Welcome Center, 969 Tahoe Blvd., Incline Village* ☎ *775/832–1606* ⊕ *travelnorthtahoenevada.com.* **Visit Lake Tahoe.** ☎ *775/588–4591, 530/542–4637* ⊕ *visitlaketahoe.com.*

Skiing and Snowboarding

Blizzards bombard the mountains around Lake Tahoe throughout the winter and often in fall and spring. With all the snowpack, 10- to 12-foot bases are common, and skiing and snowboarding can continue well into May. Check conditions at ⊕ *OntheSnow.com*, or get the inside scoop by talking to waiters and bartenders, many of whom are ski bums.

On weekends, avoid the masses by arriving and quitting early, taking a lunch break at 11 am or 1:30 pm rather than noon. Also consider skiing at areas with few high-speed lifts or limited lodging at their bases—Sugar Bowl, Mt. Rose, Sierra-at-Tahoe, Diamond Peak, and Kirkwood.

Cross-country skiing at resorts can be costly, but you get the benefits of machine grooming and trail preparation. For bargain Nordic, head to noncommercial venues such as Tahoe Meadows Snowplay Area.

When to Go

Although Lake Tahoe swells with visitors at Christmastime and during winter snowfall, high season is the summer, when the weather is crisper and cooler than in the scorched Sierra Nevada foothills and the lake's surface temperature is an invigorating 65°F to 70°F (compared with 40°F to 50°F in winter). July 4th and weekends from late May to mid-September are often packed, and beaches, lodgings, and roads become clogged. Two good times to visit are early fall and late spring, when the crowds thin and the weather's still hospitable. Travel midweek in summer and during ski season to avoid traffic congestion.

Most accommodations, restaurants, and some parks remain open year-round, but many visitor centers, mansions, parks, and beaches are closed from October through late May. Winter-sports enthusiasts pack Tahoe's downhill resorts and cross-country centers during these months. Storms often close roads and force chain requirements on the highways.

South Lake Tahoe

60 miles south of Reno, 198 miles northeast of San Francisco.

The city of South Lake Tahoe's raison d'être is tourism: the casinos of adjacent Stateline, Nevada; the ski slopes at Heavenly Mountain; the beaches, docks, bike trails, and campgrounds all around the south shore; and the backcountry of Eldorado National Forest and Desolation Wilderness. The small city's main attributes are its convenient location, bevy of services, and gorgeous lake views.

GETTING HERE AND AROUND
The main route into and through South Lake Tahoe is U.S. 50; signs say "Lake Tahoe Boulevard" in town. Arrive by car or, if coming from Reno airport, take the South Tahoe Express bus. Tahoe Transportation District operates daily bus service in the south shore area year-round.

ESSENTIALS
VISITOR INFORMATION Explore Tahoe Visitor Center. ⊠ *Heavenly Village, 4114 Lake Tahoe Blvd., South Lake Tahoe* ☎ *(530) 542–4637; (775) 588–4591* ⊕ *Visitlaketahoe.com.*

Sights

★ Heavenly Gondola

VIEWPOINT | FAMILY | Whether you ski or not, you'll appreciate the impressive view of Lake Tahoe from the Heavenly Gondola. Its eight-passenger cars travel from Heavenly Village 2.4 miles up the mountain in 15–20 minutes. When the weather's fine, you can hike around the mountaintop and have lunch at Tamarack Lodge. The thrilling gravity-powered Ridge Rider alpine roller coaster, which zips past boulders and trees, closed in 2023 because of snow damage but was expected to reopen in 2024. ✉ *4080 Lake Tahoe Blvd., South Lake Tahoe* ☎ *775/586–7000* 🌐 *www.skiheavenly.com* 🎫 *From $74 in summer* 🕒 *Check website for seasonal and other closures.*

Heavenly Village

STORE/MALL | FAMILY | This lively complex at the base of the Heavenly Gondola has good shopping, an arcade for kids, a cinema, a skating rink in winter, miniature golf in summer, and the Loft for magic shows and other live entertainment. Base Camp Pizza Co., Azul Latin Kitchen, and Kalani's at Lake Tahoe for seafood stand out among the several restaurants. ✉ *1001 Heavenly Village Way, South Lake Tahoe* 🌐 *theshopsatheavenly.com.*

Van Sickle Bi-State Park

STATE/PROVINCIAL PARK | FAMILY | Heavenly Gondola cars glide above this 756-acre day-use-only park that straddles the California–Nevada border steps south of Heavenly Village. Several trails wind up the mountain to sigh-worthy vistas. Colorful spring wildflowers and fall foliage provide further incentive to bring a picnic and hike, bike, or ride horseback. The park's Rim Trail Connector leads to the Tahoe Rim Trail, which for more than 165 miles follows the ridge lines of the mountains surrounding Lake Tahoe. ✉ *30 Lake Parkway, at Heavenly Village Way, South Lake Tahoe* ☎ *775/831–0494* 🌐 *parks.nv.gov/parks* 🎫 *Free* 🕒 *Parking lot closed Nov.–Apr. (pedestrians okay).*

Restaurants

Artemis Lakefront Cafe

$$ | MEDITERRANEAN | FAMILY | A festive marina restaurant with a heated outdoor patio, Artemis reveals its Greek influences in breakfast dishes like baklava French toast and gyros and eggs. All day, though, the menus encompass more familiar options (eggs Benedict in the morning, burgers and grilled mahimahi later on). **Known for:** heated outdoor patio; outgoing staff; marina location. [$] *Average main: $24* ✉ *900 Ski Run Blvd., South Lake Tahoe* ☎ *530/542–3332* 🌐 *www.artemislakefrontcafe.com.*

Cafe Fiore

$$$$ | ITALIAN | Inside a rough-hewn former ski cabin with an intimate six-table dining room (book two weeks ahead in winter, when two outdoor areas are closed), this restaurant serves rustic Italian cuisine that you can pair with wines from the owner's formidable list. Thin eggplant crepes stuffed with smoked salmon are among the top appetizers, with fettuccine Calabrese, swordfish, and filet mignon prepared two ways frequently on the menu. **Known for:** loyal in-town following; entrée price includes soup or salad; silky white-chocolate ice cream with seasonal berries for dessert. [$] *Average main: $43* ✉ *1169 Ski Run Blvd., off South Lake Tahoe Blvd., South Lake Tahoe* ☎ *530/541–2908* 🌐 *www.cafefiore.com* 🕒 *No lunch.*

★ Evan's American Gourmet Cafe

$$$$ | ECLECTIC | Its excellent service, world-class cuisine, and superb wine list make this intimate restaurant the top choice for high-end dining in South Lake. Inside a converted cabin, Evan's serves creative American cuisine that might include pan-seared day boat scallops and meat dishes such as rack of lamb marinated with rosemary and garlic and served with raspberry demi-glace. **Known for:** intimate atmosphere; world-class cuisine; dessert menu. [$] *Average main: $45* ✉ *536 Emerald Bay Rd., Hwy. 89, at 15th St., South Lake Tahoe* ☎ *530/542–1990* 🌐 *evanstahoe.com* 🕒 *No lunch. Closed Sun. and Mon.*

Kalani's at Lake Tahoe

$$$$ | **ASIAN** | The white-tablecloth dining room at Heavenly's sleekest (and priciest) restaurant is decked out with carved bamboo, a burnt-orange color palette, and a modern-glass sculpture, all of which complement Pacific Rim–influenced dishes like fillet of beef with miso-garlic butter and the signature Chilean sea bass with Thai-basil mashed potatoes and ponzu butter sauce. Sushi selections with inventive rolls and sashimi combos, plus less expensive vegetarian dishes, add depth to the menu. **Known for:** fresh-off-the-plane Hawaiian seafood; thoughtful wine selections; upscale setting. [$] *Average main: $43* ✉ *1001 Heavenly Village Way, Suite 26, at U.S. 50, South Lake Tahoe* ☎ *530/544–6100* 🌐 *www.kalanis.com.*

★ The Libation Lodge by South Lake Brewing Company

$ | **AMERICAN** | A floor-to-ceiling mural of Lake Tahoe scenes spans the longest wall of the South Shore's largest brewery's downtown outpost. The influences on homegrown beers, from light lagers to dark ales, come from as near as California and Mexico and as far away as New Zealand, the model as well for Pacific Rim flourishes that find their way into burgers, sliders, sandwiches, and a few apps and salads. **Known for:** beer flights; local business; outdoor patio. [$] *Average main: $16* ✉ *Tahoe Village Center, 4000 Lake Tahoe Blvd., Suite 26, South Lake Tahoe* ☎ *530/578–0087* 🌐 *www.southlakebeer.com/libation-lodge.*

★ Maggie's Restaurant and Bar

$$$$ | **AMERICAN** | The ultramodern architecture of the Desolation Hotel's third-floor restaurant raises expectations even before you take a sip or bite, but the specialty cocktails, sophisticated California-inspired cuisine, and from-the-heart hospitality more than live up to them. Appetizers like grilled tuna crudo are all about the freshness, though as with recent veal chop and Dijon-crusted salmon entrées, the deftness of the saucing heightens the satisfaction. **Known for:** osso buco chilaquiles and short ribs eggs Benedict at daily brunch; soups and salads; patio seating with heaters and fireplaces. [$] *Average main: $49* ✉ *933 Poplar St., at Manzanita St., South Lake Tahoe* ☎ *530/725–0101* 🌐 *desolationhotel.com/tahoe/maggies* 🕒 *No lunch.*

My Thai Cuisine

$ | **THAI** | Fantastic flavors and gracious owners have earned this humble roadside restaurant with river-stone columns, pine-paneled walls and ceilings, and Thai statues and ornamentation the loyalty of Tahoe residents and regular visitors. The aromatic dishes include crab pad Thai, basil lamb, sizzling shrimp, and numerous curries. **Known for:** many vegetarian options; lunch specials a good deal; lively atmosphere. [$] *Average main: $17* ✉ *2108 Lake Tahoe Blvd., ¼ mile northeast of "Y" intersection of U.S. 50 and Hwy. 89, South Lake Tahoe* ☎ *530/544–3232* 🌐 *www.mythaitahoe.com* 🕒 *Closed Tues.*

Red Hut Café

$ | **AMERICAN** | **FAMILY** | A vintage-1959 Tahoe diner, all chrome and red plastic, the Red Hut is a tiny place with a wildly popular breakfast menu featuring huge omelets; banana, pecan, and coconut waffles (cornbread, too); and other tasty vittles. A second South Lake branch has a soda fountain and is the only one that serves dinner, and there's a third location in Stateline. **Known for:** huge omelets; variety of waffles; old-school feel. [$] *Average main: $15* ✉ *2723 Lake Tahoe Blvd., near Blue Lake Ave., South Lake Tahoe* ☎ *530/541–9024* 🌐 *www.facebook.com/TheRedHut* 🕒 *No dinner.*

Scusa! Italian Ristorante

$$ | ITALIAN | This longtime favorite turns out big plates of veal scaloppine, chicken piccata, and garlicky linguine with clams—straightforward Italian American food (and lots of it), served in an intimate dining room warmed by a crackling fire on many nights. There's an outdoor patio that's open in warm weather. **Known for:** classic Italian American recipes; fritto misto, grilled radicchio, and fresh-baked mozzarella appetizers; sticky-bun bread pudding for dessert. $ *Average main: $26* ⊠ *2543 Lake Tahoe Blvd., at Sierra Blvd., South Lake Tahoe* ☎ *530/542–0100* ⊕ *scusalaketahoe.com* ◔ *No lunch.*

★ Sprouts Natural Foods Cafe

$ | AMERICAN | FAMILY | If it's in between normal mealtimes and you're hungry for something healthful, head to this order-at-the-counter café for salads, overstuffed wraps, hot sandwiches, homemade vegan soups, all-day breakfasts, and the best smoothies in town. Dine at wooden tables in the cheery contemporary indoor space or out front on the patio, or just order food to go. **Known for:** fresh, healthy cuisine; vegan and vegetarian friendly; congenial staff. $ *Average main: $12* ⊠ *3123 Harrison Ave., U.S. 50 at Alameda Ave., South Lake Tahoe* ☎ *530/541–6969* ⊕ *www.sproutscafetahoe.com.*

Hotels

Base Camp South Lake Tahoe

$ | HOTEL | FAMILY | This three-floor boutique hotel near the Heavenly Gondola, Stateline casinos, and several good restaurants provides solid value in a hip yet family-friendly setting. **Pros:** convenient location; great for groups; firepits, beer garden, rooftop mountain-view hot tub. **Cons:** near a busy area; not on the lake (five-minute walk); noise from on-site activities. $ *Rooms from: $161* ⊠ *4143 Cedar Ave., off U.S. 50, South Lake Tahoe* ☎ *530/208–0180* ⊕ *basecamptahoesouth. com* ⇆ *73 rooms* ⏺ *No Meals.*

★ Black Bear Lodge

$$$ | B&B/INN | Built in the 1990s with meticulous attention to detail, the original section of this 2-acre complex feels like an Adirondack resort, with lodge rooms and highly recommended kitchenette-equipped cabins with fine art, fireplaces, and 19th-century American antiques. **Pros:** near Heavenly skiing; within walking distance of good restaurants; wine and beer bar. **Cons:** not staffed 24/7; lacks big-hotel amenities; though upgraded with a nod to rusticity, Rubicon Building quarters aren't quite as appealing. $ *Rooms from: $279* ⊠ *1202 Ski Run Blvd., South Lake Tahoe* ☎ *530/544–4451* ⊕ *www.tahoeblackbear. com* ⇆ *31 rooms* ⏺ *No Meals.*

Camp Richardson

$ | RESORT | FAMILY | An old-fashioned family resort on 120 acres fronting Lake Tahoe, Camp Richardson earns retro cred for its 1920s log cabin–style lodge, its few dozen cabins, and its small inn—all tucked beneath giant pine trees—but wins no style points for its straightforward accommodations with a dearth of amenities. **Pros:** lakeside location; great for families; inexpensive daily and weekly rates. **Cons:** dated style; lacks modern amenities (and even phones and TVs in some rooms); some cabins available in summer only. $ *Rooms from: $125* ⊠ *1900 Jameson Beach Rd., South Lake Tahoe* ☎ *530/541–1801, 800/544–1801* ⊕ *www.camprichardson.com* ⇆ *74 units* ⏺ *No Meals.*

Desolation Hotel Hope Valley

$$ | RESORT | Known for decades as Sorensen's Resort, this 165-acre Eldorado National Forest complex with an on-site restaurant has a woodsy summer-camp charm. **Pros:** outdoor activities in gorgeous rustic setting; cabins, yurts, and tent and RV spaces; kitchen or kitchenette in most cabins. **Cons:** traffic noise in some cabins (request one away from the road); lacks amenities of larger properties; 20-minute drive from South Lake

Tahoe. $ *Rooms from: $241* ✉ *14255 Hwy. 88, Hope Valley* ☎ *530/694–2203, 800/423–9949* ⊕ *www.desolationhotel. com* ⬥ *36 units* ❙◎❙ *No Meals.*

★ Desolation Hotel Lake Tahoe

$$$ | HOTEL | Hoteliers who revere nature and luxury in equal proportions conceived this gaspworthy, glass-walled, world-un-to-itself "micro-resort" that debuted in 2022 a few-minutes' walk to a private-access beach and an even shorter one to Stateline's casinos. **Pros:** refined cuisine at Maggie's restaurant; convenient to Heavenly Village and outdoor activities; studios and town houses with kitchenettes and patios or balconies accommodate four people. **Cons:** restaurant on pricey side; high weekend rates; must park on street when on-site lot is full. $ *Rooms from: $359* ✉ *933 Poplar St., South Lake Tahoe* ☎ *530/725–0101* ⊕ *www.desolationhotel.com* ⬥ *21 rooms* ❙◎❙ *No Meals.*

Hotel Azure

$ | HOTEL | High-end motel meets boutique hotel at this revamped (to the tune of $3.5 million) property across the road from a beach. **Pros:** clean, spacious rooms; good work spaces and tech amenities; short drive to Heavenly Mountain. **Cons:** on busy Lake Tahoe Boulevard; no bell or room service; some sound bleed-through from room to room. $ *Rooms from: $190* ✉ *3300 Lake Tahoe Blvd., South Lake Tahoe* ☎ *530/542–0330, 800/877–1466* ⊕ *www.hotelazure-tahoe.com* ⬥ *99 rooms* ❙◎❙ *No Meals.*

The Landing Resort & Spa

$$$ | RESORT | Perched at the edge of a semiprivate beach that's less than a half-mile from Heavenly Village, The Landing provides luxe rooms and resort amenities in a prime location—removed from, but close to, the Stateline action. **Pros:** across the street from the beach and lake; full-service spa with six treatment rooms, pool, hot tub, fitness center; spacious rooms, most over 450 square feet. **Cons:** small lobby, lack of resort grounds; hefty resort fee; busy beach in peak season. $ *Rooms from: $389* ✉ *4104 Lakeshore Blvd., South Lake Tahoe* ☎ *855/700–5263, 530/541–5263* ⊕ *www.thelanding-tahoe.com* ⬥ *82 rooms* ❙◎❙ *No Meals.*

Marriott's Grand Residence and Timber Lodge

$$$ | RESORT | FAMILY | You can't beat the location of these two gigantic condominium complexes at the base of Heavenly Gondola, and though both are comfortable, Timber Lodge feels more like a family vacation resort, whereas Grand Residence is geared to upper-end travelers. **Pros:** smack in the center of town; great for families; near excellent restaurants. **Cons:** can be jam-packed on weekends; no room service; lacks serenity. $ *Rooms from: $371* ✉ *1001 Heavenly Village Way, South Lake Tahoe* ☎ *530/542–8400 Marriott's Grand Residence, 800/845–5279, 530/542–6600 Marriott's Timber Lodge* ⊕ *www.marriott. com* ⬥ *431 rooms* ❙◎❙ *No Meals.*

Nightlife

The Loft

THEMED ENTERTAINMENT | FAMILY | Crowd-pleasing magic shows (sometimes other entertainment) and a casual-industrial setting keep patrons happy at this Heavenly Village bar and lounge where kids are welcome. The mood is upbeat, the specialty cocktails are potent, and if you're in the mood for dinner, the kitchen turns out tapas and larger plates more tasty than one might expect at such a venue. ✉ *1001 Heavenly Village Way, South Lake Tahoe* ☎ *530/523–8024* ⊕ *thelofttahoe.com.*

McP's Taphouse Grill

BARS | You can hear live bands—rock, jazz, blues, alternative—on most nights at McP's while you sample a few of the 40 beers on draft. Lunch and dinner (Irish and California cuisine) are served daily. ✉ *4125 Lake Tahoe Blvd., Suite*

A, near Friday Ave., South Lake Tahoe
☎ *530/542–4435* ⊕ *www.mcpstahoe.net.*

 **Activities**

BIKING

Tahoe Sports Ltd.

BIKING | FAMILY | You can rent road and mountain bikes and get tips on where to ride from the friendly staff at this full-service sports store. ⊠ *Tahoe Crescent V Shopping Center, 4000 Lake Tahoe Blvd., Suite 7, South Lake Tahoe* ☎ *530/600– 4581* ⊕ *www.tahoesportsltd.com.*

FISHING

Tahoe Sport Fishing

FISHING | One of the area's largest and oldest fishing-charter services conducts morning and afternoon trips. Outings include all necessary gear and bait, and the crew cleans and packages your catch. ⊠ *900 Ski Run Blvd., off Lake Tahoe Blvd., South Lake Tahoe* ☎ *530/541–5448* ⊕ *tahoesportfishing.com* 🎫 *From $200.*

HIKING

Desolation Wilderness

HIKING & WALKING | Trails within the 63,960-acre wilderness lead to gorgeous backcountry lakes and mountain peaks. It's called Desolation Wilderness for a reason, so bring a topographic map and compass, and carry water and food. You need a permit for overnight camping (☎ *877/444–6777* ⊕ *www.recreation.gov*); bear-resistant food canisters are required. In summer you can access this area by boarding a boat taxi ($20 one-way) at Echo Chalet (⊠ *9900 Echo Lakes Rd., off U.S. 50* ☎ *530/659–7207*). The Pacific Crest Trail also traverses Desolation Wilderness. ⊠ *El Dorado National Forest Information Center, South Lake Tahoe* ☎ *530/644– 2349* ⊕ *www.fs.usda.gov.*

KAYAKING

Kayak Tahoe

KAYAKING | FAMILY | This outfit conducts excursions out of Emerald Bay and three other south shore locations. You can also rent a kayak and paddle solo on the lake. ⊠ *South Lake Tahoe* ☎ *530/544–2011* ⊕ *kayaktahoe.com* 🎫 *Rentals from $35, tours from $80.*

SKIING

★ Heavenly Mountain Resort

SKIING & SNOWBOARDING | FAMILY | Straddling two states, vast Heavenly Mountain Resort—composed of nine peaks, two valleys, and four base-lodge areas, along with the largest snowmaking system in the western United States—pairs terrain for every skier with exhilarating Tahoe Basin views. Beginners can choose wide, well-groomed trails, accessed from the California Lodge or the gondola from downtown South Lake Tahoe; kids have short and gentle runs in the Enchanted Forest area all to themselves. The Sky Express high-speed quad chair whisks intermediate and advanced skiers to the summit for wide cruisers or steep tree-skiing. Mott and Killebrew canyons draw experts to the Nevada side for steep chutes and thick-timber slopes. The ski school offers lessons for adults and children ages four and up. Summertime thrill seekers participate in Epic Discovery—fun for the whole family that includes a mountain coaster, ziplines, a climbing wall, gemstone panning, and hiking opportunities. **Facilities:** 97 trails; 4,800 acres; 3,500-foot vertical drop; 28 lifts. ⊠ *Ski Run Blvd., South Lake Tahoe* ✛ *Off U.S. 50* ☎ *775/586–7000, 800/432–8365* ⊕ *www.skiheavenly.com* 🎫 *Lift ticket from $189.*

Kirkwood Ski Resort

SKIING & SNOWBOARDING | FAMILY | Thirty-six miles south of Lake Tahoe, Kirkwood is the hard-core skiers' and boarders' favorite south-shore mountain, known for its craggy gulp-and-go chutes, sweeping cornices, steep-aspect glade skiing, and high base elevation. But there's also fantastic terrain for newbies and intermediates down wide-open bowls, through wooded gullies, and along rolling tree-lined trails. Families often head to the Timber Creek area, a good spot to learn to ski or snowboard. Tricksters can show off in two terrain parks on jumps, wall rides, rails, and a half-pipe. The mountain gets hammered with an average of 354 inches of snow annually. If you're into out-of-bounds skiing, check out Expedition Kirkwood, a backcountry-skills program that teaches basic safety awareness. If you're into cross-country, the resort has superb groomed-track skiing, with skating lanes, instruction, and rentals. The children's ski school has programs for ages 3 to 12. **Facilities:** 86 trails; 2,300 acres; 2,000-foot vertical drop; 15 lifts. ⊠ *1501 Kirkwood Meadows Dr., Kirkwood ✛ Off Hwy. 88, 14 miles west of Hwy. 89* ☎ *209/258–6000* ⊕ *www.kirkwood.com* ⊡ *Day pass from $122.*

Sierra-at-Tahoe

SKIING & SNOWBOARDING | FAMILY | Wind-protected and meticulously groomed slopes, excellent tree-skiing, and gated backcountry skiing are among the draws at this low-key but worthy resort. Popular with snowboarders, Sierra has several terrain parks, including Half-pipe, with 18-foot walls and a dedicated chairlift. **Facilities:** 46 trails; 2,000 acres; 2,250-foot vertical drop; 14 lifts. ⊠ *1111 Sierra-at-Tahoe Rd., Twin Bridges ✛ 12 miles from South Lake Tahoe off U.S. 50, past Echo Summit* ☎ *530/659–7453 information, 530/659–7475 snow phone* ⊕ *www.sierraattahoe.com* ⊡ *Lift ticket $130.*

Pope-Baldwin Recreation Area

5 miles west of South Lake Tahoe.

To the west of downtown South Lake Tahoe, U.S. 50 and Highway 89 come together, forming an intersection nicknamed "the Y." If you head northwest on Highway 89, also called Emerald Bay Road, and follow the lakefront, commercial development gives way to national forests and state parks. One of these is Pope-Baldwin Recreation Area.

GETTING HERE AND AROUND

The entrance to the Pope-Baldwin Recreation Area is on the east side of Emerald Bay Road. The area is closed to vehicles in winter, but you can cross-country ski here.

Sights

★ Tallac Historic Site

HISTORIC SIGHT | FAMILY | Three historic mansions—the Pope House, the Baldwin Museum, and the Heller Estate—open in late spring and summer, but you can stroll the grounds or picnic year-round. George S. Pope, who made his money in shipping and lumber and played host to 1920s America's business and cultural elite, commissioned the magnificent 1894 Pope House. The Baldwin Museum is in the estate that once belonged to entrepreneur "Lucky" Baldwin; today it houses a collection of family memorabilia and Washoe Indian artifacts.

With a spectacular floor-to-ceiling stone fireplace, the Heller Estate, also known as Valhalla, was occupied for years by Walter and Claire Heller. (Tidbit: after their divorce, each visited the property on alternate weekends, though she held the title.) The estate's Grand Hall, Grand Lawn, and a boathouse refurbished as a theater host the summertime Valhalla Art, Music and Theatre Festival (⊕ *valhallatahoe.com*) of concerts, plays, and cultural activities. ⊠ *Hwy. 89, Pope-Baldwin Recreation Area* ☎ *530/541–5227 late May–mid-Sept., 530/544–7383 year-round* ⊕ *tahoeheritage.org* ⊡ *Free, summer guided site walk $5, Pope House tour $10* ⊗ *House and museum closed late Sept.–late May.*

Taylor Creek Visitor Center

VISITOR CENTER | FAMILY | You can visit the site of a Washoe Indian settlement and walk self-guided trails through meadow,

Fjord-like Emerald Bay is possibly the most scenic part of Lake Tahoe.

marsh, and forest at this U.S. Forest Service center. Forest Service naturalists organize discovery walks and evening programs in summer, and you may see spawning kokanee salmon digging their nests in fall. By 2024, extensive repairs should be completed to the Stream Profile Chamber, the Rainbow Trail's underground display with windows right into Taylor Creek. ⊠ *Hwy. 89 ⊕ 3 miles north of junction with U.S. 50* ☎ *530/543–2674 late May–Oct., 530/543–2600 year-round* ⊕ *www.fs.usda.gov* ☑ *Free.*

Emerald Bay

4 miles west of Pope-Baldwin Recreation Area.

You can hike, bike, swim, camp, scuba dive, kayak, or tour a look-alike Viking castle at Emerald Bay State Park. Or simply enjoy the most popular tourist stop on Lake Tahoe's circular drive: the high cliff overlooking Emerald Bay, famed for its jewel-like shape and color. Beautiful

scenery and excellent hikes continue at the adjacent D.L. Bliss State Park.

GETTING HERE AND AROUND

The entrances to Emerald Bay and D.L. Bliss state parks are on the east side of twisting, narrow Highway 89. Caution is the keyword—pay attention to traffic when walking across the highway, and expect a ticket if your car intrudes even one inch onto the frequently patrolled roadway. Emerald Bay State Park closes to vehicles in winter; vehicles are also not allowed in D.L. Bliss when it closes for the season.

 Sights

D.L. Bliss State Park

STATE/PROVINCIAL PARK | FAMILY | This park, which shares 6 miles of shoreline with Emerald Bay State Park, takes its name from Duane LeRoy Bliss, a 19th-century lumber magnate who once owned nearly 75% of Tahoe's lakefront. Emerald Bay and D.L. Bliss parks cover 1,830 acres, 744 of which the Bliss family donated to the state. At the north end of Bliss is Rubicon Point, which overlooks one of the lake's deepest spots.

Short trails lead to an old lighthouse and the 250,000-pound Balancing Rock, perched atop a fist of granite. The 4.5-mile Rubicon Trail—a premier Tahoe hike—leads to Vikingsholm (part of Emerald Bay State Park), providing stunning views along the way. Two white-sand beaches front some of Tahoe's warmest water. ■TIP→ **When the Bliss roads close for the winter, park in the visitor center lot and hike 1 mile to the Rubicon trailhead.** ⊠ *Hwy. 89* ✢ *Entrance east side of Hwy. 89, 3 miles north of Emerald Bay State Park* ☎ *530/525–3384 visitor information (summer), 530/525–9528 winter conditions* ⊕ *www.parks.ca.gov* ⬚ *$10 per vehicle, day-use.*

★ **Emerald Bay State Park**

STATE/PROVINCIAL PARK | Millions of years ago, a massive glacier carved this 3-mile-long and 1-mile-wide fjord-like inlet. Famed for its jewel-like shape and colors, the bay surrounds Fannette, Lake Tahoe's only island. Highway 89 curves high above the lake here; from the Emerald Bay lookout, the park's centerpiece, you can survey the whole scene. The bay is one of Lake Tahoe's don't-miss views. The light is best in mid- to late morning, when the bay's colors pop. ⊠ *Hwy. 89* ☎ *530/525–3384* ⊕ *www.parks.ca.gov* ⬚ *$10 parking fee.*

Vikingsholm

HISTORIC HOME | **FAMILY** | This 38-room estate was completed in 1929, a precise copy of a 1,200-year-old Viking castle. Its original owner, Lora Knight, furnished it with Scandinavian antiques and hired artisans to build period reproductions. The sod roof sprouts wildflowers each spring. A steep 1-mile-long trail from the Emerald Bay lookout leads down to Vikingsholm. The hike back up is challenging, especially for those not acclimated to the elevation, although there are benches and stone culverts to rest on. (Avoid the

hike by taking a cruise; check the website for vendor information.)

At the 150-foot peak of Fannette Island are the ruins of a stone structure called the Tea House, built for Knight's guests to enjoy refreshments. The island is off-limits from February through mid-June to protect nesting Canada geese. The rest of the year, it's open for day use. ⊠ *Hwy. 89* ☎ *530/541–6498* ⊕ *sierrastateparks. org/vikingsholm* ⬚ *Day-use parking fee $10; mansion tour $18* ⊙ *Closed Oct.– May (can vary slightly).*

 Activities

HIKING
Eagle Falls

HIKING & WALKING | To reach these falls, leave your car in the parking lot of the Eagle Falls picnic area (near Vikingsholm; arrive early for a good spot) and walk up the short but relatively steep canyon nearby. You'll have a brilliant panorama of Emerald Bay from this spot near the boundary of Desolation Wilderness. For a strenuous full-day hike, continue 5 miles, past Eagle Lake (a good spot for an alpine swim), to Upper and Middle Velma lakes. ⚠ **Heed warnings about not getting too close to the falls or cliff edges.** ⊠ *Hwy. 89 at Emerald Bay State Park.*

Tahoma

9 miles north of D.L. Bliss State Park, 9 miles south of Tahoe City.

With its rustic waterfront vacation cottages, Tahoma exemplifies life on the lake in its quiet early days before bright-lights casinos and huge crowds proliferated. In 1960, Tahoma hosted the Olympic Nordic-skiing competitions. Today, there's little to do here except stroll by the lake at Ed Z'Berg Sugar Pine Point State Park and listen to the wind in the trees. The 1903 Hellman-Ehrman Mansion is the park's main attraction.

A classic lake view at Ed Z'berg Sugar Pine Point State Park

GETTING HERE AND AROUND

Approach Tahoma by car on Highway 89, called West Lake Boulevard in this section. TART buses provide service from some communities. A bike trail links the town and Tahoe City.

 Sights

Ed Z'berg Sugar Pine Point State Park

STATE/PROVINCIAL PARK | FAMILY | Summer visitors love to hike, swim, fish, and tour the Hellman-Ehrman Mansion at this park named for a state politician who championed conservation, but it's also popular in winter, when a small campground remains open. Nearly 12 miles of cross-country ski and snowshoe trails allow beginners and experienced enthusiasts alike to whoosh through pine forests and glide past the lake. Rangers lead full-moon snowshoe tours from January to March. With 2,000 densely forested acres and nearly 2 miles of shore frontage, this is Lake Tahoe's largest state park. ⊠ *7360 W. Lake Blvd., Tahoma* ☎ *530/525–7982 summer,* *530/525–9528 year-round* ⊕ *www.parks. ca.gov* ✉ *May–Sept. $10 per vehicle, day-use ($5 Oct.–Apr.).*

Hellman-Ehrman Mansion

HISTORIC HOME | FAMILY | A 1903 stone-and-shingle summer residence furnished in period style, the mansion, originally called Pine Lodge, was erected by businessman I.W. Hellman of San Francisco and inherited by his daughter, Florence Hellman Ehrman. The structure, designed by Wayne Danforth Bliss (the son of nearby D.L. Bliss State Park's namesake), had electric lights and full indoor plumbing, the height of modernity for its day. Docents lead tours in summer. The estate and grounds are open year-round. ⊠ *7595 Hwy. 89, Tahoma* ☎ *530/525–7982 summer, 530/525–9528 year-round, 530/583–9911 house tours* ⊕ *www. parks.ca.gov* ✉ *$10 per vehicle, day-use; mansion tour $15 (purchase tickets at Sugar Point's nature center)* ⊗ *No tours Oct.–late May.*

Tahoe City

9 miles north of Tahoma, 14 miles south of Truckee.

Tahoe City is the only lakeside town with a downtown area good for strolling and window-shopping. Stores, restaurants, and the 1908 Watson Log Cabin—at 560 North Lake Boulevard and worth a peek on the few summer days it's open—are all within walking distance of the Outlet Gates, where water is spilled into the Truckee River to control the lake's surface level. The Gatekeeper's Museum has information about the cabin and gates.

GETTING HERE AND AROUND

Tahoe City lies at the junction of Highway 89 (West Lake Boulevard) and Highway 28 (North Lake Boulevard). TART buses serve the area. A bike trail connects Tahoe City and Tahoma.

ESSENTIALS

VISITOR INFORMATION North Lake Tahoe Visitor Center. ✉ *100 N. Lake Tahoe Blvd., Tahoe City* ☎ *530/581–6900* 🌐 *www.gotahoenorth.com.*

👁 Sights

Gatekeeper's Museum

HISTORY MUSEUM | FAMILY | This museum preserves a little-known part of the region's history. Between 1912 and 1968, the gatekeeper who lived on this site was responsible for monitoring the lake level, using a winch system (still used today and visible just outside the museum) to keep the water at the correct height. Also here, the Marion Steinbach Indian Basket Museum displays intricate baskets from 85 tribes. ✉ *130 W. Lake Blvd., Tahoe City* ☎ *530/583–1762* 🌐 *www.northtahoemuseums.org* 🎟 *$10* 🕒 *Closed Mon. and Tues.*

🍴 Restaurants

★ Christy Hill

$$$$ | MODERN AMERICAN | Huge windows reveal stellar lake views at this intimate Euro–Cal restaurant serving seafood, beef, and vegetarian entrées—Moroccan-spiced lamb loin is a signature dish—along with small plates like Jamaican jerk hamachi poke. The gem-laden wine list and exceptional desserts earn accolades; the service is low-key professional. **Known for:** tasting menu a good deal; romantic choice; dinner on the deck in fine weather. [$] *Average main: $46* ✉ *115 Grove St., at N. Lake Blvd., Tahoe City* ☎ *530/583–8551* 🌐 *www.christyhill.com* 🕒 *No lunch. Closed Mon. and Tues.*

★ Fire Sign Cafe

$ | AMERICAN | FAMILY | There's often a wait for breakfast and lunch at this great little diner with pine paneling, hardwood floors, and an exposed-beam ceiling, but it's worth it. The pastries are made from scratch, the salmon is smoked in-house, the salsa is hand cut, and there's real maple syrup for the many types of pancakes and waffles. **Known for:** breakfast and lunch classics; fruit cobbler; casual atmosphere. [$] *Average main: $15* ✉ *1785 W. Lake Blvd., Tahoe City* ✥ *Hwy. 89, 2 miles south of downtown Tahoe City at Fountain Ave.* ☎ *530/583–0871* 🌐 *www.firesigncafe.com* 🕒 *No dinner.*

★ Tahoe House Bakery & Gourmet

$ | AMERICAN | FAMILY | Pastries, breakfast sandwiches, and robust regular and espresso coffees are the morning specialties of this bakery whose lineup expands at lunch to include hefty salads (spinach, tuna, Chinese chicken, and a Caesar among them), chicken potpies, and dense, flavorful sandwiches served on a half dozen breads baked that day. Stand in line to order, then choose seating indoors or on a shaded patio fronting the building. **Known for:** grab-and-go items; cakes, cookies, and pies; sweet and savory scones. [$] *Average main:*

$11 ✉ 625 W. Lake Blvd., Tahoe City ☎ 530/583–1377 🌐 www.tahoe-house.com ⏲ No dinner.

Wolfdale's
$$$$ | ECLECTIC | Consistent, inspired cuisine served in an elegantly simple dining room or an outdoor deck makes Wolfdale's one of the top restaurants on the lake, albeit among the most expensive. Entrées that might include a Thai seafood stew or Tuscan risotto merge Asian and European cooking in imaginative ways. **Known for:** multiple martinis; lake-view setting; most items gluten-free. [$] *Average main: $44 ✉ 640 N. Lake Blvd., near Grove St., Tahoe City ☎ 530/583–5700 🌐 www.wolfdales.com ⏲ Closed Mon. and Tues. (except some Mon. holidays). No lunch.*

Hotels

Basecamp Tahoe City
$$ | HOTEL | FAMILY | A downtown motel for the 21st century, Basecamp charms with a mix of industrial, retro, and rustic styles, as well as simple but modern rooms with high-speed Wi-Fi, flat-screen TVs, and original artwork. **Pros:** lively public spaces; stylish rooms; convenient to commercial strip with restaurants and grocery stores. **Cons:** some road noise; lacks amenities of large properties; eight-minute walk to local beach. [$] *Rooms from: $219 ✉ 955 N. Lake Blvd., Tahoe City ☎ 530/580–8430 🌐 basecamptahoecity.com 🛏 24 rooms 🍴 No Meals.*

Cottage Inn
$$ | B&B/INN | Avoid the crowds by staying in one of these charming, circa-1938 log cottages under towering pines on the lake's west shore. **Pros:** romantic, woodsy setting; all rooms have gas fireplaces, some two-person tubs; private beach access. **Cons:** guests must be older than 12; most cottages accommodate two people maximum; minimum weekend- and multiple-day stays required in peak. [$] *Rooms from: $289 ✉ 1690 W. Lake Blvd., Tahoe City ☎ 530/581–4073, 800/581–4073 🌐 thecottageinn.com 🛏 22 rooms 🍴 Free Breakfast.*

Granlibakken Tahoe
$ | RESORT | FAMILY | Far enough off the highway to feel secluded, this 74-acre condo community (its name in Norwegian means "a hillside sheltered by fir trees") provides an in-the-woods Tahoe experience convenient to outdoor activities and Tahoe City dining. **Pros:** range of lodging options, from studio condos to town houses; room rate includes free breakfast for bookings through website; full kitchens in some accommodations. **Cons:** some units need updating (ask about decor, which varies); more for families than romantic interludes; conference activities and weddings. [$] *Rooms from: $190 ✉ 725 Granlibakken Rd., Tahoe City ☎ 530/583–4242 front desk, 800/543–3221 reservations 🌐 www.granlibakken.com 🛏 148 rooms 🍴 No Meals.*

★ Sunnyside Restaurant and Lodge
$$ | HOTEL | FAMILY | The views are superb and the hospitality gracious at this lakeside lodge 3 miles south of Tahoe City, where locally crafted furnishings decorate the guest rooms. **Pros:** free continental breakfast and afternoon tea; most rooms have balconies overlooking the lake; lively bar and restaurant. **Cons:** can be pricey for families; noisy in summer; some public areas could use a refresh. [$] *Rooms from: $299 ✉ 1850 W. Lake Blvd., Tahoe City ☎ 530/583–7200, 800/822–2754 🌐 www.sunnysidelodge.com 🛏 23 rooms 🍴 Free Breakfast.*

Activities

RAFTING

★ Truckee River Rafting
WHITE-WATER RAFTING | FAMILY | In summer, you can take a self-guided raft trip down a gentle 5-mile stretch of the Truckee River. This outfitter will shuttle you back to Tahoe City at the end of your

Palisades Tahoe has runs for skiers and snowboarders of all ability levels, from beginner to expert.

two- to three-hour experience. ■TIP→ On **a warm day this makes a great family outing.** ✉ *175 River Rd., near W. Lake Blvd., Tahoe City* ☎ *530/583–1111* ⊕ *www. truckeeriverrafting.com* 🎟 *From $70.*

ZIPLINING
★ Treetop Adventure Parks
ZIP LINING | FAMILY | Providing "an adventure for everyone" regardless of experience is the goal of this well-designed attraction with 97 aboveground platforms amid cedars and pines. Navigating from platform to platform involves ziplines; rope swings; tight ropes; climbing walls; and other challenges on beginner, intermediate, and advanced courses. Affiliated parks operate in Tahoe Vista and Olympic Valley. ✉ *725 Granlibakken Rd., off W. Lake Tahoe Blvd., Tahoe City* ☎ *530/807–1004* ⊕ *tahoetreetop.com* 🎟 *From $59.*

Olympic Valley

7 miles north of Tahoe City to Palisades Tahoe Rd., 8½ miles south of Truckee.

Olympic Valley got its moniker in 1960, when its ski resort, now called Palisades Tahoe, hosted the Winter Olympics. Snow sports remain the primary activity, but once summer comes, you can hike into the adjacent Granite Chief Wilderness, explore wildflower-studded alpine meadows, or lie by a swimming pool in one of the Sierra's prettiest valleys.

GETTING HERE AND AROUND
Palisades Tahoe Road, the main route into Olympic Valley, branches west off Highway 89 about 8 miles south of Truckee. TART connects the Palisades Tahoe ski area with Truckee and communities along the north and west shores. Palisades Tahoe provides a free shuttle to many stops in those same areas.

Sights

Village at Palisades Tahoe

BUSINESS DISTRICT | FAMILY | The centerpiece of Olympic Valley is a pedestrian mall at the base of several four-story ersatz Bavarian stone-and-timber buildings, where you'll find restaurants, high-end condo rentals, boutiques, and cafés. ✉ *1750 Village East Rd., Olympic Valley* ☎ *530/584–1000, 800/403–0206 information* 🌐 *www.palisadestahoe.com.*

Restaurants

Fireside Pizza Company

$$ | PIZZA | FAMILY | Adults might opt for the signature pear-and-Gorgonzola pizza at this modern Italian restaurant, but most kids clamor for the house favorite—sausage and pepperoni with a four-cheese blend. Salads and pasta dishes round out the menu. **Known for:** inventive pizzas; reasonably inexpensive dining option in a pricey area; family-friendly. [$] *Average main: $20* ✉ *The Village at Palisades Tahoe, 1985 Palisades Tahoe Rd., Suite 25, Olympic Valley* ☎ *530/829–0982* 🌐 *firesidepizza.com.*

PlumpJack Cafe

$$$$ | AMERICAN | The menu at this white-tablecloth restaurant, whose wide windows reveal Palisades Tahoe in all its glory, changes seasonally, but look for rib-eye or New York steak, cioppino or pan-seared fish, or a filling vegetarian dish. The Wagyu Angus burger is a favorite with regulars. **Known for:** specialty cocktails; apps and desserts; varied, reasonably priced wines. [$] *Average main: $43* ✉ *1920 Palisades Tahoe Rd., Olympic Valley* ☎ *530/583–1578* 🌐 *www.plumpjackcafe.com* ⏱ *Closed Mon.–Wed. No lunch.*

Hotels

Everline Resort & Spa

$$ | RESORT | A golf course, a spa, a heated swimming pool, an ice skating rink, a chairlift to the mountain, groomed cross-country ski tracks, and several restaurants please the well-heeled patrons of this full-service resort within Hyatt's Destination brand. **Pros:** breathtaking views from rooms and lobby; innumerable services and amenities; many suites with fireplaces and kitchens. **Cons:** so large it can feel impersonal; high in-season rates; some parts feel dated. [$] *Rooms from: $239* ✉ *400 Squaw Creek Rd., Olympic Valley* ☎ *530/412–7034* 🌐 *www.destinationhotels.com/everline-resort-and-spa* 🔑 *405 rooms* 🍴 *No Meals.*

PlumpJack Inn

$$ | HOTEL | Stylishly rustic, this two-story, cedar-sided inn fulfills the yearnings of Bay Area sophisticates for laid-back luxury thanks, in part to rooms that have sumptuous beds with down comforters, high-end bath amenities, iPod docks, and hooded terry robes to wear to the outdoor hot tubs. **Pros:** small and intimate; many amenities; suites sleep up to six. **Cons:** not the best choice for families with small children; not all rooms have tubs; weekend minimum-stay requirement. [$] *Rooms from: $210* ✉ *1920 Palisades Tahoe Rd., Olympic Valley* ☎ *530/583–1576, 800/323–7666* 🌐 *www.plumpjackinn.com* 🔑 *55 rooms* 🍴 *No Meals.*

The Village at Palisades Tahoe

$$ | HOTEL | FAMILY | Individually owned condominium suites, all with gas fireplaces and kitchens and many with private balconies, are the main accommodations of this complex convenient to Palisades Mountain's ski slopes. **Pros:** studio to three-bedroom suites; near Village restaurants and shops; three fitness centers, eight outdoor hot tubs. **Cons:** village often gets crowded on weekends; nicely appointed but not high style; smaller standard rooms lack the amenities of suites. $ *Rooms from: $209* ✉ *1750 Village East Rd., Olympic Valley* ☎ *530/584–1000, 800/403–0206* ⊕ *www. palisadestahoe.com* ⇆ *198 rooms* ⦿*No Meals.*

Activities

GOLF
The Links at Everline Golf Course
GOLF | Play this narrow, challenging championship course designed by Robert Trent Jones Jr. for beautiful views of Palisades Tahoe's surrounding peaks. The design emphasizes accuracy over distance, especially on the front nine. All fees include a golf cart plus valet parking; rates drop after noon and again after 3 pm. ✉ *400 Squaw Creek Rd., Olympic Valley* ☎ *530/581–6637* ⊕ *www.destina- tionhotels.com/everline-resort-and-spa* ⊠ *From $134 (weekdays before noon)* ⅄ *18 holes, 6931 yards, par 71.*

SKIING

AREAS
★**Palisades Tahoe**
SKIING & SNOWBOARDING | FAMILY | A 2.4-mile gondola connects the bases of this resort's two mountains, providing patrons access to 6,000 skiable acres. **Palisades Mountain,** known for some of the area's most challenging skiing, was the centerpiece of the 1960 Winter Olympics. Experts often head directly to the untamed terrain of the infamous KT-22 face, which has bumps, cliffs, and gulp- and-go chutes, or to the nearly vertical Palisades, where many extreme-skiing films have been shot. Beginners and intermediates have plenty of wide-open, groomed trails atop the mountain and around the more challenging Snow King Peak. Snowboarders can tear up the five terrain parks, which include a giant superpipe.

With some of Tahoe's most reliable conditions, **Alpine Mountain** is a great place for kids or adults to learn to ski.

The two peaks here are well suited to intermediate skiers, with a few dozen runs for experts only. Snowboarders and hot-dog skiers will find a terrain park with a superpipe, rails, tabletops, and a boarder-cross course. ■TIP→ **A same- day lift ticket to one mountain is good at the other; in addition to the Base to Base Gondola, free shuttles run all day between the two parks. Facilities:** 170-plus trails, 3,600 acres, 2,850-foot vertical drop, 29 lifts at Palisades Mountain; 100-plus trails, 2,400 acres, 1,802-foot vertical drop, 13 lifts at Alpine Mountain. ✉ *1960 Palisades Tahoe Rd., Olympic Valley* ✛ *Off Hwy. 89, 7 miles northwest of Tahoe City* ☎ *800/403–0206* ⊕ *www.palisadestahoe. com* ⊠ *Lift tickets from $159 (but can vary by day).*

EQUIPMENT RENTALS
Tahoe Dave's Skis and Boards
SKIING & SNOWBOARDING | FAMILY | To avoid paying resort prices, rent and tune downhill skis and snowboards at this shop. ✉ *3039 Hwy. 89, Olympic Valley* ☎ *530/583–5665* ⊕ *tahoedaves.com.*

Truckee

14 miles north of Tahoe City.

Long past its days as a decrepit railroad town, Truckee is the trendy first stop for many Tahoe visitors. Established circa 1863, within a decade it had evolved from a stagecoach station into a major transcontinental railroad stop; these days, freight trains and Amtrak's *California Zephyr* still idle briefly at the depot in the middle of town. The visitor center inside the depot has a walking-tour map of historic Truckee.

Across from the station, where Old West facades line the main drag, you'll find galleries, gift shops, boutiques, a wine-tasting room, old-fashioned diners, and several good restaurants.

GETTING HERE AND AROUND

Truckee is off I–80 between Highways 89 and 267. Greyhound and Amtrak stop here, and TART buses serve the area.

ESSENTIALS

VISITOR INFORMATION Truckee Chamber Visitor Center & California Welcome Center. ✉ *Amtrak depot, 10065 Donner Pass Rd., Truckee* ☎ *530/587–2757* 🌐 *truckee.com.*

👁 Sights

Donner Memorial State Park and Emigrant Trail Museum
STATE/PROVINCIAL PARK | FAMILY | The park and museum commemorate the 89 members of the Donner Party, westward-bound pioneers who became trapped in the Sierra in the winter of 1846–47 in snow 22 feet deep. Barely more than half survived, some by resorting to cannibalism. The absorbing Emigrant Trail Museum in the visitor center contains exhibits about the Donner Party, regional Native Americans, and railroad and transportation development in the area. In the park, you can picnic, hike, camp, and go boating, fishing, and waterskiing in summer; winter brings cross-country skiing and snowshoeing on groomed trails. ✉ *12593 Donner Pass Rd., Truckee* ✣ *Off I–80, Exit 184, 2 miles west of Truckee* ☎ *530/582–7892* 🌐 *www.parks.ca.gov* 🎟 *$10 parking, day-use ($5 in winter).*

🍴 Restaurants

★ Full Belly Deli
$ | AMERICAN | FAMILY | Truckee residents and visitors jam this strip-mall restaurant for diverse breakfast fare like the biscuits-and-gravy burrito and hot lunch sandwiches that include Cubans, cheesesteaks, the Southwest chicken pepper jack on focaccia, and the formidable Dirka Dirka (corned beef, pastrami, Swiss cheese, jalapeño cole slaw). Salads, subs, and wraps are also on the menu, and there's a good beverage selection, from aloe water to Red Bull. **Known for:** outdoor dining in good weather; pasta, macaroni, and potato salad sides; order online to save time. [$] *Average main: $13* ✉ *10825 Pioneer Trail, Truckee* ☎ *530/550–9516* 🌐 *eatfullbellydeli.com* ⏲ *Closed Sun. No dinner.*

★ Great Gold Modern American Italian Kitchen
$$$ | MODERN ITALIAN | Making a reservation is the smart move at this Neapolitan-style pizzeria, which has a snappy industrial look and was opened by esteemed San Francisco restaurateurs during the pandemic. Each day they prepare several pasta dishes and a half dozen wood-fired pizzas—burrata Margherita, perhaps, or maitake mushroom, or chicken Parmesan with mozzarella—that patrons supplement with prosciutto, pepperoni, sausage, anchovies, and other toppings. **Known for:** special pizzas each week; smoked chicken, steak, and grilled fish among possible entrées; mostly Italian wine list. [$] *Average main: $33* ✉ *11025 Pioneer Trail, off Truckee Way, Truckee* ☎ *530/582–9510* 🌐 *greatgoldtahoe.com* ⏲ *No lunch.*

Moody's Bistro, Bar & Beats
$$$$ | ECLECTIC | Head here for contemporary-Cal cuisine in a sexy dining room with pumpkin-color walls, burgundy velvet banquettes, and art-deco fixtures. The earthy, sure-handed cooking showcases organically grown ingredients: look for ahi poke, snazzy pizzas bubbling-hot from a brick oven, braised lamb shanks, pan-roasted wild game, fresh seafood, and organic beef. **Known for:** lighter fare for lunch; summer alfresco dining; live music in bar some nights. [$] *Average main: $46* ✉ *10007 Bridge St., at Donner Pass Rd., Truckee* ☎ *530/587–8688* 🌐 *www.moodysbistro.com.*

Pianeta Ristorante
$$$ | ITALIAN | A longtime town favorite, Pianeta serves high-style Italian cuisine in a warmly lit, bilevel, redbrick space on Truckee's historic main drag. Start

with a beef carpaccio antipasto plate or perhaps house-made spicy-fennel and mild sausages, following up with a pasta course of ravioli Bolognese (both pasta and sauce made in-house), an entrée of ragout with spicy sausage and Mexican prawns—or both. **Known for:** welcoming atmosphere; tiramisu and panna cotta for dessert; West Coast and Italian wine selections. [$] *Average main: $39* ✉ *10096 Donner Pass Rd., Truckee* ☎ *530/587–4694* 🌐 *www.pianetarestauranttruckee.com* 🕓 *Closed Sun. No lunch.*

★ Trokay

$$$$ | MODERN EUROPEAN | The high, exposed and rough-hewn ceiling, stone walls, heavy wood shelving, and orblike contemporary metal chandeliers of special-occasion Trokay split the difference between Western high-country style and industrial chic. The four-course prix-fixe menu and 10-course tasting option also diverge from the expected in dishes that might include sea-urchin bisque, dry-aged duck with kumquat and anise, and diver scallops with bacon *dashi* (fish broth). **Known for:** chic setting; superior wine list; artful presentation. [$] *Average main: $145* ✉ *10046 Donner Pass Rd., Truckee* ☎ *530/582–1040* 🌐 *www.restauranttrokay.com* 🕓 *Closed Tues.–Thurs. No lunch.*

Truckee Tavern and Grill

$$$ | AMERICAN | The wood-fired grill of this second-floor downtown restaurant turns out steaks, chicken, chops, and fish dishes that might include halibut with coal-roasted tomato and braised fennel. As with the food, the decor is New West contemporary—bricks line the wall behind the bar, where mixologists craft drinks like the Magnolia (tequila, macadamia nut, lemon, pineapple, and bitters) and, in tribute to Truckee's bootlegging past, pour artisanal small-batch gin and whiskey. **Known for:** family-style dinner for three or four; pasta and fish entrées; deck overlooking downtown action. [$] *Average main: $38* ✉ *10118 Donner Pass Rd., near Spring St., Truckee* ☎ *530/587–3766* 🌐 *www.truckeetavern.com* 🕓 *No lunch.*

Coffee and Quick Bites

Squeeze In

$ | AMERICAN | FAMILY | Adherents flock to this downtown spot for breakfast to sample dozens of omelets, several variations on eggs Benedict, banana-walnut pancakes, and French toast oozing with cream cheese. At lunch, they savor homemade soups and sandwiches. **Known for:** cheeseburger omelet; homemade soups; gluten-free options. [$] *Average main: $15* ✉ *10060 Donner Pass Rd., near Bridge St., Truckee* ☎ *530/587–9814* 🌐 *squeezein.com/truckee* 🕓 *No dinner.*

Hotels

★ Donner Lake Inn Bed and Breakfast

$ | B&B/INN | Across from Donner Lake several miles west of Truckee's historic downtown, this lodgelike property amid the trees earns repeat business for its secluded creekside location and husband-and-wife hosts' bountiful breakfasts. **Pros:** homey ambience; gas fireplaces in all rooms; convenient to several North Tahoe ski resorts. **Cons:** low on style; must drive to downtown Truckee restaurants; often sells out. [$] *Rooms from: $199* ✉ *10070 Gregory Pl., Truckee* ☎ *530/587–5574* 🌐 *www.donnerlakeinn.com* 🛏 *5 rooms* 🍴 *Free Breakfast.*

Gravity Haus Truckee-Tahoe

$$ | HOTEL | The clean, spare lines of the Gravity Haus's wooden exterior evoke a modern European feel; energy-saving heating, cooling, and lighting systems demonstrate a commitment to sustainability; and rooms in the three two-story satellite buildings are understatedly sexy, with Merlot-and-camel color schemes and mod-Italian overtones. **Pros:** environmentally friendly; Stella restaurant for breakfast and dinner; coworking space in lobby. **Cons:** some bathrooms are small;

not all bathrooms have tubs; about a mile from historic downtown. $ *Rooms from: $224* ✉ *10918 Brockway Rd., Truckee* ☎ *530/582–5655, 866/582–5655* ⊕ *gravityhaus.com* ➥ *42 rooms* ⏽⊘⏽ *No Meals.*

Northstar California Resort
$$ | RESORT | FAMILY | The area's most complete destination resort entices with lodgings that ranges from hotel rooms and condos to private houses and ski-in, ski-out units. **Pros:** array of lodging types; on-site shuttle; several dining options in Northstar Village. **Cons:** family accommodations can be pricey; lacks intimacy; some units not as attractive as others. $ *Rooms from: $213* ✉ *5001 Northstar Dr., Truckee* ✛ *Off Hwy. 267, 6 miles southeast of Truckee* ☎ *530/562–1010, 800/466–6784* ⊕ *www.northstarcalifornia.com* ➥ *250 units* ⏽⊘⏽ *No Meals.*

Ritz-Carlton, Lake Tahoe
$$$ | RESORT | Nestled mid-mountain on the Northstar ski resort, the four-story Ritz-Carlton has plush accommodations with floor-to-ceiling windows, fireplaces, cozy robes, and down comforters. **Pros:** superb service; gorgeous setting; ski-in, ski-out convenience. **Cons:** in-season prices as breathtaking as the views; resort fee and mandatory valet parking add to cost of stay; must go off-site for golf and tennis. $ *Rooms from: $499* ✉ *13031 Ritz-Carlton Highlands Court, Truckee* ☎ *530/562–3000* ⊕ *www.ritzcarlton.com* ➥ *170 rooms* ⏽⊘⏽ *No Meals.*

🍸 Nightlife

Bar of America
BARS | In a 19th-century redbrick building that's been everything from a hotel to a bank to a bus station, this bustling bar opened in the 1970s. These days, it serves craft beers and specialty cocktails you can pair with booze-friendly appetizers, pizzas, and comfort food (or have a big ole rib eye with Bulleit bourbon peppercorn sauce). Open later than most downtown bars, BofA presents live music one night

a week or more year-round. ✉ *10040 Donner Pass Rd., Truckee* ☎ *530/587–2626* ⊕ *www.barofamerica.com.*

Cottonwood Restaurant and Bar
BARS | Perched above town on the site of North America's first chairlift, this local institution has a bar decked out with old wooden skis, sleds, skates, and photos of Truckee's early days. A superb spot to enjoy a local brew or craft cocktail and not bad at all should you stay for dinner, Cottonwood serves pasta dishes and grilled meats and fish. ✉ *10142 Rue Hilltop Rd., off Brockway Rd., ¼ mile south of downtown, Truckee* ☎ *530/587–5711* ⊕ *www.cottonwoodrestaurant.com.*

FiftyFifty Brewing Company
BREWPUBS | At the high-ceilinged brewpub of Truckee's pioneering craft-beer producer, opened in 2007, the soothing gray tones plus a pint of the Donner Party porter or Eclipse barrel-aged imperial stout will take the edge off a cold day on the slopes. The food lineup includes salads, burgers, inventive pizzas, barbecued ribs, pan-seared salmon, and the house specialty: a pulled pork sandwich. ✉ *11197 Brockway Rd., near Martis Valley Rd., Truckee* ☎ *530/587–2337* ⊕ *www.fiftyfiftybrewing.com.*

Activities

GOLF
Coyote Moon Golf Course
GOLF | With pine trees lining the fairways and no houses to spoil the view, this course is as beautiful as it is challenging. Fees include a shared cart; the greens fee drops at 1 pm and dips again at 3. ✉ *10685 Northwoods Blvd., off Donner Pass Rd., Truckee* ☎ *530/587–0886* ⊕ *www.coyotemoongolf.com* 💲 *$190* 🏌 *18 holes, 7177 yards, par 72* ⊙ *Closed late fall–late spring.*

Northstar Golf
GOLF | Robert Muir Graves designed this course, which combines hilly terrain and open meadows. The front nine holes

here are open-links style, while the challenging back nine move through tight, tree-lined fairways. Rates, which include a cart, drop successively between 1 pm and 4 pm. ⊠ *168 Basque Dr., Truckee* ⊹ *Off Northstar Dr., west off Hwy. 267* ☎ *530/562–3290* ⊕ *www.northstarcalifornia.com* ⊒ *From $119* ⅄. *18 holes, 6781 yards, par 72.*

MOUNTAIN BIKING
Northstar California Bike Park
BIKING | FAMILY | From late May or early June through September Northstar's ski slopes transform into a lift-served bike park with 100 miles of challenging terrain, including the aptly named Livewire trail. Guided tours, multiday camps, and races are available for riders of all abilities. ⊠ *Northstar Dr., off Hwy. 267, Truckee* ☎ *530/562–1010* ⊕ *www.northstarcalifornia.com* ⊒ *Lift tickets from $64.*

SKIING
AREAS
★ Northstar California Ski Resort
SKIING & SNOWBOARDING | FAMILY | Meticulous grooming and long cruisers make this resort a paradise for intermediate skiers and a fine choice for families. Although most trails are intermediate, advanced skiers and riders can access Lookout Mountain's more than two dozen expert trails and 347 acres of gated terrain and steeps, making it easy for families and groups with varying skills to hang out with each other. The eight terrain parks here are considered among North America's best. The Cross Country, Telemark, and Snowshoe Center, located mid-mountain, is the starting point for a network of 24 km (15 miles). Instructors conduct group and private ski and snowboard lessons for adults and children. **Facilities:** 100 trails; 3,170 acres; 2,280-foot vertical drop; 20 lifts. ⊠ *5001 Northstar Dr., Truckee* ☎ *530/562–2267* ⊕ *www.northstarcalifornia.com* ⊒ *Lift tickets from $91.*

★ Royal Gorge
SKIING & SNOWBOARDING | FAMILY | If you love to cross-country ski, don't miss Royal Gorge, which serves up 140 km (124 miles) of track for all abilities, 92 trails on 6,000 acres, a ski school, and eight warming huts. Because the complex, affiliated with Sugar Bowl, sits right on the Sierra Crest, the views are drop-dead gorgeous. ⊠ *9411 Pahatsi Dr., Soda Springs* ⊹ *Off I–80, Soda Springs/Norden exit* ☎ *530/426–3871* ⊕ *www.royalgorge.com* ⊒ *Day pass $50.*

Sugar Bowl Ski Resort
SKIING & SNOWBOARDING | FAMILY | Opened in 1939 by Walt Disney, this is Tahoe's oldest—and one of its best—resorts. Atop Donner Summit, it receives an incredible 500-plus inches of snowfall annually. Four peaks are connected by 1,650 acres of skiable terrain, with everything from gentle groomed corduroy to wide-open bowls to vertical rocky chutes and outstanding tree skiing. Snowboarders can hit two terrain parks with numerous boxes, rails, and jumps. More compact than the area's megaresorts, the comparatively genteel Sugar Bowl is a great place for families and a low-pressure place to learn to ski. It's not huge, but there's challenging terrain. Base-area lodgings are limited. **Facilities:** 100 trails; 1,650 acres; 1,500-foot vertical drop; 12 lifts. ⊠ *629 Sugar Bowl Rd., Norden* ⊹ *Off Donner Pass Rd., 3 miles east of I–80 Soda Springs/Norden exit, 10 miles west of Truckee* ☎ *530/426–9000, 530/426–1111 snow phone* ⊕ *www.sugarbowl.com* ⊒ *Lift tickets from $130.*

Tahoe Donner Cross Country Ski Center
SKIING & SNOWBOARDING | FAMILY | Just north of Truckee, this center, which ranks among the nation's best cross-country venues for both the skiing and the magnificent Sierra Crest views, includes 65 trails on 100 km (62 miles) of groomed tracks on more than 2,800 acres. In addition to cross-country skiing and tubing and sledding sessions, there are mountain-biking and dog trails. ⊠ *Alder Creek*

Adventure Center, 15275 Alder Creek Rd., Truckee ☎ 530/587–9484 🌐 www.tahoedonner.com.

EQUIPMENT RENTALS

BackCountry

SKIING & SNOWBOARDING | FAMILY | If you plan to ski or board the backcountry, you'll find everything from crampons to transceivers at this shop. ✉ *11400 Donner Pass Rd., Truckee* ☎ *530/582–0909* 🌐 *www.thebackcountry.com.*

Tahoe Dave's

SKIING & SNOWBOARDING | FAMILY | In business since 1977, this shop has skis and accessories, and staffers repair and tune equipment. ✉ *10200 Donner Pass Rd., near Spring St., Truckee* ☎ *530/582–0900* 🌐 *tahoedaves.com.*

Carnelian Bay to Kings Beach

5–10 miles northeast of Tahoe City.

The small lakeside commercial districts of Carnelian Bay and Tahoe Vista service the thousand or so locals who live in the area year-round and the thousands more who have summer residences or launch their boats here. Kings Beach, the last town heading east on Highway 28 before the Nevada border, has basic motels, rental condos, restaurants, and shops.

GETTING HERE AND AROUND

To reach Kings Beach and Carnelian Bay from the California side, take Highway 89 north to Highway 28 north and then east. From the Nevada side, follow Highway 28 north and then west. TART provides public transportation in this area.

Beaches

Kings Beach State Recreation Area

BEACH | FAMILY | The north shore's 28-acre Kings Beach State Recreation Area, one of the largest such areas on the lake, is open year-round. The sandy beach gets crowded in summer with people swimming, sunbathing, Jet Skiing, riding in paddleboats, spiking volleyballs, and tossing Frisbees. If you're going to spend the day, come early to snag a table in the picnic area; there's also a good playground. **Amenities:** food and drink; parking (fee); toilets; water sports. **Best for:** sunrise; sunset; swimming; windsurfing. ✉ *8318 N. Lake Blvd., Kings Beach* ☎ *530/523–3203* 🌐 *www.parks.ca.gov* 🎫 *$10 parking fee ($5 off-season).*

🍴 Restaurants

Gar Woods Grill and Pier Restaurant

$$$$ | ECLECTIC | The view's the thing at this lakeside stalwart, where you can watch the sun shimmer on the water through the dining room's plateglass windows or from the outdoor deck. Price wise, Gar Woods is a better bet for lunch, when fish tacos and crab and prime-rib French dip sandwiches are on the menu, than dinner, at which grilled steak and fish are the mainstays. **Known for:** lake views; signature Wet Woody cocktail, original-recipe Trader Vic's mai tais; dessert menu. [$] *Average main: $48* ✉ *5000 N. Lake Blvd., Carnelian Bay* ✣ *Hwy. 28, 2 miles west of Tahoe Vista* ☎ *530/546–3366* 🌐 *www.garwoods.com.*

Jason's Beachside Grille

$$ | AMERICAN | FAMILY | If the kids want burgers, but you want bourbon, Jason's has a full bar along with nachos, wings, and fried calamari starters; French onion soup and clam chowder; a dozen-plus sandwiches and burgers; and steak, chicken, seafood, and baby back ribs entrées. The whole place is wood, from floor to ceiling, lending it an ultrarustic feel. **Known for:** house Bloody Mary and other specialty cocktails; summer dining on deck overlooking the lake; tables by fireplace in winter. [$] *Average main: $23* ✉ *8338 N. Lake Blvd., Kings Beach* ☎ *530/546–3315* 🌐 *jasonsbeachsidegrille.com.*

Lanza's

$$ | **ITALIAN** | **FAMILY** | When you're craving spaghetti and meatballs, this wood-paneled roadside spot with a cordial staff and loyal clientele is the place to go. Other good old-fashioned Italian American classics—served to tables with red-and-white-checked cloths—include lasagna, ravioli, chicken and veal piccata, eggplant Parmesan, and Sicilian-style pizzas. **Known for:** generous portions; create your own pasta-and-sauce combination; spumoni for dessert. [$] *Average main: $25* ✉ *7739 N. Lake Blvd., next to Safeway, Kings Beach* ☎ *530/546–2434* 🌐 *www.lanzastahoe.com* 🕒 *No lunch.*

★ **Soule Domain**

$$$ | **ECLECTIC** | Rough-hewn wood beams, a vaulted wood ceiling, and a roaring fireplace in winter lend romance to this cozy 1927 pine-log cabin where chef-owner Charlie Soule skillfully prepares French- and Asian-inspired cuisine. Pan-roasted duck breast à l'orange with Grand Marnier, sea scallops poached in champagne with a kiwi-and-mango cream sauce, a Thai curry-chicken noodle bowl, and a vegan sauté judiciously flavored with ginger, jalapeños, sesame seeds, and teriyaki sauce frequently appear on the menu. **Known for:** romance by candlelight; old-style service; bread pudding for dessert. [$] *Average main: $36* ✉ *9983 Cove St., ½ block up Stateline Rd. off Hwy. 28, Kings Beach* ✣ *Restaurant is steps west of California–Nevada border* ☎ *530/546–7529* 🌐 *souledomain.com* 🕒 *No lunch.*

Spindleshanks American Bistro and Wine Bar

$$$ | **AMERICAN** | A local favorite on the Old Brockway Golf Course, Spindleshanks serves classic American cuisine—ribs, steaks, house-made ravioli, and seafood with adventurous sauces. Savor a drink from the full bar or wine from the extensive list while enjoying views of Lake Tahoe or the historic greens where Bing Crosby hosted his first golf tournament in 1934. **Known for:** chicken-fried steak, huevos rancheros, and omelets for breakfast; salads and sandwiches for lunch; three outdoor decks. [$] *Average main: $32* ✉ *400 Brassie Ave., Kings Beach* ✣ *At Hwy. 267 and N. Lake Tahoe Blvd.* ☎ *530/546–2191* 🌐 *spindleshankstahoe.com.*

Hotels

Cedar Glen Lodge

$$ | **HOTEL** | Cedar-shingled cottages and a two-story lodge form a horseshoe around this compact, woodsy property's central pool, picnic, and play areas. **Pros:** solicitous hosts; appealing classic alpine-rustic look; some cottages have kitchens and fireplaces. **Cons:** lacks amenities of larger properties; can seem expensive in summer for what you get; must cross Highway 28 for beach access. [$] *Rooms from: $255* ✉ *6589 N. Lake Blvd., Tahoe Vista* ☎ *530/546–4281* 🌐 *www.tahoecedarglen.com* 🛏 *31 rooms* 🍴 *No Meals.*

★ **Crown Motel**

$ | **HOTEL** | **FAMILY** | For years a lakeside favorite of travelers willing to trade style and amenities for below-average rates—and impressive water views from some rooms—the Crown is emerging from a property makeover with a sportier look but still budget-friendly pricing. **Pros:** family-friendly; an especially good value off-season; lakefront pool and beach. **Cons:** lake-view rooms the costliest; pool only open seasonally (hot tub year-round); thin walls. [$] *Rooms from: $195* ✉ *8200 N. Lake Blvd., Kings Beach* ☎ *530/546–3388* 🌐 *tahoecrown.com* 🛏 *71 rooms* 🍴 *No Meals.*

Mourelatos Lakeshore Resort

$$ | **B&B/INN** | **FAMILY** | At first glance, this family-run waterfront property looks like a slightly above-average two-story motel, but it legitimately lays claim to the title of resort thanks to a private beach; two hot tubs; alluring lake and mountain vistas; and summertime barbecuing, kayaking, and other extras.

Pros: multinight discounts; some rooms have full kitchens; additional cabins and cottages across the highway. **Cons:** modest style; books up quickly for summer; minimum-stay requirement on weekends in-season. [$] *Rooms from: $265* ✉ *6834 N. Lake Blvd., Tahoe Vista* ☎ *530/546–9500* 🌐 *www.mlrtahoe.com* 🛏 *32 rooms* 🍴 *No Meals.*

Activities

KAYAKING

★ Tahoe Adventure Company

KAYAKING | FAMILY | The seasoned guides of this well-established outfitter emphasize having fun and maintaining safety on kayaking excursions that include the leisurely Discovery paddle just off the north shore and ones incorporating a tour at the historic Thunderbird Lodge and lunch at Gar Woods restaurant. Biking, hiking, and rock climbing experiences take place in summer, snowshoe tours in winter. ✉ *Tahoe Vista Recreation Area (summer kiosk; most, but not all, tours leave from here), 7010 N. Lake Blvd., Tahoe Vista* ☎ *530/913–9212* 🌐 *tahoeadventurecompany.com* 🎟 *Kayak tours from $75.*

Wild Society

KAYAKING | FAMILY | Gaze at the underwater world while paddling a clear-bottom kayak around Kings Beach. Rentals include (on request) wireless waterproof speakers with a USB plug, waterproof phone cases, binoculars, goggles, snorkels, cooler, cup holders, selfie sticks, and safety equipment. ✉ *8612 N. Lake Blvd., Kings Beach* ✣ *At Raccoon St.* ☎ *530/553–1771* 🌐 *www.wildsocietylt.com* 🎟 *From $65.*

SNOWMOBILING

Lake Tahoe Snowmobile Tours

SNOW SPORTS | FAMILY | This company conducts two-, three-, and four-hour group and private guided cross-country tours, mostly along nearby Tahoe National Forest trails. You can rent suits, gloves, boots, mandatory helmets, and goggles (or bring your own goggles). ✉ *Hwy. 267, 3 miles north of Hwy. 28, Brockway Summit, Tahoe Vista* ☎ *530/546–4280* 🌐 *laketahoesnowmobile.com* 🎟 *From $230.*

Incline Village

5½ miles northeast of Kings Beach.

Incline Village dates from the early 1960s, when an Oklahoma developer bought 10,000 acres north of Lake Tahoe. His idea was to sketch a plan for a town without a central commercial district, hoping to prevent congestion and preserve the area's natural beauty. One-acre lakeshore lots initially cost $12,000 to $15,000; today, you couldn't buy the same land for less than several million.

GETTING HERE AND AROUND

From the California side, take Highway 89 or 267 to Highway 28. From South Lake Tahoe, take U.S. 50 north to Highway 28 north. TART provides public transportation along Lake Tahoe's north and west shores.

ESSENTIALS

VISITOR INFORMATION North Tahoe Nevada. ✉ *Welcome Center, 969 Tahoe Blvd., Incline Village* ☎ *775/832–1606* 🌐 *travelnorthtahoenevada.com.*

Sights

★ Tahoe East Shore Trail

TRAIL | FAMILY | A photogenic 3-mile cycling and walking path linking Incline Village and Sand Harbor State Park, this paved lakeside trail edges classic patches of turquoise water, giving way to cobalt blue, with the mountains as a backdrop. You can traverse portions of the trail by stopping at Highway 28 vista points, but parking is for only 20 minutes. Park at the Tunnel Creek Road pay lot for longer walks, less expensive than Sand Harbor's day-use fee. ✉ *Pay lot, 1115 Tunnel Creek Rd. B, Incline Village.*

★ Tahoe Science Center

SCIENCE MUSEUM | **FAMILY** | Learn how Lake Tahoe was formed, why it's so blue, and how its ecosystem is changing at Tahoe's only science center. Hands-on exhibits include aquariums, a virtual ecology lab and research boat, a watershed map with the 63 streams that flow into the lake (and the only one that flows out, the Truckee River), tables that teach how to identify trees, and a theater projecting an intriguing 3D movie. Visitors ages eight and older will gain the most from the experience. ✉ *Tahoe Center for Environmental Sciences, 291 Country Club Dr., Suite 320, Incline Village* ☎ *775/881–7560* 🌐 *tahoe.ucdavis.edu/tahoesciencecenter* 🎟 *$5* 🕒 *Closed Sun. and Mon.*

★ Thunderbird Lodge

HISTORIC HOME | George Whittell, a San Francisco socialite who once owned 40,000 acres of property along the lake, began building this lodge in 1936, completing it in 1941. Arriving via bus or boat (reservations essential), you can tour the mansion and grounds, and though it's pricey to do so, you'll be rewarded with a rare glimpse into a time when only the very wealthy had spectacular lakeside homes. ✉ *5000 Hwy. 28, Incline Village* ☎ *800/468–2463 tours, 775/832–8750 lodge* 🌐 *thunderbirdtahoe.org* 🎟 *Tours from $75* 🕒 *Closed mid-Oct.–late May and Sat.–Mon., Wed., and Thurs. late May–mid-Oct.*

Beaches

Lake Tahoe–Nevada State Park and Sand Harbor Beach

BEACH | **FAMILY** | Protecting much of the lake's eastern shore from development, this park consists of several sections that stretch from Incline Village to Zephyr Cove. Beaches and trails provide access to a wilder side of the lake, whether you're into cross-country skiing, hiking, or just relaxing at a picnic. With a gently sloping beach for lounging, crystal clear water for swimming and snorkeling, and a picnic area shaded by cedars and pines, **Sand Harbor Beach** sometimes reaches capacity by 11 am on summer weekends. A handicap-accessible nature trail has interpretive signs and beautiful lake views. Pets are not allowed on the beach from mid-April through mid-October. Parking is $10 for cars with Nevada plates, $15 for out-of-state cars. **Amenities**: food and drink; parking (fee); toilets; water sports. **Best for**: snorkeling; sunset; swimming; walking. ✉ *Sand Harbor Beach, Hwy. 28, 3 miles south of Incline Village, Incline Village* ☎ *775/831–0494* 🌐 *parks.nv.gov/parks/lake-tahoe-nevada-state-park.*

Restaurants

Azzara's

$$ | **ITALIAN** | **FAMILY** | This dependable if not fabulous Italian family restaurant serves a dozen pasta dishes, many pizzas, and chicken, veal, shrimp, and beef entrées. All dinners include soup or salad and garlic bread, making Azzara's a pretty good value. **Known for:** family-run; daily specials; excellent tiramisu. [$] *Average main: $24* ✉ *Raley's Shopping Center, 930 Tahoe Blvd., near Village Blvd., Incline Village* ☎ *775/831–0346* 🌐 *www.azzaras.com* 🕒 *Closed Mon. No lunch.*

★ Bite Tahoe

$$$ | **MODERN AMERICAN** | The strip-mall location and offhand, mildly industrial decor of this "American tapas" haven scarcely hint at the artistry involved in transforming comfort-food staples into tantalizing small bites. The chefs frequently change up the preparations, but deviled eggs topped with crispy prosciutto, lobster sliders, arugula and kale salad, pork ribs with Korean barbecue or tamarind chipotle honey sauce are typical of the two dozen items that pair well with specialty cocktails on a creative par with the cuisine. **Known for:** dozen-plus global wines by the glass; flavorful non-meat items; on-point waitstaff. [$] *Average*

main: $34 ✉ *Incline Plaza, 907 Tahoe Blvd., Incline Village* ☎ *775/831–1000* 🌐 *bitetahoe.com* 🕓 *Closed Sun. and Mon. No lunch.*

Fredrick's Fusion Bistro

$$$ | **ECLECTIC** | Copper-top tables lend a chic look to the dining room at this intimate, under-the-radar strip-mall bistro. Incline Villagers extol Fredrick's for its *karaage* (Japanese fried chicken), sushi rolls, braised short ribs, pan-seared salmon with Asian slaw, and similar small and large European- and Asian-influenced dishes. **Known for:** intimate space; fireside tables; ginger martini to start. [$] *Average main: $35* ✉ *907 Tahoe Blvd., at Village Blvd., Incline Village* ☎ *775/832–3007* 🌐 *www.fredricksfusion.com* 🕓 *Closed Sun.–Tues. No lunch.*

★ Le Bistro

$$$$ | **FRENCH** | Incline Village's hidden gem—this restaurant is hard to find, so ask for directions when you book—serves French-country cuisine in a romantic dining room with single-stem roses adorning linen-dressed tables. The menu, offered prix fixe (a good deal) or à la carte, might include starters like flame broiled eggplant with ratatouille or escargots, several salads (try the Caesar with white anchovies), and rack of lamb with lentils and tamarind jus or *coquille St.-Jacques* (scallops in cream sauce). **Known for:** romantic setting; wine pairings; gracious service. [$] *Average main: $42* ✉ *120 Country Club Dr., Suite 29, Incline Village* ✥ *Off Lakeshore Blvd.* ☎ *775/831–0800* 🌐 *www.lebistrotahoe.com* 🕓 *Closed Sun. and Mon. No lunch.*

Sage Leaf

$$ | **MODERN AMERICAN** | Chefs emphasizing sustainably and humanely raised local ingredients prepare three squares a day at this storefront restaurant with a contemporary interior and a shaded patio out front. The house-made sage-and-cheddar biscuits are the must-try for breakfast, and the ⅓-pound burger with bacon and fried egg is a village favorite for lunch; pasta dishes, pork chops, steaks, and pan-roasted fish are top dinner choices. **Known for:** Bloody Mary with jalapeño vodka and candied bacon; smoked-salmon on flatbread and other starters; good spot for brunch. [$] *Average main: $29* ✉ *Village Plaza, 893 Tahoe Blvd., Suite 600, Incline Village* ✥ *Garage entrance on E. Enterprise St.* ☎ *775/413–5005* 🌐 *www.sageleaftahoe.com* 🕓 *Closed Tues. and Wed.*

★ Sam Choy's Ohana Diner

$$ | **ASIAN FUSION** | **FAMILY** | The fare's as delectable as the setting is incongruous at the casual spot that Hawaii's "godfather of poke" opened inside a neon-lit 21st-century bowling alley replete with video poker; an arcade; pool tables; three bars; and a patio with firepits, cornhole, and bocce. The kinetic venue's a hoot, but the poke tacos and nachos and Sam Choy's signature Spam musabi—not to mention the burgers, salads, bowls, wraps, pizzas, and sandwiches—are seriously good. **Known for:** taco Tuesday, Tiki Thursday; potent frozen "baller" cocktails; family-friendly. [$] *Average main: $25* ✉ *Bowl Incline, 920 Southwood Blvd., off Lake Tahoe Blvd., Incline Village* ☎ *775/831–1900* 🌐 *www.samchoysohanadiner.com.*

Coffee and Quick Bites

Mountain High Sandwich Company

$ | **AMERICAN** | **FAMILY** | A casual, plank-floored, all-natural deli serving breakfast and lunch, Mountain High may well be the only place in Tahoe to find coconut chia seed pudding and similar delicacies. More familiar fare—biscuits and gravy (sausage or veggie) for breakfast, house-smoked tri-tip sandwiches (also tofu barbecue) for lunch—is also on the menu. **Known for:** grab-and-go items; inventive soups; gluten-free, vegan, and vegetarian choices. [$] *Average main: $12* ✉ *120 Country Club Dr., Suite 28, Incline Village* ☎ *775/298–2636* 🌐 *www.mountainhighsandwichco.com* 🕓 *Closed Mon. No dinner.*

Get to Sand Harbor Beach in Lake Tahoe–Nevada State Park early; the park sometimes fills before lunchtime in summer.

Tunnel Creek Cafe

$ | AMERICAN | FAMILY | The multilevel outdoor deck of this order-at-the-counter restaurant cradled in a hillside below the Ponderosa Ranch from TV's *Bonanza* entices weary East Shore hikers and bikers with filling fare fit for a ranch hand. Along with breakfast standards, there's a "power bowl" of eggs, avocado, cheese, and black beans—salads, sandwiches (including a tasty turkey club), and burgers appear for lunch. **Known for:** crème brûlée French toast; well-made coffee drinks; eight beers on tap, plus ciders and kombucha. [$] *Average main: $15* ✉ *1115 Tunnel Creek Rd., off Ponderosa Ranch Rd. at Hwy. 28, Incline Village* ☎ *775/298–2502* 🌐 *www.tunnelcreekcafe.com* ⏲ *No dinner Mon.–Thurs.*

Hotels

Hyatt Regency Lake Tahoe Resort, Spa and Casino

$$$ | RESORT | FAMILY | This full-service 26-acre destination resort is undergoing a two-year renovation of its lakeside cottages and main restaurant, with beach access, a significant part of the Hyatt's appeal, unavailable until at least April 2026; that said, accommodations in the green-glass tower and resort facilities elsewhere (several restaurants, heated pool, hot tubs, fitness center, casino, the Stillwater Sap) will remain open. **Pros:** luxurious accommodations; 20,000-square-foot spa with 16 treatment rooms; low-key casino. **Cons:** pricey (especially for families); feels corporate; loss of lake access and some activities until 2026. [$] *Rooms from: $404* ✉ *111 Country Club Dr., Incline Village* ☎ *775/832–1234* 🌐 *www.hyatt.com* 🛏 *398 rooms* 🍴 *No Meals.*

Nightlife

Alibi Ale Works Incline Public House

BEER GARDENS | The taps at the pub of this local brewery flow with 20 or so beers (including several stouts) that you can enjoy inside an industrial-style space with an open-truss ceiling, on a deck just outside, or in an adjacent beer garden. The food's decent, with the mustache-shaped pretzel (best with beer mustard and beer cheese) the most popular app and a pizza or Wagyu cheeseburger the best choice for something more filling. ⊠ *931 Tahoe Blvd., Incline Village* ☎ *775/831–8300* ⊕ *alibialeworks.com/incline-public-house.*

 Performing Arts

Lake Tahoe Shakespeare Festival

THEATER | In July and August, actors perform works by the Bard and others outdoors at Sand Harbor, with the lake as the backdrop. ⊠ *Hwy. 28, 3 miles south of Incline Village, Incline Village* ☎ *800/747–4697* ⊕ *laketahoeshakespeare.com.*

🏃 Activities

GOLF

Incline Championship

GOLF | Robert Trent Jones Sr. designed this challenging course of tightly cut, tree-lined fairways laced with water hazards that demand accuracy and distance skills. The greens fee includes a cart. ⊠ *955 Fairway Blvd., at Northwood Blvd., north off Hwy. 28, Incline Village* ☎ *775/832–1146* ⊕ *www.yourtahoeplace.com/golf-incline* 🏌 *From $146 depending on season, time of day* 🏌 *18 holes, 7106 yards, par 72* ⊗ *Closed mid-Oct.–mid-May.*

Incline Mountain

GOLF | This executive (shorter) course designed by Robert Trent Jones Jr. requires accuracy more than distance skills. The greens fee includes a cart. ⊠ *690 Wilson Way, at Golfer's Pass, south off Hwy. 431, Incline Village* ☎ *775/832–1150* ⊕ *www.yourtahoeplace.com/golf-incline* 🏌 *From $61 depending on season, time of day* 🏌 *18 holes, 3527 yards, par 58* ⊗ *Closed early Oct.–late May.*

MOUNTAIN BIKING

★ Flume Trail Bikes

BIKING | FAMILY | You can rent bikes from this company that operates a bike shuttle to the Flume Trail in Spooner Lake State Park. From there, adventurous types (many aboard e-bikes) take in some jaw-dropping views cycling 14 miles back to the parking lot. For a more leisurely ride, bike the Tahoe East Shore Trail, which starts south of the lot. ⊠ *1115 Tunnel Creek Rd., at Ponderosa Ranch Rd., off Hwy. 28, Incline Village* ☎ *775/298–2501* ⊕ *flumetrailtahoe.com* 🚲 *Bike rentals from $50, shuttle $20.*

SKIING

Diamond Peak

SKIING & SNOWBOARDING | FAMILY | Snowmaking covers 75% of affordable Diamond Peak, whose runs are groomed nightly. The ride up the 1-mile Crystal Express rewards you with fantastic views. Less crowded than Tahoe's larger ski parks and a fine place for beginners and intermediates—though there are steep-aspect black-diamond runs, advanced skiers may find the options too limited—the resort provides free shuttles to nearby lodgings. For snowboarders, there's the Village Terrain Park. Area insiders recommend having lunch mid-mountain at the Snowflake Lodge (casual food, and oh what views). **Facilities:** 40 trails; 655 acres, 1,840 vertical drop; 6 lifts. ⊠ *1210 Ski Way, off Country Club Dr., Incline Village* ☎ *775/832–1177* ⊕ *www.diamondpeak.com* 🎿 *From $145.*

Mt. Rose Ski Tahoe

SKIING & SNOWBOARDING | Here you can ski some of Tahoe's highest slopes and enjoy bird's-eye views of Reno, the lake, and Carson Valley. Though more compact than other Tahoe resorts, Mt. Rose has the area's highest base elevation and, consequently, the driest snow. The mountain has a wide variety of terrain, some accessible by the $7.5 million Lakeview Express lift, which speeds you to your destination in less than half the time of its predecessor. The most challenging area is the Chutes, 200-plus acres of gulp-and-go advanced-to-expert vertical. Intermediates can choose steep groomers or mellow, wide-open boulevards. Beginners have their own corner of the mountain, with gentle, wide slopes. The two terrain parks are on opposite sides of the mountain so boarders can follow the sun as it tracks across the resort. The mountain gets hit hard in storms; check conditions before heading up on windy or inclement days. **Facilities:** 70 trails; 1,200 acres; 1,800-foot vertical drop; 8 lifts. ✉ *22222 Mt. Rose Hwy., Reno* ✣ *Hwy. 431, 11 miles north of Incline Village* ☎ *800/754–7673* 🌐 *skirose.com* 🎟 *Lift ticket $175.*

Tahoe Meadows Snowplay Area

SKIING & SNOWBOARDING | FAMILY | This is the most popular area near the north shore for noncommercial cross-country skiing, sledding, tubing, snowshoeing, and snowmobiling. ✉ *Off Hwy. 431, Incline Village* ✣ *From Hwy. 28 at Incline Village, head north about 6½ miles on Hwy. 431 toward Mt. Rose Ski Area.*

Zephyr Cove

22 miles south of Incline Village.

The largest settlement between Incline Village and the Stateline area is Zephyr Cove, a tiny resort. It has a beach, marina, campground, picnic area, coffee shop in a log lodge, rustic cabins, and nearby riding stables.

GETTING HERE AND AROUND

From the north shore communities, reach Zephyr Cove by following Highway 28 along the eastern side of the lake. From South Lake Tahoe, take U.S. 50 north and then west. Public transportation isn't available in Zephyr Cove.

Sights

Cave Rock State Park

STATE/PROVINCIAL PARK | FAMILY | Seventy-five feet of solid stone, Cave Rock is the throat of an extinct volcano. The impressive outcropping, pierced by two U.S. 50 tunnels, towers over a parking lot, a lakefront picnic ground, a small beach, and a boat launch. The views are some of the lake's best; this is an excellent spot to snap a photo. The rock itself is a sacred burial site for the Washoe Indians. Hiking to it from the state park is prohibited. ✉ *U.S. 50, 4 miles north of Zephyr Cove, Zephyr Cove* ☎ *775/588–7975* 🌐 *parks.nv.gov/parks* 🎟 *$10 ($15 for non-NV vehicles).*

Hotels

Zephyr Cove Resort

$$ | HOTEL | FAMILY | Beneath towering pines at the lake's edge stand 28 cozy, modern, vacation cabins with peaked knotty-pine ceilings, and although they're not fancy, they come in various sizes, some perfect for families. **Pros:** family-friendly old-school ambience; cozy cabins; range of on-site outdoor activities. **Cons:** lodge rooms are basic; can be noisy in summer; not all cabins have fireplaces. [$] *Rooms from: $280* ✉ *760 U.S. 50, 4 miles north of Stateline, Zephyr Cove* ☎ *775/589–4906, 800/238–2463* 🌐 *www.zephyrcove.com* 🔑 *32 units* 🍴 *No Meals.*

Stateline

5 miles south of Zephyr Cove.

Stateline is the archetypal Nevada border town. Its four high-rise casinos are as vertical and contained as the commercial district of the California side's South Lake Tahoe is horizontal and sprawling. And, except for Edgewood Tahoe's lakeshore golf course, Stateline is as relentlessly indoors-oriented as the rest of the lake is outdoors-focused.

This small strip is where you'll find Lake Tahoe's most concentrated action: restaurants, showrooms with semi-famous headliners and razzle-dazzle revues, tower-hotel rooms and suites, and 24-hour casinos. The Tahoe Blue Center, which hosts conventions, concerts, and other events, opened in 2023 at U.S. 50 and Lake Parkway.

GETTING HERE AND AROUND

From South Lake Tahoe take U.S. 50 north across the Nevada border to reach Stateline and its casinos. If coming from Reno's airport, take I–580 south to U.S. 50 west to the lake and then south. Tahoe Transportation District operates daily bus service.

Beaches

Nevada Beach

BEACH | FAMILY | Although less than a mile long, this is the widest beach on the lake and especially good for swimming (many Tahoe beaches are rocky). You can boat and fish here, and there are picnic tables, barbecue grills, and a campground beneath the pines. The beach is the best place to watch the July 4th or Labor Day fireworks, but most of the summer the subdued atmosphere attracts families and those seeking a less-touristy spot. **Amenities:** parking (fee); toilets; water sports. **Best for:** sunrise; swimming; walking. ✉ *Elk Point Rd., Stateline* ✥ *Off U.S. 50, 3 miles north of Stateline* ☎ *530/543–2600* 🌐 *www.fs.usda.gov* 🎟 *$10 day-use fee* ☞ *Dogs permitted on leash in picnic areas but not on beach.*

Restaurants

★ Edgewood Tahoe

$$$$ | AMERICAN | The three restaurants at Stateline's classy resort, all in spaces that make the most of the lakeside setting, deliver some of the area's best dining, if on the pricey side. Head to the Bistro for casual-fancy breakfast, lunch, and dinner; Brooks Bar & Grill for inventive lunch and dinner comfort food; and the Edgewood Restaurant for evening fine dining with views across the lake to Mt. Tallac. **Known for:** a venue for all moods; Bistro patio excellent for a sunny-day lunch; golf-course views from outdoor deck at Brooks. [$] *Average main: $54* ✉ *Edgewood Tahoe, 180 Lake Pkwy., Stateline* ☎ *888/769–1924* 🌐 *edgewoodtahoe.com/dine.*

Hotels

Harrah's Tahoe Hotel/Casino

$ | HOTEL | FAMILY | The 18-story hotel's major selling point is that every room has two full bathrooms, a boon if you're traveling with family. **Pros:** lake and mountain views from upper-floor rooms; good midweek values; top-floor steak house with good views from all tables. **Cons:** can get noisy; room decor needs an update; lacks intimacy. [$] *Rooms from: $145* ✉ *15 U.S. 50, at Stateline Ave., Stateline* ☎ *775/588–6611, 800/427–7247* 🌐 *www.caesars.com/harrahs-tahoe* 🛏 *512 rooms* 🍴 *No Meals.*

Harveys Lake Tahoe Resort Hotel and Casino

$ | HOTEL | This resort began as a cabin in 1944, and now it's Tahoe's largest casino-hotel, where premium rooms have custom furnishings, oversize marble baths, minibars, and excellent lake views. **Pros:** live entertainment; on-site restaurants; lake views from upper-floor rooms. **Cons:** can get loud at night; rates jump on summer weekends; large property. [$] *Rooms from: $132* ✉ *18 U.S. 50, at Stateline Ave., Stateline* ☎ *775/588–2411, 800/648–3361* 🌐 *www.caesars.com/harveys-tahoe* 🛏 *740 rooms* 🍴 *No Meals.*

★ The Lodge at Edgewood Tahoe

$$$$ | RESORT | On a prime lakefront parcel, this hotel makes a bold impression with its stone-and-walnut Great Hall, whose four-story wall of windows frames views across Lake Tahoe to grand Mt. Tallac. **Pros:** prime lakefront location; haute-rustic design; all rooms have balconies and fireplaces. **Cons:** high rates in-season; some rooms have no lake views; long walk to pool and hot tub from some rooms. [$] *Rooms from: $549* ✉ *180 Lake Pkwy., Stateline* ☎ *775/588–2787, 888/769–1924* 🌐 *edgewoodtahoe.com/lodge* 🛏 *168 rooms* 🍴 *No Meals.*

Nightlife

Lake Tahoe AleWorX

BARS | Self-serve taps let you control the flow of this peppy alehouse's regional to international brews. The craft beer lineups and menus of apps, salads, and wood-fired pizzas and sandwiches are similar at the two locations, in Stateline and 5 miles southwest in South Lake Tahoe, so where to go depends on your mood: in the evening, the former is more barlike and stays open later than the family-friendly latter (see website for address), which has two casual outdoor areas. Both present live music some days. ✉ *31 U.S. 50, Suite 105, Stateline* ☎ *775/580–6163* 🌐 *laketahoealeworx.com.*

Performing Arts

Harveys Outdoor Summer Concert Series

CONCERTS | Headliners such as Neil Young, Dierks Bentley, Miranda Lambert, the Foo Fighters, and Sammy Hagar have performed at this weekend concert series. ✉ *Harveys Lake Tahoe, 18 U.S. 50, Stateline* ☎ *775/588–2411* 🌐 *www.caesars.com/harveys-tahoe/shows.*

South Shore Room

CONCERTS | Acts like Dave Mason, Les Claypool, and Sheila E. play Harrah's big showroom, along with the psychedelic Pink Floyd Laser Spectacular show and comedians like Rob Schneider. ✉ *Harrah's Lake Tahoe, 15 U.S. 50, Stateline* ☎ *775/586–6244* 🌐 *www.caesars.com/harrahs-tahoe/shows.*

Activities

Edgewood Tahoe

GOLF | Golfers of all skill levels enjoy this fabulously scenic lakeside course that's home to the American Century Championship tournament each July. Designed by George Fazio and renovated a generation later by his nephew, Tom Fazio, it has four sets of tees for a variety of course lengths. The greens fee includes an optional cart. ✉ *180 Lake Pkwy., at U.S. 50, Stateline* ☎ *775/588–3566* 🌐 *edgewoodtahoe.com/golf* 🎫 *From $250 (varies throughout season)* ⛳ *18 holes, 7529 yards, par 72.*

Reno

38 miles northeast of Incline Village.

Established in 1859 as a trading station at a bridge over the Truckee River, Reno grew along with the silver mines of nearby Virginia City and the transcontinental railroad that chugged through town. Gambling—legalized in 1931—put Reno on the map. This is still a gambling town, but outdoor activities and attractions like the National Automobile Museum and the Nevada Museum of Art also draw visitors.

Parts of downtown are sketchy, but sections like the Riverwalk District along the Truckee River have revitalized the area. With more than 300 days of sunshine annually, temperatures year-round in this high-mountain-desert climate are warmer than at Tahoe, though rarely as hot as in Sacramento and the Central Valley. Some of the town's best restaurants—among them the Atlantis Steakhouse—are in casinos.

GETTING HERE AND AROUND

Interstate 80 bisects Reno east–west, U.S. 395 north–south (south of town the road is signed U.S. 395/I–580). Greyhound and Amtrak stop here, and several

airlines fly into Reno-Tahoe International Airport. RTC Ride provides bus service.

ESSENTIALS
BUS CONTACT RTC Ride. ⊠ *4th St. Station, E. 4th and Lake Sts., Reno* ☎ *775/348–7433* ⊕ *www.rtcwashoe.com.*

VISITOR INFORMATION Reno Tahoe Visitor Center. ⊠ *135 N. Sierra St., Reno* ☎ *775/682–3800* ⊕ *www.visitrenotahoe. com.*

Sights

★ Atlantis Casino
CASINO | The classiest of Reno's gaming operations, the Atlantis draws high rollers seeking the allure and sophistication of Las Vegas. The casino packs a dizzying array of table games and 1,500 slots with a loose(ish) reputation into its 60,000 square feet. ⊠ *3800 S. Virginia St., Reno* ☎ *775/825–4700* ⊕ *atlantiscasino.com/ casino.*

Eldorado Resort Casino
CASINO | Action-packed, with lots of slots and popular bar-top video poker, the best of the downtown casinos has good coffee-shop and food-court fare. Choose from more than 100 martinis at Roxy's Bar and Lounge. The kitschy Fountain of Fortune is worth checking out for its massive Florentine-inspired sculptures. ⊠ *345 N. Virginia St., Reno* ☎ *775/786–5700* ⊕ *www.caesars.com/ eldorado-reno.*

★ National Automobile Museum
HISTORY MUSEUM | FAMILY | Antique and classic cars made by obscure and familiar companies fill this engaging facility. Celebrity vehicles include the Lana Turner Chrysler (one of only six made), an Elvis Presley Cadillac, and the Mercury coupe James Dean drove in the movie *Rebel Without a Cause.* Hard to miss are the experimental and still futuristic-looking 1938 Phantom Corsair and a gold-plated 1981 DeLorean. ⊠ *10 S. Lake St., at Mill St., Reno* ☎ *775/333–9300* ⊕ *automuseum.org* 🖃 *$15.*

Nevada Museum of Art
ART MUSEUM | A dramatic four-level structure designed by Will Bruder houses this splendid museum's collection, which focuses on themes such as the Sierra Nevada/Great Basin and altered-landscape photography. The exterior's torqued walls are sided with a black zinc-based material that has been fabricated to resemble textures found in the Black Rock Desert. ⊠ *160 W. Liberty St., and Hill St., Reno* ☎ *775/329–3333* ⊕ *www. nevadaart.org* 🖃 *$15* 🕐 *Closed Mon.*

Peppermill Casino
CASINO | Slots and video-poker players flock to the Peppermill, whose neon-filled casino generates plenty of glitz. High-limit slots and table games are among the other draws at this hot spot a few miles from downtown. ⊠ *2707 S. Virginia St., Reno* ☎ *866/821–9996* ⊕ *www.peppermillreno.com/gaming.*

Riverwalk District
PROMENADE | FAMILY | A formerly dilapidated section of Reno's waterfront is now the toast of the town. The Riverwalk itself is a ½-mile promenade on the north side of the Truckee River, which flows around Wingfield Park, where festivals and other events take place. On the third Saturday afternoon of each month, local merchants host Wine Walk tastings ($30). The monthlong Artown festival in July presents outdoor art, opera, dance, live music, and kids' performances, most at Wingfield Park. ⊠ *North side of Truckee River between Lake and Ralston Sts., Reno* ☎ *775/825–9255* ⊕ *www. renoriver.org.*

 Restaurants

Beaujolais Bistro
$$$$ | FRENCH | Across from the Truckee River, this Reno favorite serves earthy, country-style French food—escargots, cassoulet, steak frites with red wine sauce, sweetbreads with Madeira, and

fish and vegetarian selections—with zero pretension. Wooden floors, large windows, and brick walls with a fireplace create a welcoming and intimate atmosphere. **Known for:** inventive cocktails; intimate atmosphere; more casual experience at the bar. [$] *Average main: $47* ✉ *753 Riverside Dr., Reno* ☎ *775/323–2227* 🌐 *beaujolaisbistro.com* 🕒 *Closed Sun. and Mon. No lunch.*

Great Full Gardens Café and Eatery

$$ | AMERICAN | FAMILY | The owners of this bright-and-chipper, health-oriented restaurant open for breakfast, lunch, and dinner aim to please all palates, from carnivore to vegan. The ingredients—grass-fed burger meat, organic chicken, wild-caught seafood, and a wide range of produce—are sourced as locally as possible. **Known for:** menu accommodates most dietary needs; six Benedict recipes for breakfast; flavorful Gino the Soup Man offerings. [$] *Average main: $25* ✉ *555 S. Virginia St., Reno* ☎ *775/324–2013* 🌐 *www.greatfullgardens.com/midtown* 🕒 *No dinner Sun.*

Hotels

★ Atlantis Casino Resort Spa

$ | HOTEL | The smallest rooms at this colorful, aquatic-theme, high-rise hotel start at 375 square feet, with the penthouses more than quadruple that size. **Pros:** luxurious upper-tier rooms; Atlantis Steakhouse and Sky Terrace Sushi & Oyster Bar among Reno's top restaurants; highly praised spa. **Cons:** expensive on weekends; convention action; costly restaurants. [$] *Rooms from: $117* ✉ *3800 S. Virginia St., Reno* ☎ *775/825–4700* 🌐 *atlantiscasino.com* 🛏 *824 rooms* 🍴 *No Meals.*

Peppermill Reno

$ | HOTEL | A few miles removed from downtown's flashy main drag, this property set a high standard for luxury in Reno, especially in the Tuscany Tower, whose 600 baroque suites have plush king-size beds, marble bathrooms, and European soaking tubs. **Pros:** luxurious rooms; casino decor; good coffee shop. **Cons:** deluge of neon may be off-putting to some; enormous size; mostly expensive dining. [$] *Rooms from: $119* ✉ *2707 S. Virginia St., Reno* ☎ *775/826–2121, 866/821–9996* 🌐 *www.peppermillreno.com* 🛏 *1,623 rooms* 🍴 *No Meals.*

Nightlife

Fireside Lounge

BARS | Amid the neon-bright gambling areas at the Peppermill Casino, this lounge is a blast for its over-the-top decor and equally exotic cocktails. The signature drink, the 64-ounce Scorpion, leads with Myers's dark rum and vodka, with cherry brandy and grenadine disguising the concoction's potency. ✉ *2707 S. Virginia St., Reno* ☎ *775/826–2121* 🌐 *www.peppermillreno.com.*

Mo's By the River

WINE BARS | Patrons of this under-the-radar wine bar in a residential area a block from the Truckee River tend to linger over the affordable wines by the glass or bottle, especially on temperate days when the outdoor patio beckons. California wines are well represented, but the selection encompasses the major world regions. It's best to call ahead before coming here. ✉ *718 Jones St., Reno* ☎ *775/830–3043* 🕒 *Closed Mon. and Tues.*

Chapter 10

SAN FRANCISCO

Updated by
Trevor Felch
and Denise M. Leto

● Sights	🍴 Restaurants	🛏 Hotels	🛍 Shopping	▼ Nightlife
★★★★★	★★★★☆	★★★★★	★★★★☆	★★★☆☆

WELCOME TO SAN FRANCISCO

TOP REASONS TO GO

★ **The bay:** It's hard not to gasp as you catch sight of sunlight dancing on the water when you crest a hill, or watch the Golden Gate Bridge vanish and reemerge in the summer fog.

★ **The food:** San Franciscans are serious about what they eat, and with good reason. Home to some of the nation's best chefs, top restaurants, and finest local produce, it's hard not to eat well here.

★ **The shopping:** Shopaholics visiting the city will not be disappointed—San Francisco is packed with browsing destinations, everything from quirky boutiques to massive malls.

★ **The good life:** A laid-back atmosphere, beautiful surroundings, and oodles of cultural, culinary, and aesthetic pleasures … if you spend too much time here, you might not leave.

★ **The great outdoors:** From Golden Gate Park to sidewalk cafés in North Beach, San Franciscans relish their outdoor spaces.

1 **Union Square.** Has hotels and upscale stores aplenty.

2 **Chinatown.** A dense neighborhood full of shops and restaurants.

3 **SoMa.** A once-industrial, still-in-transition district anchored by SFMOMA and Yerba Buena Gardens.

4 **Civic Center.** Marked by monumental government buildings.

5 **The Tenderloin.** Situated just north of the Civic Center.

6 **Hayes Valley.** South of the Civic Center is this chic district.

7 **Nob Hill.** Old-money San Francisco.

8 **Russian Hill.** Steep streets lace this classy, au courant district.

9 **Polk Gulch.** A tiny area next door to Russian Hill.

10 **Pacific Heights.** Has some of the city's grand Victorians.

11 **Japantown.** A tight-knit Japanese American community with shopping and dining.

12 **Western Addition.** South of Japantown is this vibrant residential area.

13 **North Beach.** The city's small, historically Italian neighborhood.

14 **Fisherman's Wharf.** A tourist mecca.

15 **Embarcadero.** The famous Ferry Building is at the foot of Market Street.

16 **Financial District.** A district of towering buildings inland from Embarcadero.

17 **The Marina.** Home to many young professionals.

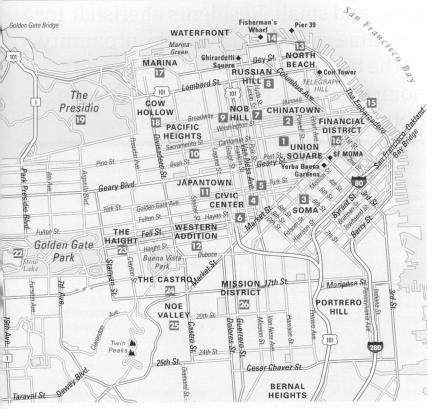

18 Cow Hollow. Affluent and residential.

19 The Presidio. A huge, wooded, shoreline park in the shadow of the Golden Gate Bridge.

20 The Richmond. Residential district north of Golden Gate Park.

21 The Sunset. The city's largest residential and commercial area.

22 Golden Gate Park. San Francisco's backyard.

23 The Haight. Still marked by a '60s atmosphere.

24 The Castro. Rainbow-flag-waving, in-your-face fab.

25 Noe Valley. A cute, pricey neighborhood favored by young families.

26 Mission District. A prime destination for restaurants and hip bars.

On a 46½-square-mile strip of land between San Francisco Bay and the Pacific Ocean, San Francisco has charms great and small. Residents cherish it for the same reasons visitors do: proximity to the bay, rows of hillside Victorian homes, sunsets framed by the Golden Gate Bridge, world-class cuisine.

You can spend hours exploring downtown, Chinatown, North Beach, the northern and western waterfronts, and Golden Gate Park, along with colorful neighborhoods like the Haight, the Mission, and the Castro. That said, San Francisco's allure—the reason why many people can't imagine calling any other place home despite a high cost of living and chilly summers—is more than surface deep. Among the attractions are the city's free-spirited tolerance and the diversity of its neighborhoods.

If you're a shopper, for instance, you'll find that each area has its own distinctive finds, whether it's 1960s housewares, cheeky stationery, or vintage Levi's. Serious shoppers head straight to Union Square, the site of most department stores and nearby haute-couture boutiques. Indeed, if San Francisco shopping here has a downside, it's that—outside of thrift shops in the Lower Haight and Mission districts—real bargains can be few and far between.

After hours, you can join the city's costume-clad partygoers, hippies, hipsters, downtown divas, and frat boys for a nightlife experience that will, again, vary by neighborhood. Downtown and the Financial District are pretty serious even after dark, and Nob Hill is staid, though you can't beat views from penthouse lounges. Nearby North Beach is livelier, with everything from comedy clubs to bars showcasing the city's bohemian past. In addition to brewpubs, SoMa has hot dance clubs and saucy gay bars. Union Square's options tend to be trendy and swanky.

Day or night, however, the diverse wonders of this beautiful metropolis inspire at every turn—even if you just focus on the highlights: riding a cable car over Nob Hill, walking down the Filbert Street Steps, gazing at the thundering Pacific from the cliffs of Lincoln Park, cheering the San Francisco Giants to *beat L.A.* in lively Oracle Park, enjoying freshly shucked oysters at the Ferry Building.

Planning

Getting Here and Around

AIR
The major gateway to San Francisco is San Francisco International Airport (SFO), 15 miles south of the city off U.S. 101. Oakland International Airport (OAK) is across the bay, not much farther away

from downtown San Francisco (via I-80 East and I-880 South), but traffic on the Bay Bridge lengthens travel times considerably.

Transportation signage at SFO is color-coded by type and is quite clear. A taxi ride to downtown costs around $60, and rideshare (e.g. Lyft and Uber) rates start around $25 for a shared ride. A 30-minute ride on BART will only cost you $10. Buses and shuttles are also available. From OAK to downtown San Francisco, a taxi costs around $80, rideshare rates are about $50, and BART costs $10.25.

AIRPORTS Oakland International Airport. (OAK) ⊠ 1 Airport Dr., Oakland ☎ 510/563-3300 ⊕ www.oaklandairport. com. **San Francisco International Airport.** (SFO) ⊠ McDonnell and Links Rds., San Francisco ☎ 800/435-9736, 650/821-8211 ⊕ www.flysfo.com.

BOAT

Alcatraz Cruises operates the ferries to Alcatraz Island ($42) from Pier 33. Boats leave 14 times a day (more in summer), and the journey itself takes 30 minutes. Allow at least 2½ hours for a round-trip jaunt.

Blue & Gold Fleet operates a number of tours, plus service to Sausalito ($14.25 one-way). Tickets are sold at Pier 39; boats depart from Pier 41. Golden Gate Ferry has daily service to and from Sausalito and Larkspur ($14 and $13.50 one-way), leaving from Pier 1, behind the Ferry Building.

The San Francisco Bay Ferry operates daily between Alameda's Main Street Terminal, Oakland's Jack London Square, and San Francisco's Ferry Building ($4.50 one-way). Purchase tickets online via the Clipper Card website or app or at terminal vending machines (tickets for the ferry to Oakland/Alameda can also be purchased on board).

CONTACTS Alcatraz Cruises. ☎ 415/981-7625 ⊕ www.alcatrazcruises.com. **Blue & Gold Fleet.** ☎ 415/705-8200 ⊕ www.blueandgoldfleet.com. **Ferry Building Marketplace.** ⊠ 1 Ferry Bldg., at foot of Market St. on Embarcadero, San Francisco ☎ 415/983-8030 ⊕ www.ferrybuildingmarketplace.com. **Golden Gate Ferry.** ☎ 415/455-2000 ⊕ www.goldengate. org/ferry. **San Francisco Bay Ferry.** ⊠ San Francisco ☎ 877/643-3779 ⊕ sanfranciscobayferry.com.

BUS

Greyhound serves San Francisco with buses from many major U.S. cities. The Greyhound depot is located at the Salesforce Transit Center in SoMa. Tickets can be purchased online; seating is first-come, first-served. Cash, checks, and credit cards are accepted.

CABLE CAR

Don't miss the sensation of moving up and down some of San Francisco's steepest hills in a clattering cable car. Jump aboard as it pauses at a designated stop, and wedge yourself into any available space. Then just hold on.

The fare (for one direction) is $8. Buy tickets in advance at the kiosks at the cable-car turnarounds at Hyde and Beach Streets and at Powell and Market Streets. Or consider MuniMobile or a Clipper Card (⊕ sfmta.com). Cash purchases require exact change.

The Powell–Mason and Powell–Hyde lines begin at Powell and Market Streets near Union Square and terminate at Fisherman's Wharf; lines for these routes can be long, especially in summer. The California Street line runs east and west from Market and California Streets to Van Ness Avenue. It's a shorter and less thrilling ride, but there's often no wait.

CAR

One-way streets, snarly traffic, and steep hills make driving in San Francisco a challenge. Be sure to leave plenty of room between your car and other vehicles when on a steep slope. This is especially important when you've braked at a stop sign on a steep incline.

Parking is also a challenge. In the Financial District and Civic Center neighborhoods, parking is forbidden on most streets between 3 or 4 pm and 6 or 7 pm. Check street signs carefully to confirm because illegally parked cars are towed immediately.

Downtown parking lots are are expensive but nevertheless often full. The city-owned Sutter-Stockton, Ellis-O'Farrell, and 5th-and-Mission garages have the most reasonable rates. Large hotels often have parking available, but many charge in excess of $40 a day. Regardless of where you park, never leave any items of value in your car.

■TIP➔ Remember to curb your wheels when parking on hills—turn wheels away from the curb when facing uphill, toward the curb when facing downhill. You can get a ticket if you don't do this.

METRO/PUBLIC TRANSPORT

Bay Area Rapid Transit (BART) trains, which run until midnight, connect San Francisco with its airport, Oakland (including its airport), Berkeley, and other communities. Within San Francisco, stations are mostly downtown and in the Mission. Trains travel frequently from early morning until evening on weekdays. After 8 pm weekdays and on weekends, there's often a 20-minute wait between trains. Intracity San Francisco fares are $2.15; intercity fares are $3.60 to $14.35.

The San Francisco Municipal Railway, or Muni, operates light-rail vehicles, the historic F-line streetcars along Fisherman's Wharf and Market Street, buses, and the world-famous cable cars. Muni provides 24-hour service on select lines to all areas of the city.

The fare for buses and streetcars is $3 ($2.50 with a Clipper Card). Exact change is required, and dollar bills are accepted in the fare boxes. Except for cable cars, transfers are free upon request (at the time the fare is paid) and are valid for 120 minutes. You can also buy one-day ($13), three-day ($31), and seven-day ($41) Visitor Passports valid on the entire Muni system. The San Francisco CityPass ($76), a discount ticket booklet to several major city attractions, also covers all Muni travel for seven consecutive days.

■TIP➔ Save money by purchasing your Passports on MuniMobile, the mobile ticketing app of the San Francisco Metropolitan Transportation Authority (SFMTA).

CONTACTS Bay Area Rapid Transit. (*BART*) ☎ 510/465–2278 ⊕ www.bart.gov. San Francisco Municipal Transportation Agency. (*Muni*) ☎ 311, 415/701–2311 ⊕ www. sfmta.com.

TAXI AND RIDE SHARE

Finding a cab in San Francisco can be frustrating. Popular nightlife locales, such as the Mission, SoMa, North Beach, and the Castro, are the easiest places to hail one on the street; hotel taxi stands are also an option. It costs $4.15 for the first 0.2 mile, 65¢ for each additional 0.2 mile, and 65¢ per minute in stalled traffic. A $5.50 surcharge is added for trips from the airport, but there aren't charges for additional passengers or for luggage. For trips farther than 15 miles outside city limits, multiply the metered rate by 1.5; tolls and tip are extra.

Rideshare companies such as Uber and Lyft are prominent throughout the city. If you're willing to share a car with strangers, an in-town trip can cost as littles as $4; rates go up for private rides and during peak-demand times. Rideshares are especially economical when going to or from the airport, where a shared ride starts at about $25—half the cost of a cab. That said, many San Franciscans use rideshare apps for going *to* SFO, but often use taxis for trips *from* the airport because they're much easier to find upon landing.

CONTACTS Flywheel Taxi. ☎ *055/359–2420* ⊕ *flywheeltaxi.com.* **Luxor Cab.** ☎ *415/282–4141* ⊕ *www.luxorcab.com.* **Yellow Cab.** ☎ *415/333–3333* ⊕ *yellowcabsf.com.*

TRAIN

Amtrak's *Coast Starlight* passes through the Bay Area on the way from Los Angeles to Seattle, and its *California Zephyr* travels from Chicago to the Bay Area. Amtrak also has several routes between San Jose, Oakland, and Sacramento. San Francisco doesn't have an Amtrak station, but it does have an Amtrak bus stop at the Ferry Building, from which shuttle buses transport passengers to trains in Emeryville. Shuttles also connect the Emeryville train station with BART and other points in downtown San Francisco.

Caltrain connects San Francisco to Palo Alto, San Jose, Santa Clara, and many smaller cities en route. Trains leave from the main depot at 4th and Townsend Streets and from a rail-side stop at 22nd and Pennsylvania Streets. One-way fares are $3.75 to $15, and tickets are valid for four hours after purchase time. There are no onboard ticket sales. You must buy tickets before boarding the train or risk paying up to $230 for fare evasion. You can also buy a day pass ($7.50–$30) for unlimited travel in a 24-hour period. The system shuts down after midnight.

CONTACTS Caltrain. ☎ *800/660–4287* ⊕ *www.caltrain.com.*

Hotels

San Francisco accommodations range from cozy bed-and-breakfasts and kitschy motels to chic boutique hotels, grande dames, and sleek high-rises. Though the tech boom has caused rates to skyrocket there are still a good number of reasonably priced accommodations. There are also ways to keep costs down in general, first and foremost among them is your timing.

Many business-oriented hotels offer weekend deals (such properties are busiest from Monday through Thursday), with the opposite often true at lodgings geared more to leisure travelers. When there's a big convention in town, rates at even the humblest accommodations can double.

When pricing accommodations, always ask what's included and what entails an additional charge, like parking fees, which are off the charts here, or per-night "resort" or "amenity" fees. A seemingly expensive hotel that provides free parking and a hearty breakfast, for instance, can end up costing you less than one that charges for parking and breakfast.

Restaurants

For some, San Francisco's landmark restaurants and top chefs are as big a draw as Alcatraz. In fact, on a Saturday, the Ferry Building—a temple to local eating—might attract more visitors than the Golden Gate Bridge.

Chefs are drawn to superb local ingredients. Chances are that the Meyer lemons, fava beans, or strawberries on your plate—whether fresh, preserved, or pickled—were harvested within the last 48 hours and that the briny abalone, crab, oysters, squid, and tuna—whether poached, seared, smoked, or carpaccio'ed—were caught just offshore. Here, you'll also get to taste unusual varieties of produce like lollipop kale, agretti greens, and yuzu citrus.

The most interesting kitchens use these fresh ingredients in Korean, Japanese, Italian, South American, or other international cuisines. So get ready to dig into kung pao pastrami, porcini doughnuts with raclette béchamel, and yucca gnocchi.

What's more, the culinary hot spots are just as likely to be burger, pizza, or barbecue joints where classically trained chefs are dedicating their lives to making, say, a better margherita pie. And you can readily find superb banh mi, ramen noodles, and juicy *al pastor* tacos in the traditional kitchens of Little Saigon, Japantown, or the Mission District.

⇨ *Hotel and restaurant reviews have been shortened. For full information, visit Fodors.com. Hotel prices are the lowest cost of a standard double room in high season. Restaurant prices are the average cost of a main course at dinner, or if dinner isn't served, at lunch.*

What It Costs

	$	$$	$$$	$$$$
RESTAURANTS				
	under $20	$20–$30	$31–$40	over $40
HOTELS				
	under $200	$200–$350	$351–$500	over $500

Tours

All About Chinatown

WALKING TOURS | On a delightful two-hour, behind-the-scenes look at the neighborhood, owner Linda Lee and her guides explore historic buildings and new murals, stroll through a food market, and stop at a Buddhist temple. At herbal markets, you'll learn the therapeutic benefits of ginseng, geckos, and more. A dim sum lunch is an added option. ✉ *660 California St., Chinatown* ☎ *415/982–8839* ⊕ *allaboutchinatown.com* 💲 *From $55, $85 with lunch.*

Foot! Fun Walking Tours

WALKING TOURS | You'll likely find yourself breathless with laughter, not just gasping after a steep hill. The tour leaders are all entertainers and history buffs; they've got offerings like the Nob Hill tour "Hobnobbing with Gobs of Snobs." ✉ *San Francisco* ☎ *415/793–5378* ⊕ *www.foottours.com* 💲 *From $30 for adults.*

Local Tastes of the City Tours

WALKING TOURS | If you want to snack your way through a neighborhood as you walk it, consider hanging with cookbook author Tom Medin or one of his local guides. You'll learn why certain things just taste better in San Francisco—like coffee and anything baked with sourdough. You'll also gorge yourself into oblivion: the North Beach tour, for instance, might include multiple stops for coffee and baked goods. ✉ *San Francisco* ☎ *415/665–0480* ⊕ *www.sffoodtour.com* 💲 *From $69.*

★ San Francisco City Guides

WALKING TOURS | An outstanding free service supported by the San Francisco Public Library since 1978, these walking tours have themes that range from individual neighborhoods to local history (the gold rush, the 1906 quake, ghost walks) to architecture. Although the tours are free and the knowledgeable guides are volunteers, it's appropriate to make a donation for these nonprofit programs. ✉ *San Francisco* ☎ *415/375–0468* ⊕ *www.sfcityguides.org* 💲 *Free; $20 donation suggested.*

Visitor Information

CONTACTS San Francisco Visitor Information Center. ✉ *Moscone Center, 749 Howard St., between 3rd and 4th Sts., SoMa* ☎ *415/391–2000* ⊕ *www.sftravel.com.*

When to Go

You can visit San Francisco comfortably any time of year. The climate feels Mediterranean—albeit with occasional fog and/or chill. Still, the temperature rarely drops below 40°F, and anything warmer than 80°F is considered a heat wave.

Though the weather can vary from cold and wet to very hot in May and June, spring is generally dry and pleasant. Summer is high season for leisure travelers, especially families with children. Possibly the best months are September and October, when outdoor concerts and festivals take advantage of the still-temperate weather. Note, however, that this is also fire season in parts of Northern California. Be prepared for rain in winter, especially December and January. Winds off the ocean can add to the chill factor.

Union Square

The city's marquee destination for big-name shopping and within walking distance of many hotels, Union Square is home base for many visitors. Four globular contemporary lamp sculptures by the artist R. M. Fischer preside over the landscaped, 2½-acre park anchored by the monument to Admiral George Dewey. The area also has a café with outdoor seating, an open-air stage, and the city's favorite holiday season ice-skating rink.

The square hosts a kaleidoscope of characters: office workers sunning and brown-bagging, street musicians, shoppers taking a rest, kids chasing pigeons, and a fair number of homeless people. The constant clang of cable cars traveling up and down Powell Street helps maintain a festive mood.

Sights

Lotta's Fountain

FOUNTAIN | Saucy gold rush–era actress, singer, and dancer Lotta Crabtree so excited the city's miners that they were known to shower her with gold nuggets and silver dollars after her performances. This peculiar, rather clunky gold-colored fountain adorned with regal lions was her way of saying thanks to her fans. Given to the city in 1875, the fountain became a meeting place for survivors after the 1906 earthquake; each April 18, the anniversary of the quake, San Franciscans gather here. An image of redheaded Lotta herself, in a very pink, rather risqué

dress, appears in one of the Anton Refregier murals in Rincon Center. ⊠ *Traffic triangle at intersection of 3rd, Market, Kearny, and Geary Sts., Union Sq.*

Maiden Lane

STREET | Known as Morton Street in the raffish Barbary Coast era, this former red-light district reported at least one murder a week during the late 19th century, though things cooled down after the 1906 fire. These days Maiden Lane is a chic, designer-boutique-lined pedestrian mall. Wrought-iron gates close the street to traffic most days between 11 and 5, when the lane becomes an alfresco hot spot dotted with umbrella-shaded tables. It's also popular with photographers and Instagrammers for its quaint-chic aesthetic. At 140 Maiden Lane is the only Frank Lloyd Wright building in San Francisco, fronted by a large brick archway. The curving ramp and skylights of the interior, which houses exclusive Italian menswear boutique Isaia, are said to have been his model for the Guggenheim Museum in New York. ⊠ *Between Stockton and Kearny Sts., Union Sq.*

🍴 Restaurants

Beanstalk Cafe

$ | SANDWICHES | Robin's-egg-blue banquettes and metal chairs in different colors add to the cheer at this sunny spot. Drop in for hearty local coffee and excellent breakfast and lunch sandwiches, including those on the popular cragel, a combination of a croissant and a bagel. **Known for:** cragel (croissant and bagel) sandwiches; quality coffee drinks; pleasant, airy space. $ *Average main: $13* ⊠ *724 Bush St., Union Sq.* ⊗ *No dinner.*

★ Kin Khao

$$$ | THAI | Casual eaters of Americanized Thai food probably won't recognize much at this modern, Michelin-star restaurant, but travelers to Thailand will likely see a few familiar items on the short, focused menu. Ingredients are sourced—more

The epicenter of high-end shopping, Union Square is lined with department stores.

accurately, tracked down with dedication—from regional purveyors to create a range of powerful, unique dishes ranging from a mushroom curry mousse with crispy rice cakes to spicy charred squid. **Known for:** fish sauce chicken wings; sharp cocktails and wine program; odd location in the back of a hotel. $ *Average main: $38* ✉ *Parc 55 Hotel, 55 Cyril Magnin St., Union Sq.* ☎ *415/362–7456* ⊕ *www.kinkhao.com* ⊘ *Closed Mon. and Tues. No lunch.*

★ Liholiho Yacht Club

$$$$ | **MODERN AMERICAN** | Inspired but not defined by the chef's native Hawaii, Ravi Kapur's lively restaurant is known for big-hearted, high-spirited cooking. It offers contemporary riffs on staples like poke and Spam, as well as squid served with crispy tripe and manila clams in coconut curry. **Known for:** beef tongue on poppy-seed steamed buns; giant mains that serve two to four people; beautifully composed cocktails. $ *Average main: $42* ✉ *871 Sutter St., Union Sq.*

☎ *415/440–5446* ⊕ *lycsf.com* ⊘ *Closed Sun. No lunch.*

Mensho Tokyo SF

$ | **JAPANESE** | Look for the lines on busy Geary Street where Union Square blurs into the edges of the Tenderloin, and you'll find what eager ramen fans consider the city's best bowl. This was the first U.S. outpost of a prominent Tokyo-based ramen shop, and the quality and consistency of its noodles and broths continue to be spectacular. **Known for:** "tori paitan" chicken ramen; excellent vegan ramen; open late. $ *Average main: $18* ✉ *672 Geary St., Union Sq.* ☎ *415/800–8345* ⊕ *mensho.tokyo* ⊘ *No lunch.*

Hotels

★ Axiom Hotel San Francisco

$$ | **HOTEL** | Green, pet-friendly, and equipped with high-speed fiber-optic Wi-Fi, the tech-oriented Axiom nimbly provides a boutique experience business and leisure travelers applaud. **Pros:** fun, hip vibe; nicely designed rooms and

bathrooms; on-site café open morning to night. **Cons:** the smallest rooms are notably tiny; somewhat congested area; nearby panhandlers. [$] *Rooms from: $229* ✉ *28 Cyril Magnin St., Union Sq.* ☎ *415/392–9466* 🌐 *www.axiomhotel.com* 🛏 *152 rooms* 🍴 *No Meals.*

Beresford Arms

$ | HOTEL | FAMILY | Fancy moldings and 10-foot-tall windows grace the red-carpeted lobby of this brick Victorian listed on the National Register of Historic Places that has rooms of varying size and setup. **Pros:** good value for the neighborhood; suites with kitchenettes and Murphy beds; excellent bathrooms. **Cons:** no a/c; older architecture and design; can be noisy at night. [$] *Rooms from: $169* ✉ *701 Post St., Union Sq.* ☎ *415/673–2600* 🌐 *www.beresford.com* 🛏 *95 rooms* 🍴 *Free Breakfast.*

★ Cornell Hotel de France

$ | HOTEL | In their six-story structure dating back to 1910, hosts Claude and Micheline Lambert have created a bit of Paris a few blocks from Union Square, with rooms individually decorated with pastel colors, a stenciled ceiling, and prints of works by Picasso, Chagall, Klimt, and other European artists. **Pros:** excellent room quality and design; updated bathrooms; special packages and discounts. **Cons:** several blocks from the center of things; surrounding area mildly dodgy after dark; small lobby. [$] *Rooms from: $165* ✉ *715 Bush St., Union Sq.* ☎ *415/421–3154* 🌐 *www.cornellhotel.com* 🛏 *50 rooms* 🍴 *Free Breakfast.*

Hotel Adagio, Autograph Collection

$$ | HOTEL | The Spanish-colonial facade of this 16-story theater-row hotel complements its chic interior, with good-size rooms that have beautiful sea-blue carpets and plenty of tech amenities. **Pros:** Marriott-run property with boutique-hotel charm; central location for sightseeing; good drinks and scene at lobby bar, the Mortimer. **Cons:** street noise; area can be dicey at night; adjacent to a popular outdoor bar. [$] *Rooms from: $246* ✉ *550 Geary St., Union Sq.* ☎ *415/775–5000* 🌐 *www.hoteladagiosf.com* 🛏 *171 rooms* 🍴 *No Meals.*

Hotel Emblem San Francisco

$ | HOTEL | Inspiration is everywhere at this intimate hotel, with a prominent literary theme that celebrates San Francisco's Beat poets, from its lobby wall of books and poetry-laced carpet to in-room libraries and typewriters. **Pros:** fun, creative vibe; solid eating and drinking options; amenities available by request include diffusers, a humidifier, and bath bombs. **Cons:** some guests might feel the hotel is trying too hard to be hip; no on-site fitness option; some small rooms. [$] *Rooms from: $159* ✉ *562 Sutter St., Union Sq.* ☎ *415/433–4434* 🌐 *www.viceroyhotelsandresorts.com/en/emblem* 🛏 *96 rooms* 🍴 *No Meals.*

Hotel Triton

$ | HOTEL | With a strong location at the convergence of Chinatown, the Financial District, and Union Square, this boutique anchor attracts a design-conscious crowd and is highlighted by its intricately decorated lobby featuring marble floors, a wood-beam ceiling, and art from around the world. **Pros:** arty environs; exceptionally pet-friendly; beautiful Café de la Presse next door offers discount for guests. **Cons:** small rooms and baths; cramped hallways; dated room decor. [$] *Rooms from: $195* ✉ *342 Grant Ave., Union Sq.* ☎ *415/394–0500* 🌐 *www.hoteltriton.com* 🛏 *140 rooms* 🍴 *No Meals.*

The Westin St. Francis San Francisco on Union Square

$$ | HOTEL | The survivor of two major earthquakes, some headline-grabbing scandals, and even an attempted presidential assassination, this richly appointed and superbly located grande dame dating to 1904 is comprised of the landmark building, renovated in 2018, and a modern 32-story tower whose glass elevators reveal Union Square views

Union Square and Chinatown

KEY

- 1 Exploring Sights
- 1 Restaurants
- 1 Hotels
- b BART station

from the upper floors. **Pros:** prime Union Square location; correctly named Heavenly Bed; Chateau Montelena wine-tasting room and the excellent Clock Bar. **Cons:** rooms in original building can be small; public spaces lack the panache of days gone by; no dinner at on-site Oak Room Restaurant. $ *Rooms from: $279* ✉ *335 Powell St., Union Sq.* ☎ *415/397–7000, 888/627–8546* ⊕ *www.marriott.com* ⇆ *1,195 rooms* ⦿ *No Meals.*

ⓨ Nightlife

Iron Horse Cocktails

COCKTAIL LOUNGES | Tucked away on lovely Maiden Lane, this warm and welcoming two-level space offers respite from the bustle of Union Square. Talented bartenders make good use of fresh fruit in reasonably priced seasonal cocktails, while muted jazz, dim lighting, and oil paintings in gilded frames create an intimate vibe. Upstairs tables overlooking the lane are particularly cozy. ✉ *25 Maiden La., Union Sq.* ⊕ *www.ironhorsesf.com.*

Redwood Room

COCKTAIL LOUNGES | Opened in 1933, this lounge at the Clift Hotel is a San Francisco icon. The art-deco bar itself and the wood-paneled room are constructed from a single old redwood tree, giving a distinct only-in-California sense of place. Cocktails are a mix of high-quality classics and slightly creative newcomers. ✉ *The Clift Royal Sonesta Hotel, 495 Geary St., Union Sq.* ☎ *415/929–2372 table reservations* ⊕ *redwoodroomsf.com.*

🛍 Shopping

Cable Car Clothiers

MEN'S CLOTHING | This classic British menswear store, open since 1939, is so fully stocked that a whole room is dedicated to hats, pants are cataloged like papers in file cabinets, and entire displays showcase badger-bristle shaving brushes. The cable-car logo gear, from silk ties to pewter banks, makes for dashing souvenirs. ✉ *110 Sutter St., Suite 108, Union Sq.* ☎ *415/397–4740* ⊕ *cablecarclothiers.com.*

Levi's

MIXED CLOTHING | A San Francisco icon, founded in 1853, Levi's offers every style, size, color, and cut of 501s for men and women at its massive flagship store. You can even get a custom fitting if you book ahead of time. ✉ *815 Market St., Union Sq.* ☎ *415/501–0100* ⊕ *www.levi.com.*

Samuel Scheuer

HOUSEWARES | A San Francisco staple since the 1930s, this decadent shop draws designers and other fans for its luxurious bed and bath items and linens. The pretty tablecloths, runners, napkins, fragrant candles, and luxurious bath accessories are popular gifts. ✉ *340 Sutter St., between Grant Ave. and Stockton St., Union Sq.* ☎ *415/392–2813* ⊕ *www.scheuerlinens.com* ⊙ *Closed Sun.*

Chinatown

A few blocks uphill from Union Square is the abrupt beginning of dense and insular Chinatown—the oldest such community in the country. This is very much both a residential *and* a tourist neighborhood, with some overly tourist-focused souvenir shops. Yet it is still an incredibly unique, welcoming place that residents love to share. Each day sees a joyful mix of curious visitors eating pork buns and gazing at the architecture, while longtime locals walk by after to shop for the night's dinner. Join the flow along Grant Avenue and its side streets: good-luck banners of crimson and gold hang beside dragon-entwined lampposts and pagoda roofs, and honking cars chime in with shoppers bargaining in Cantonese or Mandarin.

Sights

Chinatown Gate

NOTABLE BUILDING | At the official entrance to Chinatown, stone lions flank the base of the pagoda-topped gate; the lions, dragons, and fish up top symbolize wealth, prosperity, and other good things. The four Chinese characters immediately beneath the pagoda represent the philosophy of Sun Yat-sen, the leader who unified China in the early 20th century. Sun Yat-sen, who lived in exile in San Francisco for a few years, promoted the notion of friendship and peace among all nations based on equality, justice, and goodwill. The vertical characters under the left pagoda read "peace" and "trust," the ones under the right pagoda "respect" and "love." The whole shebang telegraphs the internationally understood message of "photo op." Immediately beyond the gate, dive into souvenir shopping on Grant Avenue, Chinatown's tourist strip. ⊠ *Grant Ave. at Bush St., Chinatown.*

Golden Gate Fortune Cookie Factory

FACTORY | **FAMILY** | Follow your nose down Ross Alley to this tiny but fragrant cookie factory. Two workers sit at circular motorized griddles and wait for dollops of batter to drop onto a tiny metal plate, which rotates into an oven. A few moments later, out comes a cookie that's pliable and ready for folding. It's easy to peek in for a moment, and hard to leave without getting a few free samples and then buying a bagful of fortune cookies for snacks and wisdom later. ⊠ *56 Ross Alley, between Washington and Jackson Sts., west of Grant Ave., Chinatown* ☎ *415/781–3956* ⊕ *www.goldengatefortunecookies.com* 🍽 *Free.*

Portsmouth Square

PLAZA/SQUARE | Chinatown's living room buzzes with activity: the square, with its pagoda-shape structures, is a favorite spot for morning tai chi, and by noon dozens of men huddle around Chinese chess tables, engaged in competition. Kids scamper about the square's two grungy playgrounds. Back in the late 19th century this land was near the waterfront. The square is named for the USS *Portsmouth*, the ship helmed by Captain John Montgomery, who in 1846 raised the American flag here and claimed the then-Mexican land for the United States. A couple of years later, Sam Brannan kicked off the gold rush at the square when he waved his loot and proclaimed, "Gold from the American River!" Robert Louis Stevenson, the author of *Treasure Island,* often dropped by, chatting up the sailors who hung out here. Some of the information he gleaned about life at sea found its way into his fiction. A bronze galleon sculpture, a tribute to Stevenson, anchors the square's northwest corner. A plaque marks the site of California's first public school, built in 1847. ⊠ *Bordered by Walter Lum Pl. and Kearny, Washington, and Clay Sts., Chinatown* ⊕ *sfrecpark.org.*

★ Tin How Temple

TEMPLE | In 1852, Day Ju, one of the first three Chinese to arrive in San Francisco, dedicated this temple to the Queen of the Heavens and the Goddess of the Seven Seas, and the temple looks largely the same today as it did more than a century ago. Duck into the inconspicuous doorway, climb three flights of stairs, and be surrounded by the aroma of incense in this tiny, altar-filled room. In the entryway, elderly ladies can often be seen preparing "money" to be burned as offerings to various Buddhist gods or as funds for ancestors to use in the afterlife. Hundreds of red-and-gold lanterns cover the ceiling; the larger the lamp, the larger its donor's contribution to the temple. Gifts of oranges, dim sum, and money left by the faithful, who kneel while reciting prayers, rest on altars to different gods. Tin How presides over the middle back of the temple, flanked by one red and one green lesser god. Taking photographs is not allowed. ⊠ *125 Waverly Pl., between Clay and Washington Sts., Chinatown* 🍽 *Free, donations accepted.*

🍴 Restaurants

China Live

$$ | **CHINESE** | It's been compared to a Chinatown version of Eataly, but George Chen's ultra-ambitious market, restaurant, bar, and fine-dining-experience project is its own unique place. The main ground-floor Market Restaurant excels at a wide variety of specialties from dumplings to duck, served in a refined, industrial-style dining room surrounded by different cooking areas; upstairs, the intimate Eight Tables is one of San Francisco's most elaborate special-occasion tasting-menu experiences. **Known for:** sheng jian bao pork dumplings; "nine essential flavors of Chinese cuisine" dish at Eight Tables; outstanding tea selection. $ *Average main: $26* ⊠ *644 Broadway, Chinatown* ☎ *415/788–8188* ⊕ *chinalivesf.com* ⊗ *No lunch.*

Hang Ah Dim Sum Tea House

$ | **CHINESE** | Enjoying the barbecue pork buns and curry chicken at this Chinatown icon dating to 1920 is a bite into both culinary history and San Francisco's past. Located on an alley, it's one of the smaller, more homey, and less frenetic sit-down dim sum choices in the city, with a small dining room simply decorated with pieces of Chinese art and a few Bruce Lee movie posters. **Known for:** the country's first dim sum house; soup dumplings; red-bean bun desserts decorated like cute animals. $ *Average main: $15* ⊠ *1 Pagoda Pl., between Sacramento and Clay Sts., Chinatown* ☎ *415/982–5686* ⊕ *hangahdimsumsf.com.*

Mister Jiu's

$$$$ | **CHINESE** | Brandon Jew's ambitious, graceful restaurant offers the chef's delicious contemporary, farm-to-table interpretation of Chinese cuisine that sometimes tweaks classic dishes with a California spin (hot-and-sour soup with nasturtiums) or enhances fresh produce with unique Chinese flavors (local asparagus with smoked tofu). The elegant dining room—accented with plants and a chrysanthemum chandelier—provides beautiful views of Chinatown, while the menu breathes new life into it. **Known for:** sea urchin cheong fun (rice noodle rolls); standout cocktails; large-format roast duck with pancakes. $ *Average main: $49* ⊠ *28 Waverly Pl., Chinatown* ☎ *415/857–9688* ⊕ *misterjius.com* ⊗ *Closed Sun. and Mon. No lunch.*

Sam Wo Restaurant

$ | **CHINESE** | Few restaurants in San Francisco can match the history of this city treasure that has been around since 1908. You'll want to try as much as possible from the menu, which is a unique mix of Cantonese dishes, a few items from other regions of China, a couple Southeast Asia–inspired noodles, and more familiar Chinese American fare. **Known for:** iconic sign; jook (rice porridge); barbecue pork noodle roll. $ *Average main: $13* ⊠ *713 Clay St., Chinatown* ☎ *415/989–8898* ⊕ *samworestaurant.com* ⊗ *Closed Tues.*

🛍 Shopping

Kim + Ono

SOUVENIRS | Hand-painted robes, kimonos, formal dresses, and jackets are sold at this second-generation family-owned spot. Chic Asia-inspired gifts and smaller items make great souvenirs. ⊠ *729 Grant Ave., Chinatown* ☎ *415/989–8588* ⊕ *kimandono.com.*

★ Vital Tea Leaf

OTHER FOOD & DRINK | Tea enthusiasts will feel at peace in this bright, spacious haven for sipping. You'll find more than 400 different varieties of tea here, and the staff is extremely knowledgeable on the health benefits of each and every one. ⊠ *1044 Grant Ave., between Jackson St. and Pacific Ave., Chinatown* ☎ *415/981–2388* ⊕ *vitaltealeaf.net.*

SoMa

SoMa (short for "south of Market") is less a neighborhood than a sprawling area of wide, traffic-heavy boulevards lined with office skyscrapers and ultra-chic condo high-rises. It's noteworthy primarily for its cultural offerings and concentration of bars and eateries, including a number of destination restaurants. The gigantic and impressive SFMOMA is a must-see, as are the cultural museums of the Yerba Buena arts district.

Sights

Contemporary Jewish Museum (CJM)

OTHER MUSEUM | Architect Daniel Libeskind designed the postmodern CJM, whose impossible-to-ignore diagonal blue cube juts out of a painstakingly restored power substation. A physical manifestation of the Hebrew toast *l'chaim* (to life), the cube may have obscure philosophical origins, but Libeskind created a unique, light-filled space that merits a stroll through the lobby even if the current exhibits (the museum is non-collecting and does not have permanent holdings) don't entice you into the galleries. Exhibits, usually two or three at a time, vary, from a look at the history of famous puppeteer Frank Oz (*Star Wars* and the Muppets) to an immersive series about the 19th-century Jewish immigrant and photographer Shimmel Zohar. ■TIP➜ **San Francisco's best Jewish deli, Wise Sons, operates a counter in the museum. Try their smoked salmon bagel sandwich or a slice of chocolate babka.** ⊠ *736 Mission St., SoMa* 🖾 *415/655–7800* ⊕ *www.thecjm.org* 🖃 *$16* ⊘ *Closed Mon.–Wed.*

Museum of the African Diaspora (MoAD)

OTHER MUSEUM | Dedicated to the influence that people of African descent have had in places all over the world, MoAD focuses on temporary exhibits in its four galleries over three floors. With floor-to-ceiling windows onto Mission Street, the museum fits perfectly into the cultural scene of Yerba Buena and is well worth a 30-minute foray. Most striking is its front window centerpiece: a three-story mosaic, made from thousands of photographs, that forms the image of a young girl's face. ■TIP➜ **Walk up the stairs inside the museum to view the mosaic photographs up close—Malcolm X and Muhammad Ali are there, along with everyday folks—but the best view is from across Mission Street.** ⊠ *685 Mission St., SoMa* 🖾 *415/358–7200* ⊕ *www.moadsf. org* 🖃 *$12* ⊘ *Closed Mon. and Tues.*

★ San Francisco Museum of Modern Art (SFMOMA)

ART MUSEUM | Opened in 1935, the San Francisco Museum of Modern Art was the first museum on the West Coast dedicated to modern and contemporary art, and after a three-year expansion designed by Snøhetta, it emerged in 2016 as one of the largest modern art museums in the country and the revitalized anchor of the Yerba Buena arts district. With gallery space over seven floors, the museum displays only a portion of its more than 33,000-work collection and has numerous temporary exhibits. Allow at least two hours here; you could spend a full day. The museum's holdings include art from the Doris and Donald Fisher Collection, one of the world's greatest private collections of modern and contemporary art. Highlights include deep collections of works by German abstract expressionist Gerhard Richter and American painter Ellsworth Kelly and an Agnes Martin gallery. The third floor is dedicated to photography. Also look for seminal works by Diego Rivera, Alexander Calder, Matisse, and Picasso. Don't miss the third-floor sculpture terrace. The first floor is free to the public and contains a handful of works. Save time by reserving timed tickets online. ⊠ *151 3rd St., SoMa* 🖾 *415/357–4000* ⊕ *www.sfmoma.org* 🖃 *$25* ⊘ *Closed Wed.*

Yerba Buena Gardens
GARDEN | FAMILY | These two blocks encompass the Yerba Buena Center for the Arts, the Metreon, and Moscone Convention Center, but the gardens themselves are the everyday draw. Office workers and convention-goers escape to the green swath of the East Garden, the focal point of which is the memorial to Martin Luther King Jr. Powerful streams of water surge over large, jagged stone columns, mirroring the enduring force of King's words, which are carved on the stone walls and on glass blocks behind the waterfall. Moscone North is behind the memorial, and an overhead walkway leads to Moscone South and its rooftop attractions.

■ TIP→ The gardens are liveliest during the week and during the Yerba Buena Gardens Festival, from May through October (🌐 *www.ybgfestival.org*), with free performances.

Atop the Moscone Center perch a few lures for kids. The historic Looff carousel (🎟 *$5 for 2 rides; $3 with museum admission*) twirls daily 10–5. The carousel is attached to the Children's Creativity Museum (🌐 *creativity.org*), an interactive arts-and-technology center (🎟 *$15*) geared to children ages 3–12. Outside in the children's garden, kids adore the slides, including a 25-foot tube slide, at the play circle. Also part of the complex are an ice-skating rink and a bowling alley. ✉ *Bordered by 3rd, 4th, Mission, and Folsom Sts., SoMa* ☎ *415/651–3684* 🌐 *yerbabuenagardens.com* 🎟 *Free.*

🍴 Restaurants

Bar Agricole
$$ | MODERN AMERICAN | This sharply designed spot is just as notable for its food menu as its renowned mixed drinks. Owner Thad Vogler is the city's leading voice on single-origin spirits, so any visit should include a few sips of Bar Agricole's own spirits. **Known for:** sourdough with tinned fish or duck liver; exciting vegetable-centric dishes; impeccable spirit-forward cocktails. [$] *Average main: $25* ✉ *1540 Mission St., SoMa* ☎ *415/341–0101* 🌐 *baragricole.com* 🕒 *Closed Sun. and Mon. No lunch.*

★ Benu
$$$$ | MODERN AMERICAN | Chef Corey Lee's three-Michelin-star fine dining mecca is a must-stop for those who hop from city to city collecting memorable meals. Lee, formerly of French Laundry, meticulously ties together cooking techniques and ingredients commonly seen in different cuisines of Asia—such as *xiaolongbao* (soup dumplings) and kimchi—with a deft gastronomic touch. **Known for:** high-end dining; phenomenal wine pairings; stellar service. [$] *Average main: $375* ✉ *22 Hawthorne St., SoMa* ☎ *415/685–4860* 🌐 *www.benusf.com* 🕒 *Closed Sun. and Mon. No lunch.*

★ Californios
$$$$ | MODERN MEXICAN | This Californian-Mexican tasting-menu concept by chef Val M. Cantu continues to be one of the hottest tickets in the entire Bay Area. Cantu and his team's creations, along with Charlotte Randolph's acclaimed wine program, remain as special as ever (the restaurant had a great run in smaller Mission District digs before moving to SoMa), crafting what is possibly the country's leading Mexican-influenced fine dining experience. **Known for:** housemade tortillas used in brilliant ways; wonderful patio; grilled banana with cold-smoked caviar. [$] *Average main: $307* ✉ *355 11th St., SoMa* ☎ *415/757–0994* 🌐 *www.californiossf.com* 🕒 *Closed Sun. and Mon. No lunch.*

Marlowe
$$$ | AMERICAN | Hearty American bistro fare and hip design draw crowds to this neighborhood favorite that's ambitious enough to be a citywide draw. The menu boasts one of the city's best burgers, and the dining room gleams with white penny-tile floors and marble countertops.

Sights ▼

1 Asian Art Museum.................. **D6**
2 City Hall **C6**
3 Contemporary Jewish
    Museum (CJM) **H4**
4 Museum of the
    African Diaspora (MoAD)......... **H4**
5 San Francisco Museum of
    Modern Art (SFMOMA)............ **I4**
6 Yerba Buena Gardens............. **H4**

Restaurants ▼

1 Bar Agricole......................... **C8**
2 Benu.................................. **I4**
3 Bodega SF........................... **F4**
4 Californios **E9**
5 Hayes Street Grill **B7**
6 Marlowe **J7**
7 Rich Table **B8**
8 Saigon Sandwich................... **D5**
9 Saison................................ **J6**
10 Suppenküche **A7**
11 Zuni Café............................ **B8**

Hotels ▼

1 Hotel Zelos San Francisco........ **G4**
2 Hotel Zetta San Francisco........ **G5**
3 Inn at the Opera.................... **B7**
4 Palace Hotel San Francisco...... **H3**
5 The St. Regis San Francisco **H4**

SoMa, Civic Center,
The Tenderloin,
and Hayes Valley

Known for: refined takes on comfort food like roast chicken and deviled eggs; strong drinks; festive atmosphere. [$] *Average main: $36* ✉ *500 Brannan St., SoMa* ☎ *415/777–1413* 🌐 *marlowesf.com* ⏲ *Closed Mon. No lunch Tues. and Wed.*

Saison

$$$$ | **MODERN AMERICAN** | This two-Michelin-starred restaurant is one of the city's greatest dining destinations. The culinary team teases the deepest flavors from premium ingredients in a tasting-menu that may highlight fire-grilled duck followed by a broth of its grilled bones, or the signature, showstopping sea urchin on grilled bread. **Known for:** elegant decor; world-class wine list; polished start-to-finish experience. [$] *Average main: $298* ✉ *178 Townsend St., SoMa* ☎ *415/828–7990* 🌐 *www.saisonsf.com* ⏲ *Closed Sun. and Mon.*

Hotels

Hotel Zelos San Francisco

$ | **HOTEL** | A high-style haven on the top five floors of the green-tiled Pacific Building, the Zelos offers a luxurious oasis above the busiest part of town, with spacious rooms decked out with modern art pieces, eye-catching textured carpeting, and sleek furniture echoing a 1930s sensibility. **Pros:** snappy design; convenient to public transit; home to one of the city's premier cocktail bars. **Cons:** allergenic down comforters; can be too much of a scene; chaotic street entrance. [$] *Rooms from: $167* ✉ *12 4th St., SoMa* ☎ *415/348–1111* 🌐 *zhotelssf.com* 🛏 *202 rooms* 🍴 *No Meals.*

Hotel Zetta San Francisco

$ | **HOTEL** | With a playful lobby lounge, London-style brasserie The Cavalier, and slick-yet-homey tech-friendly rooms, this trendy spot behind a stately 1913 neoclassical facade is a leader on the SoMa hotel scene. **Pros:** tech amenities and arty design; in-room spa services; noteworthy fitness center. **Cons:** lots of hubbub and traffic; need to leave the building for breakfast; frenetic aesthetic. [$] *Rooms from: $196* ✉ *55 5th St., SoMa* ☎ *415/543–8555* 🌐 *zhotelssf.com* 🛏 *116 rooms* 🍴 *No Meals.*

★ Palace Hotel San Francisco

$$$ | **HOTEL** | Open since 1875 and rebuilt after the 1906 earthquake, this legendary hotel continues to be one of the city's elite places to stay, with a prominent location at the border of SoMa and downtown plus a delightful mix of modern amenities (an indoor lap pool beneath a glass-domed ceiling) and deluxe architectural details of a bygone era. **Pros:** oozes history and Gilded Age grandeur; well-trained staff; excellent fitness center. **Cons:** entrance is frequently understaffed; small bathrooms; street noise (ask for an upper-floor room). [$] *Rooms from: $360* ✉ *2 New Montgomery St., SoMa* ☎ *415/512–1111* 🌐 *marriott.com* 🛏 *556 rooms* 🍴 *No Meals.*

★ The St. Regis San Francisco

$$$$ | **HOTEL** | Across from Yerba Buena Gardens and SFMOMA, the luxurious and modern St. Regis is favored by celebrities and others drawn to guest rooms and suites decorated with gold rush–inspired colors of silver, iron, and copper; leather-paneled headboards; 3D graphic art pieces by Christo Saba; and lots of natural light from windows offering city views. **Pros:** outstanding service; wonderful pool and spa; large rooms and bathrooms. **Cons:** expensive rates; no coffee machines; hectic lobby and entrance area. [$] *Rooms from: $585* ✉ *125 3rd St., SoMa* ☎ *415/284–4000* 🌐 *marriott.com* 🛏 *260 rooms* 🍴 *No Meals.*

Nightlife

AsiaSF

CABARET | Saucy, sexy, and fun, this is one of the best places in town for dinner with a show. The entertainment, as well as the gracious food service, is provided by some of the city's most gorgeous

Oracle Park: Where Giants Tread

The size of Oracle Park hits you immediately—the field, McCovey Cove, and the Lefty O'Doul drawbridge all look like miniature models. At just under 13 acres, the San Francisco Giants' ballpark is one of the country's smallest. After Boston's Fenway Park, Oracle Park has the shortest distance to the wall; from home plate it's just 309 feet to the tall right-field wall. But there's something endearing about its petite stature—not to mention its location, with yacht masts poking up over the outfield and the blue bay sparkling beyond.

In 2000 the Giants played their first game at Oracle Park (then called Pacific Bell Park and later SBC Park and AT&T Park). All told, $357 million was spent on the facility, and it shows in the retro redbrick exterior, the quaint clock tower, handsome bronze statues, and above-average food. There isn't a bad seat in the house, and the park has an unusual level of intimacy and access. Concourses circle the field on one level, and in some ticketed areas you can stand inches from players as they exit the locker rooms. At street level, non-ticket-holders can get up close outside a gate in right field. The giant Coke bottle and mitt you see beyond the outfield are part of the Coca-Cola Fan Lot playground. Don't miss the edible garden, the model cable car, and the specialty Crazy Crab sandwich, all located in the centerfield area. Park tours are led daily at 10:30 and 12:30 and cost $25.

The Famous "Splash Hit"

Locals show up in motorboats and inflatable rafts, ready to scoop up home-run balls that clear the right-field wall and land in McCovey Cove. Hitting one into the water isn't easy: the ball has to clear a 25-foot wall, the elevated walkway, and the promenade outside. Barry Bonds had the first "splash hit" on May 1, 2000.

Getting There

Parking is very limited and pricey ($35 and up), plus traffic can be gridlock before games. Take public transportation. Muni lines N and T (to CalTrain/Mission Bay and Sunnydale, respectively) stop in front of the park, and Muni bus lines 30 and 45 stop a block away. Or arrive in style—take the ferry from Jack London Square in Oakland (⊕ www.sanfranciscobay-ferry.com).

transgender women, who strut in impossibly high heels on top of the catwalk bar, vamping to tunes like "Cabaret" and "Big Spender." The creative Asian-influenced cuisine is surprisingly good. Make reservations, and go on a weekday to avoid the bachelorette parties. ⊠ 201 9th St., SoMa ☏ 415/255–2742 ⊕ asiasf.com.

The EndUp

DANCE CLUBS | With an all-night (and most of the morning) dance party starting at 10 pm on Saturday, the EndUp is SF's most popular after-hours place, with possibly the best sound system in the city. Weekends often see day parties that make it so 3 am and 3 pm seem to blur together. It can be a bit of a meat market, but this San Francisco institution doesn't adhere to any particular scene, with DJs playing a variety of music styles. ■ TIP→ Said sound system is cranked. Even the cool kids wear earplugs. ⊠ 401 6th St., SoMa ⊕ theendupsf.com.

The House of Shields

BARS | History and great cocktails collide at one of the city's most legendary bars. There are rumors that President Warren G. Harding met his final fate here, but other accounts say that happened across the street at the Palace Hotel. Today, it's a favorite watering hole for the Financial District happy hour set, then a quieter, casual date spot later on. The cocktails are prepared with the same care and quality as at its flashier, newer peers. ✉ *39 New Montgomery St., SoMa* ☎ *415/769–8109* 🌐 *thehouseofshields.com.*

Shopping

★ Chronicle Books

BOOKS | A local beacon of publishing produces inventively designed fiction, cookbooks, art books, and other titles, as well as postcards, planners, and address books—all of which you can purchase at its home near Oracle Park. ✉ *680 2nd St., SoMa* ☎ *415/537–4200* 🌐 *www.chroniclebooks.com* ⏲ *Closed weekends.*

K&L Wine Merchants

WINE/SPIRITS | This wine shop has an ardent cult following around town. The friendly staffers promise to sell only what they taste themselves, and weekly events (Thursday through Saturday) open the tastings to customers. The best-seller list for varietals and regions for both the under- and over-$30 categories appeals to the wine lover in everyone. ✉ *855 Harrison St., SoMa* ☎ *415/896–1734* 🌐 *www.klwines.com.*

Civic Center

San Francisco's eye-catching, gold-domed City Hall presides over this patchy neighborhood bordered roughly by Franklin, McAllister, Hyde, and Grove Streets. The optimistic "City Beautiful" movement of the early 20th century produced the Beaux Arts–style complex for which the district is named, including City Hall, the War Memorial Opera House, and the old public library, now the home of the Asian Art Museum.

Sights

★ Asian Art Museum

ART MUSEUM | You don't have to be a connoisseur of Asian art to appreciate this newly expanded museum, whose monumental exterior conceals a light, open, and welcoming space. The fraction of the museum's collection on display (about 2,500 pieces out of 18,000-plus total) is laid out thematically and by region, making it easy to follow historical developments.

Begin on the third floor, where highlights of Buddhist art in Southeast Asia and early China include a large, jewel-encrusted, exquisitely painted 19th-century Burmese Buddha and clothed rod puppets from Java. On the second floor you can find later Chinese works, as well as exquisite pieces from Korea and Japan. The ground floor is devoted to temporary exhibits and the museum's wonderful gift shop. During spring and summer, visit on Thursday evenings for extended programs and sip drinks while a DJ spins tunes. ✉ *200 Larkin St., Civic Center* ☎ *415/581–3500* 🌐 *asianart.org* 🎟 *$20, free 1st Sun. of month; $10 Thurs. 5–8* ⏲ *Closed Tues. and Wed.*

★ City Hall

GOVERNMENT BUILDING | This imposing 1915 structure with its massive gold-leaf dome—higher than the U.S. Capitol's—is as close to a palace as you'll find in San Francisco: the classic granite-and-marble behemoth was modeled after St. Peter's Basilica in Rome. Architect Arthur Brown Jr., who was also behind Coit Tower and the War Memorial Opera House, designed an interior with grand columns and a sweeping central staircase. The 1899 structure it replaced had taken 27 years to erect, but it collapsed in about 27 seconds during the 1906 earthquake.

City Hall was seismically retrofitted in the late 1990s, but the sense of history remains palpable, and you can learn about it on a free tour. Some noteworthy events that have taken place here include the hosing of civil-rights and freedom-of-speech protesters (1960); the assassi nations of Mayor George Moscone and Harvey Milk (1978); the torching of the lobby by angry members of the gay community in response to the light sentence given to their killer (1979); and the first domestic partnership registrations of gay couples (1991). In 2004, Mayor Gavin Newsom took a stand against then-current state and federal law by issuing marriage licenses to same-sex partners.

Across Polk Street from City Hall is Civic Center Plaza, with an outdoor café, flower beds, and a playground. This sprawling space is generally clean but somewhat grim, as many homeless people hang out here. ⊠ 1 Dr. Carlton B. Goodlett Pl., Civic Center ☎ 415/554–4000, 415/554–6139 tour reservations ⊕ sfgov.org/cityhall/city-hall-tours ☜ Free ⊗ Closed weekends.

⊕ Performing Arts

★ San Francisco Ballet
BALLET | For ballet lovers, the nation's oldest professional company is reason alone to visit San Francisco. The primary season runs from January through May with a repertoire including full-length ballets such as Don Quixote and Sleeping Beauty; the December presentation of The Nutcracker is truly spectacular. The company also performs bold new dances from star choreographers such as William Forsythe and Mark Morris, alongside modern classics by George Balanchine and Jerome Robbins. ⊠ War Memorial Opera House, 301 Van Ness Ave., Civic Center ☎ 415/865–2000 ⊕ www.sfballet. org.

★ San Francisco Opera
OPERA | Founded in 1923, this internationally recognized organization has occupied the War Memorial Opera House since the building's completion in 1932. From September–December and June–July, the company presents a wide range of operas, from Carmen to an operatic version of It's a Wonderful Life. The opera often takes on ambitious world premieres as well as unconventional, edgy projects designed to attract younger audiences. Translations are projected above the stage during most non-English productions. ⊠ War Memorial Opera House, 301 Van Ness Ave., Civic Center ☎ 415/864–3330 tickets ⊕ sfopera.com.

★ San Francisco Symphony
MUSIC | One of America's top orchestras performs from September through May, with additional summer performances of light classical music and show tunes. The symphony is known for its daring programming of 20th-century American works, often performed with soloists of the caliber of André Watts, Gil Shaham, and Renée Fleming. ⊠ Louise M. Davies Symphony Hall, 201 Van Ness Ave., Civic Center ☎ 415/864–6000 ⊕ www.sfsymphony.org.

The Tenderloin

Stretching west of Union Square and north of Civic Center, the Tenderloin is the poster child for the city's challenges: low-income families huddle in tiny apartments; single-room-occupancy hotels offer shelter a step up from living on the street; drug dealing and prostitution are common; and very few green spaces break up the monotony of high-rises. So why come here? Well, exceptional Vietnamese food, for one thing, but these days more than just the great pho is luring people. Trendy watering holes and coffee shops are springing up and intrepid hipsters are moving in.

⚠ **Wander with care: some parts of the Tenderloin are more dangerous than others, and a single street can change from block to block.**

🍴 Restaurants

Bodega SF
$$$ | **VIETNAMESE** | Chef Matthew Ho cut his teeth at his family's excellent, bare-bones Bodega Bistro, an anchor of the Little Saigon restaurant scene for years. This new incarnation elevates traditional Vietnamese recipes with a modern twist and the freshest ingredients. **Known for:** complex and delightful beef carpaccio; hopping late-night dining scene; well-paired cocktails. [$] *Average main: $32* ✉ *138 Mason St., Tenderloin* 🌐 *bodegarestaurants.com* 🕑 *Closed Tues.*

Saigon Sandwich
$ | **VIETNAMESE** | Stop by this hole in the wall for some of the best—and cheapest!—takeout banh mi in the city. Favorites include *thit* (roast pork) and *ga* (roast chicken). **Known for:** generous portions; really low prices; bare-bones storefront. [$] *Average main: $5* ✉ *560 Larkin St., between Eddy and Turk Sts., Tenderloin* ☎ *415/474–5698* 🌐 *www.facebook.com/saigonsandwich* 🕑 *No dinner.*

🍸 Nightlife

Great American Music Hall
LIVE MUSIC | You'll find top-drawer entertainment at this eclectic venue. Acts range from the best in blues, folk, and jazz to up-and-coming alternative artists. The colorful marble-pillared club, built in 1907 as a bordello, accommodates dancing at some shows. Pub grub is available most nights. ✉ *859 O'Farrell St., Tenderloin* ☎ *415/885–0750* 🌐 *gamh.com.*

Hayes Valley

A chic neighborhood near the Civic Center, Hayes Valley has terrific eateries, cool watering holes, and great browsing in its funky clothing, home-decor, and design boutiques. Locals love this quarter, but without any big-name draws it remains off the radar for many visitors.

🍴 Restaurants

Hayes Street Grill
$$$ | **SEAFOOD** | You'll snag a table if you arrive at this longtime (since 1979) standby just as music lovers are folding their napkins and heading off for a show at the nearby Opera House or SFJAZZ Center. Fresh, sustainable, often local seafood lures the faithful here, as well as peak seasonal produce from the nearby region. **Known for:** simple yet excellent fish preparations; choice of sauces; white-tablecloth dining in timeless atmosphere. [$] *Average main: $36* ✉ *320 Hayes St., Hayes Valley* ☎ *415/863–5545* 🌐 *www.hayesstreetgrill.com* 🕑 *Closed most Mon.–Wed. except opera and symphony performance days.*

★ **Rich Table**
$$$ | **MODERN AMERICAN** | Sardine chips and porcini doughnuts are popular bites at co-chef Evan and Sarah Rich's lively, creative restaurant; mains are also clever stunners, including pastas like the sea urchin cacio e pepe. The room's weathered-wood wallboards, repurposed from a Northern California sawmill, give it a homey vibe. **Known for:** tough-to-get reservations; freshly baked bread; seasonal ingredients. [$] *Average main: $34* ✉ *199 Gough St., Hayes Valley* ☎ *415/355–9085* 🌐 *www.richtablesf.com* 🕑 *Closed Sun. and Mon. No lunch.*

Suppenküche
$$ | **GERMAN** | Nobody goes hungry—and no beer drinker goes thirsty—at this lively, hip outpost of simple German cooking. The hearty food—bratwurst and

sauerkraut, potato pancakes with house-made applesauce, meat loaf, braised beef, pork loin, schnitzel, spaetzle—is tasty and kind to your wallet, and the imported brews are first-rate. **Known for:** seating at common tables; variety of sausages; quick service. $ *Average main: $26 ⊠ 525 Laguna St., Hayes Valley* ☎ *415/252–9289* ⊕ *www.suppenkuche. com* ⊗ *Closed Mon. No lunch weekdays.*

★ Zuni Café
$$$ | MODERN AMERICAN | After one bite of Zuni's succulent brick-oven-roasted whole chicken with warm bread salad, you'll understand why the two-floor café is a perennial star. Its long copper bar is a hub for a disparate mix of patrons who commune over oysters on the half shell and cocktails and wine. **Known for:** seasonal Californian cooking at its best; under-the-radar lunch and late-night burger; beloved margarita. $ *Average main: $39 ⊠ 1658 Market St., Hayes Valley* ☎ *415/552–2522* ⊕ *zunicafe.com* ⊗ *Closed Mon. and Tues.*

Hotels

Inn at the Opera
$$ | B&B/INN | Within walking distance of Davies Symphony Hall and the War Memorial Opera House, this inn with small rooms with dark wood furnishings caters to season-ticket holders for the opera, ballet, and symphony; it's also been the choice for stars from Luciano Pavarotti to Mikhail Baryshnikov. **Pros:** staff goes the extra mile; prime location but a quiet block; good nearby dining. **Cons:** no air-conditioning; sold out far in advance during opera season; difficult parking. $ *Rooms from: $249 ⊠ 333 Fulton St., Hayes Valley* ☎ *415/863–8400* ⊕ *www.extraholidays.com/san-francisco-california/inn-at-the-opera* ⇒ *48 rooms* ⦿ *No Meals.*

Nightlife

Fig & Thistle
WINE BARS | The Golden State's wines are the specialty at this relaxed, rustic-feeling bar. Natural and biodynamic wines from the greater West Coast and around the world are also poured, pairing nicely with cheese selections. Their eponymous and popular cannabis dispensary is just around the corner. ⊠ *429 Gough St., Hayes Valley* ☎ *415/651–9905* ⊕ *www. figandthistlesf.com.*

The Mint Karaoke Lounge
THEMED ENTERTAINMENT | A mixed gay-straight crowd that's drop-dead serious about its karaoke—to the point where you'd think an *American Idol* casting agent was in attendance—comes here seven nights a week. Do *not* walk onstage unprepared! Cash only. ⊠ *1942 Market St., Hayes Valley* ☎ *415/626–4726* ⊕ *themint.net.*

 Performing Arts

★ SFJAZZ Center
MUSIC | Jazz legends Branford Marsalis and Herbie Hancock have performed at the snazzy center, as have Rosanne Cash, Dianne Reeves, and world-music favorite Esperanza Spalding. The sight lines and acoustics here are impressive, as are the second-floor tile murals. ⊠ *201 Franklin St., Hayes Valley* ☎ *866/920–5299* ⊕ *www.sfjazz.org.*

Nob Hill

Nob Hill was officially dubbed during the 1870s when the "Big Four"—Charles Crocker, Leland Stanford, Mark Hopkins, and Collis P. Huntington, who were involved in the construction of the trans-continental railroad—built their hilltop estates. The lingo is thick from this era: those on the hilltop were referred to as "nabobs" (originally meaning a provincial governor from India) and "swells," and

Nob Hill, Russian Hill, and Polk Gulch

KEY

- ❶ Exploring Sights
- ❶ Restaurants
- ❶ Hotels
- 🅑 BART station

0 — 300 m
0 — 1,000 ft

the hill itself was called Snob Hill, a term that survives to this day.

By 1882 so many estates had sprung up on Nob Hill that Robert Louis Stevenson called it "the hill of palaces." The 1906 earthquake and fire, though, destroyed all the palatial mansions except for portions of the James Flood brownstone. History buffs may choose to linger here, but for most visitors, a casual glimpse from a cable car will be enough.

Sights

Cable Car Museum

OTHER MUSEUM | FAMILY | One of the city's best free offerings, this museum is an absolute must for kids and compelling for adults too. You can even ride a cable car here—all three lines stop between Russian Hill and Nob Hill. The facility, which is inside the city's last remaining cable-car barn, takes the top off the system to show you how it all works. Eternally humming and squealing, the massive powerhouse cable wheels steal the show. You can also climb aboard a vintage car and take the grip, let the kids ring a cable-car bell, and check out vintage gear dating from 1873. ✉ *1201 Mason St., Nob Hill* ☎ *415/474–1887* 🌐 *www.cablecarmuseum.org* 🎫 *Free* 🕒 *Closed Mon.*

★ Grace Cathedral

CHURCH | Not many churches can boast an altarpiece by Keith Haring and two labyrinths, but this one, the country's third-largest Episcopal cathedral, does. The soaring Gothic-style structure took 14 (often interrupted) years to build, beginning in 1927 and eventually wrapping up in 1964. The gilded bronze doors at the east entrance were taken from casts of Lorenzo Ghiberti's incredible *Gates of Paradise*, designed for the Baptistery in Florence, Italy. A sculpture of St. Francis by Beniamino Bufano greets you as you enter.

The 34-foot-wide limestone labyrinth is a replica of the 13th-century stone maze on the floor of Chartres Cathedral. All are encouraged to walk the ⅛-mile-long labyrinth, a ritual based on the tradition of meditative walking. There's also a granite outdoor labyrinth on the church's northeast side. The AIDS Interfaith Chapel, to the right as you enter Grace, contains a bronze triptych by the late artist Keith Haring (a gift from Yoko Ono) and panels from the AIDS Memorial Quilt. The church offers self- and docent-led tours. **■ TIP→ Especially dramatic times to view the cathedral are during Tuesday-evening yoga (6:15 pm), Thursday-night evensong (5:15 pm), and special holiday programs.** ✉ *1100 California St., Nob Hill* ☎ *415/749–6300* 🌐 *www.gracecathedral.org* 🎫 *Entrance and self-guided tours $12, docent-led tours $20.*

Restaurants

The Coffee Movement

$ | CAFÉ | Nob Hill's design and architecture tend to be resolutely old-school, except with this impossibly hip coffee shop. Coffee and espresso drinks are excellent, plus there's a tasting flight of the day's offerings for the most avid coffee nerd. **Known for:** perfect cappucinos; popular with the Instagram set; friendly baristas. [$] *Average main: $5* ✉ *1030 Washington St., Nob Hill* ☎ *415/237–3375* 🌐 *thecoffeemovement.com.*

★ Sons & Daughters

$$$$ | AMERICAN | The constantly evolving tasting menu that chef-owner Teague Moriarty serves at his standout, Michelin-star restaurant serves as a primer for how to do highly seasonal cuisine right. Though the preparations are intricate and often luxurious, there is a pretension-free, contemporary elegance that makes this one of the most relaxed (and fun) fine-dining experiences in the city. **Known for:** cozy but chic dining room anchored by an ornate fireplace; excellent house-made bread; attentive service. [$] *Average main: $225* ✉ *708 Bush St., Nob Hill* ☎ *415/994–7933* 🌐 *www.*

sonsanddaughterssf.com ⌚ *Closed Mon. and Tues. No lunch.*

 Hotels

Fairmont San Francisco

$$ | HOTEL | Dominating the top of Nob Hill like a European palace, the Fairmont indulges guests in luxury: rooms in the main building, adorned in sapphire blues with platinum and pewter accents, have high ceilings, decadent beds, and marble bathrooms, while rooms in the newer Tower, many with fine views, have a neutral color palette with bright-silver notes. **Pros:** huge bathrooms; stunning lobby; great location. **Cons:** some older rooms are small; challenging hills for those on foot; $35 per night amenity fee. Ⓢ *Rooms from: $301* ✉ *950 Mason St., Nob Hill* ☎ *415/772–5000, 866/550–4491* ⊕ *www.fairmont.com/san-francisco* ⇥ *606 rooms* ⦿ *No Meals.*

★ The Ritz-Carlton, San Francisco

$$$ | HOTEL | A tribute to beauty and attentive, professional service, the Ritz-Carlton emphasizes luxury and elegance, which are evident in the Ionic columns that grace the neoclassical facade and the crystal chandeliers that illuminate marble floors and walls in the lobby. **Pros:** terrific service; beautiful furnishings; lobby wine-tasting lounge. **Cons:** nothing is a bargain; hilly location; no pool. Ⓢ *Rooms from: $450* ✉ *600 Stockton St., Nob Hill* ☎ *415/296–7465, 800/542–8680* ⊕ *www. ritzcarlton.com/sanfrancisco* ⇥ *336 rooms* ⦿ *No Meals.*

Russian Hill

Essentially a tony residential neighborhood of spiffy pieds-à-terre, Victorian flats, Edwardian cottages, and boxlike condos, Russian Hill has some of the city's loveliest stairway walks, hidden garden ways, and steepest streets—not to mention those bay views.

 Sights

★ Lombard Street

STREET | The block-long "Crookedest Street in the World" makes eight switchbacks down the east face of Russian Hill between Hyde and Leavenworth Streets. Join the line of cars waiting to drive down the steep hill, or avoid the whole mess and walk down the steps on either side of Lombard. You take in super views of North Beach and Coit Tower either way—though if you're the one behind the wheel, you'd better keep your eye on the road lest you become yet another of the many folks who ram the garden barriers. ■**TIP**➜ **Can't stand the traffic? Thrill seekers of a different stripe may want to head two blocks south of Lombard to Filbert Street. At a gradient of 31.5%, the hair-raising descent between Hyde and Leavenworth Streets is one of the city's steepest. Go slowly!** ✉ *Lombard St. between Hyde and Leavenworth Sts., Russian Hill.*

★ Macondray Lane

STREET | San Francisco has no shortage of impressive, grand homes, but Macondray Lane is the quintessential hidden garden. Enter under a lovely wooden trellis and proceed down a quiet, cobbled pedestrian lane lined with Edwardian cottages and flowering plants and trees. A flight of steep wooden stairs at the end of the lane leads to Taylor Street—on the way down you can't miss the bay views. If you've read any of Armistead Maupin's Tales of the City books, you may find the lane vaguely familiar; it's the thinly disguised setting for parts of the series. ✉ *Between Jones and Taylor Sts., and Union and Green Sts., Russian Hill.*

★ Vallejo Steps

VIEWPOINT | Several Russian Hill buildings survived the 1906 earthquake and fire and remain standing. Patriotic firefighters

Continued on page 293

SAN FRANCISCO'S CABLE CARS

Van Ness Ave.. California
59
& Market Streets

The moment it dawns on you that you severely underestimated the steepness of the San Francisco hills will likely be the same moment you look down and realize those tracks aren't just for show—or just for tourists.

Sure, locals rarely use the cable cars for commuting these days. (That's partially due to the $8 fare—hear that, Muni?) So you'll likely be packed in with plenty of fellow sightseers. You may even be approaching cable-car fatigue after seeing its image on so many souvenirs. But if you fear the magic is gone, simply climb on board, and those jaded thoughts will dissolve. Grab the pole and gawk at the view as the car clanks down an insanely steep grade toward the bay. Listen to the humming cable, the clang of the bell, and the occasional quip from the gripman. It's an experience you shouldn't pass up, whether on your first trip or your fiftieth.

HOW CABLE CARS WORK

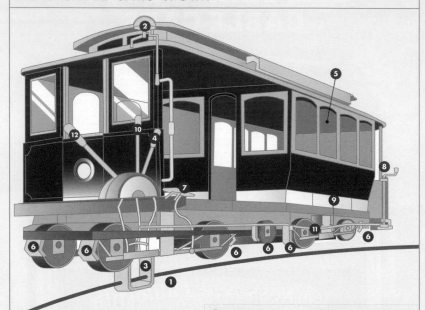

The mechanics are pretty simple: cable cars grab a moving subterranean cable with a "grip" to go. To stop, they release the grip and apply one or more types of brakes. Four cables, totaling 9 miles, power the city's three lines. If the gripman doesn't adjust the grip just right when going up a steep hill, the cable will start to slip and the car will have to back down the hill and try again. This is an extremely rare occurrence—imagine the ribbing the gripman gets back at the cable car barn!

Gripman: Stands in front and operates the grip, brakes, and bell. Favorite joke, especially at the peak of a steep hill: "This is my first day on the job, folks . . ."

Conductor: Moves around the car, deals with tickets, alerts the grip about what's coming up, and operates the rear wheel brakes.

❶ **Cable:** Steel wrapped around flexible sisal core; 2 inches thick; runs at a constant 9½ mph.

❷ **Bells:** Used for crew communication; alerts other drivers and pedestrians.

❸ **Grip:** Vice-like lever extends through the center slot in the track to grab or release the cable.

❹ **Grip Lever:** Left-hand lever; operates grip.

❺ **Car:** Entire car weighs 8 tons.

❻ **Wheel Brake:** Steel brake pads on each wheel.

❼ **Wheel Brake Lever:** Foot pedal; operates wheel brakes.

❽ **Rear Wheel Brake Lever:** Applied for extra traction on hills.

❾ **Track Brake:** 2-foot-long sections of Monterey pine push down against the track to help stop the car.

❿ **Track Brake Lever:** Middle lever; operates track brakes.

⓫ **Emergency Brake:** 18-inch steel wedge, jams into street slot to bring car to an immediate stop.

⓬ **Emergency Brake Lever:** Right-hand lever, red; operates emergency brake.

ROUTES

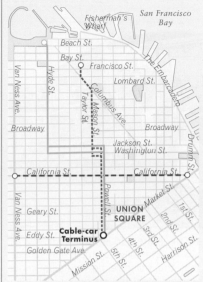

Cars run at least every 15 minutes, from around 6 am to about 1 am.

Powell–Hyde line: Most scenic, with classic Bay views. Begins at Powell and Market streets, then crosses Nob Hill and Russian Hill before a white-knuckle descent down Hyde Street, ending near the Hyde Street Pier.

Powell–Mason line: Also begins at Powell and Market streets, but winds through North Beach to Bay and Taylor streets, a few blocks from Fisherman's Wharf.

California line: Runs from the foot of Market Street, at Drumm Street, up Nob Hill and back. Great views (and aromas and sounds) of Chinatown on the way up. Sit in back to catch glimpses of the bay. ■TIP→ **Take the California line if it's just the cable-car experience you're after—the lines are shorter, and the grips and conductors say it's friendlier and has a slower pace.**

RULES OF THE RIDE

Tickets. There are ticket booths at all three turnarounds. You must purchase your ticket in advance.

■TIP→ **If you're planning to use public transit a few times, or if you'd like to ride back and forth on the cable car without worrying about the price, consider a one-day (or multiday) Muni Visitor Passport. You can get passports online, at the Powell Street turnaround, the TIX booth on Union Square, or the Fisherman's Wharf cable-car ticket booth at Beach and Hyde streets. Also consider Muni Mobile or a Clipper Card; see sfmta.com. Cash purchases require exact change.**

All Aboard. You can board on either side of the cable car. It's legal to stand on the running boards and hang on to the pole, but keep your ears open for the gripman's warnings. ■TIP→ **Grab a seat on the outside bench for the best views.**

Most people wait (and wait) in line at one of the cable car turnarounds, but you can also hop on along the route. Board wherever you see a white sign showing a figure climbing aboard a brown cable car; wave to the approaching driver, and wait until the car stops.

Riding on the running boards can be part of the thrill.

CABLE CAR HISTORY

HALLIDIE FREES THE HORSES

In the 1850s and '60s, San Francisco's streetcars were drawn by horses. Legend has it that the horrible sight of a car dragging a team of horses downhill to their deaths roused Andrew Smith Hallidie to action. The English immigrant had invented the "Hallidie Ropeway," essentially a cable car for mined ore, and he was convinced that his invention could also move people. In 1873, Hallidie and his intrepid crew prepared to test the first cable car high on Russian Hill. The anxious engineer peered down into the foggy darkness, failed to see the bottom of the hill, and promptly turned the controls over to Hallidie. Needless to say, the thing worked . . . but rides were free for the first two days because people were afraid to get on.

SEE IT FOR YOURSELF

The Cable Car Museum (✉ *1201 Mason St.* ⊕ *cablecarmusem.org*) is one of the city's best free offerings and an absolute must for kids. (You can even ride a cable car there, since all three lines stop between Russian Hill and Nob Hill.) The museum, which is inside the city's last cable-car barn, takes the top off the system to let you see how it all works. Eternally humming and squealing, the massive powerhouse cable wheels steal the show. You can also climb aboard a vintage car and take the grip, let the kids ring a cable-car bell (briefly, please!), and check out vintage gear dating from 1873.

■ **TIP→ The gift shop sells cable car paraphernalia, including an authentic gripman's bell (it'll sound like Powell Street in your house every day). For significantly less, you can pick up a key chain made from a piece of worn-out cable. Books, T-shirts, hats, and models are also on sale.**

CHAMPION OF THE CABLE CAR BELL

Each fall (though the month can vary widely : check ⊕ *sfmta.com* for update) the city's best and brightest come together to crown a bell-ringing champion at Union Square. The crowd cheers gripmen and conductors as they stomp, shake, and riff with the rope. But it's not a popularity contest; the ringers are judged by former bell-ringing champions and others who take each ping and gong very seriously.

saved what's become known as the Flag House (✉ *1652–56 Taylor St.*) when they spotted the American flag on the property. The owner, a flag collector, fearing the house would burn, wanted it to go down with "all flags flying." At the southwest corner of Ina Coolbrith Park, it is one of a number of California shingle–style homes in this neighborhood, several of which the architect Willis Polk designed.

Polk drew up the plans for the nearby Polk-Williams House (✉ *Taylor and Vallejo Sts.*) and lived in one of its finer sections, and he was responsible for 1034–1036 Vallejo, across the street. He also laid out the Vallejo Steps themselves, which climb the steep ridge across Taylor Street from the Flag House. The precipitous walk up to Ina Coolbrith Park and beyond is possibly the most pleasurable thing to do while on Russian Hill. **■ TIP→ If the walk up the steps will be too taxing, park at the top by heading east on Vallejo from Jones and enjoy the scene from there.** ✉ *Taylor and Vallejo Sts., Russian Hill* ✣ *Steps lead up toward Jones St.*

Polk Gulch

Polk Gulch, the microhood surrounding north-south Polk Street, hugs the western edges of Nob Hill and Russian Hill but is nothing like either. It's actually two microhoods: Upper Polk Gulch, fairly classy in its northern section, runs from about Union Street south to California Street; Lower Polk Gulch, the rougher southern part, continues down from California to Geary or so.

Polk Gulch was the city's gay neighborhood into the 1970s, hosting San Francisco's first Pride parade in 1972 and several festive Halloween extravaganzas. Today the friendly saloon the Cinch, the last remnant of gay Polk, and a few holdovers from that earlier time share space with newer mid-range restaurants, a passel of bars and nightclubs, and some browsable, funky stores, plus two great doughnut shops.

🍴 Restaurants

★ Acquerello

$$$$ | **ITALIAN** | Chef and co-owner Suzette Gresham has elicited swoons over the years with high-end but soulful Italian cooking that is worth every penny. Her cuttlefish "tagliatelle" is a star of the menu, which features both classic and cutting-edge dishes. **Known for:** sensational prix-fixe dining; city's premier Italian cheese selection; extensive Italian wine list. [$] *Average main: $165* ✉ *1722 Sacramento St., Polk Gulch* ☎ *415/567–5432* 🌐 *www.acquerellosf.com* ⏲ *Closed Sun. and Mon. No lunch.*

Bob's Donuts

$ | **BAKERY** | **FAMILY** | This legendary 24-hour doughnut shop has been a neighborhood anchor since the 1960s. The homemade doughnuts, whether an apple fritter or classic raised maple, are always excellent, at 10 am or 10 pm. **Known for:** cake crumb doughnut; Bob's Challenge for devoted doughnut lovers; timeless, low-key atmosphere. [$] *Average main: $3* ✉ *1621 Polk St., Polk Gulch* ☎ *415/776–3141* 🌐 *www.bobsdonutssf.com.*

★ Swan Oyster Depot

$$ | **SEAFOOD** | Half fish market and half diner, this small, slim, family-run seafood operation, open since 1912, has no tables, just a narrow marble counter with about 18 stools. Some locals come in to buy perfectly fresh salmon, halibut, crabs, and other seafood to take home; everyone else hops onto one of the rickety stools to enjoy a dozen oysters, other shellfish, or a bowl of clam chowder—the only hot food served. **Known for:** memorable Dungeness crab Louie salad; fresh oysters and seafood; clam chowder. [$] *Average main: $29* ✉ *1517 Polk St., Polk Gulch* ☎ *415/673–1101* 🌐 *swanoysterdepot.us* 💳 *No credit cards* ⏲ *Closed Sun. No dinner.*

Nightlife

The Cinch Saloon

BARS | This Wild West–motif neighborhood gay bar has pinball machines, pool tables, a smoking patio, and several theme nights and drag shows on the schedule. The Cinch is not the least bit trendy, which is part of the charm for regulars of this landmark 1970s bar. ⊠ *1723 Polk St., Polk Gulch* ☎ *415/776–4162* ⊕ *www.facebook.com/thecinchsaloon.*

Pacific Heights

Pacific Heights defines San Francisco's most expensive and dramatic real estate. Grand Victorians line the streets, mansions and town houses are priced in the millions, and there are magnificent views from almost any point in the neighborhood. Old money and new, personalities in the limelight and those who prefer absolute media anonymity live here, and few outsiders see anything other than the pleasing facades of Queen Anne charmers, English Tudor imports, and baroque bastions.

Two of the city's most spectacular parks are located in the area. The boutiques and restaurants along Fillmore Street, which range from glam to funky, are a draw as well.

Sights

★ Alta Plaza Park

CITY PARK | FAMILY | Golden Gate Park's longtime superintendent, John McLaren, designed this 12-acre park in the early 1900s, modeling its steep south-facing terracing on that of the Grand Casino in Monte Carlo. At any time of day, you're guaranteed to find San Francisco's exercise warriors running up the park's south steps. From the top of those steps, you can see Marin to the north, downtown to the east, Twin Peaks to the south, and Golden Gate Park to the west.

■ TIP→ **Kids love the many play structures at the large, enclosed playground at the top; dogs love the off-leash area in the park's southeast corner.** ⊠ *Bordered by Clay, Steiner, Jackson, and Scott Sts., Pacific Heights* ⊕ *www.altaplazapark.com.*

Haas-Lilienthal House

HISTORIC HOME | A small display of photographs on the bottom floor of this elaborate, gray 1886 Queen Anne house makes clear that despite its lofty stature and striking, round third-story tower, the 11,500-square-foot house was modest compared with some of the giants that fell victim to the 1906 earthquake and fire. San Francisco Heritage, a foundation to preserve San Francisco's architectural history, operates the home, whose carefully kept rooms provide a glimpse into late-19th-century life through period furniture, authentic details (like the antique dishes in the kitchen built-in), and photos of the Haas family, who occupied the house for three generations until 1972.

■ TIP→ **You can admire hundreds of gorgeous San Francisco Victorians from the outside, but this is the only one that's open to the public, and it's worth a visit.**

You can download free maps of two nearby walking tours highlighting the neighborhood's historic architecture on the house's website. ⊠ *2007 Franklin St., between Washington and Jackson Sts., Pacific Heights* ☎ *415/441–3000* ⊕ *www. haas-lilienthalhouse.org* ◻ *Tours $10.*

Lafayette Park

CITY PARK | FAMILY | Clusters of trees dot this four-block-square oasis for sunbathers and dog-and-Frisbee teams. On the south side of the park, squat but elegant 2151 Sacramento Street, a private condominium, is the site of a home occupied by Sir Arthur Conan Doyle in the late 19th century. Coats of arms blaze in the front stained-glass windows. Across from the park's eastern edge is another eye-catching historic home: the Queen Anne (and

A Pacific Heights Walk

Start at **Broadway and Webster Streets**, where four notable estates stand within a block of one another. Two are on the north side of Broadway west of the intersection, one is on the same side to the east, and the last is half a block south on Webster. Head south down Webster and hang a right onto Clay to **Alta Plaza Park**, or skip the park and turn left on Jackson to the **Whittier Mansion**, at Jackson and Laguna Streets. Head south down Laguna and cross Washington Street to **Lafayette Park**. Walk on Washington along the edge of the park, past the formal French **Spreckels Mansion** at the corner of Octavia Street, and continue east two more blocks to Franklin Street. Turn left (north); halfway down the block stands the handsome **Haas-Lilienthal House**. Head back south on Franklin Street, stopping to view a grand Georgian-style residence (✉ *1735 Franklin St.*) and the Queen Anne–style Coleman House with a gorgeous purple stained-glass window on the home's north side (✉ *1701 Franklin St.*). At California Street, turn right (west) to see two **Italianate Victorians** and the **Atherton House**. Continue west to Laguna Street and turn left (south); past Pine Street sits a sedate block of **Laguna Street Victorians**.

distinctly yellow) C. A. Belden House at 2004 Gough Street.

The park's northern border is anchored by the stately Spreckels Mansion, built originally for sugar heir Adolph B. Spreckels and his wife, Alma. It is now the 55-room home of celebrated romance novelist Danielle Steel. Giant, immaculately trimmed hedges hide most of the mansion from public view—and have been quite the topic of debate among locals for many years. The park itself is a lovely neighborhood space where Pacific Heights residents laze in the sun or exercise their pedigreed canines while gazing at downtown's skyline or the Bay and Marin County hills in the distance to the north. ✉ *Bordered by Laguna, Gough, Sacramento, and Washington Sts., Pacific Heights* 🌐 *sfrecpark.org.*

🍴 Restaurants

★ Octavia

$$$ | **MODERN AMERICAN** | Regardless of the time of year, Melissa Perello's upscale restaurant is a perennial favorite for diners seeking out what California cuisine really tastes like. The warm, immaculate dining room is a perfect setting for edgier dishes like the chilled squid-ink noodles starter, along with more comforting produce-driven small plates and entrées. **Known for:** exciting preparations with peak-of-season produce; spicy deviled egg starter; truly professional service. [$] *Average main: $35* ✉ *1701 Octavia St., Lower Pacific Heights* ☎ *415/408–7507* 🌐 *www.octavia-sf.com* 🕒 *Closed Sun. and Mon. No lunch.*

Sociale

$$$ | **NORTHERN ITALIAN** | The COVID-19 pandemic's outdoor dining requirement led San Franciscans to discover the city's premier patios—like the one at this Presidio Heights stalwart. Whether you're dining on that patio or in the elegant dining room, Italian and seasonal Californian cooking mingle together on the menu. **Known for:** fantastic pastas; chocolate oblivion cake; Barolo and Barbaresco wine choices. [$] *Average main: $31* ✉ *3665 Sacramento St., Presidio Heights* ☎ *415/921–3200* 🌐 *sfsociale.com* 🕒 *Closed Sun. and Mon. No lunch Tues. and Wed.*

Hotels

★ Hotel Drisco
$$$$ | HOTEL | You can pretend you're a denizen of one of San Francisco's wealthiest neighborhoods at this understated, elegant Edwardian hotel built in 1903. **Pros:** gorgeous rooms and public spaces; great service and amenities; quiet residential neighborhood. **Cons:** not a close walk to restaurants or major sights; steep prices; no complimentary chauffeur service in the afternoon or evening. [$] *Rooms from: $520* ✉ *2901 Pacific Ave., Pacific Heights* ☎ *415/346–2880, 800/634–7277* 🌐 *hoteldrisco.com* 🛏 *48 rooms* 🍴 *Free Breakfast.*

Shopping

Browser Books
BOOKS | FAMILY | Opened in 1976, one of the city's most beloved independent bookstores resides quietly among the chic fashion boutiques lining Fillmore Street. All ages will find ample choices, from contemporary fiction to children's books to a large selection of Buddhist Dharma literature. The store is owned by Inner Richmond favorite Green Apple Books. ✉ *2195 Fillmore St., Lower Pacific Heights* ☎ *415/567–8027* 🌐 *www.greenapplebooks.com.*

★ Margaret O'Leary
WOMEN'S CLOTHING | If you can only buy one piece of clothing in San Francisco, make it a hand-loomed cashmere sweater by this Irish-born local legend. The perfect antidote to the city's wind and fog, the sweaters are so beloved by San Franciscans that some of them never wear anything else. Pick up an airplane wrap for your trip home. ✉ *2400 Fillmore St., Pacific Heights* ☎ *415/771–9982* 🌐 *www.margaretoleary.com.*

Japantown

Whereas Chinatown is densely populated and still largely Chinese, Japantown, though still the spiritual center of San Francisco's Japanese American community, struggles to retain its unique character. Nevertheless, when several key properties were sold in the aughts, a group rallied to "save Japantown," and the area has since been infused with new energy.

⚠ **Japantown is a relatively safe area, but the Western Addition, south of Geary Boulevard, can be dangerous even during the daytime. Also avoid going too far west of Fillmore Street on either side of Geary.**

Sights

Japan Center
STORE/MALL | FAMILY | Cool and curious trinkets, noodle houses and sushi joints, a destination bookstore, and a peek at Japanese culture high and low await at this 5-acre complex designed in 1968 by noted American architect Minoru Yamasaki. The Japan Center includes the shop- and restaurant-filled Kintetsu Mall and Kinokuniya Building; the excellent Kabuki Springs & Spa; the Hotel Kabuki; and the AMC Kabuki cinema.

The Kinokuniya Bookstore, in the Kinokuniya Building, has an extensive selection of Japanese-language books, manga, English-language translations, books on Japanese topics, and fun gifts. Afterwards, enjoy a crepe with green tea gelato, red bean paste, and matcha from Sophie's Crepes. Just outside, on the bridge connecting the buildings, check out Asakichi and its tiny incense shop for wind chimes and teakettles. Continue into the Kintetsu Mall for a *taiyaki* (fish-shape) cone at Uji Time.

Between the West Mall and the East Mall are the five-tier, 100-foot-tall Peace Pagoda and the Peace Plaza, where seasonal festivals are held. The pagoda, which draws on the 1,200-year-old tradition of miniature round pagodas dedicated to eternal peace, was designed in the late 1960s by Yoshirō Taniguchi to convey the "friendship and goodwill" of the Japanese people to the people of the United States. ✉ *Bordered by Geary Blvd. and Fillmore, Post, and Laguna Sts., Japantown* 🌐 *www.sfjapantown.org/japan-center-malls.*

🍴 Restaurants

Marufuku Ramen

$ | **RAMEN** | Hakata-style *tonkotsu* (pork) and extra-intense chicken *paitan* ramen are the specialties of this modern-looking Japan Center restaurant that serves what many consider the city's finest bowl of ramen. As a result, long lines can be daunting, but tables move pretty quickly inside the bustling yet relaxed space decorated with wood design elements and dangling Edison bulbs. **Known for:** superb ramen; gyoza and pork buns; lively, contemporary vibe. [$] *Average main: $18* ✉ *Kinokuniya Bldg., 1581 Webster St., Suite 235, Japantown* ☎ *415/872–9786* 🌐 *www.marufukuramen.com.*

Sasa

$$ | **SUSHI** | Japantown has a host of sushi options at all price points, but this longtime staple on the second floor of the Japan Center stands out for its excellent rolls, nigiri, and sashimi. The omakase menu, with eight pieces of sushi and nigiri, is a fraction of the cost of its downtown peers, but close to equal in quality and diner satisfaction. **Known for:** "mystery box" mini chirashi bowl; uni spoon with quail egg and ikura (cured salmon roe); an oasis in a busy mall. [$] *Average main: $30* ✉ *Japan Center East Mall, 22 Peace Plaza, Suite 530, Japantown* ☎ *628/600–6945* 🌐 *sasasf.com* 🕒 *No lunch Mon.*

🏃 Activities

★ Kabuki Springs & Spa

SPAS | The serene spa is one Japantown destination that draws locals from all over town, from hipsters to grandmas, Japanese American or not. Balinese urns decorate the communal bath area of this house of tranquility. The extensive service menu includes facials, salt scrubs, and mud and seaweed wraps, in addition to massage. You can take your massage in a private room with a bath or in a curtained-off area. The communal baths ($45) contain hot and cold tubs, a large Japanese-style bath, a sauna, a steam room, and showers. The clothing-optional baths are open for men only on Thursday and Saturday; women bathe on Wednesday, Friday, and Sunday. Bathing suits are required on Tuesday, when the baths are coed. Men and women can reserve a private room daily. ✉ *1750 Geary Blvd., Japantown* ☎ *415/922–6000* 🌐 *kabukisprings.com* 🕒 *Closed Mon.*

Western Addition

Some areas of the Western Addition struggle with poverty and gang violence; other areas are trendy, like the dining-rich Divisadero corridor, or classic, like Alamo Square Park with its iconic Painted Ladies. In its post–World War II heyday, the area known as Lower Fillmore was considered the Harlem of the West for its profusion of jazz nightspots, where such legends as Billie Holliday, Duke Ellington, and Charlie Parker would play. These days the ties to that heritage include the Fillmore Jazz Festival in June; the Fillmore Auditorium, made famous in the 1960s by Bill Graham and the iconic bands he booked there; and the blues-centric Boom Boom Room.

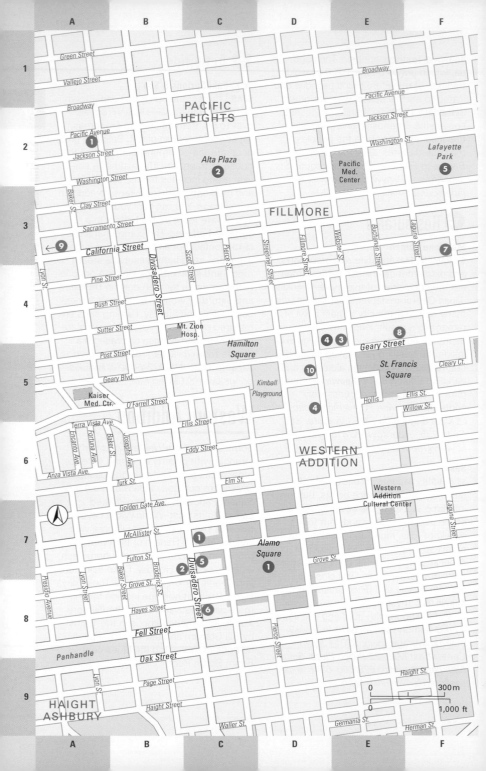

Pacific Heights, Japantown, and Western Addition

10

Sights ▼

1 Alamo Square Park............... **D7**
2 Alta Plaza Park..................... **C2**
3 Haas-Lilienthal House............. **G1**
4 Japan Center...................... **E4**
5 Lafayette Park..................... **F2**

Restaurants ▼

1 Che Fico............................. **C7**
2 4505 Burgers & BBQ **B7**
3 Marufuku Ramen **E4**
4 Merchant Roots.................... **D5**
5 The Mill ....,,,.................... **C7**
6 Nopa **C8**
7 Octavia............................. **F3**
8 Sasa................................ **E4**
9 Sociale............................. **A3**
10 State Bird Provisions............. **D5**

Hotels ▼

1 Hotel Drisco **A2**

Broadway

Clay Street

Van Ness Avenue

Polk St.

Sacramento Street

California Street

Cable Car

POLK GULCH

Pine Street

Franklin Street

Gough Street

Bush Street

Larkin Street

Hyde Street

Leavenworth Street

Sutter Street

Post Street

Geary Street

O'Farrell Street

Ellis Street

THE TENDERLOIN

101

Eddy Street

Jefferson Square

Van Ness Avenue

Turk Street

Golden Gate Ave.

McAllister Street

Polk Street

Fulton St.

CIVIC CENTER

CIVIC CENTER

Grove Street

8th Street

HAYES VALLEY

Hayes Street

9th Street

Mission St.

Minna St.

Natoma St.

Fell Street

10th Street

Oak St.

Octavia Blvd.

Page St.

11th Street

Market Street

Van Ness Avenue

Minna St.

Natoma St.

Washburn St.

Grace St.

Howard Street

Dore St.

Haight St.

Gough St.

Lafayette St.

12th St.

Valencia St.

Mission St.

101

KEY

1 Exploring Sights
1 Restaurants
1 Hotels
🅱 BART station

Sights

★ Alamo Square Park

CITY PARK | FAMILY | Whether you've seen them on postcards or on the old TV show *Full House,* the colorful "Painted Ladies" Victorian houses are some of San Francisco's world-renowned icons. The signature view of these beauties with the downtown skyline in the background is from the east side of this hilly park. Tourists love the photo opportunities, but locals also adore the park's tennis courts, dog runs, and ample picnic area—with great views, of course. After taking plenty of photos, swing by the park's northwest corner and admire the William Westerfeld House (✉ *1198 Fulton St.*), a splendid five-story late-19th-century Victorian mansion. ■ **TIP→ If it's a sunny day, grab picnic provisions from Bi-Rite Market. Thursday through Sunday, the Lady Falcon Coffee Club truck is stationed in the park, offering a great caffeine pick-me-up.** ✉ *Bordered by Steiner, Hayes, Scott, and Fulton Sts., Western Addition* 🌐 *sfrecpark.org.*

Restaurants

Che Fico

$$$ | MODERN ITALIAN | This consistently popular spot sets itself apart with homemade charcuterie, plus antipasti, pastas, and pizza that often take traditional standbys for a creative spin or a California slant from local produce. The clever, beautifully balanced cocktails and fun twists on homey desserts are must-orders. **Known for:** pineapple pizza; hard-to-get reservations; Roman Jewish specialties. [$] *Average main: $39* ✉ *838 Divisadero St., Western Addition* ☎ *415/416–6959* 🌐 *www.chefico.com* 🕘 *Closed Sun. and Mon. No lunch.*

4505 Burgers & BBQ

$$ | BARBECUE | FAMILY | The smoker works overtime from noon to night at this hipster-chic barbecue shack, churning out an array of succulent meats that can be had by the plate, the pound, or as a sandwich. Every plate comes with two sides, and you should certainly make the frankaroni one of them: possibly the work of the devil, this is macaroni-and-cheese with pieces of hot dog … deep fried. **Known for:** partially outdoor seating in shipping containers; decadent sides; self-named and possibly correct "Best Damn Cheeseburger." [$] *Average main: $20* ✉ *705 Divisadero St., Western Addition* ☎ *415/231–6993* 🌐 *www.4505burgersandbbq.com.*

Merchant Roots

$$$$ | CONTEMPORARY | After starting as part grocer/part lunch café/part tasting menu, this tiny Fillmore spot is now fully devoted to the elaborate tasting menus of chef-owner Ryan Shelton. Themes and dishes change every few months (it could be "flowers" or "Alice in Wonderland"), but the one constant is Shelton's incredible imagination and ability to transform those themes into elaborate, technique-driven composed dishes. **Known for:** SF's best chocolate chip cookies; warm and welcoming ambience; excellent wine program. [$] *Average main: $168* ✉ *1365 Fillmore St., Western Addition* ☎ *530/574–7365* 🌐 *www.merchantroots.com* 🕘 *Closed Mon., Tues., and every other Sun. No lunch.*

★ The Mill

$ | BAKERY | "Four-dollar toast" is a phrase used around San Francisco referring to gentrification—and it was inspired by this sun-drenched, Wi-Fi-less café. At this project between one of the city's leading bakers, Josey Baker, and the Mission's Four Barrel Coffee, toasts slathered with jam or spreads are the specialty during the day. **Known for:** stellar loaves of bread; precious, post-yoga vibe; one pizza topping served Monday nights. [$] *Average main: $8* ✉ *736 Divisadero St., Western Addition* ☎ *415/345–1953* 🌐 *www.themillsf.com* 🕘 *No dinner Tues.–Sun.*

★ Nopa

$$$ | AMERICAN | This is the good-food granddaddy of the hot corridor of the same name. The Cali-rustic fare draws dependable crowds regardless of the night, with attractions including a beloved Moroccan vegetable tagine; crisp-skin rotisserie chicken; and a juicy hamburger with thick-cut fries. **Known for:** high-quality comfort food with smart twists; lively vibe; a constant and diverse crowd. [$] *Average main: $32* ✉ *560 Divisadero St., Western Addition* ☎ *415/864–8643* 🌐 *nopasf.com* 🕒 *No lunch.*

★ State Bird Provisions

$$ | MODERN AMERICAN | It's hard to score a reservation for a normal dinner hour at Lower Fillmore's game-changing restaurant, but once you nab a golden ticket, you'll be rewarded with fascinating bites served from roving carts and an à la carte printed menu. The food has an artsy bent to it, and the colorful dining room with pegboard walls adds to a vibe that's part high-school art room, part bohemian dinner party. **Known for:** buttermilk fried quail; cart service and à la carte dining; "World Peace" peanut milk dessert drink. [$] *Average main: $29* ✉ *1529 Fillmore St., Western Addition* ☎ *415/795–1272* 🌐 *www.statebirdsf.com* 🕒 *No lunch.*

Nightlife

Boom Boom Room

LIVE MUSIC | One of San Francisco's liveliest music spots is this Fillmore blues favorite, opened in 1997 by the "King of the Boogie," John Lee Hooker. The club has a fun blend of blues, funk, and hip-hop shows most nights of the week. ✉ *1601 Fillmore St., at Geary Blvd., Western Addition* ☎ *415/673–8000* 🌐 *boomboomroom.com.*

The Fillmore

LIVE MUSIC | This is *the* club that all the big names, from Coldplay to Clapton, want to play. San Francisco's most famous rock-music hall presents national and local acts: rock, reggae, grunge, jazz, folk, acid house, and more. Go upstairs to view the amazing collection of rock posters lining the walls. At the end of each show, free apples are set near the door, and staffers hand out collectible posters.

■ TIP→ Avoid steep service charges by purchasing tickets at the club's box office on Sunday from 10 to 4. ✉ *1805 Geary Blvd., at Fillmore St., Western Addition* ☎ *415/346–6000* 🌐 *www.thefillmore.com.*

The Independent

LIVE MUSIC | Looking for the next big indie performer or hip-hop group? This Divisadero favorite is probably the best place to find them in the city. The eclectic, 500-person-capacity club/concert venue opened in 2004 and has become a key part of San Francisco's concertgoing culture. Headliner names like Zedd and Foster the People performed their first SF shows here, while marquee performers like Green Day and John Legend have appeared on stage in recent years. ✉ *628 Divisadero St., Western Addition* ☎ *415/771–1421* 🌐 *theindependentsf.com.*

North Beach

San Francisco novelist Herbert Gold called North Beach "the longest-running, most glorious, American bohemian operetta outside Greenwich Village." Indeed, to anyone who has spent some time in its eccentric old bars and cafés, North Beach evokes everything from the Barbary Coast days to the no-less-rowdy Beatnik era.

This was once an almost exclusively Italian American neighborhood, but today the area's premium rental market has driven many of these residents to other neighborhoods. Still, when it comes to Italian restaurants this area has some gems, and random aromas fill the air:

coffee beans, cured salami, Italian dolce, and—depending on the corner you've turned—pungent garlic.

Sights

Beat Museum
HISTORY MUSEUM | "Museum" might be a stretch for this tiny storefront that's half bookstore, half memorabilia collection. You can see the 1949 Hudson from the movie version of *On the Road* and the shirt Neal Cassady wore while driving Ken Kesey's Merry Prankster bus, "Further." There are also manuscripts, letters, and early editions by Jack Kerouac, Allen Ginsberg, and Lawrence Ferlinghetti. But the true treasure here is the passionate and well-informed staff, which often includes the museum's founder, Jerry Cimino: your short visit may turn into an hours-long trip through the Beat era. ■ TIP→ **Excellent walking tours go beyond the museum to take in favorite Beat watering holes and hangouts in North Beach.** ⊠ *540 Broadway, North Beach* ☎ *800/537–6822, 415/399–9626* ⊕ *www. kerouac.com* ⊑ *$8* ⊘ *Closed Tues. and Wed.*

★ City Lights Bookstore
STORE/MALL | The exterior of this famous bookstore is iconic in itself, from the replica of a revolutionary mural destroyed in Chiapas, Mexico, by military forces to the art banners hanging above the windows. Designated a landmark by the city, the hangout of Beat-era writers and independent publishers remains a vital part of San Francisco's literary scene. Browse the three levels of poetry, philosophy, politics, fiction, history, and local zines, to the beat of creaking wood floors.

Back in the day, writers like Allen Ginsberg and Jack Kerouac would read here (and even receive mail in the basement). The late poet Lawrence Ferlinghetti, who cofounded City Lights in 1953, cemented its place in history by publishing insberg's *Howl and Other Poems* in

1956. The small volume was ignored in the mainstream—until Ferlinghetti and the bookstore manager were arrested for obscenity and corruption of youth. In the landmark First Amendment trial that followed, the judge exonerated both men. *Howl* went on to become a classic.

Stroll Kerouac Alley, branching off Columbus Avenue next to City Lights, to read the quotes from Ferlinghetti, Maya Angelou, Confucius, John Steinbeck, and the street's namesake embedded in the pavement. ⊠ *261 Columbus Ave., North Beach* ☎ *415/362–8193* ⊕ *citylights.com.*

Coit Tower
VIEWPOINT | Among San Francisco's most distinctive skyline sights, this 210-foot tower is often considered a tribute to firefighters because of the donor's special attachment to the local fire company. As the story goes, a young gold rush–era girl, Lillie Hitchcock Coit (known as Miss Lil), was a fervent admirer of her local fire company—so much so that she once deserted a wedding party and chased down the street after her favorite engine, Knickerbocker No. 5, while clad in her bridesmaid finery. When Lillie died in 1929, she left the city $125,000 to "expend in an appropriate manner … to the beauty of San Francisco."

You can ride the elevator to the top of the tower to enjoy the 360-degree view of the Bay Bridge and the Golden Gate Bridge; due north is Alcatraz Island. Most visitors saunter past the 27 fabulous Depression-era murals inside the tower that depict California's economic and political life, but take the time to appreciate the first New Deal art project, supported by taxpayer money. It's also possible to walk up and down to the tower (if you're in shape): a highlight is the descent toward the Embarcadero via the Filbert Steps, a series of stairways that are a shaded green oasis in the middle of the city. ⊠ *Telegraph Hill Blvd., at Greenwich St. or Lombard St., North*

Beach ☎ 415/362–0808 ⊕ sfrecpark.org ✉ Free, elevator to top $10.

Grant Avenue

STREET | Originally called Calle de la Fundación, Grant Avenue is the oldest street in the city, but it's got plenty of young blood. Dusty bars such as The Saloon mix with independent boutiques, odd curio shops, and curated gourmet shops. While the street runs from Union Square through Chinatown, North Beach, and beyond, the fun stuff in this neighborhood is jammed into the four blocks from Columbus Avenue north to Filbert Street. ✉ North Beach.

★ Telegraph Hill and the Filbert Steps

NEIGHBORHOOD | Residents here have some of the city's best views, as well as the most difficult ascents to their aeries. The hill rises from the east end of Lombard Street to a height of 284 feet and is capped by Coit Tower. If you brave the slope, though, you'll be rewarded with a "secret treasure" San Francisco moment. Filbert Street starts up the hill, then becomes the Filbert Steps when the going gets too steep. You can cut between the Filbert Steps and another flight, the Greenwich Steps, on up to the hilltop. As you climb, you pass some of the city's oldest houses and are surrounded by beautiful, flowering private gardens. In some places the trees grow over the stairs, so it feels like you're walking through a green tunnel; elsewhere, you'll have wide-open views of the bay. The cypress trees that grow on the hill are a favorite roost of local avian celebrities, the wild parrots of Telegraph Hill; you'll hear the cries of the cherry-headed conures if they're nearby. The name comes from the hill's status as the first Morse code signal station back in 1853. ✉ Bordered by Lombard, Filbert, Kearny, and Sansome Sts., North Beach.

Washington Square

PLAZA/SQUARE | Once the daytime social heart of San Francisco's Italian district, this grassy patch has changed character numerous times over the years. The Beats hung out here in the 1950s, hippies camped out in the 1960s and early '70s, and nowadays you're more likely to see picnickers and residents doing community dance, yoga, or tai chi. You might also see homeless people hanging out on the benches and young locals sunbathing or running their dogs. Lillie Hitchcock Coit, in yet another show of affection for San Francisco's firefighters, donated the statue of two firemen with a rescued child. Camera-toting visitors focus on the Romanesque splendor of Saints Peter and Paul Church (Filbert Street side of the square), a 1924 building with Disneyesque stone-white towers that are local landmarks. Mass reflects the neighborhood; it's given in English, Italian, and Chinese. ✉ Bordered by Columbus Ave. and Stockton, Filbert, and Union Sts., North Beach ⊕ sfrecpark.org.

🍴 Restaurants

Caffe Trieste

$ | **CAFÉ** | Caffe Trieste gives a glimmer of North Beach soul, along with generous slices of cake and possibly the best cappuccino in town that isn't trying to be part of a hipster latte-art competition. Open since 1956 and claiming to be the West Coast's first espresso coffeehouse, this fixture draws a diverse crowd, from young artists writing to the tune of their espresso buzz to old-timers reading the paper as they sip their drip cup. **Known for:** Saturday afternoon music; neighborhood vibe; retail annex next door. ⑤ Average main: $5 ✉ 601 Vallejo St., at Grant Ave., North Beach ☎ 415/392–6739 ⊕ coffee.caffetrieste.com.

The Italian Homemade Company

$ | **ITALIAN** | **FAMILY** | In Italy, the bastion of fresh pasta is Emilia-Romagna, and a trio of entrepreneurs hailing from the region give respect to its claim to carb fame in a mini-empire of fast-casual pasta eateries, with the one in North Beach as its flagship. Come for treats like slabs

10

San Francisco NORTH BEACH

Sights ▼

1 Alcatraz............................. **G1**
2 Beat Museum **F6**
3 City Lights Bookstore............. **F6**
4 Coit Tower **F4**
5 Exploratorium **I4**
6 Ferry Building **J6**
7 F-line **C2**
8 Grant Avenue **F6**
9 Hyde Street Pier **B2**
10 Jackson Square
Historic District **G6**
11 Musée Mécanique **C2**
12 Pier 39............................... **E1**
13 San Francisco National
Maritime Museum................. **A2**
14 San Francisco Railway
Museum **J7**
15 Telegraph Hill and the
Filbert Steps **F4**
16 Washington Square **E5**
17 Wells Fargo
History Museum **G7**

Restaurants ▼

1 Angler................................. **J7**
2 Caffe Trieste......................... **F5**
3 Cotogna **G6**
4 Gary Danko.......................... **B3**
5 Hog Island Oyster Company....... **J6**
6 The Italian
Homemade Company **D4**
7 Stella Pastry & Cafe **F5**
8 Terminus Cafe and Bar............. **I7**
9 Tony's Pizza Napoletana **E5**
10 Tosca Cafe........................... **F6**
11 Waterbar **J7**
12 Wayfare Tavern..................... **G7**
13 Yang Sing **H8**

Hotels ▼

1 Galleria Park
2 Hotel Zoe Fish
3 Kimpton Alton

of lasagna that fool you into thinking you're calorie-loading in Bologna, as well as stuffed ravioli and gnocchi. **Known for:** varieties of piadina (Italian flatbreads with meats, cheeses, and vegetables); mix-and-match pastas and sauces; great quality for the price. [$] *Average main: $13* ✉ *716 Columbus Ave., North Beach* ☎ *415/712–8874* 🌐 *italianhomemade.com.*

Stella Pastry & Cafe
$ | **BAKERY** | For a quarter so rich in Italian history, North Beach sadly lacks authentic Italian *dolce* (sweet) offerings; indeed, this lone sweets bakery is it. Stella has been around since 1942 and has since changed hands from the original owners but still sticks to offering an array of Italian-American-style biscotti, tiramisu, and cannoli with creamy, cloyingly sweet predilections. **Known for:** Sacripantina cake, heavy with zabiglione; coffee and cappucino; American-style cannoli. [$] *Average main: $4* ✉ *446 Columbus Ave., North Beach* ☎ *415/986–2914.*

Tony's Pizza Napoletana
$$ | **PIZZA** | **FAMILY** | Repeatedly crowned the World Champion Pizza Maker at the World Pizza Cup in Naples, Tony Gemignani is a carb-friendly legend in the city for his flavorful dough and myriad versions. The multiple gas, electric, and wood-burning ovens in his casual, modern pizzeria turn out many different styles of pies—the famed Neapolitan-style Margherita, but also Sicilian, Roman, and Detroit styles—with salads, antipasti, homemade pastas, and calzone rounding out the menu. **Known for:** Cal-Italia pie with aged balsamic drizzle; NYC pizza parlor vibes; slice stand next door if you can't wait. [$] *Average main: $29* ✉ *1570 Stockton St., North Beach* ☎ *415/835–9888* 🌐 *tonyspizzanapoletana.com.*

Tosca Cafe
$$$ | **ITALIAN** | The leather booths and chairs are in high demand at this dark and clubby boho classic from 1919, where well-heeled locals and visitors delight in food that skews to the Cal-Italian genre, meaning local catches and seasonal produce as well as Italian flair in dishes such as halibut crudo and meatballs swimming in red sauce. This is also a great place to park on a stool at the bar, linger over a craft cocktail, and soak up the old–San Francisco vibe. **Known for:** Italian cocktails; raw bar and caviar menu; Tuscan fried chicken. [$] *Average main: $34* ✉ *242 Columbus Ave., North Beach* ☎ *415/986–9651* 🌐 *toscacafesf.com* ⏲ *Closed Sun. and Mon. No lunch.*

🍸 Nightlife

Specs' Twelve Adler Museum Cafe
BARS | If you're into bohemian dive bars, you can groove on this hidden hangout for artists, poets, and heavy-drinking old-timers. Specs' bar is a women-owned and -run institution and a beloved fixture. It's one of the few remaining old-fashioned watering holes in North Beach that still smack of the Beat years and the 1960s. Though it's just off a busy street, Specs' is strangely immune to the hustle and bustle outside. ✉ *12 William Saroyan Pl., off Columbus Ave., between Pacific Ave. and Broadway, North Beach* ☎ *415/421–4112* 🌐 *www.specsbarsf.com.*

Tony Nik's
BARS | For a dive bar with old San Francisco soul, go no further for a nightcap involving an old-fashioned, martini, or Negroni after a night of pizza crushing. ✉ *1534 Stockton St., North Beach* ☎ *415/693–0990* 🌐 *tonyniks.com/history.php.*

★ Vesuvio
BARS | If you're hitting only one bar in North Beach, it should be this one. The low-ceilinged second floor of this raucous boho saloon hangout, little altered since its 1960s heyday (when Jack Kerouac frequented the place), is a fine vantage point for watching the colorful Broadway and Columbus Avenue intersection. Another part of Vesuvio's appeal is its

diverse clientele, from older neighborhood regulars and young couples to bacchanalian posses. ⊠ *255 Columbus Ave., at Broadway, North Beach* ☎ *415/362–3370* ⊕ *www.vesuvio.com.*

 Shopping

San Francisco Rock Posters & Collectibles
ANTIQUES & COLLECTIBLES | The huge selection of rock-and-roll memorabilia, including posters, handbills, and original art, makes this spot a groovy cave for the nostalgic vintage '60s. Also available are posters from more recent shows, many at the legendary Fillmore Auditorium. ⊠ *1851 Powell St., between Filbert and Greenwich Sts., North Beach* ☎ *415/956–6749* ⊕ *rockposters.com.*

Fisherman's Wharf

Although it was once where families made a living off the sea, today fewer fishing boats depart from here, and more of the wharf survives on tourist dollars—hence the abundance of overpriced eateries alongside cheap T-shirt and souvenir shops.

There are, however, things worth experiencing. Explore maritime history aboard the fabulous ships of the Hyde Street Pier, amuse yourself with the early-20th-century mechanical diversions at Musée Mécanique, and grab some chowder or Dungeness crab from a stand along Jefferson Street for a taste (and distinct shellfish aroma) of what Fisherman's Wharf is really all about.

⊙ Sights

Hyde Street Pier
HISTORY MUSEUM | FAMILY | If you want to get to the heart of the Wharf, there's no better place to do it than at this pier. Don't pass up the centerpiece collection of historic vessels, part of the San Francisco Maritime National Historical Park, almost all of which can be boarded. The *Balclutha,* an 1886 full-rigged three-masted sailing vessel that's more than 250 feet long, sailed around Cape Horn 17 times. Kids especially love the *Eureka,* a side-wheel passenger and car ferry, for her onboard collection of vintage cars. The *Hercules* is a steam-powered tugboat, and the *C. A. Thayer* is a beautifully restored three-masted schooner.

Across the street from the pier and a museum in itself is the maritime park's Visitor Center (⊠ *499 Jefferson St.* ☎ *415/447–5000*), whose fun, large-scale exhibits make it an engaging stop. See a huge First Order Fresnel lighthouse lens from the Farallon Islands and a shipwrecked boat. Then stroll through time in the exhibit "The Waterfront," where you can touch the timber from a gold rush–era ship recovered from below the Financial District, peek into 19th-century storefronts, and see the sails of an Italian fishing vessel. ⊠ *Hyde and Jefferson Sts., Fisherman's Wharf* ☎ *415/447-5000* ⊕ *www.nps.gov/safr* 🎟 *Ships $15 (ticket good for 7 days)*

Musée Mécanique
OTHER MUSEUM | FAMILY | Once a staple at Playland at the Beach, San Francisco's early-20th-century amusement park, the antique mechanical contrivances at this time-warp arcade—including peep shows and nickelodeons—make it one of the most worthwhile attractions at the Wharf. Some favorites are the giant and rather creepy "Laffing Sal"; an arm-wrestling machine; the world's only steam-powered motorcycle; and mechanical fortune-telling figures that speak from their curtained boxes. Note the depictions of race that betray the prejudices of the time: stoned Chinese figures in the "Opium-Den" and clown-faced African Americans eating watermelon in the "Mechanical Farm." ■TIP→ Admission is free, but you'll need quarters to bring the machines to life. ⊠ *Pier 45, Shed A, Fisherman's Wharf* ☎ *415/346–2000* ⊕ *museemecaniquesf.com* 🎟 *Free.*

Pier 39

STORE/MALL | **FAMILY** | The city's most popular waterfront attraction draws millions of visitors each year, who come to browse through its shops and concessions hawking every conceivable form of souvenir. The pier can be quite crowded, and the numerous street performers may leave you feeling more harassed than entertained. Arriving early in the morning ensures you a front-row view of the sea lions that bask here, but be aware that most stores don't open until 9:30 or 10 (later in winter).

Follow the sound of barking to the northwest side of the pier to view the sea lions flopping about the floating docks. During the summer, orange-clad naturalists offer fascinating facts about the playful pinnipeds—for example, that most of the animals here are males.

At the Aquarium of the Bay (⊕ *aquariumofthebay.org*), moving walkways transport you through a space surrounded on three sides by water filled with indigenous San Francisco Bay marine life, from the orange Garibaldi (the state marine fish) to sharks. ⊠ *Beach St., at Embarcadero, Fisherman's Wharf* ☎ *415/705–5500* ⊕ *www.pier39.com.*

San Francisco National Maritime Museum

HISTORY MUSEUM | **FAMILY** | You'll feel as if you're out to sea when you step inside this sturdy, ship-shape (literally), Streamline-Moderne structure, dubbed the Bathhouse Building and built in 1939 as part of the New Deal's Works Progress Administration. The first floor of the museum, part of the San Francisco Maritime National Historical Park, has stunningly restored undersea dreamscape murals and some of the museum's intricate ship models. The first-floor balcony overlooks the beach and has lovely WPA-era tile designs. ■**TIP→ If you've got young kids in tow, the museum makes a great quick, free stop. Then pick up ice cream at Ghirardelli Square across the** street **and enjoy it on the beach or next door in Victorian Park, where you can watch the cable cars turn around.** ⊠ *Aquatic Park, foot of Polk St., Fisherman's Wharf* ☎ *415/447–5000* ⊕ *www.nps.gov/safr* ⊘ *Closed Mon. and Tues.*

 Restaurants

Gary Danko

$$$$ | **MODERN AMERICAN** | This classic for prix-fixe dining has earned legions of fans—and a Michelin star—for its refined and creative seasonal California cooking, displayed in dishes like glazed oysters with Ossetra caviar and juniper-crusted venison. The banquette-lined rooms, with stunning floral arrangements, are as memorable as the food and impeccable service. **Known for:** table-side cheese cart; soufflé for dessert; reservations are hard to get. Ⓢ *Average main: $122* ⊠ *800 N. Point St., Fisherman's Wharf* ☎ *415/749–2060* ⊕ *garydanko.com* ⊘ *Closed Tues. and Wed. No lunch.*

🛏 Hotels

Hotel Zoe Fisherman's Wharf

$ | **HOTEL** | A little removed from the heart of the wharf area craziness, this smart-looking boutique hotel with guest-room interiors inspired by luxury Mediterranean yachts aims for subtle contemporary elegance in the form of lightly stained woods and soft-brown and cream fabrics and walls. **Pros:** cozy feeling; nice desks and sitting areas in rooms; open-air courtyard with firepits. **Cons:** congested touristy area; smaller rooms can feel too tight; no on-site fitness center. Ⓢ *Rooms from: $190* ⊠ *425 N. Point St., at Mason St., Fisherman's Wharf* ☎ *415/561–1100, 800/648–4626* ⊕ *www.hotelzoesf.com* ⟿ *221 rooms* ❌ *No Meals.*

Kimpton Alton Hotel

$$ | **HOTEL** | **FAMILY** | A breath of fresh air in touristy Fisherman's Wharf, the popular

Thousands of visitors take ferries to Alcatraz each day to walk in the footsteps of the notorious criminals who were held on "The Rock."

and approachable boutique hotel chain is hands down the leading hotel option for travelers on the waterfront between the Presidio and the downtown area. **Pros:** outstanding in-house restaurant; a chain that doesn't feel like a chain; nicely sized rooms in all tiers. **Cons:** remote location; limited natural light; small bathroom sinks. [$] *Rooms from: $209* ✉ *2700 Jones St., Fisherman's Wharf* ☎ *771–9000, 833/642–9132 reservations* 🌐 *altonhotelsf.com* 🛏 *248 rooms* 🍴 *No Meals.*

Nightlife

★ The Buena Vista

CAFÉS | At the end of the Hyde Street cable-car line, the Buena Vista packs 'em in for its famous Irish coffee—which, according to owners, was the first served stateside (in 1952). The place oozes nostalgia with its white-jacketed bartenders and timeless atmosphere, drawing devoted locals as well as out-of-towners relaxing after a day of sightseeing. It's narrow and can get crowded, but this spot is a sip of history and provides a fine alternative to the overpriced tourist joints nearby. ✉ *2765 Hyde St., at Beach St., Fisherman's Wharf* ☎ *415/474–5044* 🌐 *www.thebuenavista.com.*

Embarcadero

San Francisco's flat, accessible waterfront invites you to get up close and personal with the bay. Most visitors are lured to the northern waterfront by Fisherman's Wharf and Pier 39. Between the wharf and Bay Bridge and South Beach Park, though, you'll find tourists and San Franciscans alike soaking up the sun, strolling out over the water on a long pier, enjoying the gastronomic pleasures of the Ferry Building, or watching street performers in Embarcadero Plaza. This area is also the departure point for cruises to Alcatraz.

Sights

★ Alcatraz

JAIL/PRISON | FAMILY | Thousands of visitors come every day to walk in the footsteps of Alcatraz's notorious criminals. The stories of life and death on "the Rock" may sometimes be exaggerated, but it's almost impossible to resist the chance to wander the cell block that tamed the country's toughest gangsters and saw daring escape attempts of tremendous desperation. Fewer than 2,000 inmates ever did time on the Rock, including Al "Scarface" Capone, Robert "The Birdman" Stroud, and George "Machine Gun Kelly."

Some tips for escaping to Alcatraz: (1) Buy your ticket in advance. Visit the website for Alcatraz Cruises to scout out available departure times for the ferry. (2) Dress smart. Bring a jacket to ward off the chill from the boat ride and wear comfortable shoes. (3) Go for the evening tour. The evening tour has programs not offered during the day, the bridge-to-bridge view of the city twinkles at night, and your "prison experience" will be amplified as darkness falls. (4) Be mindful of scheduled and limited-capacity talks.

The boat ride to the island is brief (15 minutes) but affords beautiful views of the city, Marin County, and the East Bay. The audio tour, highly recommended, includes observations by guards and prisoners about life in one of America's most notorious penal colonies. Plan your schedule to allow at least three hours for the visit and boat rides combined. ⊠ *Pier 33, Embarcadero* ☎ *415/981–7625* ⊕ *www.nps.gov/alca* ⌑ *From $42.*

★ Exploratorium

SCIENCE MUSEUM | FAMILY | Walking into this fascinating museum of "science, art, and human perception" is like visiting a mad-scientist's laboratory, but one in which most of the exhibits are super-ize and you can play with everything. gnature experiential exhibits include the Tinkering Studio and a glass Bay Observatory building, where the exhibits help visitors better understand what they see outside. Get an Alice-in-Wonderland feeling in the Distorted Room, where you seem to shrink and grow as you walk across the slanted, checkered floor. In the Shadow Box, a powerful flash freezes an image of your shadow on the wall; jumping is a favorite pose. More than 650 other exhibits focus on sea and insect life, computers, electricity, patterns and light, language, the weather, and more. Don't miss a walk around the outside of the museum afterward for superb views and a lesson about the bay's sediment and water motion in the Bay Windows presentation. ⊠ *Pier 15, Embarcadero* ☎ *415/528–4444 general information* ⊕ *www.exploratorium.edu* ⌑ *$40* ⊘ *Closed Mon.*

★ Ferry Building

MARKET | The jewel of the Embarcadero, erected in 1896 and now home to an outstanding food marketplace, is topped by a 230-foot clock tower modeled after the campanile of the cathedral in Seville, Spain. On the morning of April 18, 1906, the tower's four clock faces stopped at 5:17—the moment the great earthquake struck—and stayed still for 12 months.

Today San Franciscans flock to the street-level marketplace, stocking up on supplies from local favorites such as Acme Bread, Blue Bottle Coffee, El Porteño (empanadas), the gluten-free Mariposa Baking Company, and Humphry Slocombe (ice cream). For sit-down dining, there's the Hog Island Oyster Company and the seasonal Californian duo of Bouli Bar and Boulette's Larder. On the plaza side, the outdoor tables at Gott's Roadside and Fort Point Ferry Building offer great people-watching and excellent casual bites and sips. On Saturday morning the plazas outside the building buzz with an upscale farmers' market. Extending south from the piers north of the building to the Bay Bridge, the waterfront promenade out front is a favorite among joggers and picnickers, with a view of sailboats plying the bay. True to its name, the Ferry Building still serves actual ferries: from its eastern flank they sail to Sausalito, Larkspur, Tiburon, Angel Island, and the East Bay. ✉ *Embarcadero, 1 Ferry Bldg., at foot of Market St., Embarcadero* ☎ *415/983–8000* 🌐 *www.ferrybuildingmarketplace.com.*

F-line

TRANSPORTATION | The city's system of vintage electric trolleys, the F-line, gives the cable cars a run for their money as a beloved mode of transportation. The beautifully restored streetcars—some dating from the 19th century—run from the Castro District down Market Street to the Embarcadero, then north to Fisherman's Wharf. Each car is unique, restored to the colors of its city of origin, from New Orleans and Philadelphia to Melbourne and Milan. **■TIP→ Pay with a Clipper card or purchase tickets on board; exact change is required.** ✉ *Embarcadero* 🌐 *www.streetcar.org* 🎫 *$3.*

San Francisco Railway Museum

OTHER MUSEUM | FAMILY | A labor of love from the same vintage-transit enthusiasts responsible for the F-line's revival, this one-room museum and store celebrates the city's streetcars and cable cars with photographs, models, and artifacts. The permanent exhibit includes the replicated end of a streetcar with a working cab—complete with controls and a bell—for kids to explore; the cool, antique Wiley birdcage traffic signal; and models and display cases to view. Right on the F-line track, just across from the Ferry Building, this is a great quick stop. ✉ *77 Steuart St., Embarcadero* ☎ *415/974–1948* 🌐 *www.streetcar.org/museum* 🎫 *Free* ⏲ *Closed Sun. and Mon.*

🍴 Restaurants

Angler

$$$ | SEAFOOD | Immaculately fresh seafood and a wood-burning hearth are the centerpieces of this bustling yet luxurious sibling to Saison. The menu descriptions might be brief, but it's really all about the ingredients and impeccable technique—whether it's a grilled hand-dived scallop or the signature thinly sliced potato with Sonoma cheeses—fulfilling their full potential on the plate with a few smart embellishments. **Known for:** taxidermy-filled back room with Bay Bridge views; tuna tartare with tomato jelly; Instagram-favorite radicchio salad. [$] *Average main: $39* ✉ *132 The Embarcadero, Embarcadero* ☎ *415/872–9442* 🌐 *anglerrestaurants.com/san-francisco* ⏲ *No lunch Sun. and Mon.*

Hog Island Oyster Company

$$ | SEAFOOD | A thriving oyster farm north of San Francisco in Tomales Bay serves up its harvest at this raw bar and restaurant in the Ferry Building, where devotees come for impeccably fresh oysters and clams on the half shell. Other mollusk-centered options include first-rate clam chowder, grilled oysters, and steamed mussels and clams; the kitchen also makes one of the city's best grilled cheese sandwiches. **Known for:** crowds slurping dozens of oysters; local produce salads; superior Bloody Mary. [$] *Average main: $23* ✉ *1 Ferry Bldg., Embarcadero at Market St., Embarcadero* ☎ *415/391–7117* 🌐 *hogislandoysters.com.*

Waterbar

$$$$ | SEAFOOD | Come for seafood wi view: sky-high aquariums dominat dining room, and the bay is just but the biggest attraction is th Every fin and shell of the sea oak-roasted striped bass to from the Mendocino Coa sourced. **Known for:** cured fish and iced shellfish starters; always feels like a celebration; delightful Pat Kuleto–designed interior. [$] *Average main: $42* ⊠ *399 The Embarcadero, between Folsom and Harrison Sts., Embarcadero* ☎ *415/284–9922* ⊕ *www.waterbarsf.com.*

Financial District

In the latter half of the 19th century, when San Francisco was a brawling gold-rush town, the area that is now the Financial District (FiDi, for short) was underwater. Yerba Buena Cove reached all the way up to Montgomery Street, and what's now Jackson Square—a genteel neighborhood between North Beach and FiDi—was the heart of the Barbary Coast, home to some of the world's roughest wharves. Indeed, more than 100 ships abandoned by frantic crews and passengers caught up in gold fever are buried under the foundations of buildings along Montgomery Street.

Today the area is all office towers—including the iconic Transamerica Pyramid building—and when the sun sets, the streets empty out fast. The few sights here will appeal mainly to gold-rush history enthusiasts; others can spend time elsewhere.

◉ Sights

Jackson Square Historic District

HISTORIC DISTRICT | This was the heart of the Barbary Coast of the Gay '90s—the 90s, that is. Although most of the night district was destroyed in the fire that followed the 1906 earthquake, the old redbrick buildings, many now occupied by advertising offices, and antiques firms, the romance and rowdiness of San Francisco's early days.

Old rush–era buildings on Montgomery

Street just barely evokes the Barbary Coast days, but this was a colorful block in the 19th century and on into the 20th. Writers Mark Twain and Bret Harte were among the contributors to the spunky *The Golden Era* newspaper, which occupied No. 732 (now part of the building at No. 744).

Restored 19th-century brick buildings line Hotaling Place, which connects Washington and Jackson Streets; it's named for the A. P. Hotaling Company whiskey distillery, the largest liquor repository on the West Coast in its day. The exceptional Gold Rush City walking tour offered by City Guides (☎ *415/557–4266*) brings this area's history to life. ⊠ *Bordered by Columbus Ave., Broadway, and Washington and Sansome Sts., Financial District.*

Wells Fargo History Museum

HISTORY MUSEUM | At this fun two-story museum, you can get a taste of the early years of the gold rush when San Francisco had no formal banks and miners often entrusted their gold dust to saloon keepers. In 1852, Wells Fargo opened its first bank in the city on this block, and the company soon established banking offices in mother-lode camps throughout California. One popular exhibit is a simulated ride in a replica of an early stagecoach. The museum also displays samples of nuggets and gold dust from mines, an old telegraph machine on which you can practice sending codes, and tools the '49ers used to coax gold from the ground. ⊠ *420 Montgomery St., Financial District* ☎ *415/396–2619* ⊕ *www.wellsfargohistory.com* ⌨ *Free* ⊙ *Closed weekends.*

🍴 Restaurants

Cotogna

$$$ | **ITALIAN** | The draw at this urban trattoria is chef Michael Tusk's flavorful, rustic, seasonally driven Italian cooking, headlined by pastas, beautifully grilled or spit-roasted meats, and homemade

gelato. The look inside and outside is comfortably chic, with wood tables, quality stemware, and fantastic Italian wines by the bottle and glass. **Known for:** raviolo with brown butter and egg in center; tough to get reservations; peak seasonal produce in antipasti. $ *Average main: $38* ✉ *490 Pacific Ave., Financial District* ☎ *415/775–8508* ⊕ *www.cotognasf.com* ⊘ *Closed Sun. and Mon.*

Terminus Cafe and Bar
$ | **AMERICAN** | With coffee, sandwiches, and salads by day, and superb drinks at night, this spot right by the California St. cable car terminus is a charming place to visit. Its atmosphere is refreshingly low-key for FiDi—the rare downtown establishment that feels like a true neighborhood gathering place. **Known for:** excellent kale salad; relaxed atmosphere; not flashy yet unique cocktails. $ *Average main: $12* ✉ *16 California St., Financial District* ☎ *415/960–8405* ⊕ *terminussf.com.*

Wayfare Tavern
$$$ | **AMERICAN** | This energetic and upscale American tavern owned by TV chef and personality Tyler Florence is rich with upscale turn-of-the-20th-century Americana, including brick walls, comfortable booths, and a billiards room. It also tips its hat to tradition—and comfort—on the menu with deviled eggs, fresh seafood, and several signature dishes that are considered the best of their categories in the city (the burger with Marin Brie, for one), plus noteworthy cocktails that complete the full experience. **Known for:** buttermilk-brined fried chicken with herbs; giant warm popovers start each meal; house-made doughnuts. $ *Average main: $34* ✉ *558 Sacramento St., Financial District* ☎ *415/722–9060* ⊕ *www.wayfaretavern.com.*

Yank Sing
$ | **CHINESE** | This bustling, lunch-only restaurant serves some of San Francisco's best dim sum to office workers on weekdays and boisterous families on weekends, and the take-out counter makes a satisfying meal on the run. The several dozen varieties prepared daily include the classic and the creative; steamed pork buns, shrimp dumplings, scallop skewers, and basil seafood dumplings are among the many delights. **Known for:** Peking duck on weekends; Shanghai soup dumplings; energetic vibe. $ *Average main: $16* ✉ *49 Stevenson St., Financial District* ☎ *415/541–4949* ⊕ *yanksing.com* ⊘ *No dinner.*

Hotels

Galleria Park Hotel
$ | **HOTEL** | At the edge of the FiDi and Union Square areas, this boutique hotel manages to be both hip and welcoming, with modern touches on historical bones and smallish guest rooms with all the technological amenities modern travelers require. **Pros:** park terrace with walking track; complimentary wine at daily Sipping Hour; in-house Blue Bottle Coffee. **Cons:** relatively small deluxe rooms; city noise; no restaurant. $ *Rooms from: $179* ✉ *191 Sutter St., Financial District* ☎ *415/781-3060* ⊕ *www.galleriapark.com* ⇨ *177 rooms* ⊘| *No Meals.*

The Marina

After the 1989 Loma Prieta earthquake, affluent residents seeking more-solid ground flooded the Marina, changing the tenor of this formerly low-key neighborhood. A bank became a Williams-Sonoma store; the local grocer gave way to a Pottery Barn. Nowadays, a young, fairly homogeneous, well-to-do crowd floods area cafés and bars on weekends.

Sights

★ Palace of Fine Arts
NOTABLE BUILDING | This stunning, r rococo palace on a lagoon seem from another world—it's the so

of the many tinted-plaster structures (a temporary neoclassical city of sorts) built for the 1915 Panama-Pacific International Exposition, the world's fair that celebrated San Francisco's recovery from the 1906 earthquake and fire. The expo buildings originally extended about a mile along the shore. Bernard Maybeck designed this faux-Roman classic beauty, which was reconstructed in concrete and reopened in 1967.

The pseudo-Latin language adorning the Palace's exterior urns continues to stump scholars. The massive columns (each topped with four "weeping maidens"), great rotunda, and swan-filled lagoon have been used in countless fashion layouts, films, and wedding photo shoots. Other than its use for major events and exhibitions inside the building, it's really an outdoor architecture attraction that's perfect for an hour of strolling and relaxing. After admiring the lagoon, look across the street to the house at 3460 Baker Street. If the statues out front look familiar, they should—they're original casts of the "garland ladies" you can see in the Palace's colonnade. ✉ *3301 Lyon St., at Beach St., Marina* ☎ *415/886–1296* 🌐 *palaceoffinearts.com* 🎫 *Free.*

🍴 Restaurants

A16

$$$ | ITALIAN | Named after a highway that runs through southern Italy, this bustling contemporary trattoria specializes in the food from that region, done very, very well. The menu is stocked with pizza, rustic pastas like maccaronara with ragù Napoletano (a meat sauce), and entrées like braised short rib with polenta. **nown for:** spicy arrabbiata pizza; one of e city's best Italian wine programs; chocolate budino tart. [$] *Average $38* ✉ *2355 Chestnut St., Marina 771–2216* 🌐 *www.a16pizza.com nch Mon.–Thurs.*

Causwells

$$ | AMERICAN | There are two personalities to Chestnut Street's sleek grown-up diner—the double-stack burger that draws burger hounds from dozens of miles away, and the rest of the honest, spruced-up comfort-food menu. It's a local institution that feels partially like a bistro and partially like a modern tavern, and a place where the buzz from the innovative cocktails and delicious eats never disappears. **Known for:** banana bread "grilled cheese"; excellent brunch; always feels like a party. [$] *Average main: $22* ✉ *2346 Chestnut St., Marina* ☎ *415/447–6081* 🌐 *www.causwells.com* ⏲ *Closed Mon. No lunch Tues.–Thurs.*

Greens

$$ | VEGETARIAN | Even as diet trends come and go, this vegetable-focused icon (opened in 1979) continues to be a steadfast favorite for carnivores and vegetarians alike. Despite the lack of meat, the hearty and creative dishes—such as griddle cakes with crimson lentils and spiced cashew cream—really satisfy, and floor-to-ceiling windows give diners a sweeping view of the Marina and the Golden Gate Bridge. **Known for:** magnificent wood-heavy decor; delightful fresh spring rolls filled with locally made tofu; seasonal produce–driven pizzas. [$] *Average main: $30* ✉ *Fort Mason Center, 2 Marina Blvd., Bldg. A, Marina* ☎ *415/771–6222* 🌐 *greensrestaurant.com* ⏲ *Closed Mon.*

🍸 Nightlife

California Wine Merchant

WINE BARS | Part cluttered shop, part cozy bar, Chestnut Street's marquee wine destination is a longtime favorite for grabbing a glass or three. Featured wines come from some of the state's most highly regarded vintners of all sizes and celebrity standings. The neighborhood has many wine bars, but this is where the locals go when the focus is on the wine itself. ✉ *2113 Chestnut St., Marina*

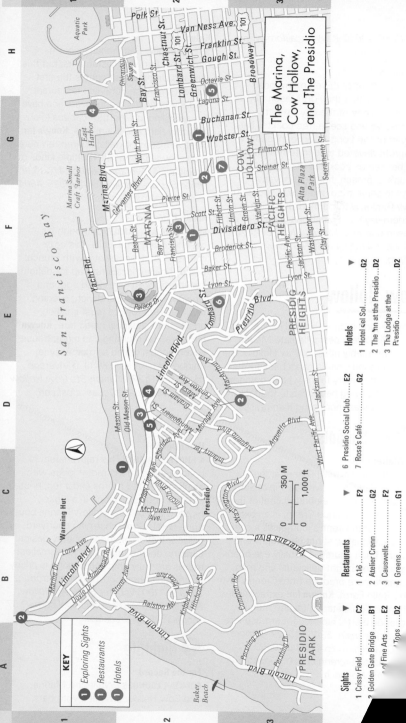

The Marina, Cow Hollow, and The Presidio

KEY

- 1 Exploring Sights
- 1 Restaurants
- 1 Hotels

San Francisco Bay

Aquatic Park

Warming Hut

Presidio

PRESIDIO PARK

Baker Beach

PRESIDIO HEIGHTS

PACIFIC HEIGHTS

COW HOLLOW

MARINA

0   350 M
0   1,000 ft

☎ *415/567–0646* ⊕ *www.californiawine-merchant.com.*

The Interval

COCKTAIL LOUNGES | Even many locals don't realize that the Fort Mason Center is home to one of the city's most impressive and scene-free cocktail bars. As part of the Long Now Foundation, a nonprofit devoted to long-term thinking, the bar serves cocktails that reflect the group's approach, finding innovative ways to serve tried-and-true libations. The Navy Gimlet with clarified lime juice is a modern-day San Francisco classic. ⊠ *Fort Mason Center, 2 Marina Blvd., Bldg. A, Marina* ☎ *415/561–6582* ⊕ *www.theinterval.org.*

Cow Hollow

Between old-money Pacific Heights and the well-heeled, postcollegiate Marina lies comfortably upscale Cow Hollow. The neighborhood's name harks back to the 19th-century dairy farms whose owners eked out a living here despite the fact that there was more sand than grass.

 Restaurants

★ **Atelier Crenn**

$$$ | **MODERN FRENCH** | Dinner at the spectacularly inventive flagship of San Francisco's most celebrated chef of the moment, Dominique Crenn, is an exploration of both Crenn's journey as a chef and California's distinct geography and history. Each course is usually eye-opening (and downright delicious) and many dishes feature produce from Crenn's own Bleu Belle Farm. **Known for:** extraordinary, whimsical pescatarian tasting menu; ˌellar desserts; hip-elegant atmosphere. ˌverage main: $365 ⊠ 3127 Fillmore ˌow Hollow ☎ 415/440–0460 ˌw.ateliercrenn.com ⊙ Closed Sun. ˌn. No lunch.

Kaiyo

$$ | **PERUVIAN** | San Francisco has a handful of Peruvian restaurants, but this uber-hip Union Street spot is the first Nikkei (Japanese-Peruvian) restaurant. Skip the pedestrian appetizers and have fun sampling around the *tiraditos* (dishes with raw fish) and sushi rolls. **Known for:** creative pisco cocktails; shrimp tempura and yellowtail Lima roll; multiple kinds of "cebiche". $ *Average main: $24* ⊠ *1838 Union St., Cow Hollow* ☎ *415/525–4804* ⊕ *kaiyosf.com* ⊙ *Closed Mon.*

Rose's Café

$$ | **AMERICAN** | **FAMILY** | Although it's open morning until night, this cozy café is most synonymous with brunch. Sleepy-headed locals turn up for delights like the smoked ham, fried egg, and Gruyère breakfast sandwich; evening favorites lean toward roast chicken, pastas, and seasonal-rustic fare. **Known for:** pizzas for morning and night; house-baked goods; grilled salmon cozy (a unique pita-like sandwich). $ *Average main: $28* ⊠ *2298 Union St., Cow Hollow* ☎ *415/775–2200* ⊕ *rosescafesf.com.*

Hotels

Hotel Del Sol

$ | **HOTEL** | **FAMILY** | This rejuvenated, beach-theme 1950s motor lodge with nicely appointed rooms and a fun, heated outdoor pool is all alone in a higher, hipper class of Cow Hollow/Marina boutique hotels. **Pros:** charming courtyard; great selection of suites; cheery design. **Cons:** no on-site fitness center; smallest rooms are truly tiny; self parking is pricey for the neighborhood. $ *Rooms from: $129* ⊠ *3100 Webster St., Cow Hollow* ☎ *415/921–5520* ⊕ *hoteldelsol.com* ⇌ *57 rooms* ❈ *Free Breakfast.*

Nightlife

For the Record

COCKTAIL LOUNGES | While the Marina and Cow Hollow are filled with bars, this throwback record album–themed charmer is surprisingly the only (non-restaurant-affiliated) craft cocktail bar in the area. The sharply designed space has a clubby meets groovy feel with tufted leather banquettes and Summer of Love floral wallpaper. Cocktails are ambitious and exciting but, like the bar's atmosphere, completely free of pretension. ⊠ 2120 Greenwich St., Cow Hollow ☎ 415/855–4607 ⊕ fortherecordsf.com ⊗ Closed Mon.

Shopping

ATYS

OTHER ACCESSORIES | Gadgets and home accessories with a sleek modern design are imported from all over Europe and Japan and sold at this charming store in a courtyard off Union Street. Among the eye-catching items are a Mies cuckoo clock and a wine rack made of leather loops. ⊠ 2149B Union St., between Fillmore and Webster Sts., Cow Hollow ☎ 415/441–9220 ⊕ atysdesign.com ⊗ Closed Mon.

Current

WOMEN'S CLOTHING | Located a few blocks off of Union Street, this shop's name perfectly sums up how in vogue its selection of women's clothing is. The boutique keeps thing edgy and comfortable but never veers too far in either direction for stylish tops, pants, skirts, dresses, and even colorful cardigans. It is without question a San Francisco favorite for contemporary, fun, but functional designs. ⊠ 3108 Fillmore St., Cow Hollow ⊕ shop-current.com.

The Presidio

At the foot of the Golden Gate Bridge, one of city residents' favorite in-town getaways is the 1,400-plus-acre Presidio, which combines accessible nature-in-the-raw with a window into the past.

Sights

Crissy Field

NATURE SIGHT | FAMILY | One of the most popular places for San Franciscans to get fresh air is this stretch of restored marshland along the sand of the bay, part of the Golden Gate National Recreation Area. Kids on bikes, folks walking dogs, and joggers share the paved path along the shore, often winding up at the Warming Hut, a combination café and fun gift store at its end, for a hot chocolate in the shadow of the Golden Gate Bridge. Midway along the Golden Gate Promenade that winds along the shore is the Greater Farallones National Marine Sanctuary Visitor Center, where kids can get a close-up view of small sea creatures and learn about the rich ecosystem offshore. Alongside the main green of Crissy Field, several renovated airplane hangars and warehouses are now home to the likes of rock-climbing gyms, an air trampoline park, and a craft brewery (the latter is not open to the public). The Quartermaster Reach Marsh by Crissy Field was reclaimed as wetland ecosystem in 2020 and is an excellent area to see some of the local bird population. ⊠ 1199 E. Beach, San Francisco ⊹ Area north of Mason St. between Baker St. and Marine Dr. ⊕ www.presidio.gov/places/crissy-field.

★ Golden Gate Bridge

BRIDGE | Instantly recognizable as an icon of San Francisco, the two reddish-orange towers of the majestic Golden Gate Bridge rise 750 feet over the Golden Gate strait at the mouth of San Francisco Bay, linking the city and Marin County. With its simple but powerful art-deco design, the 1.7-mile suspension span was built to withstand winds of more than 100 mph. It's also not a bad place to b an earthquake: designed to sway alm 28 feet, the Golden Gate Bridge (ur the Bay Bridge) was undamaged b 1989 Loma Prieta quake. If you're on the bridge when it's windy, stand still and you can feel it swaying a bit.

Crossing the Golden Gate Bridge under your own power is exhilarating—a little scary, and definitely chilly. From the bridge's eastern-side walkway, the only side pedestrians are allowed on, you can take in the San Francisco skyline and the bay islands; look west for the wild hills of the Marin Headlands, the curving coast south to Lands End, and the Pacific Ocean. On sunny days, sailboats dot the water, and brave windsurfers test the often-treacherous tides beneath the bridge. A vista point on the Marin County side provides a spectacular city panorama.

A structural engineer, dreamer, and poet named Joseph Strauss worked tirelessly for 20 years to make the bridge a reality, first promoting the idea of it and then overseeing design and construction. Though the final structure bore little resemblance to his original plan, Strauss guarded his legacy jealously, refusing to recognize the seminal contributions of engineer Charles Ellis. In 2007, the Golden Gate Bridge district finally recognized Ellis's role, though Strauss, who died less than a year after the bridge's opening day in 1937, would doubtless be pleased with the inscription on his statue, which stands sentry in the southern parking lot: "The Man Who Built the Bridge."

At the outdoor exhibits near the bridge's Welcome Center, you can learn about the features that make it art deco and read about the personalities behind its design and construction. For some pre– or post–bridge walk fuel, there is an Equator Coffees café in the historic Round House t the visitor's plaza. City Guides (⊕ sfc-guides.org) offers free walking tours he bridge every Thursday and Sunday am. ⊠ Lincoln Blvd., near Doyle Dr. rt Point, San Francisco ☎ 415/921–www.goldengate.org ⧖ Free.

★ Presidio Tunnel Tops

CITY PARK | FAMILY | With how seamlessly the Presidio Tunnel Tops landscape flows from the Presidio's Main Parade Lawn downhill to Crissy Field, it's almost impossible to envision the two not being connected. Yet, that was always the case until this impressive 14-acre green space with 1.8 miles of winding walking paths was completed in 2022. It's a park that is both function (bringing together two important areas atop a highway tunnel) and form (beautifully designed by James Corner Field Operations, the same firm that designed New York City's acclaimed High Line elevated park).

The Presidio Tunnel Tops are a marquee destination for many reasons, but there's no escaping that the park is best known for its panoramic view of the Golden Gate Bridge. There's plenty more to do, from grabbing lunch from a visiting food truck or letting kids explore the impressive 2-acre Outpost playground that tells the Presidio's extensive history and evokes its natural habitat. There are three lawn areas for picnicking, a Campfire Circle where ranger talks are given, and 200,000 plants to gaze at.

Altogether, it's a fun breath of fresh air— and it's hard to believe that you're literally on top of the busy 101 highway. After exploring the Presidio Tunnel Tops, make sure to head over to their lesser-known "above the highway" park sibling, Battery Bluff. This park doesn't have the activities or amenities that makes the Tunnel Tops such a draw, but it's worth a visit for the views and to see the four preserved historic gun batteries. ⊠ 210 Lincoln Blvd., Presidio ☎ 415/561–4323 ⊕ presidiotunneltops.gov.

Walt Disney Family Museum

HISTORY MUSEUM | FAMILY | This beautifully refurbished brick barracks is a tribute to the man behind Mickey Mouse, Disney Studios, and Disneyland. The smartly organized displays include hundreds of family photos, and well-chosen videos play throughout. Disney's legendary attention to detail is evident in the cels and footage of *Fantasia*, *Sleeping Beauty*, and other animation classics. Galleries tell the story of Disney's life from his youth in the Midwest to lesser-known bits of his professional history, like the films Walt Disney made for the U.S. military during World War II. The liveliest exhibit, and the largest gallery, documents the creation of Disneyland with a fun, detailed model of what Disney imagined the park would be. Teacups spin, the Matterhorn looms, and that world-famous castle leads the way to Fantasyland. You won't be the first to leave humming "It's a Small World." In the final gallery, a series of cartoons and quotes chronicle the world's reaction to Disney's sudden death. Worth checking for are periodic special exhibitions that take a deep dive into film themes or historical periods surrounding Disney's life. ✉ *Main Post, 104 Montgomery St., off Lincoln Blvd., San Francisco* ☎ *415/345–6800* 🌐 *www.waltdisney.org* 🎟 *$25* 🕒 *Closed Mon.–Wed.*

Beaches

★ Baker Beach

BEACH | FAMILY | West of the Golden Gate Bridge is a mile-long stretch of soft sand beneath steep cliffs, beloved for its spectacular views and laid-back vibe (read: good chance you'll see naked people here on the northernmost end). Its isolated location makes it rarely crowded, but many San Franciscans know that there is no better place to take in the sunset than this beach. Kids love climbing around the old Battery Chamberlin. This is truly one of those places that inspires local pride. **Amenities:** parking (no fee); toilets. **Best for:** nudists; solitude; sunsets. ✉ *Baker Beach, San Francisco* ✥ *Accessed from Bowley St. off Lincoln Blvd.* 🌐 *www.parksconservancy.org* 🎟 *Free.*

Restaurants

Presidio Social Club

$$ | AMERICAN | FAMILY | American comfort classics meet seasonal California cooking in this restaurant in an old barracks building at the eastern edge of the Presidio. The restaurant has a blend of the nostalgic past and the trendy present (deviled eggs with smoked salmon and furikake; grilled beef liver and onions; homemade cheesecake), as well as a lively bar and ample patio seating that allows diners to soak up the Presidio's outdoor beauty. **Known for:** East–West chicken soup; popular brunch; barrel-aged cocktails. [$] *Average main: $29* ✉ *563 Ruger St., San Francisco* ☎ *415/885–1888* 🌐 *www.presidiosocialclub.com* 🕒 *Closed Mon. and Tues. No lunch Wed.*

Hotels

The Inn at the Presidio

$$ | B&B/INN | Built in 1903, this two-story, Georgian revival–style structure once served as officers' quarters but these days is a standout boutique hotel where the rooms and suites have a nice sense of modern refinement and historical touches varying by the room, such as wrought-iron beds, vintage black-and-white photos, and Pendleton blankets. **Pros:** beautifully designed rooms, some with gas fireplaces; peaceful vibe; evening wine-and-cheese reception by firepits. **Cons:** lack of noise-blocking because of old building; two-night minimum on weekends; challenging to get a taxi. [$] *Rooms from: $350* ✉ *42 Moraga Ave., San Francisco* ☎ *415/800–7356* 🌐 *www.presidiolodging.com* 🛏 *26 rooms* 🍴 *Free Breakfast.*

★ The Lodge at the Presidio

$$ | B&B/INN | The three-story Lodge occupies former Army barracks, built in the 1890s, and is at the Main Post green's northwestern edge, allowing some rooms to have Golden Gate Bridge views; all rooms are far more upscale

Armed with only helmets, safety harnesses, and painting equipment, a full-time crew of 38 painters keeps the Golden Gate Bridge clad in International Orange.

and chic than military accommodations, with large flat-screen TVs, well-appointed bathrooms, workstations, and dreamy, custom-made pillow-top mattresses. **Pros:** gorgeous, spacious rooms; charming staff; feels like a vacation from the city. **Cons:** traffic noise; isolated from restaurants and nightlife; similar prices to downtown's more lavish luxury hotels. $ *Rooms from: $350* ✉ *105 Montgomery St., San Francisco* ☎ *415/561-1234* ⊕ *www.presidiolodging.com* ➟ *42 rooms* ❖ *Free Breakfast.*

The Richmond

In the mid-19th century, the western section of town just north of Golden Gate Park was known as the Outer Lands, covered in sand dunes and seen fit for cemeteries and little else. Today it's the Richmond, comprised of two distinct neighborhoods: the Inner Richmond, from Arguello Boulevard to about 20th Avenue, and the Outer Richmond, from to the ocean.

From Lands End in Lincoln Park, you have some of the best views of the Golden Gate and the Marin Headlands. The Great Highway and Ocean Beach run along the western edge of the city. In winter or spring, watch for migrating gray whales. The wind is often strong, summer fog can blanket the coast, and the water is cold and too dangerous for swimming. Don't forget your jacket!

Sights

★ Legion of Honor

ART MUSEUM | Built to commemorate soldiers from California who died in World War I and set atop cliffs overlooking the ocean, the Golden Gate Bridge, and the Marin Headlands, this beautiful Beaux Arts building in Lincoln Park displays an impressive collection of 4,000 years of ancient and European art. A pyramidal glass skylight in the entrance court illuminates the lower-level galleries, which exhibit prints and drawings, European porcelain, and ancient Assyrian, Greek, Roman, and Egyptian art. The 20-plus galleries on the upper level display European art (paintings, sculpture, decorative arts, and tapestries) from the 14th century to the present day. The Auguste Rodin collection includes two galleries devoted to the master and a third with works by Rodin and other 19th-century sculptors. An original cast of Rodin's *The Thinker* welcomes you as you walk through the courtyard. Also impressive is the 4,526-pipe Spreckels Organ; live concerts take advantage of the natural sound chamber produced by the building's massive rotunda. As fine as the museum is, the setting and view outshine the collection. ⊠ *100 34th Ave., at Clement St., Richmond* 🕾 *415/750–3600* ⊕ *www.famsf.org* 🎫 *$15, free 1st Tues. of month; free Sat. for Bay Area residents* 🕙 *Closed Mon.*

★ Lincoln Park

CITY PARK | Lincoln Park is a wild, 275-acre park with windswept cliffs and panoramic views. The Coastal Trail, the park's most dramatic, leads out to Lands End; pick it up west of the Legion of Honor (at the end of El Camino del Mar) or from the parking lot at Point Lobos and El Camino del Mar. Time your hike to hit Mile Rock at low tide, and you might catch a glimpse of two wrecked ships peeking up from their watery graves.

⚠ **Be careful if you hike here; landslides are frequent, and people have fallen into the sea by standing too close to the edge of a crumbling bluff top.**

Lincoln Park's 18-hole golf course (⊕ *www.lincolnparkgolfcourse.com*) is on land that in the 19th century was the Golden Gate Cemetery. (When digging has to be done in the park, human bones still occasionally surface.) Next door on 33rd Avenue and California Street are the dazzling, mosaic Lincoln Park Steps, which rival the 16th Avenue Steps and the Hidden Garden Steps in the Sunset District. They provide a delightful backdrop for contemplation or an Instagram photo op. ⊠ *Entrance at 34th Ave. and Clement St., Richmond* ⊕ *sfrecpark.org.*

🏖 Beaches

Ocean Beach

BEACH | Stretching 3 miles along the western side of the city from the Richmond to the Sunset, this sandy swath of the Pacific coast is good for flying kites, jogging, or walking the dog—but not for swimming. The water is so cold that surfers wear wet suits year-round, and riptides are strong—drownings are not infrequent. As for sunbathing, it's rarely warm enough here; think meditative walking instead of sun worshipping.

Paths on both sides of the Great Highway lead from Lincoln Way to Sloat Boulevard (near the zoo); the beachside path winds through landscaped sand dunes, and the paved path across the highway is good for biking and in-line skating (though you have to rent bikes elsewhere). The Beach Chalet restaurant and brewpub is across the Great Highway from Ocean Beach, about five blocks south of the Cliff House. **Amenities:** parking (no fee); showers; toilets. **Best for:** solitude; sunset; walking. ⊠ *San Francisco* ✛ *Along Great Hwy. from Cliff House to Sloat Blvd. and beyond* ⊕ *www.parksconservancy.org.*

🍴 Restaurants

Tenglong

$ | **CHINESE** | **FAMILY** | Plenty of locals come to this tidy space known for remarkably friendly service and the dry chicken wings fried in garlic and roasted red peppers, as well as for thinly sliced Mongolian beef and dan dan noodles. Run by two former Hong Kong restaurant owners, it specializes in mostly southern Chinese fare, like Cantonese cuisine, and has a few Sichuan specialties, too. **Known for:** honey-walnut prawns; spicy seafood noodle soup; local hot spot. 💲 *Average main: $18* ⊠ *208 Clement St., Richmond* 🕾 *415/666–3515* ⊕ *www.tenglongchinese.com* 🕙 *Closed Tues.*

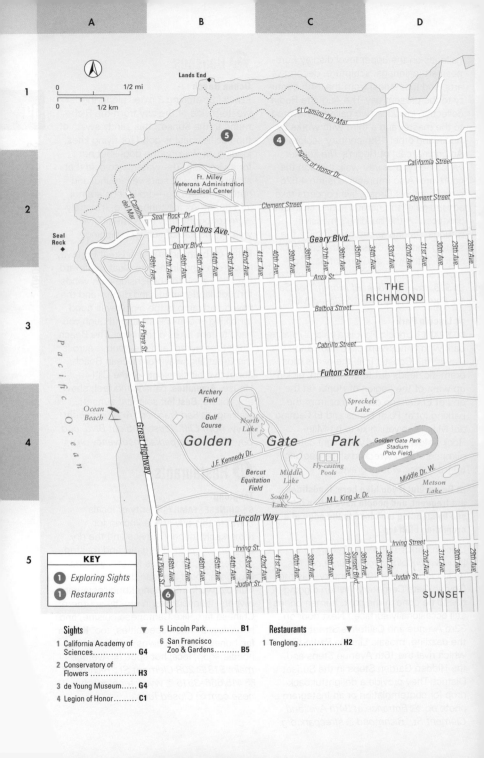

KEY

1 *Exploring Sights*

1 *Restaurants*

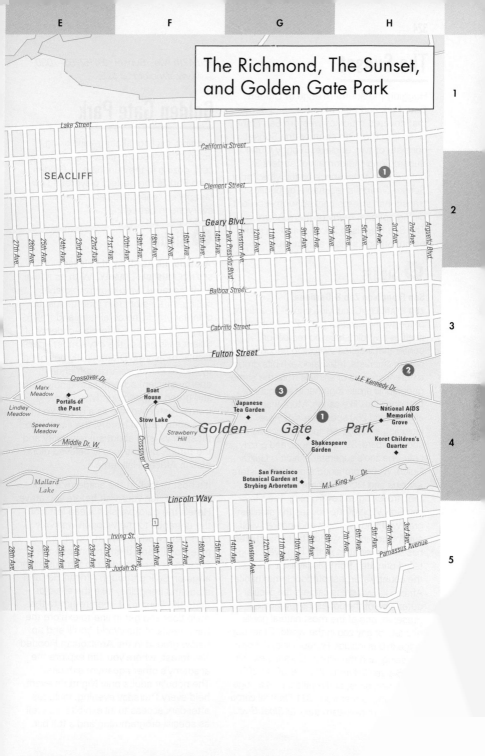

The Richmond, The Sunset, and Golden Gate Park

The Sunset

Hugging the southern edge of Golden Gate Park and built atop the sand dunes that covered much of western San Francisco into the 19th century, the Sunset consists of two enclaves. Foggy Outer Sunset, long the domain of surfers, is beloved for its laid-back beach vibe. Inner Sunset, which is reachable by public transit, has streets packed with excellent dining options, many of them Asian. The San Francisco Zoo & Gardens is the neighborhood's main attraction.

 Sights

San Francisco Zoo & Gardens

ZOO | FAMILY | Occupying prime oceanfront property, the San Francisco Zoo touts itself as a wildlife-focused recreation center that inspires visitors to become conservationists. Integrated exhibits group different species of animals from the same geographic areas together in enclosures that don't look like cages. More than 2,000 animals and 250 species reside here, including endangered species such as the snow leopard, Sumatran tiger, and grizzly bear. The zoo's superstar exhibit is Grizzly Gulch, where orphaned grizzly bear sisters Kachina and Kiona enchant visitors with their frolicking and swimming. The Mexican Gray Wolf grotto houses the smallest gray wolf and the most endangered wolf subspecies in the world. The Lemur Forest has seven varieties of the bug-eyed, long-tailed primates from Madagascar and is the country's largest outdoor lemur habitat. African kikuyu grass carpets the circular outer area of the Jones Family Gorilla Preserve, one of the most natural gorilla habitats of any zoo in the world. Other popular exhibits include Penguin Island, Koala Crossing, and the African Savanna exhibit. The 5-acre Children's Zoo has about 300 animals, birds, and reptiles, plus a huge playground, a restored 1921 Dentzel carousel, and a mini–steam train. ⊠ Sloat Blvd. and 47th Ave., Sunset ☎ 415/753–7080 ⊕ www.sfzoo.org ☜ $25.

Golden Gate Park

Jogging, cycling, skating, picnicking, going to a museum, checking out a concert, dozing in the sunshine … Golden Gate Park is the perfect playground for fast-paced types, laid-back dawdlers, and everyone in between.

 Sights

★ California Academy of Sciences

SCIENCE MUSEUM | FAMILY | With its native plant–covered living roof, retractable ceiling, three-story rain forest, gigantic planetarium, living coral reef, and frolicking penguins, the California Academy of Sciences is one of the city's most spectacular treasures. Dramatically designed by Renzo Piano, it's an eco-friendly, energy-efficient adventure in biodiversity and green architecture. Moving away from a restrictive role as a museum that cataloged natural history, the academy these days is all about sustainability and the future, but the locally beloved dioramas in African Hall remain.

It's best to look at the academy's floor plan to design your visit before you arrive. Here's the quick version: head left from the entrance to the wooden walkway over otherworldly rays in the Philippine Coral Reef, then continue to the Swamp to see Claude, the famous albino alligator. Swing through African Hall and study the penguins, take the elevator up to the living roof, then return to the main floor and get in line to explore the Rainforests of the World. You'll end up below ground in the Amazonian Flooded Rainforest, where you can explore the academy's other aquarium exhibits. The popular adults-only NightLife event, held every Thursday evening, includes after-dark access to all exhibits, as well as special programming and a full bar.

■TIP→ Considering the hefty price of admission, start early and take advantage of in-and-out privileges to take a break, and buy tickets a few days ahead for the best rate. ⊠ *55 Music Concourse Dr., Golden Gate Park* ☎ *415/379–8000* ⊕ *calacademy.org* ⚐ *From $36; save $3 if you bike, walk, or take public transit here.*

★ Conservatory of Flowers

GARDEN | FAMILY | Whatever you do, be sure to at least drive by the Conservatory of Flowers—it's too darn pretty to miss. The gorgeous, white-framed 1878 glass structure is topped with a 14-ton glass dome. Stepping inside the giant greenhouse is like taking a quick trip to the rain forest, with its earthy smell and humid warmth. The undeniable highlight is the Aquatic Plants section, where lily pads float and carnivorous plants dine on bugs to the sounds of rushing water.

On the east side of the conservatory (to the right as you face the building), cypress, pine, and redwood trees surround the **Dahlia Garden,** which blooms in summer and fall. Adding to the allure are temporary special exhibits; a recurring holiday-season model-train display punctuated with mini buildings, found objects, and dwarf plants; night blooms; and a butterfly garden that returns periodically. To the west is the **Rhododendron Dell,** which contains 850 varieties, more than any other garden of its kind in the country. It's a favorite local Mother's Day picnic spot. ⊠ *100 John F. Kennedy Dr., at Conservatory Dr., Golden Gate Park* ☎ *415/831–2090* ⊕ *conservatoryofflowers.org* ⚐ *$13 Feb.–Oct., $10 Nov.–Jan., free 1st Tues. of month, Gardens of Golden Gate Park Pass $25* ♥ *Closed Mon.* ☞ *No food, drink, tripods, or strollers are allowed inside.*

de Young Museum

ART MUSEUM | It seems that everyone in town has a strong opinion about the de Young museum: some adore its striking copper facade, while others just hope that the green patina of age will mellow the effect. Most maligned is the 144-foot tower, but the view from its ninth-story observation room, ringed by floor-to-ceiling windows and free to the public, is worth a trip here by itself. The building almost overshadows the de Young's respected collection of American, African, and Oceanic art. The museum also plays host to major international exhibitions; there's often an extra admission charge for these. The annual Bouquets to Art in June is a fanciful tribute to the museum's collection by notable Bay Area floral designers. ⊠ *50 Hagiwara Tea Garden Dr., Golden Gate Park* ☎ *415/750–3600* ⊕ *www.famsf.org* ⚐ *$15, good for same-day admittance to the Legion of Honor; free after 4:30* ♥ *Closed Mon.*

The Haight

During the 1960s, the siren song of free love, peace, and mind-altering substances lured thousands of young people to the Haight, a neighborhood just east of Golden Gate Park. By 1966, the area had become a hot spot for rock artists, including the Grateful Dead, Jefferson Airplane, and Janis Joplin. Some of the most infamous flower children, including Charles Manson and People's Temple founder Jim Jones, also called the Haight home.

Sights

Haight-Ashbury Intersection

STREET | On October 6, 1967, hippies took over the intersection of Haight and Ashbury Streets to proclaim the "Death of Hip." If they thought hip was dead then, they'd find absolute confirmation of it today—the only tie-dye in sight on the famed corner is a Ben & Jerry's storefront. ⊠ *Haight.*

A colorful mosaic mural in the Castro

Restaurants

Parada 22

$ | **PUERTO RICAN** | A small, colorful space, Parada 22 serves up heaping plates of home-style Puerto Rican cuisine—think plantains, seafood, and slow-roasted pork. There's also plenty of vegetarian fare on offer. **Known for:** delicious yuca fries; marinated meats and vegetables; lunch specials. $ *Average main: $17* ✉ *1805 Haight St., Haight* ☎ *415/750–1111* ⊕ *www.paradasf.com.*

Nightlife

Magnolia Brewing Company

BREWPUBS | Known for its food as much as its beers, Magnolia is a San Francisco institution, thanks in part to its prime location near the Haight-Ashbury intersection. Come for the smoked trout croquettes, falafel salad, and famed burgers, or just grab any one of the dozen-plus beers on tap, many brewed in-house. The brewpub occupies the site of The Drugstore Cafe, one of the first hippie hangouts in the Haight in the 1960s. ✉ *1398 Haight St., Haight* ☎ *415/864–7468* ⊕ *magnoliabrewing.com.*

Shopping

★ Amoeba Music

MUSIC | With well over a million new and used CDs, DVDs, and records at bargain prices, this warehouse-like offshoot of the Berkeley original carries titles you won't find on Amazon. No niche is ignored—from electronica and hip-hop to jazz and classical—and the stock changes frequently. In-store performances attract large crowds. ✉ *1855 Haight St., Haight* ☎ *415/831–1200* ⊕ *www.amoeba. com.*

The Castro

The Castro district—the social, political, and cultural center of San Francisco's thriving gay community—stands at the western end of Market Street. This neighborhood is one of the city's liveliest and most welcoming, especially on weekends. Streets teem with folks out shopping, pushing political causes, heading to art films, and lingering in bars and cafés. It's also one of the city's most expensive neighborhoods to live in, with an influx of tech money exacerbating an identity crisis that's been simmering for a couple of decades.

Sights

★ Castro Theatre

PERFORMANCE VENUE | Here's a classic way to join in a beloved Castro tradition: grab some popcorn and catch a flick at this 1,500-seat art-deco theater built in 1922, the grandest of San Francisco's few remaining movie palaces. The neon marquee, which stands at the top of the Castro strip, is the neighborhood's great landmark. The Castro was the fitting host of 2008's red-carpet preview of Gus Van Sant's film *Milk*, starring Sean Penn as openly gay San Francisco supervisor Harvey Milk. The theater's elaborate Spanish baroque interior is fairly well preserved. Before many shows, the theater's pipe organ rises from the orchestra pit and an organist plays pop and movie tunes, usually ending with the Jeanette MacDonald standard "San Francisco" (go ahead, sing along). The crowd can be enthusiastic and vocal, talking back to the screen as loudly as it talks to them. ⚠ **The theater's management is making renovation plans that may change the nature of the theater's offerings. Check online for updates before planning your trip.** ⊠ *429 Castro St., Castro* ☎ *415/621–6120* ⊕ *www.castrotheatre.com* ☎ *$14.*

Harvey Milk Plaza

PLAZA/SQUARE | An 18-foot-long rainbow flag flies above this plaza named for the man who electrified the city in 1977 by being elected to its Board of Supervisors as an openly gay candidate. In the early 1970s, Milk's camera store on Castro Street became the center for his campaign to open San Francisco's social and political life to gays and lesbians.

Milk hadn't served a full year of his term before he and Mayor George Moscone were shot to death in November 1978 at City Hall. The murderer was a conservative ex-supervisor named Dan White, who had resigned his post and then became enraged when Moscone wouldn't reinstate him. Milk and White had often been at odds on the board. The gay community became infuriated when the "Twinkie defense"—that junk food had led to diminished mental capacity—resulted in only a manslaughter verdict for White. During the so-called White Night Riot of May 21, 1979, gays and their allies stormed City Hall, torching its lobby.

Milk, who had feared assassination, left behind a tape recording in which he urged the community to continue his work. His legacy is the high visibility of gay people throughout city government; a bust of him was unveiled at City Hall in 2008, and the 2008 film *Milk* gives insight into his life. Keep your visiting expectations in check: this is more of a historical site than an Instagrammable spot. ⊠ *Southwest corner of Castro and Market Sts., Castro.*

Restaurants

Frances

$$$$ | **MODERN AMERICAN** | One of the hottest tickets in town, chef Melissa Perello's simple, sublime restaurant is a consummate date-night destination. Perello's seasonal California-French cooking is its own enduring love affair, with standouts including the savory bavette steak, grilled Sakura pork chop, and panisse frites. For dessert, the lumberjack cake is a perennial favor **for:** lumberjack cake; neigh reasonably priced tastin *age main: $86* ⊠ *3870* ☎ *415/621–3870* ⊕ ⊗ *Closed Sun. an*

KEY

1 Exploring Sights

Restaurants

~~RT station

Noe Valley

This upscale but relaxed enclave just south of the Castro is among the city's most desirable places to live, with laid-back cafés, kid-friendly restaurants, and comfortable, old-time shops along Church Street and 24th Street, its main thoroughfares. You can also see remnants of Noe Valley's agricultural beginnings: Billy Goat Hill (at Castro and 30th Streets), a wild-grass hill often draped in fog and topped by one of the city's best rope-swinging trees, is named for the goats that grazed here right into the 20th century.

Sights

Seward Street Slides

CITY PARK | FAMILY | A teenager designed these two long, concrete slides back in 1973, saving this mini park from development. Aimed at older kids and adults rather than little ones, the slides offer a fun, steep ride down, so wear sturdy pants. ⊠ *Seward Mini Park, 30 Seward St., Noe Valley* ⊕ *www.sfrecpark.org* ⊙ *Closed Mon.*

 Restaurants

Barney's Gourmet Hamburgers

$ | AMERICAN | FAMILY | The Noe Valley location of this family-friendly California burger chain offers a cozy indoor-outdoor dining area, the latter really a patio encased in glass windows for watching foot traffic along 24th Street. The ample menu is loaded with fancier versions of diner classics—think the Gastropub burger, with a fried egg and a pretzel bun, or ⁺he Maui Waui, with a teriyaki glaze and ⁺illed pineapple. **Known for:** all kinds of ⁺s; vegetarian options; delicious milk ⁺es. $ *Average main: $14* ⊠ *4138 ⁺t., near Castro St., Noe Valley* ⁺*282–7770* ⊕ *www.barneysham-⁺om.*

Mission District

The Mission has a number of distinct personalities. It's the Latino neighborhood, where working-class folks raise their families and where gangs occasionally clash; it's the hipster hood, where tattooed and pierced twentysomethings hold court in the coolest cafés and bars in town; it's a culinary epicenter, with the strongest concentration of destination restaurants and affordable ethnic cuisine; it's the face of gentrification, where high-tech money prices out longtime renters; and it's the artists' quarter, where murals adorn literally blocks of walls long after the artists have moved to cheaper digs. It's also the city's equivalent of the Sunshine State—this neighborhood's always the last to succumb to fog.

Sights

Balmy Alley

PUBLIC ART | Mission District artists have transformed the walls of their neighborhood with paintings, and Balmy Alley is one of the best-executed examples. Many murals adorn the one-block alley, with newer ones continually filling in the blank spaces. In 1971, artists began teaming with local children to create a space to promote peace in Central America, community spirit, and (later) AIDS awareness; since then dozens of muralists have added their vibrant works. The alley's longtime popularity has grown exponentially thanks to its Instagram appeal. Once you're done at Balmy Alley, head a couple blocks west on 24th Street to another prominent alley of murals on Cypress Street (also between 24th and 25th Streets). ⚠ **Be alert here: the 25th Street end of the alley adjoins a somewhat dangerous area.** ⊠ *24th St. between and parallel to Harrison and Treat Sts., alley runs south to 25th St., Mission District* ⊕ *balmyalley.org.*

Golden Fire Hydrant

OTHER ATTRACTION | When all the other fire hydrants went dry during the fire that followed the 1906 earthquake, this one kept pumping. Noe Valley and the Mission District were thus spared the devastation wrought elsewhere in the city, which explains the large number of pre-quake homes here. Every year on April 18th (the anniversary of the quake), folks gather here to share stories about the disaster, and the famous hydrant gets a fresh coat of gold paint. ⊠ *Church and 20th Sts., southeastern corner of intersection, across from Dolores Park, Mission.*

Mission Dolores

RELIGIOUS BUILDING | Two churches stand side by side here: a newer multi-domed basilica and the small adobe Mission San Francisco de Asís, the latter being the city's oldest standing structure along with the Presidio Officers' Club. Completed in 1791, it's the sixth of the 21 California missions founded by Franciscan friars in the 18th and early 19th centuries. Its ceiling depicts original Ohlone Indian basket designs, executed in vegetable dyes. The tiny chapel includes frescoes and a hand-painted wooden altar.

There's a hidden treasure here: a 20-by-22-foot mural with images including a dagger-pierced Sacred Heart of Jesus, painted with natural dyes by Native Americans in 1791, was found in 2004 behind the altar. Interesting fact: Mission San Francisco de Asís was founded on June 29, 1776, five days before the Declaration of Independence was signed.

The small museum in the mission complex covers its founding and history, and the pretty cemetery—which appears in Alfred Hitchcock's film *Vertigo*—contains the graves of mid-19th-century European immigrants. The remains of an estimated 5,000 Native Americans who died at the mission lie in unmarked graves. ⊠ *3321 16th St., at Dolores St., Mission District* ☎ *415/621–8203* ⊕ *www.missiondolores. org* ⊠ *$7* ⊘ *Closed Mon.*

★ Mission Dolores Park

CITY PARK | A two-square-block microcosm of life in the district, Mission Dolores Park is one of San Francisco's liveliest green spaces: dog lovers and their pampered pups congregate, kids play at the extravagant playground, and hipsters hold court, drinking beer and rosé cans on sunny days. (Fair warning: if it's over 70°F, the place can get packed like traffic at rush hour for picnic-blanket space.) During the summer, Dolores Park hosts movie nights, performances by the San Francisco Mime Troupe, and pop-up events and impromptu parties. Spend a warm day here—maybe sitting at the top of the park with a view of the city and the Bay Bridge—surrounded by locals and that laid-back, still-abundant San Francisco energy, and you may well find yourself plotting your move to the city. The best views are in the southwest corner, near the historic golden fire hydrant that saved the neighborhood after the 1906 earthquake. ⊠ *Between 18th and 20th Sts. and Dolores and Church Sts., Mission District* ⊕ *sfrecpark.org.*

Museum of Craft and Design

ART MUSEUM | Right at home in this once-industrial neighborhood now bursting with creative energy, this small, four-room space—definitely a quick view—mounts temporary art and design exhibitions. The focus might be sculpture, metalwork, furniture, or jewelry, though it might also be industrial design, architecture, the connection of scent and objects, or very on-trend subjects like data and computer encoding. The beautifully curated shop is perfect for unique souvenirs and imagination-spurring items for the home office. ⊠ *2569 3rd St., Dogpatch* ☎ *415/773–0303* ⊕ *sfmcd.org* ⊠ *$10* ⊘ *Closed Mon. and Tues.*

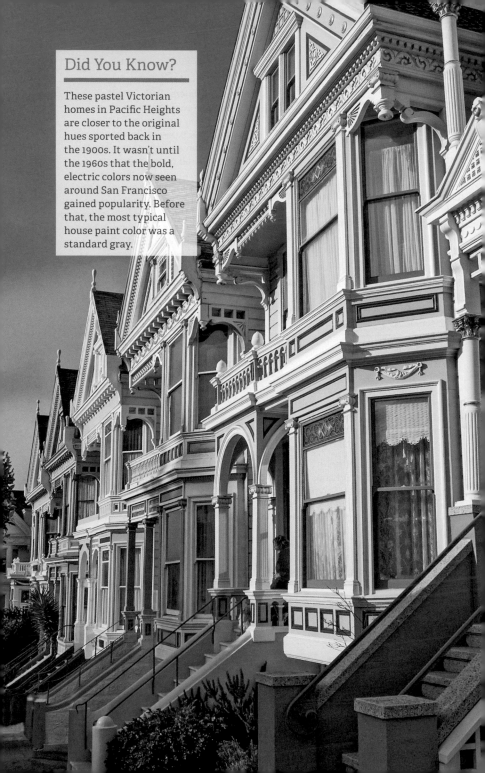

Did You Know?

These pastel Victorian homes in Pacific Heights are closer to the original hues sported back in the 1900s. It wasn't until the 1960s that the bold, electric colors now seen around San Francisco gained popularity. Before that, the most typical house paint color was a standard gray.

🍴 Restaurants

★ Delfina

$$ | **ITALIAN** | Crowds are a constant fixture at Craig and Annie Stoll's cultishly adored northern Italian spot. Deceptively simple, exquisitely flavored dishes include excellent pastas and the city's greatest panna cotta. **Known for:** signature spaghetti with plum tomatoes; hard to get reservations; Monterey Bay calamari with white bean salad. [$] *Average main: $28* ✉ *3621 18th St., Mission District* ☎ *415/552–4055* 🌐 *www.delfinasf.com* 🕒 *Closed Tues. No lunch.*

★ flour + water

$$ | **MODERN ITALIAN** | This handsome and boisterous hot spot with a tiny bar and a sleek yet rustic dining room is synonymous with pasta. The grand experience here is the seven-course pasta-tasting menu (extra charge for wine pairings) with seasonally changing dishes (the one standby is a meatless Taleggio scarpinocc with aged balsamic drizzled over the bow tie–shaped pasta). **Known for:** difficult-to-get reservations; rarely seen pasta shapes; Italian wines from small producers. [$] *Average main: $28* ✉ *2401 Harrison St., Mission District* ☎ *415/826–7000* 🌐 *www.flourandwater.com* 🕒 *No lunch.*

★ Lazy Bear

$$$$ | **MODERN AMERICAN** | There's no end to the buzz around chef David Barzelay's 12-plus-course prix-fixe seasonal and imagination-driven dinners, which might include guinea hen with English peas and morel mushrooms or delicate "sandwiches" of Wagyu 'nduja pimento cheese and fried green heirloom tomatoes. An ode to the Western lodge, the high-ceilinged, spacious dining room includes a fireplace, charred wood walls, and wooden rafters. **Known for:** freshly baked rolls with butter cultured in-house; sensational friendly yet formal service; stellar beverage program. [$] *Average main: $275* ✉ *3416 19th St., Mission District* ☎ *415/874–9921* 🌐 *www.lazybearsf.com* 🕒 *Closed Sun. and Mon. No lunch.*

SanJalisco

$ | **MEXICAN** | **FAMILY** | This sun-filled, family-run restaurant has been a neighborhood favorite since 1988, and not only because it serves breakfast all day—though the hearty chilaquiles always hits the spot. On weekends, regulars opt for birria, a spicy barbecued goat stew, or menudo, a tongue-searing soup made from beef tripe, complemented by beer and sangria. **Known for:** chilaquiles; soups change based on day of the week; friendly service. [$] *Average main: $16* ✉ *901 S. Van Ness Ave., Mission District* ☎ *415/648–8383* 🌐 *www.sanjaliscorestaurant.com.*

★ Tartine Bakery

$ | **BAKERY** | **FAMILY** | Chad Robertson is America's first modern cult baker, and this tiny Mission District outpost (along with the larger Tartine Manufactory on the eastern side of the neighborhood) is where you'll find his famed loaves of tangy country bread and beloved pastries like croissants and morning buns. You'll also find near-constant lines out the door; they're longest in the morning when locals (and plenty of tourists) need a pastry punch to start the day, and later in the afternoon when the famed loaves emerge freshly baked. **Known for:** anything bread-related; chocolate soufflé cake; fresh pastries. [$] *Average main: $16* ✉ *600 Guerrero St., Mission District* ☎ *415/487–2600* 🌐 *tartinebakery.com* 🕒 *No dinner.*

🛏 Hotels

★ The Parker Guest House

$$ | **B&B/INN** | Two yellow 1909 Edwardian houses enchant travelers wanting an authentic San Francisco experience; dark hallways and steep staircases lead to bright, earth-toned rooms with tiled baths (most with tubs), comfortable sitting areas, and cozy linens. **Pros:** handsomely

designed, affordable rooms; close to the Castro and Dolores Park; evening wine social hour. **Cons:** long walk or short car ride from the main Mission nightlife; economy rooms have private baths in a hallway; standard rooms are a little tight. $ *Rooms from: $209* ⊠ *520 Church St., Mission District* ☎ *415/621–3222* ⊕ *www.parkerguesthouse.com* ⇆ *19 rooms* |○| *Free Breakfast.*

Nightlife

ABV

BARS | One of the city's top cocktail bars offers elevated small plates (the burger has a devoted following) late into the night to pair with the excellent cocktail menu, which includes such favorites as a Mumbai Mule with saffron vodka. A knowledgeable and friendly staff serves a diverse, energetic crowd in a smart modern setting. ⊠ *3174 16th St., Mission District* ☎ *415/294–1871* ⊕ *www.abvsf. com.*

El Rio

BARS | A dive bar in the best sense, El Rio has a calendar chock-full of events, from free bands and films to Salsa Sunday (every fourth Sunday), all of which keep Mission kids coming back. No matter what day you attend, expect to find a diverse gay and straight crowd enjoying local beers and margaritas. When the weather's warm, the large patio out back is especially popular, and the midday dance parties are the place to be. ⊠ *3158 Mission St., Mission District* ☎ *415/282–3325* ⊕ *www.elriosf.com* ⊙ *Closed Mon. and Tues.*

Martuni's

PIANO BARS | A mixed crowd enjoys cocktails in the semi-refined environment of this piano bar where the Castro, the Mission, and Hayes Valley intersect; variations on the martini and different fruit-flavored lemon drops are a specialty. This is not the place for innovative mixology. In the intimate back room a pianist plays nightly, and patrons take turns boisterously singing show tunes. Martuni's often gets busy after symphony and opera performances—Davies Hall and the Opera House are both within walking distance. ⊠ *4 Valencia St., Mission District* ☎ *415/241–0205.*

★ Zeitgeist

BEER GARDENS | It's a dive but one of the city's best beer bars—there are almost 50 on tap—and a great place to relax with a cold one or an ever-popular Bloody Mary in the large "garden" (there's not much greenery) on a sunny day. Burgers and brats are available, and if you own a trucker hat, a pair of Vans, and a Pabst Blue Ribbon T-shirt, you'll fit right in. ⊠ *199 Valencia St., Mission District* ☎ *415/255–7505* ⊕ *www.zeitgeistsf.com.*

Shopping

Paxton Gate

SOUVENIRS | Elevating gardening to an art, this serene shop offers beautiful vases, succulents, decorative garden items, and coffee-table books. The collection of taxidermy and preserved bugs provides more unusual gift ideas. A couple storefronts away is too-cute Paxton Gate Curiosities for Kids, jam-packed with retro toys, books, and other stellar finds. ⊠ *824 Valencia St., Mission District* ☎ *415/824–1872* ⊕ *paxtongate.com.*

Therapy

SOUVENIRS | In addition to fun housewares, books, wellness items, and stationery that leans toward retro charm, this local company sells smart decor, linens, and accessories with San Francisco and California themes. ⊠ *545 Valencia St., Mission District* ☎ *415/865–0981* ⊕ *therapystores.com.*

Chapter 11

THE BAY AREA

11

Updated by
Trevor Felch

● Sights	⑪ Restaurants	🛏 Hotels	● Shopping
★★★★☆	★★★★☆	★★★☆☆	★★☆☆☆

WELCOME TO THE BAY AREA

TOP REASONS TO GO

★ **Berkeley's culinary mecca:** Eat your way through North Berkeley, starting with a slice of perfect pizza from Cheese Board Pizza.

★ **Point Reyes National Seashore:** Hike beautifully rugged—and often deserted—beaches at one of the most beautiful places on Earth.

★ **Sitting on a dock by the Bay:** Admire the beauty of the Bay from the rocky shores of Sausalito or Tiburon.

★ **"Beer-hopping" in Oakland's hippest hoods:** Discover the wealth of unique brewers along the Oakland Ale Trail.

★ **Giant redwoods:** Walking into Muir Woods National Monument is like entering a cathedral of nature.

★ **Elephant seals:** Few sights are as spectacular as seeing thousands of elephant seals breeding nd resting on the beach Año Nuevo State Park.

'm Drive: The ward Stanford y and the Mountains erfect.

1 **Berkeley.** Hip college town.

2 **Oakland.** Diverse city with lively arts, nightlife, and food.

3 **The Marin Headlands.** Spectacular vistas.

4 **Sausalito.** Views and bohemian vibes.

5 **Tiburon.** A quaint, scenic town.

6 **Mill Valley.** Gateway to incredible nature.

7 **Muir Beach.** Quiet beach with a local feel.

8 **Stinson Beach.** Beach town with a surfer vibe.

9 **Point Reyes National Seashore.** Dramatic coastline with sandy beaches.

10 **Palo Alto.** A residential city for Big Tech.

11 **Stanford.** Beautiful academic hot spot.

12 **Menlo Park.** Home of Meta.

13 **Sunnyvale and Mountain View.** The hip heart of Silicon Valley.

14 **San Jose.** A dynamic and intriguing city.

15 **Santa Cruz Mountains AVA.** Redwood forests and Pinot Noirs.

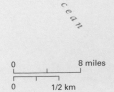

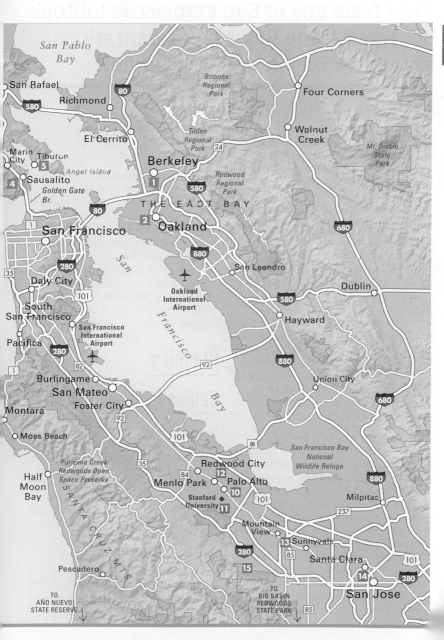

It's rare for a metropolis to compete with its suburbs for visitors, but the view from any of San Francisco's hilltops shows that the Bay Area's temptations extend far beyond the city limits.

MAJOR REGIONS

East of the city are the energetic urban centers of Berkeley and Oakland. Berkeley is famously radical yet sophisticated, while Oakland has an arts and restaurant scene so hip that it pulls San Franciscans across the bay. To the north is Marin County with its dramatic coastal beauty and chic, affluent villages.

The East Bay. The college town of Berkeley has long been known for its liberal ethos, stimulating university community (and perhaps even more stimulating coffee shops), and activist streak. But these days, the lively restaurant and arts scenes are luring even those who wouldn't be caught dead in Birkenstocks. Meanwhile, life in the diverse, harborfront city of Oakland is strongly defined by a turbulent history. Today, progressive Oakland is an incubator for artisans of all kinds, and the thriving culinary and creative scenes are taking off.

Marin County. Marin is the prettiest of the Bay Area counties, primarily because of its wealth of open space. Anchored by water on three sides, the county is mostly parkland, including long stretches of undeveloped coastline along the Marin Headlands, recognizable by the distinguished peak of Mt. Tamalpais. The coastal treasures of Muir Woods National Monument, "Mt. Tam," Stinson and Muir Beaches, and the entire Point Reyes National Seashore are among the country's greatest natural beauties. It's no wonder that the picturesque small towns here—Sausalito, Tiburon, Mill Valley, and Bolinas among them—may sometimes look rustic, but most are home to a dizzyingly high tax bracket.

The Peninsula and South Bay. Home to Silicon Valley, Stanford University, the Santa Cruz Mountains and a spectacular coastline, this is an incredibly diverse region of the Bay Area—the technology campuses and tranquil redwood forests are just minutes apart from each other. San Jose is the largest city in the region and has several interesting museums worth visiting. The Santa Cruz Mountains are home to some of the Bay Area's greatest vineyards and hiking trails.

Planning

Getting Here and Around

Seamless travel from train to ferry to bus with one fare card is possible—and often preferable to driving on congested freeways and over toll bridges. For trips from one city to the next across the bay, save time and money with a Clipper card. They work with BART, Muni, buses, and ferries. Order a Clipper card before you travel at ⊕ *www.clippercard.com*.

BART

Using public transportation to reach Berkeley or Oakland is ideal. The under- and aboveground BART (Bay Area Rapid Transit) trains make stops in both cities as well as other East Bay destinations. Trips to either take about a half hour one-way from the center of San Francisco. Trains also take passengers from the city directly to San Francisco International Airport and from the East Bay to North San Jose. BART does not serve Downtown San Jose, Marin County, or the Peninsula. ■TIP→ **Check ahead for safety measures and service advisories.**

CONTACTS BART. ☎ *510/465–2278* ⊕ *www.bart.gov.*

BOAT AND FERRY

For sheer romance, nothing beats the ferry; there's service from San Francisco to Sausalito, Tiburon, and Larkspur in Marin County, and to Alameda and Oakland in the East Bay.

The Golden Gate Ferry crosses the bay to Larkspur and Sausalito from San Francisco's Ferry Building. Blue & Gold Fleet ferries depart daily for Sausalito from Pier 41 at Fisherman's Wharf; weekday commuter ferries leave from the Ferry Building for Tiburon. The trip takes from 25 minutes to an hour. Purchase tickets from terminal vending machines.

The Angel Island–Tiburon Ferry sails to the island Wednesday–Sunday from April through October and on weekends the rest of the year. Call ahead to book and to check schedules.

The San Francisco Bay Ferry runs several times daily between San Francisco's Ferry Building and Oakland's Jack London Square, by way of Alameda. The trip lasts from 25 to 45 minutes and leads to Oakland's waterfront shopping and restaurant district. Purchase tickets on the Clipper Card app or at terminals or on board.

CONTACTS Angel Island–Tiburon Ferry. ☎ *415/435–2131* ⊕ *angelislandferry. com.* **Blue & Gold Fleet.** ☎ *415/705–8200* ⊕ *www.blueandgoldfleet.com.* **Golden Gate Ferry.** ☎ *415/921–5858* ⊕ *www. goldengate.org.* **San Francisco Bay Ferry.**

☎ *707/643–3779, 877/643–3779* ⊕ *sanfranciscobayferry.com.*

BUS

Golden Gate Transit buses travel north to Sausalito, Tiburon, and elsewhere in Marin County from the Financial District and SoMa in San Francisco. For Mt. Tamalpais State Park and West Marin (Stinson Beach, Bolinas, and Point Reyes Station), take any route to Marin City and then transfer to the West Marin Stagecoach. San Francisco Muni buses primarily serve the city.

■TIP→ **Several other bus options exist for local and regional travel throughout the Bay Area, including Amtrak and Greyhound.**

Though less speedy than BART, AC Transit bus lines serve Oakland, Berkeley, and all of Alameda County. The Peninsula is served by VTA and Samtrans bus lines.

CONTACTS AC Transit. ☎ *510/891–4777* ⊕ *www.actransit.org.* **Golden Gate Transit.** ☎ *511* ⊕ *www.goldengate.org.* **SamTrans.** ☎ *800/660–4287* ⊕ *www.samtrans. com.* **San Francisco Muni.** ☎ *311* ⊕ *www. sfmta.com.* **West Marin Stagecoach.** ☎ *511* ⊕ *marintransit.org/stagecoach.*

CAR

To reach the East Bay, take I–80 East across the San Francisco–Oakland Bay Bridge. For U.C. Berkeley, merge onto I–580 West and take Exit 11 for University Avenue. For Oakland, merge onto I–580 East. To reach downtown Oakland, take I–980 West from Interstate 580 East and exit at 14th Street. Travel time varies depending on traffic but should take about 30 minutes (or more than an hour if it's rush hour).

For all points in Marin, head north on U 101 and cross the Golden Gate Bridg Sausalito, Tiburon, the Marin Headl and Point Reyes National Seashor all accessed off U.S. 101. The sc coastal route, Highway 1, also Shoreline Highway (and brief ic Highway) for certain stre accessed off U.S. 101 as well. Follow this road to Muir Woods, Mt. Tamalpais State Park, Muir Beach, Stinson Beach, and Bolinas. From Bolinas, you can continue north on Highway 1 to Point Reyes.

From San Francisco, U.S. 101 and I–280 go straight down the Peninsula. The former is the more congested artery near the bay; the latter is closer to the Coastal Range. Both end up in San Jose.

Hotels

With a few exceptions, hotels in Berkeley and Oakland tend to be standard-issue, but many Marin hotels package themselves as cozy retreats. Summer in Marin is often booked well in advance, despite weather that can be downright chilly. Check for special packages during this season. Peninsula hotels wildly vary from basic chains on busy roads to some of the splashiest resorts in Northern California. Prices are always much steeper on weekdays here year-round, while it's the opposite on the coast.

Restaurants

The Bay Area is home to many innovative restaurants, such as Chez Panisse in Berkeley and Commis in Oakland—for which reservations must be made well in advance. There are also many casual but equally tasty eateries to test out; expect an emphasis on organic seasonal produce, locally raised meats, craft cocktails, and curated wine menus. Marin and the Peninsula's dining scene trends toward the sleepy side, so check hours ahead of time. One of the best things about the ~ion is that no matter where you are, will surely be a terrific restaurant a few minutes.

rant and hotel reviews have ened. For full information, visit Restaurant prices are the f a main course at dinner

or, if dinner is not served, at lunch. Hotel prices are the lowest cost of a standard double room in high season.

What It Costs in U.S. Dollars			
$	$$	$$$	$$$$
RESTAURANTS			
under $20	$20–$30	$31–$40	over $40
HOTELS			
under $200	$200–$350	$351–$500	over $500

When to Go

You can visit the rest of the Bay Area any time of year, though it's especially nice in late spring and fall. Unlike San Francisco, the surrounding areas are reliably sunny in summer—it gets hotter as you head inland. Even the rainy season has its charms, as otherwise golden hills turn a rich green and wildflowers become plentiful. Precipitation is usually the heaviest between November and March. Berkeley is a university town, so it's easier to navigate the streets and find parking near the university between semesters, but there's also less buzz around town then. The Marin County and Peninsular coastlines are well known for their frequent fog and fierce winds throughout the year, but a few days each month they'll have surprisingly sunny and mild conditions.

Berkeley

2 miles northeast of Bay Bridge.

Berkeley is the birthplace of the Free Speech Movement, the radical hub of the 1960s, the home of arguably the nation's top public university, and a frequent site of protests and political movements. The city of 103,000 is also a culturally diverse breeding ground for social trends, a bastion of the counterculture, and an important center for Bay Area writers, artists, and musicians, Berkeley residents, students, and faculty spend hours nursing coffee concoctions while they read, discuss, and debate at the dozens of cafés that surround campus. It's the quintessential university town, with numerous independent bookstores, countless casual eateries, myriad meet-ups, and thousands of cyclists.

Oakland may have the edge over Berkeley when it comes to ethnic diversity and cutting-edge arts, but unless you're accustomed to sipping hemp-milk lattes while taking in a spontaneous street performance prior to yoga, you'll likely find Berkeley charmingly offbeat.

GETTING HERE AND AROUND

BART is the easiest way to get to Berkeley from San Francisco. Exit at the Downtown Berkeley Station, and walk a block up Center Street to get to the western edge of campus. AC Transit buses F and FS lines stop near the university and Fourth Street shopping. By car, take I–80 East across the Bay Bridge, merge onto I–580 West, and take the University Avenue exit through downtown Berkeley or take the Ashby Avenue exit and turn left on Telegraph Avenue. Once you arrive, explore on foot. Berkeley is very pedestrian-friendly.

TOURS

Edible Excursions

FOOD AND DRINK TOURS | For an unforgettable foodie experience in Berkeley, book a culinary walking tour, maybe one of North Berkeley or a Downtown Berkeley brunch stroll. Come hungry for knowledge and noshing. Tours take place on weekends. The company also offers tours of San Francisco and Oakland. ⊠ *Berkeley* ☎ *415/806–5970* ⊕ *www.edibleexcursions.net* ⊠ *From $120.*

ESSENTIALS
CONTACTS Koret Visitor Center. ⊠ *2227 Piedmont Ave., at California Memorial Stadium, Downtown* ☎ *510/642–5215* ⊕ *Visit berkeley.edu.* **Visit Berkeley.** ⊠ *2030 Addison St., Suite 102, Downtown* ☎ *510/549–7040* ⊕ *www.visitberkeley.com.*

 Sights

★ **BAMPFA (Berkeley Art Museum and Pacific Film Archive)**
ART MUSEUM | This combined art museum, repertory movie theater, and film archive, known for its extensive collection of 28,000 works of art and 18,000 films and videos, is also home to the world's largest collection of African American quilts. Artworks span five centuries and include modernist notables Mark Rothko, Jackson Pollock, David Smith, and Hans Hofmann. The Pacific Film Archive includes the largest selection of Japanese films outside Japan and specializes in international films, offering regular screenings and performances. ⊠ *2155 Center St., Berkeley* ☎ *510/642–0808* ⊕ *bampfa.org* ⊠ *$14; free 1st Thurs. of month* ⊘ *Closed Mon. and Tues.*

Fourth Street
NEIGHBORHOOD | Once an industrial area, this walkable stretch of Fourth Street north of University Avenue has transformed into the busiest few blocks of refined shopping and eating in Berkeley. A perfect stop for lovers of design, curated taste experiences, artful living, and fashion, the vibrant district boasts more than 70 shops, specialty stores, cafés, and restaurants. Find inspiration at Castle in the Air, Builders Booksource, and Stained Glass Garden, or sip a perfect drip coffee at Artís, where you can watch small-batch coffee roasting in progress—one pound at a time. ⊠ *4th St. between*

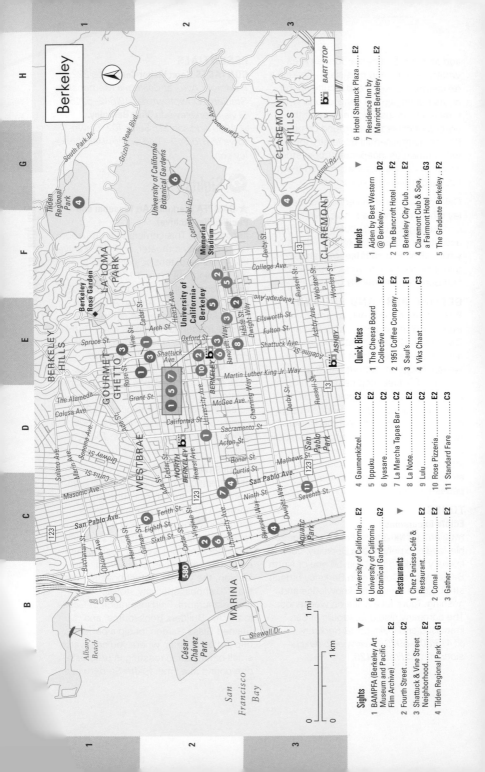

Berkeley

🧭

🚇 *BART STOP*

The University of California is the epicenter of Berkeley's energy and activism,

University Ave. and Virginia St., Berkeley ⊕ www.fourthstreet.com.

★ Shattuck & Vine Street Neighborhood

NEIGHBORHOOD | The success of Alice Waters's Chez Panisse defined California cuisine and attracted countless food-related enterprises to a stretch of Shattuck Avenue. Foodies will do well here poking around the shops, grabbing a quick bite, or indulging in a feast. **Tigerlily** (⊠ 1513 Shattuck Ave.) dishes up authentic modern Indian cuisine along with signature cocktails and light fare on the patio. Neighboring **Epicurious Garden** (⊠ 1511 Shattuck Ave.) food stands sell everything from sushi to gelato.

Across Vine Street, the **Vintage Berkeley** (⊠ 2113 Vine St.) wine shop offers tastings and reasonably priced bottles within a historic former pump house. Coffee lovers can head to the original Peet's Coffee & Tea at the corner of **Walnut and Vine** (⊠ 2124 Vine St.).

South of Cedar Street, **The Local Butcher Shop** (⊠ 1600 Cedar St.) sells locally sourced meat and hearty sandwiches of the day. For high-end food at takeout prices, try the salads, sandwiches, and signature potato puffs at **Grégoire** (⊠ 2109 Cedar St.). **Masse's Pastries** (⊠ 1469 Shattuck Ave.) is a museum of edible artwork. We could go on, but you get the idea. ⊠ Shattuck Ave. between Delaware and Rose Sts., Berkeley ⊕ www.northshattuckassociation.org.

★ Tilden Regional Park

CITY PARK | FAMILY | Stunning bay views, a scaled-down steam train, and a botanical garden with the nation's most complete collection of California plant life are the hallmarks of this 2,077-acre park in the hills just east of the UC Berkeley campus. The garden's visitor center offers weekend lectures about its plants and information about Tilden's other attractions, including its picnic spots, Lake Anza swimming site, golf course, and hiking trails (the paved Nimitz Way, at

Famed Berkeley restaurant Chez Panisse focuses on seasonal local ingredients.

Inspiration Point, is a popular hike with wonderful sunset views). ■TIP→ Children love Tilden's interactive Little Farm and vintage carousel. ✉ *Tilden Regional Park, 2501 Grizzly Peak Blvd., Berkeley* 🕾 *510/544–2747* ⊕ *www.ebparks.org* 🍽 *Free parking and botanic garden.*

University of California
COLLEGE | Known simply as "Cal," the founding campus of California's university system is one of the leading intellectual centers in the United States and a major site for scientific research. Chartered in 1868, the university sits on 178 oak-covered acres split by Strawberry Creek. Campus highlights include bustling and historic **Sproul Plaza** (✉ *Bancroft Way and Sather Rd.*), the seven floors and 61-bell carillon of **Sather Tower** (✉ *Campanile Esplanade*), hands-on **Lawrence Hall of Science** (✉ *1 Centennial Dr.*), the vibrant 34-acre **Botanical Gardens** (✉ *200 Centennial Dr.*), and the historic **Hearst Greek Theatre** (✉ *2001 Gayley Rd.*), the classic outdoor amphitheater designed by John Galen Howard. ✉ *Berkeley* 🕾 *510/642–6000* ⊕ *www.berkeley.edu.*

University of California Botanical Garden
GARDEN | FAMILY | Thanks to Berkeley's temperate climate, more than 10,000 types of plants from all corners of the world flourish in the 34-acre University of California Botanical Garden. Free garden tours are given regularly with paid admission. Benches and shady picnic tables make this a relaxing place for a snack with a breathtaking view. Call or go online before you travel to reserve your visit. ✉ *200 Centennial Dr., Berkeley* 🕾 *510/643–2755* ⊕ *botanicalgarden. berkeley.edu* 🍽 *$15* ⊙ *Closed 1st and 3rd Tues. every month.*

🍴 Restaurants

Dining in Berkeley may be low-key when it comes to dress, but it's top-of-class in quality, even in less fancy spaces. Late diners beware: Berkeley is an "early to bed" kind of town.

★ Chez Panisse Café & Restaurant

$$$$ | MODERN AMERICAN | Alice Waters's legendary eatery, the birthplace of California cuisine, first opened its doors in 1971. It's still known for a passionate dedication to locally sourced heirloom varieties of fruits and vegetables, heritage breeds, and ethically farmed or foraged ingredients. **Known for:** sustainably sourced meats; attention to detail; pizzas and fruit galettes upstairs. $ *Average main: $175* ⊠ *1517 Shattuck Ave., Berkeley* ☎ *510/548–5525 restaurant, 510/548–5049 café* ⊕ *www.chezpanisse. com* ☾ *Closed Sun. and Mon. No lunch in restaurant. No lunch Tues.–Thurs. in café.*

Comal

$ | MODERN MEXICAN | Relaxed yet trendy, Comal's cavernous indoor dining space and intimate back patio and firepit draw a diverse, casual crowd for creative Oaxacan-inspired fare and well-crafted cocktails. The modern Mexican menu centers on small dishes that lend themselves to sharing and are offered alongside more than 100 tequilas and mezcals. **Known for:** margaritas and mezcal; housemade chicharróns; wood-fired entrées. $ *Average main: $16* ⊠ *2020 Shattuck Ave., Berkeley* ☎ *510/926–6300* ⊕ *www. comalberkeley.com* ☾ *No lunch.*

Gather

$$ | MODERN AMERICAN | All things local, organic, seasonal, and sustainable harmonize at Gather. This haven for vegans, vegetarians, and carnivores alike serves up market and grain salads, shareable grilled local vegetables or cheese plates, roast chicken, and more in a vibrant, well-lit space that boasts funky light fixtures, shiny wood furnishings, and banquettes made of recycled leather belts. **Known for:** falafel burger; wood-fired pizzas; compelling cocktails. $ *Average main: $26* ⊠ *2200 Oxford St., Berkeley* ☎ *510/809–0400* ⊕ *www.gatherberkeley. com* ☾ *Closed Mon. and Tues.*

Gaumenkitzel

$$ | GERMAN | FAMILY | This award-winning, convivial locale for organic, slow-food German fare has the Bay Area's best variety of German beers. With dishes like spätzle and caramelized onions, house-made brezel with bratwurst, jägerschnitzel with braised red cabbage, and panfried catch of the day, the kitchen puts a fresh stamp on traditional German favorites. **Known for:** German wine and beer selection; house-made German breads; grass-fed beef goulash. $ *Average main: $22* ⊠ *2121 San Pablo Ave., Berkeley* ☎ *510/647–5016* ⊕ *www. gaumenkitzel.net* ☾ *Closed Mon. and Tues. No lunch Wed.–Fri.*

Ippuku

$ | JAPANESE | More Tokyo street chic than standard sushi house, this *izakaya*—the Japanese equivalent of a bar with appetizers—is decked with bamboo-screen booths. Servors pour an impressive array of sakes and shochu and serve up satisfying fare. **Known for:** baconwrapped mochi; charcoal-grilled yakitori skewers; tempura vegetables. $ *Average main: $18* ⊠ *2130 Center St., Berkeley* ☎ *510/665–1969* ⊕ *ippukuberkeley.com* ☾ *Closed Mon. and Tues. No lunch.*

Iyasare

$$ | JAPANESE | Reservations are recommended at this hot spot where the outdoor seating is ideal for people-watching and the Japanese country food is uniquely prepared. Locals come for seasonally changing, eclectic dishes made with a blend of local ingredients, such as burdock root tempura and tamari-kombu cured salmon or a wonderful salad combining various kinds of sashimi with a spicy miso dressing. **Known for:** sushi omakase; donburi (rice-bowl dishes) and small plates; ramen. $ *Average main: $27* ⊠ *1830 4th St., Berkeley* ☎ *510/845–8100* ⊕ *iyasare-berkeley.com.*

La Marcha Tapas Bar
$ | **SPANISH** | Delectable samplings of Spanish cuisine and a lively setting with expanded outdoor seating (Thursday through Sunday only) keep this tapas bar brimming with energy amid savory smells of seafood dishes and small plates of peel-and-eat prawns, cumin lamb sliders, or goat cheese–stuffed piquillos rellenos. The bar's passion for Spanish cuisine and culture is evident in the wines, the Mediterranean flavors, and the cozy setting with tile mosaics. **Known for:** paella varieties; happy hour specials; churros con chocolate. [$] *Average main: $17* ✉ *2026 San Pablo Ave., Berkeley* ☎ *510/647–9525* 🌐 *www.lamarchaberkeley.com.*

La Note
$ | **FRENCH** | A charming taste of Provence in a 19th-century locale with stone floors, country tables, and a seasonal flowering patio, La Note serves thoughtfully prepared rustic food. Enjoy breakfast and lunch outdoors with fresh, crusty breads and pastries, eggs Lucas with house-roasted tomatoes, and lemon gingerbread pancakes. **Known for:** rustic sandwiches; tempting egg preparations; brioche pain perdu. [$] *Average main: $18* ✉ *2377 Shattuck Ave., Berkeley* ☎ *510/843–1525* 🌐 *www.lanoterestaurant.com* 🕑 *No dinner.*

Lulu
$ | **MIDDLE EASTERN** | Chef-owner Mona Leena Michael channels her heritage as a first-generation Palestinian in California. Breakfast, lunch, and Friday-to-Sunday brunch are the main events here, in particular the reservation-only, prix-fixe brunch affair that might feature eight to ten compelling *mezze* (small plates). **Known for:** rose brûlée cappuccino; Turkish eggs with house chili crisp and fresh pita; outstanding freshly baked pastries. [$] *Average main: $18* ✉ *1019 Camelia St., Berkeley* ☎ *510/529–4300* 🌐 *luluberkeley.com* 🕑 *Closed Mon. No dinner.*

Rose Pizzeria
$$ | **PIZZA** | The East Bay is saturated with excellent pizzerias, but arguably the best of the esteemed group is hiding in plain sight on busy University Avenue, right by the heart of downtown Berkeley. Day and night, diners enjoy whole pies (no slices) in the cozy dining room and pleasant back patio. **Known for:** notable roster of natural wines; spicy Caesar salad; creative pizzas with several tempting vegetarian options. [$] *Average main: $22* ✉ *1960 University Ave., Berkeley* 🌐 *rosepizzeria.com* 🕑 *Closed Mon. and Tues.*

★ Standard Fare
$ | **AMERICAN** | Just look for the hungry crowds and the smell of freshly baked muffins; breakfast-lunch-brunch paradise is here in a far-flung corner of Berkeley. Kelsie Kerr's daytime-only restaurant/bakery started in 2014 and has been a sensation ever since. **Known for:** brunch salads anchored by organic pasture-raised eggs; house-made hummus plate; sourdough waffle with seasonal fruit and house-cured bacon. [$] *Average main: $15* ✉ *2701 Eighth St., Berkeley* ☎ *510/356–2261* 🌐 *standardfareberkeley.com* 🕑 *Closed Sun. and Mon. No dinner.*

Coffee and Quick Bites

★ The Cheese Board Collective
$ | **PIZZA** | A jazz combo often entertains the line that snakes down the block outside Cheese Board Pizza; it's that good. The cooperatively owned vegetarian and vegan takeout spot and restaurant draws devoted customers with the smell of just-baked garlic on the pie of the day. **Known for:** cheese varieties; green sauce; daily changing toppings. [$] *Average main: $12* ✉ *1504–1512 Shattuck Ave., Berkeley* ☎ *510/549–3183* 🌐 *cheeseboardcollective.coop/pizza* 🕑 *Closed Sun.–Tues. Pizza: no lunch; bakery: no dinner.*

1951 Coffee Company

$ | **CAFÉ** | Taking its name from the 1951 UN Refugee Convention, this nonprofit coffee shop is inspired and powered by refugees. In addition to serving high-caliber coffee drinks, local pastries, and savory bites, the colorful café also serves as an advocacy space and barista training center for refugees. **Known for:** hand-roasted blends; excellent local pastries; matcha lattes. [$] *Average main: $6* ✉ *2410 Channing Way, Berkeley* ☎ *510/280–6171* 🌐 *www.1951coffee.com.*

Saul's

$$ | **JEWISH DELI** | **FAMILY** | High ceilings and red-leather booths add to the friendly, retro atmosphere of Saul's deli, a Berkeley institution that is well known for its house-made sodas and enormous sandwiches made with Acme bread. Locals swear by the pastrami Reubens, stuffed-cabbage rolls, and challah French toast. **Known for:** hand-rolled organic bagels; chicken schnitzel; deli hash with pastrami, corned beef, and poached eggs. [$] *Average main: $22* ✉ *1475 Shattuck Ave., Berkeley* ☎ *510/848–3354* 🌐 *www.saulsdeli.com.*

Viks Chaat

$ | **INDIAN** | The Chopra family has been selling excellent chaat (Indian street food snacks) to East Bay diners since 1989. It's part market, part bustling fast-casual restaurant with more substantial meat dishes and daily specials, dosas, and the staple homemade chaat that tend to be crunchy and/or fried (like samosas or puffed puri shells filled with mint water). **Known for:** warehouse atmosphere with long waits at peak times; bhel puri (rice puffs, potato, and chutney); weekend tandoori chicken. [$] *Average main: $14* ✉ *2390 Fourth St., Berkeley* ☎ *510/644–4432* 🌐 *vikschaat.com.*

Hotels

For inexpensive lodging, investigate University Avenue, west of campus. The area can be noisy, congested, and somewhat dilapidated, but it does include a few decent motels and chain properties. All Berkeley lodgings are strictly mid-range.

Aiden by Best Western @ Berkeley

$$ | **HOTEL** | Within a mile of campus and the heart of downtown, the Aiden celebrates the culture of Berkeley with wall art showcasing the campus life and spirit the town is known for. **Pros:** private parking; rooftop terrace with firepits and Bay views; good blackout curtains. **Cons:** some rooms get street noise; rough walk to downtown and the university; not a good value for the location. [$] *Rooms from: $250* ✉ *1499 University Ave., Berkeley* ☎ *510/298–2650* 🌐 *www.best-western.com* 🛏 *39 rooms* 🍴 *No Meals.*

The Bancroft Hotel

$ | **HOTEL** | This eco-friendly boutique hotel—across from the U.C. campus—is quaint, charming, and completely green. **Pros:** closest hotel to U.C. campus; friendly staff; many rooms have good views. **Cons:** some rooms are quite small; thin walls; no elevator. [$] *Rooms from: $189* ✉ *2680 Bancroft Way, Berkeley* ☎ *510/549–1000* 🌐 *bancrofthotel.com* 🛏 *22 rooms* 🍴 *Free Breakfast.*

Berkeley City Club

$$ | **HOTEL** | Moorish design and Gothic architecture join with modern amenities at this historic locale steps from the campus, arts venues, and eateries. **Pros:** art gallery and courtyard seating; laundry facilities; boccie court. **Cons:** tiny standard rooms; old-fashioned design; no TVs in rooms. [$] *Rooms from: $235* ✉ *2315 Durant Ave., Berkeley* ☎ *510/848–7800* 🌐 *www.berkeleycityclub.com* 🛏 *38 rooms* 🍴 *Free Breakfast.*

★ Claremont Club & Spa, a Fairmont Hotel
$$$ | HOTEL | FAMILY | Straddling the Oakland–Berkeley border, this amenities-rich property dating from 1915 beckons like a gleaming white castle in the hills. **Pros:** excellent restaurant and lounge for sunset views; daily events and special programs for children; gorgeous, sharply designed rooms. **Cons:** steep resort fee; smallest rooms are truly compact; remote location. [$] *Rooms from: $369* ✉ *41 Tunnel Rd., Berkeley* ☎ *510/843–3000, 888/560–4455 reservations* 🌐 *www.fairmont.com/claremont-berkeley* 🛏 *276 rooms* 🍴 *No Meals.*

The Graduate Berkeley
$$ | HOTEL | Fresh, colorful design and Bohemian flair set the tone at this hotel in one of Berkeley's registered historic places, just steps from campus and downtown eating, shopping, and entertainment. **Pros:** convenient location; fun atmosphere; warm, nicely decorated rooms. **Cons:** rooms can be noisy; rooms can be small; restaurant isn't open every evening. [$] *Rooms from: $245* ✉ *2600 Durant Ave., Berkeley* ☎ *510/845–8981* 🌐 *www.graduatehotels.com/berkeley* 🛏 *144 rooms* 🍴 *No Meals.*

Hotel Shattuck Plaza
$$ | HOTEL | This historic boutique hotel sits amid Berkeley's downtown arts district, just steps from the U.C. campus and a short walk from North Berkeley's best bites. **Pros:** central location; special date night and B&B packages; excellent remote work desk setup. **Cons:** public and street parking only; limited on-site fitness center; street-facing rooms may be noisy. [$] *Rooms from: $229* ✉ *2086 Allston Way, Berkeley* ☎ *510/845–7300* 🌐 *www.hotelshattuckplaza.com* 🛏 *199 ooms* 🍴 *No Meals.*

idence Inn by Marriott Berkeley
OTEL | FAMILY | This new hotel in the f the city's arts and cultural district the community's dedication to green living, as evident in its Gold LEED certification, use of recycled materials, and organic design. **Pros:** views from bar and terrace on 12th floor; steps from campus, arts, fine dining, and sights; enormous suites. **Cons:** hefty pet fee; expensive parking; traffic congestion. [$] *Rooms from: $283* ✉ *2121 Center St., Berkeley* ☎ *510/982–2100* 🌐 *www.marriott.com* 🛏 *331 suites* 🍴 *Free Breakfast.*

🍸 Nightlife

East Bay Spice Company
BARS | This creative establishment pairs Indian food with excellent cocktails that are given a fun twist, often with atypical spices, liqueurs, and spirits. Try the "East Bay Indica" which partners mezcal and tequila with lemon and tamarind syrup. ✉ *2134 Oxford St., Berkeley* 🌐 *eastbayspiceco.com.*

★ The Freight & Salvage Coffeehouse
LIVE MUSIC | Since 1968, the Freight has been a venue for some of the world's finest practitioners of folk, jazz, gospel, blues, world-beat, bluegrass, and storytelling. The nonprofit grew from an 87-seat coffee house to a thriving, nearly 500-seat venue in the heart of Berkeley's Arts District. Many tickets cost less than $30. ✉ *2020 Addison St., Berkeley* ☎ *510/644–2020* 🌐 *thefreight.org.*

Tupper & Reed
BARS | Housed in the former music shop of John C. Tupper and Lawrence Reed, this cocktail haven presents a symphony of carefully crafted libations, which are mixed with live music performed by local musicians. The historic 1925 building features a balcony bar, cozy nooks, antique fixtures, a pool table, and romantic fireplaces. ✉ *2271 Shattuck Ave., Berkeley* ☎ *510/859–4472* 🌐 *www.tupperandreed.com* ⏲ *Closed Mon.*

🎭 Performing Arts

More than a hundred arts and cultural organizations championing local artists and musicians contribute to Berkeley's happening scene. Many venues have small playhouses and performance spaces, allowing for great sight lines and intimate listening experiences.

Aurora Theatre Company

THEATER | Known for critically acclaimed productions like David Mamet's *American Buffalo* and Toni Morrison's *The Bluest Eye* and frequently launching world premieres of new plays, the Aurora is at the heart of Berkeley storytelling and community engagement. The theater's Alafi Auditorium seats 150 on three sides of the stage for premium viewing, and the smaller Harry's UpStage offers a more intimate experience for 49. Beyond the stage, the company has a monthly online broadcast with members of the community and its artists. ⊠ *2081 Addison St., Berkeley* ☎ *510/843–4822* ⊕ *www.auroratheatre.org.*

★ Berkeley Repertory Theatre

THEATER | One of the region's most highly respected and innovative repertory theaters, Berkeley Rep performs the work of classic and contemporary playwrights. Well-known pieces mix with world premieres and edgier fare. The theater's complex, which includes the 400-seat Peet's Theatre and the 600-seat Roda Theatre, is in the heart of downtown Berkeley's arts district, near BART's Downtown Berkeley station. ⊠ *2025 Addison St., Berkeley* ☎ *510/647–2949* ⊕ *www.berkeleyrep.org.*

★ California Jazz Conservatory

MUSIC | What started as a music education program in 1977, offering classes with the Bay Area's best jazz players, has become the area's top concert venue for the freshest sounds in jazz from around the world. Two 100-seat performance venues across the street from each other, Hardymon Hall (⊠ *2087 Addison St.*)

and Rendon Hall (⊠ *2040 Addison St.*), offer intimate viewing of some of the world's most influential musicians. Classes and workshops continue to serve as the foundation of the conservatory, with regular, affordably priced concerts each week for the public. ⊠ *2087 Addison St., Berkeley* ☎ *510/845–5373* ⊕ *cjc.edu.*

Cal Performances

ARTS CENTERS | Based out of U.C. Berkeley, this autumn and spring series runs from September/October through May/June. It features a varied bill of internationally acclaimed artists ranging from classical soloists to the latest jazz, world-music, theater, and dance ensembles. ⊠ *101 Zellerbach Hall, Suite 4800, at Dana St. and Bancroft Way, Berkeley* ☎ *510/642–9988* ⊕ *calperformances.org.*

The UC Theatre Taube Family Music Hall

MUSIC | One of Berkeley's oldest theaters opened its doors in 1917 as a first-run movie house with seating for 1,466 filmgoers. For years it served as a famous venue for foreign and domestic classics, closing in 2001. The theater's programming is now run by the nonprofit Berkeley Music Group, dedicated to bringing local, national, and international talent to Berkeley's arts district. Limited outdoor drinks and dining are available at the street bar, Out Front at the UC. ⊠ *2036 University Ave., Berkeley* ☎ *510/356–4000* ⊕ *theuctheatre.org.*

🛍 Shopping

★ ACCI Gallery

ART GALLERIES | The Arts & Crafts Cooperative, Inc., a collective of Berkeley artists and artisans, has been a stalwart gallery and store showcasing ceramics, textiles, paintings, photography, jewelry, and various media since 1957. Explore the amazing range of local talent in a well-lit historic space, and find truly one-of-a-kind gems to take home. The gallery hosts special events featuring artist explaining their works. ⊠ *1652 Sh*

Ave., Berkeley ☎ 510/843–2527 ⊕ www.
accigallery.com.

★ Amoeba Music

MUSIC | Heaven for audiophiles and
movie collectors, this legendary shop is
the place for new and used CDs, vinyl,
cassettes, VHS tapes, Blu-ray discs, and
DVDs. The massive and ever-changing
stock includes thousands of titles for all
music tastes. ✉ 2455 Telegraph Ave.,
Berkeley ☎ 510/549–1125 ⊕ www.amoe-
ba.com ⊗ Closed Mon. and Tues.

Kermit Lynch Wine Merchant

WINE/SPIRITS | Credited with taking
American appreciation of old-world wines
to a higher level, this small shop is a
great place to peruse as you educate
your palate. The friendly salespeople will
happily direct you to the latest French
and Italian vintages, varietals, blends, and
bargains. ✉ 1605 San Pablo Ave., Berkeley ☎ 510/524–1524 ⊕ www.kermitlynch.
com ⊗ Closed Sun. and Mon.

★ Moe's Books

BOOKS | The spirit of Moe—the creative,
cantankerous late proprietor—lives on in
this world-famous house full of new and
used books. Since it first opened in 1959,
students and professors have flocked
here to browse the large selection of literary and cultural criticism, art titles, and
literature in foreign languages. ✉ 2476
Telegraph Ave., Berkeley ☎ 510/849–
2087 ⊕ www.moesbooks.com.

Oakland

*9 miles from San Francisco via Bay
Bridge.*

In contrast to San Francisco's buzz and
Berkeley's storied counterculture, Oak-
and's allure lies in its amazing diversity.
re you can find a Nigerian clothing
e, a Gothic revival skyscraper, a Bud-
meditation center, and a lively salsa
ll within the same block.

Oakland's multifaceted nature reflects
its colorful and tumultuous history. Once
a cluster of Mediterranean-style homes
and gardens that served as a bedroom
community for San Francisco, the town
had a major rail terminal and port by the
turn of the 20th century. Already a hub of
manufacturing, Oakland became a center
for shipbuilding and industry when the
United States entered World War II. New
jobs in the city's shipyards, railroads, and
factories attracted thousands of laborers
from across the country, including
sharecroppers from the Deep South,
Mexican Americans from the Southwest,
and some of the nation's first female
welders. Neighborhoods were imbued
with a proud but gritty spirit, along with
heightened racial tension. In the wake
of the civil rights movement, racial pride
gave rise to militant groups like the
Black Panther Party, but they were little
match for the economic hardships and
racial tensions that plagued Oakland.
In many neighborhoods the reality was
widespread poverty and gang violence—
subjects that dominated the songs of
such Oakland-bred rappers as the late
Tupac Shakur. The protests of the Occupy
Oakland movement in 2011 and 2012 and
the Black Lives Matter movement more
recently illustrate just how much Oakland
remains a mosaic of its past.

Oakland's affluent reside in hillside
homes and wooded enclaves like Claremont, Piedmont, and Montclair, which
provide a warmer, more spacious alternative to San Francisco. A constant flow
of newcomers ensures diversity, vitality,
and growing pains. Neighborhoods
west and south of the city center show
signs of gentrification as the renovated
downtown and vibrant arts scene inject
new life into the city. Even San Franciscans come to Uptown and Temescal
for the nightlife, arts, and restaurants.
However, much of West Oakland, East
Oakland (including the area surrounding
the Oakland Coliseum) and the long
stretch of International Boulevard remain

very dicey, so it's best to avoid walking in them.

Everyday life here revolves around the neighborhood. In some areas, such as Piedmont and Rockridge, you'd swear you were in Berkeley or Noe Valley. Along Telegraph Avenue just south of 51st Street, Temescal is littered with hipsters and pulsing with creative culinary and design energy. These are perfect places for browsing, eating, or relaxing between sightseeing trips to Oakland's architectural gems, rejuvenated waterfront, and numerous green spaces.

GETTING HERE AND AROUND

From San Francisco, take I–80 East across the Bay Bridge, then take I–580 East to the Grand Avenue exit for Lake Merritt. To reach downtown and the waterfront, take I–980 West from I–580 East and exit at 12th Street; exit at 18th Street for Uptown. For Temescal, take I–580 East to Highway 24 and exit at 51st Street.

By BART, use the Lake Merritt Station for the Oakland Museum and southern Lake Merritt; the Oakland City Center–12th Street Station for downtown, Chinatown, and Old Oakland; and the 19th Street Station for Uptown, the Paramount Theatre, and the north side of Lake Merritt.

By bus, take the AC Transit's C and P lines to get to Piedmont in Oakland. The O bus stops at the edge of Chinatown near downtown Oakland.

Oakland's Jack London Square is an easy hop on the ferry from San Francisco. Those without cars can take advantage of the free Broadway Shuttle, which runs from Jack London Square to Grand Avenue weekdays, with continued service to 27th Street weeknights from 7 to 10 pm. There's no weekend service.

Be aware of how quickly neighborhoods can change. Walking is generally safe downtown and in the Piedmont and Rockridge areas, but be mindful when walking west and southeast of downtown, especially at night.

ESSENTIALS

CONTACT Visit Oakland. ⊠ *481 Water St., Jack London Square* ☎ *510/839–9000* ⊕ *www.visitoakland.com.*

Sights

Lake Merritt

CITY PARK | In the center of Oakland just east of downtown, this tidal lagoon with its unique habitat for more than 100 bird species became the country's first wildlife refuge in 1870. Today the three-mile path around the lake is a refuge for walkers, bikers, joggers, and nature lovers. **Lakeside Park** has **Children's Fairyland** (⊠ *699 Bellevue Ave.*) and the **Rotary Nature Center** (⊠ *600 Bellevue Ave.*). The **Lake Merritt Boating Center** (⊠ *568 Bellevue Ave.*) rents kayaks and rowboats (from $18; cash only).

On the lake's south side, the **Camron-Stanford House** (⊠ *1418 Lakeside Dr.*) is the last of the grand Victorians that once dominated the area; it's open Sundays for tours. Nearby, bold **Oakland mural art** offers a more modern feast for the eyes (⊠ *Between Madison and Webster Sts. and 7th and 11th Sts.*).

The lake's necklace of lights adds allure for diners heading to **Lake Chalet** (⊠ *1520 Lakeside Dr.*), as well as to a host of tasty options along Grand Avenue, from Ethiopian cuisine at **Enssaro** (⊠ *357A Grand Ave.*) and Korean barbecue at **Jong Ga House** (⊠ *372 Grand Ave.*) to comfort gourmet at **Grand Lake Kitchen** (⊠ *576 Grand Ave.*). ⊠ *Lake Merritt* ⊠ *Free.*

★ **Oakland Museum of California** (*OMCA*) **OTHER MUSEUM** | **FAMILY** | Designed by Kevin Roche, this museum is a quintessential example of mid-century modern architecture and home to a capacious collection of nearly 2 million objects in three distinct galleries celebrating California's history, natural

11

The Bay Area **OAKLAND**

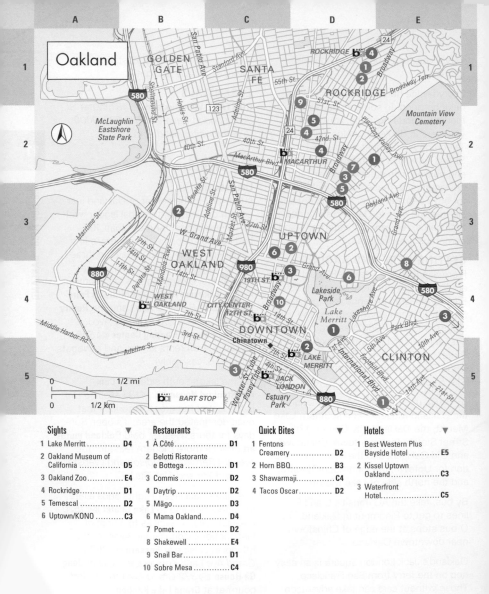

Oakland

A **B** **C** **D** **E**

GOLDEN GATE
SANTA FE
55th St.
ROCKRIDGE
ROCKRIDGE
51st St.
Broadway
Broadway Terr.
24
Mountain View Cemetery
McLaughlin Eastshore State Park
123
40th St.
40th St.
MacArthur Blvd. MACARTHUR
42nd. St.
Broadway
Oakland Ave.
Grand Ave.
580
Pleasant Valley Ave.
W. Grand Ave.
UPTOWN
WEST OAKLAND
Grand Ave.
Lakeside Park
Lake Merritt
880
980
19TH ST.
CITY CENTER 12TH ST.
14th St.
Broadway
580
WEST OAKLAND
7th St.
3rd St.
DOWNTOWN
Chinatown
LAKE MERRITT
CLINTON
Middle Harbor Rd.
Adeline St.
JACK LONDON
Estuary Park
880
International Blvd.
Foothill Blvd.
E. 21st. St.

0   1/2 mi
0   1/2 km

b BART STOP

Sights ▼	Restaurants ▼	Quick Bites ▼	Hotels ▼
1 Lake Merritt D4	1 À Côté D1	1 Fentons Creamery D2	1 Best Western Plus Bayside Hotel E5
2 Oakland Museum of California D5	2 Belotti Ristorante e Bottega D1	2 Horn BBQ B3	2 Kissel Uptown Oakland C3
3 Oakland Zoo E4	3 Commis D2	3 Shawarmaji C4	3 Waterfront Hotel C5
4 Rockridge D1	4 Daytrip D2	4 Tacos Oscar D2	
5 Temescal D2	5 Mägo D3		
6 Uptown/KONO C3	6 Mama Oakland D4		
	7 Pomet D2		
	8 Shakewell E4		
	9 Snail Bar D1		
	10 Sobre Mesa C4		

art. Listen to native species and environmental soundscapes in the Library of Natural Sounds and engage in stories of the state's past and future, from Ohlone basket making to emerging technologies. Don't miss the photographs from Dorothea Lange's personal archive and a worthy collection of Bay Area figurative painters, including David Park and Joan Brown. Stay for lunch at the Town Fare café, where chef Michele McQueen serves California-soul food dishes like Low Country shrimp and cheddar grits. ■TIP➔ On Friday evening, the museum bustles with live music, food trucks, and after-hours gallery access. ⊠ 1000 Oak St., Downtown ☎ 510/318–8400 ⊕ museumca.org ⊠ $19; free 1st Sun. of month ⊗ Closed Mon. and Tues.

Oakland Zoo

ZOO | FAMILY | One of the West Coast's leading zoos resides in the rolling hills of southeast Oakland. More than 750 animals from near and far live here, often putting on quite a show for the human visitors. The children's zoo and the California Trail are notable areas, with the latter featuring two of the most iconic animals in the Golden State: California condors and grizzly bears. The zoo has a handful of entertaining rides, but the main non-animal highlight for most guests is the Sky Ride gondola that offers incredible Bay Area views. ⊠ 9777 Golf Links Rd., Oakland ☎ 510/632-9525 ⊕ oaklandzoo.org ⊠ $24.

Rockridge

NEIGHBORHOOD | FAMILY | One of Oakland's most desirable places to live is this fashionable, upscale neighborhood. Explore the tree-lined streets that radiate out from College Avenue, just north and south of the Rockridge BART station for a look at California Craftsman bungalows at their finest. By day, College Avenue between Broadway and Alcatraz Avenue is crowded with shoppers buying fresh flowers, used books, and clothing; by night, the same folks are back for

satisfying meals filled with fresh local ingredients, artisanal wines, and locally brewed ales. There's even a cider bar, one of the few in the Bay Area (**Redfield Cider Bar & Bottle Shop**, ⊠ 5815 College Ave.). With its specialty food shops and quick bites to go, **Market Hall**, an airy European-style marketplace at Shafter Avenue, is a hub of culinary activity, including the wonderful Californian-Mediterranean cooking of the attached **Acre Kitchen & Bar** (⊠ 5655 College Ave.). ⊠ Rockridge ⊕ www.rockridgedistrict.com.

★ Temescal

NEIGHBORHOOD | Centering on Telegraph Avenue between 40th and 51st Streets, Temescal (the Aztec term for "sweat house") is a low-pretension, moneyed-hipster hood with young families and middle-aged folks in the mix. Protected bike lanes, bus islands, and a pedestrian plaza add to the vibrancy of this neighborhood. A critical mass of excellent eateries draws diners from around the Bay Area; there are newer favorites like excellent Filipino eats at **FOB Kitchen** (⊠ 5179 Telegraph Ave.) and **Smokin Woods BBQ** (⊠ 4307 Telegraph Ave.), as well as standbys like the fantastic fish tacos of **Cholita Linda** (⊠ 4923 Telegraph Ave.) and the unusually refined café-brewery **Rose's Taproom** (⊠ 4930 Telegraph Ave.). Old-timey dive bars and smog-check stations share space with public art installations of murals, sculptures, and mosaic trash cans.

Temescal Alley (⊠ Off 49th St.), a tucked-away lane of tiny storefronts, crackles with creative energy. Get an old-fashioned straight-edge shave at **Temescal Alley Barber Shop** (⊠ 470 49th St., Suite B). Don't miss grabbing a sweet scoop at **Curbside Creamery** (⊠ 482 49th St.). ⊠ Telegraph Ave. between 40th and 51st Sts., Temescal ⊕ www.temescaldistrict.org.

Uptown/KONO

NEIGHBORHOOD | Uptown and KONO (Koreatown/Northgate) is where nig and cutting-edge art merge. Doze galleries cluster around Telegraph Avenue and north of Grand Avenue into KONO, exhibiting everything from photography and installations to glasswork and fiber arts. The first Friday of each month, thousands of people descend for **Art Murmur** (🌐 *oaklandartmurmur.org*), a late-night gallery event that has expanded into **First Fridays** (🌐 *www.oaklandfirstfridays.org*), a festival of food trucks, street vendors, and live music along Telegraph Avenue.

Restaurants with a distinctly urban vibe make Uptown/KONO a dining destination every night of the week. Favorites include eclectic Japanese-inspired fare at **Hopscotch** (✉ *1915 San Pablo Ave.*), ramen and izakaya offerings at **Shinmai** (✉ *1825–3 San Pablo Ave.*), the terrific Jamaican cooking of **Kingston 11** (✉ *2270 Telegraph Ave.*), fantastic Spanish tapas and paella from celebrated chef Paul Canales at **Duende** (✉ *468 19th St.*), and sushi hand rolls offered by **Yonsei Handrolls** (✉ *1738 Telegraph Ave.*).

Toss in the bevy of bars and there's plenty within walking distance to keep you busy all evening, such as **Drake's Dealership** (✉ *2325 Broadway*), with its spacious, hipster-friendly beer garden; fantastic cocktails paired with eclectic eats and a stunning art-deco atmosphere at **Palmetto** (✉ *1900 Telegraph Ave.*); and **Somar** (✉ *1727 Telegraph Ave.*), a bar, music lounge, and art gallery in one. ✉ *Telegraph Ave. and Broadway from 14th to 27th Sts., Uptown.*

🍴 Restaurants

À Côté

$$ | **MEDITERRANEAN** | This hot spot is all about seasonal and globe-spanning small plates, family-style eating, and excellent drinks. Intimate dining nooks, natural ght, and a heated patio make this an al destination for couples, families, the after-work crowd. **Known for:** d mussels cooked in the wood latbreads; global and regional wine list. [$] *Average main: $26* ✉ *5478 College Ave., Rockridge* ☎ *510/655–6469* 🌐 *www.acoterestaurant.com* 🕘 *Closed Sun. and Mon. No lunch.*

Belotti Ristorante e Bottega

$$ | **ITALIAN** | Bay Area residents could debate for days about who truly makes the region's greatest pasta, but this Rockridge shop and restaurant from pasta whisperer Michele Belotti is more often than not on that short list. It's a perfect blend of traditional and comforting with modern influences. **Known for:** tortellini in brodo; vitello tonnato (beef with Sicilian tuna sauce); strong Italian wines roster. [$] *Average main: $22* ✉ *5403 College Ave., Oakland* ☎ *510/788–7890* 🌐 *belottirb.com* 🕘 *Closed Sun.*

★ Commis

$$$$ | **AMERICAN** | A slender, unassuming storefront houses the first East Bay restaurant with a Michelin star (two of them, in fact). The room is minimalist and polished: nothing distracts from the artistry of chef James Syhabout, who creates a multicourse prix-fixe experience based on the season and his distinctive vision of modern and classic creations. **Known for:** inventive tasting menu; fantastic wine collection; excellent bar next door with its own menu. [$] *Average main: $225* ✉ *3859 Piedmont Ave., Piedmont* ☎ *510/653–3902* 🌐 *commisrestaurant.com* 🕘 *Closed Sun. and Mon. No lunch.*

Daytrip

$$ | **MODERN AMERICAN** | A "fermentation-driven" restaurant sounds a bit odd, but you'll find a thrilling, umami-packed experience at this compact Temescal spot. With a disco ball overhead, you expect somebody to get up and dance with how groovy the vibe is. **Known for:** signature celery salad; colorful wall mural and Rubik's Cube–like counter; miso butter pasta. [$] *Average main: $22* ✉ *4316 Telegraph Ave., Oakland* 🌐 *thisisdaytrip.com* 🕘 *No lunch weekdays.*

Mägo

$$$$ | SOUTH AMERICAN | After several years as a leading chef in San Francisco, Mark Liberman crossed the Bay Bridge to open this deeply personal restaurant that channels his Colombian heritage in a contemporary way. There are two tasting menus available—a long and a short. **Known for:** affordable tasting menu; lively bar; beautiful, colorful place with big open kitchen. $ *Average main:* $75 ☒ 3762 Piedmont Ave., Oakland ☎ 510/344–7214 ⊕ magorestaurant.com ⟲ Closed Sun,–Tues. No lunch.

Mama Oakland

$$$ | MODERN ITALIAN | This classic Italian meets Californian menu is a stellar value where three courses clock in at less than $40 (the optional supplements are worth adding on). The quality is sky high, with no corners cut. **Known for:** signature meatballs; stellar wine list; homemade focaccia. $ *Average main:* $36 ☒ 388 Grand Ave., Oakland ☎ 510/974–6372 ⊕ mama-oakland.com ⟲ No lunch.

Pomet

$$ | MODERN AMERICAN | Many restaurants have direct relationships between nearby farms and the kitchen, but very few are truly co-owned. Here, with chef Alan Hsu at the helm in the kitchen, top-tier local produce is showcased in excellent contemporary Californian dishes. **Known for:** "ugly mushroom" pasta with locally made miso butter; salt-and-pepper quail; warm, quaint setting with a large open kitchen. $ *Average main:* $30 ☒ 4029 Piedmont Ave., Oakland ☎ 510/450–2541 ⊕ pomet-oakland.com ⟲ Closed Mon. and Tues. No lunch.

★ Shakewell

$$ | MEDITERRANEAN | Two *Top Chef* vets opened this stylish restaurant, which serves creative and memorable Mediterranean small plates in a lively setting with an open kitchen, wood-fired oven, communal tables, and snug seating. As the name implies, well-crafted cocktails are shaken (or stirred) and poured with panache. **Known for:** wood-oven paella; fried chicken with fenugreek yogurt; vegetarian options. $ *Average main:* $29 ☒ 3407 Lakeshore Ave., Grand Lake ☎ 510/251–0329 ⊕ www.shakewelloakland.com ⟲ Closed Mon. No dinner Sun. No lunch Tues.–Fri.

★ Snail Bar

$$ | MODERN FRENCH | The Temescal neighborhood's dining anchor is a quirky wine bar with a powerful food program. At least half of the seating is outside, lending a Parisian indoor-outdoor café vibe to the air of this appropriately named spot with a signature escargots and cashew miso dish. **Known for:** unique wines from small producers; fish and avocado tostadas; raw seafood preparations. $ *Average main:* $20 ☒ 4935 Shattuck Ave., Oakland ☎ 510/879–7678 ⊕ snailbaroakland.com ⟲ No lunch.

Sobre Mesa

$ | LATIN AMERICAN | A unique blend of African culinary influences along with flavors from various Latin American countries are the draw at chef Nelson German's restaurant. Each tapa is compelling (there are no main courses, though there are more than enough tempting dishes to satisfy a group) and nicely ties together the two geographic regions. **Known for:** ground steak picadillo empanadas; unique take on tostones; the namesake cocktail with two kinds of rum. $ *Average main:* $17 ☒ 1618 Franklin St., Oakland ☎ 510/858–7544 ⊕ sobremesaoak.com ⟲ Closed Mon. No lunch.

☕ Coffee and Quick Bites

★ Fentons Creamery

$ | AMERICAN | FAMILY | Beloved by the Bay since 1922 and featured in the Pixar film *Up*, this is the leading name locally for ice cream sundaes and good old-fashioned soda fountain fare. Kids of all ages adore the signature black-and-tan sundae with toasted almond and vanilla ice creams layered with caramel and chocolate

356

sauces. **Known for:** nostalgic atmosphere; ice cream sundaes; tuna melt. $ *Average main: $18* ✉ *4226 Piedmont Ave., Oakland* ☎ *510/658–7000* ⊕ *fentonscreamery.com.*

Horn BBQ

$$ | **BARBECUE** | It's hard to keep track of how many awards pitmaster Matt Horn has won at this point. After roving around the Bay Area for years as a pop-up with his smoker "Lucille," Horn set up shop permanently in West Oakland and has had lines out the door ever since. **Known for:** tender, irresistible smoked meats and sausages; best-in-class banana pudding; must-order pit beans on the side. $ *Average main: $20* ✉ *2534 Mandela Pkwy., Oakland* ☎ *510/225–6101* ⊕ *hornbarbecue.com* ◔ *Closed Mon.–Wed.*

Shawarmaji

$ | **MIDDLE EASTERN** | Jordan-inspired street food is not easy to find in the Bay Area. The unique Californian catch here is the use of flour tortillas, which are better for the foot-long, narrow wraps that are pressed on the flat top for an extra level of caramelized delight to each bite. **Known for:** shawarma wraps with homemade pickles and toum sauce; shawarma fries; fresh side salads. $ *Average main: $14* ✉ *2123 Franklin St., Oakland* ☎ *510/397–9817* ⊕ *theshawarmaji.com.*

★ Tacos Oscar

$ | **MEXICAN** | Arguably the most talked-about tacos in the entire Bay Area are at this colorful, cheery spot in an alley in between Uptown, Temescal, and Piedmont Ave. The fresh corn tortillas are so tender—almost a revelation. Fillings are always packed with flavor, complemented by dialed-in salsas like a peanut-arbol chile one with carefully charred broccoli. **Known for:** pork chile verde taco; fun courtyard seating; truly exciting bean and cheese taco. $ *Average main: $5* ✉ *420 [.]th St., Oakland* ⊕ *tacososcar.com* [.]losed Tues. and Wed. No lunch.

 Hotels

Best Western Plus Bayside Hotel

$$ | **HOTEL** | This relatively small-sized property has pleasant accommodations with balconies or patios, many overlooking the water and Alameda island. **Pros:** spacious rooms; no destination or amenity fees; easy access to and from airport, Jack London Square, and downtown. **Cons:** few shops or restaurants in walking distance; freeway-side rooms can be noisy; surprisingly high prices for location. $ *Rooms from: $209* ✉ *1717 Embarcadero, Oakland* ☎ *510/356–2450* ⊕ *www.bestwestern.com* ⇗ *81 rooms* ﹚ *Free Breakfast.*

Kissel Uptown Oakland

$$ | **HOTEL** | For years, Uptown Oakland was a hip neighborhood with outstanding restaurants and bars and nowhere to stay—until this ultra-chic Hyatt-flagged property came along. **Pros:** beautiful art and decorations; walking distance to all kinds of places; rooftop bar High 5ive. **Cons:** dicey neighborhood; can be too hip of a scene; smallest rooms are a bit tight. $ *Rooms from: $229* ✉ *2455 Broadway, Oakland* ☎ *510/216–1500* ⊕ *hyatt.com* ⇗ *168 rooms* ﹚ *No Meals.*

Waterfront Hotel

$ | **HOTEL** | **FAMILY** | Thoroughly modern and pleasantly appointed, this JdV by Hyatt hotel sits among the many breweries and restaurants of Jack London Square and is both a favorite place for locals' family members and a sweet spot for business travelers with its proximity to the square and downtown. **Pros:** outdoor dining in Jack London Square; lovely views, including some water views; outdoor pool. **Cons:** passing trains can be noisy on the city side; parking is pricey; long, dicey walk to downtown. $ *Rooms from: $172* ✉ *10 Washington St., Jack London Square* ☎ *510/836–3800 front desk* ⊕ *jdvhotels.com* ⇗ *145 rooms* ﹚ *No Meals.*

▼ Nightlife

BARS

★ Café Van Kleef

BARS | Long before Uptown got hot, the late Peter Van Kleef was serving stiff fresh-squeezed Greyhounds and booking live music at this funky café-bar that crackles with creative energy—there's still live music every weekend. ⊠ *1621 Telegraph Ave., Uptown* ☎ *510/763–7711* ⊕ *cafevankleef.com* ☾ *Closed Sun. and Mon.*

Friends & Family

BARS | This fantastic woman- and queer-owned bar-restaurant has an excellent compact food menu, standout cocktails, a chic interior design, and one of the best patios in the city. The house margarita is an intriguing must-try drink with mezcal and lemon instead of lime and tequila. Other drinks have eyebrow-raising elements that truly work like melon-infused gin or a coconut water popsicle. The grilled cheese and carrot cake are best in class for those comfort food staples. ⊠ *468 25th St., Oakland* ☎ *510/225–0469* ⊕ *friendsandfamilybar.com.*

★ Heinold's First and Last Chance Saloon

BARS | Arguably California's longest continuously active saloon since it opened in 1884, this watering hole, built from the hull of a flat-bottomed stern-wheeler, is where young Jack London got his start as a writer. Historic photos and artifacts hang from the crooked walls and ceilings, which have been atilt since the 1906 earthquake. Get a peek at the slanted bar, where beers on tap and bottomless stories of Oakland history abound. ⊠ *48 Webster St., Jack London Square* ☎ *510/839–6761* ⊕ *www.heinoldsfirstandlastchance.com.*

Low Bar

BARS | Unique cocktails; casual eats; and a fun space with plants and lots of natural light makes this one of the most compelling bars in Uptown Oakland. Cocktails have creative elements, like a spiced

grapefruit cordial in the mezcal-based Deadbeat Summer. ⊠ *2300 Webster St., Oakland* ⊕ *lowbaroakland.com.*

★ Viridian

BARS | Some of the most innovative, pristine cocktails in the Bay Area are at this neon-lit, energetic bar. Bar Director William Tsui previously worked at fine dining juggernaut Lazy Bear in San Francisco, and that high level of meticulous technicality and ingredient sourcing is abundantly clear here across the bay. It's almost unfair that the food menu, nodding to several Asian cuisine elements with a California touch, is so great as well. The narrow space gets packed quickly. ⊠ *2216 Broadway, Oakland* ⊕ *viridianbar.com.*

BREWPUBS AND BEER GARDENS

Brotzeit Lokal

BEER GARDENS | This tucked-away German biergarten is in Oakland's Brooklyn Basin along the waterfront Bay Trail, with lovely views of the marina, estuary, and Coast Guard Island. Known for its select German beers and delectable Bavarian dishes, including sausages, schnitzel, and homemade spaetzle, this family-friendly spot is especially popular on nice days. ⊠ *1000 Embarcadero, Lake Merritt* ☎ *510/645–1905* ⊕ *brotzeitbiergarten.com.*

Buck Wild Brewing

BREWPUBS | This chic taproom is California's first 100%-gluten-free brewery, specializing in craft beers made without rye, wheat, or barley. The brewery also has tempting gluten-free fare such as quesadillas and fish tacos. ⊠ *401 Jackson St., Jack London Square* ☎ *510/350–7938* ⊕ *www.buckwildbrew.com* ☾ *Closed Mon. and Tues.*

Federation Brewing Company

BREWPUBS | Part of Oakland's Ale Trail, the brewery has a convivial tasting room in the Jack London District with plenty of games for extended sipping of their pilsners, saisons, sours, and hoppy IPAs.

Their outdoor seating area includes booth areas made of repurposed shipping containers. The taproom hosts live music and events a few nights a month, so make sure to check their calendar. ⊠ *420 3rd St., Jack London Square* ☎ *510/496–4228* ⊕ *www.federationbrewing.com.*

Line 51 Brewing—The Terminal Taproom
BREWPUBS | This bright, airy, 7,500-square-foot brewery and taproom is a tribute to its early history, when the brewers hauled their kegs on public transit line 51 to their warehouse. Now, Oakland Ale Trail explorers can enjoy freshly tapped beer from a vintage 1971 AC transit bus that serves as a refrigeration unit for their brews. Fermentation tanks are on full display: the owners are passionate about their Red Death ale, IPAs, Short Dog ale, and porters. ⊠ *303 Castro St., Jack London Square* ☎ *510/985–4181* ⊕ *www.line51beer.com* ☾ *Closed Mon. and Tues.*

Original Pattern Brewing
BREWPUBS | The love for beer of all varieties is evident in the selection of award-winners at this employee-owned brewery. Original Pattern consistently produces the most satisfying and compelling offerings of any brewery in this beer-loving town. ⊠ *292 4th St., Jack London Square* ☎ *510/844–4833* ⊕ *www.originalpatternbeer.com.*

Sante Adairius Rustic Ales Oakland Arbor
BREWPUBS | In 2022, Sante Adairius opened a taproom in Old Oakland and the entire region rejoiced with plenty of barrel-aged saisons in tulip glasses and pints of intricate hazy IPAs. The intimate, refined saloon space also has a great rear patio. Even though the brews come from an hour away, no visit to Oakland for beer lovers is complete without a stop here. ⊠ *460 8th St., Oakland* ⊕ *rusticales.com.*

MUSIC VENUES
Fox Theater
LIVE MUSIC | This renovated 1928 theater is a remarkable feat of Mediterranean Moorish architecture and has seen the likes of Willie Nelson, the Magnetic Fields, and B.B. King. The venue boasts good sight lines, a state-of-the-art sound system, brilliant acoustics, and a bar with food. ⊠ *1807 Telegraph Ave., Uptown* ☎ *510/302–2250* ⊕ *thefoxoakland.com.*

Yoshi's
LIVE MUSIC | Opened in 1972 as a sushi bar, Yoshi's has evolved into one of the area's best jazz and live music venues. The full experience includes traditional Japanese and Asian fusion cuisine in the adjacent restaurant. ⊠ *510 Embarcadero W, Jack London Square* ☎ *510/238–9200* ⊕ *yoshis.com.*

 Performing Arts

Paramount Theatre
ARTS CENTERS | A glorious art-deco specimen, the Paramount operates as a venue for performances of all kinds, from silent films with orchestras playing the soundtrack, to the Oakland Ballet and Oakland Symphony. Docent-led tours ($5), offered the first and third Saturday of the month, are fun and informative. ⊠ *2025 Broadway, Uptown* ☎ *510/465–6400* ⊕ *paramountoakland.org.*

Shopping

Pop-up shops and stylish, locally focused stores are scattered throughout the funky alleys of Old Oakland, Uptown, and Temescal, along with Rockridge's College Ave. Meanwhile, the winding streets around Lake Merritt and Grand Lake offer more modest boutiques.

Bay-Made
SOUVENIRS | Owned and operated by women artists, this gift shop showcases the delightful works of more than 120 Oakland artisans and makers. Browse handcrafted paper and print art, collage art, chocolate, waxworks, jewelry, ceramics, herbs and oils, and quality art and printing supplies. A rotating gallery wall features the latest works from local

artists. ⊠ *3295 Lakeshore Ave., Grand Lake* ☎ *510/520–4600* ⊕ *www.bay-made. com* ⊙ *Closed Mon. and Tues.*

Maison d'Etre

HOUSEWARES | This store epitomizes the Rockridge neighborhood's funky-chic shopping scene. Look for high-end housewares along with impulse buys like whimsical watches, imported fruit-tea blends, and funky slippers. ⊠ *5640 College Ave., Rockridge* ☎ *510/658–2801* ⊕ *www.maisondetre.com.*

★ Oaklandish

MIXED CLOTHING | The ultimate place for Oakland swag started in 2000 as a public art project of local pride and has become a celebrated brand around the bay, with clothing and accessories for men, women, and kids. A portion of the proceeds from hip T-shirts and accessories supports grassroots nonprofits committed to bettering the local community. It's good-looking stuff for a good cause. ⊠ *1444 Broadway, Uptown* ☎ *510/251–9500* ⊕ *oaklandish.com.*

Ordinaire

WINE/SPIRITS | This Grand Lake stalwart deserves an enormous amount of credit for showcasing small-producer, low-intervention wines (what some like to call natural wines), and for making wine an approachable, hip subject. Whether you're enjoying a glass at the bar with some cheese or browsing the impressive selection of retail bottles, this is the local game-changer that made boutique wine as trendy as craft beer and cocktails. ⊠ *3354 Grand Ave., Oakland* ☎ *510/350–7524* ⊕ *ordinairewine.com.*

🏃 Activities

Oakland Athletics

BASEBALL & SOFTBALL | **FAMILY** | Baseball's Oakland Athletics, also called the Oakland A's, has a loyal following among locals in the East Bay and enjoys a fierce rivalry with the San Francisco Giants across the bay. The team hopes to move from its Oakland Coliseum stadium to a proposed new waterfront ballpark at Jack London Square, but that project has repeatedly stalled and fans are discouraged that it might not happen. Major League Baseball is also allowing the team to consider relocating to another city; stay tuned. ⊠ *Oakland Coliseum, 7000 Coliseum Way, Oakland* ☎ *877/638–4900* ⊕ *mlb.com/athletics.*

The Marin Headlands

Due west of the Golden Gate Bridge's northern end.

The term "Golden Gate" has become synonymous with the world-famous bridge, but it was first given to the narrow waterway that connects the Pacific and San Francisco Bay. To the north of the Golden Gate Strait lie the Marin Headlands, part of the Golden Gate National Recreation Area (GGNRA), with some of the area's most dramatic scenery.

GETTING HERE AND AROUND

Driving from San Francisco, head north on U.S. 101. Just after you cross the Golden Gate Bridge, take Exit 442 for Alexander Avenue. Keep left at the fork and follow signs for San Francisco/U.S. 101 South. Go through the tunnel under the freeway, and turn right up the hill.

Sights

Marin Headlands

NATIONAL PARK | **FAMILY** | The stunning headlands stretch from the Golden Gate Bridge to Muir Beach, drawing photographers who perch on the southern heights for spectacular shots of the city and bridge. Equally remarkable are the views north along the coast and out to the ocean, where the Farallon Islands are visible on clear days. Hawk Hill (accessed from Conzelman Road) has a trail with panoramic views and is a great place to watch the fall raptor migration; it's also home to the mission blue butterfly.

The headlands' strategic position at the mouth of San Francisco Bay made them a logical site for military installations from 1890 through the Cold War. Today you can explore the crumbling concrete batteries where naval guns once protected the area. Main attractions are centered on Forts Barry and Cronkhite, which are separated by Rodeo Lagoon and Rodeo Beach, a dark stretch of sand that attracts sandcastle builders and dog owners. ⊠ *Sausalito* ☎ *415/331–1540* ⊕ *www.nps.gov/goga* 🎟 *Free.*

Sausalito

2 miles north of Golden Gate Bridge.

Bougainvillea-covered hillsides and an expansive yacht harbor give Sausalito the feel of an Adriatic resort. The town sits on the northwestern edge of San Francisco Bay, where it's sheltered from the ocean by the Marin Headlands; the mostly mild weather here is perfect for strolling and outdoor dining. Nevertheless, morning fog and afternoon winds can roll over the hills without warning, funneling through the central part of Sausalito once known as Hurricane Gulch.

South of Bridgeway, which snakes between the bay and the hills, a waterside esplanade is lined with restaurants on piers that lure diners with good seafood and even better views. Stairs along the west side of Bridgeway and throughout town climb into wooded hillside neighborhoods filled with both rustic and opulent homes. Back on the northern portion of the shoreline, harbors shelter a community of more than 400 houseboats. As you amble along Bridgeway past shops and galleries, you'll notice the absence of basic services. Find them and more on Caledonia Street, which runs parallel to Bridgeway and inland a couple of blocks. While ferry-side shops flaunt kitschy souvenirs, smaller side streets and narrow alleyways offer eccentric jewelry and handmade crafts.

■ **TIP→ The ferry is the best way to get to Sausalito from San Francisco; you get more romance (and less traffic) and disembark in the heart of downtown.**

First occupied by the Coast Miwok tribe and later visited by Spanish explorers who called the area Saucito (Little Willow) for the trees growing along its streams, Sausalito was developed as a ranch in 1838 under the ownership of English mariner William Richardson. It served as a port for whaling ships and became a major terminus for transport by rail, ferry, and, eventually, car. By the mid-1800s, wealthy San Franciscans had made Sausalito their getaway across the bay and built lavish Victorian summer homes in the hills. Meanwhile, an influx of hardworking, fun-loving merchants and working-class folk populated the waterfront area, which grew thick with saloons, gambling dens, and bordellos. Bootleggers flourished during Prohibition, and shipyard workers swelled the town's population in the 1940s, at the height of World War II.

Sausalito developed its bohemian flair in the 1950s and '60s, when creative types, including artist Jean Varda, poet Shel Silverstein, and madam Sally Stanford, established an artists' colony and a houseboat community here (this is Otis

Marin County

0   5 mi

0   5 km

Redding's "Dock of the Bay"). Both the spirit of the artists and the neighborhood of floating homes persist. For a close-up view of the quirky community, head north on Bridgeway, turn right on Gate Six Road, park where it dead-ends, and enter through the unlocked gates.

GETTING HERE AND AROUND

From San Francisco by car or bike, follow U.S. 101 North across the Golden Gate Bridge and take Exit 442 for Alexander Avenue, just past Vista Point; continue down the winding hill toward the water to where the road becomes Bridgeway. Golden Gate Transit's Bus 130 will drop you off in downtown Sausalito, and the ferries dock downtown as well. The center of town is flat, with plenty of sidewalks and bay views. It's a pleasure and a must to explore on foot.

ESSENTIALS

CONTACT Sausalito Chamber of Commerce.
✉ *1913 Bridgeway, Sausalito* ☎ *415/331–7262* ⊕ *www.sausalito.org.*

Sights

Bay Model Visitor Center

VISITOR CENTER | FAMILY | One of the Bay Area's most unique attractions is a model of itself. It's a giant—over an acre—hydraulic model of the San Francisco Bay–San Joaquin River Delta (Sacramento area) water systems by the US Army Corps of Engineers. For visitors and tourists alike, it's a fascinating place to learn about one of the most complex, diverse environmental regions in the country. ✉ *2100 Bridgeway, Sausalito* ☎ *415/289–3007* ⊕ *www.spn.usace.army.mil/missions/recreation/bay-model-visitor-center* 🎟 *Free* ⊗ *Closed Sun. and Mon.*

The Marine Mammal Center

COLLEGE | FAMILY | This hospital for distressed, sick, and injured marine animals is a leading center for ocean conservancy in the Bay Area and the largest rehabilitation center of its kind in the world. Dedicated to pioneering education, rehabilitation, and research, the center is free and open daily to the public. Tour the facilities and see how elephant seals, sea lions, and pups are cared for and meet the scientists who care for them. Bonus: you'll catch some of the best views of the Marin Headlands and San Francisco Bay along the way. ✉ *2000 Bunker Rd., Sausalito* ☎ *415/653–1870* 🌐 *www.marinemammalcenter.org* 🎟 *Free* ☞ *Check website for tour times.*

Sally Stanford Drinking Fountain

FOUNTAIN | There's an unusual historic landmark on the Sausalito Ferry Pier—a drinking fountain inscribed "Have a drink on Sally" in remembrance of Sally Stanford, the former San Francisco brothel madam who became Sausalito's mayor in the 1970s. Sassy Sally would have appreciated the fountain's eccentric attachment: a knee-level basin with the inscription "Have a drink on Leland," in memory of her beloved dog. ✉ *Sausalito Ferry Pier, Anchor St. at Humboldt St., off southwest corner of Gabrielson Park, Sausalito* 🌐 *www.oursausalito.com.*

Viña del Mar Plaza and Park

PLAZA/SQUARE | The landmark Plaza Viña del Mar, named for Sausalito's sister city in Chile, marks the center of town. Adjacent to the parking lot and ferry pier, the plaza is flanked by two 14-foot-tall statues of elephants, which were created for the Panama–Pacific International Exposition World's Fair held in San Francisco in 1915. A picture-perfect fountain here is great for people-watching. ✉ *Bridgeway and El Portal St., Sausalito* 🌐 *www.oursausalito.com.*

🍴 Restaurants

Arawan Thai

$ | THAI | Tucked along the restaurant row of Caledonia Street, Arawan Thai is a stalwart destination for some of the tastiest Thai dishes in Marin County. The elegant and cozy interior lends an intimate quality to this hidden gem known for its generous variety of authentic soups, salads, and grilled specialties, along with shareable dishes, such as spicy angel wings (stuffed chicken wings) and prawn and cream cheese puffs. **Known for:** panang, red, and green coconut curries; papaya and mango salads; sizzling wok dishes. [$] *Average main: $14* ✉ *47 Caledonia St., Sausalito* ☎ *415/729–9395* 🌐 *www.arawansausalito.com.*

The Joinery

$ | AMERICAN | Sausalito's popular beer hall and rotisserie offers ample, open, airy indoor seating at long tables and expanded outdoor deck dining with exceptional views of the bay. It's a relaxing spot to enjoy burgers, sandwiches, soups, and salads along with a selection of Belgian beers, IPAs, lagers, and ciders on tap. **Known for:** fried chicken sandwich and grilled cheese; Joinery burger with special sauce; dirty fries and fried Brussels sprouts. [$] *Average main: $14* ✉ *300 Turney St., Sausalito* ☎ *415/766–8999* 🌐 *www.joineryca.com.*

Le Garage

$$$ | FRENCH | Brittany-born Olivier Souvestre serves traditional French bistro fare in a relaxed, bayside setting that feels more sidewalk café than the converted garage that it is. The restaurant seats only 35 inside and 15 outside, so make reservations or arrive early. **Known for:** PEI mussels and house-cut fries; popular weekend brunch; outstanding bouillabaisse. [$] *Average main: $34* ✉ *85 Liberty Ship Way, Suite 109, Sausalito* ☎ *415/332–5625* 🌐 *www.legaragesausalito.com* 🕒 *Closed Mon. No dinner Sun.*

Poggio

$$ | **MODERN ITALIAN** | Poggio serves modern Tuscan comfort food in a handsome, old world–inspired space. An extensive and ever-changing menu, with ingredients sourced from the restaurant's garden and local farms, features local and Italian wines, fresh fish, and wood-fired pizzas. **Known for:** burrata; grilled half chicken with brown butter; spaghetti carbonara. [$] *Average main: $27* ✉ *777 Bridgeway, at Bay St., Sausalito* ☎ *415/332-7771* 🌐 *www.poggiotrattoria.com.*

Sausalito Seahorse

$$ | **ITALIAN** | Live music and dancing complement Tuscan seafood and pasta specialties here and make the Seahorse one of Sausalito's most spirited supper clubs. Sample an abundant antipasti menu and homemade gnocchi on outdoor patios or enjoy the band inside with a seafood pasta or lasagna classica. **Known for:** seafood stew; schiacciata (a type of Tuscan bread) panini; fun atmosphere. [$] *Average main: $25* ✉ *305 Harbor Dr., Sausalito* ☎ *415/331–2899* 🌐 *www.sausalitoseahorse.com* 🕒 *No dinner Mon.*

★ Sushi Ran

$$$ | **JAPANESE** | Sushi aficionados swear that this tiny, stylish restaurant is the Bay Area's finest option for raw fish, but don't overlook the excellent Pacific Rim fusions, a melding of Japanese ingredients and French techniques. Book in advance or expect a wait, which you can soften by sipping one of the bar's 30 by-the-glass sakes. **Known for:** glorious pristine raw fish preparations; local miso-glazed black cod; outstanding sake and wine list. [$] *Average main: $35* ✉ *107 Caledonia St., at Pine St., Sausalito* ☎ *415/332–3620* 🌐 *sushiran.com* 🕒 *No lunch Mon.–Thurs.*

☕ Coffee and Quick Bites

★ Fish

$$ | **SEAFOOD** | **FAMILY** | Unsurprisingly, fish—specifically, fresh, sustainably caught fish—is the focus at this gleaming dockside fish house a mile north of downtown. Order at the counter and then grab a seat by the floor-to-ceiling windows or at a picnic table on the pier, overlooking the yachts and fishing boats. **Known for:** fish taco plate; fish reuben sandwich; local tuna poke. [$] *Average main: $23* ✉ *350 Harbor Dr., at Gate 5 Rd., off Bridgeway, Sausalito* ☎ *415/331–3474* 🌐 *www.331fish.com.*

Salsalito Taco Shop

$ | **MEXICAN** | This breezy spot has been a locals' go-to for Baja Mexico–style tacos with distinct Californian influences since the early 2000s. Diners tend to choose two or three kinds of tacos for a meal, perhaps free-range chicken roasted in achiote and sautéed shrimp. **Known for:** fish tacos; tequila-free margaritas with agave wine; colorful, beach-like vibe inside and outside. [$] *Average main: $15* ✉ *1115 Bridgeway, Sausalito* ☎ *415/331–5595* 🌐 *salsalitotacoshop.com* 🕒 *Hrs and closures vary seasonally.*

🛏 Hotels

Cavallo Point

$$$ | **HOTEL** | With a striking setting almost at the foot of the Golden Gate Bridge, this refined, upscale destination is truly the closest countryside getaway to San Francisco. **Pros:** can't beat the setting and urban proximity combination; excellent restaurant, bar, and spa; activities like guided hikes and yoga classes. **Cons:** long walk to anything; very hard to get rideshares; not as luxurious as some of its peers. [$] *Rooms from: $425* ✉ *601 Murray Circle, Sausalito* ☎ *888/651–2003, 415/339–4700* 🌐 *cavallopoint.c* 🔑 *142 rooms* 🍴 *No Meals.*

The Inn Above Tide
$$$ | B&B/INN | The balconies at the inn literally hang over the water, and each of its rooms has a "perfect 10" view that takes in wild Angel Island as well as the city lights across the bay. **Pros:** generous continental breakfast; walking distance to lots of sights and restaurants; beautiful beach meets urbane room decor. **Cons:** expensive; some rooms are on the small side; ferry-side rooms can be noisy. [$] *Rooms from: $465* ✉ *30 El Portal, Sausalito* ☎ *415/332–9535, 800/893–8433* 🌐 *www.innabovetide.com* 🛏 *33 rooms* 🍴 *Free Breakfast.*

Tiburon

7 miles north of Sausalito, 11 miles north of Golden Gate Bridge.

On a peninsula that was named Punta de Tiburón (Shark Point) by 18th-century Spanish explorers, this beautiful Marin County community retains the feel of a village—it's more low-key than Sausalito—despite the encroachment of commercial establishments from the downtown area. The harbor faces Angel Island across Raccoon Strait, and San Francisco is directly south across the bay, making the views from the decks of harbor restaurants major attractions. Since 1884, when the San Francisco and North Pacific Railroad relocated their ferry terminal facilities to the harbor town, Tiburon has centered on the waterfront. The ferry is the most relaxing (and fastest) way to get here and allows you to skip traffic and parking problems.

One of the bay's best secrets in plain sight, Angel Island State Park (🌐 *www.parks.ca.gov*) offers 13 miles of roads nd trails from the perimeter up to Mt. vermore (788 feet), with magnifi- t panoramic views. The 12-minute ride to Angel Island from Tiburon *740 round-trip*) includes the cost of mission.

■ **TIP→ To see the sites by bike, rent on the island (🌐 *www.angelisland.com/bike-rentals*).**

GETTING HERE AND AROUND

The Golden Gate Ferry travels between San Francisco and Tiburon daily. By car, head north from San Francisco on U.S. 101 and get off at CA 131/Tiburon Boulevard/East Blithedale Avenue (Exit 447). Turn right onto Tiburon Boulevard and drive just over 4 miles to downtown. Note that there is no bus service directly to Tiburon; ferry is the only public transit available. Tiburon's Main Street is perfect for wandering, as are the footpaths that frame the water's edge.

ESSENTIALS

CONTACT destination: Tiburon. ✉ *Town Hall, 1505 Tiburon Blvd., Tiburon* ☎ *415/435–2298* 🌐 *www.destinationtiburon.org.*

Sights

Ark Row
STREET | The historic second block of Main Street is known as Ark Row and has a tree-shaded walk lined with antiques shops, restaurants, and specialty stores. The quaint stretch gets its name from the 19th-century ark houseboats that floated in Belvedere Cove before being beached and transformed into stores. ■ **TIP→ If you're curious about architectural history, the Tiburon Heritage & Arts Commission has a self-guided walking-tour map, available online and at local businesses.** ✉ *Ark Row, Main St., south of Juanita La., Tiburon* 🌐 *www.townoftiburon.org.*

Old St. Hilary's Landmark and John Thomas Howell Wildflower Preserve
CHURCH | The architectural centerpiece here is a stark-white 1888 Carpenter Gothic church that overlooks the town and the bay from its hillside perch. Surrounding the church, which was dedicated as a historical monument in 1959, is a wildflower preserve that's spectacular in May and June, when the

rare Tiburon paintbrush and Tiburon black jewel flower bloom. Expect a steep walk uphill to reach the preserve. The Landmarks Society arranges guided tours by appointment. ■ **TIP→ The hiking trails behind the landmark wind up to a peak that has views of the entire Bay Area.** ✉ *201 Esperanza St., Tiburon* ☎ *415/435–1853* 🌐 *landmarkssociety.com* 🕒 *Church closed Mon.–Sat. and Nov.–Mar.*

Railroad & Ferry Depot Museum

HISTORY MUSEUM | A short waterfront walk from the ferry landing, this free museum in Shoreline Park is a well-preserved time capsule of the city's industrial history, complete with working trains. The landmark building has a detailed scale model of Tiburon and its 43-acre rail yard at the turn of the 20th century, when the city served as a major railroad and ferry hub for San Francisco Bay. The Depot House Museum on the second floor showcases a restoration of the stationmaster's living quarters. ✉ *1920 Paradise Dr., Tiburon* ☎ *415/435–1853* 🌐 *landmarkssociety.com* 🕒 *Closed Mon.–Sat. and Oct.–Apr.*

🍴 Restaurants

Bungalow Kitchen

$$$ | **MODERN AMERICAN** | Tiburon's low-key, mostly casual dining scene received a jolt of energy when celebrity chef Michael Mina and partner Brent Bolthouse opened this hip restaurant right next to the ferry dock in 2021. It's certainly a scene and a place to dress up, yet it's also a compelling destination for terrific eats that don't adhere to many rules or cuisines other than high-quality ingredients. **Known for:** tuna tartare and yellowtail sashimi preparations; festive, prix-fixe weekend brunch; the rare Marin restaurant with food on weekends until midnight. [$] *Average main: $39* ✉ *5 Main St., Tiburon* ☎ *415/366–4088* 🌐 *bungalowkitchen.com* 🕒 *Closed Mon. and Tues. No lunch weekdays.*

★ Luna Blu

$$$ | **SICILIAN** | Friendly, informative staff serve Sicilian-inspired seafood in this lively Italian restaurant just a stone's throw from the ferry. Enjoy views on the expansive heated patio overlooking the bay, or cozy up with friends on one of the high-sided booths near the bar. **Known for:** sustainably caught seafood and local, organic ingredients; homemade pastas; rock crab bisque. [$] *Average main: $30* ✉ *35 Main St., Tiburon* ☎ *415/789–5844* 🌐 *lunablurestaurant.com* 🕒 *Closed Tues. No lunch weekdays.*

Salt & Pepper

$$ | **AMERICAN** | **FAMILY** | Bright and welcoming, this American bistro on Ark Row is known for its seafood starters (oyster poppers, crab stacks, scallops, and steamers) and salads as well as shareable dishes and burgers, chops, and ribs. The airy, rustic space has a pleasant café-like atmosphere that makes it easy to stay and even consider returning for a breakfast of Dungeness crab omelet or ricotta pancakes. **Known for:** clam chowder; kabocha squash and vegetable curry; Mongolian pork chops and rib-eye steaks. [$] *Average main: $27* ✉ *38 Main St., Tiburon* ☎ *415/435–3594* 🌐 *www.saltandpeppertiburon.com.*

★ Sam's Anchor Cafe

$$ | **AMERICAN** | Open since 1920, this beloved dockside restaurant is the town's most famous eatery, and after 99 years, a bright remodel includes floor-to-ceiling sliding-glass doors and an 80-foot heated bench for deck views on cool days. Remnants of Sam's history are evident in some vintage decor, the hamburger and Champagne specials, and the free popcorn. **Known for:** excellent raw bar; pink lemonade and margarita "bowls"; Dungeness crab Louie. [$] *Average main: $26* ✉ *27 Main St., Tiburon* ☎ *415/435–4527* 🌐 *samscafe.com.*

Coffee and Quick Bites

Waypoint Pizza
$ | PIZZA | FAMILY | A nautical theme and a tasty "between the sheets" pizza-style sandwich are signatures of this creative pizzeria, which is housed in the 19th-century landmark building that was once home to the Pioneer Boathouse. Indoor deck chairs and a picnic table complete with umbrella add a playful air. **Known for:** pizza-style sandwiches; wild shrimp pesto pizza; soft-serve organic ice cream. [$] *Average main: $15* ✉ *15 Main St., Tiburon* ☎ *415/435–3440* 🌐 *www.waypointpizza.com.*

Hotels

Waters Edge Hotel
$$ | B&B/INN | This stylish downtown hotel feels like an inviting retreat by the water—the views are stunning, and the lighting is perfect. **Pros:** complimentary wine and cheese every evening; restaurants and sights are steps away; free bike rentals. **Cons:** downstairs rooms lack privacy and balconies; paid self-parking; two-night minimum weekends, three-night minimum holidays. [$] *Rooms from: $319* ✉ *25 Main St., Tiburon* ☎ *415/789–5999* 🌐 *watersedgehotel.com* 🛏 *23 rooms* 🍴 *Free Breakfast.*

Shopping

Local Spicery
FOOD | This is the place for spices of all varieties from around the world, from aji amarillo chili to za'atar. The apothecary-like storefront features an aromatic library of loose teas and spices milled in small quantities and prepared in small-batch hand blends to obtain maximum freshness and quality. ✉ *80 Main St., Tiburon* ☎ *415/435–1100* 🌐 *www.local-spicery.com* 🕑 *Closed Tues. and Wed.*

hoenberg Guitars
IC | Chockablock with handmade rs alongside vintage classics, this shop is a treat even for those who don't play music. Dozens of guitars varying in size, shape, and color hang from the walls and stand against the polished wood floor. There's an organized beauty to the layout and a comforting sense of musical harmony. You may even enjoy an impromptu concert or workshop. ✉ *Ark Row Shopping Center, 106 Main St., Tiburon* ☎ *415/789–0846* 🌐 *www.om28.com* 🕑 *Closed Sun. and Mon.*

Tiburon Wine
WINE/SPIRITS | Some 200 regional and international wines as well as local Skywalker wines (from George Lucas's ranch) line the walls of this cozy shop, which has an indoor tasting room and outdoor seating for sipping by the glass or bottle. ✉ *84 Main St., Tiburon* ☎ *415/435–3499* 🌐 *tiburonwine.net.*

Mill Valley

2 miles north of Sausalito, 4 miles north of Golden Gate Bridge.

Chic and woodsy Mill Valley has a dual personality. Here, as elsewhere in the county, the foundation is a superb natural setting. Virtually surrounded by parkland, the town lies at the base of Mt. Tamalpais and contains dense redwood groves traversed by countless creeks. But this is no lumber camp. Smart restaurants and chichi boutiques line streets that have been roamed by more rock stars than one might suspect.

The rustic village flavor is a holdover from the town's early days as a center for the lumber industry. In 1896, the Mt. Tamalpais Scenic Railroad—dubbed the "Crookedest Railroad in the World" because of its curvy tracks—began transporting visitors from Mill Valley to the top of Mt. Tam and down to Muir Woods, and the town soon became a vacation retreat for city slickers. The trains stopped running in the 1930s as cars became more popular, but the old railway depot still serves as the center of town: the 1929 building has been transformed into the popular Depot Café & Bookstore, at ⊠ *87 Throckmorton Avenue.*

The small downtown area has the constant bustle of a leisure community; even on weekdays people are out shopping for fancy cookware, eco-friendly home furnishings, and boutique clothing.

GETTING HERE AND AROUND

By car from San Francisco, head north on U.S. 101 and get off at CA 131/Tiburon Boulevard/East Blithedale Avenue (Exit 447). Turn left onto East Blithedale Avenue and continue west to Throckmorton Avenue; turn left to reach Depot Plaza, then park. Golden Gate Transit buses serve Mill Valley from San Francisco. Once here, explore the town on foot.

ESSENTIALS

CONTACT Mill Valley Chamber of Commerce & Visitor Center. ⊠ *85 Throckmorton Ave., Mill Valley* ☎ *415/388–9700* ⊕ *www. millvalley.org.*

Sights

Lytton Square

PLAZA/SQUARE | FAMILY | Mill Valley locals congregate on weekends to socialize in the coffeehouses and cafés near the town's central square, but it's buzzing most of any day of the week with the lunchtime crowd, tourists, and Marin residents running errands. The Mill Valley Depot Café & Bookstore at the hub of it all is the place to grab a coffee and sweet treat while reading or playing a game of chess. Shops, restaurants, and cultural venues line the nearby streets. ⊠ *Miller and Throckmorton Aves., Mill Valley.*

★ Marin County Civic Center

NOTABLE BUILDING | A wonder of arches, circles, skylights, and an eye-catching blue roof just 10 miles north of Mill Valley, the Civic Center was Frank Lloyd Wright's largest public project (and his final commission) and has been designated

a national and state historic landmark. It's a performance venue and is adjacent to where the always-fun Marin County Fair is held each summer. Ninety-minute docent-led tours begin Friday mornings at 10:30 am. ⊠ *3501 Civic Center Dr., San Rafael* ☎ *415/473–6400 Cultural Services department* ⊕ *www.marincounty.org* ⊠ *Free; tour $12* ⊗ *Closed weekends.*

Mill Valley Lumber Yard

NEIGHBORHOOD | FAMILY | The lumber yard, once a vital center of the region's logging industry, is now a vibrant micro-village of craftsfolk, bread bakers, textile makers, and lifestyle designers, and their boutiques and restaurants. You'll even find a chocolate art studio where custom-designed chocolates and truffles may look almost too good to eat. The preserved brick-red historic structures are hard to miss along Miller Avenue, and with plenty of parking in the area, plus picnic tables and outdoor space, it's well worth a visit. ⊠ *129 Miller Ave., Mill Valley* ⊕ *www.millvalleylumberyard.com.*

★ Mt. Tamalpais State Park

MOUNTAIN | FAMILY | The view of Mt. Tamalpais from all around the bay can be a beauty, but that's nothing compared to the views from the mountain, which take in San Francisco, the East Bay, the coast, and beyond. Although the summit of Mt. Tamalpais is only 2,571 feet high, the mountain rises practically from sea level, dominating the topography of Marin County. For years the 6,300-acre park has been a favorite destination for hikers, with more than 200 miles of trails. The park's major thoroughfare, Panoramic Highway, snakes its way up from U.S. 101 to the Pantoll Ranger Station and down to Stinson Beach. Parking is free along the roadside, but there's an $8 fee (cash or check only) at the ranger station and additional charges for walk-in campsites and group use.

The Mountain Theater, also known as the Cushing Memorial Amphitheatre, is a natural 3,750-seat amphitheater

Did You Know?

The gorgeous old-growth redwood trees in Muir Woods are often enveloped in fog, which provides the moisture to help them survive the dry summers.

that has showcased summer Mountain Plays since 1913. The Rock Spring Trail starts at the Mountain Theater and gently climbs for 1½ miles to the West Point Inn, where you can relax at picnic tables before forging ahead via Old Railroad Grade Fire Road and the Miller Trail to Mt. Tam's Middle Peak.

From the Pantoll Ranger Station, the precipitous Steep Ravine Trail brings you past stands of coastal redwoods. Hike the connecting Dipsea Trail to reach Stinson Beach. ■ **TIP→ If you're too weary to make the 3½-mile trek back up, Marin Transit Bus 61 takes you from Stinson Beach back to the ranger station.** ✉ *Pantoll Ranger Station, 3801 Panoramic Hwy., Mill Valley* ☎ *415/388–2070* 🌐 *www.parks.ca.gov.*

★ Muir Woods National Monument

NATIONAL PARK | FAMILY | One of the last old-growth stands of redwood (*Sequoia sempervirens*) giants, Muir Woods is nature's cathedral: awe-inspiring and not to be missed. The nearly 560 acres of Muir Woods National Monument contain some of the most majestic redwoods in the world—some more than 250 feet tall.

Part of the Golden Gate National Recreation Area, Muir Woods is a pedestrian's park. The popular 2-mile main trail begins at the park headquarters and provides easy access to streams, ferns, azaleas, and redwood groves. Summer weekends can prove busy, so consider taking a more challenging route, such as the Dipsea Trail, which climbs west from the forest floor to soothing views of the ocean and the Golden Gate Bridge.

Picnicking and camping aren't allowed, and neither are pets. Crowds can be large, especially from May through October, so come early in the morning or late in the afternoon. The Muir Woods Visitor Center has books and exhibits about redwood trees and the woods' history as well as the latest info on trail conditions; the Muir Woods Trading Company serves hot food, organic pastries, and other tasty snacks, and the gift shop offers plenty of souvenirs.

■ **TIP→ Muir Woods has no cell service or Wi-Fi, so plan directions and communication ahead of time.**

For parking reservations (required) and shuttle information, visit 🌐 *gomuirwoods.com.* To drive directly from San Francisco, take U.S. 101 North across the Golden Gate Bridge to Exit 445B for Mill Valley/Stinson Beach, then follow signs for Highway 1 North and Muir Woods. ✉ *1 Muir Woods Rd., off Panoramic Hwy., Mill Valley* ☎ *415/561–2850 park reservations* 🌐 *www.nps.gov/muwo* 🎟 *$15.*

Old Mill Park

CITY PARK | FAMILY | To see one of the outdoor oases that make Mill Valley so appealing, follow Throckmorton Avenue west from Lytton Square to Old Mill Park, a shady patch of redwoods that shelters a playground and reconstructed sawmill. The park also hosts September's annual Mill Valley Fall Arts Festival. From the park, Cascade Way winds its way past creek-side homes to the trailheads of several forest paths. ✉ *Throckmorton Ave. and Cascade Dr., Mill Valley* ☎ *415/383–1370 for rental information* 🌐 *www.millvalleyrecreation.org.*

🍴 Restaurants

Buckeye Roadhouse

$$ | AMERICAN | House-smoked meats and fish, grilled steaks, classic salads, and decadent desserts bring locals and visitors back again and again to this 1937 lodge–style roadhouse. Enjoy a Marin martini at the cozy bar or sip local wine beside the river-rock fireplace. **Known for:** oysters bingo; chili-lime "brick" chicken; ribs and chops. [$] *Average main: $30* ✉ *15 Shoreline Hwy., Mill Valley* ☎ *415/331–2600* 🌐 *www.buckeyeroadhouse.com* ⏲ *No lunch weekdays.*

Bungalow 44

$$ | MODERN AMERICAN | An open, well-lit space with booths and countertop seating from which diners can watch the cooks in action sets the scene at this lively eatery, which serves contemporary California cuisine and inventive cocktails. The menu focuses on locally sourced veggies and seafood. **Known for:** $1 oyster happy hour; root beer–braised short rib; kickin' fried chicken. $ *Average main: $27* ⊠ *44 E. Blithedale Ave., Mill Valley* ☎ *415/381–2500* ⊕ *www.bungalow44. com* ☾ *No lunch.*

La Ginestra

$$ | ITALIAN | FAMILY | In business since 1964, La Ginestra—named for the flowers that grow on Mt. Vesuvius, in the owners' homeland—is a Mill Valley institution renowned for its no-pretense, family-style Italian meals and impressive wine list. The Sorrento Bar, off the dining room, serves up a delectable array of bar bites, pizzas, and sweets to enjoy while sipping wines and cocktails. **Known for:** handmade pasta and gnocchi; excellent ravioli; daily fish and small plates. $ *Average main: $24* ⊠ *127 Throckmorton Ave., Mill Valley* ☎ *415/388–0224* ⊕ *www. laginestramv.com* ☾ *Closed Mon. and Tues. No lunch.*

Paseo: A California Bistro

$$$ | MODERN AMERICAN | In a cozy setting down a quiet alley with a beautiful brick-walled courtyard, peak seasonal produce and Northern California farms and artisans are highlighted on chef Brandon Breazeale. Start with one of the beautifully fresh salads before continuing on to a rustic yet refined main like duck breast with yellow mole and squash blossom tamale. **Known for:** locally rooted menu with exciting global influences; fantastic selection of wines and cocktails; weekend brunch dishes like huevos rancheros homemade chorizo. $ *Average $36* ⊠ *17 Throckmorton Ave., Mill*

Valley ☎ *415/888–3907* ⊕ *paseobistro. com* ☾ *Closed Mon. No lunch weekdays.*

Piazza D'Angelo

$$ | ITALIAN | FAMILY | Busy D'Angelo's is known for its authentic and fresh pastas; there are even gluten-free options. Another draw is the scene, especially in the lounge area, which hosts a lively cocktail hour in a traditional trattoria setting. **Known for:** fresh seafood; homemade pasta; top-notch tiramisu. $ *Average main: $23* ⊠ *22 Miller Ave., Mill Valley* ☎ *415/388–2000* ⊕ *www.piazzadangelo.com* ☾ *No lunch Mon.–Thurs.*

Playa

$ | MODERN MEXICAN | Modern Mexican farm-to-table creations and inspired cocktails are the focus of this festive indoor-outdoor space that's popular for its firepit, made-to-order masa station, and happy hour. An open kitchen serves up locally sourced, organic, and sustainable dishes like ceviche and flautas, grilled fresh fish tacos, and braised pork tortas. **Known for:** tacos with creative fillings like scallops; rare tequilas and mezcals; moles and salsas. $ *Average main: $18* ⊠ *41 Throckmorton Ave., Mill Valley* ☎ *415/384–8871* ⊕ *www.playamv.com* ☾ *Closed Mon. No lunch Tues.–Thurs.*

☕ Coffee and Quick Bites

Avatar's Restaurant

$ | INDIAN | The lines can get long at this hole-in-the-wall, no-frills kitchen, where Indian curries are served burrito-style while you wait. Punjabi burritos or rice plates come with savory lamb, chicken, fish, vegetarian, and vegan ingredients flavored with seasonal fruit chutneys, tamarind sauce, and aromatic blends. **Known for:** curried pumpkin; smoked eggplant; Avatar's Dream fusion dessert. $ *Average main: $12* ⊠ *15 Madrona St., Mill Valley* ☎ *415/381–8293* ⊕ *avatarsrestaurant.square.site* ⊟ *No credit cards.*

Equator Coffees

$ | **CAFÉ** | This is the prime spot for a pick-me-up over a picturesque view of downtown Mill Valley and Mt. Tam. The owners are as serious about coffee as they are about social responsibility, from their fair-chain single-origin beans and organic loose teas down to the locally recycled wood and metal decor. **Known for:** espresso and cappuccino drinks; breakfast sandwiches; strawberry and chocolate waffles. [$] *Average main: $9* ✉ *2 Miller Ave., Mill Valley* ☎ *415/383–1651* 🌐 *www.equatorcoffees.com* ⏲ *No dinner.*

Hotels

Acqua Hotel

$$ | **HOTEL** | Alongside Richardson Bay, this stylish boutique hotel has modern, elegant rooms decorated in soft Zen-like color schemes. **Pros:** evening wine service; free parking and easy to get to San Francisco; hearty breakfast buffet. **Cons:** next to freeway; traffic audible in rooms facing east; several rooms are truly cramped. [$] *Rooms from: $289* ✉ *555 Redwood Hwy., Mill Valley* ☎ *415/380–0400* 🌐 *acquahotel.com* 🛏 *49 rooms* 🍴 *Free Breakfast.*

Mill Valley Inn

$$ | **B&B/INN** | The only hotel in downtown Mill Valley comprises one of the area's first homes, the Creek House, which has smart-looking Victorian rooms, and two small cottages nestled in a grove beyond a creek. **Pros:** unique rooms in private yet central location; some rooms have balconies, soaking tubs, and fireplaces; free mountain bikes. **Cons:** some rooms feel dated; dark in winter; no attached restaurant. [$] *Rooms from: $349* ✉ *165 Throckmorton Ave., Mill Valley* ☎ *415/389–6608* 🌐 *millvalleyinn.com* 🛏 *25 rooms* 🍴 *Free Breakfast.*

Mountain Home Inn

$$ | **B&B/INN** | Abutting 40,000 acres of state and national parks, this airy wooden inn sits on the skirt of Mt. Tamalpais, where you can follow hiking trails all the way to Stinson Beach. **Pros:** amazing terrace and views; peaceful, remote setting; handsome, rustic room design. **Cons:** nearest town is a 12-minute drive away; restaurant can get crowded on sunny weekend days; some rooms are tiny and have no TVs. [$] *Rooms from: $228* ✉ *810 Panoramic Hwy., Mill Valley* ☎ *415/381–9000* 🌐 *www.mtnhomeinn.com* 🛏 *10 rooms* 🍴 *Free Breakfast.*

Nightlife

BREWPUBS AND BEER GARDENS

The Junction Beer Garden & Bottle Shop

BEER GARDENS | With more than a hundred styles of canned and bottled beers and 30 beers on tap, plus wine and hard kombucha, this enormous indoor and outdoor beer garden is perfectly situated along the Dipsea Trail for a visit before or after a Mt. Tam hike or Tennessee Valley beach visit. The brewers partnered with PizzaHacker, a cult-favorite pizzeria in San Francisco's Bernal Heights, to provide classic pies like their "top-shelf" Margherita, as well as salads and meatballs. The landscaped outdoor space is lined with picnic tables, Adirondack chairs, and firepits. ✉ *226 Shoreline Hwy., Mill Valley* ☎ *415/888–3544* 🌐 *thejunc.com.*

MUSIC VENUES

Sweetwater Music Hall

LIVE MUSIC | With the gracious help of Bob Weir of the Grateful Dead, this renowned nightclub and café reopened in a historic Masonic Hall in 2012. Famous and up-and-coming bands play on most nights, and local stars such as Bonnie Raitt and Huey Lewis sometimes stop in for a pickup session. ✉ *19 Corte*

Madera Ave., Mill Valley ☎ *415/388–3850* 🌐 *sweetwatermusichall.com.*

Performing Arts

★ Throckmorton Theatre

ARTS CENTERS | A vibrant cultural hub in the region, the restored cinema and vaudeville house in Mill Valley is known for fostering exceptional arts and education. The darling playhouse seats upward of 260 and features live theater, comedy, and concerts. Two smaller street-side halls, the Tivoli and Crescendo, feature Tuesday night comedy shows, along with improvisation workshops, jazz performances, and new art exhibits every month. ✉ *142 Throckmorton Ave., Mill Valley* ☎ *415/383–9600* 🌐 *www.throckmortontheatre.org* 🎟 *Tickets from $20.*

Shopping

Mill Valley Market

FOOD | This family-owned market is the go-to stop for specialty foods, groceries, deli items, and hot food. Known for the notable beer and wine selection alongside local and organic produce and healthy grab-and-go foods, this is an ideal place to prepare for a picnic or seek out gourmet gifts, like imported chocolates and 100-year-old balsamic vinegars. ✉ *12 Corte Madera Ave., Mill Valley* ☎ *415/388–3222* 🌐 *millvalleymarket.com.*

Muir Beach

12 miles northwest of Golden Gate Bridge, 6 miles southwest of Mill Valley.

Except on the sunniest of weekends, Muir Beach is relatively quiet, but the drive to this community and beach is a scenic adventure.

GETTING HERE AND AROUND

car is the best way to reach Muir ach. From Highway 1, follow Pacific southwest a quarter mile.

Beaches

Muir Beach

BEACH | FAMILY | Small but scenic, this beach—a rocky patch of shoreline off Highway 1—is a good place to stretch your legs and gaze out at the Pacific Ocean. Locals often walk their dogs here; families and cuddling couples come for picnicking and sunbathing. At the northern end of the beach are waterfront homes (and occasional nude sunbathers), and at the other are the bluffs of the Golden Gate National Recreation Area. A land bridge connects directly from the parking lot to the beach, as well as to a short trail that leads to a scenic overlook and connects to other coastal paths. There are no lifeguards on duty and the currents can be challenging, so swimming is not advised. **Amenities:** parking (no fee); toilets. **Best for:** solitude; sunset; walking. ✉ *100 Pacific Way, off Shoreline Hwy., Muir Beach* ☎ *415/561–4700* 🌐 *www.nps.gov/goga.*

Hotels

The Pelican Inn

$$ | **B&B/INN** | From its slate roof to its whitewashed plaster walls, this Tudor-style inn built in the 1970s is English to the core, with its cozy upstairs guest rooms (no elevator) and draped half-tester beds, a sun-filled solarium, and bangers and grilled tomatoes for breakfast. **Pros:** five-minute walk to the beach; great bar and restaurant; peaceful setting with a fun personality. **Cons:** 20-minute drive to nearby attractions; rooms are quite small and rustic; prices are as steep as more luxurious destinations. [$] *Rooms from: $285* ✉ *10 Pacific Way, off Hwy. 1, Muir Beach* ☎ *415/383–6000* 🌐 *www.pelicaninn.com* 🛏 *7 rooms* 🍴 *Free Breakfast.*

Stinson Beach

20 miles northwest of Golden Gate Bridge.

This laid-back hamlet is all about the beach, and folks come from all over the Bay Area to walk its sandy, often windswept shore. An ideal day trip would include a morning hike at Mt. Tamalpais followed by lunch at one of Stinson's unassuming eateries and a leisurely beach stroll.

GETTING HERE AND AROUND

If you're driving, take U.S. 101 to the Mill Valley/Stinson Beach/Highway 1 exit and follow the road west and then north. By bus, take Golden Gate Transit to Marin City and then transfer to the West Marin Stagecoach (61) for Bolinas.

Beaches

Stinson Beach

BEACH | FAMILY | When the fog hasn't rolled in, this expansive stretch of sand is about as close as you can get in Marin to the stereotypical feel of a Southern California beach. There are several clothing-optional areas, among them a section south of Stinson Beach called Red Rock Beach. Pets are not allowed on the national park section of the beach.

⚠ **Swimming at Stinson Beach can be dangerous; the undertow is strong, and shark sightings, though infrequent, have occurred. Lifeguards are on duty July–September.**

On any hot summer weekend, roads to Stinson are packed and the parking lot fills, so factor this into your plans. The town itself—population 600, give or take—has a nonchalant surfer vibe, with a few good eating options and pleasant hippie-craftsy browsing. **Amenities:** food and drink; lifeguards (summer); parking (no fee); showers; toilets. **Best for:** nudists; sunset; surfing; swimming; walking; windsurfing. ✉ *Hwy. 1, 1 Calle Del Sierra, Stinson Beach* ☎ *415/561–4700* ⊕ *www.nps.gov/goga.*

Restaurants

★ **Parkside Cafe**

$$ | AMERICAN | FAMILY | Though this place is popular for its 1950s beachfront snack bar, the adjoining café, coffee bar, marketplace, and bakery shouldn't be missed either. The full menu serves up fresh ingredients, local seafood, and wood-fired pizzas. **Known for:** espresso and pastry bar; tasty fish-and-chips; rustic housemade breads. $ *Average main: $28* ✉ *43 Arenal Ave., Stinson Beach* ☎ *415/868–1272* ⊕ *www.parksidecafe. com.*

Stinson Beach Breakers Cafe

$$ | AMERICAN | Hard to miss along the tiny stretch of Main Street, this café is an easy destination for a pre-beach sandwich or post-surf bar bites and cocktails on the heated patio in the afternoon. Beach-cottage hardwood floors and a woodstove add to the warmth of the rustic seaside interior, while a mountain view and firepit enhance the deck. **Known for:** Dungeness crab melt; fresh oysters; crispy fish tacos. $ *Average main: $22* ✉ *3465 Hwy. 1, Stinson Beach* ☎ *415/868–2002* ⊕ *stinsonbeachbreakerscafe.com* ⊗ *Closed Tues. and Wed.*

🛏 Hotels

Sandpiper Lodging

$$ | B&B/INN | FAMILY | Recharge, rest, and enjoy the local scenery at this ultrapopular lodging that books up months in advance. **Pros:** beach chairs, towels, and toys provided; lush garden with grill; minutes from the beach and town. **Cons:** thin walls; limited amenities; charge for rollaway beds. $ *Rooms from: $220* ✉ *1 Marine Way, Stinson Beach* ☎ *415/868–1632* ⊕ *www.sandpiperstinsonbeach. com* ⊐ *11 rooms* ‖⊙‖ *No Meals.*

Point Reyes National Seashore

Bear Valley Visitor Center is 14 miles north of Stinson Beach.

With sandy beaches stretching for miles, a dramatic rocky coastline, a spectacular lighthouse, and idyllic, century-old dairy farms, Point Reyes National Seashore is one of the most varied and strikingly beautiful corners of the Bay Area.

GETTING HERE AND AROUND

From San Francisco, take U.S. 101 North, head west at Sir Francis Drake Boulevard (Exit 450B) toward San Anselmo, and follow the road just under 20 miles to Bear Valley Road. From Stinson Beach or Bolinas, drive north on Highway 1 and turn left on Bear Valley Road. If you're going by bus, the West Marin Stagecoach takes riders to Bolinas from Marin City via the 61 bus and to Point Reyes Station and Inverness via the 68 bus.

Sights

Bear Valley Visitor Center

VISITOR CENTER | FAMILY | Tucked in the Olema Valley, this welcoming center is a perfect point of orientation for trails and roads throughout the region's unique and diverse ecosystem. It offers a rich glimpse of local cultural and natural heritage with engaging exhibits about the wildlife, history, and ecology of the Point Reyes National Seashore. The rangers at the barnlike facility share their in-depth knowledge about beaches, whale-watching, hiking trails, and camping. Restrooms are available, as well as trailhead parking and a picnic area. Hours vary seasonally; call or check the website for details. ⊠ *Bear Valley Visitor Center, Bear Valley Rd., Point Reyes Station* 📞 *415/464–5100* ⊕ *www.nps.gov/pore.*

★ Duxbury Reef

NATURE PRESERVE | FAMILY | Excellent tide-pooling can be had along the 3-mile shoreline of Duxbury Reef; it's one of the largest shale intertidal reefs in North America. Look for sea stars, barnacles, sea anemones, purple urchins, limpets, sea mussels, and the occasional abalone. But check a tide table (⊕ *usharbors.com*) or the local papers if you plan to explore the reef—it's accessible only at low tide. The reef is a 30-minute drive from the Bear Valley Visitor Center. Take Highway 1 South from the center, turn right at Olema Bolinas Road (keep an eye peeled; the road is easy to miss), left on Horseshoe Hill Road, right on Mesa Road, left on Overlook Drive, and then right on Elm Road, which dead-ends at the Agate Beach County Park parking lot. ⚠ **Avoid areas rich with fragile Monterey shale, which are prone to erosion from human disturbance. It is illegal to collect anything from this protected marine area.** ⊠ *Bolinas* ✛ *At Duxbury Point, 1 mile west of Bolinas* ⊕ *wildlife.ca.gov* 🖭 *Free.*

Heidrun Meadery

WINERY | Northern California is known for wine, but it's a different buzz at this meadery situated just outside the center of Point Reyes Station. All of the meads are sparkling, made in the Champagne production style. The honey comes from local hives owned by the meadery and from hives around the country and the world. Flavors can vary from Tanzanian miombo wildflower to Oregon radish blossom. The tasting room is open daily. ⊠ *11925 Rte. 1, Point Reyes Station* ⊕ *heidrunmeadery.com* 🖭 *Tastings $25.*

Point Reyes Bird Observatory

WILDLIFE REFUGE | FAMILY | Birders adore Point Blue Conservation Science, which maintains the Point Reyes Bird Observatory, located in the southernmost part of Point Reyes National Seashore. The surrounding woods harbor some 200 bird species. As you hike the quiet trails through forest and along ocean cliffs, you're likely to see biologists banding birds to aid in the study of their life cycles. ■TIP➜ Visit Point Blue's website for detailed directions and to find out how to make an appointment to attend a banding demonstration. ✉ 999 Mesa Rd., Bolinas 🕾 415/868–0655 field station ⊕ www. pointblue.org.

★ Point Reyes Lighthouse & Visitor Center

LIGHTHOUSE | FAMILY | In operation since 1870, this lighthouse—which was decommissioned in 1975—occupies the tip of Point Reyes, 21 miles from the Bear Valley Visitor Center, a scenic 40-minute drive over hills scattered with longtime dairy farms. The lighthouse originally cast a rotating beam lighted by four concentric wicks that burned lard oil. Keeping the wicks lighted and the 6,000-pound Fresnel lens soot-free in Point Reyes's perpetually foggy climate was a constant struggle that reputedly drove a few attendants to madness.

The lighthouse is one of the best spots on the coast for watching gray whales. On both legs of their annual migration, the magnificent animals pass close enough to see with the naked eye. Southern migration peaks in mid-January, and the whales head back north in March; see the slower mothers and calves in late April and early May. Humpback whales can be spotted feeding in the summer months.

Parking is limited, and there's a quarter-mile one-way path from the parking lot to the visitor center. Once there, it's time to decide if you have it in you to walk down—and, more importantly, up—the 308 steps to the lighthouse. The view from the bottom is worth the effort, but the whales are also visible from the cliffs above the lighthouse. Keep in mind that the lighthouse steps are open only during visitor center hours. ■TIP➜ Winds can be chilly, and food, water, gas, and other resources are scarce, so be sure to come prepared. ✉ Lighthouse Visitor Center, 27000 Sir Francis Drake Blvd., Inverness

🕾 415/669–1534 visitor center ⊕ www. nps.gov/pore/planyourvisit/lighthouse. htm ⊙ Closed Mon.–Thurs.

★ Point Reyes National Seashore

NATIONAL PARK | FAMILY | One of the Bay Area's most spectacular treasures and the only national seashore on the West Coast, the 71,000-acre Point Reyes National Seashore encompasses hiking trails, secluded beaches, and rugged grasslands, as well as Point Reyes itself, a triangular peninsula that juts into the Pacific. The Point Reyes Lighthouse occupies the peninsula's tip and is a scenic 21-mile drive from Bear Valley Visitor Center.

When Sir Francis Drake sailed along the California coast in 1579, he allegedly missed the Golden Gate Strait and San Francisco Bay, but he did land at what he described as a convenient harbor. In 2012 the federal government recognized Drake's Bay, which flanks the point on the east, as that harbor, designating the spot a National Historic Landmark.

The infamous San Andreas Fault runs along the park's eastern edge; take the Earthquake Trail from the visitor center to see the impact near the epicenter of the 1906 earthquake that devastated San Francisco. A half-mile path from the visitor center leads to Kule Loklo, a reconstructed Miwok village of the region's first known inhabitants.

You can experience the diversity of Point Reyes's ecosystems on the scenic Coast Trail through eucalyptus groves and pine forests and along seaside cliffs to beautiful and tiny Bass Lake.

The 4.7-mile-long (one-way) Tomales Point Trail follows the spine of the park's northernmost finger of land through the Tule Elk Preserve, providing spectacular ocean views from high bluffs. ✉ Bear Valley Visitor Center, 1 Bear Valley Rd., Point Reyes Station ✛ West of Hwy. 1 🕾 415/464–5100 ⊕ www.nps.gov/por ✑ Free.

🍴 Restaurants

Cafe Reyes
$ | **PIZZA** | **FAMILY** | Sunny patio seating, hand-tossed pizza, and organic local ingredients are the selling points of this laid-back café. The semi-industrial dining room, built around a brick oven, features glazed concrete floors, warm-painted walls, and ceilings high enough to accommodate full-size market umbrellas. **Known for:** wood-fired pizzas; Tomales Bay fresh oysters; good salads. $ *Average main: $15* ✉ *11101 Hwy. 1, Point Reyes Station* ☎ *415/663–9493* 🌐 *cafereyes.biz* 🕓 *Closed Mon.–Wed.*

Due West
$$ | **AMERICAN** | A convivial atmosphere and local, sustainable culinary provisions make this classic Point Reyes tavern a favorite stop among locals. Refurbished and modernized since its days as a horse-and-wagon stop in the 1860s, it now has a farm-to-fork seasonal menu including American classics from burgers and brick-roasted chicken to seafood specialties like cioppino and fish-and-chips. **Known for:** fried chicken sandwich; steak frites; excellent wine list including the hotel's own label. $ *Average main: $27* ✉ *10005 Coastal Hwy. 1, Olema* ☎ *415/663–1264* 🌐 *olemahouse.com/due-west-restaurant* 🕓 *Closed Mon.*

Eleven
$ | **WINE BAR** | For a true taste of local culture, this sisters-owned venture welcomes you to relax, sip some wine, and enjoy the flavors and scene Bolinas is known for, from the town's laid-back lifestyle and quirky decor to the natural beauty and the fresh coastal air. The wine bar and bistro's short but ever-changing creative and thoughtful Californian-Italian menus change daily and reflect the richness of this region's foodshed—con-
dered one of the nation's most diverse.
own for: house-made, locally sourced
edients; natural wine selections;
s and oysters. $ *Average main: $17* ✉ *11 Wharf Rd., Bolinas* ☎ *415/868–1133* 🌐 *www.11wharfroad.com* 🕓 *Closed Sun.–Wed. No lunch.*

★ **Hog Island Oyster Co. Marshall Oyster Farm and the Boat Oyster Bar**
$$ | **SEAFOOD** | **FAMILY** | Take a short trek north on Highway 1 to the gritty mecca of Bay Area oysters—the Hog Island Marshall Oyster Farm. Here, the Boat Oyster Bar is an informal outdoor café that serves raw and grilled oysters, local snacks, and tasty beverages. **Known for:** fresh, raw, and grilled oysters; local fish crudo; Hog Shack shellfish to go. $ *Average main: $21* ✉ *20215 Shoreline Hwy., Marshall* ☎ *415/663–9218* 🌐 *hogislandoysters.com* 🕓 *Oyster Bar closed Tues. No dinner.*

Inverness Park Market & Tap Room
$ | **AMERICAN** | An organic oasis, this deli, restaurant, and taproom offers a true taste of the Point Reyes foodshed. Classic sandwiches, breakfast bites, burritos, grilled Niman Ranch beef, wild-caught salmon, and vegan burgers are all prepared with fresh local ingredients. **Known for:** Wednesday sushi and Thursday Thai specials; breads, pies, and morning pastries baked in-house; grilled oysters. $ *Average main: $19* ✉ *12301 Sir Francis Drake Blvd., Inverness Park* ☎ *415/663–1491* 🌐 *invernessparkmarket.com* 🕓 *Closed Sun. Taproom closed Mon. No lunch.*

★ **The Marshall Store**
$ | **SEAFOOD** | It's oyster bliss at this very friendly daytime restaurant along Tomales Bay. There are a few indoor seats, but the in-demand spots are on the outside deck, where heaters keep guests somewhat warm even on the chilliest days. **Known for:** pristine Pacific Preston Point oysters; local bread, cheeses, and dairy soft-serve; chorizo fish stew and clam chowder. $ *Average main: $18* ✉ *19225 Highway 1, Point Reyes Station* ☎ *415/663–1339* 🌐 *themarshallstore.com* 🕓 *Closed Tues.–Thurs. No dinner.*

Saltwater Oyster Depot

$$ | **SEAFOOD** | Oysters shucked moments after they're taken out of Tomales Bay and French and California wines sourced from minimal-intervention small producers are the keystones of this neighborhood oyster bar. With indoor and outdoor patio seating and a creative menu, this spot makes for a welcome post-hike or post-beach indulgence. **Known for:** broiled and raw oysters; unique rendition of clam chowder; local fish and seafood. [$] *Average main: $23* ✉ *12781 Sir Francis Drake Blvd., Inverness* ☎ *415/669–1244* 🌐 *saltwateroysterdepot.com* 🕒 *Closed Tues.–Thurs. No lunch Mon.*

★ **Side Street Kitchen**

$ | **AMERICAN** | **FAMILY** | Rotisserie meats and veggies sourced from local farms steal the show at this former mid-20th-century truck stop and diner. It's a go-to for tri-tip and pork belly sandwiches or house-seasoned roasted chicken, best eaten with a host of sides, sips, and sweets, like crispy Parmesan Brussels sprouts, New Orleans–style cold brew coffee, and butterscotch pudding. **Known for:** rotisserie chicken and lots of vegetarian dishes; dog-friendly outdoor patio; apple fritters. [$] *Average main: $18* ✉ *60 4th St., Point Reyes Station* ☎ *415/663–0303* 🌐 *sidestreet-prs.com* 🕒 *Closed Mon. and Tues. No dinner after 6 pm.*

★ **Station House Café**

$ | **AMERICAN** | The Station House Café has been a stalwart venue for local music and a staunch supporter of local farms and food artisans. The community-centric eatery serves a blend of modern and classic California dishes comprised of organic seasonal ingredients, sustainable hormone-free meats, and wild-caught seafood. **Known for:** signature popovers; special weekend brunch items; fresh local seafood. [$] *Average main: $19* ✉ *11180 Hwy. 1, at 3rd St., Point Reyes Station* ☎ *415/663–1515* 🌐 *stationhouse-cafe.com* 🕒 *Closed Wed. and Thurs.*

Hotels

Nick's Cove

$$$ | **HOTEL** | On the shore of Tomales Bay, these cottages (some are quite grand, others are typical hotel room–sized) are warm and homey with wooden stoves and a decor that nicely balances an old maritime aesthetic with a contemporary edge. **Pros:** bucolic setting; rural luxury; tons of nearby activities including kayaking on-site. **Cons:** can't walk to anything; hefty prices; restaurant closes early. [$] *Rooms from: $455* ✉ *23240 Hwy. 1* ☎ *415/663–1033* 🌐 *nickscove.com* 🛏 *12 rooms* 🍴 *No Meals.*

★ **Olema House**

$$ | **B&B/INN** | **FAMILY** | Once a historic 1860s stagecoach stopover, this luxurious getaway offers as many reasons to stay on-property—with its views of Mt. Wittenberg and garden setting—as to explore the 71,000 acres of national seashore just steps away. **Pros:** steps from trails; convenient parking and horse hitching; friendly and informative staff. **Cons:** steps to some rooms are steep; street-facing rooms may be noisy; spotty Wi-Fi and cell service. [$] *Rooms from: $328* ✉ *10021 Coastal Hwy. 1, Olema* ☎ *415/663–9000* 🌐 *olemahouse.com* 🛏 *25 rooms* 🍴 *No Meals.*

Shopping

Gospel Flat Farm Stand

FOOD | This combination art gallery, farm stand, and flower shop captures the true essence of the area, with its dedication to community arts and a bounty of local organic vegetables, fruits, and eggs. The colorful self-serve site is open 24 hours, but what makes it truly special is that the entire stand operates on the honor system. Weigh and log your produce, a slip your payment (cash or check) in t box. The ever-rotating local art on e adds to the allure. ✉ *140 Olema-B Rd., Bolinas.*

★ **Toby's Feed Barn**

OTHER SPECIALTY STORE | The heart of the community since 1942, the barn has a bounty of local gifts and produce, plus an art gallery, yoga studio, and Toby's Coffee Bar for espresso drinks and sell-out pastries. See and hear what's happening locally, catch a live band or literary event, and explore the garden. The internationally renowned all-local, all-organic Point Reyes Farmers' Market is held here on Saturdays during the growing season (even King Charles and Queen Camilla visited it in 2005). ⊠ *11250 Hwy. 1, Point Reyes Station* ☎ *415/663–1223* ⊕ *www. tobysfeedbarn.com.*

Palo Alto

33 miles south of San Francisco.

Despite being a midsized residential community, Palo Alto enjoys an outsized reputation as one of the premier cities to live and work in—with eye-popping real estate figures to complement that. It's the home of many tech companies and neighbor to that great bastion of research and learning, Stanford University. Palo Alto is somewhat split between its historic northern half, anchored by the always exciting University Avenue, and its "other downtown" centered on California Avenue, where most of the city's science and technology offices are located. Throughout the city, there are pleasant little parks and a variety of homes from modern mansions to quirky bungalows to the unique mid-century Eichlers that are like large suburban cabins.

It's a progressive, environmentally-centered city where bikes, electric cars and ybrid cars seem to outnumber regular s. That green focus possibly dates to the city's namesake, a giant ood tree that still stands proudly etly in a little forest by the San ito Creek.

GETTING HERE AND AROUND

From San Francisco, drivers can take U.S. 101 South to a trio of different exits: University Avenue, Embarcadero Road, and Oregon Expressway. Alternatively, the more scenic route takes I–280 to the Page Mill Road exit.

By Caltrain, it's roughly 45 minutes to an hour (depending on if it's an express or a local train) to Palo Alto's downtown station and California Avenue station.

ESSENTIALS

CONTACTS Destination Palo Alto. ⊕ *destinationpaloalto.com.* **City of Palo Alto.** ⊕ *cityofpaloalto.org.*

 Sights

California Avenue

STREET | **FAMILY** | Palo Alto's "second downtown" actually was its own town named Mayfield until it joined the neighboring city in 1925. Back then, the main difference between the towns was that Palo Alto was dry and Mayfield was predominantly saloons. Things are quite different a century later; the old Mayfield's main thoroughfare, California Avenue, is now a favorite dining and shopping destination for the nearby Page Mill Road tech workers and Stanford students.

Térun's (⊠ *448 California Ave.*) Neapolitan pizzas are among the best on the Peninsula, while the Latin cuisine and rum cocktails at **La Bodeguita del Medio** (⊠ *463 California Ave.*), named for Ernest Hemingway's favorite bar in Havana, have a devoted following. **Bistro Elan** (⊠ *2363 Birch St.*) and **Protégé** (⊠ *250 California Ave.*) are the two fine-dining standard bearers on the street. **Mediterranean Wraps's** (⊠ *443 California Ave.*) lamb and beef shawarma plates and falafel wraps are a popular choice for the lunchtime crowds. A pair of coffee shops are the morning heart of the corridor, with **Backyard Brew** (⊠ *444 California Ave.*) serving excellent coffees in a hidden garden setting, and the quirky **Zombie**

Runner (✉ *344 California Ave.*) producing a terrific chai tea in addition to coffee from beans roasted by the café (it was previously a running shoe store with a small coffee kiosk, then fully switched and no longer sells shoes). California Avenue really shines every Saturday morning when it hosts what most residents consider the Peninsula's most impressive farmers' market. And every day of the week, there's a fun European vibe because it's now permanently pedestrian-only to expand restaurants' outdoor seating options. ✉ *California Ave., between El Camino Real and Park Blvd., Palo Alto* 🌐 *destinationpaloalto.com/california-avenue.*

University Avenue

STREET | Downtown Palo Alto's main street is a continuation of Stanford's Palm Drive after the university stretch reaches the Caltrain station. Shops, restaurants, and an always popular Apple Store (it's no different than other stores but considered special since Steve Jobs lived nearby) line the blocks of the street until it becomes residential.

The crown jewel is the **Stanford Theatre** (✉ *221 University Ave.*), a magnificent ode to classic Hollywood. Across the street is **Lytton Plaza**, a spacious, eclectic gathering place where surely somebody will be putting on an impromptu concert or protest. Toward the eastern end of the downtown area is what previously was another Hollywood Golden Age cinema, the **Varsity Theatre**. Its classic Colonial Spanish and Mission Revival–influenced architecture is still stunning as a tech shared workspace and a **Blue Bottle Coffee** café (✉ *456 University Ave.*).

There are dining highlights up and down University Avenue, led by contemporary Vietnamese stalwart **Tamarine** (✉ *546 University Ave.*) and the silky hummus specialty at **Oren's Hummus** (✉ *261 University Ave.*). The quieter side streets off University Avenue also feature several standout restaurants including **Ramen Nagi** (✉ *541 Bryant St.*), the Georgian cooking of **Bevri** (✉ *530 Bryant St.*), craft cocktails with excellent French bistro fare at **Zola** and **BarZola** (✉ *565 and 585 Bryant St.*), contemporary Indian cuisine in lavish surroundings at **Ettan** (✉ *518 Bryant St.*), **Taverna's** (✉ *800 Emerson St.*) excellent modern and rustic Greek dishes, and **Bird Dog's** (✉ *420 Ramona St.*) captivating contemporary Californian menu. ✉ *University Avenue, between El Camino Real and Middlefield Rd., Palo Alto* 🌐 *destinationpaloalto.com.*

🍴 Restaurants

Bevri

$$ | **EASTERN EUROPEAN** | As one of the few Georgian restaurants in the Bay Area, many diners from around the region come to this small, cheery spot to learn all about the Caucasus Mountains–region country's important culinary heritage. Every table has an order of the two iconic dishes from Georgia: *kinkhali* (juicy dumplings filled with various meats) and the "cheese boat" of *khachapuri*, which is a trapezoid-shaped, ultra-moist, somewhat puffy bread with cheese in the center and an egg yolk. **Known for:** extensive Georgian wine list; grilled whole rainbow trout; kebabs and hand-chopped beet and spinach "pkhali" dips. [$] *Average main: $23* ✉ *530 Bryant St., Palo Alto* ☎ *650/600–0433* 🌐 *bevri.com* ⏲ *Closed Mon. and Tues.*

Bird Dog

$$ | **MODERN AMERICAN** | It's a little strange for a chic, contemporary-minded restaurant to be best known for an avocado dish. However, that's the case at chef Robbie Wilson's suave downtown restaurant where the delicately grilled avocado has its own devoted following. **Known fo** inventive dishes with unique spices an sauces; best cocktails in town; fish c do. [$] *Average main: $27* ✉ *420 Ra St., Palo Alto* ☎ *650/656–8180* 🌐 *pa.com* ⏲ *Closed Sun.–Mon. No*

Bistro Elan

$$$ | MODERN FRENCH | One of the Peninsula's leading examples of a small, farm-to-table-driven, local ingredients–centric establishment is this homey dining room with sidewalk seating just off California Avenue. For more than 25 years, Bistro Elan has been the understated gathering place for many business and celebratory meals, where professors, CEOs, and longtime residents enjoy the signature potato waffle with smoked salmon and a smartly curated wine list. **Known for:** cast iron–seared steak frites; tiny dining room; exquisite almond cake. ⓢ *Average main: $37* ✉ *2363A Birch St., Palo Alto* ☎ *650/327–0284* ⊕ *bistroelan.com.*

★ Protégé

$$$$ | MODERN AMERICAN | A pair of French Laundry alums—protégés of some of the culinary world's greatest chefs—are the driving forces of this fine-dining standout near the train station on California Avenue. The restaurant is split into two parts: the main formal restaurant with an elaborate tasting menu at a high price point; and the sleek lounge area where the menu is à la carte. **Known for:** unique "fish and chips" dish; sleek design; cocktails that are as notable as the wine list. ⓢ *Average main: $225* ✉ *250 California Ave., Palo Alto* ⊕ *protegepaloalto.com* ⊘ *Closed Sun. and Mon. No lunch.*

Sundance The Steakhouse

$$$$ | STEAKHOUSE | It's almost a rite of passage for Stanford students and visiting families to visit this steak-house stalwart. Since 1974, it's been the place to go for shrimp cocktail followed by juicy prime rib. **Known for:** steaks with loaded baked potatoes; martinis and margaritas; Dungeness crab cakes and oysters Rockefeller. ⓢ *Average main: $48* ✉ *1921 El Camino Real, Palo Alto* ☎ *650/321–6798* ⊕ *sundancethesteakhouse.com* ⊘ *No weekends.*

Vina Enoteca

$$ | MODERN ITALIAN | Palo Alto is filled with Italian restaurants, but the best in town resides in Leland Stanford's old brick barn (where Stanford's own wines were produced), on the edge of campus. Homemade pastas are served with an idyllic toothsome al dente texture. **Known for:** mezze maniche pasta cacio e pepe; excellent global wine list; daytime Italian market. ⓢ *Average main: $25* ✉ *700 Welch Rd., Suite 110, Palo Alto* ☎ *650/646–3477* ⊕ *vinaenoteca.com* ⊘ *Closed Sun. and Mon. No lunch.*

☕ Coffee and Quick Bites

Backyard Brew

$ | CAFÉ | Palo Alto's eclectic past meets its digital present at California Avenue's outdoor-only coffee shop/roaster that is hidden from the main street by a narrow alleyway. With plenty of mismatched tables, lo-fi jazz on the stereo, and flowers growing on a wall next to a wall with drawings of its many regular dog visitors, it's easy to feel Palo Alto's old bohemian personality alive and well here. **Known for:** Nutella latte; single-origin drip coffees; beautiful setting. ⓢ *Average main: $6* ✉ *444 California Ave., Palo Alto* ☎ *650/704–7785* ⊕ *backyardbrew.com.*

🛏 Hotels

Hotels in Palo Alto vary dramatically, from some of the most glamorous accommodations anywhere in the Bay Area, to quiet chain hotels on nondescript blocks of El Camino Real. A Westin and a Sheraton reside by downtown's Caltrain station, but the few hotels within the main downtown area are smaller boutique hotels.

The Clement Palo Alto

$$$$ | ALL-INCLUSIVE | Palo Alto doesn't exactly strike travelers as an all-inclusive luxury getaway like Cancun, but that's what this impeccable hotel offers. **Pros:**

rooftop pool and hot tub; beautifully designed, spacious rooms; outstanding food program. **Cons:** not a great business model for encouraging city exploration; only some rooms have great views; limited dining options. [$] *Rooms from: $854* ✉ *711 El Camino Real, Palo Alto* ☎ *650/322–7111* 🌐 *theclementpaloalto.com* 🛏 *23 suites* 🍴 *All-Inclusive.*

★ El Prado Hotel

$$$ | HOTEL | This elegant boutique hotel is an extremely welcome breath of fresh air of non-gimmicky, non-tech-oriented space. **Pros:** sharp, friendly service; great cocktails and bites in the tapas bar; unique design. **Cons:** noise from courtyard; rooms aren't as luxurious as the public spaces; no in-room coffee. [$] *Rooms from: $365* ✉ *520 Cowper St., Palo Alto* ☎ *650/322–9000* 🌐 *elpradopaloalto.com* 🛏 *62 rooms* 🍴 *No Meals.*

Four Seasons Hotel Silicon Valley at East Palo Alto

$$$ | HOTEL | There is luxury at every turn in this stalwart accommodation for the Silicon Valley power players from the prestigious global brand. **Pros:** outstanding attention to detail everywhere; great bar and Quattro Restaurant; quiet, spacious rooms with comfortable beds. **Cons:** can't walk to anything; pool needs a renovation; uninspiring views. [$] *Rooms from: $475* ✉ *2050 University Ave., Palo Alto* ☎ *650/566–1200* 🌐 *fourseasons.com* 🛏 *200 rooms* 🍴 *No Meals.*

Graduate Palo Alto

$$ | HOTEL | There are many hotels with bland, corporate décor—and then there's the Graduate Palo Alto, where every square inch of space seems to have some form of elaborate design or decoration. **Pros:** outstanding rooftop bar; great blend of past and modern architecture; excellent Lou & Herbert's café. **Cons:** cluttered and over-designed; some rooms feel small; hectic lobby. [$] *Rooms from: $295* ✉ *488 University Ave., Palo Alto* ☎ *650/843–9755* 🌐 *graduatehotels.com* 🛏 *100 rooms* 🍴 *No Meals.*

Nobu Hotel Palo Alto

$$$$ | HOTEL | When Silicon Valley tech money meets the country's biggest celebrity sushi chef, you get this ultra-contemporary luxury hotel with, of course, a Nobu restaurant included. **Pros:** top-quality in-house restaurant; beautifully designed rooms; some rooms have balconies facing the Santa Cruz Mountains. **Cons:** relatively small rooms; feels more like Vegas than Palo Alto; comparatively limited amenities. [$] *Rooms from: $503* ✉ *180 Hamilton Ave., Palo Alto* ☎ *650/531–8888* 🌐 *paloalto.nobuhotels.com* 🛏 *73 rooms* 🍴 *No Meals.*

🍸 Nightlife

The Rose & Crown

PUBS | A true English pub, this is Palo Alto's best place for a proper pint of Old Speckled Hen or a pour of a locally-produced double IPA. Evenings bring tech workers and graduate students out to play darts and have lively conversations at the wooden tables inside or at the picnic benches on the narrow patio. Trivia nights are particularly popular in this scholarly area. ✉ *547 Emerson St., Palo Alto* ☎ *650/327–7673* 🌐 *therosepa.com.*

The Wine Room

WINE BARS | Palo Alto's favorite gathering spot for wines from around the world is this cozy, quirky cottage that looks as if it was lifted out of the Cotswolds. Seating arrangements include several comfortable couches that are popular with date nights. The staff is very knowledgeable about the wines and happy to offer recommendations since the extensive menu can be wonderfully intimidating. ✉ *520 Ramona St., Palo Alto* ☎ *650/462–1968* 🌐 *thepawineroom.com.*

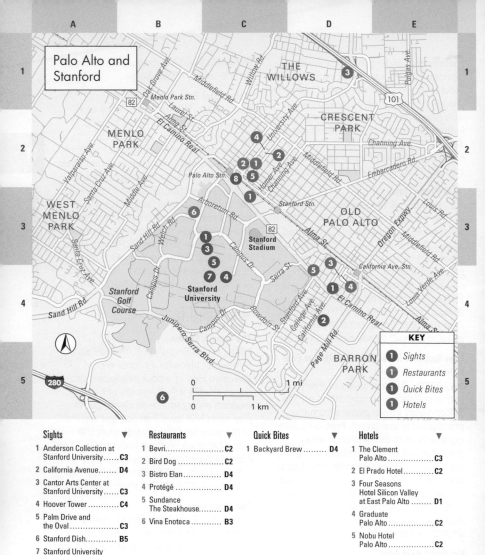

Palo Alto and Stanford

KEY

1 Sights
1 Restaurants
1 Quick Bites
1 Hotels

Sights ▼

1 Anderson Collection at
  Stanford University......C3
2 California Avenue.......D4
3 Cantor Arts Center at
  Stanford University......C3
4 Hoover Tower C4
5 Palm Drive and
  the Oval C3
6 Stanford Dish............B5
7 Stanford University
  Main Quad...............C4
8 University Avenue C2

Restaurants ▼

1 Bevri.....................C2
2 Bird Dog C2
3 Bistro Elan..............D4
4 Protégé D4
5 Sundance
  The Steakhouse.........D4
6 Vina Enoteca B3

Quick Bites ▼

1 Backyard Brew D4

Hotels ▼

1 The Clement
  Palo Alto C3
2 El Prado Hotel............C2
3 Four Seasons
  Hotel Silicon Valley
  at East Palo Alto D1
4 Graduate
  Palo Alto C2
5 Nobu Hotel
  Palo Alto C2

🎭 Performing Arts

CINEMA

★ Stanford Theatre

FILM | FAMILY | A cinematic treasure since 1925, University Avenue's grande dame is a time-traveling spectacle not to be missed—an oasis of Hollywood Golden Age glamour in the center of this relentlessly future-minded region. Everything here is majestic: the grand marquee, the bi-level interior, the intricate interior architecture and chandeliers, and the crisp screen and audio quality often showing black-and-white films still in mint condition. Films are often shown as a themed double-feature, perhaps Fred Astaire and Ginger Rogers or 1929 silent films. Arguably the highlight for any night is when the Mighty Wurlitzer organ player strikes a tune during the intermission between films. ✉ 221 University Ave., Palo Alto ☎ 650/324–3700 ⊕ stanfordtheatre.org.

Stanford

34 miles from San Francisco.

Few names are as recognizable in higher education as Stanford University—or technically Leland Stanford Jr. University, named for the deceased son of its founder, a railroad tycoon and former California governor. Stanford's campus resides on 8,180 acres, one of the largest universities in terms of land size in the entire country. Its academic specialties are too numerous to count and its alums have gone on to make a tremendous impact on the world across dozens of disciplines. There are athletes like Tiger Woods, John Elway, and John McEnroe. Former President Herbert Hoover graduated from here, as did Sandra Day O'Connor and Rishi Sunak. In business, science, and technology, there are alums including Sally Ride, Phil Knight, Sergey Brin, and Charles Schwab.

It's commonly referred to as "The Farm" since it resides on what was Leland Stanford's farm before the university was founded in 1885. Today, the old red horse barn is still used by the equestrian team and the other brick "barn" (back then a wine-making facility) now houses restaurants and offices. Even though Stanford is renowned for its serious academic prowess, students also definitely know how to have fun. The Stanford Band is famous (and sometimes maligned) for its freewheeling style, complemented by a dancing redwood tree mascot (the school's mascot is the Cardinal—the color, not the bird).

The university is an architectural and natural marvel. Its signature style is a unique mix of Mission and Romanesque styles called Richardsonian Romanesque, named for Henry Hobson Richardson whose protégé, Charles Allerton Coolidge, was the primary architect. Its defining characteristics are dramatic arched hallways connected with textured sandstone buildings and eye-catching red-tiled roofs. Spend just one minute in the Main Quad and it's easy to understand the style.

GETTING HERE AND AROUND

Stanford's campus can be reached from San Francisco via Highway 101's University Avenue exit, which drives across Palo Alto and becomes Palm Drive once it reaches the university. From Interstate 280, use the Alpine Road or Sand Hill Road exits.

Caltrain's University Avenue station in Downtown Palo Alto is the closest stop. VTA buses and SamTrans also stop here (known as the Palo Alto Transit Center).

Stanford's campus is huge, so most students bike here. The university has a free shuttle running several routes around campus known as the Marguerite. Note that parking is extremely restricted around the Stanford c... Most visitor parking is in selec...

or paid parking near the art museums and the Oval.

ESSENTIALS

CONTACT Visit Stanford. ✉ *295 Galvez St., Stanford* ⊕ *visit.stanford.edu.*

 Sights

Anderson Collection at Stanford University

ART MUSEUM | Modern, post–World War II art shines at the neighbor to the Cantor Arts Center, where the impressive collection from Harry W. and Mary Margaret Anderson and Mary Patricia Anderson Pence is displayed. Marquee mid-century artists including Richard Diebenkorn, Jackson Pollock, and Ellsworth Kelly are showcased in a gleaming concrete and glass-heavy building that smartly reflects the contemporary ethos of the artwork inside. ✉ *314 Lomita Dr., Stanford* ☎ *650/721–6055* ⊕ *anderson.stanford. edu* 🆓 *Free* ⊘ *Closed Mon. and Tues.*

Cantor Arts Center at Stanford University

ART MUSEUM | Stanford's main art museum is a wonderful indoor-outdoor mix, where it's easy to linger for two or three hours. Outside is the acclaimed Rodin Sculpture Garden, home to the one of the largest collections of the legendary French sculptor's works in the U.S. Inside, beyond the ornate opening steps and grand entry hall are two levels of galleries that mix modern works with rotating exhibitions, indigenous American art, and classical European and American paintings. ✉ *328 Lomita Dr., Stanford* ☎ *650/723–4177* ⊕ *museum.stanford. edu* 🆓 *Free* ⊘ *Closed Mon. and Tues.*

Hoover Tower

NOTABLE BUILDING | It's hard to miss Stanford's iconic building named for the first president of the United States and of 1895 alum, Herbert Hoover. -feet tall, it's the closest thing insula has to a skyscraper. The -tile roof with a Belgian carillon underneath it can be seen for miles. Visitors of Stanford-affiliated individuals can take the elevator up to the top for a panoramic view from San Francisco to the bay and East Bay Hills, and to the Santa Cruz Mountains. Unfortunately, the general public can only visit the exhibition galleries at the base of the tower. ✉ *550 Jane Stanford Way, Stanford* ☎ *650/723– 3563* ⊕ *hoover.org.*

★ Palm Drive and the Oval

STREET | **FAMILY** | Few streets in the Bay Area can match the dramatic scenery of Stanford's entrance from downtown Palo Alto. For about ⅔ mile, palm trees line the street, which runs in a direct straight line towards Memorial Church. The Santa Cruz Mountains emerge on the horizon, and it all looks as if it was framed intentionally for postcards. Palm Drive runs into a giant grass area called the Oval, named for its distinct shape, which revolves around flower plantings shaped as an "S" for Stanford. On sunny days, Stanford students are always out in force studying on the grass or playing Frisbee. It can appear like a university admissions brochure in real life. ✉ *The Oval, 20 Palm Dr., Stanford.*

Stanford Dish

NATURE PRESERVE | **FAMILY** | Known by locals as The Dish, this radio telescope has served many purposes over the years, including some for the government; it's run by a local research institute, not the university itself. The main reason that everyone comes to The Dish is because of its series of hiking and jogging trails that wind their way around the classic Northern California landscape full of oak trees, poppy flowers, and local wildlife, rewarding each workout with stellar views. ✉ *Stanford* ✛ *Trailhead at Stanford Ave. and Junipero Serra Blvd.* ⊕ *dish.stanford.edu.*

★ Stanford University Main Quad

COLLEGE CAMPUS | The heart of the Stanford University campus is its distinct Richardsonian Romanesque quad. Stanford's signature look revolves around red-tiled roofs and palm trees. The focal point of the quad is Memorial Church, a striking memorial built by Jane Stanford to her late husband Leland. The interior boasts stunning mosaics and stained-glass windows. There was originally a bell and clock tower, but that was destroyed by the powerful 1906 earthquake, just three years after the church completed construction. Docent-led tours of the church are held Friday mornings at 11. ✉ *Bldg. 500, 450 Jane Stanford Way, Stanford* ☎ *650/723-1762* ⊕ *orsl.stanford, edu* 🎫 *Free.*

Performing Arts

Bing Concert Hall

CONCERTS | Stanford's stunning main performing arts center is a wonder of distinct curves, sharp modern design, and top-notch acoustics; it's pleasing both to eyes and ears. Concerts are split between various Stanford orchestras, symphonies, and other groups, and musicians visiting from outside the university. ✉ *327 Lasuen St., Stanford* ☎ *650/724-2464* ⊕ *live.stanford.edu.*

Menlo Park

30 miles south of San Francisco.

Not to be confused with lightbulb inventor Thomas Edison's New Jersey hometown, this bedroom community centers on a small downtown strip of restaurants and shops on Santa Cruz Avenue. Menlo Park's global profile received an enormous boost in 2015 when Facebook (now Meta) opened its headquarters at the edge of the city (with the help of legendary architect Frank Gehry). The campus is actually not close to Downtown Menlo Park, but the residual effect can certainly be felt in the real estate prices and enormous amount of construction closer to town. Sand Hill Road lies along the edge of the city with Stanford's campus and Palo Alto, and its name is synonymous with the powerful venture capitalist firms that call it home. Woodside is Menlo Park's mostly pastoral northern home, where there are a couple excellent destination-worthy restaurants and the lavish Filoli Estate's mansion and gardens.

👁 Sights

Allied Arts Guild

ARTS CENTER | A popular site for photo shoots, weddings, and events, this landmark built in 1929 is known for its gardens, gorgeous Colonial Spanish architecture, and artist studios, where you can buy directly from the artists. The main Artisan Shop continues the guild's mission to help the community, with profits going to the children's hospital at Stanford. Docent tours are given six days a week, and the on-site Café Wisteria is a picturesque choice for a leisurely lunch. ✉ *75 Arbor Rd., Menlo Park* ☎ *650/322-2405* ⊕ *alliedartsguild.org* 🕐 *Closed Sun.*

★ Filoli

HISTORIC HOME | **FAMILY** | The Bay Area's definitive early-20th-century mansion and gardens reside in a quiet area along the beautiful Crystal Springs Reservoir at the base of the Santa Cruz Mountains, just a short drive from Menlo Park on I–280. The East Coast has several of these lavish estates from the titans of the Gilded Age with all kinds of Rockefeller and Vanderbilt family homes on view today to the public. However, it's very rare to find those in Northern California. Part of the National Trust for Historic Preservation, Filoli dates back to 1917 when it was built for the Bourn family based on a fortune from gold mining, along with investing in water and electricity (investing Silicon Valley was much more humble back then). The estate was purcha-

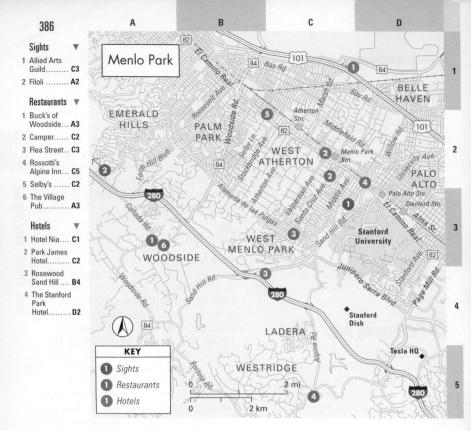

William Roth and Lurline Matson Roth, the latter the daughter of Captain William Matson, who founded the still-important namesake shipping company.

The Roths continued maintaining the impeccable estate, both inside and outside, before handing it over to the public after William's death in the 1970s. Across 654 acres, the estate features several beautiful gardens, farmland, different ecosystems, and even crosses the San Andreas Fault (the source of many Northern California earthquakes). A 1-mile trail gives a good general overview of the grounds. For most visitors, the enchanting gardens are the highlights, particularly in spring when the daffodils and myriad other flowers are in full bloom. Summer sees the rose garden at its stunning peak. The holiday season is also wonderful when the gardens include festive light displays, but it's truly special any time of year. The house is quite spectacular, as well, with beautiful terraces facing the gardens, and the interior features 10 bedrooms for the family, 15 bathrooms, and 17 fireplaces. The Georgian Revival–style architecture is very impressive throughout the home, particularly in the grand ballroom with a mural of Ireland's Muckross House, the posh reception room, and the warm, mahogany-paneled library. ⊠ *86 Cañada Rd., Woodside* ☎ *650/364–8300* ⊕ *filoli. org* ⊠ *$34.*

🍴 Restaurants

Buck's of Woodside
$ | **AMERICAN** | **FAMILY** | One of the Peninsula's best-known restaurants is this funky, family-friendly brunch specialist in the heart of tiny downtown Woodside. The restaurant is a gathering spot for the tech company executives and venture capitalists who live nearby, but it's ultimately a blend of a saloon and a diner, where many hungry locals come looking for omelets and tuna melts. **Known for:** eclectic decor; coffee cake; smash burger. [$] *Average main: $19* ✉ *3062 Woodside Rd., Woodside* ☎ *650/851–8010* 🌐 *buckswoodside.com.*

★ Camper
$$$ | **MODERN AMERICAN** | If there's such a genre as refined camping fare, then that is what chef Greg Kuzia-Carmel offers guests at his warm, bustling restaurant. Local fish, meats, and produce are highlighted, with dishes that beautifully blend pastoral with contemporary. **Known for:** cast-iron buttermilk cornbread; smoked half chicken from Petaluma; excellent wine list. [$] *Average main: $34* ✉ *898 Santa Cruz Ave., Menlo Park* ☎ *650/321–8980* 🌐 *campermp.com* 🕒 *Closed Sun. No lunch.*

Flea Street
$$$ | **MODERN AMERICAN** | Restaurants in Berkeley and San Francisco tend to get most of the credit for launching the local ingredient–focused farm-to-table California cuisine movement in the 1970s and 1980s. However, chef Jesse Cool played an enormous role in that as well when she opened this venerable restaurant in 1980. **Known for:** local-ingredient salads; grass-fed slow-braised short ribs; strong local-centric wine list. [$] *Average main: $38* ✉ *3607 Alameda de las Pulgas, Menlo Park* ☎ *650/854–1226* 🌐 *cooleatz.com* 🕒 *Closed Sun. and Mon. No lunch.*

Rossotti's Alpine Inn
$ | **AMERICAN** | **FAMILY** | On sunny weekend afternoons, the enormous tree-covered, creekside beer garden of this countryside dining icon feels like the epicenter of Silicon Valley. It's a popular destination for professors and graduate students to enjoy brews and sandwiches, located just beyond campus in the pastoral town of Portola Valley. **Known for:** fun, bucolic setting; barbecue sandwiches; wood-fired pizzas. [$] *Average main: $15* ✉ *3915 Alpine Rd., Menlo Park* ☎ *650/854–4004* 🌐 *alpineinnpv.com* 🕒 *Closed Mon.*

Selby's
$$$$ | **MODERN AMERICAN** | It's a trip back in time at this elegant retro sibling to the Village Pub. Dishes are grand and elaborate, often with luxurious flourishes, yet deeply rooted in the seasonal focus that is the hallmark of California cuisine. **Known for:** crisp, stiff martinis; polished design; divine midnight chocolate cake. [$] *Average main: $98* ✉ *3001 El Camino Real, Redwood City* ☎ *650/546–7700* 🌐 *selbysrestaurant.com* 🕒 *No lunch.*

★ The Village Pub
$$$$ | **MODERN AMERICAN** | This Woodside institution actually is a Michelin-starred fine dining destination; the only similarity with an actual pub is that the bar has its own casual menu (the main dining room is prix-fixe with multiple choices per each course) and is frequently a gathering place for well-heeled regulars. The suave dining room with red velvet chairs and booths is a beautiful backdrop for intricate dishes that often feature produce from the nearby organic SMIP Ranch. **Known for:** chocolate soufflé; pub burger on an English muffin; deep wine list. [$] *Average main: $100* ✉ *2967 Woodside Rd., Woodside* ☎ *650/851–9888* 🌐 *thevillagepub.net* 🕒 *No lunch Mon.–Thurs.*

Hotels

Hotel Nia
$$ | HOTEL | One of the first of the new wave Silicon Valley hotels, this Autograph Collection property is the closest place to stay near Meta's campus. **Pros:** wonderfully incorporates nature into indoor and outdoor design; large rooms; on-site Porta Blu restaurant. **Cons:** substantial drive to sights and restaurants; hard to reach at rush hour; rooms facing highway don't block out all noise. [$] *Rooms from: $256* ✉ *200 Independence Dr., Menlo Park* ☎ *650/900–3434* 🌐 *hotelnia.com* 🛏 *250 rooms* 🍴 *No Meals.*

Park James Hotel
$$ | HOTEL | There's an exciting energy in the courtyard of this charming boutique hotel. **Pros:** terrific restaurant and bar; great beds and workspaces; enthusiastic, helpful staff. **Cons:** bare room design; small bathrooms; not a pleasant walk to train station and downtown. [$] *Rooms from: $262* ✉ *1400 El Camino Real, Menlo Park* ☎ *650/304–3880* 🌐 *parkjames.com* 🛏 *61 rooms* 🍴 *No Meals.*

Rosewood Sand Hill
$$$$ | HOTEL | Synonymous with the relentless pursuit of exquisite luxury and exorbitant prices, few hotels in Northern California can match the gravitas and sheer delight of this gem near the northeastern base of the Santa Cruz Mountains. **Pros:** terrific upscale California cuisine at Madera restaurant; enormous, well-appointed rooms that all have balconies; beautiful grounds and views. **Cons:** hard to rationalize the price tag; the location is an office park at a highway exit; rooms don't always block out exterior noise. [$] *Rooms from: $1,030* ✉ *2825 Sand Hill Rd., Menlo Park* ☎ *650/561–1500* 🌐 *rosewoodhotels.com* 🛏 *121 rooms* 🍴 *No Meals.*

★ The Stanford Park Hotel
$$$ | HOTEL | With the university in its name and images of esteemed alums throughout the hallways, it's clear why many guests stay at this upscale boutique stalwart. **Pros:** large, nicely decorated rooms; excellent outdoor pool and fitness center; oozes charm and personality. **Cons:** have to drive to everything except shopping center; rooms have small windows; annoying noise from adjacent train tracks. [$] *Rooms from: $399* ✉ *100 El Camino Real, Menlo Park* ☎ *650/322–1234* 🌐 *stanfordparkhotel.com* 🛏 *162 rooms* 🍴 *No Meals.*

Nightlife

Dutch Goose
BEER GARDENS | For a true taste of Peninsula life, visit this longtime locals' favorite for burgers and beers on a fun patio or inside the well-worn restaurant space. There's always a lively game of pool going on and any Bay Area sports team will surely be on the TVs. Families, beer league softball teams, and many other regulars (including several celebrities who live nearby) come by for fun parties or a quick pizza dinner. The deviled eggs are not to be missed. ✉ *3567 Alameda de las Pulgas, Menlo Park* ☎ *650/854–3245* 🌐 *dutchgoose.net.*

Shopping

Kepler's Books
BOOKS | FAMILY | Since 1955, this bookstore has been the heart of Menlo Park. The store has many mainstream books, yet also maintains the independent, intellectual side that made it popular with the Beat Generation and activists (even the Grateful Dead's Jerry Garcia would play his guitar here). Author talks are a big draw at what continues to be one of the Bay Area's definitive local bookstores.

✉ 1010 El Camino Real, Menlo Park
☎ 650/324–4321 ⊕ keplers.com.

Sunnyvale and Mountain View

38 miles south of San Francisco.

Originally a stagecoach stop on the Peninsula for travelers between San Francisco and San Jose, Mountain View's technology certainly has evolved in the century and a half since its founding. Castro Street is the main downtown area, where bars, restaurants, coffee shops, and boutiques are frequented throughout the day. The iconic heart of the city, though, is out toward the Bay, where Internet giant Google's sprawling campus and headquarters are located. It's located right next to the Shoreline Amphitheatre (a popular concert venue) and the NASA Ames Research Center that opened in 1939, three decades before Neil Armstrong first set foot on the moon. Mountain View's neighbor is Sunnyvale, which is a quaint downtown stretch on Murphy Avenue by its Caltrain station but other than that is a quiet suburb with lots of tech company office parks. Together, these two cities are often considered the center of Silicon Valley since they reside in the geographic middle of the region.

GETTING HERE AND AROUND

From San Francisco, drivers can choose between U.S. 101 and I–280 for reaching Mountain View and Sunnyvale. Both routes will take between 45 minutes and a little over an hour depending on traffic.

Via U.S. 101, the main exits are Shoreline Boulevard and Rengstorff Avenue. From U.S. 280, El Monte Avenue is the primary exit. However, from both freeways, drivers often use Highway 85 to bisect Mountain View and exit at El Camino Real or Evelyn Avenue to reach downtown.

For Sunnyvale, use the Mathilda Avenue exit from U.S. 101 and the Sunnyvale-Saratoga Road exit from I–280.

Caltrain services stations in the heart of both cities' downtowns. Trains take between an hour and 1 hour 20 minutes depending on if it's an express train or a local train. Both cities also have light rail and bus service from the VTA.

ESSENTIALS

CONTACTS City of Mountain View. ⊕ *mountainview.gov.* **Mountain View Chamber of Commerce.** ⊕ *chambermv.org.* **City of Sunnyvale.** ⊕ *sunnyvale.ca.gov.* **Sunnyvale Chamber of Commerce.** ⊕ *svcoc.org.*

Sights

Castro Street

STREET | The heart of Downtown Mountain View, this constantly bustling street runs from the Caltrain station (where a few blocks are pedestrian-only for outdoor dining because of the COVID-19 pandemic) to the City Hall complex that includes the Mountain View Center for the Performing Arts. Fast-casual restaurants and ramen shops tend to be the main destinations during the daytime, while the bar scene in the evening is livelier than in any other city between San Jose and San Francisco.

A pair of excellent coffee shops anchor the ends of Castro Street: **Red Rock Coffee** (✉ *201 Castro St.*) and **1 Oz Coffee** (✉ *650 Castro St.*). Once you're caffeinated, make sure to try downtown's two premier French bakery/pastry shops: **Alexander's Patisserie** (✉ *209 Castro St.*) and **Maison Alyzée** (✉ *212 Castro St.*). **Doppio Zero** (✉ *160 Castro St.*) is the best restaurant of the crowd directly on the street, serving superb Neapolitan pizzas with an irresistible soft, lightly charred crust. Just off Castro Street are a pair of dramatically different establishments, both worth a visit: **Steins Beer Garden & Restaurant** (✉ *895 Villa St.*) and longtime fine-dining icon **Chez TJ** (✉ *938 Villa St.*

where the careers of many top Bay Area chefs began. ✉ *Mountain View ✣ Castro Street between Yosemite Ave. and Central Expy.* ☎ *650/968–8378* 🌐 *chambermv.org.*

Los Altos

TOWN | FAMILY | Arguably best known for its remaining apricot orchards, Mountain View's neighbor, Los Altos, is one of the most charming, Main Street USA–evoking downtowns in the Bay Area—well worth a stroll and a lunch break. Anchored by a grand clock at the intersection of its two main streets, the small business area is split between Main Street and State Street, where both run for roughly five blocks. **Linden Tree Books** (✉ *265 State St.*) is the signature boutique in town, and families drive from many miles away to browse the children's book selection and attend the book talks and other events a few days each month.

Popular breakfast and lunch spots along Main Street include **Red Berry Coffee** (✉ *145 Main St.*), **Manresa Bread** (✉ *271 State St.*), **Tal Palo** (✉ *149 Main St.*) and **The American Italian Delicatessen** (✉ *139 Main St.*). In the evening, crowds descend upon the contemporary farm-to-table cooking at **ASA** (✉ *242 State St.*) and **Cetrella** (✉400 Main St.), contemporary Indian cuisine at **Aurum** (✉ *132 State St.*), yakitori specialist **Sumika** (✉ *236 Plaza Central*), and craft cocktails at **Amandine Lounge** (✉ *235 1st St.*). A five-minute drive from downtown takes you to **Chef Chu's** (✉ *1067 N. San Antonio Rd., Suite 1300*), an institution for excellent Chinese cooking. ✉ *145 Main St., Los Altos* ☎ *650/949–5282* 🌐 *downtownlosaltos.org.*

Coffee and Quick Bites

Zareen's

$ | INDIAN | Serving a mix of contemporary Indian and Pakistani fare, this popular fast-casual restaurant started near Google in Mountain View in 2014 and now has two other Silicon Valley locations. Flavors are bold and riveting, whether it's a handheld lunch like a paratha roll filled with chicken *boti* (a spice-marinated kebab) or a comforting slow-cooked lamb stew. **Known for:** chicken biryani on Fridays; paneer cheese paratha roll; Peshawar-style beef chapli kebab as a burger. [$] *Average main: $15* ✉ *1477 Plymouth St., Mountain View* ☎ *650/628–6100* 🌐 *zareensrestaurant.com* 🕓 *Closed Mon.*

Hotels

★ The Ameswell Hotel

$$ | HOTEL | Just a freeway exit away from the NASA Ames Research Center and Google Headquarters, this fun, sharp hotel nicely balances being a dressed-up business hotel with a playful side. **Pros:** comfortable, nicely designed rooms; outdoor Airstream bar; great wellness focus with spa and fitness center. **Cons:** sinks are weirdly designed; not walking distance to anything; mediocre coffee at café. [$] *Rooms from: $209* ✉ *800 Moffett Blvd., Mountain View* ☎ *650/880–1000* 🌐 *theameswellhotel.com* 🛏 *255 rooms* 🍴 *No Meals.*

Shashi Hotel Mountain View

$$ | HOTEL | The closest hotel to Google's campus feels more like Palm Springs than Silicon Valley. **Pros:** plenty of great amenities and dining options; hip, relaxed vibe; short drive to Silicon Valley offices and attractions. **Cons:** pool almost never sees sunlight; room prices soar on weekdays; hardwood floors in rooms. [$] *Rooms from: $299* ✉ *1625 N. Shoreline Blvd., Mountain View*

☎ 650/420 ?600 ⊕ shashihotel.com
⬅ 200 rooms ⦿ No Meals.

Tetra Hotel, Autograph Collection
$$ | HOTEL | With a sleek Japanese-inspired modern design, this is definitely one of Silicon Valley's top hotel destinations. **Pros:** Adrestia restaurant on-site is the best in Sunnyvale; spacious rooms; nice architecture. **Cons:** beds could be more comfortable; minimalist aesthetic; surrounded by office parks. $ *Rooms from: $259* ⌧ *400 W. Java Dr., Sunnyvale* ☎ *408/734–2300* ⊕ *marriott.com* ⬅ *200 rooms* ⦿ *No Meals.*

 Performing Arts

TheatreWorks Silicon Valley
THEATER | Bay Area theater legend Robert Kelley founded this company in 1970, and today it continues to be one of the most thrilling performing arts destinations in the region. Performances are split between the intimate Lucie Stern Theatre in Palo Alto and the grander, newer Mountain View Center for the Performing Arts. The fare is never overly edgy yet is always full of innovative touches. The cast and set designs are consistently top-tier. ⌧ *500 Castro St., Mountain View* ☎ *877/662–8978* ⊕ *theatreworks.org* 🎟 *From $30.*

San Jose

55 miles south of San Francisco.

California's third-largest city, San Jose is often thought of as a smaller Los Angeles because of its relentless sprawl and valley setting surrounded by mountains and water. However, there is really nothing small about San Jose. It has a large downtown area that is home to the Plaza de Cesar Chavez, San Jose State University, and several small but enjoyable museums, including the San Jose Museum of Art and Children's Discovery Museum. About a 10-minute drive from downtown is a charming residential area that includes the Municipal Rose Garden (one of the best in the region when it's in bloom) and the Rosicrucian Egyptian Museum, both popular with families from around the South Bay and Peninsula. While San Jose doesn't have the iconic tourist sights and fascinating topography of its friendly twin to the north San Francisco, it has a lot of unique neighborhoods and an energetic vibe that reflects its position as the largest city (and the southern end) of Silicon Valley.

GETTING HERE AND AROUND
From San Francisco, both Highway 101 and I–280 go directly to San Jose. To reach the heart of downtown from either 101 or 280, take the Highway 87/Guadalupe Parkway exit, which runs parallel to the river that the highway is named after. Then take the exit for West Santa Clara Street, and that approach will land you in the center of downtown San Jose.

Caltrain connects San Francisco to San Jose at the San Jose Diridon station; the journey is 1 hour 16 minutes on an express train or 1 hour 39 minutes on a local train. VTA Light Rail and bus lines serve neighborhoods across San Jose.

ESSENTIALS
CONTACTS City of San Jose. ⌧ *San Jose* ⊕ *sanjoseca.gov.* **Visit San Jose.** ⌧ *San Jose* ☎ *800/726–5673* ⊕ *sanjose.org.*

Sights

San Pedro Square Market
MARKET | There is something for everyone at this longtime Downtown favorite. Dating back to 1972, it's technically still a market (there are a handful of boutiques), but it's really a lively, vast food hall with more than a dozen tempting choices and plenty of places to sit and watch sports on TVs or enjoy live music outside. ⌧ *87 N. San Pedro St., San Jose* ⊕ *sanpedrosquaremarket.com.*

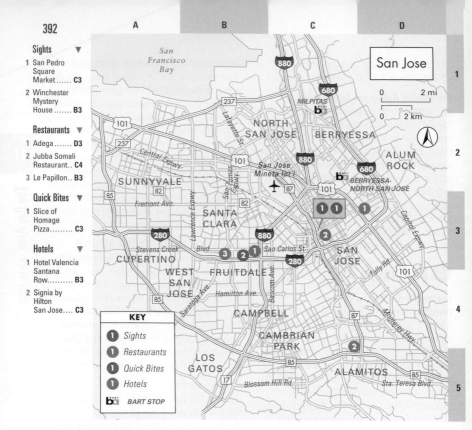

Sights ▼

1 San Pedro Square Market...... **C3**

2 Winchester Mystery House **B3**

Restaurants ▼

1 Adega **D3**

2 Jubba Somali Restaurant.. **C4**

3 Le Papillon.. **B3**

Quick Bites ▼

1 Slice of Homage Pizza **C3**

Hotels ▼

1 Hotel Valencia Santana Row.......... **B3**

2 Signia by Hilton San Jose.... **C3**

KEY

1 *Sights*

1 *Restaurants*

1 *Quick Bites*

1 *Hotels*

bã **BART STOP**

Winchester Mystery House

HISTORIC HOME | One of the Bay Area's grandest and strangest attractions is the 24,000-square-foot, 160-room Victorian mansion once owned by Sarah Winchester, the heiress to a firearms manufacturing fortune. Much of its mystique centers around the tragedies that Winchester faced in her life, and the mystery of what drove her to build and live as a recluse in this sprawling mansion after the deaths of her husband and young daughter. The mystery name, though, came after she passed away and the famous magician Harry Houdini visited the home in 1924 to investigate the stories of ghostly visitors. Apparently even Houdini was spooked by the home, and so what was the Llanada Villa became known as the Winchester Mystery House. ◿ *525 S. Winchester Blvd., San Jose*

☏ *408/247–2000* ⊕ *winchestermystery-house.com* ✉ *Tickets from $20.*

🍴 Restaurants

Adega

$$$$ | **PORTUGUESE** | San Jose's only Michelin-starred restaurant and the most ambitious destination for Portuguese-influenced cuisine in the Bay Area is this fantastic tasting menu-only spot. Seven-course dinners weave together meat and seafood plates, where the Portuguese fish staple of bacalhau (codfish) might be incorporated into a cannelloni, before leading to a delicately seared A5 Wagyu dish. **Known for:** San Jose's most ambitious restaurant; enormous selection of Portuguese wines; fantastic pastries and desserts. ⑤ *Average main: $229* ✉ *1614 Alum Rock Ave., San Jose*

☎ 408/926–9075 🌐 adegarest.com
🕑 *Closed Mon. and Tues. No lunch.*

Jubba Somali Restaurant
$ | **AFRICAN** | Diners enjoy sampling the unique specialties presented by this friendly eatery, one of the few Somali restaurants in the Bay Area. The go-to dish is "kay kay," a sweet-and-savory stir-fry of chopped chapatti bread, spice-rubbed beef or chicken, African tea, onions, and bananas—and yes, you read that last one right. **Known for:** roast goat cutlet rice plate; grilled spice-rubbed chicken suqaar; wraps filled with beef, chicken, or fish. [$] *Average main: $19* ✉ *5330 Terner Way, San Jose* ☎ *408/440–1504* 🕑 *Closed Wed.*

Le Papillon
$$$$ | **MODERN FRENCH** | For those who think that French-influenced fine dining is passé, San Jose's gastronomic stalwart will change a few opinions. It's the best of both culinary worlds, where timeless luxury meets a contemporary approach. **Known for:** soufflés; roast duck breast and pavé of leg; outstanding service. [$] *Average main: $110* ✉ *410 Saratoga Ave., San Jose* ☎ *408/296–3730* 🌐 *lepapillon.com* 🕑 *Closed Mon. and Tues. No lunch* 👔 *Business casual.*

Coffee and Quick Bites

Slice of Homage Pizza
$$ | **PIZZA** | San Jose's most well-known dining destination might be this Detroit-style square pizza specialist that only found a full-time home in 2022 after being a pop-up in a nightclub. Now it's part of a multipurpose entertainment space called San Pedro Social, just a block away. **Known for:** incredible caramelized crust for Detroit and Sicilian pies; pepperoni pies; three wings options. [$] *Average main: $27* ✉ *163 W. Santa Clara St., San Jose* ☎ *408/490–4477* 🌐 *sohpizza.com* 🕑 *Closed Mon.*

Hotels

Hotel Valencia Santana Row
$$$ | **HOTEL** | This outpost of a Texas-based boutique hotel group is located in the glossy, Disneyland-ish Santana Row shopping area on the outskirts of San Jose. **Pros:** pedestrian-friendly; comfortable beds with soft Egyptian linens; unique architecture in public spaces. **Cons:** bar becomes a loud, crowded nightclub on weekends; lobby elevator is painfully slow; basic room decor. [$] *Rooms from: $419* ✉ *355 Santana Row, San Jose* ☎ *855/596–3396 reservations, 408/551–0010* 🌐 *hotelvalencia-santanarow.com* 🛏 *233 rooms* 🍴 *No Meals.*

Signia by Hilton San Jose
$$ | **HOTEL** | Downtown San Jose's massive signature hotel recently switched brands and underwent a renovation, changing from Fairmont to this Hilton label. **Pros:** great Japanese-Peruvian restaurant and classic steak house; beautiful marble bathrooms; fitness classes daily. **Cons:** area gets a little edgy at night; high price for a downtown convention hotel; large and intimidating. [$] *Rooms from: $342* ✉ *170 S. Market St., San Jose* ☎ *408/998–1900* 🌐 *hilton.com* 🛏 *541 rooms* 🍴 *No Meals.*

Nightlife

Haberdasher
BARS | This sharply dressed speakeasy is one of the South Bay's gold standards for craft cocktails. Drinks are intricate without being fussy, and the bartenders are always quick to offer insight into what cocktails might fit your taste. The cozy, low-ceilinged space is filled with velvet curtains and plush booths, continuing the 1920s feeling. ✉ *43 W. San Salvador St., San Jose* ☎ *408/792–7356* 🌐 *haberdashersj.com.*

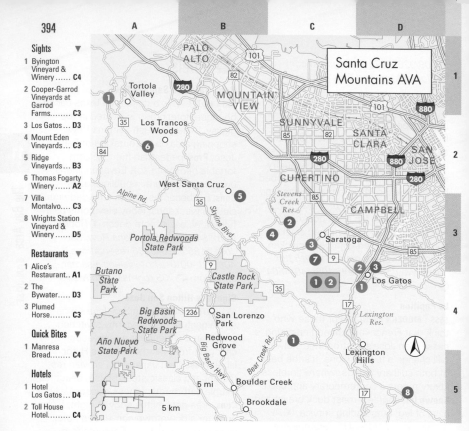

★ Paper Plane

BARS | This cocktail bar with a stunning brick back bar easily competes with the best in the Bay Area. Cocktails are creative and compelling, frequently incorporating atypical ingredients like Thai tea or a syrup made of pepitas (pumpkin seeds). The short food menu revolving around spruced up comfort food is less inventive than the cocktails but far more interesting than standard bar grub. ⊠ *72 S. 1st St., San Jose* ☎ *408/713–2625* ⊕ *paperplanesj.com.*

🏃 Activities

Levi's Stadium

FOOTBALL | The NFL's San Francisco 49ers don't actually play in San Francisco—in 2014, they relocated 40 miles south to this magnificent 68,500-seat stadium. In addition to Niners games each autumn,

it's also the leading concert venue for the Bay Area, where stars like Beyoncé and Taylor Swift perform. Getting to games and events can be an enormous hassle, but the VTA Light Rail stops next to the stadium and connects with Caltrain at Mountain View. ⊠ *4900 Marie P. DeBartolo Way, Santa Clara* ☎ *415/464–9377 box office* ⊕ *levisstadium.com.*

SAP Center at San Jose

HOCKEY | **FAMILY** | Known by fans as the Shark Tank, the South Bay's marquee arena is home to the NHL's San Jose Sharks, in addition to being a major stop for concert tours. With a capacity of just over 17,000 hockey fans, it's one of the most exciting places to see the puck on ice in the country. Younger fans always enjoy meeting SJ Sharkie, the franchise's mascot. ⊠ *525 W. Santa Clara St., San Jose* ☎ *408/287–7070* ⊕ *sapcenter.com.*

Santa Cruz Mountains AVA

Los Gatos is 50 miles south of San Francisco.

Napa Valley and Sonoma County might get most of the winery tourists, but the massive Santa Cruz Mountains AVA is often cited by locals and wine snobs alike as their favorite wine-growing region in the Bay Area. The vineyards here reside on steep, redwood tree–shaded mountains instead of in sun-drenched valleys, and are also much closer to the ocean.

The appellation is split between Santa Cruz County and Santa Clara County (and a tiny bit of San Mateo County) at the top of Highway 17 around Summit Road, an area best known as the epicenter of the 1989 Loma Prieta Earthquake. Skyline Boulevard, the main artery through the mountains, is full of hiking parking lots and panoramic viewpoints. At the base of the mountains are a pair of beautiful small towns, Los Gatos and Saratoga, full of great restaurants and a few tasting rooms. The mountains are much more narrow up the Peninsula, as the vineyards conclude in the terrain above the town of Woodside and then the mountain range fades into the ground several miles before San Francisco.

GETTING HERE AND AROUND

Don't rely on public transit or rideshares here. This is the wilderness—phone reception and Internet are spotty at best. A car is all but necessary.

From San Francisco, take I–280 either to Woodside Road to reach the northern part of the range, or continue to Highway 85 in Cupertino. From Highway 85, the exits for Saratoga Avenue or Highway 17 will take you towards the mountains. If you're driving the Highway 17 route, take the State Route 9/Saratoga–Los Gatos Road exit, which arrives directly into downtown Los Gatos. Alternatively,

Highway 17 continues further south to the Summit Road exit, where several wineries reside at the summit of the Santa Cruz Mountains.

Skyline Boulevard/State Route 35 runs along the top of the mountain range from south to north with many thrilling curves. Saratoga–Los Gatos Road/State Route 9 connects the two most important cities at the base of the mountains.

ESSENTIALS

CONTACTS Santa Cruz Mountains Winegrowers Association. ☎ 831/685–8463 ⊕ *winesofthesantacruzmountains.com.* **Los Gatos.** ⊕ *www.losgatosca.gov/3/visiting-los-gatos.* **Saratoga Chamber of Commerce.** ☎ 408/867–0753 ⊕ *saratogachamber.org.*

Sights

Byington Vineyard & Winery

WINERY | About as isolated as it gets, this winery rewards visitors with outstanding Pinot Noirs from the 8 acres of vineyards on property and views that can extend over the mountains to Monterey Bay on a clear day. You'll feel like you're on top of the world. Wines from the estate and much further afield are across the board enjoyable in the tastings. ⊠ 21850 Bear Creek Rd., Los Gatos ☎ 408/354–1111 ⊕ *byington.com* 🍷 Tastings from $25 🕐 Closed Mon.–Thurs.

★ Cooper-Garrod Vineyards at Garrod Farms

WINERY | Horseback riding and wine tasting makes a great combination for a day in the mountains; it's that duo that draws visitors to this longtime farm and winery above Saratoga. A former test pilot, George Cooper founded the winery in 1972 and all of the wine continues to be sourced exclusively from the 28 acres of vines on the estate. Don't miss the unique Test Pilot red blends and the quiet specialty of the winery: Cabernet Franc ⊠ 22645 Garrod Rd. ☎ 408/867–7116 ⊕ *garrodfarms.com* 🍷 Tastings from

Los Gatos

TOWN | Situated at the southern end of the San Jose sprawl as the last city stop in the Bay Area before Santa Cruz and the gateway to the Santa Cruz Mountains, Los Gatos is a fun, exciting city that has also maintained its small-town vibe. The downtown area is almost L-shaped, where Santa Cruz Avenue connects with Main Street for two different thoroughfares that feel like one together. Along Santa Cruz, there's the beautifully renovated art-deco-style **Los Gatos Theatre** (✉ *43 Santa Cruz Ave.*). Excellent cocktails and seasonal eats are served at **The Lexington House** (✉ *40 Santa Cruz Ave.*); standout pizzas at **Oak & Rye** (✉ *303 Santa Cruz Ave.*); notable pastas are offered at **The Pastaria & Market** (✉ *27 Santa Cruz Ave.*); fantastic breads and pastries from **Manresa Bread** (✉ *40 Santa Cruz Ave.*); and house-made brews are showcased at **Loma Brewing Company** (✉ *130 Santa Cruz Ave.*). Elsewhere in downtown on the small side streets are creative cocktails from **Los Gatos Soda Works** (✉ *21 College Ave.*), the unique gluten-free Italian cooking of **Polenteria** (✉ *10 Victory La.*), and modern Spanish tapas at **Telefèric Barcelona** (✉ *50 University Ave., Suite B270*).

Beyond downtown, Los Gatos is a residential city with a variety of neighborhoods and parks. **Vasona Lake** is a beautiful reservoir within a county park (⊕ *parks.sccgov.org*) that includes a children's railroad pulled by a steam engine and is a must-visit for families. At the far northern tip of the city is the headquarters of Netflix. ✉ *40 Santa Cruz Ave., Los Gatos* ⊕ *visitlosgatosca.com.*

Mount Eden Vineyards

WINERY | This longtime producer above Saratoga is widely considered the region's Pinot Noir whisperer. Its vineyards date back to 1945 when one of the most iconic names in California wine, winery founder Martin Ray, planted them at elevation of roughly 2,000 feet.

Mount Eden also produces outstanding estate Chardonnay and Cabernet Sauvignon. Tastings on the veranda include three wines and are by appointment only. ✉ *22020 Mount Eden Rd., Saratoga* ☎ *408/867–5832* ⊕ *mounteden.com* 🍷 *Tastings $35* ⊘ *Closed weekends.*

★ Ridge Vineyards

WINERY | One of the most iconic names in American wine, Ridge's 1971 Monte Bello Cabernet Sauvignon participated in the famous 1976 Judgement of Paris tasting between French and Californian wines. See that celebrated Monte Bello Vineyard here, a stunning hillside of wine royalty with a mesmerizing view over the South Bay. Longtime winemaker Paul Draper was a visionary for prioritizing single-vineyard expressions and a minimal-intervention approach to crafting wines, and the winery continues that tradition. Visitors can usually purchase a taste of Ridge's signature Monte Bello wine (a red Bordeaux-style blend), but fair warning, it's one of the country's most expensive wines. ✉ *17100 Montebello Rd., Cupertino* ☎ *408/868–1320* ⊕ *ridgewine.com* 🍷 *Tastings $30.*

Thomas Fogarty Winery

WINERY | The northernmost winery open to the public in the Santa Cruz Mountains is named after its founder, a legendary heart surgeon. Pinot Noir is the specialty here, but tastings often include a few wild cards like Nebbiolo. The tasting room is surrounded by rolling vineyards, yet the real postcard views are in the adjacent area where weddings are held with a panoramic backdrop of what must be close to half of the Bay Area. ✉ *19501 Skyline Blvd., Woodside* ☎ *650/851–6777* ⊕ *fogartywinery.com* 🍷 *Tastings $35.*

Villa Montalvo

ARTS CENTERS | **FAMILY** | Tuscany meets Northern California at this nonprofit arts center and 166-acre park, where a beautiful villa stands proudly amidst a forest of redwood trees. It's a special place for a lawn picnic in the sunshine, and holds concerts in its hillside amphitheater. ✉ *15400 Montalvo Rd., Saratoga* ☎ *408/961–5800* 🌐 *montalvoarts.org.*

Wrights Station Vineyard & Winery

WINERY | Near Loma Prieta, as high as one can go in the Santa Cruz Mountains, this fun winery balances high-quality wines with a more laid back atmosphere that encourages relaxing all afternoon. There's a boccie court, splendid vineyard views, and excellent estate Chardonnay and Pinot Noir. Charcuterie boards are sold for hungry tasting groups, and once a month or so there's a food truck on hand. This is one of the few local wineries that welcomes both children and dogs. ✉ *24250 Loma Prieta Ave., Los Gatos* ☎ *408/560–9343* 🌐 *wrightsstation.com* 🍷 *Tastings $20* 🕒 *Closed Mon.–Thurs.*

🍴 Restaurants

Alice's Restaurant

$ | **AMERICAN** | At the prominent intersection of Skyline Boulevard and Highway 84, this indoor-outdoor restaurant is a landmark for weekend breakfast and lunch. Alice's is surrounded by redwood trees, so sitting outside at the picnic benches is beautiful but almost always on the chilly side. **Known for:** vast menu including several burgers; French toast and blueberry pancakes; dog-friendly outdoor deck. [$] *Average main: $15* ✉ *17288 Skyline Blvd.* ☎ *650/851–0303* 🌐 *alicesrestaurant.com.*

The Bywater

$$ | **CAJUN** | Legendary farm-to-table fine dining chef David Kinch co-owns this casual restaurant. It's a loving ode to the good times and great cuisine of New Orleans. **Known for:** beignets covered in powdered sugar; shrimp and avocado remoulade; broiled oysters. [$] *Average main: $21* ✉ *532 N. Santa Cruz Ave., Los Gatos* ☎ *408/560–9639* 🌐 *thebywaterca.com* 🕒 *Closed Tues.*

Plumed Horse

$$$$ | **MODERN AMERICAN** | Plumed Horse is a venerable institution for outstanding luxury mixed with the brightness and freshness of local ingredients. The posh, shimmering space is highlighted by a giant glass wine storage area. **Known for:** incredible Champagne collection, black pepper and Parmesan soufflé; lively and well-heeled crowd. [$] *Average main: $54* ✉ *14555 Big Basin Way, Saratoga* ☎ *408/867–4711* 🌐 *plumedhorse.com* 🕒 *Closed Mon. and Tues. No lunch.*

☕ Coffee and Quick Bites

★ Manresa Bread

$ | **BAKERY** | **FAMILY** | In a region with several outstanding destinations for fresh baguettes and levain breads, the freshly baked loaves here deserve some of the highest praise. Everything in the display case and on the cooling racks is absolutely dialed in, from the *kouign-amann* (like a decadent glazed dessert version of a croissant) and cookies to slices of custardy quiche and simple avocado toast. **Known for:** excellent breakfast and lunch sandwiches; almond croissant; terrific locally roasted coffee and espresso drinks. [$] *Average main: $14* ✉ *40 N. Santa Cruz Ave., Los Gatos* ☎ *408/402–5372* 🌐 *manresabread.com* 🕒 *No dinner.*

🛏 Hotels

Hotel Los Gatos

$$ | **HOTEL** | The Tuscan villa–inspired design is hard to miss at this very pleasant hotel; it's a welcome refuge from the sprawl and tech-centric culture of Silicon Valley. **Pros:** great neighborhood with several restaurants; doesn't feel like a chain; outdoor pool and Jacuzzi. **Cons:** over-the-top theme; not as luxurious as a villa should be; no in-house breakfast option. [$] *Rooms from: $289* ✉ *210 E. Main St., Los Gatos* ☎ *408/335–1700* 🌐 *hotellosgatos.com* 🛏 *72 rooms* 🍴 *No Meals.*

Toll House Hotel
$$ | **HOTEL** | On the edge of downtown Los Gatos, this beautiful contemporary hotel is a great choice for wine-tasting weekenders or business travelers looking for a calmer, more charming locale than most of Silicon Valley. **Pros:** nice indoor-outdoor fitness center; spacious bathrooms; quiet but central location. **Cons:** lacks personality; destination fee; not many amenities. [$] *Rooms from: $259* ✉ *140 S. Santa Cruz Ave., Los Gatos* ☎ *800/238–6111* 🌐 *tollhousehotel.com* 🛏 *115 rooms* 🍴 *No Meals.*

Nightlife

Loma Brewing Company
BREWPUBS | Many baseball fans make the trip to Los Gatos just to visit this brewery owned by former MLB infielder Kevin Youkilis. However, the brewery deserves many accolades in its own right for producing some of the top beers in the South Bay, such as the hops-packed Greek God of Hops, a double IPA that riffs on Youkilis's nickname in the book *Moneyball*. At this family-friendly brewpub, everyone can enjoy refined pub grub with or without the house beers. ✉ *130 N. Santa Cruz Ave., Los Gatos* ☎ *408/560–9626* 🌐 *lomabrew.com.*

Mountain Winery
LIVE MUSIC | This gorgeous property is centered around the summer concert series at its beautiful amphitheater. Many notable musicians, often popular singers and groups from past decades, make a stop here. The winery was built by the iconic Paul Masson (one of the true pioneers of California wine in the late 19th century and early 20th century) and tastings are held each weekend. ✉ *14831 Pierce Rd., Saratoga* ☎ *408/741–2822* 🌐 *mountainwinery.com.*

Sidecar Modern Tavern
BARS | A throwback atmosphere meets the modern craft cocktail movement at this excellent "tavern" that shows how much the concept of one has evolved. Cocktails might include a unique house-made tonic for a standout gin and tonic or a tiki drink incorporating aged rum, mango, and rooibos. ✉ *25 E. Main St., Los Gatos* ☎ *408/399–5180* 🌐 *sidecar7.com.*

Chapter 12

NAPA AND SONOMA

Updated by
Daniel Mangin

👁 **Sights**
★★★★★

🍴 **Restaurants**
★★★★★

🛏 **Hotels**
★★★★☆

🛍 **Shopping**
★★★☆☆

🌙 **Nightlif**
★★★☆

WELCOME TO NAPA AND SONOMA

TOP REASONS TO GO

★ **Touring wineries:** Let's face it: this is the reason you're here, and the range of excellent sips to sample would make any oenophile (or novice drinker, for that matter) giddy.

★ **Biking:** Gentle hills and vineyard-laced farmland make Napa and Sonoma perfect for combining leisurely back-roads cycling with winery stops.

★ **Spa treatments:** Work-hard, play-hard types and inveterate sybarites flock to Wine Country spas for pampering.

★ **Fine dining:** A meal at a top-tier restaurant can be a revelation about the level of artistry intuitive chefs can achieve and how successfully quality wines pair with food.

★ **Viewing the art:** Several wineries, among them Napa Valley's Hall St. Helena and The Donum Estate in Sonoma display museum-quality artworks indoors and on their grounds.

1 **Napa.** Good base, with tasting rooms, dining, shopping, nightlife.

2 **Yountville.** Walkable downtown, must-visit restaurants.

3 **Oakville.** Cabernet central.

4 **Rutherford.** Find out what "Rutherford dust" is.

5 **St. Helena.** Genteel downtown amid wineries.

6 **Calistoga.** Spas—from rustic to chic.

7 **Sonoma.** Anchored by a historic mission and plaza.

8 **Glen Ellen.** Creekside village with a rural flavor.

9 **Kenwood.** Top of Sonoma Valley.

10 **Petaluma.** Farming town, proud of it.

11 **Healdsburg.** Northern Sonoma's swank hub.

12 **Geyserville.** Alexander Valley wineries, fun downtown.

13 **Forestville.** Woodsy river enclave.

14 **Guerneville.** A Russian River vacation spot.

15 **Sebastopol.** West County's HQ.

16 **Santa Rosa.** Sonoma County's largest city.

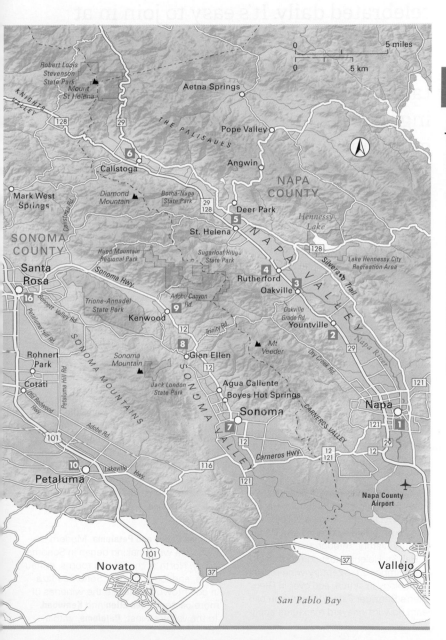

In California's premier wine region, the pleasures of eating and drinking are celebrated daily. It's easy to join in at famous wineries and rising newcomers off country roads, or at trendy in-town tasting rooms. Chefs transform local ingredients into feasts, and gourmet groceries sell perfect picnic fare.

Yountville, Healdsburg, and St. Helena have small-town charm as well as luxurious inns, hotels, and spas. Yet the natural setting is equally sublime, whether experienced from a canoe on the Russian River or the deck of a winery overlooking endless rows of vines.

The Wine Country is also rich in history. In Sonoma you can explore California's Spanish and Mexican pasts at the Sonoma Mission, and the origins of modern California wine making at Buena Vista Winery. Some wineries, among them St. Helena's Beringer and Rutherford's Inglenook, have cellars or tasting rooms dating to the late 1800s. Calistoga is a flurry of late-19th-century Steamboat Gothic architecture, though the town's oldest-looking building, the medieval-style Castello di Amorosa, is a 21st-century creation.

Visits to the Napa Valley's Beringer, Robert Mondavi, and Inglenook—and at Buena Vista in the Sonoma Valley—provide an entertaining overview of Wine Country history. Through the glass walls at Hall St. Helena's tasting room you may glimpse 21st-century wine-making technology in action, and over in Glen Ellen's Benziger Family Winery you can learn how its vineyard managers apply biodynamic farming principles to grape growing. At numerous facilities you can play winemaker at seminars in the fine art of blending wines. If that strikes you as too much effort, you can always pamper yourself at a luxury spa.

⇨ *To delve further into the fine art of Wine Country living, pick up a copy of* Fodor's Napa and Sonoma.

MAJOR REGIONS

Napa Valley. Practically speaking, the valley can be divided into its southern and northern parts. The southern Napa Valley encompasses cooler grape-growing areas and the tasting rooms, restaurants, and hotels of **Napa** and **Yountville**, along with slightly warmer **Oakville**. The northern valley begins around **Rutherford,** like Oakville blessed with Cabernet-friendly soils. Beyond it lies hotter **St. Helena,** whose downtown entices with boutiques, galleries, and restaurants. Warmer still is **Calistoga,** known for spas and hot springs.

Sonoma Valley and Petaluma. Modern California wine making began in Sonoma Valley. North of the tasting rooms, restaurants, and lodgings near Sonoma Plaza in downtown **Sonoma** lie the wineries of more pastoral **Glen Ellen** and **Kenwood.** To the valley's west, **Petaluma,** with a burgeoning dining scene, has come into its own as a Wine Country destination.

Northern Sonoma, Russian River, and West County. Its walkable downtown, swank hotels, and restaurant scene make **Healdsburg** the tourist hub of Sonoma County's northern section. North of Healdsburg, mostly rural **Geyserville** has a small, engaging downtown. The Russian River winds through or near **Forestville, Guerneville,** and **Sebastopol,** three West County towns where Chardonnay and Pinot Noir grow well. The county's largest city, **Santa Rosa,** contains nonwine attractions and affordable lodgings.

Planning

Getting Here and Around

AIR

Wine Country regulars often bypass San Francisco and Oakland and fly into Santa Rosa's Charles M. Schulz Sonoma County Airport (STS), which receives direct flights from several western cities. The airport is 15 miles from Healdsburg.

■TIP→ **Alaska Airlines allows passengers flying out of STS to check up to one case of wine for free.**

BUS

Bus travel is an inconvenient way to explore the Wine Country, though it is possible. Take Golden Gate Transit from San Francisco to connect with Sonoma County Transit buses. VINE connects with BART commuter trains in the East Bay and the San Francisco Bay Ferry in Vallejo. VINE buses serve the Napa Valley.

CAR

A car is the most convenient way to navigate Napa and Sonoma. If you're flying into the area, it's almost always easiest to pick up a car at the airport. You'll also find rental companies in major Wine Country towns. A few rules to

note: smartphone use for any purpose is prohibited, including mapping applications unless the device is mounted to a car's windshield or dashboard and can be activated with a single swipe or finger tap. A right turn after stopping at a red light is legal unless posted otherwise.

Hotels

The fanciest accommodations are concentrated in the Napa Valley towns of Yountville, Rutherford, St. Helena, and Calistoga; Sonoma County's poshest lodgings are in Healdsburg. The cities of Napa, Petaluma, and Santa Rosa are the best bets for budget hotels and inns. On weekends, two- or even three-night minimum stays are commonly required at smaller lodgings. Book well ahead for stays at such places in summer or early fall. Some accommodations aren't suitable for kids, so ask before you book.

Restaurants

Top Wine Country chefs tend to apply French and Italian techniques to dishes incorporating fresh, local products. Menus are often vegan- and vegetarian-friendly, with gluten-free options. At pricey restaurants you can save money by having lunch instead of dinner. With a few exceptions (noted in individual restaurant listings), dress is informal.

⇨ *Restaurant and hotel reviews have been shortened. For full information, visit Fodors.com. Restaurant prices are the average cost of a main course at dinner, or if dinner is not served, at lunch. Hotel prices are the lowest cost of a standard double room in high season.*

What It Costs

	$	$$	$$$	$$$$
RESTAURANTS				
	under $20	$20–$30	$31–$40	over $40
HOTELS				
	under $200	$200–$350	$351–$500	over $500

When to Go

High season extends from late May through October. In summer, expect the days to be hot and dry. Hotel rates are highest during the height of harvest, in September and October. Then and in summer, book lodgings well ahead. November, except for Thanksgiving week, and December before Christmas are less busy. The weather in Napa and Sonoma is pleasant nearly year-round. Daytime temperatures average from about 55°F during winter to the 80s and 90s (occasionally 100s) in summer. April, May, and October are milder but still warm. The rainiest months are usually from December through March.

Napa

46 miles northeast of San Francisco.

After many years as a blue-collar burg detached from the Wine Country scene, the Napa Valley's largest town (population about 80,000) has evolved into its shining star. Masaharu Morimoto and other chefs of note operate restaurants here, swank hotels and inns can be found downtown and beyond, and the nightlife options include the West Coast edition of the famed Blue Note jazz club. A walkway that follows the Napa River has made downtown more pedestrian-friendly, and the Oxbow Public Market, a complex of high-end food purveyors, is popular with locals and tourists. The market is named for the nearby oxbow bend in the Napa River, a bit north of where Napa was founded in 1848. The first wood-frame building was a saloon, and the downtown area still projects an old-river-town vibe.

GETTING HERE AND AROUND
Downtown Napa lies a mile east of Highway 29—take the 1st Street exit and follow the signs. Ample parking, much of it free for the first three hours and some for the entire day, is available on or near Main Street. Several VINE buses serve downtown and beyond.

 Sights

Arch & Tower
WINERY | While its Oakville winery undergoes renovations, a project expected to last until summer 2025, the Robert Mondavi Winery will pour its wines (along with a few other luxury brands) in downtown Napa's 1877 Borreo Building. Erected using stone quarried a few miles away in Soda Canyon, the two-story Italian Renaissance–style building has large windows and an outdoor terrace with views west to Main Street. A tireless promoter of the Napa Valley as California's preeminent winegrowing region, the late Robert Mondavi elevated Sauvignon Blanc by labeling his bottlings with the more exotic name Fumé Blanc and made Bordeaux-style reds of renown from To Kalon Vineyard in Oakville. Visits to taste these and other selections, many of them winery exclusives, require a reservation. At time of writing, there was no plan to keep the Borreo Building location open after the Oakville winery reopens in 2025. ✉ *930 3rd St., at Soscol Ave., Napa* ☎ *888/766–6328* ⊕ *robertmondaviwinery.com* 🍷 *Tastings from $65.*

CIA at Copia
COLLEGE | Food fanatics and the merely curious achieve gastronomical bliss at the Culinary Institute of America's Oxbow District campus, its facade brightened by a wraparound mural inspired by the

colorful garden that fronts the facility. You could easily spend a few hours checking out the wine and culinary options; visiting the well-curated shop, theme exhibitions, and Vintners Hall of Fame wall; or attending (book ahead) classes and demonstrations. Head upstairs to the Chuck Williams Culinary Arts Museum. Named for the Williams-Sonoma kitchenwares founder, it holds a fascinating collection of cooking, baking, and other food-related tools, tableware, gizmos, and gadgets, some dating back more than a century. ⊠ *500 1st St., Napa* ⊹ *Near McKinstry St.* ☎ *707/967–2500* ⊕ *www.ciaatcopia.com* ✉ *Facility/museum free, class/demo fees vary.*

★ Domaine Carneros

WINERY | A visit to this majestic château is an opulent way to enjoy the Carneros District—especially in fine weather, when the vineyard views are spectacular. The château was modeled after an 18th-century French mansion owned by the Taittinger family. Carved into the hillside beneath the winery, the cellars produce sparkling wines reminiscent of those made by Taittinger, using only Los Carneros AVA grapes. Enjoy flights of sparkling wine or Pinot Noir with cheese and charcuterie plates, caviar, or smoked salmon. Tastings are by appointment only. ⊠ *1240 Duhig Rd., at Hwy. 121, Napa* ☎ *707/257–0101, 800/716–2788* ⊕ *www.domainecarneros.com* ✉ *Tastings from $40.*

Etude Wines

WINERY | You're apt to see or hear hawks, egrets, Canada geese, and other wildlife on the grounds of Etude, known for sophisticated Pinot Noirs. Although the winery and its light-filled tasting room are in Napa County, the grapes for its flagship Carneros Estate Pinot Noir come from the Sonoma portion of Los Carneros, as do those for the rarer Heirloom Carneros Pinot Noir. Longtime winemaker Jon Priest also excels at single-vineyard Napa Valley Cabernets. In good weather, hosts pour Priest's reds, plus Chardonnay and Pinot Gris, on the patio outside the contemporary tasting room. Hosts of A Study of Pinot Noir, a private, seated experience, pour Pinot Noirs from different areas to illustrate how soil, climate, and growing conditions affect the finished wines. ⊠ *1250 Cuttings Wharf Rd., Napa* ⊹ *1 mile south of Hwy. 121* ☎ *707/257–5782* ⊕ *www.etudewines.com* ✉ *Tastings from $50.*

★ Fontanella Family Winery

WINERY | Six miles from the downtown Napa whirl, husband-and-wife Jeff and Karen Fontanella's hillside spread seems a world apart. In addition to his formal studies, Jeff learned about wine making at three prestigious wineries before he and Karen, a lawyer, established their own operation on 81 south-facing Mt. Veeder acres. The couple braved an economic recession, an earthquake, and wildfires in the first decade but emerged tougher, if no less gracious to guests lucky enough to find themselves tasting Viognier, Chardonnay, Zinfandel, and Cabernet Sauvignon on the patio here. Tastings often end with a Zinfandel-based port-style wine. ■**TIP**➔ **Weather permitting, the reserve tasting includes the opportunity to stroll the estate, whose views south to San Francisco and east to Atlas Peak are terrific.** ⊠ *1721 Partrick Rd., Napa* ⊹ *1st St. to Browns Valley Rd. west of Hwy. 29* ☎ *707/252–1017* ⊕ *www.fontanellawinery.com* ✉ *Tastings from $65.*

★ Mayacamas Downtown

WINERY | Cabernets from Mayacamas Vineyards placed second and fifth respectively on *Wine Spectator* magazine's 2019 and 2020 "Top 100" lists of the world's best wines, two accolades among many for this winery founded atop Mt. Veeder in 1889. One of Napa's leading viticulturists, Annie Favia farms the organic vineyards, elevation 2,000-plus feet, without irrigation; her husband, Andy Erickson, the consulting winemaker. The grape

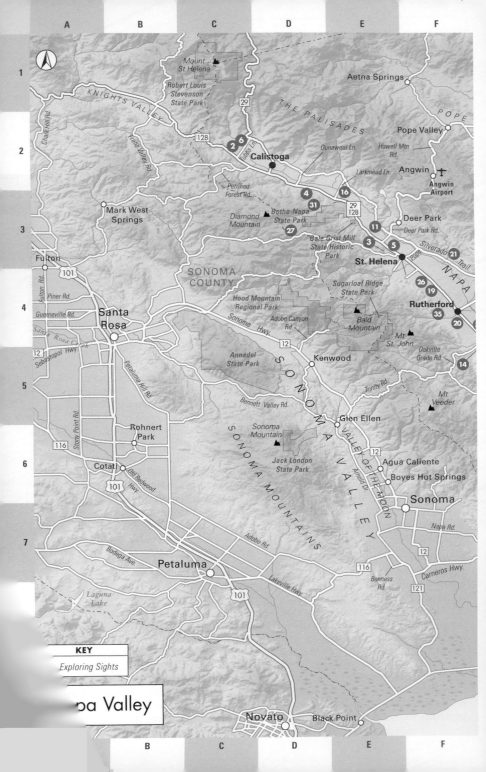

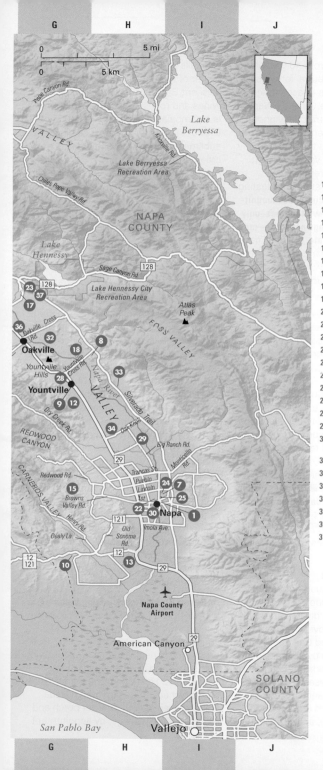

Sights ▼

the Chardonnay come from 40-year-old vines. Aged in mostly neutral (previously used) French oak barrels to accentuate mountain minerality, the wine is a Napa Valley marvel. The Cabernet Sauvignon ages for three years, spending part of the time in oak barrels more than a century old. Erin Martin, a Napa Valley resident with a hip international reputation, designed the light-filled storefront tasting space. ■TIP➜ Experiencing these magnificent wines downtown—white wines–only and red wines–only tastings possible—may entice you to visit the estate. ⊠ First Street Napa, 1256 1st St., at Randolph St., Napa ☎ 707/294–1433 ⊕ www.mayacamas. com ⊠ Tastings from $35 ⊙ Closed Mon. and Tues.

Napa Valley Wine Train

TRAIN/TRAIN STATION | Guests on this Napa Valley fixture travel the corridor established in 1864 to transport passengers as far north as Calistoga's spas. The rolling stock includes restored Pullman cars and a two-story Vista Dome coach with a curved glass roof. The train travels a leisurely, scenic route between Napa and St. Helena. Patrons on some tours enjoy a multicourse meal and tastings at one or more wineries. Some rides involve no winery stops, and themed trips are occasionally scheduled. ■TIP➜ It's best to make this trip during the day, when you can enjoy the vineyard views. ⊠ 1275 McKinstry St., Napa ⊹ Off 1st St. ☎ 707/253–2111, 800/427–4124 ⊕ www.winetrain. com ⊠ From $225.

★ Oxbow Public Market

MARKET | The 40,000-square-foot market's two dozen stands provide an introduction to Northern California's diverse artisanal food products. Swoon over decadent charcuterie at the Fatted Calf (great sandwiches, too), slurp oysters at Hog Island, or enjoy empanadas at El Porteño. Sample wine (and cheese) at the Oxbow Cheese & Wine Merchant, ales at Fieldwork Brewing's taproom (at ⊠ 1046 McKinstry, near Fatted Calf), and barrel-aged cocktails at the Napa Valley Distillery. The owner of Kara's Cupcakes operates the adjacent Bar Lucia for (mostly) sparkling wines and rosés. Milestone Provisions is a combination butchery, restaurant (California country cuisine including sublime fried-chicken sandwiches), and creamery known for velvety ice cream. Among the few nonfood vendors here is Napa Bookmine, which also operates a larger store elsewhere downtown. ⊠ 610 and 644 1st St., at McKinstry St., Napa ⊕ www.oxbowpublicmarket.com.

★ Robert Biale Vineyards

WINERY | Here's a surprise: a highly respected Napa Valley winery that doesn't sell a lick of Cabernet. Zinfandel from heritage vineyards, some with vines more than 100 years old, holds the spotlight, with luscious Petite Sirahs in supporting roles. Nearly every pour comes with a fascinating backstory, starting with the flagship Black Chicken Zinfandel. In the 1940s, the Biale family sold eggs, walnuts, and other farm staples, with bootleg Zinfandel a lucrative sideline. Because neighbors could eavesdrop on party-line phone conversations, "black chicken" became code for a jug of Zin. These days the wines are produced on the up-and-up, steps from the 10-acre property's tasting area. A stone's throw from Zinfandel vines, with far-off views of two mountain ranges, the open-air space has a back-porch feel. Visits are by appointment; call ahead for same-day. ⊠ 4038 Big Ranch Rd., at Salvador Ave., Napa ☎ 707/257–7555 ⊕ biale.com ⊠ Tastings from $50.

★ Robert Craig Winery Tasting Salon

WINERY | Based way up Howell Mountain but with meticulously farmed hillside sources on both sides of the valley, Robert Craig has established a loyal following for its textured, full-flavored Cabernet Sauvignons. Hosts pour the wines inside a refurbished 1890s downtown Napa Folk Victorian and on its front porch and redbrick patio. Tastings, by appointment but usually possible on short notice, often begin with a Sonoma County Chardonnay or, while it lasts, La Fleur Craig Grenache Rosé from Howell Mountain. One trait all the wines share is how well they age. The Zinfandel from Howell Mountain's Black Sears Vineyard does its varietal proud. ⊠ *1553 2nd St., at Church St.* ☎ *707/252–2250* ⊕ *robertcraigwine. com* 🍷 *Tastings from $35.*

Stag's Leap Wine Cellars

WINERY | A 1973 Stag's Leap Wine Cellars S.L.V. Cabernet Sauvignon put this winery and the Napa Valley on the enological map by placing first in the famous Judgment of Paris tasting of 1976. The grapes for that wine came from a vineyard visible from the stone-and-glass Fay Outlook & Visitor Center, which has broad views of a second fabled Cabernet vineyard (Fay) and the promontory that gives both the winery and the Stags Leap District AVA their names. The top-of-the-line Cabernets from these vineyards are poured at appointment-only tastings (call ahead for same-day visits), some of which include perceptive food pairings by the winery's executive chef. ■**TIP➜ When the weather's right, two patios with the same views as the tasting room fill up quickly.** ⊠ *5766 Silverado Trail, at Wappo Hill Rd., Napa* ☎ *707/261–6410* ⊕ *www.stagsleap-winecellars.com* 🍷 *Tastings from $75.*

★ Trefethen Family Vineyards

WINERY | Superior estate Chardonnay, dry Riesling, Cabernet Sauvignon, Merlot, Pinot Noir, and the Malbec-heavy Dragon's Tooth blend are the trademarks of this family-run winery founded in 1968. To find out how well Trefethen wines age, book a reserve tasting, which includes pours of limited-release wines and one or two older vintages. The terra-cotta-color historic winery on-site, built in 1886, was designed with a gravity-flow system, with the third story for crushing, the second for fermenting the resulting juice, and the first for aging. The wooden building suffered severe damage in the 2014 Napa earthquake, but after extensive renovations it reopened as the main tasting room. The early-1900s Arts and Crafts–style Villa, situated amid gardens, hosts reserve and elevated tastings. All visits require a reservation. ⊠ *1160 Oak Knoll Ave., Napa* ✛ *Off Hwy. 29* ☎ *707/255–7700* ⊕ *www.trefethen.com* 🍷 *Tastings from $50.*

🍴 Restaurants

★ Angèle

$$$ | **FRENCH** | A vaulted wood-beamed ceiling and paper-topped tables set the scene for romance at this softly lit French bistro inside an 1890s boathouse. Look for clever variations on classic dishes such as croque monsieur (grilled Parisian ham and Gruyère) and salade niçoise for lunch, with veal sweetbreads, cassoulet, beef bourguignon, and, in season, steamed mussels for dinner. **Known for:** classic bistro cuisine; romantic setting; outdoor seating under bright-yellow umbrellas. $ *Average main: $38* ⊠ *540 Main St., at 5th St., Napa* ☎ *707/252–8115* ⊕ *www.angelerestaurant.com.*

Grace's Table

$$ | **ECLECTIC** | A dependable, varied menu makes this modest corner restaurant occupying a brick-and-glass storefront many Napans' go-to choice for a simple meal. Empanadas and iron-skillet cornbread with lavender honey and butter show up at all hours, with buttermilk pancakes and chilaquiles scrambled eggs among the brunch staples and cassoulet and roasted heirloom chicken popular for dinner. **Known for:** congenial staffers; good beers on tap; eclectic menu focusing on France, Italy, and the Americas. $ *Average main: $30* ⊠ *1400 2nd St., at Franklin St., Napa* ☎ *707/226–6200* ⊕ *www.gracestable.net.*

★ Kitchen Door

$$ | **ECLECTIC** | Todd Humphries has overseen swank haute-cuisine kitchens in Manhattan, San Francisco, and the

Napa Valley, but he focuses on multicultural comfort plates at his high-ceilinged industrial-contemporary restaurant downtown. The signature dishes include a silky cream of mushroom soup, flatbreads, pho, Thai fisherman's stew, duck banh mi sandwiches (go for the voluptuous duck jus add-on), and sweet, spicy, and succulent chicken wings among many other crowd-pleasers that keep this place hopping even in the off-season. **Known for:** specialty cocktails (bar a casual hangout); seasonally changing apps and entrées; outdoor patio. $ *Average main: $25* ✉ *First Street Napa, 1300 1st St., Suite 272, Napa* ✛ *Near Clay St.* ☎ *707/226–1560* ⊕ *www.kitchendoornapa.com.*

★ La Toque

$$$$ | **MODERN AMERICAN** | Chef Ken Frank's La Toque is the complete package: his French-inspired cuisine, served in a formal dining space, is complemented by a wine lineup that consistently earns the restaurant a coveted *Wine Spectator* Grand Award. Ingredients appearing on the à la carte and prix-fixe tasting menus often include caviar, Alaskan halibut, Wagyu beef, and rich cheeses in dishes prepared and seasoned to pair with wines jointly chosen by the chefs and master sommelier. **Known for:** chef's tasting menu; astute wine pairings; vegetarian tasting menu. $ *Average main: $50* ✉ *Westin Verasa Napa, 1314 McKinstry St., Napa* ✛ *Off Soscol Ave.* ☎ *707/257–5157* ⊕ *www.latoque.com* ⊘ *Closed Mon. and Tues. No lunch.*

Morimoto Napa

$$$$ | **JAPANESE** | *Iron Chef* star Masaharu Morimoto is the big name behind this downtown Napa restaurant where everything is delightfully over the top, including the desserts. Organic materials such as twisting grapevines above the bar and rough-hewn wooden tables seem simultaneously earthy and modern, creating a fitting setting for the gorgeously plated Japanese fare, from straightforward sashimi to more elaborate seafood, chicken, pork, and beef entrées. **Known for:** theatrical ambience; gorgeous plating; cocktail and sake menu. $ *Average main: $55* ✉ *610 Main St., at 5th St., Napa* ☎ *707/252–1600* ⊕ *www.morimotonapa.com.*

Oenotri

$$ | **ITALIAN** | Often spotted at local farmers' markets and his restaurant's gardens, Oenotri's ebullient chef-owner and Napa native Tyler Rodde is ever on the lookout for fresh produce to incorporate into his rustic southern Italian cuisine. His restaurant, a brick-walled contemporary space with tall windows and wooden tables, is a lively spot to sample house-made *salumi* and pastas, thin-crust pizzas, and entrées that might include seared fresh fish or grilled rib eye. **Known for:** lively atmosphere; Margherita pizza with San Marzano tomatoes; desserts with flair. $ *Average main: $26* ✉ *1425 1st St., at Franklin St., Napa* ☎ *707/252–1022* ⊕ *www.oenotri.com* ⊘ *Closed Mon. No lunch weekdays.*

★ Scala Osteria & Bar

$$$ | **ITALIAN** | The brightly lit dining room's mural map of the Naples coastline signals the chef's focus on *frutti di mare* (seafood) at this downtown homage to southern Italian cuisine the folks behind valley-fave Bistro Don Giovanni opened in 2023. Raw oysters, cooked whole fish, skillet-sautéed mussels, and halibut soup were among the early hits, along with pizzas hot out of a wood-fired oven. **Known for:** shareable plates and pasta dishes; Italian wine selection; late-night pizza, small bites, and desserts. $ *Average main: $30* ✉ *1141 1st St., Napa* ✛ *Near Coombs St.* ☎ *707/637–4380* ⊕ *scalaosteria.com.*

★ Torc

$$$$ | **MODERN AMERICAN** | Torc means "wild boar" in an early Celtic dialect, and owner-chef Sean O'Toole, who formerly helmed kitchens at top Manhattan, San Francisco, and Yountville establishments, occasionally incorporates the restaurant's

namesake beast into his eclectic offerings. A recent menu featured tuna tartare, squash risotto, three hand-cut pasta dishes, a side of mushrooms foraged by a local pro, and Maine diver scallops in a lobster emulsion, all prepared by O'Toole and his team with style and precision. **Known for:** jolly only-at-the-bar happy hour (4–6 pm, nine seats total); specialty cocktails; Bengali sweet-potato pakora and deviled-egg appetizers. [$] *Average main: $42* ✉ *1140 Main St., Napa* ✣ *At Pearl St.* ☎ *707/252–3292* 🌐 *www.torcnapa.com* 🕒 *Closed Sun. and Mon. No lunch.*

★ ZuZu

$$$ | SPANISH | The owner of this four-storefront empire touts it as a "mid-block party": ZuZu for paella, tapas, and other northern Spanish favorites; next door a gin bar (the spirit is big in Spain); third, a takeout window; and finally La Taberna for beer, wine, and *pintxos* (bar bites). The anchor, which opened in 2002, is still drawing crowds, who come for shareable plates that might include flounder ceviche, tender wood-fired octopus, *jamón ibérico,* and lamb chops with Moroccan barbecue glaze. **Known for:** range of gin flavors and tonics; paella of the day with bomba rice, chorizo, and shellfish; energetic crowds at gin bar and La Taberna. [$] *Average main: $35* ✉ *829 Main St., Napa* ✣ *Near 3rd St.* ☎ *707/224–8555* 🌐 *www.zuzunapa.com* 🕒 *Closed Mon. and Tues.*

Hotels

Andaz Napa

$$$ | HOTEL | Part of the Hyatt family, this boutique hotel with an urban-hip vibe has spacious guest rooms with white-marble bathrooms stocked with high-quality products. **Pros:** casual-chic feel; proximity to downtown restaurants, theaters, and tasting rooms; cheery, attentive service. **Cons:** unremarkable views from some rooms; expensive on weekends in high season; renovations might be ongoing so ask for a room not affected by them. [$] *Rooms from: $458* ✉ *1450 1st St., Napa* ☎ *707/687–1234* 🌐 *andaznapa.com* 🛏 *141 rooms* 🍴 *No Meals.*

★ Archer Hotel Napa

$$$ | HOTEL | Ideal for travelers seeking design pizzazz, a see-and-be-seen atmosphere, and first-class amenities, this five-story downtown Napa property fuses New York City chic and Las Vegas glamour. **Pros:** restaurants by chef Charlie Palmer; Sky & Vine rooftop bar; great views from upper-floor rooms (especially south and west). **Cons:** not particularly rustic; expensive in high season; occasional service and hospitality lapses. [$] *Rooms from: $459* ✉ *1230 1st St., Napa* ☎ *707/690–9800, 855/200–9052* 🌐 *archerhotel.com/napa* 🛏 *183 rooms* 🍴 *No Meals.*

★ Carneros Resort and Spa

$$$$ | RESORT | A winning combination of glamour, service, and pastoral seclusion makes this resort with freestanding board-and-batten cottages the perfect getaway for active lovebirds or families and groups seeking to unwind. **Pros:** cottages have lots of privacy; views from hilltop pool and hot tub; heaters on private patios. **Cons:** long drive to upvalley destinations; least expensive accommodations pick up highway noise; pricey pretty much year-round. [$] *Rooms from: $1,099* ✉ *4048 Sonoma Hwy./Hwy. 121, Napa* ☎ *707/299–4900, 888/400–9000* 🌐 *www.carnerosresort.com* 🛏 *100 rooms* 🍴 *No Meals.*

★ The Inn on First

$$$ | B&B/INN | Guests gush over the hospitality at this inn, where the painstakingly restored 1905 mansion facing 1st Street contains five rooms, with five additional accommodations, all suites, in a building behind a secluded patio and garden. **Pros:** full gourmet breakfast by hosts-with-the-most owners; gas fireplaces and whirlpool tubs in all rooms; away from downtown but not too far. **Cons:** no TVs; owners "respectfully request no children, no exceptions"; lacks pool, fitness center, and other amenities of larger properties. $ *Rooms from: $430* ✉ *1938 1st St., Napa* ☎ *707/253–1331* ⊕ *www.theinnonfirst.com* ⇨ *10 rooms* ⦿I *Free Breakfast.*

★ Inn on Randolph

$$$ | **B&B/INN** | A few calm blocks from the downtown action on a nearly 1-acre lot with landscaped gardens, the Inn on Randolph—with a Gothic revival–style main house and its five guest rooms plus five historic cottages out back—is a sophisticated haven celebrated for its gourmet gluten-free breakfasts and snacks. **Pros:** quiet residential neighborhood; spa tubs in cottages and two main-house rooms; romantic setting. **Cons:** a bit of a walk from downtown; expensive in-season; weekend minimum-stay requirement. $ *Rooms from: $420* ✉ *411 Randolph St., Napa* ☎ *707/257–2886* ⊕ *www.innonrandolph.com* ⇨ *10 rooms* ⦿I *Free Breakfast.*

Nightlife

Blue Note Napa

LIVE MUSIC | The famed New York jazz room's intimate West Coast club hosts national headliners such as Kenny Garrett, KT Tunstall, and Jody Watley. At Locals Night on many Wednesdays, homegrown talent performs. There's a full bar, and you can order a meal or small bites from the kitchen. The larger JaM Cellars Ballroom upstairs books similar artists. ✉ *Napa Valley Opera House, 1030 Main St., at 1st St., Napa* ☎ *707/880–2300* ⊕ *www.bluenotenapa.com.*

Cadet Wine + Beer Bar

WINE BARS | Cadet plays things urban-style cool with a long bar, high-top tables, and a low-lit, loungelike feel. California wines and beers predominate, but the lineup circles the globe. Artisanal tequilas in cocktails or on their own will be the focus of Chispa, a new bar a few blocks away on 1st Street the same owners plan to open in 2023. ✉ *930 Franklin St., Napa* ✛ *At end of pedestrian alley between 1st and 2nd Sts.* ☎ *707/224–4400* ⊕ *www.cadetbeerandwinebar.com.*

Shopping

First Street Napa

MALL | The Archer Hotel Napa anchors this open-air downtown complex of mostly ground-level restaurants, tasting rooms, and national (Anthropologie, Lululemon) and homegrown (The Bennington Napa Valley, Habituate Lifestyle + Interiors, Napa Stäk) design, clothing, housewares, and culinary shops. Copperfield's Books and the Visit Napa Valley Welcome Center are also here, along with Milo and Friends for pet necessities and accessories. ✉ *1300 1st St., between Franklin and Coombs Sts., Napa* ☎ *707/257–6900* ⊕ *www.firststreetnapa.com.*

Activities

Napa Valley Gondola

ENTERTAINMENT CRUISE | Rides in authentic gondolas that seat up to six depart from downtown Napa's municipal dock. You'll never mistake the Napa River for the Grand Canal, but this is a diverting excursion that often includes a serenade. ✉ *Main St. Boat Dock, 700 Main St., Napa* ✛ *Riverfront Promenade, south of 3rd St. Bridge* ☎ *707/373–2100* ⊕ *napavalleygondola.com* 🎟 *From $169 (up to 6 people).*

Yountville

9 miles north of the town of Napa.

Yountville (population 3,000) is something like Disneyland for food lovers. You could stay here several days and not exhaust all the options—a few of them owned by The French Laundry's Thomas Keller—and the tiny town is full of small inns and high-end hotels that cater to those who prefer to walk (not drive) after an extravagant meal. It's also well located for excursions to many big-name Napa wineries, especially those in the Stags Leap District, from which big, bold Cabernet Sauvignons helped make the Napa Valley's wine-making reputation.

GETTING HERE AND AROUND

Downtown Yountville sits just off Highway 29. Approaching from the south take the Yountville exit—from the north take Madison—and proceed to Washington Street, home to the major shops and restaurants. Yountville Cross Road connects downtown to the Silverado Trail, along which many noted wineries do business. The free Yountville Trolley serves the town daily 10–7 (on-call service until 11 pm except on Sunday).

Sights

★ Cliff Lede Vineyards

WINERY | Inspired by his passion for classic rock, owner and construction magnate Cliff Lede named the blocks in his Stags Leap District vineyard after hits by the Grateful Dead and other bands. Two other Lede obsessions are rock memorabilia and contemporary art like Jim Dine's outdoor sculpture *Twin 6' Hearts*, a magnet for the Instagram set. The vibe at this efficient, high-tech winery is anything but laid-back, however. Cutting-edge agricultural and enological science informs the vineyard management and wine making here. Lede produces Sauvignon Blanc, Cabernet Sauvignon, and Bordeaux-style red blends. All the wines are well crafted, though the Cabs truly rock. ■TIP→ **Book a Backstage Tasting Lounge session to sip top-tier wines amid a rock music–related art exhibition.** ✉ *1473 Yountville Cross Rd., Yountville* ✛ *Off Silverado Trail* ☎ *707/944–8642* ⊕ *cliffledevineyards. com* 🍷 *Tastings from $60.*

Cornerstone Cellars

WINERY | Inside Yountville's whitewashed 19th-century passenger train depot, Cornerstone shares a space with an apparel shop and displays contemporary art curated by Aerena Galleries. The winery, started on something of a whim more than three decades ago (a Howell Mountain grower offered the founders some excess fruit late in the 1991 season), produces Cabernet Sauvignon from the valley's benchland and mountain sections. Because each Cabernet receives similar treatment from winemaker Kari Auringer, the wines express what's unique about their sub-appellations, vineyard sources, and vintages. Cornerstone is a good place to find out what type of Napa Valley Cabernet you prefer—perhaps the smooth Benchlands blend, in recent years softened with Merlot and Cabernet Franc, or maybe the sturdier yet still lush Howell Mountain offering, usually 100% Cabernet or nearly so. ✉ *6505 Washington St., Yountville* ☎ *707/945–0388* ⊕ *www.cornerstonecellars.com* 🍷 *Tastings from $40.*

★ Elyso Winery

WINERY | One of his colleagues likens Elyse's winemaker, Russell Bevan, to "a water witch without the walking stick" for his ability to assess a vineyard's weather, soil, and vine positioning and intuit how particular viticultural techniques will affect wines' flavors. Bevan farms judiciously during the growing season, striving later in the cellar to preserve what nature and his efforts have yielded rather than rely on heavy manipulation. Elyse makes highly praised small-lot single-vineyard Zinfandels and Cabernet Sauvignons. Red blends containing as many as five varietals are another strong suit. A country lane edged by vines leads to this unassuming winery, whose unhurried tastings, often outdoors, have a backyard-casual feel. ■TIP→ **Costing much less than the average Napa Valley Cab, Elyse's Holbrook Mitchell Cabernet Sauvignon holds its own against peers priced appreciably higher.** ✉ *2100 Hoffman La., Napa* ✛ *1¾ miles south of central Yountville, off Hwy. 29 or Solano Ave.* ☎ *707/944–2900* ⊕ *elysewinery.com* 🍷 *Tastings from $55.*

Goosecross Cellars

WINERY | Large retractable west-facing windows in this boutique winery's barn-like tasting space open up behind the bar to views of Cabernet Sauvignon vines—in fine weather, guests on the outdoor deck can practically touch them. Farther in the distance lie the Mayacamas Mountains. Goosecross makes Chardonnay and Pinot Noir from Carneros grapes, but the soul of this cordial operation is its 12-acre State Lane Vineyard, the 9.2 planted acres mostly Cabernet Sauvignon and Merlot with some Cabernet Franc, Malbec, and Petit Verdot. The State Lane Cabernet and Merlot are the stars, along with the Holly's Block 100% Cab and the Aeros Bordeaux-style blend of the vineyard's best grapes. The last two aren't always poured, but the intentionally big Branta red wine (the blend changes with each vintage), a crowd-pleaser, usually is. Visits to Goosecross are by appointment only. ⊠ *1119 State La., Yountville ✛ Off Yountville Cross Rd.* ☎ *707/944–1986* ⊕ *www.goosecross.com* ⊠ *Tastings from $60.*

RH Wine Vault

WINERY | Gargantuan crystal chandeliers, century-old olive trees, and strategically placed water features provide visual and aural continuity at Restoration Hardware's quadruple-threat food, wine, art, and design compound. An all-day café fronts two steel, glass, and concrete home-furnishings galleries, with a bluestone walkway connecting them to the wine salon. Centered on a two-story 1904 manor house constructed from Napa River stone, it's an excellent spot to learn about small-lot Napa and Sonoma wines, served by the glass, flight, or bottle. Collector-revered labels like Corison, Fisher, Lail, Matthiasson, Mayacamas, and Spottswoode are all represented, the wines in good weather poured in "outdoor living rooms" behind the stone structure. Oozing RH fabulousness as it does, the Wine Vault can feel like a scene on a busy day, but the wines are the real deal. All tastings are by appointment. ⊠ *6725 Washington St., at Pedroni St., Yountville* ☎ *707/339–4654* ⊕ *rh.com/yountville/winevault* ⊠ *Tastings from $20 glass, $65 flight.*

🍴 Restaurants

Ad Hoc

$$$$ | **AMERICAN** | At this low-key dining room with zinc-top tables, superstar chef Thomas Keller offers a changing daily fixed-price menu that might include smoked beef short ribs with creamy herb rice and charred broccolini or sesame chicken with radish kimchi and fried rice (check the website for that day's offerings). Ad Hoc also serves a small but decadent Sunday brunch, and Keller's Addendum annex, in a separate small building behind the restaurant, sells boxed lunches to go (including moist buttermilk fried chicken) from Thursday to Saturday except in winter. **Known for:** casual cuisine; don't-miss buttermilk-fried-chicken night; good prices for a Thomas Keller restaurant. $ *Average main: $64* ⊠ *6476 Washington St., at Oak Circle, Yountville* ☎ *707/944–2487* ⊕ *www.thomaskeller.com/adhoc* ⊘ *Closed Tues. and Wed. No lunch weekdays and Sat.*

★ Bistro Jeanty

$$$ | **FRENCH** | Escargots, cassoulet, steak au poivre (pepper steak), and other French classics are prepared with precision inside this tan-brick country bistro whose flower-filled window boxes, extra-wide shutters, and red-and-white-striped awning hint at the old-world flair and joie de vivre that infuse the place. Regulars often start with the rich tomato soup in a flaky puff pastry before proceeding to sole meunière or coq au vin, completing the French sojourn with crème brûlée *au chocolat* or another authentic dessert. **Known for:** traditional preparations; oh-so-French atmosphere; patio seating. $ *Average main: $34* ⊠ *6510 Washington St., at Mulberry St., Yountville* ☎ *707/944–0103* ⊕ *www.bistrojeanty.com.*

Bottega

$$$ | **ITALIAN** | At his softly lit, exposed-redbrick downtown trattoria, which occupies sections of the 19th-century former Groezinger Winery, chef Michael Chiarello (Food Network, etc.) and his team transform local, seasonally changing ingredients into regional Italian cuisine. Staples like ricotta gnocchi with tomato sauce and smoked/braised short rib in espresso *agrodolce* (sweet-and-sour sauce) served with creamy ancient-grain polenta show the chef at his most rustic yet sophisticated. **Known for:** romantic setting; soulful craft cocktails; Italian and California wines. $ *Average main: $33* ⊠ *6525 Washington St., Yountville* ⊹ *Near Mulberry St.* ☎ *707/945–1050* ⊕ *www.botteganapavalley.com.*

★ Bouchon Bistro

$$$ | **FRENCH** | The team that created The French Laundry is also behind this place, where everything—the zinc-topped bar, antique sconces, suave waitstaff, and traditional French onion soup—could have come straight from a Parisian bistro. Pan-seared flat iron steak with caramelized shallots and mussels steamed with white wine, saffron, and Dijon mustard—both served with crispy, addictive fries—are among the perfectly executed entrées. **Known for:** bistro classics; raw bar; Bouchon Bakery next door. $ *Average main: $36* ⊠ *6534 Washington St., Yountville* ⊹ *Near Humboldt St.* ☎ *707/944–8037* ⊕ *thomaskeller.com/bouchonyountville.*

★ Coqueta Napa Valley

$$$ | **SPANISH** | From pintxos and paellas to Iberian cheeses and fish *à la plancha* (flat-grilled), the chefs at this Wine Country offspring of Michael Chiarello's successful San Francisco restaurant Coqueta reimagine Spanish classics with a 21st-century farm-to-table sensibility. The frenetic pace in the flame-happy open kitchen, inside Yountville's redbrick former railroad depot, keeps the mood lively in the relatively small dining space, with the vibe on the patio out back even more so. **Known for:** sensual flavors; dynamic spicing; seasonal cocktails inspired by Spain and the Napa Valley. $ *Average main: $33* ⊠ *6525 Washington St., Yountville* ⊹ *Near Yount St.* ☎ *707/244–4350* ⊕ *www.coquetanv.com.*

★ The French Laundry

$$$$ | **AMERICAN** | Inside an ivy-laced old stone building and atop many a Napa Valley visitor's bucket list, chef Thomas Keller's destination restaurant lives up to the hype with intricate yet not over-thought cuisine. Some courses on the two prix-fixe menus, one of which highlights vegetables, rely on luxe ingredients such as white quail; others take humble elements like carrots or fava beans and elevate them to art. **Known for:** signature starter "oysters and pearls"; "supplements" like white truffles, caviar, and Wagyu beef; superior wine list. $ *Average main: $400* ⊠ *6640 Washington St., at Creek St., Yountville* ☎ *707/944–2380* ⊕ *www.frenchlaundry.com* ⊘ *No lunch Mon.–Thurs.* ⚎ *Jacket required* ☞ *Reservations essential wks ahead.*

Mustards Grill

$$$ | **AMERICAN** | Cindy Pawlcyn's Mustards Grill fills day and night with fans of her hearty cuisine, equal parts updated renditions of traditional American dishes—what Pawlcyn dubs "deluxe truck stop classics"—and fanciful contemporary fare. Barbecued baby back pork ribs and a lemon-lime tart piled high with brown-sugar meringue fall squarely in the first category, and sweet corn tamales with tomatillo-avocado salsa and wild mushrooms represent the latter. **Known for:** roadhouse setting; convivial mood; hoppin' bar. $ *Average main: $31* ⊠ *7399 St. Helena Hwy./Hwy. 29, Napa* ⊹ *1 mile north of Yountville* ☎ *707/944–2424* ⊕ *www.mustardsgrill.com.*

★ Regiis Ova Caviar & Champagne Lounge

$$$ | **WINE BAR** | Even restaurateurs as famous as Thomas Keller test out concepts via pop-ups, though in retrospect

his pairing of mostly French sparkling wines with caviar from a company (Regiis Ova) the chef co-owns was always destined for permanent glory. Intended as a palate-cleansing pit stop between Cab tasting and dinner, the place, furnished in insouciant, faintly decadent style by Bay Area celeb designer Ken Fulk, tempts patrons to stay put, order more bubbly and roe, and call it a meal. **Known for:** live jazz most days; chilled oysters, tartares, and crudités; sommelier-selected French Champagnes. [$] *Average main: $35 ✉ 6480 Washington St., at Oak Circle, Yountville ☎ 707/947–7181 🌐 regiisovalounge.com ⏲ Closed Mon. and Wed. No lunch (but check).*

Hotels

★ Bardessono

$$$$ | RESORT | Tranquility and luxury with a low carbon footprint are among the goals of this ultragreen wood, steel, and glass resortlike property in downtown Yountville, but there's nothing spartan about the accommodations, arranged around four landscaped courtyards. **Pros:** large rooftop lap pool; in-room spa treatments; three luxury villas for extra privacy. **Cons:** expensive year-round; limited view from some rooms; a bit of street traffic on hotel's west side. [$] *Rooms from: $1,100 ✉ 6526 Yount St., Yountville ☎ 707/204–6000 🌐 www.bardessono.com 🛏 65 rooms 🍴 No Meals.*

Maison Fleurie

$$ | B&B/INN | A stay at this comfortable, reasonably priced inn, said to be the oldest hotel in the Napa Valley, places you within walking distance of Yountville's fine restaurants. **Pros:** smallest rooms a bargain; outdoor hot tub and pool; free bikes. **Cons:** lacks amenities of a full-service hotel; some rooms pick up noise from nearby Bouchon Bakery; hard to book in high season. [$] *Rooms from: $260 ✉ 6529 Yount St., Yountville ☎ 707/944–2056 🌐 www.maisonfleurienapa.com 🛏 13 rooms 🍴 Free Breakfast.*

Napa Valley Lodge

$$$ | HOTEL | Clean rooms in a convenient motel-style setting draw travelers willing to pay more than at comparable lodgings in the city of Napa to be within walking distance of Yountville's tasting rooms, restaurants, and shops. **Pros:** well-maintained rooms; vineyard-view rooms on north and west sides; large pool area. **Cons:** no elevator; nice enough but lacks panache; pricey on weekends in high season. [$] *Rooms from: $450 ✉ 2230 Madison St., Yountville ☎ 707/944–2468, 888/944–3545 🌐 www.napavalleylodge.com 🛏 55 rooms 🍴 Free Breakfast.*

★ North Block Hotel

$$$$ | HOTEL | A two-story boutique property near downtown Yountville's northern edge, the North Block attracts sophisticated travelers who appreciate the clever but unpretentious style and offhand luxury. **Pros:** extremely comfortable beds; personalized service; spacious bathrooms. **Cons:** outdoor areas get some traffic noise; weekend minimum-stay requirement; rates soar on high-season weekends. [$] *Rooms from: $662 ✉ 6757 Washington St., Yountville ☎ 707/944–8080 🌐 northblockhotel.com 🛏 20 rooms 🍴 No Meals.*

Vintage House

$$$$ | RESORT | Part of the 22-acre Estate Yountville complex—other sections include sister lodging Hotel Villagio, the 13,000-square-foot Spa at The Estate, and shops and restaurants—this downtown hotel consists of two-story brick buildings along verdant landscaped paths shaded by mature trees. **Pros:** aesthetically pleasing accommodations; private patios and balconies; secluded feeling yet near shops, tasting rooms, and restaurants. **Cons:** highway noise audible in some exterior rooms; very expensive on summer and fall weekends; weekend minimum-stay requirement. [$] *Rooms from: $800 ✉ 6541 Washington St., Yountville ☎ 707/927–2130, 877/351–1153 🌐 www.vintagehouse.com 🛏 80 rooms 🍴 Free Breakfast.*

Activities

BALLOONING

Napa Valley Aloft

BALLOONING | Passengers soar over the Napa Valley in balloons that launch from downtown Yountville. Flights are from 40 minutes to an hour-plus, depending on the wind speed, with the entire experience taking from three to four hours. ⊠ *The Estate Yountville, 6525 Washington St., Yountville ✛ Near Mulberry St.* ☎ *707/944–4400, 855/944–4408* ⊕ *www.nvaloft.com* ✆ *From $295.*

BICYCLING

Napa Valley Bike Tours

BIKING | With dozens of wineries within 5 miles, this shop makes a fine starting point for guided and self-guided vineyard and wine-tasting excursions. Rental bikes are also available. ⊠ *6500 Washington St., at Mulberry St., Yountville* ☎ *707/251–8687* ⊕ *www.napavalleybiketours.com* ✆ *From $169.*

SPAS

The Spa at The Estate

SPAS | The joint 13,000-square-foot facility of Vintage House and the Hotel Villagio is a five-minute walk from the former's lobby, even less from the latter's. Private spa suites are popular with couples, who enjoy the separate relaxation areas, indoor and outdoor fireplaces, steam showers, saunas, and extra-large tubs. Therapists customize the signature Estate Massage based on clients' needs. Other massages and treatments involve hot stones, grape-seed extract, mud, magnesium, CBD, or aromatherapy. Several types of facials are offered as well. The ground-floor retail area, open to the public, is well stocked with beauty products. ⊠ *The Estate Yountville, 6481 Washington St., at Oak Circle, Yountville* ☎ *707/948–5050* ⊕ *www.theestateyountville.com/spa* ✆ *Treatments from $225.*

Oakville

2 miles northwest of Yountville.

A large butte that runs east–west just north of Yountville blocks the cooling fogs from the south, facilitating the myriad microclimates of the Oakville AVA, home to several high-profile wineries.

GETTING HERE AND AROUND

Driving along Highway 29, you'll know you've reached Oakville when you see the Oakville Grocery on the east side of the road. You can reach Oakville from the Sonoma County town of Glen Ellen by heading east on Trinity Road from Highway 12. The twisting route, along the mountain range that divides Napa and Sonoma, eventually becomes the Oakville Grade. The views on this drive are breathtaking, though the continual curves make it unsuitable for those who suffer from motion sickness.

Sights

Far Niente

WINERY | Hamden McIntyre, a prominent winery architect of his era also responsible for Inglenook and what's now the Culinary Institute of America at Greystone, designed the centerpiece 1885 stone winery here. Abandoned in the wake of Prohibition and only revived beginning in 1979, Far Niente now ranks as one of the Napa Valley's most beautiful properties. Guests participating in the Estate Tasting learn some of this history while sipping the flagship wines, a Chardonnay and a Cabernet Sauvignon blend, along with Russian River Valley Pinot Noir from the affiliated EnRoute label and Dolce, a late-harvest white dessert wine. The Extended Estate Tasting takes in the winery and its aging caves, while the Cave Collection library tasting pairs older vintages with seasonal bites. ■ **TIP→ Fall, when nearly 200 ginkgo trees lining the driveway glow yellow, is a fine time to visit.** ⊠ *1350 Acacia Dr., Oakville ✛ Off Oakville*

Frog's Leap's picturesque country charm extends all the way to the white picket fence.

Grade Rd. ☎ 707/944–2861 ⊕ www.farniente.com 🖼 Tastings from $100.

★ Silver Oak

WINERY | The first review of this winery's Napa Valley Cabernet Sauvignon declared the debut 1972 vintage not all that good and overpriced at $6 a bottle. Oops. The now-celebrated Bordeaux-style blend, still the only Napa Valley Cab bearing the winery's label each year, evolved into a cult favorite, and founders Ray Duncan and Justin Meyer received worldwide recognition for their signature use of exclusively American oak to age the wines. Tastings take place in a hospitality center constructed out of reclaimed stone and other materials from a 19th-century Kansas flour mill. The standard session includes sips of the current Napa Valley vintage, its counterpart from Silver Oak's Alexander Valley operation in Sonoma County, and a library wine. Hosts of vertical tastings pour six Cabernet vintages. All visits require an appointment. ⊠ 915 Oakville Cross Rd., Oakville ✛ Off Hwy.

29 ☎ 707/942–7022 ⊕ www.silveroak.com 🖼 Tastings from $60.

★ Turnbull Cellars

WINERY | It'd be easy to confuse this winery for its more famous neighbor to the north, Cakebread Cellars—William Turnbull designed the original buildings at each. Founded by the architect in 1979 and owned since 1993 by Patrick O'Dell, Turnbull produces richly textured Cabernets from Oakville and Calistoga vineyards. Winemaker Peter Heitz plays light with French oak or, in some cases, handmade Italian amphorae. Guests sip his estate wines indoors among curated shows of works from O'Dell's art and photography collection or outside on landscaped patios surrounded by vineyards. The hospitality exceeds millennials' expectations, and social media–friendly backdrops make for enticing shots, but there's an older-Napa gentility to this appointment-only winery that even many locals haven't gotten around to visiting. Beat them to the punch. This place is worth it. ⊠ 8210 St. Helena Hwy.,

Oakville ⊹ ¼ mile south of Glos La.
☎ 707/963–5839 ⊕ *www.turnbullwines.*
com 🍷 *Tastings from $65.*

Rutherford

2 miles northwest of Oakville.

With its singular microclimate and soil, Rutherford is an important viticultural center, with more big-name wineries than you can shake a corkscrew at. Cabernet Sauvignon is king here. The well-drained, loamy soil is ideal for those vines, and since this part of the valley gets plenty of sun, the grapes develop exceptionally intense flavors.

GETTING HERE AND AROUND

Wineries around Rutherford are dotted along Highway 29 and the parallel Silverado Trail north and south of Rutherford Road/Conn Creek Road, on which wineries can also be found.

Sights

★ Frog's Leap

WINERY | If you're a novice, the tour at eco-friendly Frog's Leap is a fun way to begin your education. Conducted by hosts with a sense of humor, the tour stops by a barn built in 1884, an acre of organic gardens, and a frog pond topped with lily pads. The winery produced its first vintage, small batches of Sauvignon Blanc and Zinfandel, in 1981, adding Chardonnay and Cabernet Sauvignon the next year. Merlot, Petite Sirah, and the Heritage Blend of classic Napa Valley varietals including Charbono and Valdiguié are among the other reds these days. All visits require a reservation, but walk-ins are accommodated when possible. ■ **TIP**➜ **The tour is recommended, but you can forgo it and taste on a garden-view porch.** ✉ *8815 Conn Creek Rd., Rutherford* ☎ *707/963–4704* ⊕ *www.frogsleap. com* 🍷 *Tastings from $45.*

★ Inglenook

WINERY | *Wine Enthusiast* magazine bestowed a lifetime-achievement award on vintner-filmmaker Francis Ford Coppola, whose wine-world contributions include resurrecting the historic Inglenook estate. Over the decades, he reunited the original property acquired by Inglenook founder Gustave Niebaum, remodeled Niebaum's ivy-covered 1880s château, and purchased the rights to the Inglenook name. Just in time for the 2022 harvest, the winery unveiled a 22,000-square-foot wine cave and production facility. The eco-friendly cave and Inglenook's place in Napa Valley history are among the topics discussed at tastings, some involving food pairings. Most sessions see a pour of the signature Rubicon, a Cabernet Sauvignon–based blend with a classic Rutherford profile. All visits require an appointment; call the winery or check at the visitor center for same-day availability. ■ **TIP**➜ **In lieu of a tasting, you can book a table at The Bistro, a wine bar with a picturesque courtyard, to sip wine by the glass or bottle.** ✉ *1991 St. Helena Hwy./Hwy. 29, at Hwy. 128, Rutherford* ☎ *707/968–1179* ⊕ *www. inglenook.com* 🍷 *Tastings from $75* ☼ *Closed Tues. and Wed., except for bistro.*

Mumm Napa

WINERY | When Champagne Mumm of France set about establishing a California sparkling-wine outpost, its winemaker chose the Napa Valley, where today the winery sources grapes from more than 50 local producers. Made in the *méthode traditionnelle* style from Chardonnay, Pinot Noir, Pinot Meunier, and occasionally Pinot Gris, the wines are all fermented in the bottle. Most guests enjoy them alfresco, by the glass or flight, on a patio above the surrounding vineyards or one at eye level. Book an Oak Terrace Tasting to sample top-of-the-line cuvées under the sprawling branches of a blue oak nearly two centuries old. Tasting is by appointment only, but walk-ins are accommodated when possible. ✉ *8445 Silverado Trail, Rutherford* ✢ *1 mile south of Rutherford Cross Rd.* ☎ *707/967–7700* 🌐 *www.mummnapa.com* 🎫 *Tastings from $40.*

ZD Wines

WINERY | Founded in 1969 and still run by the same family, this winery specializing in Chardonnay, Pinot Noir, and Cabernet Sauvignon is respected for its organic practices, local philanthropy, and Abacus blend. Made "solera-style," Abacus contains wine from every ZD Reserve Cabernet Sauvignon vintage since 1992. The Chardonnay and Pinot Noir come from a Carneros property, the Cabernet from the winery's Rutherford estate, where the wines are made and presented to the public. Appointment-only tastings (same-day often possible, but call ahead) take place in a second-floor space with broad valley views west to the Mayacamas Mountains. Book a current-release flight for an introduction to ZD and its wine-making philosophy. Barrel tastings, small bites, and small-batch reserve wines are all part of the Abacus Experience, which concludes with a current and older Abacus blend. ✉ *8383 Silverado Trail, Rutherford* ☎ *800/487–7757* 🌐 *www.zdwines.com* 🎫 *Tastings from $50.*

🍴 Restaurants

★ Restaurant at Auberge du Soleil

$$$$ | **AMERICAN** | Possibly the most romantic roost for brunch, lunch, or dinner in all the Wine Country is a terrace seat at the Auberge du Soleil resort's illustrious restaurant, and the Mediterranean-inflected cuisine more than matches the dramatic vineyard views. The prix-fixe dinner menu (three or four courses), relying mainly on local produce, might include caviar or diver scallop starters, delicately prepared fish or vegetable middle-course options, and mains like prime beef pavé with béarnaise, spiced lamb loin, or Japanese Wagyu A5. **Known for:** six-course chef's tasting menu; comprehensive wine list; special-occasion feel. [$] *Average main: $150* ✉ *Auberge du Soleil, 180 Rutherford Hill Rd., Rutherford* ✢ *Off Silverado Trail* ☎ *707/963–1211* 🌐 *www.aubergedusoleil.com* ⏲ *Closed Mon. and Tues.*

Rutherford Grill

$$ | **AMERICAN** | Dark-wood walls, subdued lighting, and red-leather banquettes make for a perpetually clubby mood at this Rutherford hangout where the patio, popular for its bar, fireplace, and rocking chairs, opens for full meal service or drinks and appetizers when the weather's right. Many entrées—steaks, burgers, fish, rotisserie chicken, and barbecued pork ribs—emerge from an oak-fired grill operated by master technicians. **Known for:** iron-skillet cornbread direct from the oven; signature French dip sandwich; reasonably priced wine list. [$] *Average main: $29* ✉ *1180 Rutherford Rd., at Hwy. 29, Rutherford* ☎ *707/963–1792* 🌐 *www.rutherfordgrill.com.*

🛏 Hotels

★ Auberge du Soleil

$$$$ | **RESORT** | Taking a cue from the olive-tree-studded landscape, this hotel with a renowned restaurant and spa cultivates a luxurious look that blends French and California style. **Pros:** stunning valley views; spectacular pool and spa areas; Deluxe-category suites fit for a superstar. **Cons:** stratospheric prices; least expensive rooms get some noise from the bar and restaurant; weekend minimum-stay requirement. [$] *Rooms from: $1,575* ✉ *180 Rutherford Hill Rd., Rutherford* ☎ *707/963–1211, 800/348–5406* 🌐 *www.aubergedusoleil.com* 🛏 *52 rooms* 🍽 *Free Breakfast.*

★ Rancho Caymus Inn

$$$ | **HOTEL** | A romantic hacienda-away-from-home that off-season may be the Napa Valley's best value in its price range, this upscale-contemporary boutique hotel near Inglenook and the Rutherford Grill contains rooms whose decor and artworks evoke the area's Mexican heritage. **Pros:** courtyard pool area; smallest rooms are 400 square feet, with several 600 or more; well-trained staff. **Cons:** all rooms have only showers (albeit nice ones); king beds in all rooms (no sofa beds, though a few rollaways available); no spa or fitness center. $ *Rooms from: $475* ✉ *1140 Rutherford Rd., Rutherford* ☎ *707/963–1777* ⊕ *www.ranchocaymusinn.com* ⤳ *26 rooms* ⦿ *Free Breakfast.*

St. Helena

2 miles northwest of Oakville.

Downtown St. Helena is the very picture of good living in the Wine Country: sycamore trees arch over Main Street (Highway 29), where visitors flit between boutiques, cafés, and storefront tasting rooms housed in sun-faded redbrick buildings. The genteel district pulls in rafts of tourists during the day, though like most Wine Country towns St. Helena more or less rolls up the sidewalks after dark.

The Napa Valley floor narrows between the Mayacamas and Vaca mountains around St. Helena. The slopes reflect heat onto the vineyards below, and since there's less fog and wind, things get pretty toasty. This is one of the valley's hottest AVAs, with midsummer temperatures often reaching the mid-90s. Bordeaux varietals are the most popular grapes grown here—especially Cabernet Sauvignon but also Merlot, Cabernet Franc, and Sauvignon Blanc.

GETTING HERE AND AROUND

Downtown stretches along Highway 29, called Main Street here. Many wineries lie north and south of downtown along Highway 29. More can be found off Silverado Trail, and some of the most scenic spots are on Spring Mountain, which rises southwest of town.

◉ Sights

Beringer Vineyards

WINERY | Brothers Frederick and Jacob Beringer opened the winery that still bears their name in 1876. One of California's earliest bonded wineries, it's the oldest one in the Napa Valley never to have missed a vintage—no mean feat, given Prohibition. Some tastings take place inside or on the veranda of Frederick's grand Rhine House Mansion, completed in 1886 and surrounded by mature landscaped gardens worth a stroll themselves. Beringer is known for several widely distributed wines, but many poured here are winery exclusives. The Legacy Tasting & Tour surveys Beringer's history; the tasting takes place where the brothers crafted their first vintage. The winery prefers that all guests make a reservation, but same-day visits are often possible when no food is involved. ✉ *2000 Main St./Hwy. 29, St. Helena* ✛ *Near Pratt Ave.* ☎ *707/257–5771* ⊕ *www.beringer.com* ⤳ *Tastings from $20 glass, $45 flight.*

Charles Krug Winery

WINERY | A historically sensitive renovation of its 1874 Redwood Cellar Building transformed the former production facility of the Napa Valley's oldest winery into an epic hospitality center. Charles Krug, a Prussian immigrant, established the winery in 1861 and ran it until his death in 1892. Italian immigrants Cesare Mondavi and his wife, Rosa, purchased Charles Krug in 1943, operating it with their sons Peter Sr. and Robert (who later opened his own winery). Still run by Peter Sr.'s family, Charles Krug specializes in small-lot Yountville and Howell Mountain Cabernet Sauvignons plus Sauvignon Blanc, Chardonnay, Merlot, and Pinot Noir. All visits are by appointment. ✉ *2800 Main St./Hwy. 29, St. Helena* ✛ *Across from Culinary Institute of America* ☎ *707/967–2229* ⊕ *www.charleskrug.com* ⤳ *Tastings from $50.*

Duckhorn Vineyards

WINERY | Merlot's moment in the sun may have passed, but you wouldn't know it at Duckhorn, whose Three Palms Merlot was crowned wine of the year by *Wine Spectator* as recently as 2017. Duckhorn also makes Cabernet Sauvignon, Cabernet Franc, Chardonnay, Sauvignon Blanc, and a few other wines you can sip in the high-ceilinged tasting room or on a fetching wraparound porch overlooking carefully tended vines. "Elevated" experiences, some not offered daily, include a tasting of estate and single-vineyard wines and private hosted tastings guests can customize to suit their preferences. All visits are by appointment. ⊠ *1000 Lodi La., at Silverado Trail N, St. Helena* ☎ *707/963–7108* ⊕ *www.duckhorn.com* ⌕ *Tastings from $60.*

Hall St. Helena

WINERY | The Cabernet Sauvignons produced here are works of art born of the latest in organic-farming science and wine-making technology. A glass-walled tasting room allows guests to see some of the high-tech equipment winemaker Megan Gunderson employs to craft wines that also include Merlot, Cabernet Franc, and Sauvignon Blanc. Looking westward from the second-floor tasting area, rows of neatly spaced Cabernet vines capture the eye, and beyond them the tree-studded Mayacamas Mountains. Hard to miss as you arrive along Highway 29, Lawrence Argent's 35-foot-tall *Bunny Foo Foo,* a stainless-steel sculpture of a rabbit leaping out of the vineyard, is one of many museum-quality artworks on display at appointment-only Hall (call for same-day). The Art of Cabernet tasting provides a solid introduction to this prominent producer's output. Another worthwhile tour takes in the grounds and the artworks. ■TIP➜ **Sister winery Hall Rutherford hosts an exclusive wine-and-food pairing atop a Rutherford hillside.** ⊠ *401 St. Helena Hwy./Hwy. 29, St. Helena* ⚓ *Near White La.* ☎ *707/967–2626* ⊕ *www.hallwines.com* ⌕ *Tastings from $60.*

★ Joseph Phelps Vineyards

WINERY | In 2022, LVMH's Moet Hennessy division purchased the winery the late Joseph Phelps founded a half-century before, a changing of the guard that reinforced Napa's stature as an international luxury-lifestyle player. Phelps produces excellent whites, along with Pinot Noir from its Sonoma Coast vineyards, but the blockbusters are the Bordeaux reds, particularly the Cabernet Sauvignons and Insignia, a luscious-yet-subtle Cab-dominant blend. Insignia, which often receives high-90s scores from respected wine publications, is always among the current releases poured at the one-hour seated Terrace Tasting overlooking grapevines and oaks. Other experiences, including one involving food pairings, unfold inside the main redwood structure, a classic of 1970s Northern California architecture. Participants in the Insignia Retrospective Tasting, offered a few times a month, sample several vintages of the flagship wine. ⊠ *200 Taplin Rd., St. Helena* ⚓ *Off Silverado Trail* ☎ *707/963–2745, 800/707–5789* ⊕ *www.josephphelps.com* ⌕ *Tastings from $115.*

Prager Winery & Port Works

WINERY | "If door is locked, ring bell," reads a sign outside the weathered-redwood tasting shack at this family-run winery known for red, white, and tawny ports. The sign, the bell, and the thousands of dollar bills tacked to the walls and ceilings inside are your first indications that you're drifting back in time with the old-school Pragers, who have been making regular and fortified wines in St. Helena since 1979. Five members of the second generation run this homespun operation founded by Jim and Imogene Prager. In addition to ports, the winery makes Petite Sirah and Sweet Claire, a late-harvest Riesling dessert wine. Some tastings take place in a garden outside the tasting room or on the crush pad.

Visits are by appointment; call for same-day. ✉ *1281 Lewelling La., St. Helena* ✣ *Off Hwy. 29* ☎ *707/963–7678* 🌐 *www.pragerport.com* 🎫 *Tastings $40 (includes glass).*

★ Pride Mountain Vineyards

WINERY | This winery 2,200 feet up Spring Mountain straddles Napa and Sonoma counties, confusing enough for visitors but even more complicated for the wine-making staff: government regulations require separate wineries and paperwork for each side of the property. It's one of several Pride Mountain quirks, but the winery's "big red wines," including a Cabernet Sauvignon that earned 100-point scores from a prominent wine critic two years in a row, are serious business. On a visit, by appointment only, you can learn about the farming and cellar strategies behind Pride's acclaimed Cabs. The winery also produces Syrah, a Cab-like Merlot, Claret, Cabernet Franc, and noteworthy Chardonnay and Viognier whites. **■ TIP→ The views here are knock-your-socks-off gorgeous.** ✉ *4026 Spring Mountain Rd., St. Helena* ✣ *Off St. Helena Rd. (extension of Spring Mountain Rd. in Sonoma County)* ☎ *707/963–4949* 🌐 *www.pridewines.com* 🎫 *Tastings from $30* 🕓 *Closed Tues.*

★ Tres Sabores Winery

WINERY | A long, narrow lane with two sharp bends leads to workaday Tres Sabores, where the sight of sheep, golden retrievers, guinea hens, pomegranate and other trees and plants, a slew of birds and bees, and a heaping compost pile reinforces a simple point: despite the Napa Valley's penchant for glamour this is, first and foremost, farm country. Owner-winemaker Julie Johnson specializes in single-vineyard wines that include Cabernet Sauvignon and Zinfandel from estate-grown certified-organic Rutherford bench vines. She also excels with Petite Sirah from dry-farmed Calistoga fruit, Sauvignon Blanc, and the zippy ¿Por Qué No? (Why not?) red blend. *Tres sabores* is Spanish for "three flavors," which to Johnson represents the land, her vines, and, as she puts it, "the spirit of the company around the table." Tastings by appointment only are informal and usually held outside. ✉ *1620 S. Whitehall La., St. Helena* ✣ *West of Hwy. 29* ☎ *707/967–8027* 🌐 *www.tressabores.com* 🎫 *Tastings from $55.*

🍴 Restaurants

Brasswood Bar + Bakery + Kitchen

$$$ | ITALIAN | After Napa Valley fixture Tra Vigne lost its lease, many staffers regrouped a few miles north at the restaurant (the titular Kitchen) of the Brasswood complex, which also includes a bakery, shops, and a wine-tasting room. Along with dishes developed for the new location, the chefs incorporate Tra Vigne favorites such as mozzarella-stuffed arancini (rice balls) into the Mediterranean-leaning menu. **Known for:** mostly Napa-Sonoma wine list; bakery a good lunch stop for pizzas, salads, and sandwiches; patio seating. [$] *Average main: $33* ✉ *3111 St. Helena Hwy. N, St. Helena* ✣ *Near Ehlers La.* ☎ *707/302–5101* 🌐 *brasswood.com/brasswoodbarkitchen.*

The Charter Oak

$$$ | MODERN AMERICAN | Christopher Kostow's reputation rests on his swoon-worthy haute cuisine for the Meadowood resort, but he and his Charter Oak team adopt a more straightforward approach—fewer ingredients chosen for maximum effect—at this high-ceilinged, brown-brick downtown restaurant. With exceedingly fresh produce from Meadowood's nearby farm, this strategy might translate into dishes like red kuri squash with pickled peppers, almonds, and goat cheese; or pork collar with fermented pepper jam (or just go for the cheeseburger and thick hand-cut fries). **Known for:** monthly changing wings appetizer; patio dining in brick courtyard; weekday happy hour 2:30–5. [$] *Average main: $32* ✉ *1050 Charter Oak Ave., at Hwy. 29, St. Helena*

☎ *707/302–6996* 🌐 *www.thecharteroak.com.*

★ Cook St. Helena

$$ | **ITALIAN** | A curved marble bar spotlit by contemporary art-glass pendants adds a touch of style to this downtown restaurant whose northern Italian cuisine pleases with understated sophistication. Mussels with house-made sausage in a spicy tomato broth, chopped salad with pancetta and pecorino, and the daily changing risotto are among the dishes regulars revere. **Known for:** top-quality ingredients; reasonably priced local and international wines; intimate dining. [$] *Average main: $30* ✉ *1310 Main St., St. Helena* ✥ *Near Hunt Ave.* ☎ *707/963–7088* 🌐 *www.cooksthelena.com* 🕒 *Closed weekends.*

★ Farmstead at Long Meadow Ranch

$$$ | **AMERICAN** | In a high-ceilinged former barn with plenty of outside seating, Farmstead revolves around an open kitchen whose chefs prepare meals with grass-fed beef and lamb, fruits and vegetables, and eggs, olive oil, wine, honey, and other ingredients from nearby Long Meadow Ranch. Entrées might include wood-grilled trout with fennel and bacon-mustard vinaigrette; caramelized beets with goat cheese and chimichurri; or a wood-grilled heritage pork chop with jalapeño grits. **Known for:** heritage St. Louis–style ribs; Sunday brunch; on-site general store, café, and Long Meadow Wines tasting space. [$] *Average main: $33* ✉ *738 Main St., at Charter Oak Ave., St. Helena* ☎ *707/963–4555* 🌐 *www.longmeadowranch.com/eat-drink/restaurant.*

Goose & Gander

$$$$ | **AMERICAN** | A Craftsman bungalow whose 1920s owner reportedly used the cellar for bootlegging during Prohibition houses this restaurant where the pairing of food and drink is as likely to involve a craft cocktail as a sommelier-selected wine. Main courses such as wood-grilled chicken or salmon, wet-aged black Angus rib eye, and the grass-fed G&G burger with Gruyère follow starters that might include corn croquettes, sticky pig ears, and harissa sausage with fry bread and baba ghanoush. **Known for:** intimate main dining room with fireplace; alfresco patio dining; basement bar among Napa's best watering holes. [$] *Average main: $41* ✉ *1245 Spring St., at Oak St., St. Helena* ☎ *707/967–8779* 🌐 *www.gooseganer.com* 🕒 *No lunch.*

Gott's Roadside

$ | **AMERICAN** | A 1950s-style outdoor hamburger stand goes upscale at this spot whose customers brave long lines to order breakfast sandwiches, juicy burgers, root-beer floats, and garlic fries. Choices not available a half century ago include ahi-tuna and Impossible burgers and kale and Vietnamese chicken salads. **Known for:** tasty 21st-century diner cuisine; shaded picnic tables (arrive early or late for lunch to get one); second branch at Napa's Oxbow Public Market. [$] *Average main: $16* ✉ *933 Main St./Hwy. 29, St. Helena* ✥ *Near Charter Oak Ave.* ☎ *707/963–3486* 🌐 *www.gotts.com.*

★ Press

$$$$ | **AMERICAN** | For years this cavernous casual-chic restaurant with a contempo-barn interior and wraparound patio steps from neighboring vineyards was northern Napans' preferred stop for a top-shelf cocktail, dry-aged steak, and high-90s-scoring local Cabernet. You can still order a tomahawk or New York strip, but chef Philip Tessier, formerly of Yountville's The French Laundry and Bouchon Bistro and New York City's Le Bernardin, has introduced more refined cuisine, much of whose produce is grown nearby. **Known for:** impressive craft cocktails for pairing with dozen-plus apps; *Wine Spectator* Grand Award for wide-ranging list; prix-fixe tasting menu highly recommended. [$] *Average main: $56* ✉ *587 St. Helena Hwy./Hwy. 29, at White La., St. Helena* ☎ *707/967–0550* 🌐 *www.pressnapavalley.com* 🕒 *No lunch.*

Hotels

★ Alila Napa Valley

$$$$ | HOTEL | An upscale-casual ultracontemporary adults-only resort formerly known as Las Alcobas Napa Valley but now in the Hyatt Alila brand's fold, this hillside gem sits adjacent to Beringer Vineyards six blocks north of Main Street shopping and dining. **Pros:** vineyard views from most rooms; Acacia House restaurant; pool, spa, and fitness center. **Cons:** expensive much of the year; hotel is only for guests 18-plus; sizable resort fee. [$] *Rooms from: $767* ✉ *1915 Main St., St. Helena* ☎ *707/963–7000* 🌐 *www.alilanapavalley.com* 🛏 *68 rooms* 🍴 *No Meals.*

El Bonita Motel

$$ | MOTEL | A classic 1950s-style neon sign marks the driveway to this roadside motel that during the off-season offers solid value to budget-minded travelers. **Pros:** cheerful rooms; family friendly; microwaves and mini-refrigerators. **Cons:** noise issues in roadside and ground-floor rooms; expensive in high season; lacks amenities of fancier properties. [$] *Rooms from: $339* ✉ *195 Main St./Hwy. 29, St. Helena* ☎ *707/963–3216* 🌐 *www.elbonita.com* 🛏 *52 rooms* 🍴 *Free Breakfast.*

Harvest Inn

$$$ | HOTEL | Although this inn sits just off Highway 29, its patrons remain mostly above the fray, strolling 8 acres of gardens, enjoying views of the vineyards adjoining the property, and drifting to sleep in beds adorned with fancy linens and down pillows. **Pros:** garden setting; spacious rooms; near choice wineries, restaurants, and shops. **Cons:** fair amount of wedding action; rooms could be nicer for the high-season price; occasional service lapses. [$] *Rooms from: $399* ✉ *1 Main St., St. Helena* ☎ *707/963–9463* 🌐 *www.harvestinn.com* 🛏 *81 rooms* 🍴 *No Meals.*

Meadowood Napa Valley

$$$$ | RESORT | This elite 250-acre resort's celebrated restaurant and more than half its accommodations were destroyed in the 2020 Glass Fire, but the spa, pools, tennis courts, fitness center, and a fair number of cottages in one part survived, with continuing reconstruction in other areas not expected to affect the guest experience. **Pros:** scrupulously maintained rooms; all-organic spa; gracious service. **Cons:** still recovering from fire; far from downtown St. Helena; weekend minimum-stay requirement. [$] *Rooms from: $1,025* ✉ *900 Meadowood La.* ☎ *707/531–4788* 🌐 *meadowood.com* 🛏 *36 rooms* 🍴 *No Meals.*

Wine Country Inn

$$$ | B&B/INN | Vineyards flank the three buildings, containing 24 rooms and five cottages, of this pastoral retreat where blue oaks, maytens, and olive trees provide shade and gardens feature lantana (small butterflies love it) and lavender. **Pros:** no resort fee; good-size swimming pool; vineyard views from most rooms. **Cons:** some rooms let in noise from neighbors; expensive in high season; weekend minimum-stay requirement. [$] *Rooms from: $429* ✉ *1152 Lodi La., St. Helena* ✥ *East of Hwy. 29* ☎ *707/963–7077, 888/465–4608* 🌐 *www.winecountryinn.com* 🛏 *29 rooms* 🍴 *Free Breakfast.*

★ Wydown Hotel

$$$ | HOTEL | This smart boutique hotel near downtown shopping and dining delivers comfort with a heavy dose of style: the storefront lobby's high ceiling and earth tones, punctuated by rich-hued splashes of color, hint at the relaxed grandeur owner-hotelier Mark Hoffmeister and his design team achieved in the rooms upstairs. **Pros:** well run; eclectic decor; downtown location. **Cons:** lacks the amenities of larger properties; large corner rooms pick up some street noise; two-night minimum stay on weekends. [$] *Rooms from: $374* ✉ *1424 Main*

St., St. Helena ☎ *707/963–5100* ⊕ *www.wydownhotel.com* ⊷ *12 rooms* ⊙ *No Meals.*

Nightlife

The Saint

WINE BARS | This high-ceilinged downtown wine bar occupies a stone-walled late-19th-century former bank. Lit by chandeliers and decked out in contemporary style with plush sofas and chairs and Lucite stools at the bar, it's a classy, loungelike space to expand your enological horizons. ⊠ *1351 Main St., St. Helena* ✛ *Near Adams St.* ☎ *707/302–5130* ⊕ *www.thesaintnapavalley.com* ⊘ *Closed Mon.*

Calistoga

3 miles northwest of St. Helena.

With false-fronted, Old West–style shops and 19th-century inns and hotels lining its main drag, Lincoln Avenue in Calistoga comes across as more down-to-earth than its more polished neighbors. Don't be fooled, though. On its outskirts lie some of the Wine Country's swankest (and priciest) resorts and its most fanciful piece of architecture, the medieval-style Castello di Amorosa winery.

Calistoga was developed as a spa-oriented getaway from the start. Sam Brannan, a gold rush–era entrepreneur, planned to use the area's natural hot springs as the centerpiece of a resort complex. His venture failed, but old-time hotels and bathhouses—along with some glorious new spas—still operate. You can come for an old-school mud bath, or go completely 21st century and experience lavish treatments based on the latest innovations in skin and body care.

GETTING HERE AND AROUND

Highway 29 heads east (turn right) at Calistoga, where in town it is signed as Lincoln Avenue. If arriving via the Silverado Trail, head west at Highway 29/Lincoln Avenue.

Sights

Bennett Lane Winery

WINERY | Winemaker Rob Hunter of Bennett Lane strives "to create the greatest Cabernet Sauvignon in the world." At this appointment-only winery's tastefully casual salon in the far northern Napa Valley, you can find out how close he and his team come. Although known for valley-floor Cabernet, Bennett Lane also produces Merlot and the Maximus Red Feasting Wine, a Cab-heavy red blend nicely priced considering the quality. On the lighter side are Chardonnay and the Maximus White Feasting Wine blend of Sauvignon Blanc, Chardonnay, and Muscat. The basic flight surveys current-release whites and reds. There's also a Cab-focused offering. Many tastings take place in a garden whose pergola frames vineyard and Calistoga Palisades views. ⊠ *3340 Hwy. 128, Calistoga* ✛ *3 miles north of downtown* ☎ *707/942–6684* ⊕ *www.bennettlane.com* 🍷 *Tastings from $35.*

Castello di Amorosa

WINERY | An astounding medieval structure complete with drawbridge and moat, chapel, stables, and secret passageways, the Castello commands Diamond Mountain's lower eastern slope. Some of the 107 rooms contain artist Fabio Sanzogni's replicas of 13th-century frescoes (cheekily signed with his website address), and the dungeon has an iron maiden from Nuremberg, Germany. You must pay for a tour to see most of Dario Sattui's extensive eight-level property, though with general admission you'll have access to part of the complex. Bottlings of note include Sangiovese and other Italian-style wines and Il Barone, a deliberately big Cab. All visits are by appointment. ⊠ *4045 N. St. Helena Hwy./Hwy. 29, Calistoga* ✛ *Near Maple La.*

The astounding Castello di Amorosa has 107 rooms.

☎ 707/967–6272 ⊕ www.castellodiamorosa.com ☐ Tastings from $55.

Chateau Montelena

WINERY | Set amid a bucolic northern Calistoga landscape, this stately winery whose stone winery building was erected in 1888 helped establish the Napa Valley's reputation for high-quality wine making. At the pivotal Paris tasting of 1976, the Chateau Montelena 1973 Chardonnay took first place, beating out four white Burgundies from France and five other California Chardonnays, an event immortalized (with some liberties taken) in the 2008 movie *Bottle Shock*. A 21st-century Napa Valley Chardonnay is always part of A Taste of Montelena—the winery also makes Sauvignon Blanc, Riesling, a fine estate Zinfandel, and Cabernet Sauvignon—or you can opt for the Montelena Estate Collection tasting of Cabernets from several vintages. All visits require a reservation. ⊠ 1429 Tubbs La., Calistoga ⊕ Off Hwy. 29 ☎ 707/942–5105 ⊕ www.montelena.com ☐ Tastings from $60.

Frank Family Vineyards

WINERY | Former Disney film and telovioion oxooutivo Rich Frank founded his namesake winery in 1992, but the wine-making history here dates to the 19th century—portions of an original 1884 structure, reclad in stone in 1906, remain standing today. From 1952 until 1990, Hanns Kornell made sparkling wines on this site. Frank Family, since 2022 part of the Treasury Wine Estates portfolio, also makes sparklers, but the high-profile wines are the Carneros Chardonnay and several Cabernet Sauvignons, particularly the Rutherford Reserve and the Winston Hill red blend. Tastings, some held in the glass-walled, vineyard's-edge The Miller House hospitality barn, which debuted in 2023, are sit-down affairs, with reservations required. ⊠ 1091 Larkmead La., Calistoga ⊕ Off Hwy. 29 ☎ 707/942–0859 ⊕ www.frankfamilyvineyards.com ☐ Tastings from $60.

★ Schramsberg

WINERY | On a Diamond Mountain site the German-born Jacob Schram planted to grapes in the early 1860s, Schramsberg pours its esteemed *méthode traditionnelle* sparkling wines. Author Robert Louis Stevenson was among Schram's early visitors. After the vintner's death in 1905, the winery closed and fell into disrepair, but in 1965 Jack and Jamie Davies purchased the 200-acre Schramsberg property and began restoring its buildings and caves. Chinese laborers dug some of the latter in the 1870s. In the 1990s, the family set about replanting the vineyard to Cabernet Sauvignon and other Bordeaux varietals for the Davies Vineyards label's still red wines. Tastings at Schramsberg can include pours of only sparkling wines, only still wines, or a combination of the two. All visits are by appointment. ✉ *1400 Schramsberg Rd., Calistoga* ✥ *Off Hwy. 29* ☎ *707/942–2469, 800/877–3623* 🌐 *www.schramsberg.com* 🎫 *Tastings with cave tour from $80.*

🍴 Restaurants

★ Lovina

$$$$ | MODERN AMERICAN | A vintage-style neon sign outside this bungalow restaurant announces "Great Food," and the chefs deliver with well-plated dishes served in two buildings, one a Craftsman gem, or on street-side patios that are especially festive during weekend brunch. The offerings at women-owned and -run Lovina change often, but a recent menu's roasted Cornish hen, lobster and prawn risotto, and seared wild halibut with gnocchi and wild mushrooms are typical of the imaginative cuisine. **Known for:** no-tipping policy; varied brunch menu; Wine Wednesdays no corkage fee and discounts on wine list. [$] *Average main: $45* ✉ *1107 Cedar St., at Lincoln Ave., Calistoga* ☎ *707/942–6500* 🌐 *www.lovinacalistoga.com* 🕒 *No lunch Mon.–Wed. and Fri.*

Sam's Social Club

$$$ | AMERICAN | Tourists, locals, and spa guests—some of the latter in bathrobes after treatments—assemble inside this casual resort restaurant or on its extensive patio for breakfast, lunch, bar snacks, or dinner. Lunch options include thin-crust pizzas, sandwiches, a cheddar burger, and entrées such as chicken paillard, with the burger reappearing for dinner along with fish, steak, the house-made pasta of the day, and similar fare. **Known for:** weekend slow-roasted prime rib; cocktail-friendly starters; hearty salads. [$] *Average main: $36* ✉ *Indian Springs Resort and Spa, 1712 Lincoln Ave., at Wappo Ave., Calistoga* ☎ *707/942–4969* 🌐 *www.samssocialclub.com.*

★ Solbar

$$$$ | AMERICAN | The restaurant at Solage attracts the resort's clientele, upvalley locals, and guests of nearby lodgings for sophisticated farm-to-table cuisine served in the high-ceilinged dining area or alfresco on a sprawling patio warmed by shapely heaters and a mesmerizing firepit. Dishes on the lighter side might include house-made pasta or sake-marinated fish, with duck breast, crispy pork, or a tomahawk steak among the heartier options. **Known for:** artisanal cocktails; festive patio; lunchtime salads and sandwiches. [$] *Average main: $48* ✉ *Solage, 755 Silverado Trail, at Rosedale Rd., Calistoga* ☎ *707/226–0860* 🌐 *aubergeresorts.com/solage/dine.*

☕ Coffee and Quick Bites

★ Calistoga Depot

$ | AMERICAN | Calistoga's flashy 19th-century entrepreneur Sam Brannan built the depot in 1868 to receive spa patrons, but it was looking careworn until his 21st-century equivalent, Wine Country vintner-showman Jean-Charles Boisset, restored the wood-frame building and opened a combination gourmet grocery, café, wine shop, distillery, and wine and beer garden. As at Boisset's historic Oakville Grocery, salads, artisanal sandwiches, and wood-fired pizzas headline. **Known for:** all-day breakfast; wine and craft-beer selection; patio seating. [$] *Average main: $17 ✉ 1458 Lincoln Ave., at Fair Way, Calistoga ☎ 707/963–6925 🌐 calistogadepot.com ⏲ No dinner.*

Hotels

★ Brannan Cottage Inn

$$ | B&B/INN | Stained oak floors, wainscoting, and retro bathroom fixtures recall Victorian times at this small inn whose centerpiece is an 1860s cottage from Calistoga's original spa era. **Pros:** short walk from downtown; helpful staff; Sam's General Store for coffee and light meals. **Cons:** noise from neighbors can be heard in some rooms; showers but no bathtubs in some rooms; lacks pool and other amenities of larger properties. [$] *Rooms from: $329 ✉ 109 Wappo Ave., at Lincoln Ave., Calistoga ☎ 707/942–4200 🌐 www.brannancottageinn.com 🛏 6 rooms 🍴 Free Breakfast.*

Four Seasons Resort and Residences Napa Valley

$$$$ | RESORT | Opened in 2021, this suave luxury resort entices high rollers with farmhouse-eclectic interiors and amenities that include a spa, a destination restaurant, two pools, 7-plus acres of vines, and a working winery. **Pros:** estate villa and one-bedroom suites offer maximum luxury and privacy; casual dining at indoor-outdoor Truss and five-course tasting menu at Auro; on-site vineyard and winery. **Cons:** expensive year-round; casual-chic yet may feel too formal for some guests; minimum weekend stay requirement. [$] *Rooms from: $1,491 ✉ 400 Silverado Trail N, Calistoga ☎ 707/709–2100, 800/819–5053 for reservations 🌐 www.fourseasons.com/napavalley 🛏 83 rooms 🍴 No Meals.*

Indian Springs Calistoga

$$ | RESORT | Palm-studded Indian Springs—operating as a spa since 1862—ably splits the difference between laid-back and chic in accommodations that include lodge rooms, suites, cottages, stand-alone bungalows, and two houses. **Pros:** sprawling grounds with outdoor seating areas; on-site Sam's Social Club restaurant; enormous mineral pool. **Cons:** lodge rooms are small; many rooms have showers but no tubs; two-night minimum stay on weekends (three with Monday holiday). [$] *Rooms from: $309 ✉ 1712 Lincoln Ave., Calistoga ☎ 707/709–8139 🌐 www.indianspringscalistoga.com 🛏 113 rooms 🍴 No Meals.*

★ Solage

$$$$ | RESORT | The aesthetic at this 22-acre property where health and wellness are priorities is Napa Valley barn meets San Francisco loft: guest rooms have high ceilings, sleek contemporary furniture, all-natural fabrics in soothingly muted colors, and an outdoor patio. **Pros:** great service; complimentary bikes; separate pools for kids and adults. **Cons:** scene might not suit everyone; longish walk from some lodgings to spa and fitness center; expensive in season. [$] *Rooms from: $749 ✉ 755 Silverado Trail, Calistoga ☎ 866/942–7442, 707/226–0800 🌐 www.solagecalistoga.com 🛏 89 rooms 🍴 No Meals.*

Activities

SPAS

Indian Springs Spa

SPAS | Even before Sam Brannan constructed a spa on this site in the 1860s, the Wappo Indians built sweat lodges over its thermal geysers. Treatments include a Calistoga-classic, pure volcanic-ash mud bath followed by a mineral bath and an infrared sauna, after which clients are wrapped in a flannel blanket for a 15-minute cool-down session or until called for a massage if they've booked one. Body scrubs—one with sea salt, the other with sugar—and facials are also popular. Before or following a treatment, guests unwind at the serene Buddha Pool, fed by one of the property's four geysers. ✉ *1712 Lincoln Ave., at Wappo Ave., Calistoga* ☎ *707/709–8139* ⊕ *indianspringscalistoga.com/spa-overview* ✉ *Treatments from $115.*

★ Spa Solage

SPAS | This 20,000-square-foot eco-conscious spa reinvented the traditional Calistoga mud-and-mineral-water regimen with the hour-long "Mudslide." The three-part treatment includes a mud body mask applied in a heated lounge, a soak in a thermal bath, and a power nap in a sound-vibration chair. The mud here, less gloppy than at other resorts, is a mix of clay, volcanic ash, and essential oils. Massage and other traditional services are available, along with hydration therapy, infrared saunas for exfoliation and relaxation, and wellness sessions. ✉ *755 Silverado Trail, at Rosedale Rd., Calistoga* ☎ *855/790–6023* ⊕ *aubergeresorts.com/solage/wellness/spa* ✉ *Treatments from $200.*

Sonoma

14 miles west of Napa, 45 miles northeast of San Francisco.

One of the few towns in the valley with multiple attractions unrelated to food and wine, Sonoma has plenty to keep you busy for a couple of hours before you head out to tour the wineries. And you needn't leave town to taste wine. About three dozen tasting rooms are within steps of tree-filled Sonoma Plaza. The valley's cultural center, Sonoma was founded in 1835 when California was still part of Mexico.

GETTING HERE AND AROUND

Highway 12 (signed as Broadway near Sonoma Plaza) heads north into Sonoma from Highway 121 and south from Santa Rosa into downtown Sonoma. Parking

is relatively easy to find on or near the plaza, and you can walk to many restaurants, shops, and tasting rooms. Signs point the way to several wineries a mile or more east of the plaza. Sonoma County Transit buses serve the town.

 ## Sights

Buena Vista Winery

WINERY | A local actor in top hat and 19th-century garb sometimes greets guests as Count Agoston Haraszthy at this homage to the birthplace of modern California wine making. Haraszthy's rehabilitated former press house (used for pressing grapes into wine), completed in 1864, is the architectural focal point, with photos, banners, plaques, and artifacts providing historical context. Chardonnay, Pinot Noir, Cabernet Sauvignon, and several Bordeaux-style red blends are the strong suits among the several dozen wines produced. During appointment-only visits (weekday walk-ins generally possible), you can taste some of them solo or preorder a cheese plate or box lunch from the affiliated Oakville Grocery. ✉ *18000 Old Winery Rd., Sonoma* ✛ *Off E. Napa St.* ☎ *800/926–1266* ⊕ *www. buenavistawinery.com* ✉ *Tastings from $30.*

Corner 103

WINERY | After leading an effort to revive a local winery, Lloyd Davis, an African American financier and oenophile, turned his attention to making the experience of learning about wine and food-wine pairings less daunting. To that end he opened a light-filled space, diagonally across from Sonoma Plaza, for tastings of Sonoma County wines guests can pair with cheeses or small bites. The lineup includes a brut rosé sparkler, Chardonnay and Marsanne-Roussanne whites, a rosé of Pinot Noir, and several reds. Corner 103's welcoming atmosphere, which in recent years has earned it a ranking at or near the top of *USA Today*'s Best Tasting Room list, makes it an excellent choice for wine novices seeking to expand their knowledge. Visits are by appointment, though hosts usually accommodate drop-ins seeking wine-only tastings. ✉ *103 W. Napa St., at 1st St. W, Sonoma* ☎ *707/931–6141* ⊕ *www.corner103.com* ▧ *Tastings from $30.*

★ The Donum Estate

WINERY | The team at this prominent Chardonnay and Pinot Noir producer prizes viticulture—selecting vineyards with superior soils and microclimates, planting compatible clones, and farming organically with rigor—over wine-making wizardry. Tasting areas that include a contemporary white board-and-batten structure and a pavilion with a conical multicolor glass canopy afford guests hilltop views of Los Carneros, San Pablo Bay, and beyond. The wines, from several Sonoma County appellations and one in Mendocino County, continue to exhibit the "power yet elegance" that sealed the winery's fame in the 2000s. Tastings are by appointment only (last-minute unlikely). The more than three dozen large-scale museum-quality contemporary sculptures placed amid the vines, including works by Ai Weiwei, Lynda Benglis, Louise Bourgeois, Keith Haring, and Anselm Kiefer, add a touch of high culture to a visit here. ✉ *24500 Ramal Rd., Sonoma* ✛ *Off Hwy. 121/12* ☎ *707/732–2200* ⊕ *www.thedonumestate.com* ▧ *Tastings from $125.*

Gloria Ferrer Caves and Vineyards

WINERY | On a clear day this Spanish hacienda–style winery's Vista Terrace lives up to its name as guests at seated tastings sip delicate sparkling wines while taking in east-facing views of Los Carneros AVA and beyond it San Pablo Bay. The Chardonnay and Pinot Noir grapes from the vineyards in the foreground are the product of old-world wine-making knowledge—generations of the founding Ferrer family made cava in Spain—but also contemporary soil management techniques and clonal research. Hosts well-acquainted with the winery's sustainability practices and history as the Carneros District's first sparkling-wine house serve the wines, either solo or accompanied by food that varies from cheese and charcuterie to caviar or a full lunch. Except on Wednesday, visits are by appointment. ■**TIP**➔ **On Wednesday only, the winery is open for by-the-glass pours and bottle service (no flights), reservations not required.** ✉ *23555 Carneros Hwy./Hwy. 121, Sonoma* ☎ *707/933–1986* ⊕ *www.gloriaferrer.com* ▧ *Tastings from $65* ☉ *Closed Tues. No flights (only bottle and by-the-glass service) Wed.*

Hanson of Sonoma Distillery

DISTILLERY | The Hanson family makes grape-based organic vodkas, one traditional, the rest infused with cucumbers, ginger, mandarin oranges, Meyer lemons, or habañero and other chili peppers. A surprise to many visitors, the Hansons make a blended white wine before distilling it into vodka. The family pours its vodkas and a single-malt whiskey in an industrial-looking tasting room heavy on the steel, with wood reclaimed from Deep South smokehouses adding a rustic note. In good weather, some sessions take place on the landscaped shore of a small pond. Per state law, there's a limit to the amount poured, but it's sufficient to get to know the product. ✉ *22985 Burndale Rd., at Carneros Hwy./Hwy. 121, Sonoma* ☎ *707/343–1805* ⊕ *hansonofsonoma.com* ▧ *Tastings from $35, tours from $75 (includes tasting).*

★ Sangiacomo Family Wines

WINERY | Several dozen wineries produce vineyard-designate Chardonnays and Pinot Noirs from grapes grown by the Sangiacomo family, whose Italian ancestors first started farming in Sonoma in 1927. The family didn't establish its own label until 2016, but its cool-climate wines and a Napa Valley Cabernet quickly earned critical plaudits. Chardonnay vines and the Carneros District's western hills form the backdrop for tastings, usually outdoors, at the 110-acre Home Ranch,

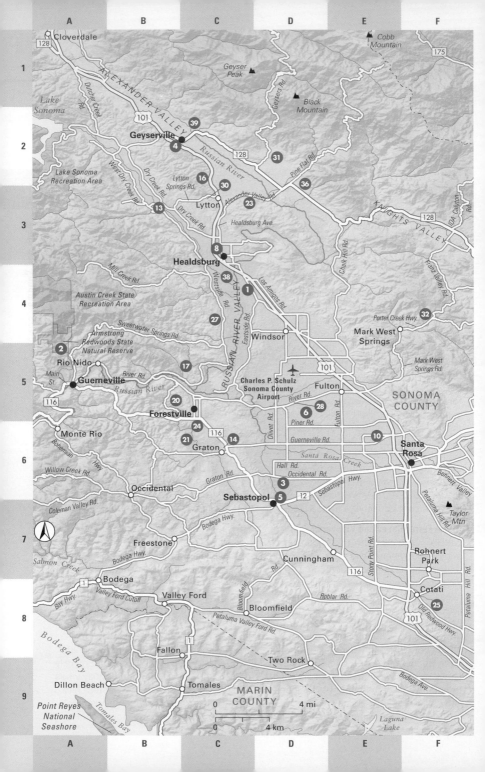

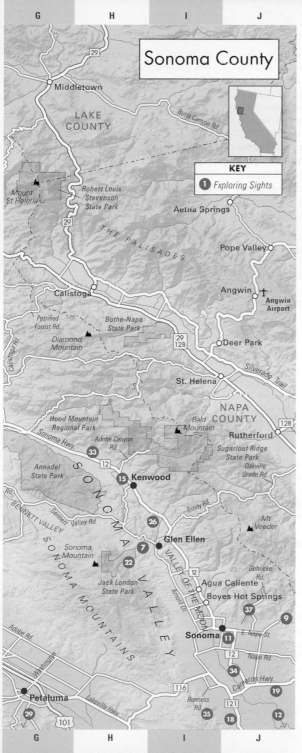

Sonoma County

KEY

① Exploring Sights

12

Napa and Sonoma **SONOMA**

the first of a dozen-plus vineyards the Sangiacomos acquired or lease. At appointment-only visits, you're apt to encounter one or more third-generation members, all of whom enjoy meeting guests and sharing their family's legacy. **■ TIP→ On Friday from May through September, the winery hosts Sunset on the Terrace, with wines served by the glass, carafe, or bottle (no flights) from 3:30 pm until sundown.** ✉ *21545 Broadway, Sonoma* ✥ *2½ miles south of Sonoma Plaza* ☎ *707/934–8445* 🌐 *www.sangiacomowines.com* 🎫 *Tastings from $30.*

Schug Carneros Estate Winery

WINERY | As a young lad in Germany, the late Walter Schug made Pinot Noir, inspiring a lifelong preoccupation with the Burgundian varietal. The founding winemaker at Joseph Phelps, where he developed the flagship Insignia Bordeaux-style blend, in the 1980s he established his namesake winery in the far western reaches of Los Carneros AVA. His children continue his legacy, focusing on Chardonnay, Pinot Noir, Cabernet Sauvignon, and other Bordeaux varietals. There's also a wine from the St. Laurent grape, an offspring of Pinot. To sample current releases with a vineyard view, book a Classic Wine Tasting. The more comprehensive Cave Tour and Tasting includes a brief property walk, seasonal small bites, and current and library wines. ✉ *602 Bonneau Rd., Sonoma* ✥ *East off Hwy. 116 at Hwy. 121* ☎ *707/939–9363* 🌐 *schugwinery.com* 🎫 *Tastings from $35* ⏲ *Closed Mon.*

Sonoma Mission

CHURCH | The northernmost of the 21 missions established by Franciscan friars in California, Sonoma Mission was founded in 1823 as Mission San Francisco Solano. These days it serves as the centerpiece of Sonoma State Historic Park, which includes several other sites in Sonoma and nearby Petaluma. Some early mission structures fell into ruin, but all or part of several remaining buildings date to the era of Mexican rule over California. The Sonoma Barracks, a half block west of the mission at 20 East Spain Street, housed troops under the command of General Mariano Guadalupe Vallejo, who controlled vast tracts of land in the region. General Vallejo's Home, a Victorian-era structure, is a few blocks west. ✉ *114 E. Spain St., at 1st St. E, Sonoma* ☎ *707/938–9560* 🌐 *www.parks.ca.gov* 🎫 *$3, includes same-day admission to other historic sites.*

🍴 Restaurants

★ Cafe La Haye

$$ | **AMERICAN** | In a postage-stamp-size open kitchen (the dining room, its white walls adorned with contemporary art, is nearly as compact), chef Jeffrey Lloyd turns out understated, sophisticated fare emphasizing seasonably available local ingredients. Meats, pastas, and seafood get deluxe treatment without fuss or fanfare—and the daily risotto special is always worth trying. **Known for:** Napa-Sonoma wine list with French complements; signature butterscotch pudding; owner Saul Gropman on hand to greet diners. [$] *Average main: $27* ✉ *140 E. Napa St., Sonoma* ✥ *East of Sonoma Plaza* ☎ *707/935–5994* 🌐 *www.cafelahaye.com* ⏲ *Closed Sun. and Mon. No lunch.*

El Dorado Kitchen

$$ | **MODERN AMERICAN** | This restaurant owes its visual appeal to its clean lines and svelte decor, but the eye inevitably drifts westward to the open kitchen, where longtime executive chef Armando Navarro's team crafts dishes full of subtle surprises. The menu might include ceviche or roasted maitake mushrooms as starters and pan-roasted salmon, fettuccine carbonara, or paella awash with seafood among the entrées. **Known for:** subtle tastes and textures; truffle-oil fries with Parmesan; takeout window for Mexican (plus the spicy burger). [$] *Average main: $29* ✉ *El Dorado Hotel, 405 1st St.*

W, at W. Spain St., Sonoma ☎ 707/996–3030 🌐 eldoradokitchen.com.

★ The Girl & the Fig

$$ | **FRENCH** | At this hot spot for inventive French cooking inside the historic Sonoma Hotel bar, you can always find a dish with the signature figs on the menu, whether it's a fig-and-arugula salad or an aperitif blending sparkling wine with fig liqueur. Also look for duck confit, a burger with matchstick fries, and wild flounder meunière. **Known for:** Rhône-wines emphasis; artisanal cheese and charcuterie platters; weekly changing three-course prix-fixe option. [$] *Average main: $30 ✉ Sonoma Hotel, 110 W. Spain St., at 1st St. W, Sonoma ☎ 707/938–3634 🌐 www.thegirlandthefig.com.*

★ LaSalette Restaurant

$$$ | **PORTUGUESE** | Born in the Azores and raised in Sonoma, chef-owner Manuel Azevedo serves cuisine inspired by his native Portugal in this warmly decorated spot with a heated patio out front. The wood-oven whole-roasted fish is always worth trying, and there are usually boldly flavored pork dishes, along with a casserole, pot roast, stew, salted cod, and other hearty fare. **Known for:** authentic Portuguese cuisine; sophisticated spicing; rice pudding with Madeira-braised fig for dessert. [$] *Average main: $31 ✉ 452 1st St. E, Sonoma ✣ Near E. Spain St. ☎ 707/938–1927 🌐 www.lasaletterestaurant.com ⏲ Closed Wed.*

★ Wit & Wisdom Tavern

$$$ | **MODERN AMERICAN** | A San Francisco culinary star with establishments worldwide, Michael Mina debuted his first Wine Country restaurant in 2020, its interior of charcoal grays, browns, and soft whites dandy indeed, if by evening vying with outdoor spaces aglow with firepits and lighted water features. Seasonal regional ingredients—Pacific Coast fish, pasture-raised meats, freshly plucked produce—go into haute-homey dishes, prepared open-fire, that include pizzas, handmade pastas, and the signature lobster potpie with brandied lobster cream and black truffle. **Known for:** 3–5 happy hour's beverage and app selections; many local wines on award-winning list; prix-fixe Night at the Tavern tasting menu. [$] *Average main: $35 ✉ The Lodge at Sonoma, 1325 Broadway, at Leveroni Rd., Sonoma ☎ 707/931–3405 🌐 www.witandwisdomsonoma.com ⏲ Closed Mon. and Tues. No lunch.*

Hotels

Inn at Sonoma

$$ | **B&B/INN** | Little luxuries delight at this well-run inn ¼ mile south of Sonoma Plaza whose guest rooms, softly lit and done in pastels, have comfortable beds topped with feather comforters and plenty of pillows. **Pros:** last-minute specials can be a great deal; freshly baked cookies, afternoon wine and cheese; good soundproofing blocks out Broadway street noise. **Cons:** on a busy street rather than right on the plaza; pet-friendly rooms book up quickly; some rooms on the small side. [$] *Rooms from: $275 ✉ 630 Broadway, Sonoma ☎ 707/939–1340 🌐 www.innatsonoma.com 🛏 27 rooms 🍴 Free Breakfast.*

★ Ledson Hotel

$$$ | **B&B/INN** | With just six rooms the Ledson feels intimate, and the furnishings and amenities—down beds, mood lighting, gas fireplaces, whirlpool tubs, and balconies for enjoying breakfast or a glass of wine—stack up well against Wine Country rooms costing more, especially in high season. **Pros:** convenient Sonoma Plaza location; spacious, individually decorated rooms; whirlpool tub in all rooms. **Cons:** two people maximum occupancy in all rooms; children must be at least 12 years old; front rooms have plaza views but pick up some street noise. [$] *Rooms from: $395 ✉ 480 1st St. E, Sonoma ☎ 707/996–9779 🌐 www.ledsonhotel.com 🛏 6 rooms 🍴 No Meals.*

★ **MacArthur Place Hotel & Spa**
$$$$ | HOTEL | Guests at this 7-acre boutique property five blocks south of Sonoma Plaza bask in ritzy seclusion in plush accommodations set amid landscaped gardens. **Pros:** verdant garden setting; great for a romantic getaway; appealing common areas. **Cons:** a bit of a walk from the plaza; some traffic noise audible in street-side rooms; pricey in high season. [$] *Rooms from: $705* ✉ *29 E. MacArthur St., Sonoma* ☎ *707/938–2929, 800/722–1866* 🌐 *www.macarthurplace.com* 🛏 *64 rooms* 🍴 *No Meals.*

Nightlife

Sigh!
WINE BARS | From the oval bar and walls the color of a fine blanc de blancs to retro chandeliers that mimic Champagne bubbles, everything about this sparkling-wine bar's frothy space screams "have a good time." That owner Jayme Powers and her posse are trained in the fine art of *sabrage* (opening a bottle of sparkling wine with a saber) only adds to the festivity. **■ TIP→ Sigh! opens at noon, so it's a good daytime stop, too.** ✉ *120 W. Napa St., at 1st St. W, Sonoma* ☎ *707/996–2444* 🌐 *www.sighsonoma.com.*

Activities

BIKING

Sonoma Adventures
BIKING | Mount a regular bike or one with "pedal assist" on this company's half- and full-day guided tours to area wineries. You can also rent a bike and head off on your own. ✉ *1254 Broadway, Sonoma* ↔ *1/5 mile north of Napa Rd.* ☎ *707/938–2080* 🌐 *www.sonoma-adventures.com* 🎫 *½-day tour from $119, not including tasting fees.*

SPAS

The Spa at the Lodge
SPAS | A restful haven in the rear of the 10-acre Lodge at Sonoma property, the spa contains 11 treatment rooms including two for couples. The signature 80-minute Celestial Body Renewal Ritual begins with an exfoliating shea-butter body scrub, followed by a body wrap and a CBD deep-tissue massage, and there are several other 50- or 80-minute options. Facials, eye and lip treatments, and waxing are also on the menu. Before or after sessions, guests can relax in a landscaped outdoor garden with a pool, a hot tub, and a barrel sauna. ✉ *Lodge at Sonoma, 1325 Broadway, at Leveroni Rd., Sonoma* ☎ *707/931–3434* 🌐 *www.thelodgeatsonoma.com/spa* 🎫 *Treatments from $210.*

Glen Ellen

7 miles north of Sonoma.

Craggy Glen Ellen epitomizes the difference between the Napa and Sonoma valleys. Whereas small Napa towns like St. Helena get their charm from upscale boutiques and restaurants lined up along well-groomed sidewalks, Glen Ellen's crooked streets are shaded with stands of old oak trees and occasionally bisected by the Sonoma and Calabazas creeks. Tucked among the trees of a narrow canyon where Sonoma Mountain and the Mayacamas pinch in the valley floor, Glen Ellen looks more like a town of the Sierra foothills gold country than a Wine Country village.

GETTING HERE AND AROUND

Glen Ellen sits just off Highway 12. From the north or south, take Arnold Drive west and follow it south less than a mile. The walkable downtown straddles a half-mile stretch of Arnold Drive. Sonoma County Transit buses serve Glen Ellen.

Benziger tram tours take to the fields to show biodynamic farming techniques in action.

Sights

Benziger Family Winery

WINERY | One of the best-known Sonoma County wineries sits on a sprawling estate in a bowl with 360-degree sun exposure. Hosts conducting popular tram tours explain the benefits of the vineyard's natural setting and how biodynamic farming yields healthier, more flavorful fruit. The eco-friendly agricultural practices include extensive plantings to attract beneficial insects and the deployment of sheep to trim vegetation between the vines while simultaneously tilling the soil with their hooves and fertilizing to boot. Known for Chardonnay, Cabernet Sauvignon, Merlot, Pinot Noir, and Sauvignon Blanc, the winery is a beautiful spot for an alfresco tasting, whether you take the tour or not. All visits are by appointment; reserve a tram tour at least a day or two ahead in summer and early fall. ⊠ *1883 London Ranch Rd., Glen Ellen ⊹ Off Arnold Dr.* ☎ *888/490–2739* ⊕ *www.benziger.com* 🍷 *Tastings from $40* 🕐 *Closed Tues. and Wed.*

★ Jack London State Historic Park

STATE/PROVINCIAL PARK | The pleasures are pastoral and intellectual at author Jack London's beloved Beauty Ranch, where you could easily spend the afternoon hiking some of the 30-plus miles of trails that loop through meadows and stands of oaks, redwoods, and other trees. Manuscripts and personal artifacts depicting London's travels are on view at the House of Happy Walls Museum, which provides an overview of the writer's life, literary passions, humanitarian and conservation efforts, and promotion of organic farming. His wife Charmian's equally compelling story is also documented. A short hike away lie the ruins of Wolf House, which burned down just before London was to move in. Also open to visitors are a few outbuildings and the restored wood-frame cottage where London penned many of his later works. He's buried on the property. ■ **TIP→ The park hosts hot-ticket musical revues and comedies produced by Transcendence Theatre Company each summer.** ⊠ *2400 London Ranch Rd., Glen Ellen ⊹ Off Arnold Dr.*

☏ *707/938–5216* ⊕ *www.jacklondonpark.
com* 🅿 *Parking $10 ($5 walk-in or bike).*

★ Lasseter Family Winery

WINERY | Immaculately groomed grape-vines dazzle the eye at John and Nancy Lasseter's secluded winery, and it's no accident: Phil Coturri, Sonoma Valley's premier organic vineyard manager, tends them. Even the landscaping, which includes an insectary to attract beneficial bugs, is meticulously maintained. Come harvest time, the wine-making team oversees gentle processes that transform the fruit into wines of purity and grace, among them a Sémillon–Sauvignon Blanc blend, the Enjoué rosé, and Bordeaux and Rhône reds. Evocative labels illustrate the tale behind each wine. In good weather, guests hear these well-told stories at tastings on the winery's outdoor patio, whose views include the vineyard and the Mayacamas Mountains, where the Lasseters purchased a second vineyard. All visits to the Glen Ellen property are by appointment. ✉ *1 Vintage La., Glen Ellen* ✛ *Off Dunbar Rd.* ☏ *707/933–2800* ⊕ *www.lasseterfamilywinery.com* 🅿 *Tastings from $40.*

 Restaurants

★ Glen Ellen Star

$$$ | **ECLECTIC** | Chef Ari Weiswasser honed his craft at The French Laundry, Daniel, and other bastions of culinary finesse, but his Sonoma Valley outpost revolves around haute-rustic cuisine, much of it emerging from a wood-fired oven. In 2022, Weiswasser turned the day-to-day reins over to a new chef de cuisine, but the mainstay crisp-crusted, richly sauced Margherita and other pizzas continue to thrive in the oven's torrid heat, as do tender whole fish entrées and vegetables roasted in small iron skillets. **Known for:** outdoor dining area; prix-fixe Wednesday "neighborhood night" menu with free corkage; Weiswasser's sauces, emulsions, and

spices. 💲 *Average main: $33* ✉ *13648 Arnold Dr., at Warm Springs Rd., Glen Ellen* ☏ *707/343–1384* ⊕ *glenellenstar. com* 🕐 *No lunch.*

★ Les Pascals

$ | **CAFÉ** | A bright-yellow slice of France in downtown Glen Ellen, this combination pâtisserie, boulangerie, and café takes its name from its husband-and-wife owners, Pascal and Pascale Merle. Pascal whips up croissants, breads, turnovers, and sweet treats like Napoleons, galettes, and eclairs, along with quiches, potpies, and other savory fare; Pascale creates a cordial environment for customers to enjoy them. **Known for:** memorable French onion soup; shaded back patio; high-test French and Italian coffee drinks. 💲 *Average main: $12* ✉ *13758 Arnold Dr., Glen Ellen* ✛ *Near London Ranch Rd.* ☏ *707/934–8378* ⊕ *www.lespascalspatisserie.com* 🕐 *Closed Wed. No dinner.*

Hotels

★ Gaige House

$$$ | **B&B/INN** | There's no other place in Sonoma or Napa quite like the Gaige House, which blends the best elements of a traditional country inn, a boutique hotel, and a secluded hideaway. **Pros:** short walk to Glen Ellen restaurants, shops, and tasting rooms; idyllic swimming pool and hot tub area; full breakfast with two hot items. **Cons:** sound carries in the main house; least expensive rooms are on the small side; oriented more toward couples than families with children. 💲 *Rooms from: $351* ✉ *13540 Arnold Dr., Glen Ellen* ☏ *707/935–0237, 866/207–7146* ⊕ *www.thegaigehouse. com* 🛏 *23 rooms* 🍽 *Free Breakfast.*

★ Olea Hotel

$$$ | **HOTEL** | Husband-and-wife team Ashish and Sia Patel operate this country-casual yet sophisticated boutique lodging. **Pros:** beautiful style; complimentary wine; filling two-course breakfasts. **Cons:** minor road noise in some rooms;

fills up quickly on weekends; weekend minimum-stay requirement. **$** *Rooms from: $387* ✉ *5131 Warm Springs Rd., Glen Ellen* ✛ *West off Arnold Dr.* ☎ *707/996–5131* ⊕ *www.oleahotel.com* ⤳ *15 rooms* ⦿ *Free Breakfast.*

Kenwood

4 miles north of Glen Ellen.

Tiny Kenwood consists of little more than a few restaurants, shops, tasting rooms, and a historic train depot, now used for private events. But hidden in this pretty landscape of meadows and woods at the north end of Sonoma Valley are several good wineries, most just off the Sonoma Highway. Varietals grown here at the foot of the Sugarloaf Mountains include Sauvignon Blanc, Chardonnay, Zinfandel, and Cabernet Sauvignon.

GETTING HERE AND AROUND

To get to Kenwood from Glen Ellen, head northeast on Arnold Drive and north on Highway 12. Sonoma Transit buses serve Kenwood from Glen Ellen and Sonoma.

⊙ Sights

★ En Garde Winery

WINERY | Sommeliers, critics, and collectors extol the Pinot Noirs and Cabernet Sauvignons of Csaba Szakál, En Garde's Hungarian-born winemaker and owner. To create what he describes as "aromatic, complex, lush, and juicy" wines, Szakál selects top Sonoma County vineyards for the Pinots and the Napa Valley's Diamond Mountain, Mt. Veeder, and other high-elevation sites for the Cabernets. Not afraid to heavy up the oak on the Cabernets, he nevertheless achieves elegance as well. The winemaker is equally precise about hiring staffers for his modest highway's-edge tasting room along Kenwood's brief commercial strip. Well-acquainted with his goals and methods, they provide a wealth of knowledge

about wine making and California viticulture. If you're lucky, Szakál will be around to discuss his wines (he loves to), which also include Chardonnay, other whites, and rosé of Pinot Noir. Visits are by reservation, with same-day appointments sometimes possible. ✉ *9077 Sonoma Hwy., at Shaw Ave., Kenwood* ☎ *707/282–9216* ⊕ *www.engardewinery. com* ⛾ *Tastings from $40.*

St. Francis Winery

WINERY | Nestled at the foot of Mt. Hood, St. Francis has earned national acclaim for its pairings of wines and small bites. With its bell tower, red-tile roof, and views of the Mayacamas Mountains to the east, the winery's California Mission–style visitor center occupies one of Sonoma County's most scenic locations. The charm of the surroundings is matched by the wines, among them Cabernet Sauvignon and rich, earthy Zinfandels from the Dry Creek, Russian River, and Sonoma Valleys. The five-course pairings might include Chardonnay with lobster bisque or Cabernet Sauvignon with wine-braised beef ribs. ✉ *100 Pythian Rd., Kenwood* ✛ *Off Hwy. 12* ☎ *707/833–0242* ⊕ *www. stfranciswinery.com* ⛾ *Tastings from $35.*

⦿ Restaurants

Salt & Stone

$$$ | MODERN AMERICAN | The menu at this upscale roadhouse with a sloping wood-beamed ceiling focuses on seafood and meat—beef, lamb, chicken, duck, and other options—with many dishes in both categories grilled. Start with the classics, perhaps a martini and oysters Rockefeller, before moving on to well-plated contemporary entrées that might include crispy-skin salmon or duck breast, a fish stew, or grilled rib eye. **Known for:** mountain-view outdoor seating area; weekend brunch; weekday happy hour 2:30–5 except holidays. **$** *Average main: $31* ✉ *9900 Sonoma Hwy., at Kunde Winery Rd., Kenwood* ☎ *707/833–6326* ⊕ *www.saltstonek-enwood.com* ⊘ *No lunch Tues. and Wed.*

Hotels

★ Kenwood Inn and Spa
$$$ | B&B/INN | Fluffy feather beds, custom Italian furnishings, and French doors in most cases opening onto terraces or balconies lend this inn's uncommonly spacious guest rooms a romantic air—more than a few guests are celebrating honeymoons or anniversaries. **Pros:** large rooms; lavish furnishings; romantic setting. **Cons:** far from nightlife; expensive in high season; geared more to couples than families with children. [$] *Rooms from: $420* ✉ *10400 Sonoma Hwy./Hwy. 12, Kenwood* ☎ *707/833–1293, 800/353–6966* 🌐 *www.kenwoodinn.com* 🛏 *29 rooms* 🍴 *Free Breakfast.*

Petaluma

24 miles southwest of Kenwood, 39 miles north of San Francisco.

The first thing you should know about Petaluma is that this is a farm town—with more than 62,500 residents, a large one—and the residents are proud of it. Recent years have seen an uptick in the quality of Petaluma cuisine, fueled in part by the proliferation of local organic and artisanal farms and boutique wine production. With the 2018 approval of the Petaluma Gap AVA, the city even has its name on a wine appellation.

GETTING HERE AND AROUND

Petaluma lies west of Sonoma and southwest of Glen Ellen and Kenwood. From Highway 12 or Arnold Drive, take Watmaugh Road west to Highway 116 west. Sonoma Transit buses serve Petaluma. From San Francisco take U.S. 101 (or Golden Gate Transit Bus 101) north.

Sights

Lagunitas Brewing Company
BREWERY | These days owned by Heineken International, Lagunitas began as a craft brewery in Marin County in 1993 before moving to Petaluma in 1994. In addition to its large facility, the company operates a taproom, the Schwag Shop for gifts, and an outdoor beer garden that in good weather bustles even midday. Guides leading the brewery tour, which includes a beer flight, provide an irreverent version of the company's rise to international acclaim. An engaging tale involves the state alcohol board's sting operation commemorated by Undercover Investigation Shut-down Ale, one of several small-batch brews made here. ✉ *1280 N. McDowell Blvd., Petaluma* ✥ *½ mile north of Corona Rd.* ☎ *707/778–8776* 🌐 *lagunitas.com/taproom/petaluma* 🎟 *Tour $10* 🕒 *Taproom closed Mon. and Tues.*

★ McEvoy Ranch
FARM/RANCH | The late Nan McEvoy's retirement project after departing as board chair of the *San Francisco Chronicle,* the ranch produces organic extra-virgin olive oil as well as Pinot Noir and other wines, the estate ones from the Petaluma Gap AVA. In good weather, relaxing tastings of oils or wines unfold on a pond's-edge flagstone patio with views of alternating rows of Syrah grapes and mature olive trees. You can preorder lunch to accompany any tasting; for a more private experience, book a pond-side cabana. Walkabout Ranch Tours of four guests or more take in vineyards, gardens, and a Chinese pavilion. All visits require an appointment. ✉ *5935 Red Hill Rd., Petaluma* ✥ *6½ miles south of downtown* ☎ *707/778–2307* 🌐 *www.mcevoyranch.com* 🎟 *Tastings from $25 (olive oil), $35 (wine); tours from $55.*

🍴 Restaurants

★ Central Market
$$ | **MODERN AMERICAN** | A participant in the Slow Food movement, Central Market serves creative, upscale Cal-Mediterranean dishes—many of whose ingredients come from the restaurant's organic farm—in a century-old building with an exposed brick wall and an open kitchen. The menu, which changes daily depending on chef Tony Najiola's inspiration and what's ripe and ready, might include spicy duck wings as a starter, a slow-roasted-beets salad, pizzas, stews, two or three pasta dishes, and wood-grilled fish and meat. **Known for:** happy hour (5–6) apps, beer, and wine specials; superior wine list; historic setting.
[$] *Average main: $27* ✉ *42 Petaluma Blvd. N, Petaluma* ✣ *Near Western Ave.* ☎ *707/778–9900* 🌐 *www.centralmarket-petaluma.com* 🕒 *Closed Mon. and Tues. No lunch.*

★ Pearl Petaluma
$$ | **MEDITERRANEAN** | Regulars of this southern Petaluma "daytime café" with indoor and outdoor seating rave about its eastern Mediterranean–inflected cuisine—then immediately downplay their enthusiasm lest this unassuming gem become more popular. The menu changes often, but mainstays include *shakshuka* (a tomato-based stew with baked eggs) and a lamb burger dripping with fennel tzatziki. **Known for:** weekend brunch; fun beverage lineup, alcoholic and non; menu prices include gratuity.
[$] *Average main: $23* ✉ *500 1st St., at G St., Petaluma* ☎ *707/559–5187* 🌐 *pearl-petaluma.com* 🕒 *Closed Tues. and Wed. No dinner.*

Healdsburg

17 miles north of Santa Rosa, 32 miles northwest of Petaluma.

Sonoma County's ritziest town and the star of many a magazine spread or online feature, Healdsburg is located at the intersection of the Dry Creek Valley, Russian River Valley, and Alexander Valley AVAs. Several dozen wineries bear a Healdsburg address, and around downtown's plaza you'll find fashionable boutiques, spas, hip tasting rooms, and art galleries, and some of the Wine Country's best restaurants.

Especially on weekends, you'll have plenty of company as you tour the downtown area. You could spend a day just exploring the tasting rooms and shops surrounding Healdsburg Plaza, but be sure to allow time to venture into the surrounding countryside. With orderly rows of vines alternating with beautifully overgrown hills, this is the setting you dream about when planning a Wine Country vacation.

GETTING HERE AND AROUND

Healdsburg sits just off U.S. 101. Heading north, take the Central Healdsburg exit to reach Healdsburg Plaza; heading south, take the Westside Road exit and pass east under the freeway. Sonoma County Transit buses serve Healdsburg from Santa Rosa.

👁 Sights

★ Aperture Cellars
WINERY | As a youth, Jesse Katz tagged along with his photographer father, Andy Katz, to wineries worldwide, stimulating curiosity about wine that led to stints at august operations like the Napa Valley's Screaming Eagle and Bordeaux's Petrús. In 2009, still in his 20s, Katz started Aperture, a success from the get-go

for his single-vineyard Cabernets and Bordeaux blends. Among the whites are Sauvignon Blanc and an old-vine Chenin Blanc that's one of California's best. Katz's wines, which benefit from rigorous farming and cellar techniques, are presented by appointment only in an ultracontemporary hospitality center about 2½ miles south of Healdsburg Plaza. One tasting explores Aperture's various wine-growing sites and their soils, the other the single-vineyard wines. The center's shutterlike windows and other architectural elements evoke Andy Katz's photography career; his images of the Russian River Valley and beyond hang on the walls. ⊠ *12291 Old Redwood Hwy., Healdsburg ⊹ ¼ mile south of Limerick La.* ☎ *707/200–7891* ⊕ *www. aperture-cellars.com* ▥ *Tastings from $60* ⊗ *Closed Tues. and Wed.*

Breathless Wines

WINERY | The mood's downright bubbly (pardon that pun) at the oasis-like garden patio of this sparkling-wine producer tucked away in an industrial park northwest of Healdsburg Plaza. Established by three sisters in memory of their mother, Breathless sources grapes from appellations in Sonoma, Napa, and Mendocino Counties that find their way into sparklers and a few still wines. The small indoor tasting area was fashioned out of shipping containers, though nearly everyone sips in the umbrella-shaded garden in fine weather. You can sample wine by the glass, flight, or bottle; all visits require an appointment, with same-day reservations sometimes possible. ■ TIP→ **Splurge on the Sabrage Experience to learn how to open a bottle with a saber, a tradition supposedly initiated by Napoléon's soldiers.** ⊠ *499 Moore La., Healdsburg ⊹ Off North St.* ☎ *707/395–7300* ⊕ *www. breathlesswines.com* ▥ *Tastings from $28* ⊗ *Closed Tues. and Wed.*

Dry Creek Vineyard

WINERY | Loire-style Sauvignon Blanc marketed as Fumé Blanc brought instant success to the Dry Creek Valley's first new winery since Prohibition, but this stalwart established in 1972 also does well with Zinfandel and Cabernet Sauvignon and other Bordeaux-style reds. Founder David Stare's other contributions include leading the drive to develop the Dry Creek Valley appellation and coining the term "old-vine Zinfandel." The winery's history and wine-making evolution are among the topics addressed at tastings—outdoors under the shade of a magnolia and several redwood trees or in the nautical-theme tasting room. ⊠ *3770 Lambert Bridge Rd., Healdsburg ⊹ Off Dry Creek Rd.* ☎ *707/433–1000* ⊕ *www. drycreekvineyard.com* ▥ *Tastings from $30.*

★ Gary Farrell Vineyards & Winery

WINERY | Pass through an impressive metal gate and wind up a steep hill to reach this winery with knockout Russian River Valley views from the two-tiered tasting room and terrace outside. In 2017 *Wine Enthusiast* magazine named a Gary Farrell Chardonnay wine of the year, one among many accolades for this winery known for sophisticated single-vineyard Chardonnays and Pinot Noirs. Farrell departed in the early 2000s, but current winemaker Theresa Heredia acknowledges that her philosophy has much in common with his. For the Pinots, this means picking on the early side to preserve acidity and focusing on "expressing the site." The Elevation Tasting of single-vineyard wines provides a good introduction; other tastings involve a winery tour or library wines. Visits are by appointment; same-day reservations are possible on weekdays, but call ahead. ⊠ *10701 Westside Rd., Healdsburg* ☎ *707/473–2909* ⊕ *www.garyfarrellwinery.com* ▥ *Tastings from $55.*

★ Jordan Vineyard and Winery

WINERY | Founders Tom and Sally Jordan erected the French-style château here in part to emphasize their goal of producing Sonoma County Chardonnays and Cabernet Sauvignons—one of each annually—to rival those from the Napa Valley and France itself. Their son John, now at the helm, has instituted numerous improvements, among them the replanting of many vines and a shift to all-French barrels for aging. The signature winery tour and tasting includes a peek at the tank room and its towering oak barrels. The pièce de résistance of the three-hour Estate Tour & Tasting, hosted from spring to early fall, is a stop at a 360-degree vista point overlooking the 1,200-acre property's vines, olive trees, and countryside. As part of these experiences and other seasonal events, the executive chef prepares small bites and dishes whose ingredients come mainly from Jordan's organic garden. Visits are strictly by appointment. ⊠ *1474 Alexander Valley Rd., Healdsburg* ✛ *1½ miles east of Healdsburg Ave,* ☎ *707/431–5250* ⊕ *www.jordanwinery.com* ⊠ *Tastings from $90* ⊗ *Closed Tues. and Wed. Dec.–Mar.*

MacRostie Estate House

WINERY | A driveway off Westside Road curls through undulating vineyard hills to this longtime Chardonnay and Pinot Noir producer's steel, wood, and heavy-on-the-glass tasting space. Moments after you've arrived and a host has offered a glass of wine, you'll already feel transported into a genteel realm. Hospitality is clearly a priority, but so, too, is seeking out top-tier grape sources—30 for the Chardonnays, 15 for the Pinots—among them Dutton Ranch, Sangiacomo, and owner Steve MacRostie's Wildcat. With fruit this renowned, current winemaker Heidi Bridenhagen downplays the oak and other tricks of her trade, letting the vineyard settings, grape clones, and vintage do the talking. Tastings, inside or on balcony terraces with views across the Russian River Valley, are all seated and by appointment. ⊠ *4605 Westside Rd., Healdsburg* ✛ *Near Frost Rd.* ☎ *707/473–9303* ⊕ *macrostiewinery.com* ⊠ *Tastings from $35.*

★ Ridge Vineyards

WINERY | Ridge stands tall among local wineries, and not merely because its 1971 Monte Bello Cabernet Sauvignon rated second-highest among California reds competing with French ones at the famous Judgment of Paris blind tasting of 1976. The winery built its reputation on Cabernets, Zinfandels, and Chardonnays of unusual depth and complexity, but you'll also find blends of Rhône varietals. Ridge makes wines using grapes from several California locales—Sonoma County, Dry Creek Valley, the Napa Valley, and Paso Robles among them—but the focus is on single-vineyard estate wines such as the Lytton Springs Zinfandel from fruit grown near the tasting room. In good weather, you can sit outside, taking in views of rolling vineyard hills while you sip. ■**TIP**→ **The educational Century Tour & Library Tasting, a solid value, begins with a spin around the property in an electric cart, followed by a comparative tasting of current and older wines.** ⊠ *650 Lytton Springs Rd., Healdsburg* ✛ *Off U.S. 101* ☎ *408/867–3233* ⊕ *www.ridgewine.com/visit/lytton-springs* ⊠ *Tastings from $30.*

★ Silver Oak

WINERY | The views and architecture are as impressive as the wines at the 113-acre Sonoma County outpost of the same-named Napa Valley winery. As in Napa, the Healdsburg facility—an ultramodern, environmentally sensitive winery with a glass-walled tasting pavilion—produces just one wine each year: a well-balanced Alexander Valley Cabernet Sauvignon aged in American rather than French oak barrels. One tasting includes the current Alexander Valley and Napa Valley Cabernets, plus an older vintage. Two or more wines of sister operation Twomey Cellars, which produces Sauvignon Blanc, Pinot Noir, and Merlot, begin a second offering that concludes with the current Cabernets. Hosts at a third pour current and older Cabernets from Napa and Sonoma. Make a reservation for all visits. ✉ *7300 Hwy. 128, Healdsburg* ⊕ *Near Chaffee Rd.* ☎ *707/942–7082* 🌐 *www.silveroak.com* 🎫 *Tastings from $50.*

★ Tongue Dancer Wines

WINERY | Down a country lane less than 2 miles south of Healdsburg Plaza, James MacPhail's modest production facility seems well away from the upscale fray. MacPhail makes wines for The Calling, Sangiacomo, and other labels, but Tongue Dancer's Chardonnays and Pinot Noirs are his handcrafted labors of love. Made from small lots of grapes from choice vineyard sites, the wines impress, sometimes stun, with their grace, complexity, and balance. The flagship Sonoma Coast Pinot Noir, a blend from two or more vineyards, is poured at most tastings, in a mezzanine space above oak-aging barrels or on an outdoor patio. Either the winemaker or his co-owner and wife, Kerry Forbes-MacPhail—she's credited on bottles as the "Knowledge-able One" (and she is)—will host you. As James describes it, they aim to "create an approachable experience for guests we hope will leave as friends." Appointment-only visits are best made a day or more ahead. ✉ *851 Magnolia Dr., Healdsburg* ⊕ *Off Westside Rd.* ☎ *707/433–4780* 🌐 *tonguedancerwines.com* 🎫 *Tastings $30* ⏲ *Closed Sun. and Mon.*

🍴 Restaurants

★ Barndiva

$$$$ | **AMERICAN** | Not one to rest on her laurels, the creative director of this urban-rustic restaurant responded to winning a prestigious fine-dining award by welcoming a new chef, mixologist, and wine lead, all with impressive credentials themselves. The worth-the-splurge cuisine, hinging on hyperfresh local ingredients from superstar purveyors, comes off even more intricate than before in dishes that might include kanpachi crudo or goat-cheese croquette apps or a smoked pork chop with Japanese sweet potato entrée. **Known for:** open-air front and back patios; ornate, well-built cocktails; Friday and weekend brunch. [$] *Average main: $45* ✉ *231 Center St., Healdsburg* ⊕ *Near Matheson St.* ☎ *707/431–0100* 🌐 *www.barndiva.com* ⏲ *Closed Mon. and Tues. No lunch weekdays.*

Bravas Bar de Tapas

$$$ | **SPANISH** | Spanish-style tapas and an outdoor patio in perpetual party mode make this restaurant, headquartered in a restored 1920s bungalow, a popular downtown perch. Contemporary Spanish mosaics set a perky tone inside, but unless something's amiss with the weather, nearly everyone heads out back for flavorful croquettes, paella, *jamón ibérico, pan tomate* (tomato toast), grilled octopus, skirt steak, and crispy fried chicken. **Known for:** casual small plates; specialty cocktails, sangrias, and beer; Spanish and Sonoma County wines. [$] *Average main: $33* ✉ *420 Center St., Healdsburg* ⊕ *Near North St.* ☎ *707/433–7700* 🌐 *www.barbravas.com.*

Little Saint

$$ | **VEGETARIAN** | Inside a metal-and-glass structure design writers have described as industrial grange-hall chic, the chefs at this "farm-forward gathering place" prepare satisfying plant-based cuisine supporting the founders' goal of creating Healdsburg's first entirely vegan restaurant. With most ingredients rushed over from Little Saint's nearby 8-acre Russian River farm, the menu items change often. **Known for:** sensitive wine pairings, plus beers, ciders, and cocktails alcoholic and non; coffee bar, wine shop, and mercantile with made-to-go salads, sandwiches, and dips; live music and events upstairs some nights. [$] *Average* *main: $29 ✉ 25 North St., at Foss St., Healdsburg ☎ 707/433–8207 🌐 www.littlesainthealdsburg.com 🕒 Closed Tues. and Wed.*

★ The Matheson

$$$$ | MODERN AMERICAN | The location of Dustin Valette's farm-to-table restaurant holds a special place in his heart: the bar and its Wine Wall taps dispensing mostly Sonoma County wines occupy the space where the Geyserville native's great-grandfather ran a bakery a century ago. Valette describes the menu—aged meats creatively adorned, local fish with recently plucked vegetables—as a "love letter" to local agriculture, a point driven home by the large, bright paintings of farm and culinary activity hanging above the dining-room floor. **Known for:** rooftop bar for craft cocktails and bar bites; see-and-be-seen dining; ingredients harvested for peak ripeness. [$] *Average main: $43 ✉ 106 Matheson St., Healdsburg ✣ Near Healdsburg Ave. ☎ 707/723–1106 🌐 www.thematheson.com 🕒 No lunch.*

★ SingleThread Farm Restaurant

$$$$ | ECLECTIC | The seasonally oriented Japanese dinners known as kaiseki inspire the 10-course prix-fixe vegetarian, meat, and seafood menu at the spare, elegant restaurant—redwood walls, walnut tables, mesquite-tile floors, muted-gray yarn-thread panels—of internationally renowned culinary artists Katina and Kyle Connaughton (she farms, he cooks). As Katina describes the endeavor, the micro-seasons of their nearby farm plus SingleThread's rooftop garden of fruit trees and greens dictate Kyle's rarefied fare, prepared in a theatrically lit open kitchen. **Known for:** impeccable wine pairings; dishes customized based on guests' preferences; instinctive service. [$] *Average main: $425 ✉ 131 North St., at Center St., Healdsburg ☎ 707/723–4646 🌐 www.singlethread-farms.com 🕒 Closed Tues. and Wed. No lunch.*

Hotels

★ Harmon Guest House

$$$$ | HOTEL | A boutique sibling of the h2hotel two doors away, this downtown delight that debuted in 2018 earned instant LEED Gold status for its eco-friendly construction and operating practices. **Pros:** rooftop bar's cocktails, food menu, and views; connecting rooms and suites; similarly designed sister property h2hotel two doors south. **Cons:** minor room-to-room noise bleed-through; room gadgetry may flummox some guests; minimum-stay requirements some weekends. [$] *Rooms from: $519 ✉ 227 Healdsburg Ave., Healdsburg ☎ 707/922–5262 🌐 harmonguesthouse.com 🛏 39 rooms 🍴 Free Breakfast.*

★ Hotel Trio Healdsburg

$$ | HOTEL | Named for the three major wine appellations—the Russian River, Dry Creek, and Alexander Valleys—whose confluence it's near, this Residence Inn by Marriott 1¼ miles north of Healdsburg Plaza caters to families and extended-stay business travelers with spacious rooms equipped with full kitchens. **Pros:** cute robot room service; full kitchens; rooms sleep up to four or six. **Cons:** 30-minute walk to downtown; corporate feel; pricey in high season. [$] *Rooms from: $282 ✉ 110 Dry Creek Rd., Healdsburg ☎ 707/433–4000 🌐 www.hoteltrio.com 🛏 122 rooms 🍴 Free Breakfast.*

★ Montage Healdsburg

$$$$ | RESORT | Its bungalow-like guest rooms deftly layered into oak- and Cabernet-studded hills a few miles north of Healdsburg Plaza, this architectural sensation that opened fully in 2021 significantly upped Sonoma County's ultraluxury game. **Pros:** vineyard views from spa, restaurant, and swimming pool; outdoor living spaces with daybeds and firepits; recreational options on-property or nearby. **Cons:** expensive year-round; hefty resort fee; car trip required for off-property visits. $ Rooms from: $1,000 ✉ 100 Montage Way, Healdsburg ☎ 707/979–9000 ⊕ www.montagehotels.com/healdsburg ⇥ 130 bungalows ⦿ No Meals.

★ River Belle Inn

$$$ | B&B/INN | An 1875 Victorian with a storied past and a glorious colonnaded wraparound porch anchors this boutique Russian River property affiliated in 2022 with SingleThread Farms. **Pros:** riverfront location near tasting rooms; cooked-to-order full breakfasts; attention to detail. **Cons:** about a mile from Healdsburg Plaza; minimum-stay requirement on weekends; lacks pool, fitness center, and other amenities. $ Rooms from: $425 ✉ 68 Front St., Healdsburg ☎ 707/955–5724 ⊕ www.riverbelleinn.com ⇥ 11 rooms ⦿ Free Breakfast.

Nightlife

★ Lo & Behold Bar and Kitchen

BARS | Two cocktail all-stars and a chef with a fascination for international comfort food opened this bar where patrons wash down fish tacos, kimchi noodles, crispy pork spare ribs, and chicken tenders with craft cocktails that include the Phatty Margarita ("phattened" up with avocado and coconut oil). Good beer and wine list, too. Everything's best enjoyed out back on the patio. ✉ 214 Healdsburg Ave., Healdsburg ✛ Near Mill St. ☎ 707/756–5021 ⊕ loandbeholdca.com ◔ Closed Tues. and Wed.

Shopping

ART GALLERIES
★ Gallery Lulo

ART GALLERIES | A collaboration between a local artist and jewelry maker and a Danish-born curator, this gallery presents changing exhibits of jewelry, sculpture, and objets d'art. ✉ 303 Center St., at Plaza St., Healdsburg ☎ 707/433–7533 ⊕ www.gallerylulo.com.

FOOD AND WINE
Dry Creek General Store

FOOD | For breakfasts, sandwiches, bread, cheeses, and picnic supplies, stop by the general store, established in 1881 and still a popular spot for locals to hang out on the porch or in the bar. Beer and wine are also for sale, along with artisanal sodas, ciders, and juices. ✉ 3495 Dry Creek Rd., at Lambert Bridge Rd., Healdsburg ☎ 707/433–4171 ⊕ www.drycreekgeneralstore1881.com.

Activities

BICYCLING
Getaway Adventures / Wine Country Bikes

BIKING | This shop several blocks southeast of Healdsburg Plaza is perfectly located for setting up single or multiday treks into the Dry Creek and Russian River valleys by bike, kayak, or both. Private and group tours might include winery stops. If you prefer to explore on your own, you can rent equipment. ✉ 61 Front St., at Hudson St., Healdsburg ☎ 800/499–2453 ⊕ getawayadventures.com ☞ Daily rentals from $39 per day, full-day tours from $144.

SPAS
★ A Simple Touch Spa

SPAS | Skilled in Swedish, deep-tissue, sports, and other massage modalities, this soothing but unpretentious day spa's therapists routinely receive post-session raves. The most popular treatment involves heated basalt stones applied to the client's body, followed by a massage of choice. Foot reflexology, reiki, and facials are among the other specialties. ■TIP→ **Couples can enjoy any of the massages performed side-by-side by two therapists.** ✉ 239 Center St., Suite C, Healdsburg ✛ Near Matheson St. ☎ 707/433–6856 ⊕ asimpletouchspa.com ☞ Treatments from $60.

Geyserville

8 miles north of Healdsburg.

Several high-profile Alexander Valley AVA wineries, including the splashy Francis Ford Coppola Winery, can be found in the town of Geyserville, a small part of which stretches west of U.S. 101 into northern Dry Creek. Not long ago this was a dusty farm town, and downtown Geyserville retains its rural character, but the restaurants, shops, and tasting rooms along the short main drag hint at Geyserville's growing sophistication.

GETTING HERE AND AROUND

From Healdsburg, the quickest route to downtown Geyserville is north on U.S. 101 to the Highway 128/Geyserville exit. Turn right at the stop sign onto Geyserville Avenue and follow the road north to the small downtown. For a more scenic drive, head north from Healdsburg Plaza along Healdsburg Avenue. About 3 miles north, jog west (left) for a few hundred feet onto Lytton Springs Road, then turn north (right) onto Geyserville Avenue. In town the avenue merges with Highway 128. Sonoma County Transit buses serve Geyserville from downtown Healdsburg.

◉ Sights

Bannister Wines

WINERY | Brook Bannister's appreciation for his mother's wine-industry achievements inspired him to, as he puts it, forsake his career as a furniture maker "to keep her dream alive." That dream, which Martha "Marty" Bannister initiated in 1989, was to make layered, graceful age-worthy wines. Brook continues this tradition with the core lineup of Chardonnay, Riesling, several Pinot Noirs, and Zinfandel, supplemented in recent years by wines from lesser-known grapes. In 2022, Bannister Wines opened a gallery-style tasting room in the 1901 Geyserville Bank structure. Full of stories all its own, it's a fanciful space to sample Brook's well-crafted wines and learn more about this multigenerational labor of love. ⊠ *21035 Geyserville Ave., at Hwy. 128, Geyserville* ☎ *707/387–0124* ⊕ *bannisterwines.com* 🍷 *Tastings from $35* ⊘ *Closed Tues. and Wed.*

Francis Ford Coppola Winery

WINERY | The fun at what the film director has called his "wine wonderland," since 2021 owned by Delicato Family Wines, is all in the excess. You may find it hard to resist having your photo snapped standing next to Don Corleone's desk from *The Godfather* or beside other movie memorabilia. A bandstand reminiscent of one in *The Godfather Part II* is the centerpiece of a large pool area where you can rent a changing room, complete with shower, and lounge poolside, perhaps ordering food from the adjacent café. A more elaborate restaurant, Rustic, overlooks the vineyards. As for the wines, the excess continues in the cellar, where the team produces several dozen single-varietal bottlings and blends. You don't need an appointment to taste at the bar but do for seated experiences. All memorabilia may not be on display when you visit—items are sometimes on loan. ⊠ *300 Via Archimedes, Geyserville* ⊹ *Off U.S. 101* ☎ *707/857–1400* ⊕ *www.franciscoppolawinery.com* 🍷 *Tastings from $30.*

★ Robert Young Estate Winery

WINERY | Panoramic Alexander Valley views unfold at Scion House, the stylish yet informal knoll-top tasting space of this longtime Geyserville grower. The first Youngs began farming this land in the mid-1800s, raising cattle and growing wheat, prunes, and other crops. In the 1960s the late Robert Young, of the third generation, began cultivating grapes, eventually planting two Chardonnay clones now named for him. Grapes from them go into the Area 27 Chardonnay, among the best whites. The reds—small-lot Cabernet Sauvignons plus individual bottlings of Cabernet Franc, Malbec, Merlot, and Petit Verdot—shine even brighter. Tastings at Scion House, named for the fourth generation, whose members built on Robert Young's legacy and established the winery, are by appointment. Call ahead for same-day reservations. ■ **TIP→ Cab fanatics should consider the Ultimate Cabernet Lovers Experience of top-tier estate wines.** ✉ *5120 Red Winery Rd., Geyserville* ✣ *Off Hwy. 128* ☎ *707/431–4811* 🌐 *www.ryew.com* 🎫 *Tastings from $40* ⏲ *Closed Tues.*

★ Zialena

WINERY | Sister-and-brother team Lisa and Mark Mazzoni (she runs the business, he makes the wines) debuted their small winery's first vintage in 2014, but their Italian American family's wine-making heritage stretches back more than a century. Named for the siblings' great aunt Lena, known for her hospitality, Zialena specializes in estate-grown Zinfandel and Cabernet Sauvignon, some of whose lush mouthfeel derives from techniques Mark absorbed while working for the international consultant Philippe Melka. The Zin and Cab grapes, along with Chardonnay and Sangiovese for the seductive rosé, come from the 120-acre Mazzoni Vineyard, from which larger labels like Jordan also source fruit. Tastings are by appointment only, with same-day visits often possible. ✉ *21112 River Rd., Geyserville* ✣ *Off Hwy. 128* ☎ *707/955–5992* 🌐 *www.zialena.com* 🎫 *Tastings from $30.*

🍴 Restaurants

★ Cyrus

$$$$ | **MODERN AMERICAN** | A decade after his beloved, same-named Healdsburg restaurant closed, celebrity chef Douglas Keane of *Top Chef Masters* and other fame reopened a "2.0" version inside an 8,000-square-foot steel, glass, and concrete structure set in an Alexander Valley vineyard. Keane bills his prix-fixe culinary experience as a "dining journey," with guests (couples'-rate only; single diners charged double) changing rooms a few times for multiple internationally inspired courses based on hyper-seasonal mostly Northern California ingredients. **Known for:** architectural stunner in a rural setting; reservations (essential) released in monthly blocks two months in advance; Bubbles Lounge for cocktails and small bites à la carte (no reservations). [$] *Average main: $295* ✉ *275 Hwy. 128, Geyserville* ✣ *Near Railroad Ave.* ☎ *707/318–0379* 🌐 *www.cyrusrestaurant.com* ⏲ *Closed Mon.–Wed. No lunch.*

Diavola Pizzeria & Salumeria

$$ | **ITALIAN** | A dining area with hardwood floors, a pressed-tin ceiling, and exposed-brick walls provides a fitting setting for the rustic cuisine at this Geyserville mainstay. Chef Dino Bugica studied with artisanal cooks in Italy before opening this restaurant specializing in wood-fired pizzas and house-cured meats, with a few salads and meaty main courses rounding out the menu. **Known for:** talented chef; prime rib sandwich for lunch, chicken under a brick for dinner; outdoor patio. [$] *Average main: $26* ✉ *21021 Geyserville Ave., at Hwy. 128, Geyserville* ☎ *707/814–0111* 🌐 *www.diavolapizzeria.com.*

Forestville

13 miles southwest of Healdsburg.

To experience the Russian River Valley AVA's climate and rusticity, follow the river's westward course to the town of Forestville, home to a highly regarded restaurant and inn and a few wineries producing Pinot Noir from the Russian River Valley and well beyond.

GETTING HERE AND AROUND

To reach Forestville from U.S. 101, drive west from the River Road exit north of Santa Rosa. From Healdsburg, follow Westside Road west to River Road and then continue west. Sonoma County Transit buses serve Forestville.

Sights

★ Hartford Family Winery

WINERY | Pinot Noir lovers appreciate the subtle differences in the wines Hartford's team crafts from grapes grown in several Sonoma County AVAs, along with fruit from nearby Marin and Mendocino Counties and Oregon. The winery also produces highly rated Chardonnays and old-vine Zinfandels. If the weather's good, enjoy a flight on the patio outside the main winery building. At private library tastings, guests sip current and older vintages. All visits are by appointment; call ahead on the same day. ✉ *8075 Martinelli Rd., Forestville* ✥ *Off Hwy. 116 or River Rd.* ☎ *707/904–6950* 🌐 *www.hartfordwines.com* 🎟 *Tastings from $40.*

★ Joseph Jewell Wines

WINERY | Pinot Noirs from the Russian River Valley and Humboldt County to the north are the strong suit of this winery sourcing from prestigious vineyards like Bucher and Hallberg Ranch. Owner-winemaker Adrian Manspeaker, a Humboldt native, spearheaded the foray into Pinot Noir grown in the coastal redwood country. His storefront tasting room in downtown Forestville (visits by appointment; walk-ins welcomed when possible) provides the opportunity to experience what's unique about the varietal's next Northern California frontier. Manspeaker also makes two Zinfandels; lighter wines include two Chardonnays, Pinot Gris, Vermentino, a sparkling Vermentino, and rosé of Pinot Noir. ■ **TIP→ From spring to mid-fall, a private wine educator accompanies small parties on engaging vineyard tastings involving a tour or picnic lunch.** ✉ *6542 Front St., Forestville* ✥ *Near 1st St.* ☎ *707/820–1621* 🌐 *www.josephjewell.com* 🎟 *Tastings from $35* 🕓 *Closed Mon.–Wed.*

Hotels

★ The Farmhouse Inn

$$$$ | **B&B/INN** | With a farmhouse-meets-modern-loft aesthetic, this low-key but upscale getaway with a pale-yellow exterior contains spacious rooms filled with king-size four-poster beds, whirlpool tubs, and hillside-view terraces. **Pros:** on-site Farmhouse Inn Restaurant (fine dining) and Farmstand (upscale casual); luxury bath products; full-service spa. **Cons:** mild road noise audible in rooms closest to the street; two-night minimum on weekends; pricey, especially during high season. [$] *Rooms from: $1,182* ✉ *7871 River Rd., Forestville* ☎ *707/887–3300, 800/464–6642* 🌐 *www.farmhouseinn.com* 🛏 *25 rooms* 🍴 *Free Breakfast.*

Activities

Burke's Canoe Trips

CANOEING & ROWING | You'll get a real feel for the Russian River's flora and fauna on a leisurely 10-mile paddle downstream from Burke's to Guerneville. A shuttle bus returns you to your car at the end of the journey, which is best taken on a weekday—summer weekends can be crowded and raucous. ✉ *8600 River Rd., at Mirabel Rd., Forestville* ☎ *707/887–1222* 🌐 *www.burkescanoetrips.com* 🎟 *From $55 (kayak), $90 (canoe)* 🕓 *Closed mid-Oct.–late May.*

Guerneville

7 miles northwest of Forestville, 15 miles southwest of Healdsburg.

Guerneville's tourist demographic has evolved over the years—Bay Area families in the 1950s, lesbians and gays starting in the 1970s, and these days a mix of both groups, plus techies and outdoorsy types—with coast redwoods and the Russian River always central to the town's appeal. The area's most famous winery is Korbel Champagne

Cellars, established nearly a century and a half ago. Even older are the stands of trees that except on the coldest winter days make Armstrong Redwoods State Natural Reserve such a perfect respite from wine tasting.

GETTING HERE AND AROUND

To get to Guerneville from Healdsburg, follow Westside Road south to River Road and turn west. From Forestville, head west on Highway 116; alternatively, you can head north on Mirabel Road to River Road and then head west. Sonoma County Transit buses serve Guerneville.

Sights

★ Armstrong Redwoods State Natural Reserve

STATE/PROVINCIAL PARK | FAMILY | Here's your best opportunity in the western Wine Country to wander amid *Sequoia sempervirens,* also known as coast redwood trees. The oldest example in this 805-acre state park, the Colonel Armstrong Tree, is thought to be more than 1,400 years old. A half mile from the parking lot, the tree is easily accessible, and you can hike a long way into the forest before things get too hilly. ■TIP→ **During hot summer days, Armstrong Redwoods's tall trees help the park keep its cool.** ✉ *17000 Armstrong Woods Rd., Guerneville* ⚓ *Off River Rd.* ☎ *707/869–2015* ⊕ *www.parks.ca.gov* 💲 *$10 per vehicle, free to pedestrians and bicyclists.*

🍴 Restaurants

★ boon eat+drink

$$ | AMERICAN | A casual storefront restaurant on Guerneville's main drag, boon eat+drink has a menu built around salads, smallish shareable plates, and entrées that might include a vegan bowl, chili-braised pork shoulder, and local cod with shiitakes. Like many of chef-owner Crista Luedtke's dishes, the signature polenta lasagna—creamy ricotta salata

cheese and polenta served on greens sautéed in garlic, all of it floating upon a spicy marinara sauce—deviates significantly from the lasagna norm but succeeds on its own merits. **Known for:** adventurous culinary sensibility; Sonoma County wine selection; sister restaurant Brot for German cuisine in same block. 💲 *Average main: $25* ✉ *16248 Main St., at Church St., Guerneville* ☎ *707/869–0780* ⊕ *eatatboon.com* ⊘ *Closed Mon. and Tues.*

Hotels

★ Dawn Ranch

$$$ | RESORT | A historic, woodsy 15-acre property that reopened in 2022 as a deluxe, reconnect-with-nature variation on mid-century roadside resorts, Dawn Ranch provides accommodations ranging from one-room, cedar-shingled cabins and larger "chalets" with sitting areas to a cottage and a bungalow. **Pros:** high-quality beds, linens, and bath products; on-site restaurant and full bar with live music some nights; emphasis on unplugging and unwinding. **Cons:** some cabins are small; no TVs or phones in rooms (but solid Wi-Fi); two-night minimum for some stays. 💲 *Rooms from: $399* ✉ *16467 Hwy. 116, Guerneville* ☎ *707/869–0656* ⊕ *www.dawnranch.com* ⇋ *53 rooms* ⊘ *No Meals.*

Sebastopol

14 miles southeast of Guerneville.

A stroll through downtown in Sebastopol—formerly known more for Gravenstein apples than for grapes but these days a burgeoning wine hub—reveals glimpses of the past and, perhaps, the future, too. Many hippies settled here in the '60s and '70s and, as the old Crosby, Stills, Nash & Young song goes, they taught their children well: the town remains steadfastly countercultural.

GETTING HERE AND AROUND

From Guerneville, take Highway 116 south. From Santa Rosa, head west on Highway 12. Sonoma County Transit buses serve Sebastopol.

 Sights

★ The Barlow

MARKET | A multibuilding complex on a 12½-acre former apple-cannery site, The Barlow celebrates Sonoma County's "maker" culture with tenants who produce or sell wine, beer, spirits, crafts, clothing, art, and artisanal foods. The anchor wine tenant, Kosta Browne, receives only club members and allocation-list guests, but other tasting rooms are open to the public, among them Region wine bar, which promotes small Sonoma County producers. Crooked Goat Brewing makes and sells ales, Golden State Cider pours apple-driven beverages, and you can have a nip of vodka, gin, sloe gin, or wheat and rye whiskey at Spirit Works Distillery. Over at Fern Bar, the zero-proof (as in nonalcoholic) cocktails entice as much as the traditional ones. The bar serves food, as do Blue Ridge Kitchen (Southern-influenced comfort fare), Acme Pizza, Red Bird Bakery (excellent breakfast and lunch fare), Sushi Koshō, and the affiliated Oyster Bar, and a few other spots. ⊠ *6770 McKinley St., at Morris St., off Hwy. 12, Sebastopol* ☎ *707/824–5600* ⊕ *www.thebarlow.net* ☒ *Complex free; fees for tasting.*

★ Dutton-Goldfield Winery

WINERY | An avid cyclist whose previous credits include developing the wine-making program at what's now Hartford Family Winery, Dan Goldfield teamed up with fifth-generation farmer Steve Dutton to establish this small operation devoted to cool-climate wines. Goldfield modestly strives to take Dutton's meticulously farmed fruit and "make the winemaker unnoticeable," but what impresses the most about these wines, which include Chardonnay, Pinot Blanc, Pinot Noir, and Zinfandel, is their sheer artistry. Among the ones to seek out are the Angel Camp Pinot Noir, from Anderson Valley (Mendocino County) grapes, and the Morelli Lane Zinfandel, from fruit grown on the remaining 1.8 acres of an 1880s vineyard Goldfield helped revive. Lauded as a top Sonoma County winery by *Wine & Spirits* and *Food & Wine* magazines, Dutton-Goldfield is open by appointment but accepts walk-ins when possible. ⊠ *3100 Gravenstein Hwy. N/Hwy. 116, at Graton Rd., Sebastopol* ☎ *707/827–3600* ⊕ *www.duttongoldfield.com* ☒ *Tastings from $40.*

★ Iron Horse Vineyards

WINERY | A meandering one-lane road leads to this winery known for its sparkling wines and estate Chardonnays and Pinot Noirs. The sparklers have made history: Ronald Reagan served them at his summit meetings with Mikhail Gorbachev; George H. W. Bush took some along to Moscow for treaty talks; and Barack Obama included them at official state dinners. Despite Iron Horse's brushes with fame, a casual rusticity prevails at its outdoor tasting area (large heaters keep things comfortable on chilly days), which gazes out on acres of rolling, vine-covered hills. Tastings are by appointment only. ⊠ *9786 Ross Station Rd., Sebastopol* ⊕ *Off Hwy. 116* ☎ *707/887–1507* ⊕ *www.ironhorsevineyards.com* ☒ *Tastings from $35.*

🍴 Restaurants

Handline

$ | MODERN AMERICAN | FAMILY | Sebastopol's former Fosters Freeze location, now a 21st-century fast-food palace, won design awards for its rusted-steel frame and translucent panel-like windows. The menu, a paean to coastal California cuisine, includes oysters raw and grilled, fish tacos, ceviche, tostadas, three burgers (beef, vegetarian, and fish), and, honoring the location's previous incarnation, chocolate and vanilla soft-serve ice cream. **Known for:** upscale comfort food; outdoor patio; sustainable seafood and other ingredients. [$] *Average main: $17* ✉ *935 Gravenstein Hwy. S, Sebastopol* ✥ *Near Hutchins Ave.* ☎ *707/827–3744* 🌐 *www.handline.com.*

Ramen Gaijin
$$ | JAPANESE | Inside a tall-ceilinged, brick-walled, industrial-looking space with reclaimed wood from a coastal building backing the bar, the chefs at Ramen Gaijin turn out richly flavored ramen bowls brimming with pork belly, wood ear mushrooms, seaweed, and other well-proportioned ingredients. *Izakaya* (Japanese pub grub) dishes like *donburi* (meat and vegetables over rice) are another specialty, like the ramen made from mostly local proteins and produce. **Known for:** artisanal cocktails, beer, wine, and cider; gluten-free, vegetarian options on request; karaage (fried chicken) and other small plates. [$] *Average main: $21* ✉ *6948 Sebastopol Ave., Sebastopol* ✥ *Near Main St.* ☎ *707/827–3609* 🌐 *www.ramengaijin.com* ⏲ *Closed Sun. and Mon.*

Santa Rosa

6 miles east of Sebastopol, 55 miles north of San Francisco.

Urban Santa Rosa isn't as popular with tourists as many Wine Country destinations—not surprising, as there are more office parks than wineries within its limits. Still, this hardworking town has a couple of interesting cultural offerings and a few noteworthy restaurants and vineyards. The city's chain motels and hotels can be handy if everything else is booked, especially since Santa Rosa is roughly equidistant from Sonoma, Healdsburg, and the western Russian River Valley, three of Sonoma County's most popular wine-tasting destinations.

GETTING HERE AND AROUND

From Sebastopol, drive east on Highway 12. From San Francisco, cross the Golden Gate Bridge and continue north on U.S. 101. Santa Rosa's hotels, restaurants, and wineries are spread over a wide area; factor in extra time when driving around the city, especially during rush hours. From San Francisco or Marin County, take Golden Gate Transit Bus 101. Sonoma County Transit buses serve Santa Rosa and the surrounding area.

Sights

Balletto Vineyards
WINERY | A few decades ago Balletto was known more for quality produce than grapes, but the new millennium saw vineyards emerge as the core business. About 90% of the fruit from the family's 800-plus acres goes to other wineries, with the remainder destined for Balletto's estate wines. The house style is light on the oak, high in acidity, and low in alcohol content, a combination yielding exceptionally food-friendly wines. Sipping Pinot Gris, rosé of Pinot Noir, or a brut rosé sparkler on the outdoor patio can feel transcendent on a warm day, though the Chardonnays and Pinot Noirs steal the show. The winery also makes Gewürztraminer, Sauvignon Blanc, Syrah, and Zinfandel. ✉ *5700 Occidental Rd., Santa Rosa* ✥ *2½ miles west of Hwy. 12* ☎ *707/568–2455* 🌐 *www.ballettovineyards.com* 🎫 *Tastings from $25.*

★ Benovia Winery
WINERY | Winemaker-partner Mike Sullivan's Chardonnays and Pinot Noirs would taste marvelous even in a toolshed, but guests to Benovia's unassumingly chic Russian River Valley ranch house will never know. Appointment-only tastings of his acclaimed wines—Benovia also produces Grenache, Zinfandel, and Cabernet Sauvignon—take place in the brown-hued living room or on the open-air patio. From either vantage point, views of the estate Martaella Vineyard all the way to Mt. St.

Helena draw the eye. Wine educators leading vineyard tours focus on Benovia's earth-friendly farming practices; a production tour tracks the wine-making process from vineyard to barrel to glass. Sullivan's handling of two Chardonnays from Martinelli-family grapes typifies his minimalistic approach. He subtly emphasizes minerality in a wine from the Three Sisters Vineyard in the coastal Fort Ross–Seaview AVA. By contrast, a hint of California ripeness emerges in La Pommeraie, from Zio Tony Ranch in the warmer Russian River Valley. ⊠ *3339 Hartman La., Santa Rosa* ✛ *Off Piner Rd.* ☎ *707/921–1040* ⊕ *benoviawinery.com* 🍷 *Tastings from $45.*

★ Charles M. Schulz Museum

ART MUSEUM | FAMILY | Fans of Snoopy and Charlie Brown will love this museum dedicated to the late Charles M. Schulz, who lived his last three decades in Santa Rosa. Permanent installations include a re-creation of the cartoonist's studio, and temporary exhibits often focus on a particular theme in his work. ■**TIP→ Children and adults can take a stab at creating cartoons in the Education Room.** ⊠ *2301 Hardies La., at W. Steele La., Santa Rosa* ☎ *707/579–4452* ⊕ *www.schulzmuseum. org* 🍷 *$14* ⊙ *Closed Tues. early Sept.– late May.*

Martinelli Winery

WINERY | In a century-old hop barn with the telltale triple towers, Martinelli has the feel of a traditional country store, but sophisticated wines are made here. The winery's reputation rests on its complex Pinot Noirs, Syrahs, and Zinfandels, including the Jackass Hill Vineyard Zin, made with grapes from vines planted mainly in the 1880s by the current owners' ancestors. Noted winemaker Helen Turley set the Martinelli style— fruit-forward, easy on the oak, reined-in tannins—in the 1990s, and the 21st-century team continues this approach. Tastings held (weather permitting) on a vineyard's-edge terrace survey the current releases. All visits are by appointment, best made online. ■**TIP→ Terrace and Hop Barn tastings survey the portfolio, but serious wine drinkers should consider the Collector's Flight of top-drawer Chardonnays, Pinot Noirs, and Zinfandels.** ⊠ *3360 River Rd.* ✛ *East of Olivet Rd.* ☎ *707/525–0570, 800/346–1627* ⊕ *www. martinelliwinery.com* 🍷 *Tastings from $35.*

★ Safari West

WILDLIFE REFUGE | FAMILY | An unexpected bit of wilderness in the Wine Country, this preserve with African wildlife covers 400 acres. Begin your visit with a stroll around enclosures housing lemurs, cheetahs, giraffes, and rare birds like the brightly colored scarlet ibis. Next, climb with your guide onto open-air vehicles that spend about two hours combing the expansive property, where more than 80 species—including gazelles, cape buffalo, antelope, wildebeests, and zebras—inhabit the hillsides. ■**TIP→ If you'd like to extend your stay, lodging in semi-glam Botswana-made tent cabins is available.** ⊠ *3115 Porter Creek Rd., Santa Rosa* ✛ *Off Mark West Springs Rd.* ☎ *707/579–2551, 800/616–2695* ⊕ *www. safariwest.com* 🍷 *From $105 Sept.–May, from $126 June–Aug.*

🍽 Restaurants

The Spinster Sisters

$$$ | MODERN AMERICAN | The versatile chef of this concrete-and-glass grazing spot anchoring the SOFA Santa Rosa Arts District satisfies her diverse devotees with American standards and playful variations on international cuisines. Separated on the menu into three main categories—ocean, garden, and pasture, each with a selection of appetizers, salads, and entrées—the dishes change often but might include trout with French lentils, hanger steak with kale gratin, Tuscan-style St. Louis ribs, and mushroom hand pie with leeks and ricotta. **Known for:** thought-provoking flavors; dessert pastries; local and international wines. [$] *Average main: $31 ✉ 401 S. A St., at Sebastopol Ave., Santa Rosa ☎ 707/528–7100 🌐 thespinstersisters.com ⏲ Closed Sun. and Mon. No lunch.*

★ Walter Hansel Wine & Bistro

$$$$ | FRENCH | Tabletop linens and lights softly twinkling from this ruby-red roadhouse restaurant's low wooden ceiling raise expectations the Parisian-style bistro cuisine consistently exceeds. A starter of cheeses or French onion soup awakens the palate for entrées like chicken cordon bleu, steak au poivre, or seafood dishes that might include scallops in a rich yet somehow delicate gastrique or subtly sauced wild Alaskan halibut. **Known for:** romantic setting for classic cuisine; prix-fixe option; vegan and vegetarian dishes. [$] *Average main: $38 ✉ 3535 Guerneville Rd., at Willowside Rd., Santa Rosa ✣ 6 miles northwest of downtown ☎ 707/546–6462 🌐 walter-hanselbistro.com ⏲ Closed Mon. and Tues. No lunch.*

Hotels

★ Vintners Resort

$$$ | HOTEL | With a countryside location, a reserved sense of style, and spacious rooms with comfortable beds, the Vintners Resort further seduces with a slew of amenities and a scenic vineyard landscape. **Pros:** café and John Ash & Co. restaurant; vineyard jogging and walking path; facials, massages at Vi La Vita spa. **Cons:** occasional noise from adjacent events center; trips to Healdsburg or downtown Santa Rosa require a car; pricey on summer and fall weekends. [$] *Rooms from: $364 ✉ 4350 Barnes Rd., Santa Rosa ☎ 800/421–2584 🌐 www.vintnersresort.com 🛏 78 rooms 🍴 No Meals.*

Chapter 13

THE NORTH COAST

Updated by
Daniel Mangin

⊙ Sights   🍴 Restaurants   🛏 Hotels   🛍 Shopping   🍸 Nightlife
★★★★★   ★★★★☆   ★★★★★   ★☆☆☆☆   ★☆☆☆☆

WELCOME TO
THE NORTH COAST

TOP REASONS TO GO

★ **Scenic coastal drives:** There's hardly a road here that *isn't* scenic.

★ **Wild beaches:** This stretch of California is one of nature's masterpieces. Revel in the unbridled, rugged coastline, without a building in sight.

★ **Dinnertime:** When you're done hiking the beach, refuel with delectable food; you'll find everything from fresh-off-the-boat seafood to haute French-inspired cuisine.

★ **Fine wine:** Sip wines at family-owned tasting rooms—cool-climate Pinot Noirs and Chardonnays in the Anderson Valley, then wines from Zinfandel and other heat-loving varietals as you move inland.

★ **Wildlife:** Watch for migrating whales, sunbathing sea lions, and huge Roosevelt elk with majestic antlers.

It's all but impossible to explore the Northern California coast without a car. Indeed, you wouldn't want to—driving here is half the fun. The main road is Highway 1, two lanes that twist and turn (sometimes 180 degrees) up cliffs and down through valleys in Sonoma and Mendocino counties. U.S. 101 proceeds parallel inland until the two roads join northward in the Redwood Country of Humboldt County.

1 Bodega Bay. Harbor seals bask on Bodega Bay's windswept beaches.

2 Jenner. Cliffs here overlook the estuary where the Russian River empties into the Pacific.

3 Point Arena. A lighthouse and a wildlife preserve supply daytime thrills you can extend overnight.

4 Elk. Perched high above the ocean, Elk entices with a sandy public beach and two ultraluxurious resorts.

5 Little River. Bask in breathtaking ocean views at restaurants in Little River and nearby Albion.

6 Mendocino. Artsy Mendocino is all about aesthetics, from coastal vistas to stylishly plated cuisine.

7 Fort Bragg. Travelers love this down-to-earth town for its botanical gardens, working harbor, and water's-edge trail.

8 Philo. Chardonnay and Pinot Noir star in scenic Philo.

9 Boonville. Sip beer at a famous brewery or drop by family-owned wineries at this town with a certified language all its own.

10 Hopland. This wisp of a town has acquired a hip cachet for its tasting rooms, restaurants, and lodgings.

11 Ukiah. Wine making in and around Mendocino County's largest city dates back a century-plus.

12 Avenue of the Giants. This glorious stretch of redwoods passes through tiny Weott.

13 Eureka. Ornate Victorians line downtown blocks of this gateway to national and state parks.

14 Trinidad. A former trading post, Trinidad trades these days on its beauty and proximity to ocean and redwoods.

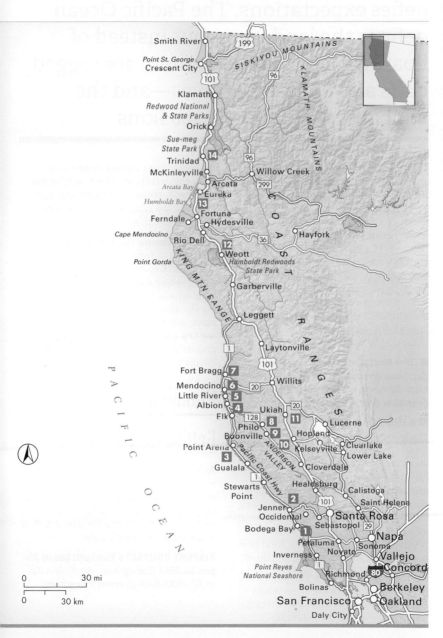

The spectacular coastline of Sonoma, Mendocino, and Humboldt counties defies expectations. The Pacific Ocean defines the landscape, but instead of boardwalks and bikinis there are ragged cliffs and pounding waves—and the sunbathers are mostly sea lions.

Two-lane Highway 1 follows the fickle shoreline. Although coastal towns vary from deluxe spa retreat to hippie hideaway, all are reliably sleepy—and that's precisely why many Californians escape here to enjoy nature unspoiled. On a detour inland, you can explore redwoods and sip wines at tasting rooms rarely too crowded or pricey. When you travel the North Coast, turn off your phone; you won't have much of a signal anyway, and this stretch of Highway 1 has numerous little worlds, each different from the last, waiting to be discovered.

■ TIP→ **Don't plan to travel too far in one day. Some drivers stop frequently to appreciate the views, and you can only safely drive 30 or 40 mph on many stretches.**

MAJOR REGIONS
The Sonoma Coast. As you enter Sonoma County from the south on Highway 1, you pass through rolling pastureland. North of Bodega Bay dramatic shoreline takes over. The road snakes up, down, and around sheer cliffs and steep inclines—some without guardrails—where cows seem to cling precariously. Stunning vistas (or cottony fog) and hairpin turns make for an exhilarating drive.

The Mendocino Coast. The timber industry gave birth to most of the small towns along this stretch of coastline. Although tourism now drives the economy, the region has retained much of its old-fashioned charm. The beauty of the landscape, of course, has not changed. Inland lie the wineries of the Anderson Valley, Hopland, and Ukiah.

Redwood Country. For a pristine encounter with giant redwoods, make the trek to Humboldt County's national and state parks, where even casual visitors have easy access to thick redwood forests. Eureka and nearby Arcata, both former ports, are sizable, but otherwise towns are tiny and nestled in the woods, and people have an independent spirit that recalls the original homesteaders.

Planning

Getting Here and Around

AIR
Humboldt County Airport (ACV), 14 miles north of Eureka in McKinleyville, is served by United and Avelo. Most visitors rent a car, with ride-sharing (about $25 to Eureka) the next best option.

AIRPORT CONTACTS Humboldt County Airport. ⊠ *3561 Boeing Ave., McKinleyville* ☎ *707/839–5401* ⊕ *www.flyacv.com.*

GROUND TRANSPORTATION CONTACTS
City Cab. ☎ 707/442–4551 ⊕ citycabhumboldt.com.

BUS
Greyhound buses serve Eureka. Mendocino Transit Authority serves its county. Humboldt Transit Authority connects Eureka and Trinidad.

BUS CONTACTS Humboldt Transit Authority. ☎ 707/443–0826 ⊕ www.hta.org. **Mendocino Transit Authority.** ☎ 800/696–4682 ⊕ mendocinotransit.org.

CAR
Twisting Highway 1 is the scenic route to Mendocino from San Francisco, but the fastest one is U.S. 101 north to Highway 128 west (from Cloverdale) to Highway 1 north. The quickest route to the far North Coast is straight up U.S. 101 past Cloverdale to Hopland and Ukiah and into Humboldt County.

■TIP➔ **U.S. 101 has excellent services, but long stretches separate towns along Highway 1. Stop for a refill if you're running low on fuel and see a gas station.**

ROAD CONDITIONS Caltrans. ☎ 800/427–7623 ⊕ quickmap.dot.ca.gov.

Hotels

Restored Victorians, rustic lodges, country inns, and vintage motels are among the accommodations available here. Few have air-conditioning (ocean breezes make it unnecessary), and many lack in-room phones or TVs. Budget accommodations are rare except in Fort Bragg and a few other towns, but you're likely to find reduced rates in winter. Make reservations at small inns as far ahead as possible in summer and on weekends—rooms at the best places sometimes sell out months in advance.

Restaurants

Restaurants here entice diners with dishes fashioned from fresh seafood and locally grown vegetables and herbs. Attire is usually informal, though dressy casual is the norm at pricier places. Most kitchens close at 8 or 8:30 pm, and only a few places serve past 9:30 pm.

⇨ *Restaurant and hotel reviews have been shortened. For full information, visit Fodors.com. Restaurant prices are the average cost of a main course at dinner, or if dinner is not served, at lunch. Hotel prices are the lowest cost of a standard double room in high season.*

What It Costs			
$	$$	$$$	$$$$
RESTAURANTS			
under $20	$20–$30	$31–$40	over $40
HOTELS			
under $200	$200–$350	$351–$500	over $500

Visitor Information

CONTACTS Humboldt County Visitors Bureau. ✉ Eureka ☎ 707/443–5097, 800/346–3482 ⊕ www.visitredwoods.com. **Sonoma County Tourism.** ☎ 707/522–5800, 800/576–6662 ⊕ www.sonomacounty.com. **Visit Mendocino County.** ☎ 707/964–9010, 866/466–3636 ⊕ www.visitmendocino.com.

When to Go

The North Coast is a year-round destination, though when you go determines what you will see. The migration of Pacific gray whales lasts from November through April. Wildflowers follow the winter rain, as early as January in southern areas through June farther north.

Surfers check out the waves near Bodega Bay on the Sonoma Coast.

Summer is the high season, but spring and fall are arguably better times to visit. The pace is slower, towns are quieter, and lodging is cheaper.

The coastal climate is similar to San Francisco's, although winter nights are colder than in the city. In July and August, thick fog can drop temperatures to the high 50s, but fear not: you need only drive inland a few miles to find temperatures often 20 degrees higher.

Bodega Bay

23 miles west of Santa Rosa.

Pockets of modernity notwithstanding, this commercial fishing town retains the workaday vibe of its cinematic turn in Alfred Hitchcock's *The Birds* (1963). Little from the film's era remains save the windswept bay and ocean views. To the east in the town of Bodega, the film's schoolhouse still stands, at Bodega Lane off Bodega Highway.

GETTING HERE AND AROUND

To reach Bodega Bay, exit U.S. 101 at Santa Rosa and take Highway 12 west (called Bodega Highway west of Sebastopol) 23 miles to the coast. A scenic alternative is to take U.S. 101's East Washington Street/Central Petaluma exit and follow signs west to Bodega Bay; just after you merge onto Highway 1, you'll pass through down-home Valley Ford, where Valley Ford Cheese & Creamery is worth a stop if it's open. Mendocino Transit Authority buses serve Bodega Bay.

Sights

Sonoma Coast Vineyards

WINERY | This winery with an ocean-view tasting room makes small-lot wines from grapes grown close to the Pacific. The Petersen Vineyard Chardonnay and Antonio Mountain Pinot Noir stand out among cool-climate bottlings that also include Sauvignon Blanc, rosé of Pinot Noir, and a Blanc de Noirs sparkler. ⊠ *555 Hwy. 1, Bodega Bay* ☎ *707/921–2860* ⊕ *www.*

sonomacoastvineyards.com 🎫 *Tastings from $10 per glass.*

Beaches

★ Sonoma Coast State Park

BEACH | FAMILY | The park's gorgeous sandy coves stretch for 17 miles from Bodega Head to 4 miles north of Jenner. Bodega Head is a popular whale-watching perch in winter and spring, and Rock Point, Duncan's Landing, and Wright's Beach, at about the halfway mark, have good picnic areas. Rogue waves have swept people off the rocks at Duncan's Landing Overlook, so don't stray past signs warning you away. About 2 miles north, calmer Shell Beach is known for beachcombing, tide-pooling, and fishing. Walk part of the bluff-top Kortum Trail or drive about 2½ miles north of Shell Beach to Blind Beach. Near the mouth of the Russian River just north of here at Goat Rock Beach, you'll find harbor seals; pupping season is from March through August. Bring binoculars and walk north from the parking lot to view the seals. Lifeguards are on duty at some beaches during summer, but strong rip currents and heavy surf keep most visitors onshore. **Amenities:** parking (fee); toilets. **Best for:** solitude; sunset; walking. ✉ *Park Headquarters/Salmon Creek Ranger Station, 3095 Hwy. 1* ✣ *2 miles north of Bodega Bay* ☎ *707/875–3483* 🌐 *www.parks.ca.gov* 🎫 *$8 per vehicle.*

Restaurants

Fisherman's Cove

$ | SEAFOOD | Brave the lines at this seafood shack that doubles as a bait-and-tackle store to feast on crab sandwiches on sourdough, catch-of-the-day fish tacos, and fresh Tomales Bay oysters raw or barbecued (the latter with sauces that include piquant chorizo butter). The family owners place a premium on quality and sustainably produced ingredients. **Known for:** indoor and outdoor seating; hearty clam chowder and Portuguese fish stew; vegetarian options including salads and beer-batter avocado and fries. [$] *Average main: $16* ✉ *1850 Bay Flat Rd., Bodega Bay* ✣ *Follow Eastshore Rd. west from Hwy. 1* ☎ *707/377–4238* 🌐 *www.fishermanscovebodegabay.com* 🕓 *No dinner.*

★ Ginochio's Kitchen

$ | ECLECTIC | The eye-level bay perspective steals the show at this low-slung self-described barbecue and Italian restaurant whose outdoor seating areas fill up quickly in good weather. For breakfast the kitchen turns out oh-so-moist caramel-bacon monkey bread and burritos with scrambled eggs and brisket; lunchtime brings Italian-style scallop-and-clam chowder, fish tacos, pulled-pork sandwiches, and, in season, Dungeness crab sandwiches awash in molten Havarti cheese. **Known for:** Alicia's Crackling Nachos with or without meat; 14-hour cherrywood-smoked beef and brisket; wine list favoring small Sonoma County producers. [$] *Average main: $18* ✉ *1410 Bay Flat Rd., Bodega Bay* ✣ *Off Eastshore Rd. west off Hwy. 1* ☎ *707/377–4359* 🌐 *ginochioskitchen.com* 🕓 *No dinner.*

Spud Point Crab Company

$ | SEAFOOD | Crab sandwiches, New England or Manhattan clam chowder, and homemade crab cakes with roasted red-pepper sauce star on this food stand's brief menu. Place your order and enjoy your meal to go or, when possible, at one of the marina-view picnic tables outside. **Known for:** family operation; opens at 9 am; seafood cocktails, superb chowder. [$] *Average main: $14* ✉ *1910 Westshore Rd., Bodega Bay* ✣ *West off Hwy. 1, Eastshore Rd. to Bay Flat Rd.* ☎ *707/875–9472* 🌐 *www.spudpointcrab-co.com* 🕓 *No dinner.*

★ Terrapin Creek Cafe & Restaurant

$$$ | MODERN AMERICAN | Intricate but not fussy cuisine based on locally farmed ingredients and *fruits de mer* has made this casual yet sophisticated restaurant with an open kitchen a West County darling. Start with raw oysters, rich potato-leek soup, or (in season) Dungeness crab before moving on to halibut or other fish pan-roasted to perfection. **Known for:** intricate cuisine of chefs Liya and Andrew Truong; many locally sourced ingredients; signature hamachi crudo and Mediterranean fish stew. $ *Average main: $36* ✉ *1580 Eastshore Rd., Bodega Bay* ✛ *Off Hwy. 1* ☎ *707/875–2700* ⊕ *www.terrapincreekcafe.com* ☾ *Closed Tues. and Wed. No lunch.*

Hotels

Bodega Harbor Inn
$ | **HOTEL** | Rooms at this humble property are small and clean, and some are decorated with tile or wood laminate flooring. **Pros:** budget choice; rooms for larger groups; ocean views from public areas and some rooms. **Cons:** older facility; nondescript rooms; behind a shopping center. $ *Rooms from: $145* ✉ *1345 Bodega Ave., Bodega Bay* ☎ *707/875–3594* ⊕ *www.bodegaharborinn.com* ⇦ *16 rooms* ℃ *No Meals.*

★ The Lodge at Bodega Bay
$$$ | **HOTEL** | Looking out to the ocean across a wetland, the lodge's shingle-and-river-rock buildings contain Bodega Bay's finest accommodations. **Pros:** spacious rooms with ocean views; on-site Drakes Sonoma Coast restaurant for sunsets and seafood; fireplaces and patios or balconies in most rooms. **Cons:** pricey in-season; parking lot in foreground of some rooms' views; must drive to other fine dining. $ *Rooms from: $349* ✉ *103 Coast Hwy. 1, Bodega Bay* ☎ *707/875–3525* ⊕ *www.bodegabaylodge.com* ⇦ *83 rooms* ℃ *No Meals.*

Activities

★ Bodega Bay Sailing Adventures
RAFTING | **FAMILY** | Part salty dog and part jolly entertainer, Captain Rich conducts three-hour Bodega Bay tours on his 33-foot sailboat. Whales are often sighted from winter into spring, and sea lions and harbor seals commonly appear. ✉ *1410 Bay Flat Rd., Bodega Bay* ✛ *Off Hwy. 1; meet in front of sport fishing center* ☎ *707/318–2251* ⊕ *www.bodegabaysailing.com* ⛵ *From $95 per person (4-person minimum).*

Jenner

10 miles north of Bodega Bay.

The Russian River empties into the Pacific Ocean at Jenner, a wide spot in the road where houses dot a mountainside high above the sea. The village looks south across the river's mouth to Sonoma Coast State Park's Goat Rock Beach. North of town, Fort Ross State Historic Park provides a glimpse into Russia's early-19th-century foray into California. South of the fort, a winery named for it grows Chardonnay and Pinot Noir above the coastal fog line. North of the fort lie more beaches and redwoods to hike and explore.

GETTING HERE AND AROUND
Jenner is north of Bodega Bay on Highway 1. From Guerneville head west on Highway 116 (River Road). Mendocino Transit Authority buses serve Jenner.

Sights

Fort Ross State Historic Park
STATE/PROVINCIAL PARK | **FAMILY** | With its reconstructed Russian Orthodox chapel, stockade, and officials' quarters, Fort Ross looks much the way it did after the Russians made it their major California coastal outpost in 1812. Russian settlers established the fort on land they leased from the Kashia people. The Russians hoped to gain a foothold in the Pacific coast's warmer regions and to produce crops and other supplies for their Alaskan fur-trading operations. In 1841, with the local marine mammal population depleted and farming

having proven unproductive, the Russians sold their holdings to John Sutter, later of gold-rush fame. The land, privately ranched for decades, became a state park in 1909. One original Russian-era structure remains, as does a cemetery. The rest of the compound has been reconstructed to look much as it did during Russian times. An excellent small museum documents the history of the fort, the Kashia people, and the ranch and state-park eras. No dogs are allowed past the parking lot and picnic area. ✉ *19005 Hwy. 1, Jenner* ✣ *11 miles north of Jenner village* ☎ *707/847–3437* 🌐 *www.fortross.org* 🎟 *$10 per vehicle.*

Fort Ross Vineyard & Winery

WINERY | The Russian River and Highway 116 snake west from Guerneville through redwood groves to the coast, where Highway 1 twists north past rocky cliffs to this windswept ridgetop winery. Many experts deemed the weather this far west too chilly even for cool-climate varietals, but Fort Ross Vineyard and other Fort Ross–Seaview AVA wineries proved that Chardonnay and Pinot Noir could thrive above the fog line. The sea air and rocky soils here produce wines generally less fruit-forward than their Russian River Valley counterparts but equally sophisticated and no less vibrant. With its barnlike tasting room and outdoor patio overlooking the Pacific, Fort Ross provides an appealing introduction to its region's wines. Tastings include small bites (vegetarian options possible). Appointments are required; for same-day visits, call before 11 am. ✉ *15725 Meyers Grade Rd., Jenner* ✣ *Off Hwy. 1, 6 miles north of Jenner* ☎ *707/847–3460* 🌐 *www.fortrossvineyard.com* 🎟 *Tastings from $60* ⏲ *Closed Wed. and Thurs.*

🍴 Restaurants

★ River's End

$$$ | **AMERICAN** | The hot tip at this low-slung cliff's-edge restaurant is to come early or reserve a window table, where the Russian River and Pacific Ocean views alone, particularly at sunset, might make your day (even more so if you're a birder). Seafood is the specialty—during the summer the chef showcases local king salmon—but filet mignon, duck, elk, a vegetarian napoleon, and pasta with prawns are often on the dinner menu. **Known for:** majestic setting; raw oysters and wine pairing; burgers, fish-and-chips for lunch. [$] *Average main: $37* ✉ *11048 Hwy. 1, Jenner* ✣ *1½ miles north of Hwy. 116* ☎ *707/865–2484* 🌐 *www.ilovesunsets.com* ⏲ *Closed Wed. and Thurs.*

🛏 Hotels

★ Timber Cove Resort

$$$ | **RESORT** | Restored well beyond its original splendor, this resort anchored to a craggy oceanfront cliff is by far the Sonoma Coast's coolest getaway. **Pros:** dramatic sunsets; grand public spaces; patio dining at Coast Kitchen restaurant. **Cons:** some service lapses; pricey ocean-view rooms; far from nightlife. [$] *Rooms from: $467* ✉ *21780 Hwy. 1, Jenner* ☎ *707/847–3231* 🌐 *www.timbercoveresort.com* 🛏 *46 rooms* 🍴 *No Meals.*

Point Arena

52 miles north of Jenner.

A former timber town, Point Arena is part New Age and part rowdy. The one road going west out of downtown will lead you to the harbor, where fisherfolk unload their catch, and someone's nearly always riding the waves.

GETTING HERE AND AROUND

From Jenner, follow Highway 1 north; from Mendocino follow it south. Mendocino Transit Authority serves the area.

👁 Sights

★ B Bryan Preserve

NATURE PRESERVE | **FAMILY** | Guides helming vintage Land Rovers conduct

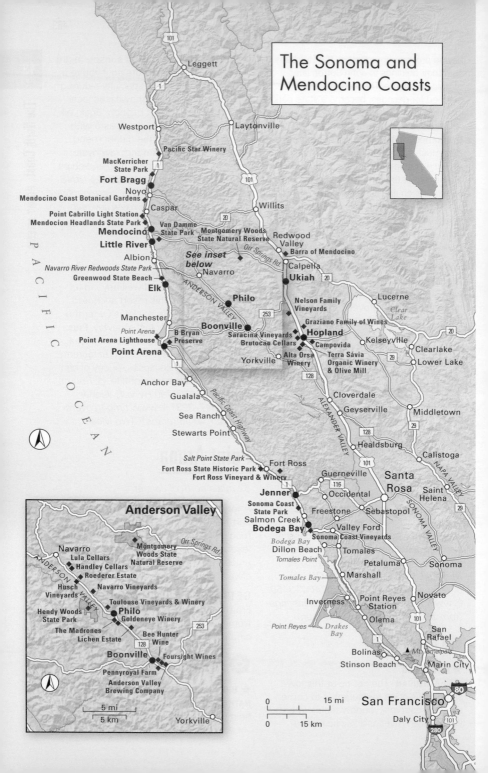

The Sonoma and Mendocino Coasts

Leggett

Westport

Laytonville

Pacific Star Winery

MacKerricher State Park
Fort Bragg
Noyo
Mendocino Coast Botanical Gardens
Caspar
Willits
Point Cabrillo Light Station
Mendocion Headlands State Park
Mendocino
Van Damme State Park
Montgomery Woods State Natural Reserve
Redwood Valley
Little River
Orr Springs Rd.
Barra of Mendocino
Albion
See inset below
Navarro
Calpella
Navarro River Redwoods State Park
Greenwood State Beach
Ukiah
Elk
ANDERSON VALLEY
Lucerne
Philo
Nelson Family Vineyards
Clear Lake
Manchester
Graziano Family of Wines
Point Arena Lighthouse
B Bryan Preserve
Boonville
Hopland
Kelseyville
Point Arena
Saracina Vineyards
Brutocao Cellars
Campovida
Clearlake
Yorkville
Alta Orsa Winery
Terra Sávia Organic Winery & Olive Mill
Lower Lake

PACIFIC OCEAN

Anchor Bay
Pacific Coast Highway
Cloverdale
Gualala
Geyserville
Middletown
Sea Ranch
Stewarts Point
ALEXANDER VALLEY
Healdsburg
Calistoga
Salt Point State Park
Fort Ross
NAPA VALLEY
Fort Ross State Historic Park
Fort Ross Vineyard & Winery
Guerneville
Santa Rosa
Jenner
Sonoma Coast State Park
Salmon Creek
Bodega Bay
Occidental
Freestone
Sebastopol
Saint Helena
SONOMA VALLEY
Bodega Bay
Dillon Beach
Valley Ford
Sonoma Coast Vineyards
Tomales Point
Tomales
Sonoma
Tomales Bay
Petaluma
Marshall
Inverness
Point Reyes Station
Novato
Point Reyes
Drakes Bay
Olema
San Rafael
Bolinas
Mt. Tamalpais
Stinson Beach
Marin City
San Francisco
Daly City

Anderson Valley

Navarro
Montgomery Woods State Natural Reserve
Lula Cellars
Handley Cellars
Roederer Estate
Orr Springs Rd.
Husch Vineyards
Navarro Vineyards
Toulouse Vineyards & Winery
Hendy Woods State Park
Philo
Goldeneye Winery
The Madrones
Bee Hunter Wine
Lichen Estate
Boonville
Foursight Wines
Pennyroyal Farm
Anderson Valley Brewing Company

5 mi
5 km

Yorkville

0   15 mi

0   15 km

spellbinding tours of this sanctuary for zebras, giraffes, antelopes, and other endangered African hoof stock. The self-guided tour in your own car costs less, but the guided one, slightly more expensive, is recommended for the personal touch and closer-up access and timing to giraffe-feeding time. ■ **TIP→ Reservations are a must for visits to the preserve, which maintains three cottages for overnight stays.** ✉ *130 Riverside Dr., Point Arena* ✣ *East of Main St.* ☎ *707/882–2297* 🌐 *www.bbryanpreserve.com* 🎟 *Tours from $25 (self-guided).*

★ Point Arena Lighthouse

LIGHTHOUSE | FAMILY | For an outstanding view of the ocean and, in winter, migrating whales, take the marked road off Highway 1 to this 115-foot lighthouse completed in 1908. On tours (last one at 3 pm), the 145-step climb rewards participants with a 360-degree panorama. The ground-level museum displays the original Fresnel lens and other maritime artifacts. ■ **TIP→ Six cottages with full kitchens can be booked for overnight stays.** ✉ *45500 Lighthouse Rd., Point Arena* ✣ *Off Hwy. 1* ☎ *707/882–2809, 877/725–4448* 🌐 *www.pointarenalighthouse.com* 🎟 *$5 site, $10 tour and site.*

🍴 Restaurants

★ Gama

$$$ | JAPANESE | Japanese gastropubs known as *izakaya* inspired the menu and ambience of this sedate wood-paneled restaurant serving pickle, sashimi, gyoza, miso soup, and *karaage* (fried chicken) appetizers and slightly larger skewered items that might include mushrooms, pork belly, various chicken parts, and Wagyu beef. The husband and wife owners contributed to top Northern California restaurants before embarking on this well-received venture. **Known for:** ramen night last Sunday of month; beers and sakes; vegan and gluten-free options. [$] *Average main: $31* ✉ *150 Main St., Point Arena* ☎ *707/485–9232* 🌐 *izakaya-gama.com* 🕒 *Closed Mon. and Tues. No lunch.*

☕ Coffee and Quick Bites

★ Franny's Cup and Saucer

$ | CAFÉ | FAMILY | Aided by her mother, Barbara, a former pastry chef at famed Chez Panisse in Berkeley, Franny, turns out sophisticated and inventive baked goods. Morning favorites include scones and sweet and savory pastries; there are fruit tarts and strawberry-apricot crisps, plus a mouthwatering assortment of cookies, candy, jams, and jellies for indulging anytime. **Known for:** dazzling specialty cakes; delightful ambience; cash-only, closes at noon on Sunday. [$] *Average main: $8* ✉ *213 Main St., Point Arena* ☎ *707/882–2500* 🌐 *www.frannyscupandsaucer.com* 💳 *No credit cards* 🕒 *Closed Mon. and Tues. No lunch Sun. No dinner.*

Elk

19 miles north of Point Arena, 17 miles south of Mendocino.

In this quiet town on the cliff above Greenwood Cove, just about every spot has a view of the rocky coastline and stunning Pacific sunsets. A few restaurants and inns do business here, but the main attraction is highly walkable Greenwood State Beach.

GETTING HERE AND AROUND

Elk is along Highway 1, 6 miles south of Highway 128. Mendocino Transit Authority buses serve Elk.

⛱ Beaches

Greenwood State Beach

BEACH | FAMILY | The easiest access to the sandy shore below Elk's cliff-top lodgings is at this state beach, whose parking lot sits across Highway 1 from the town's general store. A trail leads from the lot down to the shore, where the waves crashing against the huge offshore rocks are the perfect backdrop. **Amenities:** parking (no fee). **Good for:** sunset; walking. ✉ *6150 Hwy. 1, Elk* ☎ *707/937–5804* 🌐 *www.parks.ca.gov* 🎟 *Free.*

🍴 Restaurants

★ Greenwood Restaurant

$$$$ | **MODERN AMERICAN** | At the Sand Rock Inn's fine-dining restaurant, meals are served in intimate room with an open-truss ceiling, hardwood floors, and tables inlaid with abalone-shell fragments. The chef prepares seasonal California coastal cuisine based on garden-grown and foraged produce sourced from impeccable purveyors, and the menu usually includes duck, fish, beef, and vegetarian dishes. **Known for:** ocean views from some tables; wine list favors Mendocino County producers; Elk House steps away for elevated pub fare. [$] *Average main: $44* ✉ *5926 S. Hwy. 1, Elk* ☎ *707/877–3422* 🌐 *sacredrockinn.com/dining* 🕒 *Closed Wed. and Thurs. (but check).*

★ Harbor House Inn Restaurant

$$$$ | **MODERN AMERICAN** | The chef at this ocean-bluff inn's redwood-paneled dining room describes the Mendocino Coast's most intricate meal—an 8- to 12-course, prix-fixe extravaganza—as "hyperlocal" seasonal cuisine revolving around seafood and vegetables (many of the latter grown on-site). The artistry displayed in every dish lives up to the raves the restaurant has received from local and national food writers. **Known for:** breathtaking views; astute wine pairings; five-course prix-fixe lunch ($95). [$] *Average main: $295* ✉ *5600 S. Hwy. 1, Elk* ☎ *707/877–3203* 🌐 *theharborhouseinn.com/dine* 🕒 *Closed Tues. and Wed. (except in-room dinner for guests).*

☕ Coffee and Quick Bites

Elk Store

$ | **AMERICAN** | You'll often see cyclists sitting on benches outside Elk's general store, wolfing down well-made salads and deli sandwiches after scaling the coastal highway's hills. The staffers at this modest pit stop for all travelers are consistently welcoming, and the ocean views is a bonus. **Known for:** picnic fixings; beer and wine selection; bakery items. [$] *Average main: $14* ✉ *6101 S. Hwy. 1, Elk* ☎ *707/877–3544* 🌐 *www.theelkstore.com* 🕒 *Closed Tues. No dinner.*

🛏 Hotels

★ Elk Cove Inn & Spa

$$ | **B&B/INN** | Perched on a bluff above pounding surf and a driftwood-strewn beach, this property has stunning views from most of its accommodations, which include seven rooms, five suites, and four cottages. **Pros:** gorgeous views; filling breakfast included, optional French-inspired dinners (also available to nonguests as space permits); off-season specials and packages on website. **Cons:** rooms in main house are smallish; not suitable for young children; spa's massage calendar often full. [$] *Rooms from: $265* ✉ *6300 S. Hwy. 1, Elk* ☎ *707/877–3321, 800/275–2967* 🌐 *www.elkcoveinn.com* 🔑 *16 units* 🍽 *Free Breakfast.*

★ Harbor House Inn

$$$$ | **B&B/INN** | Prepare to be bowled over by every aspect of this showcase property with a rugged Pacific-cliff setting, destination restaurant, sterling hospitality, and luxurious accommodations in a 1916 redwood Craftsman-style house and a few newer cottages. **Pros:** romantic, ocean-view setting; luxurious base for wine tasting and outdoor activities; destination restaurant. **Cons:** not ideal for kids; 16 miles from Mendocino; best accommodations expensive for the area. [$] *Rooms from: $550* ✉ *5600 S. Hwy.*

1, Elk ☎ *707/877–3203, 800/720–7474* 🌐 *www.theharborhouseinn.com* 🛏 *11 rooms* 🍴 *Free Breakfast.*

★ Sacred Rock Inn

$$$ | HOTEL | A communal hot tub that seems to float above the crashing waves a few hundred feet below typifies the reorientation of this luxury resort, completed in 2023 after a half decade–plus of renovations, to its gasp-worthy setting. **Pros:** ocean views; varied room choices include cottages, inn rooms, and architecturally stunning multilevel units; Greenwood Restaurant for fine dining. **Cons:** on the expensive side; two-night minimum on weekends; one structure with four rooms must be booked whole. $ *Rooms from: $495* ✉ *5920 Hwy. 1, Elk* ☎ *707/877–3422* 🌐 *sacredrockinn.com* 🛏 *22 rooms* 🍴 *No Meals.*

Little River

13½ miles north of Elk.

The town of Little River is not much more than a post office and a convenience store; Albion, its neighbor to the south, is even smaller. Along winding Highway 1 you'll find numerous inns and restaurants, all situated to take advantage of the breathtaking ocean views.

GETTING HERE AND AROUND

Little River is along Highway 1, 7 miles north of Highway 128. Mendocino Transit Authority buses serve the area.

Sights

Van Damme State Park

STATE/PROVINCIAL PARK | FAMILY | Best known for its quiet beach, a prime diving spot, this park is also popular with day hikers. A ¼-mile stroll on a boardwalk leads to the bizarre Pygmy Forest, where acidic soil and poor drainage have produced mature cypress and pine trees no taller than a person. Hike the moderate 4¼-mile Pygmy Forest and Fern Canyon Loop past the forest and sword ferns that grow as tall as 4 feet. The visitor center has displays on ocean life and the historical significance of the redwood lumber industry along the coast. ✉ *Little River Park Rd., off Hwy. 1, Little River* ☎ *707/937–5804* 🌐 *www.parks.ca.gov* 🎟 *$8 per vehicle, walk-ins free (park at beach).*

Restaurants

Ledford House

$$$ | FRENCH | The only thing separating this bluff-top wood-and-glass restaurant from the Pacific Ocean is a great view. Entrées evoke the flavors of southern France and include hearty bistro dishes—stews, cassoulet, and pastas—and large portions of grilled meats and freshly caught fish (though the restaurant is also vegetarian friendly). **Known for:** outdoor deck; Mendocino-centric wine list; daily three-course bistro specials a true bargain. $ *Average main: $31* ✉ *3000 N. Hwy. 1, Albion* ☎ *707/937–0282* 🌐 *www.ledfordhouse.com* 🕒 *Closed Mon. and Tues. and late-Feb.–early Mar. and mid-Oct.–early Nov. No lunch.*

★ Little River Inn Restaurant

$$$ | AMERICAN | Straightforward seafood preparations and seasonal cocktails best sipped from the ocean-view Whale Watch Bar rank high among the pleasures of a visit to the Little River Inn resort, opened in 1939 and still run by members of the same family. Start with clam chowder, flash-fried calamari, or Dungeness crab cakes before settling into cioppino, the day's catch, or a steak. **Known for:** step-back-in-time feel; alfresco dining in garden courtyard; 67-room inn with varied accommodations from lodge rooms to cottages. $ *Average main: $31* ✉ *7901 N. Hwy. 1, Little River* ☎ *707/937–5942* 🌐 *littleriverinn.com* 🕒 *No lunch.*

Mendocino

3 miles north of Little River.

A flourishing logging town in the late-19th century, Mendocino seduces 21st-century travelers with windswept cliffs, phenomenal Pacific Ocean views, and boomtown-era New England–style architecture. Following the timber industry's mid-20th-century decline, artists and craftspeople began flocking here, and so did Hollywood: Mendocino served as a backdrop for *East of Eden* (1955), starring James Dean, and the town stood in for fictional Cabot Cove, Maine, in the TV series *Murder, She Wrote*. Today, shops, galleries, inns, and cafés predominate in the small downtown area.

GETTING HERE AND AROUND

Main Street is off Highway 1 about 10 miles north of Highway 128. Mendocino Transit Authority buses serve the area.

Sights

★ Mendocino Headlands State Park
STATE/PROVINCIAL PARK | FAMILY | A 3-mile, easy-to-walk trail leads across the spectacular seaside cliffs bordering Mendocino. The restored Ford House, built in 1854, serves as the visitor center for the park and the town. The house has a scale model of Mendocino as it looked in 1890, when it had 34 water towers and a 12-seat public outhouse. ✉ *45035 Main St., Mendocino* ☎ *707/937–5397* 🌐 *mendoparks.org/mendo-parks* 🎟 *Free.*

Point Cabrillo Light Station
STATE/PROVINCIAL PARK | FAMILY | Completed in 1909 and noteworthy for its original, third-order Fresnel lens that glows like a jewel day or night, the still-active station inhabits a breezy plateau 3 miles north of Mendocino village. Dirt and paved paths lead ½-mile downhill from the parking lot to the station. **■ TIP→ The lighthouse museum and other historic buildings are worth a peek if open, but the park merits a visit for its views alone.** ✉ *45300 Lighthouse Rd., Mendocino* ⊕ *Point Cabrillo Dr. off Hwy. 1* ☎ *707/937–6123* 🌐 *pointcabrillo.org* 🎟 *Park free, museum $5, lens tours $10.*

🍴 Restaurants

Cafe Beaujolais
$$ | AMERICAN | A garden of heirloom and exotic plantings surrounds this popular restaurant inside a yellow Victorian cottage. Local ingredients find their way into dishes that might include Oaxacan-style ceviche, smash burgers, pizzas from a wood-fired brick oven, fish and prawn tacos, beef bourguignon, and oven-roasted cauliflower with house-made mole verde. **Known for:** garden dining in fine weather; bowls and other vegan and vegetarian selections; "Waiting Room" for morning pastries and other grab-and-go fare. [$] *Average main: $28* ✉ *961 Ukiah St., Mendocino* ☎ *707/937–5614* 🌐 *www.cafebeaujolais.com* 🕒 *Closed Mon. and Tues.*

Fog Eater Cafe
$$ | VEGETARIAN | The culinary influences are Deep South and Californian at this vegetarian (mostly vegan) restaurant with salmon-color walls, teal tables, and white trim. The chefs' flair for the dramatic might exhibit itself in carrot-cake waffles at Sunday brunch, hush puppies and beet-dyed deviled eggs as happy-hour nibbles, and dinnertime fried-green-tomato biscuit sliders and Mississippi Delta–style hot tamales. **Known for:** all-organic Mendocino and Sonoma produce; outdoor dining; natural wines and local beers. [$] *Average main: $20* ✉ *45104 Main St., at Albion St., Mendocino* ☎ *707/397–1806* 🌐 *fogeatercafe.com* 🕒 *Closed Mon. and Tues. No lunch Wed.–Sat. No dinner Sun.*

Trillium Cafe
$$$ | AMERICAN | The term "light rustic" applies equally well to this comely café's decor—plank flooring, wood-top tables,

gas fireplace with a brick hearth—and its cuisine, which emphasizes local produce and seafood. The menu changes seasonally, with the grilled flatbread, albacore appetizer, Point Reyes blue cheese salad, and grilled organic pork chop among the year-round crowd-pleasers. **Known for:** outdoor patio area with garden and ocean views; wine list favoring Northern California wines, particularly Mendocino; organic grass-fed meats. $ *Average main: $33* ⊠ *10390 Kasten St., Mendocino* ☎ *707/937–3200* ⊕ *www.trilliummendocino.com* ☽ *Closed Wed. and Thurs. (but check).*

Hotels

★ Brewery Gulch Inn

$$ | **B&B/INN** | The feel is modern yet tasteful at this inn with stained-wood and leather furnishings and plush beds; two rooms have whirlpool tubs with views, and there's a stand-alone cottage. The luxury is in tune with the surrounding nature. **Pros:** luxury in tune with nature; peaceful ocean views; complimentary wine hour and light dinner buffet. **Cons:** a mile from Mendocino village; expensive in-season; two-night minimum on weekends. $ *Rooms from: $425* ⊠ *9401 N. Hwy. 1, Mendocino* ☎ *707/937–4752, 800/578–4454* ⊕ *www.brewerygulchinn.com* ☞ *12 rooms* ⓄⓁ *Free Breakfast.*

Inns of Mendocino

$$ | **B&B/INN** | Each of the three Victorian properties managed by California-based Four Sisters Inns has its appeal—Blue Door for its garden, Packard House for its serene setting, JD House for its ocean views—with all three worth consideration for their proximity to restaurants, shops, and the Mendocino Headlands. **Pros:** historic properties with modern decor; service-oriented staff; range of prices and room types. **Cons:** some rooms are on the small side; lacks personal touch of on-site owner-inn-keeper; two-night minimum for all stays. $ *Rooms from: $265* ⊠ *10481 Howard St., Mendocino* ☎ *707/937–4892* ⊕ *www.innsofmendocino.com* ☞ *19 rooms* ⓄⓁ *Free Breakfast.*

MacCallum House

$$ | **HOTEL** | A historic boutique property set on 2 flower-filled acres in the middle of town, MacCallum House strikes the perfect balance between Victorian charm and modern luxury. **Pros:** 10 modern luxury suites a few blocks away; private outdoor hot tub or a sauna-equipped bathroom in some rooms; outstanding restaurant. **Cons:** cottages and rooms in main house less luxurious than others (though a good bargain); some rooms pick up street noise; two-night minimum on weekends. $ *Rooms from: $239* ⊠ *45020 Albion St., Mendocino* ☎ *707/937–0289, 800/609–0492* ⊕ *www.maccallumhouse.com* ☞ *29 rooms* ⓄⓁ *Free Breakfast.*

Stanford Inn by the Sea

$$$ | **HOTEL** | This woodsy yet luxurious family-run property a few minutes south of town feels like the Northern California version of an old-time summer resort but with an ecologically friendly twist. **Pros:** lovely grounds; on-site bike and kayak rentals; plant-based cuisine. **Cons:** minimum two-night stay some weekends (three if a holiday); carnivores may find all-vegan menus challenging (or not); many rooms lack ocean views. $ *Rooms from: $351* ⊠ *44850 Comptche Ukiah Rd., Mendocino* ☎ *707/937–5615, 800/331–8884* ⊕ *www.stanfordinn.com* ☞ *41 rooms* ⓄⓁ *Free Breakfast.*

▼ Nightlife

Patterson's Pub

BARS | An Irish-style watering hole, Patterson's is a friendly if occasionally boisterous gathering place, with good pub grub and nearly two dozen beers on tap. ⊠ *10485 Lansing St., Mendocino* ☎ *707/937–4782* ⊕ *www.pattersonspub.com.*

Shopping

Highlight Gallery

ART GALLERIES | The Highlight exhibits artworks and crafts in various media, along with exquisite handmade furniture, much of it by Mendocino County wood-workers. ⊠ *45094 Main St., Mendocino* ☎ *707/937–3132* ⊕ *www.thehighlightgallery.com.*

Mendo Vino

WINE/SPIRITS | Find out what makes Mendocino County wines special at this shop and tasting space, whose owner enthusiastically supports area boutique producers. Enter through the Mendocino Country Store, which sells local and regional food, crafts, and art. ⊠ *10481 Lansing St., Mendocino* ☎ *707/397–1414* ⊕ *mendovino.org.*

 ## Activities

Catch-A-Canoe and Bicycles Too

KAYAKING | **FAMILY** | Rent kayaks and regular or outrigger canoes here year-round, as well as mountain and suspension bicycles. The outfit's tours explore Big River and its 8-mile estuary. ⊠ *Stanford Inn by the Sea, 1 S. Big River Rd., Mendocino* ⊹ *Off Hwy. 1, 1 mile south of town* ☎ *707/937–0273* ⊕ *www.catchacanoe. com* ⬚ *From $55.*

Fort Bragg

10 miles north of Mendocino.

Fort Bragg is a working-class town many feel is the most authentic place on the coast. The city maintains a local vibe since most people who work at the area hotels and restaurants also live here, as do many artists and commercial anglers. The pleasures of a visit are mainly outdoors, a stroll through the botanical gardens or along the town's coastal trail, touring by train or boat, tide-pooling or fishing at the state park, or tasting wine within steps of the ocean.

GETTING HERE AND AROUND

Highway 20 winds west 33 miles from Willits to Highway 1 just south of Fort Bragg. Mendocino Transit Authority buses serve the town.

 ## Sights

Fort Bragg Coastal Trail

TRAIL | **FAMILY** | A multiuse path, much of it flat and steps from the rocky and highly photogenic shoreline, stretches the length of Fort Bragg. An enjoyable section lined with benches created by local artists follows the coast north about 2 miles between Noyo Headlands Park in southern Fort Bragg and Glass Beach. You can continue into MacKerricher State Park from the beach. ⊠ *Fort Bragg* ⊹ *Noyo Headlands Park, W. Cypress St. off S. Main St. (Hwy. 1); Glass Beach, W. Elm St. off N. Main St.* ⬚ *Free.*

★ **Mendocino Coast Botanical Gardens**

GARDEN | Something beautiful is always abloom in these marvelous gardens. Along 4 miles of trails, including pathways with ocean views and observation points for whale-watching, lie a profusion of flowers. The rhododendrons are at their peak from April through June; the dahlias begin their spectacular show in July and last through September. In winter, the heather and camellias add more than a splash of color. The main trails are wheelchair accessible. ⊠ *18220 N. Hwy. 1, 2 miles south of Fort Bragg, Fort Bragg* ☎ *707/964–4352* ⊕ *www.gardenbythesea.org* ⬚ *$20.*

Pacific Star Winery

WINERY | When the sun's out and you're sipping wine while viewing whales or other sea creatures swimming offshore, this bluff-top winery's outdoor tasting spaces feel mystical and magical, but the site's equally beguiling on brooding stormy days. The engaging owner-winemaker, Sally Ottoson, makes whites that include Viognier and Semillon. Charbono, Sangiovese, Tempranillo, and a Zinfandel, Barbera, Charbono, and Petite Sirah blend count among the reds. Walk-ins are welcome. ✉ *33000 N. Hwy. 1, Fort Bragg ✣ 12 miles north of downtown* ☎ *707/964–1155* 🌐 *www.pacificstarwinery.com* 🎫 *Tastings from $14* 🕒 *Closed Mon.–Thurs. (but check).*

Skunk Train and Rail Bikes

TRAIN/TRAIN STATION | FAMILY | A reproduction train travels a few miles of the route of its 1920s predecessor, a fume-spewing gas-powered motorcar that shuttled passengers along a rail line dating from the 1880s logging days. Nicknamed the Skunk Train, the original traversed redwood forests inaccessible to automobiles. There are also excursions from the town of Willits and seasonal and holiday-theme tours.

■ **TIP→ For a separate fee you can pedal the same rails as the Skunk Train on two-person, side-by-side, reclining bikes outfitted for the track, an experience many patrons find more diverting (albeit pricier) than the train trip.** ✉ *100 W. Laurel St., at Main St., Fort Bragg* ☎ *707/964–6371* 🌐 *www.skunktrain.com* 🎫 *Train rides from $54; rail bikes from $265 for 2 people (no single-rider fee)* 🕒 *Days, hrs vary; call or check website.*

Beaches

MacKerricher State Park

STATE/PROVINCIAL PARK | FAMILY | This park starts at Glass Beach, its draw an unfortunately dwindling supply of sea glass best spotted at low tide. Beginning with rocky headlands that taper into dunes and sandy beaches, MacKerricher stretches north for 9 miles, its cliff tops excellent for whale-watching from November through April. Fishing, canoeing, hiking, tide-pooling, jogging, bicycling, beachcombing, camping, and harbor seal watching at Laguna Point are among the popular activities, many accessible to the mobility-impaired. ⚠ **Be vigilant for rogue waves—don't turn your back on the sea. Amenities:** parking; toilets. **Best for:** solitude; sunset; walking. ✉ *24100 MacKerricher Park Rd., Fort Bragg* ✣ *Off Hwy. 1, 3 miles north of town* ☎ *707/937–5804* 🌐 *www.parks.ca.gov* 🎫 *Free.*

🍴 Restaurants

KW SaltWater Grill

$$$ | SEAFOOD | The chef at this small downtown restaurant with a clean but no-nonsense decor serves fresh-off-the-boat seafood, some caught locally but never too far afield. The emphasis on letting the main ingredient speak for itself extends to the meats and produce, which come from respected area purveyors. **Known for:** Dungeness crab several ways when in season; raw oyster bar; shareable "Seafood Charcuterie Platter" starter with oysters, tempura, ceviche, mussels or clams, and smoked fish. [$] *Average main: $39* ✉ *542 N. Main St., Ft. Bragg* ☎ *707/900–1667* 🌐 *kw-saltwater-grill.squarespace.com* 🕒 *Closed Mon. No lunch.*

Mayan Fusion

$$ | MEXICAN FUSION | The tastefully eclectic Mayan decor at this restaurant near the Skunk Train depot hints at the layers of complexity in the Yucatán-inflected cuisine based on the chef-owner's family recipes. Tamales, empanadas, sweet Mexican corn, fish tacos, and pork slow-roasted in banana leaves form the menu's backbone, with pork osso buco and the meatless, mildly spicy Thai burrito (or add coconut prawns) typical of the fusion plays. **Known for:** family restaurant vibe; Mayan clam chowder and Yucatán cioppino; mojitos, margaritas, and other specialty drinks. [$] *Average main: $26* ✉ *418 N. Main St., Fort Bragg* ✣ *Near E. Laurel St.* ☎ *707/961–0211* 🌐 *www.mayanfusion.com.*

Noyo River Grill

$$ | **SEAFOOD** | The Noyo River Bridge looms high above this family-owned harborside restaurant, whose outdoor tables have views of the river emptying (via Noyo Bay) into the Pacific. No surprises with the straightforward, beer-friendly, seafood-oriented cuisine—fried calamari, fish-and-chips, prawns scampi, and the like—but it's executed well, especially the grilled local salmon. **Known for:** harbor-watching from outdoor tables; po'boys and homemade tacos at lunch; shellfish apps at lunch and dinner. *Average main: $23 ✉ 32150 N. Harbor Dr., Fort Bragg ✣ Off S. Main St. (Hwy. 1) almost 1 mile, rear of Snug Harbor Resort ☎ 707/962–9050 🌐 www.noyorivergrill.com ⏲ Closed Thurs.*

★ Princess Seafood Restaurant

$ | **SEAFOOD** | Captain Heather Sears leads her all-woman crew of "girls gone wild for wild-caught seafood" that heads oceanward on the *Princess* troller, returning with some of the seafood served at their harbor-view restaurant under the Noyo River Bridge. Chowder, crab or lobster bisque, crab rolls, shrimp po'boys, raw or barbecued oysters, and seasonal wild seafood plates that might include sablefish, salmon, rock cod, or prawns count among the stars here. **Known for:** fresh, sustainable seafood; dozen beers on tap; crew members who clearly love their jobs. *Average main: $19 ✉ 32096 N. Harbor Dr., Fort Bragg ✣ Off S. Main St. (Hwy. 1) about 1 mile (¼-mile past Princess market) ☎ 707/962–3046 🌐 fvprincess.com/p/the-res ⏲ Closed Mon.–Wed.*

Coffee and Quick Bites

Cowlick's Ice Cream

$ | **AMERICAN** | **FAMILY** | Candy-cap mushroom (tastes like maple syrup) and black raspberry chocolate chunk are among this fun ice-cream shop's top-selling flavors. Chocolate, mocha almond fudge, and ginger appear year-round, supplemented by blackberry-cheesecake, pumpkin, eggnog, and other seasonal offerings. **Known for:** handmade ice cream; chai, yellow-cake batter, and other wiggy flavors; sodas, sundaes, and root-beer floats. *Average main: $7 ✉ 250 N. Main St., Fort Bragg ☎ 707/962–9271 🌐 www.cowlicksicecream.com.*

Hotels

★ The Inn at Newport Ranch

$$$$ | **B&B/INN** | Attention to detail in design and hospitality makes for an incomparable stay at this 2,000-acre working cattle ranch with 1½ miles of private coastline. **Pros:** mesmerizing Pacific views; superb on-site chef; UTV ranch tour, 25 miles of hiking, jogging, and horseback trails. **Cons:** all this design and glamour comes at a price; lengthy drive back from Mendocino and Fort Bragg restaurants at night; coast can be foggy in summer. *Rooms from: $650 ✉ 31502 N. Hwy. 1, Fort Bragg ☎ 707/962–4818 🌐 theinnatnewportranch.com ⇨ 10 rooms 🍽 Free Breakfast.*

★ Noyo Harbor Inn

$$ | **HOTEL** | Craftsman touches abound in this luxury inn's lavishly restored 1868 main structure, which overlooks Noyo Harbor, and in a nearby newer wing with Pacific Ocean views. **Pros:** landscaped grounds; warm service; brunch or dinner on harbor-view deck. **Cons:** barking of sea lions in harbor at certain times of year; expensive during high season; some rooms lack water views. *Rooms from: $295 ✉ 500 Casa del Noyo Dr., Fort Bragg ☎ 707/961–8000 🌐 noyoharborinn.com ⇨ 15 rooms 🍽 No Meals.*

Surf and Sand Lodge

$ | **HOTEL** | As its name implies, this six-building, two-story property, whose owners run two similar lodgings nearby, sits practically on the beach; pathways lead from the accommodations down to the rock-strewn shore. **Pros:** beach location; gorgeous sunsets from decks and patios of ocean-side rooms; very affordable in the off-season. **Cons:** motel style; no restaurants close by; least expensive rooms lack view. $ *Rooms from: $179* ⊠ *1131 N. Main St., Fort Bragg* ☎ *707/964–9383* ⊕ *www.surfsandlodge.com* ↝ *30 rooms* ⊙*I No Meals.*

Nightlife

Overtime Brewing

BREWPUBS | Murals depicting logging, fishing, and other local industries adorn the walls of this small-batch brewery opened by two childhood pals. You'll find the expected range of ale types, along with novelties like the Jasmine Green Tea Ale and Overkill Chocolate Raspberry Imperial Stout. ⊠ *190 E. Elm St., Fort Bragg* ☎ *707/962–3040* ⊕ *www.overtimebrewing.com* ⊙ *Closed Sun. and Mon.*

Activities

All Aboard Adventures

WILDLIFE-WATCHING | FAMILY | Captain Tim of All Aboard operates whale-watching trips from late December through April. He also heads out to sea on fishing excursions. ⊠ *Noyo Harbor, 32410 N. Harbor Dr., Fort Bragg* ☎ *707/964–1881* ⊕ *www.allaboardadventures.com* ↝ *$50 whale-watching, $120 fishing.*

★ Noyo Harbor Tours with Captain Dan

WILDLIFE-WATCHING | FAMILY | The genial Captain Dan has piloted commercial fishing boats on the high seas, but for his gentle tours of Noyo Harbor from the river up to (but not into) the ocean, he ordered a custom-built, 18-foot, eco-friendly Duffy electric boat. Having been in Fort Bragg for decades, he knows everyone and everyone's story, including those of the harbor seals, sea lions, birds, and other wildlife you'll see on his excursion. ⊠ *32399 Basin St., Fort Bragg* ✣ *From S. Main St. (Hwy. 1), take Hwy. 20 east ¼ mile, S. Harbor Dr. north ¼ mile, and Basin St. northeast 1 mile*

☎ *707/734–0044* ⊕ *www.noyoharbortours.com* ↝ *From $35.*

Ricochet Ridge Ranch

HORSEBACK RIDING | FAMILY | Come here for private and group trail rides through the redwood forest and on the beach. ⊠ *24201 N. Hwy. 1, Fort Bragg* ☎ *707/964–7669, 888/873–5777* ⊕ *www.horse-vacation.com* ↝ *From $65.*

Philo

43 miles southeast of Fort Bragg, 34 miles southeast of Mendocino, 5 miles northwest of Boonville.

Many wineries straddle Highway 128 in Philo, where the tasting rooms are more low-key than their counterparts in Napa. The wineries here, however, produce world-class Pinot Noirs, Chardonnays, Rieslings, and Gewürztraminers, whose grapes thrive in the moderate coastal climate.

GETTING HERE AND AROUND

Take Highway 128 east from Highway 1 and west from Boonville to Philo. Mendocino Transit Authority buses serve the area.

Sights

Goldeneye Winery

WINERY | Established in 1996 by the founders of what's now The Duckhorn Portfolio, Goldeneye makes Pinot Noirs from estate grapes, along with a Brut Rosé sparkling wine, Gewürztraminer, and a blush Vin Gris of Pinot Noir. Leisurely tastings, some by appointment only, take place in a restored farmhouse or on a patio with vineyard views. ⊠ *9200 Hwy. 128, Philo* ☎ *800/208–0438, 707/895–3202* ⊕ *www.goldeneyewinery.com* ↝ *Tastings from $25.*

Handley Cellars

WINERY | International folk art collected by founding winemaker the late Milla Handley adorns the tasting room at this

Anderson Valley pioneer, whose lightly oaked Chardonnays and Pinot Noirs earn high praise from wine critics. The winery, which has an arbored outdoor patio picnic area, also makes Gewürztraminer, Pinot Gris, Riesling, Zinfandel, sparklers, and several others. ⊠ *3151 Hwy. 128, Philo* ☎ *707/895–3876* ⊕ *www.handleycellars.com* ᴸ *Tastings from $20.*

Hendy Woods State Park

STATE/PROVINCIAL PARK | FAMILY | Two groves of ancient redwoods accessible via short trails from the parking lot are the main attractions at this 945-acre park also perfect for a picnic. ⊠ *18599 Greenwood Rd., Philo* ✛ *½ mile southwest of Hwy. 128* ☎ *707/895–3141* ⊕ *www.hendywoods.org* ᴸ *$8 per vehicle.*

Husch Vineyards

WINERY | A century-old former pony barn houses the tasting room of the Anderson Valley's oldest winery. Founded in 1968, Husch prides itself on its conservation efforts in the vineyard and winery. Wines of note include Gewürztraminer, Chardonnay, Pinot Noir, and old-vine Zinfandel. You can picnic on the deck or at tables under grape arbors. ⊠ *4400 Hwy. 128, Philo* ☎ *800/554–8724* ⊕ *www.huschvineyards.com* ᴸ *Tastings free.*

★ Lula Cellars

WINERY | Fun, relaxing, and pet-friendly Lula is among the Anderson Valley wineries closest to the coast. Lula produces Chardonnay, Gewürztraminer, Sauvignon Blanc, rosé of Pinot Noir, Cabernet Sauvignon, Zinfandel, and a red blend, but the several Pinot Noirs, each flavorful and with its own personality, are the highlights. ⊠ *2800 Guntly Rd., at Hwy. 128, Philo* ☎ *707/895–3737* ⊕ *www.lulacellars.com* ᴸ *Tastings from $15* ◷ *Closed Tues. and Wed.*

The Madrones

OTHER ATTRACTION | Expand your palate and perhaps your mind at this engaging complex. Chardonnay and Pinot Noir from Anderson Valley grapes are the focus at the Long Meadow Ranch tasting room. The decorous, 1920s-inspired Bohemian Chemist bills itself as a "curated cannabis apothecary" for quality sun-grown marijuana products. Sun & Cricket Curiosity Shoppe next door carries clever and whimsical gifts. The chef at Wickson incorporates local ingredients into his Iberian-inspired cuisine. ⊠ *9000 Hwy. 128, Philo* ☎ *707/895–2955* ⊕ *www.themadrones.com* ◷ *Days closed vary.*

Navarro Vineyards

WINERY | A visit to this family-run winery that opened in 1974 is a classic Anderson Valley experience, with tastings in fine weather on several perches overlooking sustainably farmed vineyards. Best known for Alsatian varietals such as Gewürztraminer and Riesling, Navarro also makes Chardonnay, Pinot Noir, and other wines. ⊠ *5601 Hwy. 128, Philo* ☎ *707/895–3686, 800/537–9463* ⊕ *www.navarrowine.com* ᴸ *Tastings free.*

Roederer Estate

WINERY | The Anderson Valley is particularly hospitable to Pinot Noir and Chardonnay grapes, the two varietals used to create Roederer's sparkling wines. The view of vineyards and rolling hills from the patio is splendid. ⊠ *4501 Hwy. 128, Philo* ☎ *707/895–2288* ⊕ *www.roedererestate.com* ᴸ *Tastings from $25.*

Toulouse Vineyards & Winery

WINERY | The view west across the Anderson Valley from this winery's tasting room and deck is captivating enough to warrant a visit, but the wines don't disappoint either. Tastings begin with whites that might include Pinot Gris, Riesling, or Gewürztraminer—there's also a rosé of Pinot Noir that sells out quickly each spring—followed by Pinot Noir from estate and sourced fruit and perhaps another red. ⊠ *8001 Hwy. 128, Philo* ☎ *707/895–2828* ⊕ *www.toulousevineyards.com* ᴸ *Tastings $20.*

Restaurants

Wickson Restaurant

$$$ | MODERN AMERICAN | A wood-fired oven anchors the small kitchen of this contempo-rustic restaurant, whose chef references the Iberian peninsula in entrées that might include seafood *cataplana* (a fisherman's stew in the cioppino vein) or port-braised short ribs. Small offerings like marinated olives, house-baked focaccia, mushroom (cultivated and foraged) bisque, and imported tinned seafood served with hot sauce whet the appetite for the main event. **Known for:** Iberian Caesar with anchovies; Monday-night pizzas to go; alfresco lunch on the patio. $ *Average main: $38* ⊠ *The Madrones, 9000 Hwy. 128, Philo* ☎ *707/895–2955* ⊕ *wicksonrestaurant. com* ⊗ *Closed Tues. and Wed. (but check). No lunch Mon. and Thurs.*

🛏 Hotels

★ The Madrones Guest Quarters

$$ | B&B/INN | The centerpiece of a 2-acre spread that includes tasting rooms, a gift shop, an apothecary-style cannabis dispensary, and a restaurant, this property has nine eclectically decorated accommodations that range from apartment-like studios to duplex cottages, some with patios or balconies facing landscaped gardens. **Pros:** location near wineries and Hendy Woods State Park; on-site Wickson Restaurant; nearby sister property The Brambles set among redwoods for a more casual experience. **Cons:** weekend minimum-stay requirement; pricey on summer weekends; yogurt, cereal, and coffee/tea provided in-room but no breakfast served. $ *Rooms from: $255* ⊠ *9000 Hwy. 128, Philo* ☎ *707/895–2955* ⊕ *www.themadrones.com* ⇌ *9 rooms* ⏉ *No Meals.*

The Philo Apple Farm

$$$ | HOTEL | Relatives of the family that owns the Boonville Hotel are involved in this farm with three inviting cottages and one guest room set in an organic heirloom apple orchard. **Pros:** contemporary touches in cottages and room; working farm; relaxing back-to-nature experience. **Cons:** occasionally hot in summer; few "activities"; no phones or TVs in rooms (Wi-Fi in common areas). $ *Rooms from: $375* ⊠ *18501 Greenwood Rd., Philo* ☎ *707/895–2333* ⊕ *www.philoapplefarm. com* ⇌ *4 rooms* ⏉ *Free Breakfast.*

Boonville

6 miles southeast of Philo, 28 miles west of Hopland.

At first glance Boonville, population a little more than 1,000, looks pretty much as it has for decades, with the 19th-century Boonville Hotel anchoring the few blocks downtown and sheep farms and fruit orchards fanning out on either side of Highway 128, albeit with more grapevines these days. The founding of the Anderson Valley Brewing Company in the late 1990s and the revitalization of the hotel by its current owners, the Schmitt family, jump-started the community's transformation into a haven of artisanal food, wine, and beer. Despite this, the town retains its old-school character—listen carefully and you may hear fragments of the academically recognized Boontling argot, which dates to when this stretch of the valley was even more isolated.

GETTING HERE AND AROUND

Boonville lies along Highway 128 at its junction with Highway 253. Mendocino Transit Authority buses serve the area.

Sights

Anderson Valley Brewing Company

BREWERY | Brewery tours, tastings, and cornhole, boccie, and disc golf provide an entertaining, diversified, and mainly outdoor experience at the home of Boont Amber Ale, double and triple Belgian-style ales, and other brews. Local winemakers clear their palates with the Bourbon Barrel Stout, aged in Tennessee whiskey barrels. ✉ *17700 Hwy. 253, at Hwy. 128, Boonville* ☎ *707/895–2337* 🌐 *www.avbc.com* 🎫 *Tastings from $14.*

Bee Hunter Wine

WINERY | Winemaker Andy DuVigneaud of Bee Hunter prefers vineyards close to the ocean because the cool climate requires grapes to stay longer on the vine, preventing them from ripening before their flavors fully develop. His delicious output, poured with enthusiasm in a former car repair shop, includes Sauvignon Blanc, Chardonnay, dry Riesling, rosé of Pinot Noir, several Pinot Noirs, and a few other reds. ✉ *14251 Hwy. 128, Boonville* ☎ *707/895–3995* 🌐 *www.beehunterwine.com* 🎫 *Tastings from $30.*

★ Foursight Wines

WINERY | Four generations of the Charles family have farmed the land that produces this winery's vegan-friendly, all-estate lineup of Sauvignon Blanc, Semillon, Vin Gris of Pinot Noir (aka rosé), and Pinot Noir. With the Pinots, winemaker Joe Webb employs various techniques to produce four very different wines, from the light Zero, aged solely in used oak barrels, to the "richer, riper" Paraboll, its flavors heightened by new French oak. **■ TIP→ After a tasting, you can picnic outside the casual wood-frame tasting room, enjoying a glass or bottle.** ✉ *14475 Hwy. 128, Boonville* ☎ *707/895–2889* 🌐 *www.foursightwines.com* 🎫 *Tastings $20* ⏲ *Closed Tues. and some days in Jan. and June.*

★ Lichen Estate

WINERY | Vintner Douglas Stewart takes pride in his contrarian views about farming and winemaking. Bucking accepted California wisdom, he planted his vines tightly together, mimicking French practices, and with his sparkling wine—of Pinot Gris rather than Chardonnay and/or Pinot Noir—he selects only the high-quality middle portion of the initial press. Stewart earned raves from influential critics and a loyal following for his initial Pinot Gris and later for two sparklers, a rosé, and several Pinot Noirs. ✉ *11001 County Rd. 151, at Hwy. 128, Boonville* ☎ *707/895–7949* 🌐 *www.lichenestate.com* 🎫 *Tastings from $25.*

★ Pennyroyal Farm

WINERY | FAMILY | At this ranch with a contemporary-barn tasting room and vineyard-view patio, you can sample Sauvignon Blanc, velvety Pinot Noirs, and other wines paired with award-winning artisanal cheeses made on the premises from goat and sheep milk. Engaging farmstead tours pass through the barn and by the creamery; the adorable animals win most guests' hearts. Reservations are required for the tour and suggested for tastings, though walk-ins for the latter are accepted when possible. ✉ *14930 Hwy. 128, Boonville* ☎ *707/895–2410* 🌐 *www.pennyroyalfarm.com* 🎫 *Tastings from $25* ⏲ *Closed Tues. and Wed.*

🍴 Restaurants

Lauren's at the Buckhorn

$ | AMERICAN | FAMILY | Boonville locals and frequent visitors love Lauren's for its down-home vibe and well-sourced comfort food—vegetarian and ground-beef burgers, hand-cut fries, chicken tostadas, fish-and-chips, and Thai-curry bowls. Chocolate brownies and (seasonally) apple tarts and honey-baked pears are among the desserts worth a trip on their own. **Known for:** "made-from-scratch American-International cooking"; many ingredients grown or produced nearby; Taco Tuesdays with half-price margaritas. [$] *Average main: $18* ✉ *14081 Hwy. 128, Boonville* ☎ *707/895–3869* 🌐 *laurensgoodfood.com* ⏲ *No lunch Tues.–Thurs.*

★ Restaurant at The Boonville Hotel

$$$$ | AMERICAN | This stylishly funky restaurant's chef, Perry Hoffman, got his start (at age five) working in the kitchen of Napa Valley's The French Laundry, which his grandmother founded and later sold to Thomas Keller. As an adult, Hoffman made a name for himself at three highly praised Napa and Sonoma spots before returning to Boonville in 2019 to prepare prix-fixe, California farm-to-table cuisine (including a few original French Laundry dishes) at his extended family's hotel. **Known for:** many ingredients grown on-site or nearby; superior protein sources; alfresco patio dining. $ *Average main: $75* ✉ *Boonville Hotel, 14050 Hwy. 128, Boonville* ☎ *707/895–2210* ⊕ *www. boonvillehotel.com/eat* ⊗ *Closed Mon.– Thurs. Nov.–Apr., closed Tues. and Wed. May–Oct. No lunch.*

☕ Coffee and Quick Bites

Disco Ranch Wine Bar + Specialty Market
$ | **WINE BAR** | In a rough-hewn structure that, for years, housed a beloved coffee haunt called the Horn of Zeese—the local "Boontling" lingo for a cup (horn) of coffee (zeese)—international wine expert Wendy Lamer operates this combination wine bar and gourmet mini-mart. Well versed in the local wine scene and generous with advice, she pours wines by the glass or bottle and serves up sliders and other "disco snacks." **Known for:** wines by Anderson Valley producers without tasting rooms; European and other wines complementing local selection; good stop for light lunch. $ *Average main: $8* ✉ *14025 Hwy. 128, Boonville* ☎ *707/901– 5002* ⊕ *www.discoranch.com* ⊗ *Closed Tues. and Wed. No dinner.*

Mosswood Market Café and Bakery
$ | **AMERICAN** | **FAMILY** | Pastries for breakfast; wraps, salads, hot soup, and sandwiches for lunch; and espresso drinks all day make this sweet café in downtown Boonville a fine stop for a quick bite. Order at the counter and enjoy your meal—the oven-roasted turkey and chicken mango wraps and Reuben and albacore tuna sandwiches are among the lunchtime choices—at tables inside or out front. **Known for:** empanadas;

Danishes and scones; vegan options. $ *Average main: $15* ✉ *14111 Hwy. 128, Boonville* ☎ */07/895–3635* ⊕ *www. mosswoodmarketcafe.com* ⊗ *Closed Sun. No dinner.*

Hotels

★ The Boonville Hotel
$$ | **HOTEL** | From the street, this looks like a standard small-town hotel with nine freestanding cottages and a two-room, two-story building in the back garden, but once you cross the threshold you begin to sense the laid-back sophistication that makes the entire Anderson Valley so appealing. **Pros:** stylish yet homey; beautiful gardens and grounds; restaurant's excellent prix-fixe meals. **Cons:** minimum-stay requirement most weekends; no TVs or phones, no a/c in some rooms; some rooms or days of week require one booking at restaurant. $ *Rooms from: $255* ✉ *14050 Hwy. 128, Boonville* ☎ *707/895–2210* ⊕ *www.boonvillehotel. com* ⇨ *17 rooms* ⏹ *Free Breakfast*

Hopland

28 miles east of Boonville, 14 miles south of Ukiah, 32 miles north of Healdsburg.

U.S. 101 briefly narrows to one lane in each direction to become this small town's main drag. For many years a center for the cultivation and drying of beer hops—the source of its name—Hopland these days is a center of grape growing and wine making. In-town tasting rooms of note include Blue Quail, Brutocao, and Graziano; venture into the countryside to visit Alta Orsa, Campovida, Saracina, and Terra Sávia.

GETTING HERE AND AROUND
Car travelers from Sonoma and Humboldt counties arrive in Hopland via U.S. 101. Highway 253 will get you here from

You'll find excellent wines and great places to taste them in the laid-back Anderson Valley.

Boonville. Mendocino Transit Authority buses serve the area.

ESSENTIALS
VISITOR INFORMATION Destination Hopland. ☎ 707/564–2582 ⊕ www.facebook.com/DestinationHopland.

 Sights

★ Alta Orsa Winery

WINERY | Lofty valley views and deftly crafted wines, the latter often sipped under a cork oak, are among this 160-acre boutique winery's lures. The vineyard team uses "regenerative" techniques such as no-till farming, which increases the soil's organic matter, to grow Cabernet Sauvignon, Merlot, and Syrah. Winemaker Martin Bernal-Hafner taps Sonoma County sources for Chardonnay and Pinot Noir. Reservations are a must. ⊠ 1850 Duncan Springs Rd., Hopland ✛ La Franchi Rd. off U.S. 101 ☎ 707/540–4311 ⊕ www.orsawines.com ⊠ Tastings free ☉ Closed weekends.

Brutocao Cellars

WINERY | Family-owned Brutocao produces Sauvignon Blanc, Zinfandel, Merlot, and Cabernet Sauvignon along with Chardonnay and Pinot Noir. Some of these wines, plus ones from Italian varietals like Sangiovese and Primitivo, are poured in Hopland's 1925 former high school building, whose outdoor areas have picnic tables and regulation boccie courts. ⊠ 13500 S. U.S. 101, Hopland ☎ 800/433–3689 ⊕ www.brutocaocellars.com ⊠ Tastings $10 ☉ Closed Mon. and Tues.

★ Campovida

WINERY | Gently made wines from Italian and Rhône varietals grown in Mendocino County organic, biodynamic, and sustainable vineyards are Campovida's focus. The historic 56-acre estate—previous owners include a local railroad magnate and the Fetzer wine-making clan—opens to the public on weekends, with the downtown tasting room (⊠ Stock Farm, 13441 S. U.S. 101) an option four days a week. ⊠ 13601 Old River Rd., Hopland

⌖ *Take Hwy. 175 east ¾ mile from U.S. 101* ☎ *707/744–8797* ⊕ *www.campovida. com* 🍷 *Tastings from $20 downtown, $40 estate* ⊘ *Estate closed weekdays, downtown Mon.–Wed.*

Graziano Family of Wines

WINERY | Gregory Graziano creates wines for four separate labels, one devoted to Burgundian grapes like Pinot Noir; two to Italian varietals; and the last to Zinfandel, Rhône, and a few other types. Gregory's grandfather planted the winery's oldest Mendocino County vineyard just before Prohibition. The lineup poured in the downtown Hopland tasting space might include Pinot Gris and Arneis whites and Dolcetto and Nebbiolo reds. ⊠ *13275 U.S. 101, Hopland* ☎ *707/744–8466* ⊕ *grazianofamilyofwines.com* 🍷 *Tastings $10.*

★ Saracina Vineyards

WINERY | Guests at this boutique winery's contemporary, stone-and-glass hospitality center enjoy views of landscaped outdoor picnic and tasting areas and the olive grove and vineyards beyond. The excellent Lolonis Vineyard Sauvignon Blanc's organic grapes come from California's oldest Sauvignon Blanc vines, planted in 1942. Standout reds include Zinfandel, Cabernet Sauvignon, Pinot Noir, and the Soul of Mendocino blend. Hosts conduct combination cave and vineyard tours on Friday and weekends. ⊠ *11684 U.S. 101, Hopland* ☎ *707/670–0199* ⊕ *www.saracina.com* 🍷 *Tastings from $20.*

Terra Savia Winery & Olive Mill

WINERY | Don't be surprised to find yourself whiling away a few hours at this warehouse-like operation, whose proprietors grow grapes and olives; tend gardens; display art indoors and out; and care for goats, donkeys, and other rescue animals. The owners (and critters) won't mind if you do: this is a laid-back kind of place. Estate-grown Chardonnay, Merlot, and Cabernet Sauvignon are the highlights. ⊠ *14160 Mountain House Rd., Hopland* ⌖ *Off U.S. 101* ☎ *707/744–1114*

⊕ *www.terrasavia.com* 🍷 *Tastings $10 olive oil, from $12 wine.*

🍽 Restaurants

Golden Pig

$$ | AMERICAN | Grass-fed-beef burgers, pulled-pork and pork-schnitzel sandwiches, and cod ceviche are among the popular items this hip-casual restaurant serves all day, with heritage pork chop, rotisserie chicken, and similar plates appearing for dinner. Well-selected breads and buns, crispy fries with the burgers, perfect pickles with the sandwiches, and slivers of fresh ginger in the ceviche elevate the farm-to-table comfort fare, much of it showcasing ingredients from local purveyors. **Known for:** all-day brunch; Mendocino County wines; tastings at affiliated wine shop 200 feet south. 💲 *Average main: $26* ⊠ *13380 U.S. 101, Hopland* ☎ *707/670–6055* ⊕ *www.thegoldenpig.com.*

Hopland Tap and Grill

$ | AMERICAN | A plaque out front hints at the layers of history that have unfolded in this hangout's redbrick 1880s structure. The mood's invariably upbeat in the bar, even more so in the courtyard beer garden, where patrons chow down on burgers, sandwiches, chicken wings, and other pub grub. **Known for:** California brews on tap; down-home atmosphere; live music some nights. 💲 *Average main: $16* ⊠ *13351 U.S. 101, Hopland* ☎ *707/510–0000* ⊕ *hoplandtap.com* ⊘ *Closed Mon. and Tues. (but check). No lunch Wed.*

Stock Farm

$$ | MODERN AMERICAN | Gourmet wood-fired pizzas, many with ingredients grown a mile away at Campovida winery, are the main attraction at this country-casual restaurant and bar. Menu staples include burgers; grilled vegetables; pasta dishes; and seasonal soups, stews, and salads. **Known for:** specialty cocktails; patio dining; well-made coffee drinks.

[$] *Average main: $22* ✉ *13441 U.S. 101, Hopland* ☎ *707/744–1977* 🌐 *www.stockfarmhopland.com* ⏲ *Closed Mon.–Wed. No lunch Thurs. (but check).*

Hotels

Thatcher Hotel

$$ | **HOTEL** | **FAMILY** | Among Mendocino County's finest lodgings when completed in 1890, this high-ceilinged boutique hotel in downtown Hopland received a meticulous, aesthetically pleasing makeover favoring shades of deep gray and light to medium brown. **Pros:** pool and exterior courtyard; 500-square-foot suite good for families; adjoining sister property Stock Farm Inn has additional rooms. **Cons:** some traffic noise in streetside rooms; rooms lack closets and drawers; no elevator to upper floors (one ADA room on ground floor). [$] *Rooms from: $210* ✉ *13401 U.S. 101, Hopland* ☎ *707/723–0838* 🌐 *thatcherhotel.com* 🛏 *18 rooms* 🍴 *No Meals.*

Ukiah

14 miles north of Hopland, 21 miles northeast of Boonville.

About 17,000 people live in Ukiah, the Mendocino County seat and largest town. Logging and beer hops became prominent industries starting in the late-19th century and continuing well into the 20th. Grape plantings date from the late 1800s, though many of the head-trained (no trellising) old vines were planted in the early 1900s and during and just after Prohibition. Warmer than the Anderson Valley, the Ukiah area is known for Zinfandel, Cabernet Sauvignon, and other varietals that thrive in high heat. Should you need to cool off, you can repair to the redwoods of Montgomery Woods State Natural Reserve.

GETTING HERE AND AROUND

Ukiah is off U.S. 101; if coming from Boonville, take Highway 253 northeast to U.S. 101 and head north. Mendocino Transit Authority buses serve the area.

ESSENTIALS

VISITOR INFORMATION Ukiah Visitor Center. ✉ *200 S. School St.* ☎ *707/467–5766* 🌐 *www.visitukiah.com.*

Sights

Barra of Mendocino

WINERY | Curved support beams swoop upward to a central peak at this winery, whose tasting space is as dramatic as the hospitality is down-home. The room sits amid a vineyard containing organically grown Chardonnay, Riesling, Pinot Noir, Cabernet Sauvignon, Zinfandel, and several other grapes. The founding family's deep Mendocino roots and early adoption of sustainable practices are among the topics discussed at indoor and outdoor tastings. ✉ *7051 N. State St., Redwood Valley* ☎ *707/485–0322* 🌐 *www.barraofmendocino.com* 🎟 *Tastings from $10.*

Montgomery Woods State Natural Reserve

STATE/PROVINCIAL PARK | **FAMILY** | Narrow Orr Springs Road winds 13 miles west from Ukiah to this secluded park whose 2-mile loop trail leads to serene old-growth redwood groves. Only the intermittent breezes, rustling of small wildlife, and calls of resident birds punctuate the prehistoric quiet of the most remote one. The reserve (no dogs allowed) is a place like few others in all of California. **■ TIP→ From the town of Mendocino you can access the park by taking the Comptche Ukiah Road to Orr Springs Road.** ✉ *15825 Orr Springs Rd., Ukiah* ✣ *13 miles west of N. State St.* ☎ *707/937–5804* 🌐 *www.parks.ca.gov* 🎟 *Free.*

Nelson Family Vineyards

WINERY | The grandparents of the current winemaker moved to Mendocino County in the early 1950s, establishing a ranch just north of Hopland that now encompasses 2,000 acres. About 10% of the land is devoted to grapes (Chardonnay and Cabernet Sauvignon are two strong suits), with olives and pears among the other plantings. Tastings take place inside the former family home or in an outdoor area with views of grapevines and a redwood grove. ✉ *550 Nelson Ranch Rd., Ukiah* ☎ *707/462–3755* 🌐 *www.nelsonfamilyvineyards.com* 🎟 *Tastings from $10.*

🍴 Restaurants

★ Cultivo

$$ | AMERICAN | An oasis of low-key sophistication in downtown Ukiah, Cultivo is known for inventive wood-fired pizzas (try the braised-pork or wild-boar-sausage pie, or go meatless with one starring trumpet mushrooms) but also plates up oysters on the half shell, fish tacos, a gem salad with bacon and buttermilk–blue cheese dressing, and entrées like grilled salmon and a hefty porterhouse. Meals are served on thick wooden tables in the downstairs bar area and mezzanine; there's also sidewalk dining out front. **Known for:** something for everyone; California beers on tap; well-chosen, mostly Mendocino wines. $ *Average main: $27* ✉ *108 W. Standley St., Ukiah* ✣ *Near N. State St.* ☎ *707/462–7007* 🌐 *cultivorestaurant.com* ⏲ *Closed Sun. No lunch.*

🛏 Hotels

Vichy Springs Resort

$$ | RESORT | The cottages and multiunit one-story buildings of this historic hot-springs resort—luminaries from Ulysses S. Grant to Nancy Pelosi have unwound here—surround a broad lawn shaded by mature manzanitas and oaks. **Pros:** rural solitude; naturally carbonated hot springs; some accommodations have full kitchens. **Cons:** pool is only heated part of the year; not a pampering-type spa; noise from nearby gun range. $ *Rooms from: $310* ✉ *2605 Vichy Springs Rd., Ukiah* ☎ *707/462–9515* 🌐 *www.vichysprings.com* 🛏 *26 rooms* 🍽 *Free Breakfast.*

Avenue of the Giants

98 miles north of Ukiah.

Conservationists banded together a century ago as the Save the Redwoods League and scored a crucial victory when a memorial grove was dedicated in 1921. That grove is now part of Humboldt Redwoods State Park. About a third of the park's more than 53,000 acres contain untouched old-growth coast redwoods most easily viewed while driving the 32-mile Avenue of the Giants.

GETTING HERE AND AROUND

The Avenue of the Giants is off U.S. 101 between Exits 645 and 674. Southern Humboldt Intercity (🌐 *hta.org*) buses serve the area.

👁 Sights

★ Avenue of the Giants

SCENIC DRIVE | FAMILY | Some of Earth's tallest trees tower over this magnificent 32-mile stretch of two-lane blacktop, also known as Highway 254, that follows the south fork of the Eel River through Humboldt Redwoods State Park. The highway runs more or less parallel to U.S. 101 from Phillipsville in the south to the town of Pepperwood in the north. A brochure available at either end of the highway or the visitor center, 2 miles south of Weott, contains a self-guided tour, with short and long hikes through various groves.

A trail at Founders Grove passes by several impressive trees, among them the fallen 362-foot-long Dyerville Giant, whose root base points skyward 35 feet. The tree can be reached via a short trail that begins 4 miles north of the visitor center. About 6 miles north of the center lies the 10,000-acre Rockefeller Forest, containing the world's largest concentration of old-growth coastal redwoods. ✉ *Humboldt Redwoods State Park Visitor Center, 17119 Ave. of the Giants, Weott* ☎ *707/946–2263* 🌐 *www.parks.ca.gov/humboldtredwoods* 🎫 *Free; $8 day-use fee for Williams Grove.*

Briceland Vineyards
WINERY | Lean yet flavorful Humboldt County Pinot Noirs are the specialty of this winery set amid the trees. In good weather, the low-key tastings take place in front of the weathered original winery building. Guests sip Chardonnay, Sauvignon Blanc, or other whites before sampling Pinots and perhaps Syrah or Zinfandel. Briceland hosts tastings on summer weekend afternoons and by appointment at other times. ✉ *5959 Briceland Rd., 10½ miles southwest of Ave. of the Giants southern entrance* ✥ *Take Briceland Rd. 5½ miles west from Redwood Dr. in Redway (from north, U.S. 101 Exit 642; from south, Exit 639B)* ☎ *707/923–2429* 🌐 *bricelandvineyards.com* 🎫 *Tastings $20.*

Hotels

Scotia Lodge
$ | **HOTEL** | Eureka-based entrepreneurs passionate about providing safe, legal places for patrons to enjoy cannabis products renovated a century-old logging hotel near the northern Avenue of the Giants entrance into a hip, stylish hub welcoming all travelers. **Pros:** snappy reboot of historic property; some adjoining rooms; microwaves and refrigerators in all rooms. **Cons:** some rooms a little dark; pot vibe may not work for all travelers; a tad pricey for the area. [$] *Rooms from: $185* ✉ *100 Main St., Scotia* ☎ *707/783–3059* 🌐 *www.scotia-lodge.com* 🛏 *22 rooms* 🍴 *No Meals.*

Eureka

20 miles northeast of Ferndale, 33 miles north of Avenue of the Giants north entrance.

An excellent place to fuel up, buy groceries, and learn a little about the region's mining, timber, and fishing pasts, historic Eureka was named after a gold miner's hearty exclamation. The county visitor center has maps of self-guided walking tours of the town's nearly 100 Victorians. Art galleries and antiques stores liven up the Old Town district from C to N Street between the waterfront and 4th Street, and a walking pier extends into the harbor.

GETTING HERE AND AROUND

Eureka is set along the North Coast's main north–south highway, U.S. 101.

ESSENTIALS

VISITOR INFORMATION Humboldt County Visitors Bureau. ✉ *422 1st St., Eureka* ☎ *707/443–5097, 800/346–3482* 🌐 *www.visitredwoods.com.*

Sights

★ **Blue Ox Millworks**
FACTORY | **FAMILY** | Its lead artisan's star turn on the cable-TV series *The Craftsman* has brought welcome attention to this woodshop specializing in Victorian-era architecture. The craftspeople here use antique tools—printing presses and lathes among them—to create gingerbread trim, fence pickets, and other Victorian embellishments. Visitors on guided and self-guided tours can watch the workers in action. ✉ *1 X St., Eureka* ☎ *707/444–3437* 🌐 *www.blueoxmill.com* 🎫 *Guided tours $30, self-guided $15* 🕒 *Closed weekends (but check for Sat. openings), guided tours limited in winter.*

Clarke Historical Museum
HISTORY MUSEUM | **FAMILY** | The Native American wing of this museum contains a beautiful collection of northwestern

California basketry. Artifacts from Eureka's Victorian, logging, and maritime eras fill the rest of the space. ⊠ *240 E St., Eureka* 🕾 *707/443–1947* ⊕ *www.clarkemuseum.org* 🞐 *$5* 🕁 *Closed Mon. yr-round, Tues. late fall–early spring.*

Dick Taylor Craft Chocolate

FACTORY | FAMILY | Dick Taylor specializes in small-batch dark chocolates made with beans from Africa and Central America. His factory store's on-site café serves dense European-style "drinking chocolates," along with hot chocolates, addictive fudge pops, and other delights. Book a tour (with tasting) through the company's website. ⊠ *333 1st St., Eureka* 🕾 *707/798–6010* ⊕ *dicktaylorchocolate.com* 🞐 *Samples free, café items from $3, tour $8.*

Ferndale Victorians

TOWN | FAMILY | The town of Ferndale, best known for its colorful Victorian architecture, much of it Stick-Eastlake style, is worth the 20-mile drive south from Eureka or north from the Avenue of the Giants. Many Main Street shops carry a self-guided tour map highlighting the most interesting historic buildings. Gift shops and ice-cream stores comprise a fair share of the businesses here, but Ferndale remains a fully functioning small town, and descendants of the Portuguese and Scandinavian dairy farmers who settled here continue to raise dairy cows in the surrounding pastures. If it's open, pop into the two storefronts of the **Blacksmith Shop** (⊠ *455 and 491 Main St.* 🕾 *707/786–4216* ⊕ *www.ferndaleblacksmith.com*), which celebrates the survival of the traditional blacksmithing arts in the area. ⊠ *Ferndale* ✛ *From U.S. 101, follow Hwy. 211 southwest 5 miles.*

★ Redwood Sky Walk at Sequoia Park Zoo

ZOO | FAMILY | Stroll 100 feet above the forest floor on California's oldest zoo's aerial walkway through old-growth and newer redwoods. Favorite wildlife viewing areas back on the ground include a walk-in aviary. A bear and coyote exhibit

was set to open during 2023. ⊠ *3414 W St., Eureka* 🕾 *707/441–4263* ⊕ *redwoodskywalk.com* 🞐 *$25* 🕁 *Closed Mon.*

🍴 Restaurants

★ Brick & Fire Bistro

$$ | MODERN AMERICAN | Nearly every seat in this urbane bistro has a view of its most important feature—a wood-fired brick oven used to prepare everything from local Kumamoto oysters and creatively topped pizzas to wild-mushroom cobbler. Soups, several well-constructed salads, grilled meats, and seafood round out the menu. **Known for:** house-made sausage pizza; polenta lasagna; affiliated 2 Doors Down wine bar steps away. 🖫 *Average main: $26* ⊠ *1630 F St., Eureka* 🕾 *707/268–8959* ⊕ *www.brickandfirebistro.com* 🕁 *Closed Tues. No lunch.*

Café Waterfront

$$ | SEAFOOD | Amid Old Town's vibrant dining district, this rollicking spot in a former saloon and brothel turns out consistently fresh locally caught seafood—steamed clams, grilled snapper, oyster burgers, homemade chowder, and quite a bit more. Soups, salads, steaks, and burgers are on the menu, too, and breakfast, served only on weekends, is popular. **Known for:** historic vibe; locally sourced oysters (raw and grilled); Victorian-style B&B upstairs. 🖫 *Average main: $23* ⊠ *102 F St., Eureka* 🕾 *707/443–9190* ⊕ *www.cafewaterfronteureka.com* 🕁 *Closed Tues. and Wed.*

★ Five Eleven

$$$ | MODERN AMERICAN | The chef at this colorfully lighted, contemporary, Old Town restaurant applies Western European techniques to mostly locally sourced ingredients in dishes that might include a wood-fired steak slathered in sauce au poivre, fish with saffron rice, or a mushroom-laden meatless cassoulet. Many patrons start with a classic or specialty cocktail or one of the clever

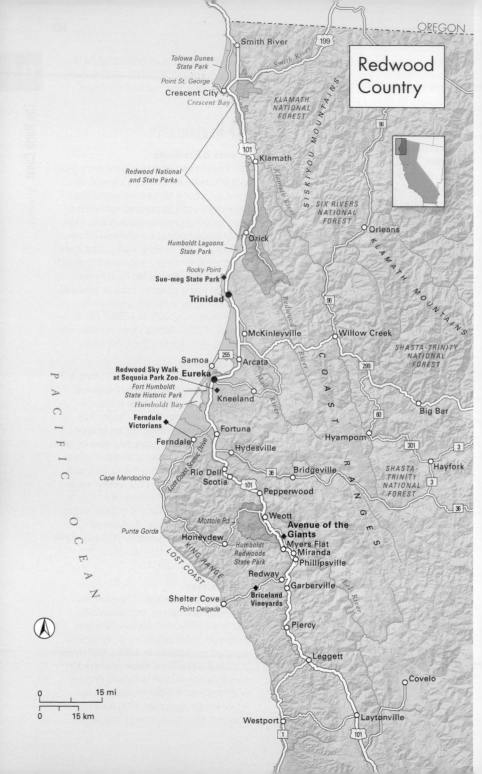

mocktails. **Known for:** small-plate and raw-bar starters; short but smart wine list; "Bananas Fosters" cake with spiced-rum caramel. [$] *Average main: $38* ✉ *511 2nd St., Eureka* ☎ *707/268–3852* 🌐 *fiveeleveneureka.com* 🕓 *Closed Sun. and Mon. No lunch.*

Samoa Cookhouse

$$ | AMERICAN | FAMILY | Eat like a mill worker at this family-style former logging cafeteria's long, communal tables. You're here more for the blast from the past than the cuisine (think biscuits and gravy for breakfast, sandwiches and pot roast for lunch and dinner). **Known for:** hearty meals; historical ambience; nearby museum. [$] *Average main: $20* ✉ *908 Vance Ave., Samoa* ✣ *Near Cookhouse Rd.* ☎ *707/442–1659* 🌐 *www.samoacookhouse.net* 🕓 *Closed Mon. and Tues.*

Hotels

★ Carter House Inns

$ | HOTEL | Richly painted and aglow with wood detailing, the inns' guest rooms, in two main Victorian buildings and several historic cottages, contain a mix of modern and antique furnishings. **Pros:** elegant ambience; whirlpool tubs and separate sitting areas in some rooms; superb Restaurant 301. **Cons:** not suitable for children; restaurant a bit pricey; two-night minimum on weekends. [$] *Rooms from: $195* ✉ *301 L St., Eureka* ☎ *707/444–8062* 🌐 *www.carterhouse.com* 🛏 *33 rooms* 🍴 *Free Breakfast.*

Inn at 2nd and C

$ | B&B/INN | By the bustling waterfront and steps from Old Town's inviting shops and restaurants, this towering, late-1880s Victorian abounds with opulent architectural details and florid period-style bedding, wallpapers, and furnishings. **Pros:** upgraded amenities; Tavern restaurant and Phatsy Kline's pub; reasonable rates. **Cons:** thin walls; least expensive rooms are small; rambling, quirky place. [$] *Rooms from: $179* ✉ *139 2nd St., Eureka* ☎ *707/444–3344* 🌐 *www.historiceaglehouse.com/the-inn-at-2nd-c* 🛏 *23 rooms* 🍴 *Free Breakfast.*

Nightlife

Lost Coast Brewery & Café

BREWPUBS | This bustling microbrewery with surf-tropical decor accents is a good place to relax with a pint of ale or porter. Soups, salads, burgers, sandwiches, tacos, and light meals are served. ✉ *617 4th St., Eureka* ☎ *707/445–4480* 🌐 *www.lostcoast.com* 🕓 *Closed Mon. and Tues.*

Trinidad

23 miles north of Eureka.

A mellow base for exploring the southern portion of Redwood National and State Parks, coastal Trinidad got its name from the Spanish mariners who entered the bay on Trinity Sunday, June 9, 1775. Formerly the principal trading post for mining camps along the Klamath and Trinity rivers, Trinidad is a quiet, charming community with several beaches, impressive restaurants, and romantic inns.

GETTING HERE AND AROUND

Trinidad sits right off U.S. 101, about 10 miles north of Highway 299.

Sights

Sue-meg State Park

STATE/PROVINCIAL PARK | FAMILY | On a forested plateau almost 200 feet above the surf, this park—until 2021 known as Patrick's Point—offers stunning views of the Pacific, great whale- and sea lion–watching spots, campgrounds, picnic areas, bike paths, and hiking trails through old-growth spruce forest. There are also tidal pools at Agate Beach, a re-created Yurok Indian village, and a small visitor center with exhibits. It's uncrowded and sublimely quiet here. Dogs are not allowed on trails or the beach. ✉ *4150*

Patricks Point Dr., Trinidad ✢ Off U.S. 101, 5 miles north of town ☎ 707/677–3570 🌐 www.parks.ca.gov 🎟 $10 per vehicle.

🍴 Restaurants

Beachcomber Cafe

$ | BAKERY | FAMILY | Before a day of hiking and exploring, fuel up on organic espresso and coffee drinks, freshly baked breads and pastries, house-made granola, frittatas, and bagels with lox, chèvre, local jams, poached eggs, and other toppings. The lunch lineup includes soups, salads, and panini. **Known for:** bagels with creative toppings; strong, organic coffee; vegetarian options. [$] *Average main: $9 ✉ 363 Trinity St., Trinidad ☎ 707/677–0106 🕑 No dinner.*

★ Larrupin' Cafe

$$$$ | AMERICAN | Set in a two-story house on a quiet country road north of town, this casually sophisticated restaurant—one of the North Coast's best places to eat—is often packed with people enjoying mesquite-grilled fresh seafood, beef brisket, St. Louis–style ribs, and vegetarian dishes. The garden setting and candlelight stir thoughts of romance. **Known for:** refined but friendly service; rosemary-crusted garlic, Cambozola cheese, and toast points appetizer; superb wine list. [$] *Average main: $42 ✉ 1658 Patricks Point Dr., Trinidad ☎ 707/677–0230 🌐 www.thelarrupin.com 🕑 No lunch.*

Trinidad Bay Eatery & Gallery

$$ | SEAFOOD | FAMILY | A short stroll from Trinidad's bayfront, this unpretentious combination gallery and seafood-oriented restaurant is known for tasty meals, starting with breakfast's buttermilk pancakes and Dungeness crab Benedict. Clam chowder, salads, burgers, and several melts star at lunch; for dinner, consider an ahi poke bowl or coconut shrimp starter, followed by more seafood (cioppino and steamed clams or mussels usually appear on the menu) or a burger or chicken dish. **Known for:** hand-punched fries; blackberry cobbler; heated patio. [$] *Average main: $23 ✉ 607 Parker St., Trinidad ☎ 707/677–3777 🌐 www.trinidadeatery.com 🕑 No dinner Tues. or Wed.*

🛏 Hotels

Lost Whale Inn

$$ | B&B/INN | For a romantic special-occasion getaway, look to this intimate luxurious inn perched on a seaside bluff near Sue-meg State Park. **Pros:** stunning ocean views; elaborate and delicious breakfast spread; spa services in some rooms or on lawn or decks. **Cons:** no pets allowed; two-night minimum stay on summer weekends; sometimes books up fully for weddings. [$] *Rooms from: $315 ✉ 3452 Patricks Point Dr., Trinidad ☎ 707/677–3425 🌐 www.lostwhaleinn.com 🛏 8 rooms 🍴 Free Breakfast.*

Trinidad Inn

$ | HOTEL | FAMILY | These quiet cottage rooms nestled in the evergreens are 2 miles north of Trinidad Bay's harbor, restaurants, and shops. **Pros:** idyllic setting; walking path through adjacent redwood grove; good for kids. **Cons:** older property; no breakfast in off-season; reservations can be made only by phone. [$] *Rooms from: $175 ✉ 1170 Patricks Point Dr., Trinidad ☎ 707/677–3349 🌐 www.trinidadinn.com 🛏 10 rooms 🍴 Free Breakfast.*

Turtle Rocks Oceanfront Inn

$$ | B&B/INN | This comfortable inn has the best view in Trinidad, with the ocean and sunning sea lions seen from private, glassed-in decks in each room. **Pros:** ocean views; a mile from Sue-meg State Park; surrounding landscape left natural and wild. **Cons:** no restaurants within walking distance; often books up well in advance; can be foggy here in summer. [$] *Rooms from: $349 ✉ 3392 Patricks Point Dr., Trinidad ☎ 707/677–3707 🌐 www.turtlerocksinn.com 🛏 6 rooms 🍴 Free Breakfast.*

Chapter 14

REDWOOD NATIONAL AND STATE PARKS

Updated by
Daniel Mangin

⛺ Camping	🏨 Hotels	🏃 Activities	👁 Scenery	👥 Crowds
★★★☆☆	★★★★☆	★★★★☆	★★★★★	★★★★☆

WELCOME TO REDWOOD NATIONAL AND STATE PARKS

TOP REASONS TO GO

★ **Giant trees:** These mature coastal redwoods, which you can hike beneath in numerous groves, are the world's tallest trees.

★ **Hiking along the sea:** The parks offer many miles of ocean access, including the Coastal Trail, which runs along the western edge.

★ **Rare wildlife:** Mighty Roosevelt elk favor flat prairie and open lands; seldom-seen black bears roam the backcountry; trout and salmon leap through streams; and Pacific gray whales swim along the coast during their spring and fall migrations.

★ **Stepping back in time:** Hike mossy, mysterious Fern Canyon Trail, and explore a prehistoric scene of lush vegetation and giant ferns—a memorable scene in *The Lost World: Jurassic Park* was shot here.

★ **Getting off-the-grid:** Amid the majestic redwoods you're usually out of cell phone range and often free from crowds, offering a rare opportunity to disconnect.

1 South. Highlights include the hikes and scenic drives along Bald Hills Road and the beautiful coastal scenery at Thomas H. Kuchel Visitor Center and the estuarial lagoons to the south. This area encompasses much of the original Redwood National Park. Here you'll find the small village of Orick, which has a gas station and a few other basic services.

2 Middle. The span from north of Orick to the Yurok tribal community of Klamath contains magnificent and accessible stands of old-growth redwoods. Start your adventures at Prairie Creek Redwoods State Park's visitor center, from which several trails emanate. Set aside time to explore the meadows inhabited by Roosevelt elk, the trail to Fern Canyon from Gold Bluffs Beach, and the gorgeous drives along Newton B. Drury Scenic Parkway and Klamath's Coastal Drive Loop.

3 North. Anchored by the region's largest community, Crescent City, this section encompasses the rugged, pristine forests of Jedediah Smith Redwoods State Park, which is slightly inland, and Del Norte Coast Redwoods State Park, which offers the chance to visit windswept beaches, steep sea cliffs, and forested ridges. On a clear day it's postcard-perfect; with fog, it's mysterious and mesmerizing.

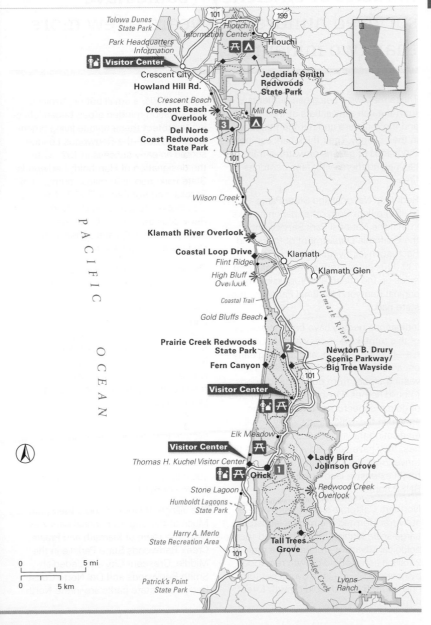

Soaring more than 375 feet high, California's coastal redwoods are miracles of efficiency—some have survived hundreds of years, a few more than two millennia.

These massive trees glean nutrients from the rich alluvial flats at their feet and the moisture and nitrogen trapped in their canopy. Their thick bark can hold thousands of gallons of water, a trait that has helped them withstand centuries of fires.

Redwood National and State Parks (RNSP) differs from other national parks in that the National Park Service and the California Department of Parks and Recreation jointly administer it. The 139,000-acre system extends nearly 50 miles up the coast, encompassing the original Redwood National Park and three state parks.

Indigenous people have been stewards of this remarkable ecosystem for millennia—hunting, fishing, and foraging early on, and, in more recent centuries, harvesting timber from downed redwoods to build homes. Despite the cruel efforts of gold prospectors and loggers who arrived in the 1850s and swiftly set about eradicating the indigenous communities, they have survived and continue to thrive. Both the Yurok and Tolowa tribes retain extensive land holdings within RNSP borders.

Northern California's gold rush immediately transformed the natural landscape. Large-scale logging, aided by rapid technological advances, reduced the region's 2 million acres of old-growth redwoods by nearly 90% in a little over a century—only about 5% of the old-growth forest remains today.

By the 1910s, a small but determined conservation-minded group began lobbying to protect these unique living organisms. The Save-the-Redwoods League scored an early success in 1921 with the designation of Humboldt Redwoods State Park, about 30 miles southeast of Eureka (and not part of RNSP). The group also lobbied to establish Del Norte Coast Redwoods and Prairie Creek Redwoods state parks in 1925 and Jedediah Smith Redwoods State Park in 1939.

Demand for lumber following World War II led to further depletion of unprotected forests, prompting the federal government to establish Redwood National Park in 1968. Finally, in 1994, federal and state agencies officially joined forces to manage the newly created Redwood National and State Parks, whose mission is to preserve uncut old-growth redwood forest and restore and replant sections lost to logging.

The easiest way to approach the RNSP system is to divide it geographically into South, Middle, and North sections. U.S. 101 is the main north–south route; U.S. 199 east of Crescent City bisects a brief portion of the North.

The village of Orick anchors the South. Much of the original national park was here. The town of Klamath and Prairie Creek Redwoods State Park lie in the Middle. Crescent City and Jedediah Smith Redwoods and Del Norte Coast Redwoods state parks are in the North.

Four other coastal parks are just south of RNSP: Humboldt Lagoons State Park, Harry A. Merlo State Recreation Area, Big Lagoon Beach and County Park, and Sue-meg State Park.

While exploring the national and three state parks, you may wonder which part you're in, but ultimately it's not all that important. Refer to the excellent map in the free RNSP brochure and visitor guide newspaper, and you'll quickly figure out where you are and how to navigate this magnificent preserve.

Planning

Getting Here and Around

AIR

United and Avelo airlines serve Humboldt County Airport, between Trinidad and Arcata in McKinleyville. Another option is Oregon's Rogue Valley International Medford Airport, served by Alaska, Allegiant, American, Avelo, Delta, and United. The drive from Rogue Valley to the RNSP's northern tip in Crescent City takes about two hours.

CAR

U.S. 101 runs north–south nearly the entire length of RNSP. You can access all the main roads via U.S. 101 and U.S. 199, which runs east–west through the northern portion. Many ancillary roads aren't paved. Winter rains can turn streets into obstacle courses; sometimes, they close entirely. Motor homes/RVs and trailers aren't permitted on some routes. The drive from San Francisco to the southern end takes about six hours via U.S. 101. It takes roughly the same time from Portland to reach the northern section via Interstate 5 to U.S. 199.

■TIP→ Don't rely solely on GPS, which is notoriously inaccurate within the parks; consult the official maps available online and at visitor centers.

Hotels

The only lodgings within the parks are the Elk Meadow Cabins, near Prairie Creek Redwoods Visitor Center. Orick, to the south of Elk Meadow, and Klamath, to the north, have basic motels. In Klamath there's also the historic Requa Inn. Victorian inns, seaside motels, and fully equipped vacation rentals are among the options in Crescent City to the north and Eureka, Trinidad, and Arcata to the south. Try to book lodgings at least a week ahead in summer.

Park Essentials

FEES AND PERMITS

Admission to Redwood National Park is free. A few areas in the state parks collect day-use fees of $8–$12, including Gold Bluffs Beach and Fern Canyon in Prairie Creek Redwoods State Park and day-use areas accessed via campground entrances in Jedediah Smith and Del Norte Coast state parks. Most state and federal passes are honored.

Overnight camping costs $35. Pick up a free permit at the Kuchel visitor center in Orick to visit the popular Tall Trees Grove. Free permits, available at the Kuchel, Crescent City, and (summer only) Hiouchi visitor centers, are also required to stay at designated backcountry camps.

HOURS

The parks are open year-round, 24 hours a day.

CELL PHONE RECEPTION

It's difficult to pick up a signal in much of RNSP, especially in camping areas or on hiking trails. The Prairie Creek and Jedediah Smith visitor centers have pay phones.

AVERAGE HIGH/LOW TEMPERATURES					
Jan.	Feb.	Mar.	Apr.	May	June
54/39	56/41	57/41	59/42	62/45	65/48
July	Aug.	Sept.	Oct.	Nov.	Dec.
67/51	67/51	68/49	64/46	58/43	55/40

Restaurants

The parks have no restaurants, but Eureka and Arcata have diverse establishments—everything from hip oyster bars to ethnic spots. More limited, though decent, dining options can be found in Crescent City and Trinidad, fewer still in Klamath and Orick. Most small-town restaurants close by 7:30 or 8 pm.

Hotel and restaurant reviews have been shortened. For full information visit Fodors.com. Hotel prices are the lowest cost of a standard double room in high season. Restaurant prices are the average cost of a main course at dinner, or if dinner is not served, at lunch.

What It Costs			
$	$$	$$$	$$$$
RESTAURANTS			
under $20	$20–$30	$31–$40	over $40
HOTELS			
under $200	$200–$350	$351–$500	over $500

Visitor Information

CONTACTS Redwood National and State Parks. ✉ *1111 2nd St., Crescent City* ☎ *707/464–6101* ⊕ *www.nps.gov/redw.*

When to Go

Campers and hikers flock to the park from mid-June to early September. The crowds disappear in winter, but you'll have to contend with frequent rains, nasty potholes, and occasional closures on side roads. Temperatures fluctuate widely: the foggy coastal lowland is much cooler than the higher-altitude interior.

The average annual rainfall is between 60 and 80 inches, most falling between November and April. During the dry summer, thick fog rolling in from the Pacific can veil the forests, providing the redwoods a large portion of their moisture intake.

South

19 miles north of Trinidad, 8 miles south of Prairie Creek Visitor Center, 44 miles south of Crescent City.

The section of the parks you'll reach first if driving up the coast from Eureka and Trinidad is home to the invaluable Thomas H. Kuchel Visitor Center, on U.S. 101 shortly after the entrance. This portion includes the town of Orick and everything else south of the turnoff onto Bald Hills Road, which leads to two significant redwood stands, the Lady Bird Johnson and Tall Trees groves.

◉ Sights

SCENIC DRIVES
Bald Hills Road
SCENIC DRIVE | FAMILY | This steep, dramatic road winding up to some of the parks' highest elevations accesses great hikes—Lady Bird Johnson Grove and Lyons Ranch among them—as well as the spur road to Tall Trees Grove. But it's wondrously scenic all on its own,

Redwood in One Day

This south-to-north day-trip itinerary hits some Redwood National and State Parks highlights. If you're approaching the parks from Crescent City, it's easy to undertake this itinerary in reverse.

Get your bearings in Orick at the **Thomas H. Kuchel Visitor Center,** a beautiful spot to enjoy ocean views. The crowds head to Lady Bird Johnson Grove, but take local guides' advice and slip farther north on U.S. 101 and west on Davison Road to **Trillium Falls Trail.** En route to the trailhead, you may see elk grazing in **Elk Meadow.** Past the meadow is its parking lot. Park and follow signs to the falls, which you'll encounter after ½ mile. From here, backtrack to the parking lot or hike the whole 2.8-mile loop past tall redwoods.

From the parking lot, continue west on Davison (unpaved in stretches) to **Gold Bluffs Beach** (day-use fee). From the beach, drive north a short way farther to the trailhead for lush, spectacular **Fern Canyon.** From mid-May to mid-September, you'll need a free parking permit for the canyon, which you can reserve online.

After the canyon hike, backtrack to U.S. 101, continuing north to the **Newton B. Drury Scenic Parkway,** a 10-mile drive through one of RNSP's best and most accessible expanses of old-growth redwood forest. Stop

at **Prairie Creek Visitor Center,** housed in a small redwood lodge. Enjoy a picnic lunch and follow the ½-mile **Revelation Trail,** an engaging tactile walk for vision-impaired visitors. If you have an hour or two, hike all or part of the stunning 3½-mile **Prairie Creek–Big Tree–Cathedral Trees Loop** instead.

Leaving Prairie Creek, continue north on the parkway and U.S. 101. Exit at Klamath Beach Road, following signs to the **Coastal Drive Loop,** which winds past redwoods toward the High Bluffs Overlook. Take in the ocean and Klamath views before continuing back to U.S. 101.

Follow U.S. 101 north to Crescent City, heading east on Elk Valley Road and Howland Hill Road to **Jedediah Smith Redwoods State Park.** Howland Hill is unpaved much of the way but is well-maintained. Follow the road to the **Stout Memorial Grove,** where you can take the short ½-mile loop trail past old-growth redwoods or the 1½-mile River Trail. Return to downtown Crescent City via U.S. 199 to U.S. 101, rewarding yourself with a pizza and a cider, microbrew, or nonalcoholic spritzer at **SeaQuake Brewing.**

■TIP➜ RVs and trailers aren't allowed on Davison Road. Even if traveling by car, check with the visitor centers about road closures before setting out.

passing through a sometimes misty redwood patch before reaching open meadows with wildflowers in spring and the chance to see Roosevelt elk and bears year-round. Do stop at Redwood Creek Overlook, a 2,100-foot elevation pullout at mile 6.6. Bald Hills Road is paved for the first 13 miles. It continues

another 4 miles unpaved to RNSP's southern boundary. From here you can continue another 20 miles or so to the small village of Weitchpec and then onward inland toward Redding or Yreka. ⊠ *Off U.S. 101, 5½ miles north of Kuchel center, Orick.*

14

Redwood National and State Parks SOUTH

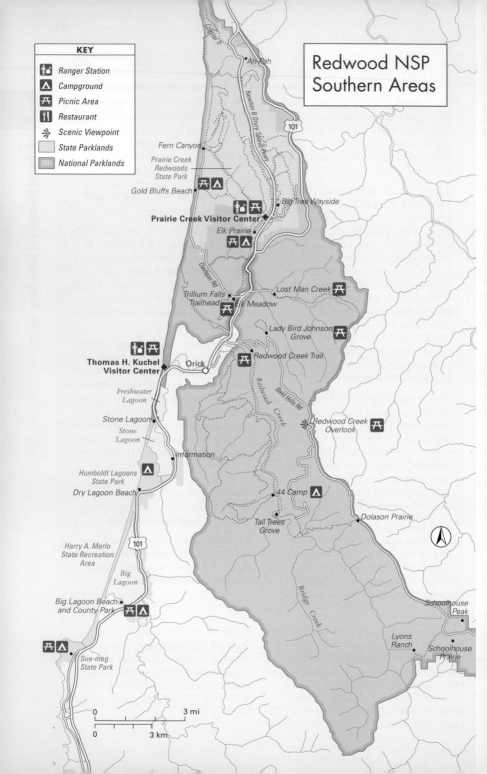

Redwood NSP Southern Areas

KEY

- 🚶 *Ranger Station*
- 🏕 *Campground*
- ⛽ *Picnic Area*
- 🍴 *Restaurant*
- ☀ *Scenic Viewpoint*
- ⬜ *State Parklands*
- ⬛ *National Parklands*

Coastal Tr

Ah-Pah

Newton B Drury Scenic Pkwy

101

Fern Canyon

Prairie Creek
Redwoods
State Park

Gold Bluffs Beach

Big Tree Wayside

Prairie Creek Visitor Center

Elk Prairie

Davison Rd

Trillium Falls
Trailhead

Lost Man Creek

Elk Meadow

Lady Bird Johnson
Grove

**Thomas H. Kuchel
Visitor Center**

Orick

Redwood Creek Trail

Freshwater
Lagoon

Redwood Creek
Overlook

Stone Lagoon

Stone
Lagoon

Bald Hills Rd

Information

Humboldt Lagoons
State Park

Dry Lagoon Beach

44 Camp

Harry A. Merlo
State Recreation
Area

Tall Trees
Grove

Dolason Prairie

Big
Lagoon

Big Lagoon Beach
and County Park

Schoolhouse
Peak

Lyons
Ranch

Schoolhouse
Prairie

Sue-meg
State Park

Redwood Creek

Bridge Creek

0   3 mi

0   3 km

TRAILS
★ Lady Bird Johnson Grove Trail
TRAIL | FAMILY | Among the most accessible spots to view big trees, this impressive grove a short drive northeast of Orick was dedicated by, and named for, the former first lady. A level, 1.4-mile nature loop crosses a neat old wooden footbridge and follows an old logging road through this often mist-shrouded forest of redwoods. *Easy.* ☒ *Orick* ⊹ *Trailhead: Bald Hills Rd., 2 miles east of U.S. 101.*

Lyons Ranch Trail
TRAIL | FAMILY | You won't see redwoods on this open, upper-elevation, 3.7-mile round-trip trail, but on summer days when the coast is socked in with rain or fog, an outing to this typically sunny prairie at Redwood National Park's southeastern boundary is highly rewarding, as is the steep—but slow—17-mile drive on Bald Hills Road. The trail leads to a former sheep and cattle ranch with a few interesting old outbuildings that date from the turn of the 20th century. *Moderate.* ☒ *Redwood National Park* ⊹ *Trailhead: Off Bald Hills Rd., 17 miles south of U.S. 101 (unpaved last few miles).*

Tall Trees Trail
TRAIL | Although this roughly 30-acre grove ranks among the parks' most beautiful old-growth stands, getting to it requires a steep and winding 14-mile drive, followed by a somewhat rigorous 4-mile round-trip hike involving an 800-foot descent into the Redwood Creek flood plain. To embark on this journey, you must obtain a free permit at the Kuchel center to access the unpaved road off Bald Hills Road. Rangers dispense a limited number per day, first come, first served. No trailers or RVs are allowed. Given the effort required, if you only have a little time, it's best to save this one for your second or third visit. *Moderate.* ☒ *Orick* ⊹ *Trailhead: Tall Trees Access Rd., off Bald Hills Rd., 7 miles from U.S. 101, then 6½ miles to trailhead.*

VISITOR CENTER
★ Thomas H. Kuchel Visitor Center
VISITOR CENTER | FAMILY | Rangers at RNSP's largest and best visitor center dispense brochures, advice, and free permits to drive up the access road to Tall Trees Grove. Whale-watchers find the center's deck an excellent observation point, and bird-watchers enjoy the nearby Freshwater Lagoon, a popular layover for migrating waterfowl. Many of the exhibits are hands-on and kid-friendly. ☒ *U.S. 101, Orick* ⊹ *Redwood Creek Beach County Park* ☎ *707/465–7765* ⊕ *www.nps.gov/redw* ⊙ *Closed Mon. and Tues. mid-Nov.–mid-May.*

Middle

8 miles north of Kuchel visitor center, 34 miles south of Crescent City.

Encompassing a relatively narrow band of coastal forest that extends north of Orick (starting around Elk Meadow) to north of Klamath (up to Requa Road), RNSP's middle section is home to one of the most magical places to stroll through a redwood forest, Prairie Creek State Park, which is laced with both easy and challenging trails and traversed by the stunning Newton B. Drury Scenic Parkway. You can often view herds of Roosevelt elk near the visitor center and in nearby Elk Meadow. The state park extends west to famously spectacular Gold Bluffs Beach and Fern Canyon. Highlights to the north include the Coastal Drive and Klamath River Overlook.

◉ Sights

SCENIC DRIVES
★ Coastal Drive Loop
SCENIC DRIVE | FAMILY | The 9-mile, narrow, and partially unpaved Coastal Drive Loop takes about 45 minutes to traverse. Weaving through redwoods, the road yields close-up Klamath River views and expansive Pacific panoramas. This

loop, closed to trailers and RVs, is all that remains of a longer drive. A spur road leads to the High Bluff Overlook, a premier whale-watching spot; a ½-mile trail leads down to the beach. A little less than a mile north of the overlook lies the B-71 Radar Station, which looks like a farmhouse, its disguise during World War II. About ½-mile farther along, hikers access the Flint Ridge section of the Coastal Trail, also possible off Klamath Beach Road. ⊠ *Klamath ⊹ Klamath Beach Rd. off U.S. 101 (follow signs); begin drive on Alder Camp Rd. across from Old Douglas Memorial Bridge Site.*

★ Newton B. Drury Scenic Parkway

SCENIC DRIVE | FAMILY | This paved 10-mile route threads through Prairie Creek Redwoods State Park and old-growth redwoods. Great stops include the 0.8-mile walk to Big Tree Wayside and a meadow where Roosevelt elk often graze—both are near the park's visitor center. ⊠ *Orick ⊹ Off U.S. 101, Exit 753 north of Orick, Exit 765 south of Klamath ☉ Closed to motorized vehicles 1st Sat. of month Oct.–May for Bike and Hike Day.*

SCENIC STOPS

★ Fern Canyon

CANYON | Enter another world and be surrounded by 50-foot canyon walls covered with sword, deer, and five-finger ferns. Allow an hour to explore the ¼-mile-long vertical garden along a 0.7-mile loop. From the northern end of Gold Bluffs Beach it's an easy walk, although you'll have to wade across or scamper along planks that traverse a small stream several times (in addition to driving across a couple of streams on the way to the parking area). But the lush, otherworldly surroundings, which appeared in *The Lost World: Jurassic Park* (1997), are a must-see when creeks aren't running too high. Motor homes/RVs and all trailers are prohibited. You can also hike to the canyon from Prairie Creek Visitor Center along the challenging West Ridge–Friendship Ridge–James Irvine Loop, 12½ miles

round-trip. ⊠ *Orick ⊹ 2¾ miles north of Orick, take Davison Rd. northwest off U.S. 101 and follow signs to Gold Bluffs Beach ⊕ www.nps.gov/redw/planyourvisit/permits.htm ⊠ $12 day-use fee, pay at Gold Bluffs Beach kiosk; mid-May–mid-Sept. free Gold Bluffs Beach timed parking reservation available only online is required.*

★ Klamath River Overlook

VIEWPOINT | FAMILY | This grassy, windswept bluff rises 650 feet above the confluence of the Klamath River and the Pacific. Among RNSP's best spots for spying migratory whales in early winter and late spring (other wildlife year-round), it accesses a section of the Coastal Trail. Warm days are ideal for picnicking at one of the tables. ⊠ *End of Requa Rd., Klamath ⊹ 2¼ miles west of U.S. 101.*

TRAILS

★ Coastal Trail

TRAIL | This gorgeous 70-mile trail, much of it along dramatic bluffs high above the crashing surf, can be tackled in short, relatively easy chunks or longer, strenuous spans that entail backcountry overnight camping. A few of the most alluring smaller sections, listed here from north to south, are accessible at well-marked trailheads. The moderate-to-difficult DeMartin section (accessed from mile marker 15.6 on U.S. 101) leads south past 6 miles of old-growth redwoods and through sweeping prairie. It connects with the moderate 5½-mile-long Klamath section, which proceeds south from Wilson Creek Picnic Area to Klamath River Overlook, with a short detour to Hidden Beach and its tide pools, providing coastal views and whale-watching opportunities. If you're up for a real workout, hike the brutally difficult but stunning Flint Ridge section (accessed from the Old Douglas Memorial Bridge Site on Klamath Beach Rd.), with its 4½ miles of steep grades and numerous switchbacks past Marshall Pond and through stands

Redwood trees and the moss that often coats them grow best in damp, shady environments.

of old-growth redwoods. *Moderate–Difficult.* ✉ *Klamath.*

★ Karl Knapp–Big Tree–Cathedral Trees Loop

TRAIL | FAMILY | This flat, well-maintained, 3½-mile loop starting and ending at the Prairie Creek Visitor Center passes beneath awe-inspiring redwoods. The 1-mile section along the Karl Knapp Trail (formerly the Prairie Creek Trail) fringes a babbling brook. You then cross Newton B. Drury Scenic Parkway, turn south onto the Cathedral Trees Trail, and detour along the 0.3-mile Big Tree Loop before meandering south and west through yet more gorgeous old-growth forest. Options for extending your hike include walking 1½ miles up Cal-Barrel Road (an old, unpaved logging route) and then looping back 2 miles on the Rhododendron Trail to rejoin Cathedral Trees. *Easy–Moderate.* ✉ *Orick* ✛ *Trailhead: Prairie Creek Visitor Center.*

★ Trillium Falls Trail

TRAIL | FAMILY | On this lush trek through a mix of old-growth redwoods, ferns, smaller deciduous trees, and some

clusters of trillium flowers, you'll encounter the pretty cascades that give the hike its name after the first ½ mile. It's worth continuing along the full 2.8-mile loop, as the walk's southern end offers the best views of soaring redwoods. Roosevelt elk sometimes roam in the meadow by the trailhead. *Easy–Moderate.* ✉ *Orick* ✛ *Trailhead: Elk Meadow parking lot, Davison Rd. off U.S. 101.*

VISITOR CENTER

★ Prairie Creek Visitor Center

VISITOR CENTER | FAMILY | A massive stone fireplace anchors this small redwood lodge whose wildlife displays include a section of a tree a young elk died beside. Due to the peculiar way the redwood grew around the elk's skull, the tree appears to have antlers. You can learn about interpretive programs at the center, which has a gift shop, a picnic area, restrooms, and exhibits on flora and fauna. Roosevelt elk often roam the vast field across the parkway, and several trails begin nearby. Stretch your legs with a stroll along Revelation Trail, a short loop that starts behind the lodge. ✉ *Prairie Creek Rd., Orick* ✥ *Off southern end of Newton B. Drury Scenic Pkwy.* ☎ *707/488–2039* 🌐 *www.nps.gov/redw.*

Hotels

★ Elk Meadow Cabins

$ | MOTEL | FAMILY | From the porches of these restored former mill workers' cottages that can be booked whole or in part (as studios occupying former garages), you often see Roosevelt elk meandering in the namesake meadow—or right outside the window. **Pros:** elks frequently congregate on the grounds; perfect for groups or families; same-day discounts up to 30%. **Cons:** a bit of a drive to restaurants; three-bedroom, two-bath cabins expensive for two occupants; no elk at Ranch House (at separate location; choose Valley Road cabins or studios). [$] *Rooms from: $152* ✉ *7 Valley Green Camp Rd., Orick* ☎ *707/302–8393* 🌐 *www.elkmeadowcabins.com* 🛏 *15 rooms* 🍴 *No Meals.*

Roosevelt Base Camp

$$ | MOTEL | FAMILY | An enthusiastic family's work-in-progress restoration of a roadside motor lodge, this property on the edge of Prairie Creek Redwoods State Park charms travelers with sanded and varnished original oak flooring and rough-hewn decorative touches. **Pros:** two-room suites sleep up to six people; proximity to Fern Canyon and other attractions; aim-to-please hospitality. **Cons:** workaday motel exterior (belies guest rooms' pleasing contemporary decor); some noise bleed-through between rooms; not all rooms have been upgraded. [$] *Rooms from: $220* ✉ *121130 U.S. 101, Orick* ☎ *707/498–3847* 🌐 *www.rooseveltbasecamp.com* 🛏 *16 rooms* 🍴 *No Meals.*

North

34 miles north of Prairie Creek Redwoods State Park, 84 miles north of Eureka, 73 miles south of Grants Pass, OR, 133 miles south of Coos Bay, OR.

Home to Crescent City, the northern section contains RNSP's headquarters and two state parks: Del Norte Redwoods and Jedediah Smith Redwoods. Del Norte lies 5 miles south of Crescent City on U.S. 101 and contains more than a dozen memorial groves and 8 miles of pristine coastline, most easily accessed at Crescent and Wilson beaches.

Jedediah Smith, 5 miles east of Crescent City on U.S. 199, is home to the legendary Stout Memorial Grove, along with some 20 miles of hiking and nature trails. In 1826, the park's namesake became the first white man to explore Northern California's interior. **■ TIP→ If coming from interior Oregon, this is your first chance to drive and hike among soaring redwood stands.**

Sights

SCENIC DRIVES

★ Howland Hill Road

SCENIC DRIVE | FAMILY | Take your time as you drive this 10-mile route that meanders within inches of old-growth redwoods' hulking trunks and follows the Smith River for a spell. Trailers and RVs are prohibited on the unpaved but well-maintained road for the roughly 7 miles that pass through Jedediah Smith Redwoods State Park. Pullouts include those for the Boy Scout Tree and Stout Memorial Grove trailheads. ✥ *Western access off U.S. 101 in Crescent City, east on Elk Valley Rd.; eastern access off U.S. 199, South Fork Rd. to Douglas Park Rd.*

SCENIC STOPS

Crescent Beach Overlook

VIEWPOINT | FAMILY | The scenery here includes views of the ocean and, in the distance, Crescent City and its working

Plants and Wildlife in Redwood

Coast redwoods, the world's tallest trees, grow in the moist, temperate climate of California's North Coast. The current record holder, Hyperion, tops out at 380 feet and was found in the Redwood Creek watershed in 2006. These ancient giants thrive in an environment that exists in only a few hundred coastal miles along the Pacific Ocean. They commonly live 600 years—though some have been around for more than 2,000 years.

Diverse, Complex

A healthy redwood forest is diverse and includes Douglas firs, western hemlocks, tan oaks, and madrone trees. The complex soils of the forest floor support a profusion of ferns, mosses, and fungi, along with numerous shrubs and berry bushes. Rhododendrons bloom all over in spring, a dazzling purple and pink contrast to the dense greenery.

Old-Growth Forests

Redwood National and State Parks hold nearly 50% of California's old-growth redwood forests, but only about a third of the forests in the parks are old-growth. Of the original 3,125 square miles (2 million acres) in the Redwoods Historic Range, only 4% survived logging that began in 1850. A quarter of these trees are privately owned and on managed land. The rest are on public tracts.

Wildlife Species

In the parks' backcountry, you might spot mountain lions, black bears, black-tailed deer, river otters, beavers, and minks. Roosevelt elk roam the flatlands, and the rivers and streams teem with salmon and trout. Gray whales, seals, and sea lions cavort near the coastline. More than 280 species of birds have been recorded in RNSP, which is located along the Pacific Flyway. In 2022, California condors were reintroduced with great fanfare.

---

harbor. In balmy weather this is a fine spot for a picnic. You may spot migrating gray whales between November and April. ⊠ *Enderts Beach Rd.* ✛ *Off U.S. 101, 4½ miles south of Crescent City.*

TRAILS

★ Boy Scout Tree Trail

TRAIL | This is the most challenging but also the most rewarding of the Howland Hill Road hikes. Give yourself about three hours to complete this 5.6-mile round-trip trek to verdant Fern Falls. The old-growth redwoods on the tranquil trail are magnificent. If you don't have enough time, the ½-mile-loop Stout Memorial Grove Trail is a nearby alternative. *Moderate.* ⊠ *Crescent City* ✛ *Trailhead: Howland Hill Rd., 3.7 miles east of Elk Valley Rd.*

Simpson-Reed Trail

TRAIL | **FAMILY** | Of the redwood hikes in Jedediah Smith Redwoods State Park, this flat, easy, 1-mile loop through an incredibly dense forest is the best fit if you have only an hour or so. The trailhead is a short hop off U.S. 199 between Crescent City and Hiouchi, and interpretative signs tell a bit about the diverse flora— you'll encounter hemlocks, huckleberries, and many ferns along this route. *Easy.* ⊠ *Crescent City* ✛ *Trailhead: Walker Rd., off U.S. 199, 2.5 miles east of U.S. 101.*

★ Stout Memorial Grove Trail

TRAIL | **FAMILY** | Civilization quickly recedes as you walk amid the grove's breathtakingly majestic standing and fallen old-growth trees. Ferns and redwood sorrel line the wide and easy path, which

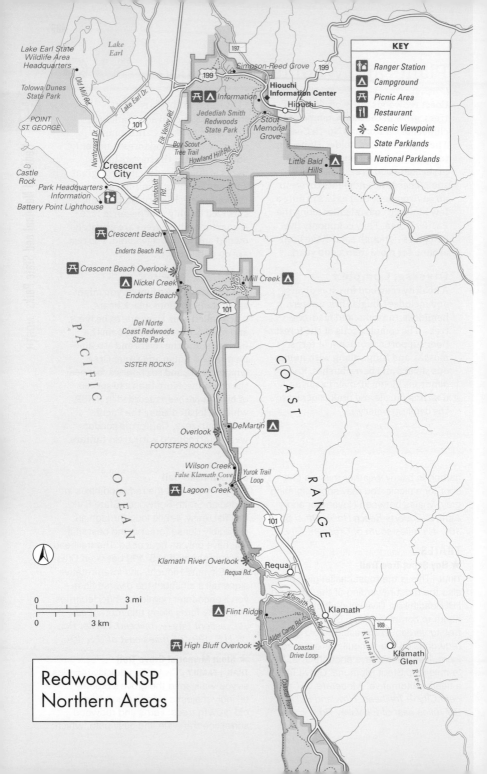

KEY

👤	Ranger Station
⛺	Campground
🍴	Picnic Area
🍽	Restaurant
⚡	Scenic Viewpoint
	State Parklands
	National Parklands

Lake Earl State Wildlife Area Headquarters

Lake Earl

197

Simpson-Reed Grove

199

199

Hiouchi Information Center

Hiouchi

Tolowa Dunes State Park

Information

Jedediah Smith Redwoods State Park

Stout Memorial Grove

POINT ST. GEORGE

Old Mill Rd.

Lake Earl Dr.

Elk Valley Rd.

101

Northcrest Dr.

Boy Scout Tree Trail

Howland Hill Rd.

Little Bald Hills

Castle Rock

Crescent City

Humboldt Rd.

Park Headquarters Information

Battery Point Lighthouse

Crescent Beach

Enderts Beach Rd.

Crescent Beach Overlook

Nickel Creek

Enderts Beach

Mill Creek

101

P A C I F I C

Del Norte Coast Redwoods State Park

SISTER ROCKS

C O A S T

O C E A N

Overlook

DeMartin

FOOTSTEPS ROCKS

R A N G E

Wilson Creek

False Klamath Cove

Yurok Trail Loop

Lagoon Creek

101

Klamath River Overlook

Requa

Requa Rd.

0   3 mi

0   3 km

Flint Ridge

Klamath Beach Rd.

Klamath

High Bluff Overlook

Alder Camp Rd.

169

Coastal Drive Loop

Klamath Glen

Coastal Trail

Klamath River

Redwood NSP Northern Areas

loops for ½ mile back to the parking lot. Extend your hike another mile following the slightly more difficult River Trail, which sidles along the Smith River. *Easy.* ⊠ *Redwood National Park* ⊹ *Trailhead: off Howland Hill Rd.*

Yurok Loop Trail

TRAIL | FAMILY | Providing a scenic opportunity to stretch your legs and breathe in fresh sea air, this 1.2-mile loop starts at the southern end of Del Norte Coast Redwoods State Park. After following the California Coastal Trail for a short stretch, the path forks off toward False Klamath Cove—keep an eye out for shorebirds and migrating whales here. Just north of False Klamath Cove, there's excellent beachcombing at Wilson Creek Beach. *Easy.* ⊠ *Klamath* ⊹ *Trailhead: Lagoon Creek Picnic Area, U.S. 101, 6.5 miles north of Klamath.*

VISITOR CENTERS

Crescent City Information Center

VISITOR CENTER | FAMILY | The headquarters of RSNP is the main information stop if you're approaching from the north. Located downtown, the center also has a gift shop and picnic area. ⊠ *1111 2nd St., Crescent City* ☎ *707/465–7335* ⊕ *www. nps.gov/redw* ⊗ *Closed Tues. and Wed. in Nov.–Mar.*

Hiouchi Visitor Center

VISITOR CENTER | FAMILY | This small center at Jedediah Smith Redwoods State Park has exhibits about the area's flora and fauna. A starting point for ranger programs (daily in summer, some weekends the rest of the year), the center has restrooms and a picnic area. ⊠ *U.S. 199, Hiouchi* ⊹ *Opposite Jedediah Smith Campground, 9 miles east of Crescent City* ☎ *707/458–3294* ⊕ *www.nps.gov/ redw* ⊗ *Closed Mon. and Tues. in winter.*

Jedediah Smith Visitor Center

VISITOR CENTER | FAMILY | Adjacent to the state park's main campground, this seasonal center has information about ranger-led walks and evening campfire programs. Also here are nature and history exhibits, a gift shop, and a picnic area. ⊠ *U.S. 199, Hiouchi* ⊹ *At Jedediah Smith Campground* ☎ *707/458–3496* ⊕ *www.nps.gov/redw* ⊗ *Closed early Sept.–mid-May.*

Activities

BIKING

In addition to roadways, you can bike on several trails, many of them along former logging roads. Best bets include the 11-mile Lost Man Creek Trail, which begins 3 miles north of Orick; the 12-mile round-trip Coastal Trail (Last Chance Section), which starts at the southern end of Enderts Beach Road and becomes steep and narrow as it travels through dense slopes of foggy redwood forests; and the 19-mile, single-track Ossagon Trail Loop in Prairie Creek Redwoods State Park, on which you're likely to see elk as you cruise through redwoods before coasting ocean side toward the end. ∎TIP→ Redwood Adventures (⇨ *see Hiking*) conducts guided e-bike tours.

BIRD-WATCHING

Many rare and striking winged specimens—chestnut-backed chickadees, brown pelicans, great blue herons, pileated woodpeckers, northern spotted owls, marbled murrelets—inhabit the area. In 2022, California condors were reintroduced.

CAMPING

Roughly 60 public and private camping facilities operate within 30 miles of the parks. For all campgrounds, check size limitations for RVs and trailers. Several primitive and backcountry sites (none drive-in) are first come, first served. All require a free permit obtainable at the Kuchel or Hiouchi visitor center. Bring drinking water—the sites have no sources.

Four developed drive-in campgrounds— Elk Prairie, Gold Bluffs Beach, Jedediah Smith, and Mill Creek, operate within state-park boundaries. There are no RV hookups, though Jedediah Smith and Mill Creek have dump stations. Fees are $35 nightly. Call ☎ 800/444–7275 or visit ⊕ www.reservecalifornia.com to book a site.

CANOEING

Redwood Yurok Canoe Tours

CANOEING & ROWING | FAMILY | Guides knowledgeable about Yurok traditions and the upper North Coast's natural splendor lead two- and four-hour Klamath River tours in authentic dugout canoes carved from redwoods. Boat-safety training precedes all excursions. ⊠ Tour check-in, 17635 U.S. 101, Redwood National Park ☎ 707/482–7775 ⊕ www.visityurokcountry.com ⊠ From $150 ⊘ Closed Mon. and Tues.

EDUCATIONAL PROGRAMS

RANGER PROGRAMS

Ranger-led programs explore the mysteries of the redwoods and the sea all summer. Topics include how the trees grow from fleck-size seeds to towering giants, what causes those weird fungi on old stumps, why the ocean fog is so essential to redwoods, and precisely what those green-tentacled creatures are that float in tide pools. Campfire programs can include slide shows, storytelling, music, and games. Check with visitor centers for offerings and times.

Junior Ranger Program

LOCAL SPORTS | FAMILY | Kids earn a badge by completing activity books available at visitor centers. Additionally, rangers lead programs for kids throughout the summer, including nature walks and lessons in bird identification and outdoor survival.

Ranger Talks

LOCAL SPORTS | FAMILY | From mid-May through mid-September, state park rangers lead discussions on the redwoods, tide pools, geology, and Native American culture. Check schedules at the visitor centers.

FISHING

Deep-sea and freshwater fishing are popular here, and a single state license (⊕ www.wildlife.ca.gov/licensing/fishing) covers both. A two-day license costs about $30. Anglers often stake out sections of the Klamath and Smith rivers seeking salmon and trout. You can go crabbing and clamming on the coast, but check the tides carefully: rip currents and sneaker waves can be deadly. Fishing from Crescent City's long B Street Pier requires no license.

Pergish Carlson's Blue Creek Guide Service

FISHING | FAMILY | Carlson, a Yurok Tribe member with years of experience, conveys the history of the Klamath River and his ancestors' connection to the waterway on guided salmon and steelhead fishing trips. His company provides rods, reels, tackle, bait, and life jackets, but you must acquire a fishing license ahead of time. He also conducts scenic river trips. ⊠ 75 Maple Rd., Klamath, Redwood National Park ☎ 707/951–1284 ⊕ fishklamathriver.com ⊠ Fishing trips $250 (2-person minimum).

HIKING

Towering redwoods may look cool from your car window, but hiking beneath them is the best way to behold their sheer immensity. The parks contain miles of trails, including short, level, easily managed treks just off the main roads. Avid hikers will find fantastic rambles with serious elevation gains and thrilling flora and fauna.

Some hikes don't pass big trees but rather hug the wild, pristine shoreline. Most famous is the Coastal Trail, which runs for about 70 miles from RNSP's northern to southern end.

Visitors without the time or inclination to research trails and sights often find booking a tour an efficient way to experience the parks' highlights.

★ **Bigfoot Adventure Academy**
HIKING & WALKING | FAMILY | "Helping visitors fulfill their outdoor dreams" is the goal of this outfit affiliated with a Eureka sporting goods store. Redwoods hiking is a particular strength, and there are several such naturalist-led excursions, as well as a foraging adventure. Bigfoot will also customize tours based on your interests. Other activities include surfing, kayaking, tide-pooling, and firearms training. ⊠ *Pacific Outfitters, 1600 5th St., Eureka, Redwood National Park* ☎ *844/926–6566* ⊕ *bigfootaa.com* ✉ *From $99 per person ($250 minimum).*

★ **Redwood Adventures**
HIKING & WALKING | FAMILY | This small outfit's passionate staff conducts half- and full-day excursions that include hikes through stunning redwood groves, a tide-pooling adventure, a Fern Canyon tour, and guided e-bike treks through the parks. ⊠ *Elk Meadow Cabins, 7 Valley Green Camp Rd., Orick* ☎ *866/733–9637* ⊕ *www.redwoodadventures.com* ✉ *From $100* ۞ *No Fern Canyon tour mid-June–Sept.*

KAYAKING
With many miles of often shallow rivers, streams, and estuarial lagoons, kayaking is a popular pastime in the parks, especially in the south near the Kuchel center, on Arcata and Humboldt bays near Eureka, up north along the Klamath and Smith rivers, and on the ocean in Crescent City.

Humboats Kayak Adventures
KAYAKING | FAMILY | You can rent kayaks and book kayaking tours that, from December to June, include whale-watching trips. Half-day river kayaking excursions pass beneath massive redwoods. ⊠ *Woodley Island Marina, 601 Startare Dr., Dock A, Eureka* ☎ *707/443–5157* ⊕ *www.humboatskayaking.com* ✉ *From $30 rentals, $55 tours.*

★ **Kayak Trinidad**
KAYAKING | FAMILY | This respected outfitter rents kayaks and stand-up paddleboards for sea kayaking or touring Humboldt Lagoons State Park. You can book guided half-day paddles around the spectacular Big Lagoon, where Roosevelt elk sometimes traipse along the shore, and raptors, herons, and waterfowl abound. You'll also see plenty of wildlife on the Trinidad Bay tour, with gray-whale sightings likely from March to May. ⊠ *Trinidad* ☎ *707/329–0085* ⊕ *www.kayaktrinidad.com.*

WHALE-WATCHING
Good vantage points for whale-watching include Crescent Beach Overlook, the Kuchel visitor center in Orick, points along the Coastal Trail, Klamath Beach Road, and Klamath River Overlook. From late November through January is the best time to see their southward migration; from February through April the whales return, usually passing closer to shore.

What's Nearby

Arcata

8 miles north of Eureka, 33 miles south of Kuchel visitor center.

Begun in 1850 as a base camp for miners and loggers, Arcata is today an artsy, progressive college town. Activity centers on the grassy Arcata Plaza, which is surrounded by restored buildings containing bars, cafés, and indie shops.

GETTING HERE AND AROUND
Arcata sits along U.S. 101 just south of its junction with Highway 299, the hilly, winding route connecting the coast and I–5 to the east.

ESSENTIALS

VISITOR INFORMATION Arcata Chamber of Commerce. ✉ *1635 Heindon Rd., Arcata* ☎ *707/897–6004* 🌐 *www.arcatachamber.com.*

Sights

Septentrio Winery & Tasting Room

WINERY | **FAMILY** | Estate Pinot Noir and sparkling and still Pinot rosés are the flagship wines of this Humboldt County producer, which also makes whites and reds from several other Northern California appellations and Oregon's Willamette Valley. The downtown tasting room—exposed beams, white walls, polished concrete floor—and its spacious gravel outdoor patio areas are highly social and family-friendly. ✉ *650 6th St., Arcata* ☎ *6707/672–2058* 🌐 *www.septentriowinery.com* 🎟 *Tastings from $18* 🕒 *Closed Mon. and Tues.*

Restaurants

★ Salt Fish House

$$ | **SEAFOOD** | A couple of blocks from Arcata's festive plaza, this hip seafood restaurant inside a beautifully converted old machine shop offers seating in an airy dining room and on a large side patio. Specialties include classic panko-crusted cod and chips and seared-rare steelhead, but you could also make a meal of small plates from the raw bar—shrimp cocktail, ceviche tostadas, and raw or grilled Pacific oysters among them. **Known for:** sharable raw-seafood trays and towers; wine and cocktail list; happy hour 3:30–5. [$] *Average main: $30* ✉ *935 I St., Arcata* ☎ *707/630–5300* 🌐 *www.saltfishhouse.com* 🕒 *Closed Mon. No lunch in winter.*

Coffee and Quick Bites

Cafe Brio

$ | **AMERICAN** | **FAMILY** | With an inviting indoor dining room and outside seating overlooking bustling Arcata Plaza, this artisan bakery and restaurant is known for savory and sweet breads. Notable noshes include quiche, ham-and-cheese breakfast croissants, croques monsieur and madame, and focaccia sandwiches with avocado and Humboldt Fog goat cheese from Arcata's Cypress Grove creamery. **Known for:** lemon cream tarts and other pastries available all day; excellent coffee and espresso drinks; grab-and-go breakfast and lunch sandwiches. [$] *Average main: $15* ✉ *791 G St., Arcata* ☎ *707/822–5922* 🌐 *www.cafebrioarcata.com* 🕒 *No dinner.*

Wildberries Marketplace

$ | **SANDWICHES** | **FAMILY** | This market with a juice bar and a small café sells prepared salads, deli items, cheeses, and picnic provisions. There's a good selection of local wine and beer. **Known for:** burgers and jerk chicken sandwiches; organic produce; pizzas, tarts, pies, and other baked goods. [$] *Average main: $9* ✉ *747 13th St., Arcata* ☎ *707/822–0095* 🌐 *www.wildberries.com.*

Klamath

13 miles north of Prairie Creek Redwoods Visitor Center, 22 miles south of Crescent City, 64 miles north of Eureka.

Surrounded by parkland, Klamath is a hub of the indigenous Yurok people, who make up nearly 50% of the town's population and operate a casino resort in its center. A few inexpensive motels and eateries, plus the Historic Requa Inn, are among the area amenities.

GETTING HERE AND AROUND

Downtown Klamath is a mile north of the Klamath River off U.S. 101. Public transit is not a viable option for touring.

ESSENTIALS

VISITOR INFORMATION Visit Yurok Country. ✉ *101 Klamath Blvd., Klamath* ☎ *707/482–1555* 🌐 *www.visityurokcountry.com.*

Sights

Trees of Mystery
FOREST | FAMILY | Since opening in 1946, this goofy but endearing roadside attraction has been doling out family fun. The kitschy thrills begin the moment you pull your car up to the 49-foot-tall talking statue of Paul Bunyan alongside Babe the Blue Ox. You can then explore a genuinely informative museum of Native American artifacts, admire intricately carved redwood figures, and browse tacky souvenirs. A six-passenger gondola glides over the redwood treetops for a majestic view of the forest canopy, which you can also experience 50–100 feet high on the Redwood Canopy Trail. At ground level, several mostly easy trails wind through the adjacent forest. ✉ *15500 U.S. 101 N, Klamath* ✥ *4½ miles north of Yurok Country Visitor Center* ☎ *800/638–3389* 🌐 *www.treesofmystery.net* 🎫 *$25.*

Restaurants

Woodland Villa Restaurant
$ | AMERICAN | FAMILY | This homey, diner-style café just north of Klamath serves the sort of hearty American fare that'll fuel you up before a big day of hiking. The cooks prepare breakfast sandwiches, Belgian waffles, and chicken-fried steaks in the morning, and deli sandwiches, salads, and pizzas throughout the rest of the day. **Known for:** craft beers and ciders; local smoked salmon in the adjacent market; closes at 5:30 or 6 pm depending on the season. [$] *Average main: $11* ✉ *15870 U.S. 101, Klamath* ☎ *707/482–2081* 🌐 *www.woodlandvillacabins.com* 🕓 *Closed Sun. (but check).*

Hotels

★ Historic Requa Inn
$ | B&B/INN | A short drive from the middle section of Redwood National and State Parks, this serene 1914 inn overlooks the Klamath River a mile east of where it meets the ocean. **Pros:** antiques-furnished guest rooms; within easy reach of trails and scenic drives; excellent seasonal restaurant (also open to nonguests). **Cons:** least expensive rooms are small; not a good choice for families with kids; room rate doesn't include additional cleaning fee. [$] *Rooms from: $159* ✉ *451 Requa Rd., Klamath* ☎ *707/482–1425* 🌐 *www.requainn.com* 🛏 *16 rooms* 🍴 *No Meals.*

Motel Trees
$ | HOTEL | FAMILY | Operated by and adjacent to the joyfully kitschy Trees of Mystery roadside attraction, this casual mid-century motel has simply furnished rooms brightened with paintings and, in some cases, wall-length photographic murals of local redwoods and coastal scenes. **Pros:** very affordable; close to beaches and trails; retro-1950s vibe. **Cons:** few frills; so-so restaurant; noise from U.S. 101. [$] *Rooms from: $119* ✉ *15495 U.S. 101, Klamath* ☎ *707/482–3152, 800/848–2982* 🌐 *www.moteltrees.com* 🛏 *23 rooms* 🍴 *No Meals.*

Crescent City

5 miles north of Del Norte Coast Redwoods State Park, 5 miles west of Jedediah Smith Redwoods State Park, 25 miles south of Brookings, OR, 82 miles southwest of Grants Pass, OR.

The headquarters of Redwood National and State Parks and its northern gateway, this small oceanfront city offers close access to Jedediah Smith's redwoods, Del Norte's sweeping, boulder-strewn beaches, and other highlights. Although often socked in by summer fog and pelted by winter storms, the town enjoys a remarkable scenic setting overlooking the Pacific. Mid-priced restaurants and accommodations predominate.

GETTING HERE AND AROUND
Crescent City straddles U.S. 101 about 20 miles south of Oregon. Public transit serves parts of downtown but service is infrequent.

ESSENTIALS
VISITOR INFORMATION Visit Del Norte County. ✉ *1001 Front St., Crescent City* ☎ *707/464–3174* 🌐 *www.visitdelnorte-county.com.*

Sights

Battery Point Lighthouse
LIGHTHOUSE | FAMILY | During low tide, you can walk from the pier across the ocean floor to this working lighthouse. Built in 1856, it houses a museum with nautical artifacts and shipwreck photographs. There's purportedly a resident ghost. ✉ *235 Lighthouse Way, Crescent City* ☎ *707/464–3089* 🌐 *www.delnortehistory.org* 🎫 *$5* ⏲ *Closed weekdays Oct.–Mar.*

Northcoast Marine Mammal Center
ZOO | FAMILY | The small center rescues and rehabilitates stranded, sick, and injured seals, sea lions, dolphins, and porpoises. Placards and kiosks provide information about marine mammals and coastal ecosystems, and even when the place is closed you can observe the rescued animals through a fence enclosing individual pools. Call the day of your visit to find out when feedings will occur. ✉ *424 Howe Dr., Crescent City* ☎ *707/465–6265* 🌐 *www.northcoastmmc.org* 🎫 *Free.*

Restaurants

Good Harvest Cafe
$$ | AMERICAN | FAMILY | A cheerful café serving hearty, delicious breakfasts and espresso drinks, Good Harvest lives up to its name with ample use of locally grown and organic ingredients. Salads, burgers, sandwiches, vegetarian specialties, and several fish entrées are on the menu for lunch and dinner. **Known for:** fish-and-chips and other local seafood; local beers and West Coast wines; vegetarian items. [$] *Average main: $24* ✉ *575 U.S. 101 S, Crescent City* ☎ *707/465–6028* 🌐 *facebook.com/thegoodharvestcafe.*

★ SeaQuake Brewing
$ | AMERICAN | Water from the cool and clean Smith River goes into the dozen or so beers poured at this microbrewery with a modern-industrial interior. They pair well with wood-fired thin-crust pizzas that include one with grilled chicken, bacon, artichoke hearts, garlic cream sauce, and cheeses from the local Rumiano Cheese Company. **Known for:** patio with heat lamps; well-crafted beers; off-menu caramel sundae. [$] *Average main: $17* ✉ *400 Front St., Crescent City* ☎ *707/465–4444* 🌐 *seaquakebrewing.com.*

Hotels

Curly Redwood Lodge
$ | HOTEL | FAMILY | A single redwood tree produced the 57,000 board feet of lumber used to build this budget 1957 motor lodge, and the mid-century modern furnishings make the most of that tree—including redwood paneling, platform beds, and built-in dressers. **Pros:** retro style; nearby restaurants; decent value. **Cons:** perfunctory welcome; sketchy Wi-Fi; no breakfast. [$] *Rooms from: $117* ✉ *701 U.S. 101 S, Crescent City* ☎ *707/464–2137* 🌐 *www.curlyredwoodlodge.com* 🛏 *36 rooms* 🍴 *No Meals.*

Ocean View Inn & Suites
$ | HOTEL | FAMILY | This clean, comfortable, reasonably priced hotel doesn't have a lot of bells and whistles, but its water's-edge location makes up for it. **Pros:** views of the water; many restaurants nearby; good value. **Cons:** on a busy road; cookie-cutter furnishings; sound of nearby foghorn. [$] *Rooms from: $135* ✉ *270 U.S. 101, Crescent City* ☎ *707/465–1111, 855/623–2611* 🌐 *www.oceanviewinncrescentcity.com* 🛏 *65 rooms* 🍴 *Free Breakfast.*

Chapter 15

THE FAR NORTH

Updated by
Daniel Mangin

15

Sights	Restaurants	Hotels	Shopping	Nightlife
★★★★☆	★★★☆☆	★★★☆☆	★★★☆☆	★★★☆☆

WELCOME TO THE FAR NORTH

TOP REASONS TO GO

★ **Mother Nature's wonders:** California's Far North has more rivers, streams, lakes, forests, and mountains than you'll ever have time to explore.

★ **Volcanoes:** With two volcanoes to view— Lassen and Shasta—you can learn firsthand what happens when a mountain blows its top.

★ **Fantastic fishing:** Whether you like casting from a riverbank or letting your line bob beside a boat, you'll find fabulous fishing in all the northern counties.

★ **Cool hops:** On a hot day there's nothing quite as inviting as a visit to Chico's world-famous Sierra Nevada Brewery. Take the tour, and then savor a chilled glass on tap at the adjacent brewpub.

★ **Shasta:** Wonderful in all its forms: lake, dam, river, mountain, forest, and town.

1 Chico. A state university and a famous brewery help set the mood in this city also known for its artisans and farmers.

2 Corning. Olive-oil tasting rooms make this small town a fun stop for travelers along I–5.

3 Redding. This northern gateway to Lassen Volcanic National Park has several points of interest within city limits, and day trips to Weaverville, Shasta Dam, and Lake Shasta Caverns National Natural Landmark are easily undertaken from here.

4 Weaverville. A 19th-century temple erected by Chinese miners is the centerpiece of this laid-back town's historic district.

5 Shasta Lake. Caverns, Shasta Dam, and vacation houseboats count among this quiet town's draws.

6 Dunsmuir. The upper Sacramento River near Dunsmuir consistently ranks among the country's best fishing spots. Most of the accommodations at a popular resort here were formerly cabooses.

7 Mt. Shasta. The town named for the peak that towers above it lures outdoorsy types year-round—hikers and golfers in summer, skiers in winter.

8 Chester. The southern gateway to Lassen Volcanic National Park sits on the forested edge of Lake Almanor.

9 Mineral. Lassen's official address is this town within the 165-square-mile national treasure.

10 Burney. President Theodore Roosevelt was among the fans of two magnificent waterfalls here.

11 Tulelake. Hundreds of underground lava tube caves make this town's Lava Beds National Monument well worth the remote drive.

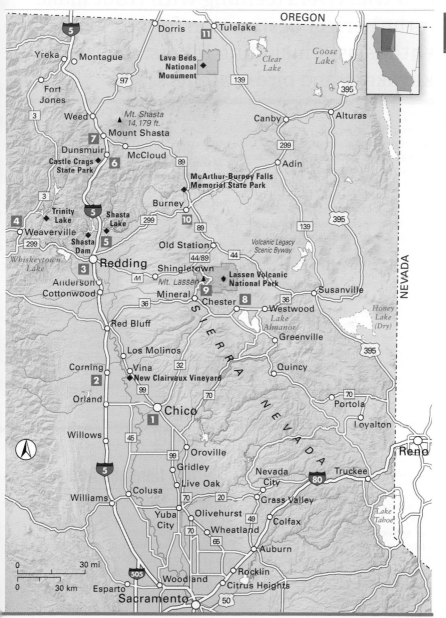

The Far North's soaring mountain peaks, trail-filled national forests, alpine lakes, and wild rivers teeming with trout make it the perfect destination for outdoor enthusiasts, including hikers, cyclists, kayakers, and bird-watchers.

You won't find many hot nightspots or cultural enclaves in this region which you'll also see branded as Upstate CA, but you will discover crowd-free national and state parks, crystal clear mountain streams, and superlative hiking and fishing, plus small towns worth exploring. And the spectacular landscapes of Lassen Volcanic National Park and Mt. Shasta are sure to impress.

The wondrous landscape of California's northeastern corner is the product of volcanic activity. At the southern end of the Cascade Range, Lassen Volcanic National Park is the best place to witness the Far North's fascinating geology. Beyond the sulfur vents and bubbling mud pots, the park owes much of its beauty to 10,457-foot Mt. Lassen and 50 wilderness lakes. Mt. Lassen and another volcano, Mt. Shasta, draw amateur geologists, weekend hikers, and avid mountain climbers to their rugged terrain. An intricate network of high-mountain watersheds feeds lakes large and small, plus streams and rivers that course through several forests.

The most enduring image of the region, though, is Mt. Shasta, whose 14,179-foot snowcapped peak beckons outdoor adventurers of all kinds. There are many versions of Shasta to enjoy—the mountain, the lake, the river, the town, the dam, and the forest—all named after the Native Americans known as the

Shatasla, or Sastise, who once inhabited the region.

MAJOR REGIONS
From Chico to Mt. Shasta. The Far North is bisected, south to north, by I–5, which passes through several historic towns and state parks, as well as miles of mountainous terrain. Halfway to the Oregon border is Lake Shasta, a favorite recreation destination, and farther north stands the spectacular snowy peak of Mt. Shasta.

The Backcountry. East of I–5, the Far North's main corridor, scenic two-lane roads crisscross the wilderness, leading to dramatic mountain peaks and fascinating natural wonders. Small towns settled in the second half of the 19th century seem frozen in time, except that they are well equipped with tourist amenities.

Planning

Getting Here and Around

AIR
For the cheapest fares, fly into Sacramento, rent a car (you'll need one anyway), and drive north. United Express and Avelo serve Redding's small airport, which has no shuttle service. Ride-sharing (starting at about $16 to downtown) is the best option.

AIR CONTACTS Redding Municipal Airport. ✉ *6751 Woodrum Circle, off Airport Rd., Redding* ☎ *530/224–4320* ⊕ *www.cityofredding.org/departments/airports.*

BUS AND TRAIN

Greyhound buses stop in Chico and Redding. STAGE buses serve Dunsmuir and Mt. Shasta. Various other agencies provide local public transit. Amtrak serves Chico, Redding, and Dunsmuir.

BUS CONTACTS STAGE. ☎ *530/842–8220* ⊕ *www.co.siskiyou.ca.us/generalservices/page/stage-schedule.*

CAR

Interstate 5 runs up the center of California through Redding and Mt. Shasta. Chico is east of I–5, where Highways 32 and 99 intersect. Lassen Volcanic National Park can be reached off I–5 by Highway 36 from Red Bluff or (except in winter) Highway 44 from Redding. Highway 299 connects Weaverville and Redding. Check weather reports and carry detailed maps, warm clothing, and tire chains if you head into mountainous terrain in winter.

ROAD CONDITIONS Caltrans. ☎ *800/427–7623* ⊕ *quickmap.dot.ca.gov.*

Hotels

Chain properties predominate in this region, with the occasional inn or restored hotel. Wilderness resorts close in fall and reopen in mid-spring after snow season ends. Book well ahead for summer visits to Mt. Shasta, Dunsmuir, Mineral, and Chester and to ensure state or national park campsite availability.

Restaurants

Redding and Chico have the most varied restaurant options. Cafés and simple eateries are the norm in smaller towns. Dress is always informal.

⇨ *Restaurant and hotel reviews have been shortened. For full information, visit Fodors.com. Restaurant prices are the average cost of a main course at dinner, or if dinner is not served, at lunch. Hotel prices are the lowest cost of a standard double room in high season.*

What It Costs			
$	$$	$$$	$$$$
RESTAURANTS			
under $20	$20–$30	$31–$40	over $40
HOTELS			
under $200	$200–$350	$351–$500	over $500

Visitor Information

CONTACTS Shasta Cascade Wonderland Association. ✉ *Shasta Outlets, 1699 Hwy. 273, off I–5, Exit 667, Anderson* ☎ *530/365–7500* ⊕ *www.upstateca. com.* **Visit Trinity County.** ✉ *509 Main St., Weaverville* ☎ *530/623–6101* ⊕ *www. visittrinity.com.*

When to Go

Heat scorches the valley in summer. Temperatures above 110°F are common, but the mountains provide cool respite. Fall throughout the Far North is beautiful, rivaled only by spring, when wildflowers bloom and mountain creeks fed by the snowmelt splash through the forests. Winter is usually temperate in the valley, but cold and snowy in the high country. As a result, some attractions are closed in winter or have sharply curtailed hours.

Chico

86 miles north of Sacramento.

Its name is Spanish for "small," but with more than 102,000 residents, Chico is the Far North's largest city. Chico State University, scores of local artisans, and area agriculture all influence life here, but the Sacramento Valley city's main claim to fame—and the premier visitor attraction—is the nationally renowned Sierra Nevada Brewery.

GETTING HERE AND AROUND

Highway 99, off I–5 from the north or south, and Highway 32 east off the interstate, intersect Chico. Amtrak and Greyhound stop here, and Butte Regional Transit's B-Line buses serve the area. Chico's downtown neighborhoods are walkable.

BUS CONTACT B-Line. ✉ *Chico* ☎ *530/342–0221* ⊕ *www.blinetransit. com.*

ESSENTIALS
VISITOR INFORMATION Chico Chamber of Commerce. ✉ *180 E. 4th St., Suite 120, Chico* ☎ *530/891–5556* ⊕ *www.chico-chamber.com.*

◉ Sights

Bidwell Mansion State Historic Park
HISTORIC HOME | FAMILY | Built between 1865 and 1868 by General John Bidwell, the founder of Chico, this mansion was designed by Henry W. Cleaveland, a San Francisco architect. Bidwell and his wife, Annie, welcomed many distinguished guests to their pink Italianate home, including President Rutherford B. Hayes, naturalist John Muir, suffragist Susan B. Anthony, and General William T. Sherman. One-hour tours take in most of the three-story mansion's 26 rooms. ✉ *525 Esplanade, at Memorial Way, Chico* ☎ *530/895–6144* ⊕ *www.parks.ca.gov* ✑ *$6* ⊘ *Closed Mon., Tues., Thurs., and Fri.*

Bidwell Park
CITY PARK | FAMILY | The 3,670-acre park straddles Big Chico Creek, where scenes from *Gone With the Wind* (1939) and *Robin Hood* (1938), starring Errol Flynn, were filmed. The region's recreational hub has a golf course; "the best urban swimming holes in California"; and biking, hiking, horseback riding, and skating trails. Chico Creek Nature Center serves as the official information site. ✉ *1968 E. 8th St., Chico* ⊹ *Off Hwy. 99* ☎ *530/891–4671* ⊕ *chicorec.com/chico-creek-nature-center* ✑ *Park free, nature center $4* ⊘ *Nature center closed Tues.– Fri. (but check).*

Museum of Northern California Art
ART MUSEUM | The Veterans Memorial Building, a handsome 1927 Classical Revival structure designed by a local architectural firm, houses this engaging museum of contemporary art. The focus is on works by artists from San Jose north to Oregon. ✉ *900 Esplanade, at E. Washington Ave., Chico* ☎ *530/487–7272* ⊕ *www.monca.org* ✑ *$5* ⊘ *Closed Mon.–Wed.*

★ Sierra Nevada Brewing Company
BREWERY | This pioneer of the microbrewery movement still has a hands-on approach to beer making. The Brewhouse Tour surveys production—from sorting hops through fermentation and bottling—and concludes with a tasting. The Beyond the Pale Tour delves even deeper into creating craft beers, Sierra Nevada's history, and the company's sustainability initiatives. ✉ *1075 E. 20th St., at Sierra Nevada St., Chico* ☎ *530/345–2739 taproom, 530/899–4776 tours* ⊕ *www.sierranevada.com* ✑ *Tours (includes tasting) from $9* ⊘ *No tours Mon. and Tues. (bar and restaurant open daily).*

🍴 Restaurants

★ 5th Street Steakhouse

$$$$ | **STEAKHOUSE** | Hand-cut steak is the star in this refurbished early 1900s building, the place to come when you're craving red meat, a huge baked potato, or some fresh seafood. Exposed redbrick walls warm the dining rooms, and a long mahogany bar catches the overflow crowds that jam the restaurant on weekends. **Known for:** alfresco dining on outdoor patio; classic and specialty cocktails; prime cuts of beef with white-tablecloth service. [$] *Average main: $43* ✉ *345 W. 5th St., at Normal Ave., Chico* ☎ *530/891–6328* 🌐 *www.5thstreetsteakhouse.com* 🕓 *Closed Mon. No lunch Sat.–Thurs.*

The Rawbar Restaurant & Sushi

$$ | **ASIAN FUSION** | For more than two decades, the chefs at this downtown pan-Asian restaurant and bar have served up sushi, sashimi, rolls, "hot bites" like Korean tacos (short ribs with kimchi aioli), and build-your-own poké bowls. Chico being an inland destination, the sushi might not always be as absolutely fresh as on the coast, but even then it's close, and the nonsushi options show flair and imagination. **Known for:** blistered shishito peppers and other starters; Thai "drunken" noodles and Korean egg-topped pork belly over rice cake; signature cocktails and wine, sake, and whiskey flights. [$] *Average main: $27* ✉ *346 Broadway St., at W. 4th St., Chico* ☎ *530/897–0626* 🌐 *www.rawbarchico.com* 🕓 *Closed Mon. and Tues. No lunch Sun.*

Red Tavern

$$ | **MODERN AMERICAN** | With its burgundy carpet, white linen tablecloths, and mellow lighting, this is one of Chico's coziest restaurants. The Mediterranean-influenced menu, inspired by fresh local produce, with vegetarian and pescatarian fare in addition to meat and poultry dishes, changes seasonally—steak au poivre, bucatini and clams, grilled meat loaf, and pan-seared halibut are among recent offerings. **Known for:** wines from California and beyond; nightly specials, happy hour Monday–Thursday; patio seating. [$] *Average main: $29* ✉ *1250 Esplanade, at E. 3rd Ave., Chico* ☎ *530/894–3463* 🌐 *www.redtavern.com* 🕓 *Closed Mon. No lunch Tues.–Sat.*

Sierra Nevada Brewery Taproom

$ | **AMERICAN** | The famous brewery's high-ceilinged, heavy-on-the-wood taproom bustles day and night with patrons washing down well-conceived gastropub grub with the best-selling Pale Ale and smaller-batch offerings, some only available here. The open kitchen turns out sandwiches, burgers, wood-oven pizzas, and fish-and-chips (the fish's batter made with Pale Ale) with remarkable speed. **Known for:** pretzel with white-cheddar beer cheese and mustard; wings and salads; draft beers. [$] *Average main: $19* ✉ *1075 E. 20th St., Chico* ✣ *½ mile west of Hwy. 99, Exit 384* ☎ *530/345–2739* 🌐 *www.sierranevada.com/visit/california/taproom.*

☕ Coffee and Quick Bites

★ Bidwell Perk

$ | **AMERICAN** | **FAMILY** | A clean and tidy, many-windowed chain alternative for coffee (several different roasts daily) and pastries, Bidwell Perk also serves full breakfasts and light lunches. Bagels, French toast, quiche, and croissant sandwiches in the morning give way to small plates, salads, panini, and sliders as the day moves along. **Known for:** beer and wine selection; outdoor patio; well-crafted espresso drinks. [$] *Average main: $14* ✉ *664 E. 1st Ave., at Mangrove Ave., Chico* ☎ *530/899–1500* 🌐 *bidwellperk.com* 🕓 *No dinner.*

🛏 Hotels

Hotel Diamond

$ | **HOTEL** | Crystal chandeliers and gleaming century-old wooden floors and banisters welcome you into the foyer of this restored 1904 boutique property two blocks from Chico State University. **Pros:** downtown location; variety of accommodations, from affordable "Petite" rooms to spacious suites; refined rooms, some with bay windows and fireplaces. **Cons:** street scene can be noisy on weekends; some rooms are small; some rooms lack tubs. [$] *Rooms from: $159* ✉ *220 W. 4th St., near Broadway, Chico* ☎ *530/893–3100* 🌐 *www.hoteldiamondchico.com* 🛏 *59 rooms* 🍴 *No Meals.*

Corning

29 miles northwest of Chico, 50 miles south of Redding.

Signs along Highway 99 and I–5 beckon you to Corning. The town's favorable soil and plentiful sunshine have made it a center of olive cultivation and olive-oil manufacturing.

GETTING HERE AND AROUND

Corning lies just off I–5 at Exit 631. From Chico take Highway 99 for 17½ miles and follow signs west to Corning. TRAX provides weekday bus service.

CONTACTS TRAX. ☎ *530/602–8282* 🌐 *www.taketrax.com.*

Sights

New Clairvaux Vineyard

WINERY | History converges in fascinating ways at this winery and vineyard, whose tale involves pioneer-rancher Peter Lassen (Mt. Lassen is named for him), railroad baron Leland Stanford, newspaper magnate William Randolph Hearst, the Napa Valley's five-generation Nichelini wine-making family, and current owners the Trappist-Cistercian monks. In the 1890s, the rambling redbrick tasting room, erected by Stanford, stored 2 million gallons of wine. These days the hosts pour Albariño, Viognier, Tempranillo, Barbera, Syrah, and other small-lot bottlings from grapes mostly grown nearby. The on-site chapel (the Hearst connection) has a convoluted story all its own. A second tasting room in downtown Redding was scheduled to open before the end of 2023. ✉ *26240 7th St., Vina* ✣ *10 miles from Corning, South Ave. east off I–5 or Hwy. 99 to Rowles Rd. north to 7th St. west* ☎ *530/839–2434* 🌐 *www.newclairvauxvineyard.com* 🎟 *Tastings $10.*

Olive Pit

OTHER ATTRACTION | Three generations of the Craig family run this combination café and store, where you can learn about California olive production and purchase olive products, craft beers, small-lot wines, and artisanal foods. Sandwich selections at the café include muffulettas and messy-good olive burgers. Tickle your palate with a balsamic shake in flavors that include peach, fig, coconut, strawberry, and chocolate. ✉ *2156 Solano St., Corning* ✣ *Off I–5, Exit 631 (Corning Rd.)* ☎ *530/824–4667* 🌐 *www.olivepit.com.*

Redding

50 miles north of Corning.

A handy gateway to Lassen Volcanic National Park, Shasta Lake, and Lake Shasta Caverns, Redding, population about 94,000, sits along the busy I–5 corridor. The photogenic Sundial Bridge in Turtle Bay Exploration Park remains Redding's marquee attraction, but the promoters of Market Center, modeled on the artisanal stalls at San Francisco's Ferry Building and Napa's Oxbow, hope to lure visitors and locals to downtown's nascent cultural district.

GETTING HERE AND AROUND

Interstate 5 is the major north–south route through Redding. Highway 299 bisects the city east–west, and Highway 44 connects Redding and Lassen Park's northwest entrance.

ESSENTIALS

VISITOR INFORMATION Visit Redding.
✉ *1321 Butte St., Suite 100, Redding*
☎ *530/225–4100* ⊕ *www.visitredding.
com.*

Sights

Moseley Family Cellars

WINERY | The Moseleys make their wines in Redding and present them downtown, but the grapes come from vineyards as far afield as Napa, Sonoma, Lodi, and Oregon's Rogue Valley. There's usually a Chardonnay, and the reds include Pinot Noir, old-vine Zinfandel, and Cabernet Sauvignon. The tasting room, in an area emerging as a mini wine hub, occupies one of Redding's oldest residences.
✉ *Thompson House, 1448 Pine St., Redding* ✛ *Near Butte St.* ☎ *530/229–9463* ⊕ *www.moseleyfamilycellars.com* 🍷 *Tastings $10* ⊙ *Closed Mon. and Tues.*

Shasta State Historic Park

STATE/PROVINCIAL PARK | **FAMILY** | Six miles west of downtown and straddling Highway 299 lies the former town of Shasta City, which thrived in the mid- to late 1800s. This park's 19 acres of half-ruined brick buildings, accessed via trails, are a reminder of the glory days of the California gold rush. The former county courthouse building (whose exhibits include rare California landscape paintings), jail, and gallows have been restored to their 1860s appearance. The Litsch General Store (1850–1950), now a museum, displays items once sold here.
■ **TIP→ Next to the store in a wooden shack, family-run Shorty's Eatery (closed Monday and Tuesday) serves up good sandwiches and Filipino dishes.** ✉ *15312 Hwy. 299, Redding* ☎ *530/243–8194* ⊕ *www. parks.ca.gov/shastashp* 🍷 *Free to park, $3 Courthouse Museum* ⊙ *Courthouse Museum closed Mon.–Wed.*

★ Turtle Bay Exploration Park

CITY PARK | **FAMILY** | This peaceful downtown park has 300 acres of walking trails, an aquarium, an arboretum and botanical gardens, and many interactive exhibits for kids. The main draw is the stunning Santiago Calatrava–designed Sundial Bridge, a metal and translucent glass pedestrian walkway, suspended by cables from a single tower and spanning a broad bend in the Sacramento River. On sunny days the 217-foot tower lives up to the bridge's name, casting a shadow on the ground below to mark time. Access to the bridge and some trails is free, but the museum and gardens charge admission. ✉ *844 Sundial Bridge Dr., Redding* ☎ *530/243–8850* ⊕ *www. turtlebay.org* 🍷 *Museum $18, gardens $5 suggested* ⊙ *Museum closed Mon. and Tues. (except holidays) early Sept.–Apr.*

🍽 Restaurants

★ Café Paradisio

$$ | **AMERICAN** | Many Reddingites consider this softly lit restaurant with black-linen-topped tables and artworks for sale adorning the walls their town's best fine-dining option. The menu tilts heavily Italian (gnocchi, lasagna, chicken Marsala) and American (braised short ribs, pan-seared fish, an elk burger), but the chef ventures across the Pacific for dishes that might include a pork-belly appetizer or Thai coconut curry entrée.
Known for: baked Brie starter; house-made meatballs; many organic ingredients. 💲 *Average main: $29* ✉ *1270 Yuba St., Redding* ✛ *Near Pine St.* ☎ *530/215–3499* ⊕ *www.cafeparadisio. com* ⊙ *Closed Sun. and Mon. No lunch.*

Moonstone Bistro

$$$ | **AMERICAN** | The chef-owner at this light-filled restaurant in a strip mall 1½ miles southwest of downtown incorporates seasonal organic produce, free-range meats, sustainable line-caught fish, and cage-free eggs in his cuisine. Staples include salads, fish tacos, pasta dishes, and burgers (standard, veggie, or teriyaki mushroom Swiss) for dinner daily and lunch except on Sunday, when buckwheat pancakes, French toast, and two variations on eggs Benedict headline the brunch menu. **Known for:** organic produce; all-day bistro menu; Sunday brunch. [$] *Average main: $33* ✉ *3425 Placer St., near Buenaventura Blvd., Redding* ☎ *530/241–3663* ⊕ *www. moonstonebistro.com* ⊗ *Closed Mon. and Tues.*

Taroko Asian Bar & Grill

$$ | **ASIAN FUSION** | With items like Shanghai dumplings and Taiwanese sausage fried rice, this pan-Asian restaurant decorated with contemporary flair tilts heavily Chinese- the chef's from the mainland, the owner is Taiwanese- but Japan and the rest of Southeast Asia are amply represented. Some dishes seem tweaked to broaden their appeal, but they're generally well executed, and even on busy nights the staffers remain pleasant and efficient. **Known for:** small bites that can add up to a meal; salads, bowls, soups, rice, and noodles; specialty cocktails and beer selection. [$] *Average main: $29* ✉ *1701 Pine St., at Placer St., Redding* ☎ *530/255–8863* ⊕ *www. tarokoredding.com.*

Vintage Public House

$$ | **AMERICAN** | Patrons of this comfort-food haven across from downtown's 1935 Cascade movie palace wash down elevated pub grub with classic and craft cocktails and wines and beers from California and beyond. The fare includes salads, sandwiches, rice bowls, a locally revered mac-and-cheese, truffle burgers, fish-and-chips, and a few heartier entrées. **Known for:** patio dining; poke appetizer with jalapeño wonton nachos; artisanal spirits. [$] *Average main: $25* ✉ *1790 Market St., at Sacramento St., Redding* ☎ *530/229–9449* ⊕ *vintageredding.com* ⊗ *Closed Sun. No lunch Sat.*

☕ Coffee and Quick Bites

From the Hearth Kitchen & Pie Shop

$ | **AMERICAN** | **FAMILY** | A homegrown variation on the Panera theme, this extremely popular operation (as in expect a wait at peak dining hours) serves pastries, eggs and other hot dishes, and good coffee drinks, juices, and smoothies for breakfast. The chefs whip up a diverse selection of wraps, panini, sandwiches, burgers, rice bowls, and soups the rest of the day. **Known for:** pork breakfast tacos; pies and other baked goods; several other locations (two drive-through). [$] *Average main: $13* ✉ *2650 Churn Creek Rd., Redding* ✛ *Near E. Cypress St.* ☎ *530/424–2233* ⊕ *www.fthcafe.com.*

Hotels

★ Hope Inn Redding

$ | **B&B/INN** | Bordering Churn Creek on a bend in a residential street secluding the property from its neighbors, this two-turreted Tudor-style inn occupies 3½ woodsy acres several miles north of downtown and Sundial Bridge. **Pros:** creek and mountain views; individually decorated rooms; aim-to-please owners. **Cons:** lacks fitness center, room service, and other hotel amenities; must drive to attractions and restaurants; no breakfast (but coffeemaker and refrigerator in each room). [$] *Rooms from: $145* ✉ *19177 Hollow La., Redding* ☎ *530/605–0589* ⊕ *hopeinnredding.com* ⤢ *5 rooms* ⚭ *No Meals.*

★ Sheraton Redding Hotel at Sundial Bridge

$$ | **HOTEL** | **FAMILY** | Stylish and modern, this hotel at the entrance to Sundial Bridge and Turtle Bay Exploration Park makes a great, family-friendly base for visiting Lassen, Whiskeytown, and other area attractions. **Pros:** pool and gym; excellent restaurant; clean, spacious guest rooms. **Cons:** neighborhood not very walkable; nearly an hour's drive to Lassen Volcanic NP; parking fee. [$] *Rooms from: $242* ✉ *820 Sundial*

Bridge Dr., Redding ☎ 530/364–2800
⊕ www.marriott.com ⟟ 130 rooms
⚲ No Meals.

Nightlife

Final Draft Brewing Company
BARS | This spacious brick-walled brew-pub receives high acclaim for its accessible ales and above-average pub grub. Try the beer-battered Sidewinder Fries instead of regular ones. While they're cooking, order a sampler flight to decide which of the brews to wash them down with. ⊠ 1600 California St., at Placer St., Redding ☎ 530/338–1198 ⊕ www.finaldraftbrewingcompany.com.

Jack's Bar & Grill
BARS | The original 1938 iteration of Jack's featured a brothel upstairs, and though it's less risqué these days, the place exudes old-school charm. Stalwarts start with a stiff martini, followed by a classic steak (A-1 and Worcestershire sauce at every table). ⊠ 1743 California St., Redding ⊹ Near Sacramento St. ☎ 530/241–9705 ⊕ www.jacksgrillredding.com ⊙ Closed Sun. No lunch.

Woody's Brewing Company
BREWPUBS | A fun downtown hangout with a party vibe, Woody's has built a loyal following for its Bavarian soft pretzels (served with beer cheese), special-recipe tater tots, and range of beers from fruited wheat ales to an unfiltered dry-hopped IPA and the Pray for Powder porter. Sandwiches, worthy burgers, pizza, and fish-and-chips are also on the menu. ⊠ 1257 Oregon St., at Shasta St., Redding ☎ 530/768–1034 ⊕ www.woodysbrewing.com ⊙ Closed Mon.

Activities

The Fly Shop
FISHING | **FAMILY** | The store that bills itself as "Northern California's fly-fishing headquarters" sells gear and other products and has information about guides, conditions, and fishing trips. ⊠ 4140 Churn Creek Rd., at Denton Way, Redding ☎ 530/222–3555, 800/669–3474 ⊕ www.theflyshop.com.

Weaverville

46 miles west of Redding on Hwy. 299.

Chinese miners erected the 1874 Joss House that anchors Weaverville's downtown historic district. The town, population about 3,700, is a popular headquarters for family vacations and hiking, fishing, and gold-panning excursions.

GETTING HERE AND AROUND
Highway 299, east from the Pacific Coast or west from Redding, becomes Main Street in central Weaverville. Trinity Transit provides bus service.

ESSENTIALS
VISITOR INFORMATION Trinity County Visitors Bureau. ⊠ 509 Main St., Weaverville ☎ 530/623–6101 ⊕ visittrinity.com.

Sights

Hal Goodyear Historical Park
HISTORY MUSEUM | **FAMILY** | For a vivid sense of Weaverville's past, visit this outdoor park of old mining equipment, and step inside the adjacent **Jake Jackson Memorial Museum**. A blacksmith shop and a stamp mill (where ore is crushed) from the 1890s are still in use during certain community events. ⊠ 780 Main St., Weaverville ☎ 530/623–5211 ⊕ www.trinitymuseum.org ⊠ Free ⊙ Museum closed various days early Sept.–late May.

★ Weaverville Joss House State Historic Park
HISTORIC SIGHT | Weaverville's main attraction is the Joss House, a Taoist temple built in 1874 and called Won Lim Miao ("the temple of the forest beneath the clouds") by Chinese miners. The oldest continuously used Chinese temple in California, it attracts worshippers from

around the world. With its golden altar, antique weaponry, and carved wooden canopies, the Joss House is a piece of California history best appreciated on a guided 30-minute tour. ✉ *630 Main St., at Oregon St., Weaverville* ☎ *530/623–5284* 🌐 *www.parks.ca.gov* 🎟 *Museum free; guided tour $5* 🕑 *Closed Mon.–Wed.*

🍴 Restaurants

Mamma Llama Eatery & Cafe

$ | **AMERICAN** | **FAMILY** | Tap into the spirit of 21st-century Weaverville at this mellow café that serves breakfast (all day) and lunch, in winter specializing in hot soups to warm body and soul. Expect all the usual suspects at breakfast, along with Country Cheesy Potatoes (topped with green chili) and sausage between two biscuits topped with homemade sausage gravy; a spicy club wrap and several vegetarian sandwiches are among the lunch offerings. **Known for:** hometown vibe; good soups; espresso drinks. [$] *Average main: $10* ✉ *490 Main St., Weaverville* ☎ *530/623–6363* 🌐 *www.mammallama.com* 🕑 *Closed Sun. (but check). No dinner.*

Trinity County Brewing Company

$ | **AMERICAN** | Craft brews, from pale ales to stout, and food that's a cut above the expected have made this brewpub with a cavernous industrial interior a hit. The cheese-curd and chicken-wing starters and burger and grilled-chicken sandwich are among the best sellers. **Known for:** community feel; outside patio; garlic fries with secret sauce. [$] *Average main: $15* ✉ *301 Main St., Weaverville* ☎ *530/423–4114* 🌐 *trinitycountybrewery.com* 🕑 *Closed Mon. and Tues.*

🛏 Hotels

Weaverville Hotel

$ | **HOTEL** | Originally built during the gold rush, this restored hotel is filled with antiques and period furniture. **Pros:** gracious on-site owners; in heart of the historic district; beautifully restored. **Cons:** no breakfast on-site; children under 12 not permitted; only one room has a TV. [$] *Rooms from: $150* ✉ *481 Main St., Weaverville* ✥ *Near Court St.* ☎ *530/623–2222* 🌐 *www.weavervillehotel.com* 🛏 *7 rooms* 🍴 *No Meals.*

🏃 Activities

Weaverville Ranger Station

HIKING & WALKING | Check here for maps, free wilderness and campfire permits, and information about local fishing and the 600 miles of hiking trails in the 500,000-acre Trinity Alps Wilderness. ✉ *360 Main St., Weaverville* ☎ *530/623–2121* 🕑 *Closed weekends.*

Shasta Lake

10 miles north of Redding.

The city of Shasta Lake, population about 10,000, is a portal to water, wilderness, and dazzling stalagmites, with the monolithic Shasta Dam in the midst of it all.

GETTING HERE AND AROUND

Shasta Lake lies at the intersection of I–5 and Highway 151. There is no local bus service.

👁 Sights

Lake Shasta

BODY OF WATER | **FAMILY** | Created when Shasta Dam corralled the Sacramento River in the 1940s, Lake Shasta evolved into a habitat for numerous types of fish, including rainbow trout, salmon, bass, brown trout, and catfish. The region also supports a large nesting population of bald eagles. You can rent houseboats, fishing boats, ski boats, sailboats, canoes, paddleboats, Jet Skis, and windsurfing boards at marinas and resorts along the 370-mile shoreline. ✉ *Shasta Lake* 🌐 *www.upstateca.com.*

★ Lake Shasta Caverns
National Natural Landmark

CAVE | FAMILY | Stalagmites, stalactites, flowstone deposits, and crystals entice visitors to the Lake Shasta Caverns. To see this impressive spectacle, you must take the two-hour tour, which includes a catamaran ride across the McCloud arm of Lake Shasta and a bus ride up North Grey Rocks Mountain to the cavern entrance. The temperature in the caverns is 58°F year-round, making them a cool retreat on a hot summer day. The most awe-inspiring of the limestone rock formations is the glistening Cathedral Room, which appears to be gilded.
■ TIP→ In summer, it's wise to purchase tickets online a day or more ahead of your visit. ⊠ 20359 Shasta Caverns Rd., Lakehead ⊕ 20 miles north of Redding (take I–5 Exit 695 and follow signs) ☎ 530/238–2341, 800/795–2283 ⊕ www.lakeshastacaverns.com ☒ $40.

Shasta Dam

DAM | FAMILY | Road-trippers traveling along I–5 often stop at the second-largest concrete dam in the United States— only Grand Coulee in Washington is bigger than Shasta Dam, completed in 1945. The visitor center's 20-minute film and exhibits explain the engineering and construction, but even if the facility isn't open, the photogenic view north to snowcapped Mt. Shasta makes the dam worth the detour. The landmark's history-laden guided tours were set to resume by 2024. ⊠ 16349 Shasta Dam Blvd., Shasta Lake ⊕ From I–5 Exit 685, take Hwy. 151/Shasta Dam Blvd. west to Lake Blvd. north ☎ 530/247–8555 ⊕ www.usbr.gov/mp/ncao/shasta-dam.html ☒ Free ☉ Visitor center closed Wed. and Thurs. (but check).

 Activities

Shasta Marina at Packers Bay

BOATING | FAMILY | Trips aboard this highly regarded operator's amenities-packed houseboats, which sleep up to 20 people, qualify as waterborne glamping. Some boats even have a hot tub on board. Smaller watercraft are also available for rent. ⊠ 16814 Packers Bay Rd., Lakehead ⊕ West from I–5, Exit 693 (see directions on website) ☎ 800/959–3359 ⊕ shastalake.net ☒ Houseboats from $1,215 per night in summer, 3-night minimum.

Dunsmuir

10 miles south of Mt. Shasta.

Surrounded by towering forests and boasting world-class upper Sacramento River fly-fishing, Dunsmuir acquired its current moniker when a Scottish coal baron built a fountain in exchange for the town renaming itself in his honor. (Fame came cheap back in the day.) An upscale restaurant, a brewpub, and a boutique hotel do business downtown. Farther out lie the restored-caboose lodgings of the Railroad Park Resort. Check with the chamber of commerce for information on local fishing guides.

GETTING HERE AND AROUND

Reach Dunsmuir via exits off I–5 at the north and south ends of town. Amtrak stops here. On weekdays, STAGE buses serve Dunsmuir.

ESSENTIALS

VISITOR INFORMATION Dunsmuir Chamber of Commerce. ⊠ 5915 Dunsmuir Ave., Suite 100, Dunsmuir ☎ 530/235–2177 ⊕ dunsmuir.com.

Sights

★ Castle Crags State Park

STATE/PROVINCIAL PARK | FAMILY | Named for its 2,000–6,500-foot glacier-polished crags, formed by volcanic activity centuries ago, this park offers fishing on the upper Sacramento River, hiking in the backcountry, and a view of Mt. Shasta. The 4,350-acre park has 28 miles of trails, including a 2¾-mile access trail to Castle Crags Wilderness, part of the Shasta-Trinity National Forest. The excellent trails at lower altitudes include the ¼-mile Vista Point Trail (near the entrance), which leads to views of Castle Crags and Mt. Shasta. ✉ *20022 Castle Creek Rd., Castella* ✣ *I–5, Exit 724, 6 miles south of Dunsmuir* ☎ *530/235–2684* 🌐 *www.castlecragspark.org* 🎫 *$10 per vehicle, day-use.*

🍴 Restaurants

★ Café Maddalena

$$ | **MEDITERRANEAN** | The chef here gained experience working in top San Francisco restaurants before moving north to prepare adventurous Mediterranean fare with a French influence. Appetizers like a recent menu's mozzarella-stuffed arancini with a piquant tomato-based sauce hint at the level of refinement on display, as do entrées that might include cassoulet or roasted steelhead trout. **Known for:** pizzas and pasta dishes; artisanal small-lot wines; outdoor dining under an arbor. [$] *Average main: $30* ✉ *5801 Sacramento Ave., Dunsmuir* ☎ *530/235–2725* 🌐 *www.cafemaddalena.com* ⏲ *Closed Mon.–Wed. and Jan.–mid-Feb. No lunch.*

Dunsmuir Brewery Works

$ | **AMERICAN** | Travelers mingle with locals at this downtown spot for microbrews and pub fare that includes vegetarian-nut, elk, and ½-pound Angus-beef burgers, along with pesto-cream mussels, duck tacos, and smoked-salmon and classic BLTs. The house brews range from pale ale to a porter, with growlers available to go. **Known for:** outdoor patio; warm pretzels, house-made beer cheese bread; clam chowder Fridays. [$] *Average main: $17* ✉ *5701 Dunsmuir Ave., Dunsmuir* ☎ *530/235–1900* 🌐 *www.dunsmuirbreweryworks.com* ⏲ *Closed Mon. (sometimes Tues.) early Sept.–late May.*

Yaks on the 5

$$ | **AMERICAN** | Beloved on social media for its sticky buns, addictive two-cheese tater tots, and bacon-jalapeño and other 100% grass-fed burgers, this festive, brightly painted joint wins most diners' hearts with its house-made ingredients, dozens of beers, and upbeat staff. You'll pay more than expected but will likely leave feeling you got your money's worth. **Known for:** pastrami sandwiches; a few meatless burgers; Yaks Shack in downtown Mt. Shasta. [$] *Average main: $21* ✉ *4917 Dunsmuir Ave., Dunsmuir* ☎ *530/678–3517* 🌐 *www.yaks.com.*

🛏 Hotels

★ Mossbrae Hotel

$ | **HOTEL** | Patrons of this urbane, two-story boutique hotel bask in au courant comfort in guest rooms with kitchenettes and either queen or California king beds. **Pros:** luxury feel; queen rooms, though small, are a good value; easy walk to Dunsmuir Brewing, Cafe Maddalena, art venues. **Cons:** costs a bit more than town's other properties (but outshines them); no elevator (one ground-floor ADA suite); some rooms have no tubs. [$] *Rooms from: $155* ✉ *5734 Dunsmuir Ave., Dunsmuir* ☎ *530/235–7019* 🌐 *mossbraehotel.com* 🛏 *7 rooms* 🍴 *No Meals.*

Railroad Park Resort

$ | **HOTEL** | **FAMILY** | The antique cabooses here were collected over several decades and converted into 23 cozy motel rooms in honor of Dunsmuir's railroad legacy; there are also four cabins. **Pros:** gorgeous setting; unique accommodations; kitschy fun. **Cons:** cabooses can feel cramped; must drive to Dunsmuir restaurants; some guests find location too remote. [$] *Rooms from: $145* ✉ *100 Railroad Park Rd., Dunsmuir* ☎ *530/235–4440* 🌐 *www.rrpark.com* 🛏 *27 rooms* 🍴 *No Meals.*

Mt. Shasta

34 miles north of Lake Shasta.

Although a snow-covered dormant volcano is the area's dazzling draw, the town of Mt. Shasta charms visitors with its small shops, friendly residents, and beautiful scenery in all seasons.

GETTING HERE AND AROUND

Three exits off I–5 lead to the town of Mt. Shasta. When snow hasn't closed Highway 89, you can take it northwest from the Lassen Park area to Mt. Shasta. Greyhound stops at Weed, 10 miles north; Amtrak stops at Dunsmuir, 10 miles south. STAGE provides bus service.

ESSENTIALS

VISITOR INFORMATION Visit Mt. Shasta.
⊠ *Visitor center, 300 Pine St., at W. Lake St., Mt. Shasta* ☎ *530/926–4865* ⊕ *visitmtshasta.com.*

Sights

★ Mt. Shasta

VOLCANO | The crown jewel of the 2½-million-acre Shasta-Trinity National Forest, Mt. Shasta, a 14,179-foot-high dormant volcano, is a mecca for day hikers. It's especially enticing in spring, when fragrant Shasta lilies and other flowers adorn the rocky slopes. A paved road, the Everitt Memorial Highway, reaches only as far as the timberline; the final 6,000 feet are a strenuous climb of rubble, ice, and snow (the summit is perpetually ice-packed). Hiking enthusiasts include this trek with those to the peaks of Kilimanjaro and Mt. Fuji in lists of iconic must-do mountain hikes. **■ TIP→ Always check weather predictions; sudden storms—with snow and freezing temperatures—have trapped climbers.** ⊠ *Mt. Shasta.*

❶ Restaurants

★ Lilys

$$ | ECLECTIC | This restaurant in a white-clapboard home, framed by a picket fence and arched trellis, offers an eclectic menu, starting with bananas Foster French toast for breakfast. The varied lunch and dinner selections might include spicy Mongolian chicken salad, herb-stuffed fresh trout, pad Thai, filet mignon, and always several burgers. **Known for:** hearty breakfast fare; brussels sprouts salad with crispy bacon and goat cheese; patio dining. Ⓢ *Average main: $29* ⊠ *1013 S. Mt. Shasta Blvd., at Holly St., Mt. Shasta* ☎ *530/926–3372* ⊕ *www.lilysrestaurant.com* ☾ *Closed Mon. and Tues.*

Yaks Shack

$ | AMERICAN | FAMILY | The northern sibling of the Yaks on the 5 restaurant in Dunsmuir begins the day serving breakfast burritos and sandwiches, staying open until mid-evening for lunch- and dinner-oriented burritos and Buddha bowls along with burgers overflowing with ingredients that might include bacon, avocado, pickled jalapeños, crispy onion strings, and one or more cheeses. Smaller than the original Yaks but similarly enlivened by colorful murals and pulsating to indie rock, the Mt. Shasta iteration benefits from zealous staffers aiming to please. **Known for:** garlic Parmesan fries; coffee and tea offerings; local and West Coast seltzers, ciders, ales, stouts, and porters. Ⓢ *Average main: $16* ⊠ *401 N. Mt. Shasta Blvd., Mt. Shasta* ⊹ *Near W. Castle St.* ☎ *530/568–8121* ⊕ *www.yaks.com/shack.*

☕ Coffee and Quick Bites

Seven Suns Coffee and Cafe

$ | CAFÉ | FAMILY | A favorite gathering spot for locals, this small coffee shop in a stone building serves specialty wraps and burritos for breakfast and lunch, plus soups and salads. Pastries, made daily, include muffins, cookies, and scones (great blackberry ones in season).

Known for: coffee, tea, spiced cider, Italian sodas; outside patio; vegetarian offerings. $ *Average main: $12* ⊠ *1011 S. Mt. Shasta Blvd., at Holly St., Mt. Shasta* ☎ *530/926–9701* ⊘ *No dinner.*

Hotels

Best Western Tree House Motor Inn
$$ | HOTEL | FAMILY | The clean, standard rooms at this motel less than a mile from downtown are decorated with natural-wood furnishings, and some of the nicer accommodations have vaulted ceilings and mountain views. **Pros:** close to ski park; heated indoor pool; lobby's roaring fireplace is a big plus on winter days. **Cons:** no elevators in two of three buildings; pricier than other chain properties; doesn't offer free breakfast like much of BW chain. $ *Rooms from: $209* ⊠ *111 Morgan Way, Mt. Shasta* ☎ *530/926–3101, 800/780–7234* ⊕ *www.bestwestern.com* ⊷ *98 rooms* ⏐◉⏐ *No Meals.*

Inn at Mount Shasta
$ | HOTEL | FAMILY | This two-story, motel-style property on Mt. Shasta's main drag wins points for its cleanliness, comfortable beds, and spacious (325 square feet minimum) rooms with Wi-Fi, microwaves, refrigerators, hair dryers, and flat-screen TVs with satellite HDTV. **Pros:** solicitous hosts; 500-square-foot family suite with three beds; convenient location. **Cons:** minimal style; some street and room-to-room noise; no elevator to second-floor rooms. $ *Rooms from: $169* ⊠ *710 S. Mt. Shasta Blvd., Mt. Shasta* ☎ *530/918–9292* ⊕ *innatmountshasta.com* ⊷ *30 rooms* ⏐◉⏐ *No Meals.*

Mount Shasta Resort
$ | HOTEL | FAMILY | The resort's Craftsman-style private chalets, all with gas-log fireplaces, are nestled among tall pine trees along the shore of Lake Siskiyou. **Pros:** incredible views (from the hotel and its 18-hole golf course); full kitchens in many lodgings; largest chalets sleep up to six people. **Cons:** chalets could use a refresh; must drive to Mt. Shasta restaurants; some hospitality lapses. $ *Rooms from: $189* ⊠ *1000 Siskiyou Lake Blvd., Mt. Shasta* ☎ *530/926–3030, 800/958–3363* ⊕ *www.mountshastaresort.com* ⊷ *65 rooms* ⏐◉⏐ *No Meals.*

Activities

Fifth Season Mountaineering Shop
MOUNTAIN CLIMBING | This shop rents bicycles and skiing and climbing equipment and operates a recorded 24-hour climber-skier report. ⊠ *300 N. Mt. Shasta Blvd., Mt. Shasta* ☎ *530/926–3606, 530/926–5555 mountain report* ⊕ *www. thefifthseason.com.*

Mt. Shasta Nordic Center
SKIING & SNOWBOARDING | FAMILY | This center, run by a nonprofit, maintains about 15 miles of groomed cross-country ski trails, plus a short snowshoeing trail. ⊠ *Ski Park Hwy., Mt. Shasta* ✛ *North off Hwy. 89, 7 miles southeast of Mt. Shasta City* ☎ *530/925–3495, 530/925–3494 grooming report* ⊕ *mtshastanordic.org.*

Mt. Shasta Ranger Station
HIKING & WALKING | Check here for current trail conditions and avalanche reports. ⊠ *204 W. Alma St., at Pine St., Mt. Shasta* ☎ *530/926–4511, 530/926–9613 avalanche conditions* ⊕ *www.fs.usda. gov/main/stnf.*

Mt. Shasta Ski Park
SKIING & SNOWBOARDING | FAMILY | More than half the trails at this ski park on Mt. Shasta's southeast flank are for beginning or intermediate skiers. A package for children, available through the ski school, includes a lift ticket, ski rental, and a lesson. The base lodge has a bar, a few dining options, a ski shop, and a ski-snowboard rental shop. **Facilities:** 38 trails; 635 skiable acres; 2,036-foot vertical drop; 6 lifts. ⊠ *4500 Ski Park Hwy., Mt. Shasta* ✛ *Hwy. 89 exit east from I–5, south of Mt. Shasta City* ☎ *530/926–8610 winter only, 530/926–8686 snow phone*

www.skipark.com ✉ Lift tickets from $79 (nonholiday weekdays).

Chester

30 miles southeast of Lassen's south-west entrance, 71 miles east of Red Bluff.

A gateway to Lassen Volcanic National Park on Lake Almanor's north shore, Chester, population 2,200, supports locals and tourists with modest restaurants, hotels, and shops. The 2021 Dixie Fire, the second-largest wildfire in California's history, consumed much of the lake's western shore, but firefighters saved Chester.

GETTING HERE AND AROUND

Chester is on Highway 36, the main route east from I–5 at Red Bluff, at the junction of Highway 89, which leads northwest to Lassen.

ESSENTIALS

VISITOR INFORMATION Lake Almanor Area Chamber of Commerce. ✉ *278 Main St., Chester* ☎ *530/208–5330* ⊕ *www.lakealmanorarea.com.*

Sights

★ Volcanic Legacy Scenic Byway

SCENIC DRIVE | FAMILY | The byway is a 500-mile scenic drive connecting Lassen with Oregon's Crater Lake National Park. The route's southern loop begins in Chester and winds for about 185 miles through the forests, volcanic peaks, hydrothermal springs, and lava fields of Lassen National Forest and Lassen Volcanic National Park. The all-day excursion into dramatic wilderness includes a detour north to 129-foot-tall Burney Falls. Note, though, that the Dixie Fire of 2021 scorched the forested areas along Highway 36 and Lassen National Park Highway near Chester. ✛ *From Chester, take Hwy. 36 west to Hwy. 89 (Lassen Volcanic National Park Hwy. within the park) north to Burney*

Falls. Backtrack south on Hwy. 89, turning southeast on Hwy. 44. At Hwy. 36 head west past Lake Almanor back to Chester ⊕ *www.volcaniclegacybyway.org* ⊗ *In most yrs, snow closes parts of the byway from mid-fall to mid-spring.*

🍽 Restaurants

★ Cravings

$ | CAFÉ | FAMILY | This casual breakfast and lunch place inside a clapboard house satisfies diners' cravings with dishes like homemade slow-roasted corned-beef hash topped with two eggs and accompanied by a slice of sourdough or gluten-free bread. You can get breakfast and excellent pastries all day, with soups, salads, sandwiches, wraps, and burgers on the menu for lunch. **Known for:** waffles with applewood-smoked bacon in the batter; outdoor patio; attached bookstore (run separately). $ *Average main: $14* ✉ *278 Main St., Chester* ☎ *530/258–2229* ⊕ *www.facebook.com/chestercravings* ⊗ *Closed Tues. and Wed. (sometimes more in winter). No dinner.*

The Ranch House

$ | AMERICAN | FAMILY | This convivial neighborhood pub stands out because of its abundance of shaded patio seating (and full horseshoes pit) in the landscaped backyard. After a long day of hiking and exploring, the restaurant is a reliable bet for hearty comfort fare—sandwiches, half-pound burgers, fish-and-chips, and tacos, plus a daily special or two. **Known for:** chicken wings, mac-and-cheese bites, and fried pickles appetizers; decadent "Sidewinder" spiral fries with cheese, pulled pork, creamy Sriracha, and sour cream; beer selection. $ *Average main: $15* ✉ *669 Main St., Chester* ☎ *530/258–4226* ⊕ *www.facebook.com/theranchhouse16* ⊗ *Closed Sun.–Tues. No lunch Wed. and Thurs.*

Hotels

Antlers Motel

$ | **MOTEL** | A spotlessly clean downtown option, this homey, two-story motel is a handy base for exploring Warner Valley and the southern end of Lassen Park Highway. **Pros:** satellite TV and electric fireplaces; coffeemakers, microwaves, and refrigerators in every room; short walk to restaurants and bars. **Cons:** no breakfast; basic decor; parking tight when motel is fully booked. $ *Rooms from: $140* ✉ *268 Main St., Chester* ☎ *530/258–2722* ⊕ *www.antlersmotel. com* ⇄ *20 rooms* ⏨ *No Meals.*

Mineral

58 miles east of Redding, 42 miles east of Red Bluff.

Fewer than 200 people live in Mineral, which serves as Lassen Volcanic National Park's official address.

GETTING HERE AND AROUND

Reach Lassen's southern entrance by turning north off Highway 36 onto Highway 89. Access the northwest entrance via Highway 44 from Redding. No buses serve the area.

Sights

★ Lassen Volcanic National Park

NATIONAL PARK | **FAMILY** | Several volcanoes have been active in this area for roughly 600,000 years, but what led to the 1916 national park designation was the activity of the largest one: the plug dome known as Lassen Peak. A 1914 eruption sent pumice, rock, and snow thundering down and hot ash billowing up. It was followed by an even more spectacular 1915 outburst that blew a cloud of ash almost 6 miles high and created a mudflow that destroyed vegetation for miles.

Although Lassen Peak settled down in 1921, it's not considered dormant, as evidenced by the park's fascinating—if dangerous—landscape of frothy mud pots, steamy fumaroles, and boiling springs. Lassen Park Road (the continuation of Highway 89 within the park) and numerous hiking trails provide access to these wonders. ⚠ **The 166-square-mile national park's coniferous forests and alpine meadows also offer abundant opportunities for hiking, as well as for camping and wildlife photography. Note, too, that the café at the main Kohm Yah-mah-nee Visitor Center, in the park's southern section, serves pizza, salads, sandwiches, burgers, and a variety of beverages, including beer from local producer, Lassen Ale Works.**

Although the Dixie Fire of 2021 ravaged more than two-thirds of the park, the visitor center, the famous Bumpass Hell Trail, and other popular spots survived. ⚠ **Heed signs about fire-related closures and warnings to stay on trails and railed boardwalks to avoid falling into boiling water or through thin-crusted areas.** ✉ *Mineral* ☎ *530/595–4480* ⊕ *www.nps.gov/lavo* ⊠ *$30 car, $25 motorcycle, $15 person not in motor vehicle (fees good for 7 days)* ☾ *Visitor center closed Mon. (except national holidays) and Tues. Nov.–Apr.*

Sulphur Works Thermal Area

NATURE SIGHT | **FAMILY** | Proof of Lassen Peak's volatility becomes evident shortly after you enter the park at the southwest entrance. Sidewalks skirt boiling springs and sulfur-emitting steam vents. This area is usually the last site to close in winter, but even when the road is closed, you can access the area via a 2-mile round-trip hike through the snow. ✉ *Lassen Park Hwy., Lassen Volcanic National Park* ⊹ *1 mile from southwest entrance.*

Restaurants

★ Highlands Ranch Restaurant and Bar

$$$ | **AMERICAN** | Dining at the Highlands Ranch Resort's contemporary roadhouse restaurant is in a stained-wood, high-ceilinged indoor space or on an outdoor

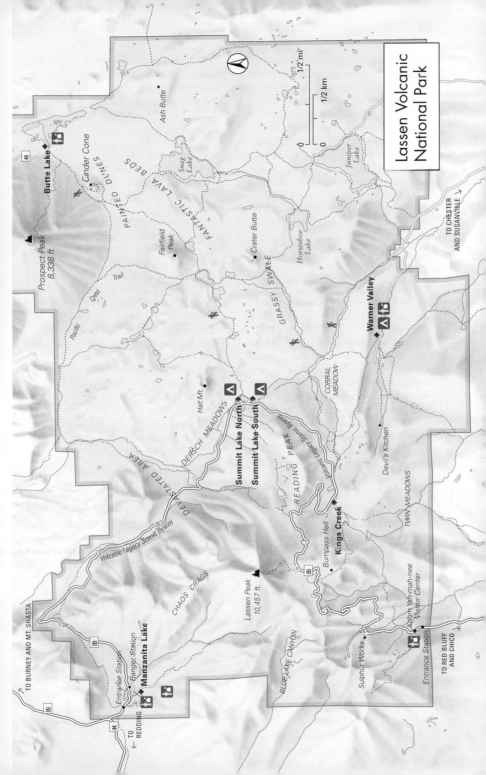

deck with striking views of a serene meadow and the hillside beyond. Among the few sophisticated eating options within Lassen Volcanic National Park's orbit, the restaurant serves updated pasta, fish, chicken, beef, and lamb dishes. **Known for:** craft cocktails, beer flights, wines by the glass; small plates and burgers in the bar; inventive sauces and preparations. $ *Average main: $37* ⊠ *41515 Hwy. 36, Mill Creek* ☎ *530/595–3388* ⊕ *www.highlandsranchresort.com/restaurant* ⊙ *Closed Mon.–Wed. (no lunch Thurs.) Nov.–late May.*

Hotels

★ Highlands Ranch Resort

$$$ | B&B/INN | In a gorgeous, 175-acre alpine meadow 10 miles from Lassen's southwest entrance, this resort's smartly designed bungalows are splurge-worthy if you want stay near the national park but don't want to rough it. **Pros:** stunning views; most luxurious accommodations near the park; friendly and helpful staff. **Cons:** pricey for the area; remote location; books up months ahead for summer stays. $ *Rooms from: $359* ⊠ *41515 Hwy. 36, Mill Creek* ☎ *530/595–3388* ⊕ *www.highlandsranchresort.com* ⊙ *Closed Mon.–Wed. Nov.–late May* ⤙ *7 cottages* ❑ *Free Breakfast.*

Mill Creek Resort

$ | RESORT | FAMILY | Set amid towering evergreens in a tranquil patch of Lassen National Forest, this delightfully unfussy 1930s cabin and camping resort feels as though it could be inside the national park, although it's actually about 10 miles south on a scenic country road. **Pros:** utterly peaceful, wooded setting; one of the closest lodging options near Lassen's southwest entrance; old-fashioned, family-friendly summer-camp vibe. **Cons:** must drive to other restaurants and services; small bedrooms and bathrooms; no cell reception or Wi-Fi (although cell phones

work 2 miles away). $ *Rooms from: $165* ⊠ *40271 Hwy. 172, Mill Creek* ☎ *530/595–4449* ⊕ *www.millcreekresort.net* ⊙ *Closed mid-Oct.–Apr.* ⤙ *9 cabins* ❑ *No Meals.*

Activities

★ Bumpass Hell Trail

HIKING & WALKING | FAMILY | This 3-mile round-trip hike leads to arguably the park's most mesmerizing feature, a wondrous landscape of hydrothermal activity characterized by boiling springs, hissing steam vents, and roiling gray mud pots. Allow two hours to complete the loop, which involves a gradual 300-foot descent into the Bumpass Hell basin, and be sure to venture to the basin's several upper viewpoints, which provide amazing views of the entire scene. Stay on trails and boardwalks near the thermal areas, as what appears to be firm ground may be only a thin crust over scalding mud. From the basin, you can continue another 1.9 miles along a scenic ridge to Cold Boiling Lake, from which you can trek farther to Kings Creek Picnic Area or Crumbaugh Lake. *Moderate.* ⊠ *Lassen Park Hwy., Lassen Volcanic National Park* ✛ *Trailhead: 6 miles from southwest entrance.*

★ Lassen Peak Trail

HIKING & WALKING | This trail winds 2.5 miles to the mountaintop. It's an arduous climb—2,000 feet uphill on a steady, steep grade—but the reward is a spectacular view. At the peak you can see into the rim and view the entire park (and much of California's Far North). Give yourself about five hours to complete this climb, and bring sunscreen, water, snacks, a first-aid kit, and a jacket—it can be windy and cold at the summit. *Difficult.* ⊠ *Lassen Park Hwy., Lassen Volcanic National Park* ✛ *Trailhead: 7 miles north of southwest entrance.*

Burney

62 miles southeast of Mt. Shasta, 41 miles north of Lassen Volcanic National Park.

One of the most spectacular sights in the Far North is Burney Falls, where countless ribbon-like streams pour from moss-covered crevices. The beauty of the falls, and the state park in which they're set, is well worth the trek along two forested highways.

GETTING HERE AND AROUND

To get to the falls, head east off I–5 on Highway 89 at Mt. Shasta. From Redding, head east on Highway 299 to Highway 89; follow signs 6 miles to the park.

 Sights

★ McArthur–Burney Falls Memorial State Park

STATE/PROVINCIAL PARK | **FAMILY** | Just inside this park's southern boundary, Burney Creek wells up from the ground and divides into two falls that cascade over a 129-foot cliff into a pool below. Countless ribbon-like streams pour from hidden moss-covered crevices; resident bald eagles are frequently seen soaring overhead. You can walk a self-guided nature trail that descends to the foot of the falls, which Theodore Roosevelt—according to legend—called "the eighth wonder of the world." On warm days, swim at Lake Britton; lounge on the beach; rent motorboats, paddleboats, and canoes; or relax at one of the campsites or picnic areas. ⊠ *24898 Hwy. 89, Burney* ✛ *6 miles north of Hwy. 299* ☎ *530/335–2777* ⊕ *www.burneyfallspark.org* ⬛ *$10 per vehicle, day-use.*

Tulelake

89 miles from Burney, 85 miles from Mt. Shasta City.

Lava Beds National Monument, the chief attraction of Tulelake, is so far north that one of the main routes to it briefly passes into Oregon before looping back into California. Stunning underground lava tube caves make the trip to this off-the-beaten-path geological site worth the detour.

GETTING HERE AND AROUND

From McArthur-Burney Falls Memorial State Park, take Highway 89 south to Highway 299 east to Bieber-Lookout Road and Highway 139 north. At Forest Service Route 97 turn left (west) and follow signs. From Mt. Shasta City, take Highway 89 to Forest Service Routes 97 and 10. There's no public transportation.

 Sights

★ Lava Beds National Monument

NATURE SIGHT | **FAMILY** | Thousands of years of volcanic activity created this rugged landscape, distinguished by cinder cones, lava flows, spatter cones, pit craters, and more than 400 underground lava tube caves. During the Modoc War (1872–73), the indigenous Modoc people, under the leadership of their chief "Captain Jack" Kintpuash, took refuge in a natural lava fortress now known as Captain Jack's Stronghold. They managed to hold off U.S. Army forces, which outnumbered them 20 to 1, for five months.

When exploring this area, wear hard-soled boots and a bump hat. Bring a flashlight with you, although some are available for borrowing at the visitor center, which is in the park's south-central reaches. This is also the departure point for summer activities such as guided walks, cave tours, and campfire programs. ■**TIP➜ Lava Beds is extremely remote; visit the website for detailed driving instructions and information about winter road closures.** ⊠ *Visitor center, 1 Indian Well, Tulelake* ✛ *Take Forest Rte. 97 to Forest Rte. 10* ☎ *530/260–0537, 530/667–8113* ⊕ *www.nps.gov/labe* ⬛ *$25 per vehicle, good for 7 days.*

Index

Photo Credits

Front Cover: Arkanto/Alamy Stock Photo [Descr.: Bixby Creek Bridge, Highway 1, and Big Sur coast of California California]. **Back cover, from left to right:** Celso Diniz/Shutterstock. Dan Harmeson/iStockphoto. Mblach/Dreamstime. **Spine:** S. Greg Panosian/iStockphoto. **Interior, from left to right:** Nikki Koehlert/Shutterstock (1). M.M Photography/Shutterstock (2-3). Pius Lee/Shutterstock (5). **Chapter 1: Experience Northern California:** Ewoerlen/iStockphoto (8-9). Stephen Moehle/Shutterstock (10-11). Lynn Yeh/Shutterstock (11). Oscity/Shutterstock (11). Mike Peters/Shutterstock (12). Jill Krueger (12). Eric Broder Van Dyke/Shutterstock (12). Chris Leschinsky/Visit California (12). Jill Krueger (13). Joseph Phelps Vineyard (13). Carol Highsmith/Visit California (14). Toms Auzins/Shutterstock (14). Amanda Marsalis/Chez Panisse (14). Courtesy of Musée Mécanique (14). Michael Lauffenburger/Shutterstock (15). Andreas Hub/Visit California (15). Remy Hale (20). Nito/Shutterstock (21). Jill Krueger (22). Jemny/Shutterstock (22). ESB Professional/Shutterstock (22). TJ Muzeni (22). Eug Png/Shutterstock (23). Kropic1/Shutterstock (23). MNStudio/Shutterstock (23). Morenovel/Shutterstock (23). **Chapter 3: Northern California's Best Road Trips:** Zack Frank/Shutterstock (35). **Chapter 4: Monterey Bay Area:** Haveseen/Shutterstock (47). Nadezhdasarkisian/Dreamstime (56). Artyart/Shutterstock (64). Wolterk/Dreamstime (74). Mike Brake/Dreamstime (84). **Chapter 5: Sequoia and Kings Canyon National Parks:** Robert Holmes (93). Urosr/Shutterstock (108). Chapter 6: Yosemite National Park: Ershov_Maks/iStockphoto (121). Sky Sajjaphot/iStockphoto (138). Jane Rix/Shutterstock (141). Simon Dannhauer/iStockphoto (144). Katrina Leigh/Shutterstock (148-149). Trekandshoot/Shutterstock (154). **Chapter 7: Eastern Sierra:** Glenn Pettersen/Shutterstock (157). Mark Sayer/Shutterstock (167). **Chapter 8: Sacramento and the Gold Country:** Heyengel/iStockphoto (177). RickC/Flickr (203). Ambient Images Inc./Alamy (212). **Chapter 9: Lake Tahoe:** MariuszBlach/iStockphoto (223). Mblach/Dreamstime (237). Thetahoeguy/Shutterstock (239). Tom Zikas/North Lake Tahoe (242). Christopher Russell/iStockphoto (254). **Chapter 10: San Francisco:** Jill Krueger (261). Scott Chernis/San Francisco Travel Association (270). Canadastock/Shutterstock (289). Pius Lee/Shutterstock (291). San Francisco Municipal Railway Historical Archives (292). Andresr/Dreamstime (309). Robert Holmes (320). Aprillilacs/Fodors Member (326). Hramirez125/iStockphoto (332). **Chapter 11: The Bay Area:** Gary Crabbe/Alamy Stock Photo (335). Bongo/California Travel and Tourism Commission (343). Nancy Lloyt Belcher/Alamy (344). Robert Holmes (368). **Chapter 12: Napa and Sonoma:** Israel Valencia/Infinity Visuals (399). Terry Joanis/Frog's Leap (418). Courtesy of Castello di Amorosa (427). Robert Holmes (437). **Chapter 13: The North Coast:** MWP/iStockphoto (455). Robert Holmes (460). Robert Holmes (478). **Chapter 14: Redwood National and State Parks:** Ericliu08/iStockphoto (487). Westphalia/iStockphoto (497). **Chapter 15: The Far North:** NPS (507). Stephen Moehle/Shutterstock (527). **About Our Writers:** All photos are courtesy of the writers.

Every effort has been made to trace the copyright holders, and we apologize in advance for any accidental errors. We would be happy to apply the corrections in the following edition of this publication.

Notes

Notes

Notes

Notes

Notes

Fodor's NORTHERN CALIFORNIA

Publisher: Stephen Horowitz, *General Manager*

Editorial: Douglas Stallings, *Editorial Director;* Jill Fergus, Amanda Sadlowski, *Senior Editors;* Brian Eschrich, Alexis Kelly, *Editors;* Angelique Kennedy-Chavannes, Yoojin Shin, *Associate Editors*

Design: Tina Malaney, *Director of Design and Production;* Jessica Gonzalez, *Senior Designer;* Jaimee Shaye, *Graphic Design Associate*

Production: Jennifer DePrima, *Editorial Production Manager;* Elyse Rozelle, *Senior Production Editor;* Monica White, *Production Editor*

Maps: Rebecca Baer, *Senior Map Editor;* David Lindroth, Mark Stroud (Moon Street Cartography), *Cartographers*

Photography: Viviane Teles, *Director of Photography;* Namrata Aggarwal, Neha Gupta, Payal Gupta, Ashok Kumar, *Photo Editors;* Jade Rodgers, *Photo Production Intern*

Business and Operations: Chuck Hoover, *Chief Marketing Officer;* Robert Ames, *Group General Manager*

Public Relations and Marketing: Joe Ewaskiw, *Senior Director of Communications and Public Relations*

Fodors.com: Jeremy Tarr, *Editorial Director;* Rachael Levitt, *Managing Editor*

Technology: Jon Atkinson, *Executive Director of Technology;* Rudresh Teotia, *Associate Director of Technology;* Alison Lieu, *Project Manager*

Writers: Cheryl Crabtree, Trevor Felch, Marlise Kast-Myers, Denise M. Leto, Daniel Mangin

Editor: Laura M. Kidder

Production Editor: Elyse Rozelle

17th Edition

ISBN 978-1-64097-677-1

ISSN 1543-1045

SPECIAL SALES

This book is available at special discounts for bulk purchases for sales promotions or premiums. For more information, e-mail SpecialMarkets@fodors.com.

PRINTED IN CHINA

10 9 8 7 6 5 4 3 2 1

About Our Writers

Native Californian **Cheryl Crabtree,** who updated the Monterey Bay Area, Sequoia and Kings Canyon National Parks, and Yosemite National Park chapters, has contributed to *Fodor's California* since 2003 and also contributes regularly to the *Fodor's Oahu, Kauai,* and *National Parks* guides. Cheryl is editor of *Montecito Magazine* and co-author of *The California Directory of Fine Wineries* hardcover book series (Napa-Sonoma and Central Coast editions). Her articles have appeared in many regional and national magazines, and she has also authored travel apps for mobile devices and content for travel websites.

Marlise Kast-Myers (⊕ *www. marlisekast.com*) has traveled to more than 80 countries; lived in Switzerland, Dominican Republic, Spain, and Costa Rica; co-authored more than 40 Fodor's guides; and written a memoir, *Tabloid Prodigy*. She also completed a surfing and snowboarding expedition across the world and has served as a photojournalist for *Surf Guide to Costa Rica*. She currently lives in San Diego County at the historic Betty Crocker Estate, where she and her husband, Benjamin, operate an antiques business, Brick n Barn, and where she writes travel features for the *San Diego Union-Tribune*. For this edition of Northern California, Marlise updated the Eastern Sierra chapter.

Daniel Mangin has been a Fodor's Travel writer and editor for more than a quarter century. The author of all five editions of *Fodor's Napa and Sonoma,* he has also written about wine and wineries for the *California Directory of Fine Wineries, Napa Valley Life,* and other print and online outlets. Daniel updated the Travel Smart, Northern California's Best Road Trips, Sacramento and the Gold Country, Lake Tahoe, Napa and Sonoma, North Coast, Redwood National and State Parks, and Far North chapters.

San Francisco chapter and The Bay Area chapter contributors: **Trevor Felch** and **Denise M. Leto.**